AVID

READER

PRESS

PARTY OF ONE

THE RISE OF XI JINPING AND CHINA'S SUPERPOWER FUTURE

CHUN HAN WONG

AVID READER PRESS

New York   London   Toronto   Sydney   New Delhi

Avid Reader Press
An Imprint of Simon & Schuster, Inc.
1230 Avenue of the Americas
New York, NY 10020

First Avid Reader Press hardcover edition May 2023

AVID READER PRESS and colophon are trademarks of Simon & Schuster, Inc.

For information about special discounts for bulk purchases, please contact Simon & Schuster Special Sales at 1-866-506-1949 or business@simonandschuster.com.

The Simon & Schuster Speakers Bureau can bring authors to your live event. For more information or to book an event contact the Simon & Schuster Speakers Bureau at 1-866-248-3049 or visit our website at www.simonspeakers.com.

Interior design by Wendy Blum

Manufactured in the United States of America

1   3   5   7   9   10   8   6   4   2

ISBN 978-1-9821-8573-2
ISBN 978-1-9821-8575-6 (ebook)

To my parents, my siblings, and my wife.

The Yangtze's roaring waters roll ever eastward,
Their spray washes away gallant heroes.
Rights and wrongs, triumphs and failures, all ebb into emptiness,
But the lush hills remain, and the scarlet sunsets repeat.

—From "Linjiangxian · Gungun Changjiang Dongshishui," or
"Immortal by the River · The Yangtze's Roaring Waters Roll Ever Eastward,"
a verse by Ming dynasty poet Yang Shen[1]

CONTENTS

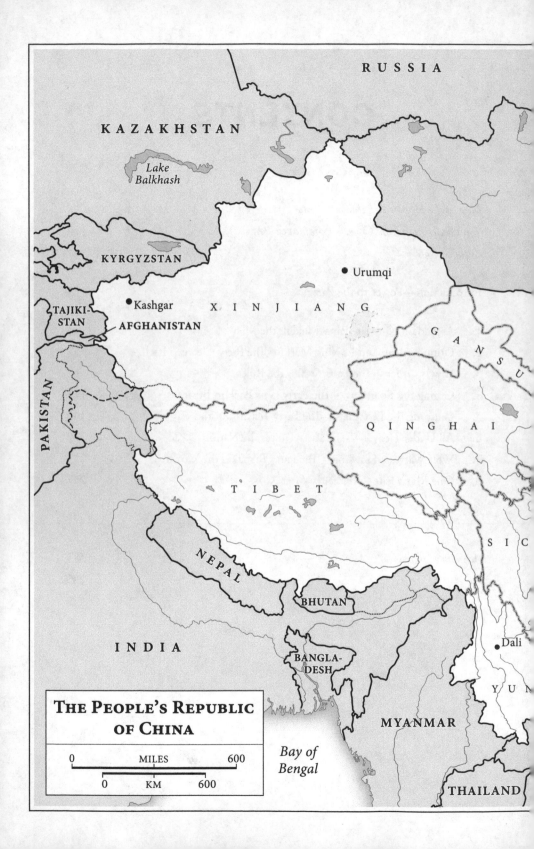

THE PEOPLE'S REPUBLIC
OF CHINA

| 0 | MILES | 600 |

| 0 | KM | 600 |

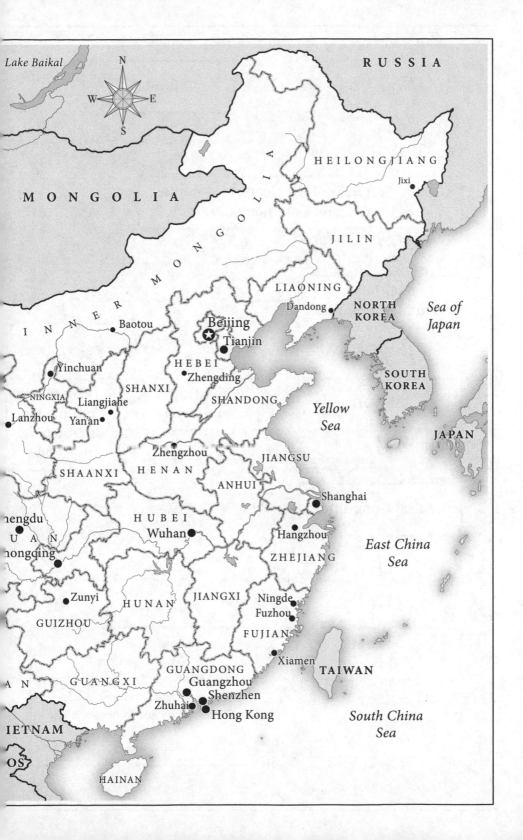

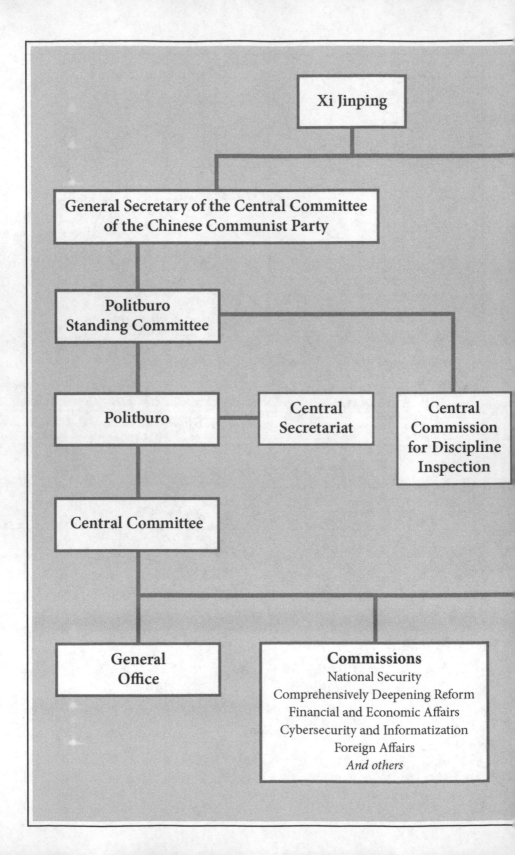

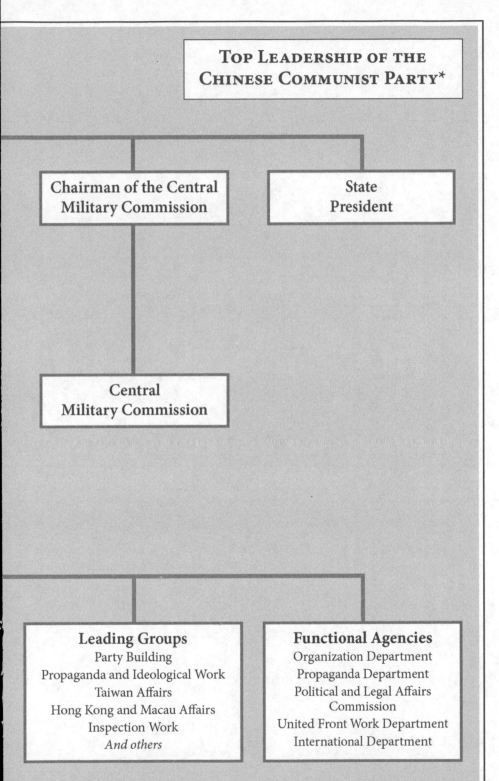

TOP LEADERSHIP OF THE CHINESE COMMUNIST PARTY*

Chairman of the Central Military Commission

State President

Central Military Commission

Leading Groups
Party Building
Propaganda and Ideological Work
Taiwan Affairs
Hong Kong and Macau Affairs
Inspection Work
And others

Functional Agencies
Organization Department
Propaganda Department
Political and Legal Affairs Commission
United Front Work Department
International Department

*As of February 2023

AUTHOR'S NOTE

This book draws on my firsthand reporting as a China correspondent for the *Wall Street Journal* since 2014. I worked in Beijing for five years before moving to Hong Kong in 2019, when the Chinese government declined to renew my press credentials and forced me to leave the mainland.

The Communist Party and its black-box bureaucracy are notoriously hard to penetrate. Even privileged insiders can struggle to pry beyond their immediate environs within a secretive Leninist system. And covering Chinese politics gets harder the farther one operates from the seat of national power, as it becomes more difficult to arrange the face-to-face meetings that are most conducive for candid conversations, and to experience tactile shifts in the political climate and public mood. Reporting for this book, therefore, required resourcefulness and humility—making use of contacts and research techniques that I had cultivated throughout my five years in mainland China, and understanding that any attempt to examine the party's inner workings can yield only partial glimpses of a complex picture.

Xi Jinping, since becoming China's paramount leader, has rarely given face-to-face interviews or fielded questions from foreign journalists. Nonetheless, a detailed account of Xi's life, influences, ideas, and policies can be constructed from a wide variety of primary and secondary sources. The materials I consulted include Xi's writings, public speeches, internal remarks; interviews from his earlier career; as well as authorized biographies and memoirs of people who knew him, including his father and maternal uncle. I also reviewed party and state documents, official histories, memoirs, archival papers, state-media reports, as well as academic literature published in China and elsewhere. Notwithstanding the discernment that reporters and researchers must apply when handling open-source material often crafted for propaganda purposes, there is much knowledge that can be distilled from scrutinizing what

Xi and the party say—both plainly and implicitly—among themselves and to the 1.4 billion people they govern.

I also used information gleaned from conversations with party insiders, officials, diplomats, academics, lawyers, business executives, and ordinary people whom I met in China. Many of them spoke on the record, though many more preferred anonymity, given the sensitivities of discussing political matters. Where sources can't be precisely identified, I provide contextual details—either within the text or in endnotes—to help readers understand where the information came from, and assess its reliability.

PARTY OF ONE

INTRODUCTION

POWER TO THE PARTY

"The party, government, military, society, education; north, south, east, west, center—the party leads everything."

—Xi Jinping

Weeks after becoming general secretary of China's Communist Party, Xi Jinping summoned hundreds of top officials to an elite political academy in northwestern Beijing, a cluster of austere buildings embellished with wide lawns and a willow-lined lake, near old imperial gardens where Qing emperors once lived. Here, in early January 2013, amid wintry hues of yellow and brown, Xi laid out his priorities as China's new leader.

His speech was somber. He recalled the crumbling of the Iron Curtain more than two decades ago and warned that Communist China could suffer the same fate. "Why did the Soviet Union disintegrate? Why did the Soviet Communist Party collapse? An important reason was that their ideals and convictions wavered," Xi told officials at the Central Party School.[1] "Their ideology became confused, party groups at all levels became virtually ineffective, even the military was no longer under the party's leadership. In the end, a party as vast as the Soviet Communist Party scattered like birds and beasts, and a socialist state as colossal as the Soviet Union fell to pieces. This is a warning from the past!"

At the time there were few signs suggesting an imminent collapse of the People's Republic, already the world's second-largest economy and a superpower-in-waiting. The party's embrace of pragmatic politics and market-style reforms more than three decades earlier had pulled China away from the calamitous radicalism that marred

Mao Zedong's dictatorship, delivering relative stability and unprecedented prosperity. A spectacular Beijing Olympics and the implosion of the Western financial system in 2008 cemented China's ascendancy and, in the eyes of many Chinese, vindicated the country's much-maligned model of authoritarian capitalism. Bitter memories of 1989, when mass protests in Beijing and other cities shook the party, had faded from public consciousness. China's pivot—from socialist dogma to state capitalism and from dictatorship to collective rule—seemed unquestionable. Xi himself, soon after taking power, declared that the "China Dream" of restoring national glory was at hand. "We are more confident and capable of achieving it than at any other time in history," he said.

But this seeming stability masked turbulent undercurrents. Economic expansion was slowing, as the excesses of debt-driven growth took their toll. Income inequality widened, corruption grew, pollution worsened, and social unrest soared. Ethnic tensions in the restive borderlands of Tibet and Xinjiang flared into deadly riots. Public intellectuals lamented that China's rapid enrichment had unmoored its spiritual anchors. As society atomizes into self-centered individuals, "all kinds of bonds and interpersonal connections will be lost," Chinese philosophy professor Tian Yipeng warned in 2012. "Selfish solipsism will be in vogue across society, causing social constraints to dissolve and pushing society toward the dangers of disorder."[2]

The Communist Party itself grappled with internal strife. Ideological cleavages divided the ruling elite. Advocates for stronger state control vied for influence against those who championed the private sector, civil society, and the rule of law. Shadowy contests for promotions and influence burst into the open in the months before the party congress in 2012 where Xi would take power. The party purged a high-flying regional leader, Bo Xilai, who supported a Maoist revival and state-led economic development, weeks after his former police chief fled to a U.S. consulate and aired allegations that Bo's wife had murdered a British businessman. The son of a top aide to the incumbent leader died in a fiery Ferrari crash, embarrassing the party and precipitating his father's downfall. Xi himself mysteriously disappeared for two weeks as the party congress neared, canceling meetings with foreign officials and sowing speculation over his health.

Xi emerged unscathed, assuming his place atop the party's new seven-man leadership. With order seemingly restored, he acknowledged that business couldn't go on as usual. "Our party faces many severe challenges, and there are also many pressing problems within the party that need to be resolved," Xi said in his first public remarks as general secretary. He described a party riddled with graft, out of touch with ordinary people, and crippled by red tape. Its sprawling ranks, numbering more than 85 million at the time, were swollen with careerist, corrupt, and indolent officials seeking sinecures and shirking duties.

The party's slide toward this moral morass dated back to Mao's death in 1976. After a brief interregnum, Deng Xiaoping became paramount leader and sought to inoculate the party from the perils of one-man rule. Senior leaders shared power, encouraged timely retirement, and made plans for orderly succession. Though Deng himself dominated politics until his death in 1997, he and his supporters tried to professionalize the government, fast-tracking capable cadres up the hierarchy. They seeded pro-market reforms that spurred China's economic miracle, bringing about three decades of breakneck growth. Millions of rural Chinese rushed into the cities to fill jobs on expanding factory floors. Private businesses flourished and living standards soared. Hundreds of millions joined the country's fast-swelling middle class. After China joined the World Trade Organization in 2001, foreign investment flooded in while exports poured out across the globe.

Along the way, the party shed its revolutionary zeal and developed a ruthless pragmatism. Deng promoted his own brand of trickle-down economics, saying the government should allow "some people and some regions to get rich first" to spur development. His use of a proverb from his native Sichuan province—a cat, whether yellow or black, is a good feline if it can catch mice—brought the celebrated "cat analogy" into the public consciousness, and encapsulated the can-do spirit that animated the "reform era." Local authorities felt empowered to experiment with new ideas, and officials were judged on their ability to deliver growth and stability, rather than their ideological rectitude.

The party loosened its totalitarian grip and a once-omnipresent state sector receded, allowing ordinary Chinese more autonomy over their lives. People could largely pursue their material aspirations as long as they didn't challenge the party's authority. Authorities grew more tolerant of intellectual diversity, as pockets of independent thinking and journalism flourished with the emergence of commercial news outlets and social media. The party diluted its socialist ideals, welcoming entrepreneurs to join its ranks in the early 2000s and rationalizing yawning wealth gaps as a necessary evil. Officials even debated whether to drop "Communist" from their party's name. Mao's most ubiquitous motto, "serve the people," became so hollow that Chinese writer Yan Lianke used it as the title of his 2005 satirical novel depicting an illicit affair between the wife of a military commander and a peasant soldier.[3]

With time the ideological decay grew so worrisome that some within the party sensed looming disaster. A year before Xi took power, dozens of his fellow "second-generation reds" assembled in Beijing's central business district for an unusual confab. It was a who's who of Communist royalty, including descendants of party grandees, ministers, and generals, and even a half sister of Xi. Officially, the occasion was a seminar marking thirty-five years since the "Gang of Four"—a radical faction led by Mao's wife—was arrested for fanning the bloody excesses of the 1966–1976 Cultural Revolution. But as with many political gatherings in China, discussing the past was a pretext for critiquing the present. Lu De, whose father had been a propaganda minister under Mao, lamented the loss of ideals and rectitude among officials, who he claimed were splurging some 37 percent of all government expenditure on personal perks like dining and travel.[4] "The Communist Party is like a surgeon who has cancer," said Ma Xiaoli, the daughter of a former labor minister. "It can't remove the tumor by itself, it needs help from others, but without help it can't survive for long."[5]

These "princelings," as the scions of revolutionary elders and senior officials are known, prescribed a range of remedies. Some demanded a thorough anticorruption purge and more democratic debate within the party leadership. Others called for efforts to foster the rule of law, using constitutional checks and balances to prevent the party from using power arbitrarily. Many of them wanted a firmer hand on the tiller, from someone who shared their commitment to the party's revolutionary legacy. But for all their demands for change, these red aristocrats brooked no question over how far reforms can go. "In today's China," Lu said, "there's no political party that can replace the Communist Party."[6]

The party has flirted with doom many times. But the 1989 protests on Tiananmen Square in Beijing, where as many as a million people rallied to demand greater political freedoms, and fall of the Soviet bloc cast a particularly long shadow over the People's Republic. While Deng crushed the protests with military force, the demise of socialist regimes across the Soviet Union and Eastern Europe shook China, where officials and scholars obsessed over the causes and debated ways to avoid a similar fate. Some traced the Soviet collapse to policy and economic stagnation under Leonid Brezhnev's leadership from 1964 to 1982. Others blamed Mikhail Gorbachev and the U.S. strategy of encouraging "peaceful evolution" in socialist regimes. "The efforts by international capitalist forces to subvert socialist systems through 'peaceful evolution' will get more and more intense," wrote Xi in late 1991, as a municipal party boss.[7] "They will never give up on subverting, infiltrating, damaging and disturbing a major socialist power like us." When Xi had started out as a county official in the early 1980s, the Cold War was raging, China stood among dozens of socialist states flying the flag for world communism, and U.S. President Ronald Reagan declared that the march of freedom and democracy "will leave Marxism-Leninism on the ash heap of history."[8] By the time Xi took power, capitalism had become global orthodoxy, only five socialist states remained, and the People's Republic was just sixty-three years old—a shade short of the Soviet Union's sixty-nine-year run.

Generations of Chinese have been schooled to channel their patriotism through a rousing revolutionary anthem: "Without the Communist Party, there would be no new China." And so it has been for Xi. Born just a few years after Mao proclaimed the People's Republic, Xi has known no political power in China but the party. A princeling son of a revolutionary hero, he enjoyed an elite upbringing that imbued him with a sense of entitlement and an ironclad commitment to Communist rule. An unelected authoritarian leader, he asserts a personal legitimacy that is inseparable from the party's moral claims to power. Whereas Mao's revolutionary exploits made him a living deity, Xi owes everything to the party that raised him, shaped him, and empowered him. His authority emanates entirely from the offices he holds and the political structures those positions command. "The party is the power in China, and Xi is only powerful through it," wrote Kerry Brown, a professor of Chinese studies at King's College London. "He has no existence separate from the culture of the party, and no autonomy from it."[9]

There are more practical considerations too. The party imposed a political monopoly so complete that it has intertwined itself with almost every fiber of Chinese society. Party members overwhelmingly staff government agencies from Beijing down to remote village offices. They control the mass media, manage state-owned companies, supervise civic and religious groups, and preside over chambers of commerce and labor unions. They command the domestic security forces and the People's Liberation Army, the ultimate enforcers of party authority. In the Chinese body politic, the party acts as the brain, nerves, sinews, and muscles. Its dysfunction imperils the state, but it can't be easily replaced. For Xi, and others invested in perpetuating Communist rule, the only option is to heal.

The maladies, as Xi diagnosed them, are multifold. He saw that a diffuse leadership was impeding the decisive governance that China needed to cope with twenty-first-century challenges. A corrupt and bloated bureaucracy was eroding the party's moral standing and ability to govern. A better educated, more pluralistic, and increasingly complex society was tearing at the party's levers of control. The main anchors of party legitimacy—economic progress and social mobility—were becoming harder to keep in place as China switched gears toward slower, more sustainable growth. Its abandonment of communism, in practice if not in name, meant new ideological glue was needed to unite its members. Such challenges, Xi warned, could "ruin the party and ruin the nation."[10]

Rejuvenating the party was an immense and risky undertaking. Vested interests must be challenged, powerful rivals subdued, and rank-and-file members antagonized. Xi signaled an appreciation of the magnitude of his task. For his first trip outside Beijing as general secretary, he traveled to the coastal province of Guangdong, echoing Deng's famous "southern tour" two decades earlier, when the elder statesman had exerted his personal influence to revive economic reforms stifled by party conservatives. Xi made a show of honoring Deng, laying a floral basket at a statue of the late leader and pledging to uphold his legacy. Away from the cameras, however, Xi revealed the true parallel between Deng's sojourn and his own "new southern tour"— a show of force against political opponents.

"Ideals and beliefs are the 'spiritual calcium' for communists. Those lacking or wavering in their ideals and belief would suffer a deficiency in 'spiritual calcium' and be plagued by soft bones," Xi said in a secret speech that filtered out weeks later through Hong Kong and foreign media. "Proportionally the Soviet Communist Party had more members than we do, but nobody was man enough to step forward and resist," he said.[11] Where Gorbachev had failed, he shall succeed.

And resist Xi did. He would centralize decision-making authority and strengthen his control over all levers of party power, from village committees to the armed forces. He would set an expansive definition of national security, directing the state's coercive apparatus to suppress threats to China's economy, social stability, territorial unity, and one-party system. He would tap the party's history for its reservoirs of legitimacy, recounting tales of triumph and sacrifice against foreign imperialists and internal enemies. He would promote Confucian philosophy and cultural traditions, stoking a sense of Chinese civilizational pride that could counter Western ideals of individual freedom and democracy. He would fan nationalist passions around Communist rule, pledging to restore China's glory as a great power. At a personal level, Xi would meld his elite pedigree with a populist touch, styling himself as a decisive leader who could inspire loyalty and win mass support.

He began with a cleansing, launching a withering crackdown on corruption that punished more than 1.6 million people during his first five years in power. He targeted everyone from rank-and-file "flies" to top-tier "tigers," including senior officials, executives, generals, and a retired member of the party leadership. He arrested China's capitalist advance, reining in private entrepreneurs who strayed from the party's interests, and reinstating the state's visible hand in shaping the economy. His administration issued a directive, known as Document Number 9, that denounced Western ideas and demanded efforts to reinforce the party's dominance of ideology. He revived Maoist slogans and practices, waging ideological purges and demanding officials engage in self-criticism. He even restored the centrality of Marxism as the party's guiding philosophy, celebrating the two hundredth anniversary of Karl Marx's birth and calling on party members and ordinary Chinese to study the *Communist Manifesto*.

In his 2010 book, *The Party*, Richard McGregor described a panopticon-like institution controlling China largely from the shadows, positioned "to keep an eye on any state or non-state agency, while shielding itself from view at the same time." Its leaders, he said, airbrushed their Marxist ideology, donned suit jackets instead of Mao-style tunics, and masked their influence over business, academia, and civil society. "When it interacts with the outside world, the party is careful to keep a low profile. Sometimes, you can't see the party at all," McGregor wrote.[12] These observations were true at the time, but they no longer hold. The party of Xi celebrates its Marxist roots, flexes its coercive powers, and hides behind no one. Its leader demands to be seen, heard, and obeyed.

Where pragmatic innovation once flourished, Xi imposed "top-level design," placing the party unequivocally in charge of policy-making and reclaiming responsibilities once delegated to technocrats and specialists. Party committees have come to the fore, setting policies in their own name and siphoning authority from government ministries. Officials and state-enterprise executives openly brandish their party roles, listing them before their professional titles. Private companies that once played down their party connections now trumpet those ties. Rank-and-file party members, once conscious of their reputations as craven careerists, increasingly showcase their identities by wearing party insignia.

The shakeup elevated Xi's powers to an apogee unseen since Mao. His name adorns every government directive, his image plastered ubiquitously across newsprint, television screens, and propaganda posters, and his ideas hailed as "Marxism of the twenty-first century." Xi himself invokes the Chairman, borrowing his slogans, rehashing his tactics, and taking on grandiose titles such as the "people's leader" that echo Mao's accolades. But there are differences between master and disciple. While Mao could mobilize the masses to "bombard the headquarters" and attack the party's fossilizing bureaucracy from the outside, Xi relies on party institutions to execute his edicts. A deified Mao could transcend the party, but a mortal Xi is nothing without it. Or as Xi describes it, "the party's in our blood."[13]

Xi sought similar preeminence by turning to the true source of the party's power—its stories. Mao was a superlative storyteller, famously invoking the ancient Chinese fable "Foolish Old Man Moves Mountains" as a rallying cry against imperialist and feudal oppression and to build a powerful, prosperous "new China."[14] Mao's successors ditched his utopian ideals but clung to his narrative of national redemption, though none could or wanted to rouse mass fervor. Deng largely governed from the shadows and urged his countrymen to "hide our light and bide our time"—or keep a low profile while building China's strengths. His successor, Jiang Zemin, exuded an ebullient persona but deviated little from Deng's doctrine of contrived modesty. Hu Jintao, Xi's predecessor, championed China's "peaceful development" and pledged to build a "harmonious society," but these amorphous aspirations fizzled in the public imagination, much like Hu's placid personality.

The Communist Party can retain power through coercion, but to flourish it must persuade. Xi emerged as storyteller-in-chief, promising a Chinese manifest destiny that only he could deliver. He cast aside Deng's gradualist approach, declaring that decisive leadership will take China back to its rightful place as a great power. He promised a more egalitarian society, girded by a vibrant and self-reliant economy, secured by a first-rate military, and led by a resilient ruling party. And while his recent predecessors kept their private lives occluded, Xi thrust his personal story into the public eye. State media mythologized him as a committed communist who inherited his parents' revolutionary spirit and earned his spurs through hardship and sacrifice. "Xi Jinping is the new architect of China's pathway to becoming a major power," said Gong Fangbin, a professor at Beijing's National Defense University. "Mao Zedong let the Chinese people stand up, Deng Xiaoping let the Chinese people get rich, Xi Jinping will let the Chinese people get strong."[15]

This exalting narrative extends far beyond China's borders. Xi styled himself as a forceful defender of Chinese sovereignty, unafraid to challenge the West and unapologetic in defying diplomatic norms. He launched the "Belt and Road" initiative, an ambitious effort to develop global trade infrastructure and export China's excess industrial capacity. His administration poured loans and aid into developing countries and established a Beijing-led multilateral lender, the Asian Infrastructure Investment Bank, to pry loose Western dominance over international development finance. Xi told officials to "tell China's stories well," portray their nation as a responsible power, and proffer Chinese solutions for global issues like poverty alleviation and climate change. Beijing lobbied successfully for Chinese officials to lead United Nations agencies overseeing civil aviation, food and agriculture, and telecommunications. China ramped up contributions to the U.N. peacekeeping program, becoming its second-biggest funder and the largest provider of peacekeepers among major powers. The People's Liberation Army flexed its growing muscles, establishing a naval base in Djibouti, sending long-range patrols into the Pacific Ocean, and conducting combat drills around the island democracy of Taiwan, which Beijing claims as its territory.

Such forward-leaning diplomacy won plaudits at home but rankled audiences abroad. Beijing's forceful assertion of territorial claims—from building artificial islands in the South China Sea to sending civilian fishing fleets and coast guard craft into disputed waters—inflamed tensions with Asian neighbors and sparked border skirmishes with India. Western democracies denounced the party's overseas outreach as influence-peddling operations, while Xi's appeals for a Chinese diaspora to rally around their motherland irked countries with large ethnic Chinese communities. Beijing's "wolf warrior" diplomats riled foreign governments with pugnacious behavior aimed at satisfying Xi's demands for a more combative statecraft. China engaged in what critics condemned as "hostage diplomacy," detaining foreign nationals for leverage in disputes with other powers. African governments that received copious Chinese aid faced domestic anger over Beijing's allegedly neocolonialist practices. Anti-China sentiment surged, particularly in the West, as the novel coronavirus emerged in the central Chinese city of Wuhan and engulfed the world—a resentment aggravated by the party's efforts to shout down criticism of its Covid-19 response and questions about the contagion's origins.

The rise of a confident, uncompromising China grated most of all on the United States, the incumbent superpower that spent decades engaging Beijing and building economic ties so deep that academics dubbed the economic relationship "Chimerica." Today, U.S. politicians and academics warn of a "new Cold War" as Washington vies with Beijing over trade, technology, military power, and global influence. Getting tough on China has become bipartisan consensus in a divided Washington. Both Democrats and Republicans have demanded action against Beijing's industrial policies and human rights abuses, particularly its treatment of

Muslim minorities in Xinjiang and the suppression of dissent in the former British colony of Hong Kong.

Xi's methods have been questioned at home too. Party insiders blame his domineering style for stifling internal debate and leading to policy blunders. His top-down leadership engenders excessive bureaucracy, as officials resort to inaction, duplicity, and other unproductive practices to please Beijing and protect their careers. Some of Xi's most ambitious programs appear to have stalled, with his Belt and Road initiative drawing backlash for saddling developing countries with debt and plans to build a new economic center—the "Xiong'an New Area" in northern China—yielding sparse progress. Despite Xi's dominance, he has struggled to enact crucial but contentious reforms to address China's declining productivity and aging population. His zero-tolerance approach to Covid-19, while successful in containing the virus during early phases of the pandemic, throttled the domestic economy and inflamed social tensions with harsh lockdowns (before unraveling in the face of faster-spreading Covid variants). On social media, where embers of political satire still flicker, detractors deride Xi as the "accelerator-in-chief," implying that his full-throttle authoritarianism will send the party careening toward collapse.

Xi has remained resolute. He renewed demands for ideological probity and patriotic zeal. He blamed policy inertia and missteps on the moral failings of individual officials, eliding the structural ills endemic in a one-party system and aggravated by his centralization of power. Those who dared question his leadership were harassed, locked up, or forced into exile. China's proclaimed success in challenging the West across economic and military fronts vindicated Xi's methods in the eyes of many Chinese. And where he recognized shortcomings in his system, he doubled down on his prescribed remedies, insisting that the party become stronger and more loyal than ever to its leader.

These maneuvers propelled Xi's authority to a new zenith in 2022. He pushed rivals into retirement, packed allies into the party leadership, took a norm-breaking third term as general secretary, and declined to designate an heir apparent—all but obliterating his predecessors' efforts to ensure regular succession. After a decade in power, Xi had cemented his status as China's most formidable leader since Mao. But while his ruling party projects imperious confidence, a seemingly stable system can prove surprisingly brittle—particularly one built so inextricably around one man. His accession was only the second time the People's Republic conducted a handover of power that was triggered neither by the leader's death nor a political crisis. Now poised to rule indefinitely without a clear successor, Xi represents key-person risk like no other, a singular vulnerability that could unleash profound consequences for China and the rest of the world.

How did Xi upend decades of collective leadership and realign Chinese politics around himself? Can his autocratic turn save the party, or does it sow the seeds for future turmoil? Will he make the world safe for an increasingly authoritarian China, or return his country to the ruinous days of one-man rule? These questions have become harder to answer. Foreign journalists face growing harassment and even expulsion. Diplomats lament shrinking access to Chinese officials. Some academics now think twice about visiting the People's Republic, concerned that they may be detained. Foreign businesses are reconsidering their investments as the Chinese economy grows increasingly opaque and driven by political imperatives. Fearmongering and misinformation about China have colored public opinion and policy debates as governments around the world seek a new modus vivendi with Beijing.

For decades, deciphering the party's intentions and dissecting its inner workings have been the preserve of specialists—academics, diplomats, corporate executives, and journalists. Today, encounters with China are no longer a matter of choice. The party of Xi reaches around the globe, and its decisions affect politics, business, and ordinary lives just about anywhere—from Wall Street and Silicon Valley to far-flung factory floors intertwined with Chinese trade. Understanding China has never been more essential. To do so, one must start by seeing the world through the eyes of its most powerful leader in generations, and the political machine that he commands.

CHAPTER ONE

ASCENDANT XI

THE PARTY MAKETH THE MAN

"People who have little contact with power, who are far from it, always see these things as mysterious and novel. . . . I understand politics on a deeper level."

—Xi Jinping

"In their minds, princelings believe that 'all under heaven are ours to rule; if we don't do it, who will?'"

—Cai Xia, former Central Party School professor

"Going into politics means one cannot dream of getting rich. Just as Sun Yat-sen said, one must set their mind to do great things."

—Xi Jinping

On a chilly, overcast morning in the spring of 2018, China crowned a president who may rule for life. The gloomy skies over Beijing shed a sliver of snowfall as nearly three thousand lawmakers arrived for the occasion at the Great Hall of the People, a cavernous coliseum that has hosted some of the nation's grandest pageantry since the Mao era. These officials, soldiers, entrepreneurs, scholars, workers, and villagers had gathered from across China to ruminate on affairs of the state, an annual assembly choreographed to portray a nation united in harmony. Together they constitute the National People's Congress, a legislative body that is controlled by the Communist Party but claims to channel the collective will of 1.4 billion people. Tasked with choosing a head of state that day, they voted as one, for the only man on the ballot: Xi Jinping.

The unanimous result drew rapturous applause from lawmakers, who cheered their newly re-elected president with a standing ovation. Dressed in a dark business suit with a violet tie, Xi clapped briefly and bowed in a customary show of humility. Minutes later, after a military band played a rousing rendition of the national anthem, Xi strode toward the lectern. Raising his right fist and placing his left palm flat on a copy of China's constitution, Xi recited his oath of office with a measured cadence, vowing to "build a modern socialist power that is prosperous, strong, democratic, culturally advanced, harmonious and beautiful."[1]

For the first time in thirty-five years, a Chinese head of state was inaugurated with no limits on his tenure. And in a departure from two decades of precedent, a Chinese president was starting his second term without a deputy young enough to be his successor. Xi could stay in office indefinitely, and was in effect telling the world that he would.

China's presidency is largely ceremonial. An incumbent signs legislation into effect, appoints senior government officials, and conducts the pomp and ceremony of statecraft. In Chinese, the title literally means "state chairman," echoing Chairman Mao's most famous honorific. The head of state is China's face to the world, presented to audiences abroad as "president," a label shorn of the authoritarian aura that shrouds leaders of one-party regimes. And while he does possess the awesome executive authority wielded by counterparts in the United States and Russia, those powers come not from the presidency, but from two other roles he concurrently serves.

The first is general secretary of the Communist Party's Central Committee, the highest office in a sprawling political machine that boasts more than 96 million members and has governed China since 1949. The other is chairman of the party's Central Military Commission, a council of mostly martial men who command the armed forces. These positions are the true keys to the Middle Kingdom, controlling the most powerful organs of state in one of the world's most populous nations. It was these two posts that Xi acquired when taking power in November 2012, months before his first inauguration as president in the following spring.

Only one office in this trinity, the state presidency, had been constrained by clear term limits. Constitutional decree, until 2018, compelled the president to step aside after two five-year terms. The party positions of general secretary and military-commission chairman faced no such restraint. While the party's governing charter prohibited life tenure for its leaders, it didn't specify how long they could hold office.

The party had provisional regulations stating that officials in leadership roles couldn't stay in the same post beyond ten years, or remain at the same level of the party for more than fifteen. But these rules could be easily revised or revoked, and some insiders said they didn't apply to top leaders.[2]

The restriction on presidential terms dated back to the early 1980s, when China was still reeling from the upheavals unleashed by its last leader to rule for life. From his proclamation of the People's Republic in 1949 till his death in 1976, Mao Zedong ran a brutal dictatorship that ravaged China with mass purges, economic collapse, and one of history's deadliest famines. His despotic instincts spurred bloody suppressions of dissent and perceived class enemies. His ideological dogma drove the "Great Leap Forward," a disastrous attempt to industrialize China's agrarian economy that ended up starving tens of millions to death. His megalomania enkindled the 1966–1976 Cultural Revolution, a fanatical movement that purported to defend China against capitalist restoration but tore society asunder.

The task of healing this generational trauma fell to Deng Xiaoping, a revered revolutionary who deposed Mao's successor to become paramount leader. Already in his seventies when he took power, Deng devoted himself to stamping out the vestiges of Maoism and devising safeguards against one-man rule. In a landmark 1980 speech, he called for reforms to encourage power-sharing, promote succession, and ensure that no leadership post could be held indefinitely.[3] His demands yielded China's 1982 constitution, which imposed term limits on major offices of state—like the presidency and the premiership—that allowed appointees to serve no more than two consecutive stints of five years.

But Deng operated above his own strictures, never serving as the titular party chief or head of state even as he wielded preponderant sway until his death in 1997. He fashioned himself a trustee of the nation, whose job was to deliver a stable and prosperous China by creating power structures conducive to collective leadership and peaceful succession.[4] He allowed his protégés and peers to hold office as general secretary, premier, and president, while he kept control over the People's Liberation Army as military commission chairman. This arrangement crumbled in the heat of crisis during the 1989 Tiananmen Square protests, when divisions within the leadership hampered a decisive response. Deng ultimately decided to crush the demonstrations with deadly force, and purged the incumbent general secretary—a protégé whom he blamed for supporting the protesters and splitting the party.

Deng tried a different tack after sending the PLA to put down the protests in what became known as the June 4 massacre. He opted to centralize key powers with one man, who would be kept in check by influential peers. His choice of heir was Jiang Zemin, a compromise candidate plucked from Shanghai to replace the previous general secretary. When Jiang assumed the presidency in 1993, he became the first Chinese leader since Mao to hold office as head of the party, military, and state concurrently. Even so, Jiang often found himself hemmed in by powerful rivals and had to govern as "first among equals." He couldn't even pick his successor, a choice all but made for him by Deng.

Jiang stepped down as party chief and president on time, in late 2002 and early 2003 respectively, but clung to his military title for roughly two more years. His successor, Hu Jintao, a colorless technocrat, was even more scrupulous in abiding by the ten-year limit. Hu handed over all three posts to Xi on schedule, completing the smoothest leadership transition that Communist China had managed to date. Analysts marveled at the achievement, declaring that the party had translated constitutional procedure into established practice, and allowed Chinese politics to evince a predictability that a few decades earlier would have seemed unthinkable.

Xi started reversing this trajectory almost immediately. He named himself head of party committees overseeing economic reforms, internet policy, military overhauls, and national security—prompting Australian sinologist Geremie Barmé to call him the "Chairman of Everything."[5] Just eighteen months after taking power, Xi was appearing in the party mouthpiece *People's Daily* with a frequency unseen since Mao, and nearly twice as often as his predecessor.[6] Xi sidelined the party's number two leader, Premier Li Keqiang, and siphoned off the prime minister's traditional influence over economic affairs. The Central Committee acclaimed Xi as the "core" of the party's fifth-generation leadership, cementing his preeminence with a title that had eluded the feeble Hu.

Xi stepped up his power grab at the party's nineteenth national congress in 2017, when he rewrote the party charter to include a political slogan bearing his name: "Xi Jinping Thought on Socialism with Chinese Characteristics for a New Era." Only Mao and Deng had enjoyed such an honor previously, with "Mao Zedong Thought" and "Deng Xiaoping Theory" consecrated alongside Marxism-Leninism as the party's guiding ideologies. "Writing Xi Jinping's name into the party charter is like making his words part of the holy scripture," said Ding Xueliang, a Hong Kong–based professor and expert on Chinese politics. "As long as Xi's alive, his words would matter. He would have the final say."[7]

Just as tellingly, the congress didn't promote to the Politburo Standing Committee, the party's top decision-making body, anyone young enough to be considered

Xi's successor. For the first time in two decades, an incumbent general secretary was starting his second term without an understudy. China's chattering classes went wild with speculation that Xi would outstay his expected decade as leader. The rumors intensified when the party announced weeks later that it was drafting unspecified changes to the national constitution.

Xi revealed his hand in late February 2018, just a week before China started its annual legislative session. The government-run Xinhua News Agency issued a bulletin listing twenty-one proposed amendments, with the bombshell tucked away fourteenth on the list. Article 79, which defined the terms of office for the president and vice president, would be trimmed, removing a clause stating that the head of state and their deputy "shall serve no more than two consecutive terms."

The proposal shocked many Chinese. Their country may have attained the trappings of capitalist modernity—sleek skylines, glitzy consumer brands, and high-tech infrastructure—but their politics was backsliding toward what many considered a bygone era. Wang Gongquan, a venture capitalist turned activist, denounced the planned amendment as "a reversal in our political culture." Some social media users shared images of Winnie the Pooh—the cartoon bear whom Xi purportedly resembles—dressed as a Chinese emperor.[8] Others joked that China was becoming "West Korea" by mimicking the despotic Kim dynasty in Pyongyang. Immigration consultants noted an uptick in queries from Chinese citizens considering new lives abroad.

Censors and propagandists went into overdrive. State media justified the scrapping of presidential term limits as necessary for giving China the "centralized and unified leadership" that it needs. The *People's Daily* assured readers that "this amendment doesn't portend changes to the retirement system for leading party and state officials, nor does it mean life tenure for leading cadres."[9] Officials feted Xi with reverential labels like "helmsman" and *lingxiu*, or leader, that were closely associated with Mao. The party chief of the northwestern province of Qinghai, home to a large Tibetan Buddhist population, said authorities there encouraged resettled nomadic herders to "love their leader" by hanging Xi portraits in their new homes. Ordinary folks called Xi "a living Bodhisattva," he said, using a Buddhist term for enlightened devotees who carry out altruistic acts.[10]

When the constitutional changes were put to a vote at the National People's Congress in March 2018, just six of the 2,964 delegates present demurred, casting two dissents, three abstentions, and one invalid vote to yield a 99.8 percent approval rate. The result inspired gallows humor among some Chinese liberals, who mused that the dissenting delegates were the modern-day "six gentlemen of Wuxu," a group of intellectuals executed by the imperial Qing government in 1898 for championing ill-fated political reforms. The vast majority of lawmakers, meanwhile, fawned over their leader. "Under President Xi's leadership, we are certain to achieve the 'China Dream,'" said Song Fengnian, a septuagenarian NPC member who wore a Mao suit for the occasion, complete with a Communist Party flag pin and a Mao badge. "This is the wish of the people." Days later, the legislature voted unanimously to give Xi a second term as president.

The party now recounts Xi's rise with the teleological certitude it uses for proclaiming China's inexorable return to greatness. But there was nothing preordained about his ascent. Xi suffered political persecution during his formative years, his career in local and regional government appeared undistinguished, and his rivals sometimes seemed likelier to succeed. When he first emerged as heir apparent, some observers argued that the party's kingmakers saw in Xi a pliable puppet, crediting his rise to his perceived weakness.

Nicholas Kristof, a former China correspondent and Pulitzer Prize winner, made a bold prediction in a January 2013 op-ed for the *New York Times*: "The new paramount leader, Xi Jinping, will spearhead a resurgence of economic reform, and probably some political easing as well. Mao's body will be hauled out of Tiananmen Square on his watch, and Liu Xiaobo, the Nobel Peace Prize–winning writer, will be released from prison." Kristof was optimistic that "change is coming" to China under a new leader who inherited reformist instincts from his late father, the revolutionary hero Xi Zhongxun. "I'm betting that in the coming 10 years of Xi's reign, China will come alive again," he wrote.[11] Some Chinese intellectuals even suggested that Xi could emulate Taiwan's President Chiang Ching-kuo, who before his death in 1988 started reforms that spurred the island's transition to democracy from the military dictatorship imposed by his father, Chiang Kai-shek.

Such optimism was misplaced. Mao remained in his hallowed mausoleum. Authorities released Liu from prison in 2017, but only on medical parole before he died of cancer while receiving treatment under police guard. Xi secured a third term as party chief in 2022 and seems set to stay in power for many years to come. Change did come to China, just not the kind for which Kristof and others hoped.

Xi's first decade in power has laid bare his hyper-authoritarian doctrine. He sidelined rivals, purged corrupt and indolent officials, and demanded unstinting loyalty from the rank and file. He quashed activism, silenced dissent, and built an unprecedentedly sophisticated surveillance state to assert control over society. He padded the party's Marxist maxims with Confucian wisdoms and rallied nationalistic fervor around one-party rule. As some historians now argue, the paternal legacy that Xi inherited wasn't his father's liberal leanings, but his unstinting devotion to the party and its interests, regardless of private doubt.[12]

The misjudgment of Xi was no accident. To ascend the byzantine world of Chinese politics, where officials who advertise allegiances too firmly expose themselves to reprisals when orthodoxies change, Xi made himself inoffensive and inscrutable in his early career. He appeared amenable to friends and rivals alike, with his public remarks seldom straying from perfunctory praise for party policies and routine condemnation of corruption and red tape. Unvarnished accounts of his personal life are rare and patchy. In 2000, while he was a provincial governor, Xi said he had rejected more than one hundred interview requests.[13] Even some of Xi's fellow princelings concede to having misjudged a longtime friend.

Nonetheless, as the celebrated American biographer Robert Caro observed, power reveals. "When a man is climbing, trying to persuade others to give him power, concealment is necessary: to hide traits that might make others reluctant to give him power, to hide also what he wants to do with that power," Caro wrote in the fourth volume of his biography of U.S. president Lyndon Johnson. "But as a man obtains more power, camouflage is less necessary. The curtain begins to rise. The revealing begins."[14]

With the benefit of hindsight, Xi's words and deeds, paired with contemporary and retrospective accounts from those who knew him, offer a more complete and complex portrait of China's most dominant leader since Mao. It reveals a man fired with ambition and steeled by adversity; a red aristocrat who embraced his noblesse oblige and sees leadership as a birthright; a flexible apparatchik who trimmed his sails to prevailing orthodoxies; and a savvy streetfighter who sidestepped scandals and exploited good fortune to carve a path to power.

A PRINCELING'S BIRTH

XI JINPING WAS BORN ON June 15, 1953, in Beijing, the third of four children to a revolutionary couple.[15] His given name, a nod to the capital's old appellation of Beiping, can translate as "near peace." His father, Xi Zhongxun, was a propaganda minister at the time, brought into the central government after decades of distinguished military service against Chiang Kai-shek's Nationalist Party and the invading Japanese army. His mother, Qi Xin, joined the revolution during World War II and worked at an elite party academy. Less than four years after Mao proclaimed the People's Republic, the Communist leadership was grappling with the realities of nation-building, from formulating their first five-year plan for economic development to negotiating an armistice to end the Korean War. Those were difficult but heady years, buoyed by patriotic zeal and a sense of possibility in forging a "new China."

Many second-generation reds, or *hongerdai*, grew up in a bubble of relative luxury in central Beijing. Families of senior officials typically lived in large court-yard homes, enjoyed access to foreign books and films, and sent their children to top schools. Privileges were pegged to rank, and those who qualified could enjoy perks such as official cars, security details, superior health care, and access to exclusive entertainment venues and summer resorts.[16] In 1956, salaries for top Communist Party and government officials were 36.4 times the wages earned by the lowest-level bureaucrats—far outstripping the equivalent pay gap within Chiang's Nationalist government in 1946, when top officials out-earned the most junior ranks by 14.5 times.[17]

Even so, party histories remember Xi Zhongxun as a virtuous politician who enforced austerity and rectitude at home.[18] His marriage to Qi Xin in 1944 was his second, a union that bore two daughters—Qi Qiaoqiao in 1949 and Xi An'an in 1951—and two sons, Xi Jinping and Xi Yuanping, the latter born in 1956. Qi Xin had to live at the party academy, so the elder Xi spent more time caring for their children—bathing them, washing their clothes, and taking them on weekend out-ings.[19] The patriarch told so many stories about his revolutionary exploits that his children's ears "grew calluses," Xi Jinping later recalled.[20] "Among the children in our family, Jinping was the most mischievous and the smartest," Xi's half brother Zhengning told an acquaintance. "Father loved him the most."[21]

Xi Zhongxun was a strict and frugal parent. He often declined gifts for his children. He taught them to save water and electricity. He often forced his sons to wake up late at night and wash themselves in bathwater he had used earlier—a practice that Xi Jinping later said he feared most during his childhood.[22] The patriarch also made his sons wear their elder sisters' castoff clothes, which on one occasion made Xi Jinping cry before his father pacified him by dyeing the clothes black with ink, Qi recalled.[23] Each Xi child commuted to school by bus and received so little pocket money that if they splurged on ice sticks, they wouldn't be able to afford their bus fares and had to walk home. The elder Xi instructed his personal aide not to indulge his children if they asked for extra cash.[24] "Sometimes," Qi later wrote in an essay, "I really felt that you were too demanding of our children."[25]

Xi Zhongxun insisted that his children finish every scrap of food, even dropped rice grains, and often cited a verse from Tang dynasty poet Li Shen: "Hoeing grass under the noonday sun, his sweat drips onto the soil beneath. Who knows that the food on their plate, every grain came from hardship."[26] His children would answer with another Li verse: "A single seed sown in spring, yields ten thousand grains by autumn. No field in the world lies fallow, yet farmers still die of hunger."[27]

The elder Xi saw himself as "a son of peasants."[28] Born into a rural landown-ing family in China's northern province of Shaanxi in 1913, he encountered Marx-ism in school and joined the Communist Youth League in 1926, when he was just twelve. Two years later, Xi spent time in jail for inciting student protests and became a full-fledged party member—at the age of fourteen—during the months he spent in prison. He became a guerrilla fighter after his release, establishing himself as a young commander as he helped set up a revolutionary base in Shaanxi and its neighboring province of Gansu. His prodigious career almost ended in 1935, when party rivals accused him of disloyalty and threatened to bury him alive before Mao intervened. Undeterred by the experience, he proved his mettle in combat against Nationalist forces and Japanese invaders. Mao praised Xi for his selfless service to the revolution, and in 1943 gifted him a piece of calligraphy: "The party's interests come first."[29]

After the Communist victory, Xi oversaw political and military affairs in north-western China as a regional official, before Mao summoned him to Beijing in 1952 to become the party's propaganda minister. The following year, he took an assignment as secretary general at the State Council, as China's cabinet is known, where he assisted Premier Zhou Enlai in policy-making. He continued climbing the hierarchy through the decade, winning promotion to the party's Central Committee in 1956 and then vice premier in 1959.

Notwithstanding Xi's efforts to shield his children from morally corrosive privi-lege, they received some of the best schooling that Maoist China had to offer. A young Xi Jinping went to the Beihai Kindergarten, an elite facility that catered to offspring of senior officials, established in 1949 on the grounds of an imperial altar near the Forbidden City and the Zhongnanhai leadership compound housing the party and government's headquarters. He then attended elementary school and junior high at the exclusive Bayi School, named after the PLA's founding anniversary on August 1.[30]

Founded in 1947 to educate the children of Red Army officials as well as revolutionary veterans and martyrs, the Bayi School drew on military tradition and discipline. Students lived on campus, performed morning calisthenics, sang revolutionary songs, and formed ranks for meals and roll calls. Its Beijing premises, built in the early 1950s, comprised modern furnishings, heated classrooms and dorms, and even its own farm that supplied students with pork, eggs, milk, and watermelons.[31]

Alumni from the Mao era recall a campus steeped in machismo, where students often brawled, hurled profanities, and disdained "softness and delicateness."[32] Populated with the children of high-ranking cadres, known colloquially as *gaogan zidi*, the school also drew ridicule as an "aristocratic" institution misaligned with the party's egalitarian ideals. Many students were lackadaisical about their studies and carried themselves with a sense of entitlement, often comparing and goading each other over their fathers' ranks and relative wealth. "We didn't sense it while we were inside," Liu Huixuan, a Bayi alumnus who spent a dozen years at the school from the 1950s to the 1960s, said in an autobiographical account. "But after leaving Bayi School and comparing, only then did we realize that place was really a jar of honey."[33]

Xi was about a year younger than most of his classmates. One of his primary-school teachers, Tian Luying, remembered him as a kind and conscientious pupil who enjoyed playing soccer.[34] Chen Qiuying, who taught Xi in middle school, recalled an inquisitive student who brought questions to teachers after class and admired the ancient Chinese poet Du Fu.[35]

Political turmoil breached the Bayi bubble. Mao's Great Leap Forward, a radical program launched in 1958 to transform an agrarian society into an industrial powerhouse, instead devastated agriculture and caused mass starvation that killed tens of millions. Even Bayi's relative luxuries couldn't prevent students from going hungry during the Great Famine of 1959 to 1961. Some recalled eating spoiled buns and meals made from stale grain contaminated with rat feces.[36]

The economic disaster fueled party infighting. Senior leaders tried to rein in Mao's radical policies. Mao and his loyalists struck back, engineering intrigue against perceived rivals. Xi Zhongxun fell victim in the fall of 1962, when the leadership purged him for allegedly leading an anti-party clique that sought to seize power.[37]

The purported proof of Xi's conspiracy was his support for the publication of a novel celebrating the revolutionary martyr Liu Zhidan. The book featured characters modeled after Xi and another prominent revolutionary, Gao Gang, who fought alongside Liu in northwestern China before Liu was killed in 1936. Xi worked closely with Gao through the mid-1940s, though their paths had diverged by the time Gao was purged in 1954 for trying to oust two other party elders. Gao's name became a byword for treachery, and he killed himself later that year.

Mao's security chief, Kang Sheng, denounced the novel as a manifesto for Xi Zhongxun and his alleged co-conspirators. "Making use of a novel to carry out anti-party activities is a major invention," Kang wrote in a note to Mao, who read it aloud during a Central Committee meeting and effectively condemned Xi.[38] Despite Xi's protests of innocence, the party stripped him of his posts and revoked almost all the official perks that his family had enjoyed.

Xi struggled emotionally with his downfall, and Zhou Enlai told Qi Xin to make sure that her husband didn't try to harm himself, according to historian Joseph Torigian, who cited memoirs, unpublished diaries, and interviews with friends of the family.[39] In an essay, Qi recalled her husband sitting silently in the living room with the lights off, a puzzling sight for their younger daughter An'an, who asked: "Daddy, what's the matter?" Their younger son, Yuanping, asked: "Daddy, why aren't you going to Zhongnanhai?"[40]

Xi Jinping's Bayi classmates likely ostracized him. The party categorized people by their *jieji chengfen*, a concept of class status akin to a caste system, and Xi Zhongxun's downfall tainted his family. Liu, the Bayi alumnus, recalled a fellow student whose application to join the Communist Youth League was rejected because his father was allegedly associated with the elder Xi.[41]

The party eventually ordered Xi Zhongxun to undergo political education at the Central Party School, where he was confined inside his house and made to study writings by Marx, Lenin, and Mao, as well as avoid interaction with outsiders.[42] In summer 1965, Xi wrote to Mao asking to be sent to work in the countryside. Mao had other ideas, dispatching him instead to the central city of Luoyang to become a deputy manager at a tractor factory. Xi wouldn't see his family for seven years.

DISASTROUS DECADE

THE WORST WAS TO COME for the Xis. In May 1966, Mao launched what would become the most radical and destructive of his mass purges: the Great Proletarian Cultural Revolution. Historians believe Mao's goals were twofold. Stung by his loss of prestige from the Great Leap Forward, the Chairman wanted to reclaim his authority that other party elders had siphoned from him. The movement, as Mao envisioned, would also tear down the party's ossifying bureaucracy, cleanse its ranks of self-serving apparatchiks, and restore revolutionary fervor to China.

Mao declared that the party had been infiltrated by bourgeois elements seeking to restore capitalism, and urged his supporters to wage violent class struggle to eliminate these so-called revisionists. Militant students answered his call, forming "Red Guards" to defend the revolution. Mobs of fanatical youth hurled abuse and tortured alleged counter-revolutionaries in public "struggle sessions." Marauding Red Guards rampaged through museums, libraries, and religious sites to destroy art, books, and cultural relics regarded as the "Four Olds" of Chinese society—old customs, old culture, old habits, and old ideas. Many of their victims, from officials and their relatives to famous artists and writers, were injured, killed, or driven to suicide.

Xi Zhongxun, already a pariah, suffered further persecution, getting abused in struggle sessions and thrown into detention. Red Guards ransacked his home, and his wife and children were forced out of Beijing. Official accounts say his eldest daughter, Heping, the oldest of three children with his first wife, was "persecuted to death," which some historians and party insiders say meant that she was hounded into killing herself.

Xi Jinping was turning thirteen when the Cultural Revolution began. While many *hongerdai* formed their own Red Guard units, Xi was too young and tainted by his father to join. Peers pilloried and publicly shamed him. Chen, the Bayi teacher, recalled how Xi once told her about a physical education teacher who bullied him and denounced him for being a child of "black gangs," an epithet for politically disgraced officials. "During the 10-year catastrophe of the 'Cultural Revolution,' he endured a lot of arduous trials," Chen wrote. "But he believed the dark clouds would always disperse, and that under any circumstance, one should be full of confidence in the future."[43]

After Red Guards forced the Bayi School to shut down in 1967, Xi moved to Beijing's Number 25 Middle School along with Liu Weiping, a son of a general who had been purged for crossing one of Mao's top lieutenants. The pair befriended Nie Weiping, a student at the Number 25 school who would become a grandmaster of the ancient board game of Go. Nie himself had fallen into disgrace after his parents were accused of colluding with black gangs. Together the boys became known as the "three Pings," a nod to the common character in their names.

With little classroom education on offer, Xi often roamed the streets and read books taken from deserted schools and libraries, according to a family friend.[44] On one occasion, the trio heard that feuding Red Guard factions were gathering at a Beijing school, and they went over to see what would happen. Soon after the three arrived and joined a large group of gathered students, militants sprung their ambush from the school hall. "Hundreds of people wielding clubs came shouting and rushing out, and they beat whomever they saw," Nie wrote in a memoir.[45] "The three of us turned and ran to where we locked our bicycles," he recalled. "Xi Jinping and I moved fast and escaped, but Liu Weiping ran a step slower and was beaten into a concussion."

Xi escaped physical injury but not psychological trauma. In interviews and writings decades later, he recounted how he was jailed three to four times and pressed into struggle sessions, where Red Guards hurled slurs and threatened to execute him.[46] "Because I was stubborn and unwilling to be bullied, I offended the rebel faction," Xi told a state-run magazine in 2000.[47] "Anything that was bad was blamed upon me; they thought I was a leader." At one point, Red Guards denounced Xi as "anti-revolutionary" for allegedly speaking up against the Cultural Revolution, forced him to wear a cone-shaped dunce cap, and paraded him at a public-shaming rally, according to one of his father's associates, Yang Ping, who recounted conversations with Xi Zhongxun and other members of his family.[48] Qi Xin attended the struggle session, and "when they yelled, 'Down with Xi Jinping!' on the stage, his mother was forced to raise her arm and shout the slogan along with everyone," Yang wrote.

"They asked me how bad I thought my crimes were," Xi Jinping recalled of one encounter with Red Guards. "I said that they should make a guess, was it enough to deserve being shot? They said it would be enough to be shot 100 times over. I thought, what was the difference between being shot once and 100 times?"[49]

Xi slipped out of detention one rainy night and ran home cold and hungry, hoping his mother would make him some food. But instead of feeding her son, Qi Xin reported him, worried that she would get detained for sheltering a "counter-revolutionary" and leave two of her other children by themselves with no one to care for them. Xi understood his mother's decision and ran off to find another hiding place, but was caught the next day, Yang wrote.[50]

In interviews recounting his experiences during the Cultural Revolution, Xi suggested that his family's misfortunes taught him the brutality of politics. To survive, and one day flourish, he would have to lie low and bide his time.[51] "People who have little contact with power, who are far from it, always see these things as mysterious and novel," Xi told a party-run magazine in 2000. "But what I see is not just the su-perficial things: the power, the flowers, the glory, the applause. I see the cowsheds"—makeshift detention houses—"and how people can blow hot and cold. I understand politics on a deeper level."[52]

The Mao era left a complex mark on Xi. Some historians believe the chaos of the Cultural Revolution seeded his fixation with authoritarian order. As paramount leader, Xi would acknowledge Mao's mistakes but also quote his maxims and borrow his political tactics. The hardship Xi endured also would become an asset, placing him on the right side of this dark history while many of his peers had to conceal their involvement in Red Guard atrocities.

By late 1968, Xi had been assigned to a juvenile detention center, but the facil-ity had no spare beds and he would have to wait a month before moving in. Right around then, Mao issued a call for urban youth to get "re-educated" by living and working in rural areas, a movement known as "Up to the Mountains and Down to the Countryside." Though the program had started years before as a way to ease urban unemployment, historians believe Mao ramped up the campaign to quell the rabid Red Guards who were barreling beyond his control. More than 17 million young Chinese were rusticated, or "sent down," across China between the 1960s and 1970s. Eager to escape persecution in Beijing, Xi joined the exodus.

RUSTICATED YOUTH

NEARLY THIRTY THOUSAND BEIJING YOUTH went to the countryside around Yan'an, a desolate stretch of northern Shaanxi that served as Mao's revolutionary base between the mid-1930s and late 1940s. Perched on the windswept Loess Plateau, a dusty highland known for its loose yellow earth, Yan'an in the late 1960s was impov-erished and isolated—an unforgiving crucible for city dwellers forced into rural life.

A fifteen-year-old Xi started his journey in January 1969. He felt something close to joy as the train prepared to leave Beijing. "Everyone was crying, there wasn't anyone on the entire train who didn't cry," Xi said in a 2004 television interview. "Only I was smiling. Of course, my relatives beside the train asked me, 'Why are you smiling?' I said if I didn't leave then I'd be crying. If I didn't leave, I wouldn't even know if I'd survive staying here."[53]

The Xi family has deep roots in Shaanxi. Xi Zhongxun's first wife, Hao Ming-zhu, was a fellow Shaanxi native, while his second marriage took place there as well. Five of his seven children from both marriages were born in Shaanxi. His brother, Xi Zhongkai, held senior roles in the provincial government. That Xi Zhongxun languished in the political wilderness for a decade and a half before his rehabilitation after the Cultural Revolution "made his political associations in Shaanxi more important," wrote Cheng Li, a senior fellow at the Washington-based Brookings Institution.[54] Xi Jinping too would regard his seven years in Shaanxi as the most defining period of his life.

Conditions on the Loess Plateau were grueling. Many newcomers struggled to cope with the harsh landscape, deprivation, and physical labor. A memorial in a Yan'an park lists the names of seventy-six rusticated youth from Beijing who lost their lives, including thirty-two who died during work and more than forty who passed away from disease and unnatural causes.[55] Some of them drowned because they naively tried to escape flash floods by running alongside the river.[56]

Xi Jinping was among fifteen youths assigned to Liangjiahe, a cluster of more than sixty households living in hillside cave dwellings, located about 160 miles northeast of his father's birthplace. Locals recalled a tall, slim, and introverted teenager who arrived with two heavy cases of books. Xi's time in the village started inauspiciously. Soon after arriving, he found a piece of stale bread in his bag and fed it to a dog, drawing attention from a villager who asked him what it was. His earnest response— that it was bread—sent residents gossiping about how Xi was a pampered urbanite who wasted precious food.

Rural hardships shocked Xi. "The first test was the flea test," he recalled in the 2004 interview.[57] "When I first got there, the thing I couldn't stand the most were the fleas. I don't know if they're still there. The fleas at the time, my skin was very allergic to them, their bites would turn my skin into swathes of red sores that became blisters that burst. Ah, it was so painful you didn't want to live."

Xi lived in a cave dwelling, shared with others, and typically rose at 6 a.m. to do menial farm work. He disliked the bland meals and often shirked the hard labor in the fields, even picking up a smoking habit so that he could take rest breaks rolling cigarettes for a puff. Overwhelmed by the drudgery, he ran back to Beijing after just three months, but was soon caught and detained for nearly half a year. Xi's maternal aunt, Qi Yun, and her husband admonished him for turning his back on the masses, and regaled him with stories about how they, as revolutionaries in Shaanxi decades earlier, cultivated close ties with ordinary folk. "I listened to them," Xi later recounted, and returned to Liangjiahe determined to overcome his misgivings about rural life.[58]

By his third year in Liangjiahe, Xi had mastered farm work and could speak the local dialect fluently. He plowed fields, ferried manure, and harvested wheat. He later claimed, rather incredibly, that he could carry two hundred *jin* of wheat for ten *li*, or about two hundred twenty pounds for just over three miles, without switching shoulders.[59] Around the village, he helped fetch water, cook meals, and dig new cave dwellings. Inside his cave, he sewed blankets, mended clothes, and read books into the night, smoking cigarettes by a small oil lamp.

Official accounts described Xi as a voracious reader who devoured titles like the *Communist Manifesto*, Lenin's *The State and Revolution*, and Mao's works on revolutionary strategy. He read books while herding sheep and learned new words from a dictionary during rest breaks from tilling fields. Decades later, Xi would often mention his appetite for books, saying he once walked thirty *li*, or a little more than nine miles, just to borrow a copy of Goethe's *Faust*.

The specter of persecution loomed large even in Liangjiahe. Xi, who sometimes gossiped about party intrigue with other rusticated youth, almost landed in trouble after a local cadre discovered that a letter he wrote contained references to Mao's wife, Jiang Qing. The cadre threatened to report Xi, but a mutual acquaintance appeased him by offering a gift of two military jackets.[60] Xi credited some of the goodwill he received to his father's reputation in Shaanxi.

Xi only saw his father again in 1972, after his mother asked Premier Zhou Enlai to arrange a family reunion. The patriarch could neither recognize his sons nor tell his two daughters apart. "He wept when he saw us, and I quickly offered him a cigarette and lit one up for myself as well," the younger Xi recalled. "He asked me, 'How come you also smoke?' I said: 'I'm depressed. We've also made it through tough times over these years.' He went quiet for a moment and said, 'I grant you approval to smoke.'"[61]

Both father and son kept their faith in the party, blaming their persecution on security chief Kang Sheng and his wife Cao Yi'ou.[62] While some of his peers scorned the party, the younger Xi decided to join it. He first sought membership in the Communist Youth League, though officials repeatedly rejected his applications due to his father's sullied standing. His persistence won over local cadres, including one who burned a dossier of "black material" sent from Beijing to discredit Xi. The youth league admitted him in 1972 on his eighth attempt. It then took him ten tries before becoming a party member in January 1974, after which Liangjiahe residents elected him, still only twenty years old, as their party secretary.

Xi's embrace of the party baffled some of his friends. Yi Xiaoxiong, a son of a former revolutionary persecuted by Red Guards, later told an American diplomat that he felt betrayed by Xi at the time. But Yi came to understand that Xi had chosen "to survive by becoming redder than the red," according to a leaked U.S. diplomatic cable that summarized his remarks.[63] In Xi's own telling, he found inspiration in his belief that he and his father were honest and upright. "It was just a feeling that the more good people there were in the party and the youth league, the fewer bad people there would be," he said.[64]

Xi was an enthusiastic village secretary. He led efforts to build dams, pave roads, and construct a methane tank to supply residents with gas for cooking and lighting.[65] But he was also making plans to leave, having seen other rusticated youth drift back to the cities to fill vacancies in factories, schools, and the military. Xi had applied to Beijing's esteemed Tsinghua University in 1973, but was rejected for being a "black gang child." At the time, college-entrance examinations were suspended and universities admitted students through political screening. Administrators selected applicants for their class background and political rectitude, and those chosen were known as "worker-peasant-soldier" students, which became a pejorative epithet insinuating a lack of intellectual bona fides.

Xi reapplied two years later when Tsinghua allotted two places to youth in Yan'an. This time, he had glowing recommendations from local officials and enjoyed a stroke of luck. Tsinghua's top two administrators, who were Mao loyalists, were absent when recruiters sought guidance on whether Xi could be admitted. The decision was left to a sympathetic deputy, who gave his approval after Xi Zhongxun sent a note saying his political problems shouldn't affect his children's education.[66] Villagers waited outside Xi's cave home to send him off the morning he left Liangjiahe in October 1975. The gesture moved Xi to tears, he recalled, only the second time that he cried during his years as a rusticated youth, the first being when he received a letter telling him his half sister Heping had died. That day about a dozen villagers walked with Xi to the county seat more than twelve miles away.

Seven years in Shaanxi hardened Xi. Friends say he gained an ability to relate to ordinary people and a desire to reclaim his family's status. Official accounts depict Liangjiahe as a centerpiece in Xi's political origin story, describing a transformative experience that ingrained in him a pragmatic can-do attitude and a sense of duty to the rural poor. In his own words, Xi said he came away determined to "do practical things for the people."[67] The village itself is now a popular "red tourism" destination for travelers keen on revolutionary history.

REHABILITATION

XI WAS AMONG NEARLY TWENTY-SEVEN HUNDRED students who enrolled at Tsinghua's Beijing campus in the fall of 1975.[68] The university had been a hotbed of fanaticism nearly a decade earlier, when students at the Tsinghua-affiliated middle school formed the first militant group to take the Red Guard name. A Tsinghua undergraduate, Kuai Dafu, emerged as a Red Guard leader who waged violent skirmishes against rival factions, including an infamous "hundred day war" on the Tsinghua campus in 1968.[69]

An uneasy calm had returned by the time Xi arrived as a worker-peasant-soldier student. He pursued a degree in organic chemistry, but university education at the time was more political than academic, marred by a lack of intellectual rigor and patchy teaching.[70] One friend described Xi's Tsinghua training as a degree in applied Marxism.[71] Not that it mattered to Xi, who told another friend that he had no plans to work in the chemical industry. Xi, the friend recalled, "wanted to enter politics."[72]

While many of his peers indulged in romance, alcohol, and movies, Xi focused on politics, overseeing propaganda work as a member of his class's party committee.[73] Friends recalled a budding politician who showed savviness beyond his years. One instance came in the wake of the "April 5 Movement" in 1976, when hundreds of thousands of people gathered at Beijing's Tiananmen Square to eulogize Zhou Enlai, who had died three months earlier, and criticize Jiang Qing and other Cultural Revolution leaders later condemned as the "Gang of Four." Security forces broke up the protests and hunted participants, some of whom had written and posted poetry on the square.

While Xi didn't participate, he sympathized with fellow students who joined the demonstrations and distributed the Tiananmen poems, according to a Tsinghua classmate, Wu Xiju. Xi helped shield these students from investigations, but avoided advertising his own leanings one way or the other. When the university later urged students to write articles denouncing Deng Xiaoping, whom the Gang of Four accused of orchestrating the April 5 Movement, Wu asked Xi if he wanted to contribute. Xi declined, saying he wasn't good at writing.[74]

Mao's death in September 1976 triggered a chain of events that smoothed Xi's path into politics. A bloodless coup soon toppled the Gang of Four. Deng, twice purged during the Cultural Revolution, maneuvered his way into power by ousting Mao's designated successor, Hua Guofeng. Xi Zhongxun was another beneficiary, rehabilitated in early 1978 and given a top post in the southern province of Guangdong. For the first time in a decade and a half, Xi Jinping was free from the stigma of being a "black gang child."

The elder Xi's three years in Guangdong sealed his legacy as a pioneer in Deng's "reform and opening up" program credited for spurring China's economic miracle. As the provincial party chief, Xi helped persuade Beijing to grant Guangdong greater autonomy on economic affairs, paving the way for one of China's first "special economic zones" and other policy experiments that would transform the province into a manufacturing hub and top exporter to foreign markets. His advocacy for market-style reforms was politically fraught at the time. Leftist conservatives who championed state planning remained a potent force within the party, and their opposition to China's capitalist tilt would continue simmering for decades. Nonetheless Xi Zhongxun's reputation as an economic reformer bequeathed a priceless political inheritance to his son, who could claim a personal connection to one of the party's most successful and popular policies.

Xi Jinping tasted front-line politics while visiting his father in Guangdong in summer 1978, when he joined an inspection tour and observed his father's interactions with local cadres and residents. As paramount leader, Xi would hearken back to that trip while highlighting his own contributions to China's economic development.

MILITARY MAN

BY THE TIME XI JINPING graduated from Tsinghua in 1979, his father had secured him a job as an aide to Geng Biao, a vice premier and the newly appointed secretary-general of the Central Military Commission. An old revolutionary comrade of Xi Zhongxun, Geng had served as an ambassador, vice foreign minister, and chief of the party's international liaison department before returning to a military role. He became defense minister in 1981.

A twenty-five-year-old Xi enlisted in the PLA to serve as one of Geng's three secretaries. He put on a uniform, handled confidential documents, and attended meetings with Geng, a security-conscious boss who often barred Xi from taking notes and made him memorize sensitive information, including hundreds of telephone numbers. Under pressure not to mess up vital details, Xi sometimes secretly scribbled notes and stuffed them into his pockets.[75] He also followed Geng on domestic inspection tours and overseas trips, his first time traveling abroad. During Geng's 1979 European tour,

Xi was joined by a young foreign ministry official by the name of Yang Jiechi, who later became China's top diplomat, a Politburo member, and a foreign policy adviser to Xi.[76]

Access to top-level defense deliberations educated Xi on the intricacies of diplomacy and military strategy, as well as territorial issues, including Beijing's sovereignty claims over the South China Sea and the self-ruled island of Taiwan. He would have witnessed Deng's efforts to court PLA backing to consolidate his power, and seen how the aftermath of the 1979 Sino-Vietnamese war, which ended in stalemate, spurred efforts to overhaul China's obsolescent Soviet-style military. Xi also gleaned insights into U.S.-China relations. Beijing had only just normalized ties with Washington and wanted to develop bilateral military links as a counterweight against the Soviet Union. In 1980, Geng visited the U.S. to negotiate the purchase of American weaponry and came back with deep appreciation of the technological gap between the two militaries—an insight he relayed to colleagues and subordinates, including Xi.

Geng became a lifelong mentor for Xi. The two men often rode in Geng's official Mercedes-Benz sedan and played Go to unwind. Geng believed that Go could develop a player's ability to think strategically, and asked his aides to learn the game. Xi sought coaching help from his friend Nie Weiping, but the grandmaster declined, concerned that he would lose face if Xi played badly.[77] Xi kept in touch with Geng after they stopped working together, continuing to address him as "chief" and visiting him almost every year until Geng's death in 2000. Decades later, Xi would cite his fondness for the PLA as he pushed to modernize the military.

During his military stint, Xi married a daughter of China's then ambassador to Britain. But the couple drifted apart and fought "almost every day," according to Yi, the longtime friend, who was living directly across the hall from Xi in a Beijing housing compound at the time. Xi and his wife divorced when she left for England and he refused to go with her, Yi was quoted as telling an American diplomat in the leaked cable.[78] Official biographies of Xi are silent on this marriage.

DOWN TO THE PROVINCES

XI JINPING SHED HIS UNIFORM after three years as a military aide, and threw himself into what would become a quarter century in local government. He told friends that leaving Beijing was a strategic choice, a way to learn new skills and gain valuable grassroots experience as China entered an era of economic development. One account described Xi's decision as partly driven by PLA downsizing. Geng needed to lose one member of his staff, and Xi, the youngest and least experienced of his three secretaries, volunteered.[79]

Geng tried to dissuade him, telling Xi he could tour the grassroots within the military. Xi had every chance of rising to the PLA's senior ranks, as some of his princeling peers would do. But his mind was set. In a conversation with Yi, Xi confided that going out into the provinces was his "only path to central power."[80] Staying put would leave Xi reliant on political networks that his father and Geng built, and curtail his own career potential in the long run, said Xi, who wanted to build his own power base.

Xi asked to be assigned a people's commune, a now-defunct administrative unit equivalent to a township. But provincial officials placed him one tier higher. In March 1982, Xi became deputy party secretary of Zhengding, a poor agricultural county of about four hundred thousand people in Hebei province, located roughly 150 miles southwest from Beijing. An ancient religious center sprinkled with Buddhist temples and pagodas built as early as the sixth century, the county had faded into a backwater known for producing grain. Zhengding schooled Xi in the grueling and unglamorous work required of rural officials, who front some of the party's most unpopular policies and suffer the scorn of residents who often see local cadres as brutish and venal functionaries. Xi later described the role of county official as one of the toughest and most important jobs in Chinese politics, tending to people's most basic needs while juggling political, economic, and even cultural affairs.[81]

Some Zhengding residents greeted the twenty-eight-year-old bureaucrat from Beijing with disdain, regarding Xi as an elite outsider parachuted in to lord over the locals. "Here comes someone with no hair above his lips to boss us around," muttered Jia Dashan, a popular local novelist and public servant, when Xi visited him for the first time.[82] Xi presented himself as an approachable and earnest official, wearing old military uniforms to work and queueing for canteen meals with subordinates. While most county officials got around by car, Xi often rode his bicycle into the countryside. He said it helped him reach out to ordinary folk, save gasoline, and get some exercise. Jia was among those won over by Xi, who later nominated the novelist to become director of Zhengding's culture bureau.

Promoted to county party chief in 1983, Xi tried leveraging Zhengding's cultural heritage to earn tourism revenues. When he heard that state broadcaster China Central Television was producing an adaptation of the classic Chinese novel *Dream of the Red Chamber*, he persuaded the producers to shoot the series in Zhengding. He raised funds to help build a permanent Rongguo Mansion, the fictional home to one of two families featured in the novel, which was used for the production and retained as a tourist attraction.[83] Xi also refurbished the county's many Buddhist temples and pagodas as a way of attracting more tourist spending.[84] His efforts dovetailed with a broader shift in religious policy—a part of Xi Zhongxun's portfolio at the time—that urged a more tolerant approach to managing faith and encouraged officials to restore and repair places of worship.

In Zhengding, Xi also cemented ties with allies who would rise with him to the party leadership. He befriended Li Zhanshu, the party chief of a nearby county who became one of Xi's closest confidants.[85] Wang Qishan, who would run Xi's anticorruption campaign decades later, was working at a central government office studying rural affairs at the time, and often hosted Xi and other local officials for policy discussions.[86]

Xi's record caught the eye of the Central Organization Department, the party's powerful personnel arm. Tasked in the early 1980s to revitalize the party's aging and decimated bureaucracy, the department set up a Young Cadres Bureau to identify a "third echelon" of promising officials, who could be groomed to succeed the first two generations of party leaders. Opinions were split over the selection process. Some party elders supported a meritocratic approach while others insisted on favoring children of high-ranking officials, citing their presumed loyalty to the party. The latter attitude was captured in an oft-repeated but possibly apocryphal anecdote about how the revolutionary elder Chen Yun once said: "Letting our children take over means they wouldn't dig up the ancestral graves."[87]

Yan Huai, a section chief at the Young Cadres Bureau, encountered Xi while touring Hebei in 1983 to assess third echelon candidates. Local bureaucrats told Yan that Xi was a hardworking and conscientious official with no airs, though some veteran cadres called him a privileged upstart who often proposed fancy, even impractical, ideas. Yan, himself a son of a revolutionary and fellow Tsinghua alumnus, gave Xi a positive appraisal. The following year, Xi was selected as one of Hebei's one thousand third echelon cadres, setting him up for a fast-tracked career.[88]

Xi Zhongxun lobbied on his son's behalf as well, asking Hebei party chief Gao Yang to look after Xi Jinping. But the intervention irked Gao, who in internal meetings raised concerns about the elder Xi's actions, according to recollections by Yan and his mentor Li Rui, a former Mao aide who served as the Central Organization Department's deputy chief around that time. Gao's revelations made it untenable for Xi Jinping to remain in Hebei, so the elder Xi sought help from an old friend, Xiang Nan, then party boss in the coastal province of Fujian and a prominent advocate of pro-market reforms.[89] The younger Xi gained a new mentor in Xiang and a transfer to Fujian's port city of Xiamen, where he was to become director of the municipal tourism bureau. The posting got better before he arrived. A Xiamen vice mayor stepped aside citing health reasons, and Xi was assigned to fill the vacancy.[90]

Xi has been circumspect about his father's role in his career. "It can't be said that there's absolutely no connection, but it also can't be said that I'm someone who lives off his father," he told a Hong Kong newspaper in 1989. "Frankly speaking, currently we still haven't set up a comprehensive cadre-selection system, and it's easy for leaders to promote and use people who are close and familiar to them."[91] As Xi reminded his interviewer, he first became a village official while his father was still politically disgraced. "This was a level playing field," he said. "There was no backdoor to use."

FUJIAN YEARS

XI ARRIVED IN XIAMEN on his thirty-second birthday, kicking off what would become a seventeen-year tour of Fujian. There he built his résumé as a local administrator and honed his craft as a glad-handing politician.

A culturally diverse region with a rich history of maritime trade on China's southeastern coast, Fujian exposed Xi to economic, social, and military affairs far removed from his experiences in the northern countryside. He sought ways to entice foreign capital and promote export industries, while fighting poverty and building up an economically laggard region. He encountered Fujian's cultural connections with the Chinese diaspora, particularly in Southeast Asia, where many Fujianese migrants had settled over past centuries. Xi also gained a familiarity with Taiwan, separated from Fujian by a strait roughly 110 miles wide, and a source of much-needed investment for Fujian, which Beijing had long regarded as a military frontier.

By most accounts, Xi's Fujian record was unremarkable. He earned a reputation as a conscientious official and acquainted himself with an influential superior who later joined the party's top leadership. But Xi's stint also coincided with sluggish growth, white elephant projects, and major corruption scandals. Willy Lam, a Hong Kong–based analyst of Chinese politics, described the period as "seventeen lackadaisical years in Fujian," during which Xi's performance "could not be called meteoric nor did he leave behind any major achievements."[92]

In Xiamen, where Xi served three years as vice mayor, he got his first taste of "reform and opening up" at one of its freewheeling urban front lines, brimming with fast-growing factories, commercial buzz, and the seedy side effects of fast money. He would also witness firsthand the bitter ideological feuding within the party. In June 1985, around the time Xi arrived in the port city, the *People's Daily* published a scathing report about a fake medicine scandal in a Fujian county, kicking off a state media offensive that blamed negligence by provincial authorities and the unbridled development of private enterprises. The real target was Xiang, the Fujian party chief, whose pro-business policies had irked conservative elders in Beijing. Despite interventions by his allies, including Xi Zhongxun, the scandal forced Xiang to step down from front-line politics in February 1986.

Party conservatives claimed another scalp in January 1987, unseating the liberal-minded Hu Yaobang as general secretary for allegedly mishandling student protests and economic reforms. Some insiders say Xi Zhongxun spoke fiercely in Hu's defense at a high-level meeting, though historian Joseph Torigian has cited evidence suggesting that this outburst didn't happen. And while the elder Xi was upset with his friend's ouster, he later voiced support for the decision—likely to protect himself. Either way, the purges of Xiang and Hu would have reinforced somber lessons for Xi Jinping: lying low and biding time were the safest ways to navigate party intrigue.

Those lessons were put to the test in late 1987, when a group of municipal lawmakers nominated Xi for Xiamen mayor. The gesture reflected Xi's popularity among the local elite but pitted him against the incumbent, who was seeking a second term as the party's preferred candidate. Xi knew better than to defy his superiors. He told them he would withdraw from the mayoral contest and support the party's choice, according to a senior Fujian official at the time.[93] Xi remained vice mayor until he left Xiamen the following year.

Xi's Xiamen stint was perhaps best known for its impact on his personal life. He befriended He Lifeng, a local bureaucrat who would become one of Xi's most trusted allies and a top economic official in his administration. In late 1986, friends introduced Xi to Peng Liyuan, a popular PLA folk singer nine years his junior and, at that point, far more famous than he was. At their first meeting, Peng wore military pants to test how much her date valued a woman's appearances. Xi also came modestly attired, and his first questions to Peng, she recalled, weren't the usual quizzing about her latest hits or the fees she earned, but an almost academic question about the number of ways to perform vocal music. "I'm very sorry, I watch very little television. What songs have you sung?" Xi asked. Peng named "In the Fields of Hope," a 1981 tune that had become one of her signature songs. "Oh," Xi said, "I've heard this song before, it's quite nice."[94]

They married in September 1987 with little fanfare, celebrating with Xi's colleagues at a hastily arranged dinner. One attendee was surprised to see Peng, only finding out then that she was the bride.[95] Xi later told Peng: "Having met you for less than 40 minutes, I had already decided that you'll be my wife." The couple spent long spells apart. Peng continued her singing career in Beijing, while Xi stayed in Fujian. He missed the birth of their daughter and only child, Mingze, in 1992 as he was busy directing typhoon relief operations.[96]

Marrying Peng reinforced Xi's military connections and added a dash of glamor to his staid image. As Xi's national profile grew in the 2000s, Peng became a vocal advocate for her husband, lauding him in interviews as a loving spouse and doting father. She took on a limited role in politics, becoming a member of a government advisory body and a goodwill ambassador for HIV/AIDS prevention. Within elite circles, she often presented herself as a face of the family, even speaking on her husband's behalf in private engagements.[97] The couple emulated many of their peers in the party elite by sending their daughter to attend college in the United States. Mingze studied at Harvard under an assumed name in the early 2010s, her true identity known only to a small number of faculty. She has kept a low profile since returning to China and rarely appears in public.

In 1988, Xi returned to the countryside as party chief of Ningde, a mountainous rural district of about 2.7 million people in eastern Fujian. Mired in poverty with few natural resources, the area had dim prospects that soured further as Beijing imposed austerity measures to combat inflation across the country. Xi's first challenge was tempering expectations. When he arrived, a veteran cadre introduced him to residents as a high-ranking official's son, who would "definitely go to the central government to get a few big projects" for Ningde, he recalled in a 1989 interview. The gesture appalled Xi, who later told local officials he had never gone to Beijing to solicit projects and wouldn't be able to secure any even if he did.[98] Xi directed efforts to fight rural poverty—one of his future priorities as paramount leader—and made a show of touring the countryside, even picking up a hoe to work the fields with farmers. He resettled thousands of fisherfolk from dilapidated junks into new housing on land. He also turned to what would become a signature theme of his leadership decades later: crushing corruption.

At the time, widespread malfeasance plagued Ningde, where many officials misappropriated land to build homes for themselves.[99] Xi ordered an anti-graft clampdown that uncovered wrongdoing by nearly 7,400 cadres, drawing attention from higher-ups and scoring national headlines. In May 1990, the *People's Daily* published a report titled "Doing One Thing Well and Winning Ten Thousand Hearts," praising Ningde as a shining example of how decisive leadership overcame a vexing problem and won over skeptical residents.[100]

The crackdown proved well timed, coming amid rising resentment over inflation and corruption kicked up by Deng's economic reforms. During the 1989 Tiananmen Square protests, which inspired similar demonstrations across China, including in Fujian, Xi treaded a careful line between mollifying public wrath and defending the party. Addressing local officials in May 1989, just as the protest movement climaxed, Xi acknowledged the anger over government graft but warned against what he called misguided solutions like unfettered democracy. He cited the Cultural Revolution as an example where democratic passions, mixed with superstition and stupidity, wreaked havoc. "Can these days be allowed to repeat?" he said. "Without stability and unity, nothing else matters!"[101]

It isn't clear what Xi thought of the bloodletting that ended the protests. Some party insiders said that Xi Zhongxun, then a senior legislative official, privately opposed the use of force and was sidelined again as a result, though historians haven't found any evidence suggesting that he took active steps to prevent the crackdown. Either way, the elder Xi soon retired, spending most of his final years in Shenzhen before passing away in a Beijing hospital in 2002, aged eighty-eight.

Xi Jinping remained a filial son throughout, showing profound respect for his father's character and legacy. When the patriarch celebrated his eighty-eighth birthday in 2001, the younger Xi was too busy to attend and wrote him a letter instead. "From the time people on the streets called us 'sons of bitches,' I've already firmly believed that my father is a big hero and a father most deserving of our pride," the son wrote. "Father has unwavering faith in Communism and believes that our party is great, glorious, and correct; your words and deeds have shown us the right way forward."[102]

In 1990, Xi earned a call-up to the provincial capital of Fuzhou, where he would stay for twelve years, first as the municipal party boss, before rising to Fujian governor, the provincial number two. As before, Xi tried to make a quick impression, going on a grassroots tour within days of his arrival and ingratiating himself with superiors and foreign diplomats.[103] He demanded urgency from his subordinates, telling them to work with a spirit of *mashang jiuban*, or "do it right away"—a slogan still displayed at Fuzhou's party headquarters today.[104] In early 1991, Xi's administration proposed building a large airport to serve Fuzhou, arguing that a shortage of air-transport links was impairing the city's growth. The Changle Airport project received speedy approval and construction commenced in 1993.

Following Deng Xiaoping's 1992 "southern tour," aimed at reviving economic reforms that had stalled in the aftermath of the Tiananmen Square crackdown, Xi embraced the message, traveling to places like British Hong Kong, Singapore, and the U.S. to solicit investments and commercial tie-ups. He courted ethnic Chinese entrepreneurs in Taiwan and Southeast Asia, touting Fujian's low labor costs and appealing to a sense of kinship among those with ancestral roots in the province. Xi scored a coup by bringing in Hong Kong tycoon Li Ka-shing to redevelop Fuzhou's historic Sanfang Qixiang, or "Three Lanes, Seven Alleys," into a lavish residential and commercial zone, a deal celebrated with a grand groundbreaking ceremony that Xi hosted for Li in 1993.

Some of these "prestige projects" would later be tarred by controversy. Fuzhou's Changle Airport fell far short of usage projections after it opened in 1997, suffering hefty losses and taking on heavy debt. A government audit blamed "unscientific" policy-making and poor management, and the airport underwent restructuring before turning its first annual profit in 2005.[105] Municipal authorities suspended and overhauled the Sanfang Qixiang development in the mid-2000s due to delays and public outrage over the razing of historical buildings.[106] The magnitude of these problems only became clear after Xi left his role as Fuzhou party chief in 1996 and the negative press left him unscathed. After Xi took power as paramount leader, state media rehabilitated both projects as examples of far-sighted leadership.

Military affairs proved more profitable for Xi's résumé building. He often held concurrent military roles across his Fujian posts, including first political commissar of a reserve anti-aircraft artillery division, familiarizing him with PLA operations during a period of heightened tensions between Beijing and Taipei. In public writings, he echoed the party leadership in denouncing Taiwan's then president for allegedly trying to "split the motherland," and urged efforts to strengthen China's military.[107]

He spared little expense backing the troops, apportioning funds to upgrade equipment and facilities, supplement stipends, and even help demobilized servicemen find new work. "There are no small matters in the military," he would say whenever a subordinate asked about troop-related expenses. "To meet the army's needs, nothing is excessive."[108] Beijing named Xi a model supporter of the armed forces—a reputation that he would replicate as paramount leader.

Local officials and journalists, however, saw Xi as a cautious and somewhat nondescript administrator, one who preferred working by the book and avoiding decisions that could backfire later. "Xi was a real goody-goody who spent a lot of time cultivating relationships with the military and party elders," hosting meals and visiting them during the Lunar New Year holidays, said Alfred Wu, a politics professor who met Xi on several occasions while working as a newspaper reporter in Fuzhou during the 2000s. "Back then he was rather bland and passive—even if he had the authority to do something, he often didn't use it."[109] When a government adviser suggested using tax rebates to boost certain local industries, Xi said he would consider the idea but never followed up on it, Wu recalled. The proposal faded away.

Xi won promotion to Fujian deputy party chief in 1995, setting up a shot at national politics two years later at the fifteenth party congress, where he joined the 344-strong Central Committee as a nonvoting alternate member. The appointment gave him access to key decision-making circles, but the manner of his entry was a source of embarrassment, coming dead last among the 151 alternates chosen in an internal poll. Given that party congresses had consistently yielded an even number of alternate Central Committee members since the 1970s, rumors swirled that influential patrons had shoehorned Xi into the committee by fiat.

Some observers blamed Xi's poor showing on anti-nepotism impulses within the party, as other princelings also received tepid support.[110] The party's embrace of technocratic leadership after Mao had fueled the rise of engineers-turned-administrators like Jiang Zemin and Hu Jintao, who both hailed from relatively humble backgrounds and built careers around their training in hard science. Regardless, the 1997 party congress was more boon than bane for Xi. He gained a foothold in the Beijing beltway, where he could cultivate more patrons. One of his former bosses, Jia Qinglin, who was Fujian's party chief from 1993 to 1996, joined the elite Politburo.

Such connections likely proved vital when Xi confronted his biggest crisis in Fujian, a massive smuggling and corruption scandal that implicated officials across all levels of government. The sordid affair erupted in 1999, when investigators from Beijing unearthed a criminal conspiracy led by Lai Changxing, a Fujianese farmer turned swaggering entrepreneur, whose Xiamen-based Yuanhua Group had been smuggling billions of dollars' worth of oil, cars, cigarettes, and appliances into China since the mid-1990s with help from military and police units. Authorities arrested hundreds of officials and businessmen, and executed more than a dozen people. Lai, who fled to Canada, is now serving a life sentence after being deported back to China in 2011 on Beijing's promise that he would not be executed.

Xi, who stepped up as Fujian governor while the scandal unfolded, was tasked with managing the political cleanup. He steered clear of controversy even as former colleagues were detained, and proved his worth to patrons. When rumors swirled that Jia Qinglin's wife was implicated in the Yuanhua case, Xi issued a firm denial in a newspaper interview—remarks that would have pleased Jia, a close associate of the incumbent paramount leader, Jiang Zemin.[111]

For Xi's detractors, such gestures exposed his commitment to clean government as far from absolute. They felt his incorruptible image masked a willingness to ignore misconduct when it might be politically expedient. Some of Xi's subordinates were purged over their alleged roles in the Yuanhua scandal, as well as organized-crime cases that surfaced after Xi left Fujian, including one involving Fuzhou crime boss Chen Kai, who was sentenced to death in 2005 for running brothels and gambling dens in collusion with some fifty officials. The cases didn't implicate Xi, but he conceded to making some poor personnel choices.[112]

At this point, Xi appeared tolerant of his relatives' dabblings in business, a common practice across elite party families, even though Xi reportedly told relatives and friends to neither engage in commercial activities in places where he worked nor use his name for leverage.[113] In a 2012 report, Bloomberg News revealed that members of Xi's extended family had been accruing significant wealth since the 1990s, collectively holding more than $50 million worth of property as well as lucrative investments in a range of companies that collectively possessed more than $2 billion in assets.[114] Some of Xi's cousins also went into business in Shenzhen and Hong Kong in the 1980s and 1990s, according to a biography of Xi's maternal uncle.[115]

There was no evidence that Xi did anything to advance his relatives' business interests at any point in his career. Bloomberg's 2012 report didn't trace any assets to Xi himself, or his wife and daughter. Within the party and business elite, stories have circulated about how Qi Xin, not long before Xi took power, told her other children to dial back their business activities to avoid causing problems for the leader-in-

waiting. One well-connected businessman told me that Xi often instructed subordinates not to get involved in any commercial dealings with his siblings, particularly his
elder sister Qi Qiaoqiao, who went into business after serving in China's paramilitary
police and—along with her second husband—accumulated assets worth hundreds
of millions of dollars.[116] After Xi took office, authorities even detained one of his
maternal cousins in 2014 for alleged criminal wrongdoing, according to the cousin's
associates.[117]

In Xi's own words, as well as the words of those who knew him, his ambitions led him not to wealth, but to power. Yi Xiaoxiong, the former friend, told an
American diplomat that Xi doesn't care about money. Xi, rather, is "repulsed by the
all-encompassing commercialization of Chinese society, with its attendant nouveau
riche, official corruption, loss of values, dignity, and self-respect," according to Yi,
who predicted that Xi would tackle these evils once he became leader.[118] "Going into
politics means one cannot dream of getting rich," Xi said in a 2000 interview.[119]

By the early 2000s, Xi had acquired a breadth of experience that was rare among
officials of his rank and age. He even secured a PhD in law from Tsinghua with a
thesis on agricultural policy that many believe to be ghostwritten, joining the ranks of
high-flying officials who padded their credentials with advanced degrees.[120] Chinese
politics watchers and Hong Kong media were already identifying Xi as a potential
leader. Unlike the ostentatious Bo Xilai, a fellow princeling and regional leader with
eyes on high office, Xi avoided indulging such speculation. At a 2002 news conference, a reporter asked Xi if he was one of China's new generation of leaders to watch.
His eyes widened and his face flushed. "I nearly spilt water all down my shirt," he
said. "You trying to give me a fright?"[121]

BUSINESS AS USUAL

WHEN XI TOOK CHARGE in the coastal province of Zhejiang in late 2002, the party
was in the midst of an unlikely makeover—welcoming once-reviled capitalists into
its proletarian ranks. After two decades of economic reforms, China's entrepreneurial
classes had superseded state enterprises in driving growth and demanded more say
over policies, while middle-class Chinese were shedding their deference to party authority. General Secretary Jiang Zemin responded with a new doctrine, the "Three
Represents," to make the party more responsive to a more dynamic and pluralistic

society. The party, Jiang said, must represent people of all social classes and the needs of "advanced productive forces"—i.e., private entrepreneurs—if it were to stay relevant and in power.

Zhejiang was a pacesetter in the party's embrace of private business. Adjacent to glitzy Shanghai, the affluent region of more than 46 million people was known for its hardscrabble entrepreneurs and a growing bevy of ambitious companies, from the automaker Geely to Jack Ma's internet startup Alibaba. For Xi, his stint as Zhejiang party boss was also an audition for the nation's highest offices, with an implicit mandate to ensure that the province catch or even outpace the national economy, by then the fastest growing among major countries.

Xi abided by the party's prevailing wisdoms on development, doling out business-friendly policies and encouraging local firms to seek new markets. He traveled abroad to drum up investment and greased the wheels for foreign businesses, helping American companies like Citibank, FedEx, McDonald's, and Motorola set up or expand operations in Zhejiang.[122] In a prelude to his future campaigns to promote higher-end and sustainable industry, Xi blacklisted "backward" manufacturing sectors, which were made to either upgrade their technology or leave the province. His efforts reaped ample rewards in an era when economic indicators defined an official's worth. During Xi's tenure, Zhejiang reported solid double-digit growth each year, while the annual value of its exports more than tripled, surpassing $100 billion in 2006.

Privately, though, some Chinese observers scoffed at Xi's achievements, saying he benefited from a favorable business climate and only needed "not to mess things up."[123] As it was in Fujian, some problems that critics blamed on Xi only surfaced after he moved on. The risky private-lending markets that underpinned a thriving entrepreneurial scene in the Zhejiang city of Wenzhou unraveled in 2011, forcing thousands of small businesses to fold and driving desperate entrepreneurs to skip town or even commit suicide.[124]

Politically, Xi maintained an unobstrusive mien. Li Rui, the former Mao aide and a friend of Xi Zhongxun, recalled having a meal with the younger Xi while visiting Zhejiang during the future leader's stint there. "Now your position is different," Li told Xi, "you can offer some opinions to the higher-ups." But Xi demurred, suggesting that Li, as a respected revolutionary elder, could get away with saying things that incumbent officials could not. "How can I be compared to you?" Xi replied. "You can play on the edges and test the limits. I wouldn't dare."[125]

Xi kept up his schmoozing with party bigwigs and foreign dignitaries, as would any official on the cusp of promotion. He charmed the U.S. ambassador over dinner with his keen grasp of economic data and fondness for Hollywood movies about World War II, and plied his superiors with alcohol in the kind of extravagance that he would suppress after taking power.[126] On one occasion in 2004, as he recounted later to liquor executives, Xi hosted former party chief Jiang Zemin and his wife with a bottle of eighty-year-old Moutai liquor—a scarce and lavish treat worth at least tens of thousands of yuan at the time.[127] That same year, the company that produces Moutai, a fiery *baijiu* spirit made from red sorghum, donated a bottle of the same vintage to the permanent collection at a museum in Zhejiang's capital of Hangzhou.[128]

Jiang's support was essential for Xi. Having a powerful patron could prove decisive in his bid to become China's "fifth generation" leader, a choice to be finalized through painstaking deliberations within the party elite. By the mid-2000s, the field had narrowed to two main contenders: Xi and Li Keqiang, a provincial party boss two years his junior. Each man enjoyed backing from one of two broad camps within the party, respectively comprising officials sharing similar backgrounds, ideological leanings, and political interests.[129]

Many fellow princelings favored Xi. They believed the party must be led by born-red officials who would never renounce their revolutionary lineage, as opposed to apparatchiks of humble stock—such as Mikhail Gorbachev—who might one day betray the party. Xi's military background helped him build ties with the politically influential PLA. His pedigree as the son of a prominent economic reformer, as well as his own business-friendly record in Fujian and Zhejiang, convinced some private entrepreneurs that Xi was their man.

Li represented a more meritocratic path. The son of a low-level official, he began his party career in a rural farming unit before earning a place at the prestigious Peking University through competitive entrance exams when they resumed in 1977. Li headed the student council and graduated with a law degree before joining the Communist Youth League, where he worked with Hu Jintao while the latter led the league in the mid-1980s. After a decade and a half with the league, Li took senior posts in two impoverished provinces, first Henan in central China and then Liaoning in the northeast, though his performances were seen as patchy, marred by the perceived mishandling of mass-fatality fires and an HIV/AIDS epidemic caused by blood-selling rackets.

Some insiders say Li was the preferred successor for Hu and other senior officials with a Youth League background, collectively known as *tuanpai*, or "league faction," though the name suggests greater cohesion among its perceived members than may be warranted. A fluent English speaker with a master's degree and PhD in economics, Li boasted genuine intellectual chops, unlike Xi, whose academic credentials were less solid. Li's vocal support of Hu's policies, including efforts to reduce wealth gaps and create social safety nets, marked him as a leading figure in what some observers called the party's "populist" coalition.[130]

But some party elders eyed Li with suspicion. His undergraduate years in Peking University overlapped with the "Democracy Wall" movement that spanned the winter of 1978 and the following spring, when students put up posters expressing hopes for democratic reforms. Many *hongerdai* derided Li and other officials with non-elite backgrounds as "shopkeepers' sons," unworthy of governing the nation that their revolutionary ancestors had fought for.

Both Xi and Li were expected to win seats on the Politburo Standing Committee at the 2007 party congress. The question was who would outrank the other and claim pole position in the succession race. Whatever Xi thought of his chances, he kept it to himself. In January 2007, when a reporter asked him to rate his own performance, he responded with artful prevarication. "How can I grade myself?" Xi said. "If I gave a high score, others would say I'm boastful; if I gave a low score, others would say I lack self-esteem."[131]

SHANGHAI SOJOURN

Xi's LAST REGIONAL JOB came unexpectedly. Shanghai party boss Chen Liangyu was dismissed in September 2006 for corruption, becoming the first sitting Politburo member to be sacked in over a decade.[132] A prominent figure in Jiang Zemin's "Shanghai Gang" of loyalists, Chen later received an eighteen-year jail sentence for crimes that included shady financial dealings and misusing money from the city's pension fund for vanity real-estate projects. Within political circles, the common wisdom was that Chen had picked too many fights with Beijing in exerting Shanghai's autonomy, handing Hu Jintao an opening to strike at Jiang's camp.

Choosing Chen's full-time replacement was a weighty decision. Shanghai's party secretaries have customarily occupied a Politburo seat and gone on to join its

Standing Committee since Jiang did so in the late 1980s. The pool of candidates was therefore limited to those worthy of promotion to senior ranks, if they weren't already there. With just months to go before the party congress, a Shanghai assignment would signal an advantage for Xi or Li.

Fortune favored Xi again. Announcing the transfer in March 2007, the party's personnel chief praised the new Shanghai party boss as someone who is "fair and upright, good at uniting people, and holds himself to strict standards."[133] Xi himself told Shanghai cadres that he "had no mental preparation whatsoever" for the transfer, but pledged to shore up public confidence and tackle corruption.[134] Six days after his appointment, Xi made his first public appearance since the transfer with a pilgrimage to the party's roots—a brick house in Shanghai's French Concession where Mao and a dozen others had convened the party's founding congress in 1921. It was canny stagecraft, given his mandate to smooth over the scandal and rally the city's shaken bureaucracy.[135] The visit was a way to "commemorate the party's great achievements and learn from the lofty spirit of our revolutionary forebears," Xi said. "We must wield power impartially, maintain integrity and self-discipline, and consciously resist the corrosiveness of corrupt and backward thinking."[136]

Xi spent the next seven months identifying trusted aides he could bring to Beijing, while filling his schedule with safe engagements. Among those granted audiences were foreign dignitaries like Henry Kissinger and former Japanese prime minister Yasuhiro Nakasone, as well as business delegations who hadn't imagined that Xi would agree to meet.[137] Kerry Brown, a former British diplomat turned researcher who attended one such delegation meeting, recalled that "this was so unusual that the junior official charged with looking after us was unable to conceal his amazement that a group as relatively unimportant as ours was to be granted golden moments with someone who was expected, very soon, to become one of the most powerful people in the world."[138]

The party elite coalesced around Xi as their preferred leader-in-waiting in June, when more than four hundred senior officials gathered at the Central Party School to nominate a new Politburo. In an innovation that officials hailed as a showcase of "intra-party democracy," attendees received ballot slips and picked from a list of nearly two hundred candidates.[139] Xi performed well in this "straw poll," a result that sealed his advantage over Li, according to party insiders and official accounts.[140] Though Xi rose to power through this quasi-democratic mechanism, he would dismantle it after taking office, reverting to backroom consultations with party grandees to fill top posts.[141]

Contemporary accounts credited Jiang for engineering Xi's victory, with help from princelings eager to see one of their own reclaim power from Hu's coterie of commoners. Xi was a compromise choice, less objectionable to broader sections of the party than his rivals. There were also more practical reasons for favoring Xi, who offered a common, populist touch that the party needed but Hu lacked.[142]

The final vote in October 2007 was a formality. When the party's new nine-man ruling council filed onto a dais in the Great Hall of the People to meet the press, emerging in order of seniority, Xi appeared sixth in line, just ahead of Li.[143] China learned who their next leader was likely to be, but for many, he was just a name. "Who's Xi Jinping?" began a popular joke at the time. "Ah, he's Peng Liyuan's husband."

CROWN PRINCELING

THE ROLE OF HEIR APPARENT has been fraught with peril, across cultures and throughout history. Imperial China saw its share of crown princes waylaid or killed before claiming the throne, and the People's Republic had fared little better, with Mao and Deng each deposing would-be successors. Though Xi was priming himself for power, any mistake or misfortune could have derailed his ascension.

Xi had much to learn in his five years as Hu's understudy. He experienced first-hand the awesome responsibilities in helming the ship of state, grappling with ethnic tensions and social unrest kicked up by rapid but haphazard growth. Abroad, he confronted outbursts of anti-China sentiment, a stunning implosion of Western finance, and the social media–fueled uprisings of the Arab Spring that rumbled through the Middle East from late 2010 to 2012. As a member of the top leadership responsible for party cohesion, he helped shape Beijing's responses to these challenges, while preparing his own strategies for reinforcing authoritarian rule.

Xi's first major task was to lead a party committee supervising final preparations for the 2008 Beijing Olympics. It was a tricky test ensuring that China's grandiose "coming-out party" succeed, a soft-power extravaganza that cost $42 billion in new stadia and infrastructure, a facelift for the capital city, and a laborious effort to clean up smoggy skies by shutting and relocating factories, restricting road traffic, and planting millions of trees. Despite meticulous planning, the run-up to the games could hardly have gone worse. Bloody riots broke out in Tibet in March 2008, exposing pent-up anger among its majority Buddhist population against the party's heavy-handed rule. Two months later, a massive earthquake devastated the southwestern province of Sichuan, killing more than eighty thousand people, including countless children crushed by the collapse of shoddily built schools.

Authorities contained the domestic fallout with censorship and propaganda, including gushy reports of Xi's wife and daughter taking part in relief efforts. But they proved less adept at selling Beijing's messaging abroad. Rights activists denounced what they called the "Genocide Olympics" to pressure Beijing over its alleged role in abetting the Darfur conflict with arms shipments to Sudan.[144] Even the torch relay, envisioned as a global public relations exercise, was overshadowed by large anti-China demonstrations along the route in Western Europe and North America, where protesters criticized the party's human rights record and voiced support for Tibetan independence.

Fortunately for Xi, the games proceeded smoothly. No serious security incidents occurred and the dreaded smog stayed away, though media revelations of fakery marred the opening ceremony, where a photogenic girl lip-synched in place of the actual singer, who had crooked teeth. When a Chinese track star's injury-forced withdrawal plunged the nation into grief, Xi offered a consolatory message to the athlete—a rare gesture from a senior leader.[145] China topped the medal table for the first time, handing the party a propaganda coup.

The Olympic legacy was far less rosy for China on the global stage. Its image-building fell flat among Western countries, whose lecturing on human rights rankled Chinese officials even more as the global financial crisis exposed what Beijing saw as fundamental flaws in liberal democracies. "There are some foreigners who've nothing better to do after eating their fill, pointing fingers at our affairs," Xi said while visiting Mexico as vice president in February 2009. "China, first of all, doesn't export revolution; second, we don't export hunger and poverty; and third, we don't cause trouble for you. What else is there to say?"[146] It was an early taste of the nationalistic straight talk that Xi would deliver as paramount leader, jarring to foreign ears but refreshingly forthright to Chinese audiences. Social media users cheered his candor and compared it favorably against Hu Jintao's corseted demeanor.[147] Censors soon scrubbed the footage from the Chinese internet.[148]

Within China, social foment fueled by labor disputes, land grabs, environmental degradation, and other inequities dominated the party's domestic agenda. Despite Hu's calls to create a "harmonious society," Chinese researchers estimated that the annual volume of "mass incidents"—the official euphemism for protests, strikes, and other forms of unrest—had swelled to some 180,000 by 2010, from about 87,000 incidents in 2005, and roughly 10,000 incidents in the early 1990s. The most explosive of these erupted in the northwestern frontier region of Xinjiang, home to millions of Uyghurs, a mostly Muslim ethnic minority, many of whom resented the growing Han Chinese influence over their culture and economy. In July 2009, just weeks after Xi toured Xinjiang, bloody riots erupted in the regional capital of Urumqi between Uyghurs and Han Chinese, leaving about two hundred dead and more than seventeen hundred others injured.[149] Political turmoil abroad, particularly the Arab Spring, added to the party's unease.

Hu's administration took a hardline approach to *weiwen*, or "maintaining stability," which became a mantra for officials whose career advancement rested on their ability to keep the peace and deliver growth. China's planned spending on public security surpassed the defense budget for the first time in 2011 as the government ramped up funding for law enforcement, domestic intelligence, and judicial agencies.[150] Annual internal security expenditure would more than double over the course of Hu's second five-year term, topping 710 billion yuan—the equivalent of roughly $112 billion at the time—in 2012. Internet regulators exerted greater control over social media, particularly after a deadly high-speed train crash sparked an outpouring of anger and emotion on Chinese social media that overwhelmed government censors.[151]

Xi grasped the exigencies of *weiwen*. As president of the Central Party School, the elite training academy in Beijing, he ordered more than two thousand county chiefs to attend weeklong training courses in late 2008, with classes focused on how to handle emergencies and maintain social stability.[152] Party cadres must "strengthen their decisiveness in maintaining stability, resolve disputes in a timely manner, and handle mass incidents appropriately," Xi told officials at the Central Party School in March 2009.[153]

When then U.S. vice president Joe Biden visited China in 2011, Xi spoke with him at length about the Soviet collapse and how Ba'athist and other authoritarian leaders in the Middle East and North Africa were facing a similar fate. Xi characterized these events as "an object lesson to the CCP—it meant the party cannot get out of touch with the people, the party cannot allow unfettered corruption to rage," said Daniel Russel, a senior Obama administration official who attended dozens of meetings with Xi before and after he took power.[154] The leader-in-waiting also explained how the party must overcome infighting and excessive autonomy among officials acting like they run local fiefs. "Xi Jinping talked at length about how China's natural state is entropy, that there are forces of division and separatism within the country and also external forces trying to break it apart," Russel recalled. "He was quite straightforward about how China needs a strong, single point of leadership—and that is the Chinese Communist Party—and that the party needs a strong, single point of leadership as well."[155]

Biden offered a similar assessment years later, describing Xi as "a very smart and calculating guy" who "doesn't have a democratic—with a small 'd'—bone in his body." Through their conversations, Biden came to believe that Xi "doesn't think that democracies can be sustained in the 21st century," an era so fast-changing that "only autocracies are able to handle it," he said. "Because democracies require consensus, and it takes too much time, too much effort to get it together."[156]

Xi's views were a widely shared indictment of China's leadership under Hu and Premier Wen Jiabao, both technocrats of humble upbringing seen as competent caretakers incapable of bold action. With decision-making powers shared among officials with competing ideas and interests, the result was often policy gridlock and tepid reforms that failed to mitigate the side effects of breakneck growth. Many Chinese felt left behind even as their economy swelled into the world's second largest. Wealth gaps widened, corruption festered, pollution worsened, and consumer-safety scares increased. Some scholars called the Hu-Wen years a "lost decade," arguing that the party failed to deliver the political overhauls that China needed to cope with slowing growth and avoid economic stagnation.[157]

Within the party, discordant voices battled over what should be done. A 2008 report published by Central Party School researchers urged the leadership to pursue limited democratic reforms, warning that China risked falling into grave instability unless the party submitted to legal checks on its powers, eased censorship, tolerated a freer press, and allowed some competitive elections.[158] Some public intellectuals spoke boldly of the need for "constitutionalism," calling for legal checks and balances and separation of powers similar to liberal democracies. Many princelings, though, believed it was time for one of their own to reclaim power from the commoners. "Princelings regard the likes of Hu Jintao and Wen Jiabao as 'butlers' and 'shopkeepers' who merely help them look after the business," said Cai Xia, a former Central Party School professor who socialized in princeling circles and is herself a granddaughter of a revolutionary. "In their minds, princelings believe that 'all under heaven are ours to rule; if we don't do it, who will?' "[159]

Questions remained on whether Xi was the right man for the job. His lack of a power base, some analysts argued, would leave him vulnerable to meddling by Jiang Zemin and Hu, whose protégés could outflank Xi in the decision-making process. Party infighting could intensify, depending on how key positions were apportioned between the standard bearers of rival coalitions, ideological camps, and interest groups. The corruption and bureaucratic inertia that hobbled Hu would remain formidable challenges for his successor. One veteran Japanese journalist even published in early 2012 a book titled *Xi Jinping: Communist China's Weakest Emperor*.[160]

Whether by chance or scheming, the final lead-up to the succession in 2012 proved propitious for Xi. Potential challengers crashed out in corruption and murder scandals, tarring the party's image but also boosting officials, like Xi, who sought a root-and-branch overhaul of China's blighted bureaucracy. After months of horse-trading, the party elite agreed on a largely conservative lineup for Xi's leadership bench, easing liberal-minded contenders into less important roles, and giving the next general secretary a firm mandate to clean house.

The most dramatic downfall belonged to Bo Xilai, a princeling and regional chief gunning for a seat in the top leadership. Born in July 1949, Bo was the fourth of seven children fathered by Bo Yibo, a revolutionary hero exalted as one of the party's "eight great elders" who held sway in the post-Mao era. The younger Bo brimmed with ambition, charisma, and good looks. Throughout his career he had displayed a flair for publicity more familiar to Western politicians, as well as a single-minded ruthlessness that alienated many within the party.

Like Xi, Bo had left a desk job in Beijing to enter grassroots politics in the 1980s, becoming a county official in the northeastern province of Liaoning. Backed by his father's lobbying and his own hard-charging ways, Bo scaled the local hierarchy to become mayor of Dalian, an industrial seaport in Liaoning, and then provincial governor. He earned a reputation for splashy politics, pursuing prestige real-estate projects, staging international fashion shows, and micromanaging the media to craft a glowing personal image.[161] Named commerce minister in 2004, Bo brought his overbearing panache to the international stage, upstaging superiors in trade talks with the U.S. Though Bo secured a Politburo seat in 2007, his antics had also made him influential enemies in Beijing, who engineered his transfer to the inland megacity of Chongqing to keep him out of the corridors of power.

But Bo wasn't deterred. As Chongqing party boss, he plotted his return to national prominence by mixing Maoist nostalgia with populist policies. In a campaign known as "singing red, smashing black," he encouraged mass singing of Mao-era "red songs," saturated local airwaves with revolutionary content, and directed a vicious purge of underworld groups that also toppled entrepreneurs and local elites who opposed him. He championed a state-heavy economic program, juicing growth and addressing social inequities with debt-fueled spending on infrastructure, public housing, and welfare programs.[162]

Bo's "Chongqing model" was popular among residents, leftist intellectuals, and even some senior officials, who saw it as a way to put China back on a more egalitarian footing and boost support for the party. When Xi visited Chongqing in late 2010, he too praised the city's enthusiasm for Mao and its purge of underworld groups.[163] Some party insiders said Xi's gesture was tactical, masking his wariness of a potent rival behind his own sympathies for Bo's Maoist revivalism. "Bo and Xi were destined for a showdown," Cai Xia, the former party scholar, told me. "Both of them wanted to become China's number one."[164]

Bo seemed certain to claim a seat on the Politburo Standing Committee, until February 2012, when Chongqing's erstwhile police chief, Wang Lijun, walked into a U.S. consulate with a stunning revelation: Bo's wife had murdered a British businessman with poison. Just days earlier, Wang had been stripped of his police duties after telling Bo about his wife's role in the killing, a falling out that left Wang fearing for his life. Chinese police surrounded the consulate in the southwestern city of Chengdu soon after Wang entered, sparking online rumors that he was trying to defect. The standoff lasted some thirty hours as Wang parlayed with American diplomats and Chinese central government officials for guarantees of his safety. He eventually left the consulate on his own, escorted to Beijing by a vice minister of state security.

Chongqing authorities said Wang was receiving "vacation-style treatment" due to stress and overwork, a claim ridiculed on Chinese social media. Bo himself responded by traveling some four hundred miles to a military base in southwestern China to visit the PLA's 14th Group Army, a unit that traced its roots to guerrilla forces that Bo's father had led in the 1930s. The trip alarmed some senior leaders. They felt Bo was courting the military at a moment of personal crisis, a politically fraught maneuver that recalled the PLA's once-pervasive factionalism that the party sought to quash.[165]

When the nine-man Politburo Standing Committee convened to discuss the Wang case, deliberations centered on whether investigations should go beyond the former police chief, according to an account of the meeting that Premier Wen's wife relayed to a business associate.[166] Zhou Yongkang, an ally of Bo and the Standing

Committee member overseeing China's security services, said the probe should stop at Wang. While other leaders pondered Zhou's remarks, Xi seized his moment, arguing that investigators should also look into anyone else who might have been involved. Wen agreed with Xi, as did Hu Jintao. When the Standing Committee voted at a subsequent meeting in March 2012 on how to handle the Wang case, only Zhou opposed plans to expel Bo and open a broader probe.[167]

A week later, Wen used his final press conference as premier to declare an end to Bo's career, chastising the Chongqing leadership over the Wang scandal and rebuking its indulgence in Maoist theatrics. State media announced the next day that Bo had been stripped of his Chongqing posts.[168] Bo would be sentenced to life imprisonment in 2013 for corruption and abuses of power, while his wife, Gu Kailai, was separately convicted of murder and given a suspended death sentence, which effectively meant life in prison.

More intrigue started playing out in Xi's favor just days after Bo's dismissal. One early morning in March 2012, a black two-seater Ferrari speeding down a snow-slickened road in Beijing smashed into a bridge, broke apart, and burst into flames. The twenty-three-year-old man behind the wheel died instantly, and two female passengers suffered serious injuries. Images of the mangled wreck were splashed on local press and social media. But details about the driver's identity were suppressed, sparking speculation.[169]

The driver, as many suspected, came from privilege. His father was Ling Jihua, chief of staff to Hu Jintao and director of the Central Committee General Office, the party's nerve center that supervises scheduling, document flow, and security for top leaders. Ling ordered a cover-up, worried that revelations about his son's lavish lifestyle could torpedo his chances for a promotion to the Politburo.[170] But attempts to suppress the news only led to Ling's downfall. In September, state media announced his demotion to a less powerful post, before an influential Hong Kong broadsheet, *South China Morning Post*, identified Ling's son as the Ferrari driver.[171] Though Ling would cling on for two more years before being purged for corruption, his career was effectively over, depriving Hu of a protégé who could help him assert influence in the Xi administration.

Xi himself added to the intrigue by disappearing for two weeks in September, when he canceled meetings with U.S. secretary of state Hillary Clinton and other foreign leaders. Chinese officials told American counterparts that Xi had a back injury, but otherwise said nothing about his absence.[172] Rumors went wild, with some speculating that Xi had suffered a life-threatening ailment or even an assassination attempt. Some suggested he was in eleventh-hour negotiations with party elders. My *Wall Street Journal* colleagues Bob Davis and Lingling Wei wrote that Xi was huddling with close advisers at a riverside city in Zhejiang, deliberating policy and sketching out his "China Dream" of national renewal.[173] When Xi resurfaced at a Beijing university, Chinese officialdom carried on as if nothing had happened.

The coronation in November was almost underwhelming. Xi emerged first in the new Politburo Standing Committee, which was cut to seven members from nine. Hu turned over his party and military roles to Xi without fuss. Desmond Shum, a well-connected investor who once did business with members of high-powered families, recalled a joyous mood within princeling circles. "The elite in Beijing were saying: 'the young master has come home, now the butlers can leave.'"[174]

MAN OF THE PEOPLE

TWO WEEKS INTO HIS NEW JOB, Xi brought his colleagues to the National Museum in Beijing, an austere monolith just east of Tiananmen Square, built to mark Communist China's tenth birthday in 1959. Together they trooped through *The Road to Rejuvenation*, an exhibition that traced China's modern history from its humiliation by foreign powers during the 1839–1842 Opium War to its resurgence as a great power in the twenty-first century. It was a well-worn narrative casting the Communist Party as the savior and shepherd of the Chinese people, a story designed to rally patriotic fervor around the party's authoritarian rule.

Xi took this message a step further. After paying tribute to the Chinese people's endurance and sacrifice over more than a century of foreign bullying, invasion, and civil war, he urged his compatriots to look ahead. "Nowadays, everyone is talking about the China Dream. In my view, achieving the great rejuvenation of the Chinese nation is the greatest dream of the Chinese people since the advent of modern times," he said. "If the country does well and the nation does well, then everyone will do well." Xi was issuing his personal mission statement, distilled into one simple yet compelling idea: make China great again.

Xi offered few specifics at the time, leaving the substance of the "China Dream" to public imagination. Even so, his appeal to patriotism marked a shift in the party's vocal register.[175] For years, party leaders, scarred by Mao's rabble-rousing, had tempered their rhetoric, and come to speak a soulless dialect of stuffy slogans and economic targets. Such tedium was adequate when promises of growth and social mobility could secure tacit acceptance of authoritarian rule, but for the party to regain public trust and reclaim its centrality in people's lives, Xi saw a need to inspire. As he would later tell officials, the party must "tell China's stories well." And as storyteller-in-chief, Xi would spin grand narratives of a Chinese renaissance. But first, he would start with himself.

Two days before Christmas 2012, the official Xinhua News Agency published a fifteen-thousand-character report titled: "'The People Are the Source of Our Strength'—A Chronicle of Chinese Communist Party Central Committee General Secretary Xi Jinping."[176] By the party's opaque standards, the essay offered a remarkably intimate portrait of China's new leader. It recounted key episodes in Xi's life, depicting an honest and hardworking official who inherited his father's revolutionary spirit. Personal vignettes spotlighted Xi's childhood, his devotion to his parents, his courtship of Peng Liyuan, and even the name of their daughter. Readers learned about Xi's fondness for home-cooked dishes, his daily phone calls with his songstress wife while she was away on tour, and his occasional late nights watching sports like basketball and soccer.

Never had a Chinese leader promoted his life story so publicly, and with such emotive appeal. While Hu and Wen disappeared behind sterile speeches and monotonous résumés, Xi showcased his personal narrative to validate his rise to power. He presented himself as a humble figure who earned the right to rule through his hard-earned experiences, affinity for common folk, and loyalty to the party. His elite background, once disdained by some peers, was repackaged to portray Xi's sense of mission and filial piety. Official accounts cast his suffering during the Cultural Revolution as a tale of redemption and triumph, even though broader political and historical discussions about that period remained taboo.

Whereas Western politicians wooed voters to win power, Xi was campaigning after his victory, trying to rehabilitate the party's battered brand and promote his agenda. Xi expounded his "China Dream" with speeches and inspection tours that fleshed out an expansive vision of an economically vibrant, militarily powerful, and globally influential nation. For his first trip outside Beijing as leader, Xi traveled to Guangdong to pay homage to Deng Xiaoping and pledge further reforms to boost China's economic might. He visited rural villages and called on peasants in their homes, asking after their needs, tasting their food, and promising more efforts to alleviate poverty. He made high-profile visits to army, air force, navy, space-program, and strategic-missile facilities within his first hundred days in office, something Jiang and Hu didn't do.[177]

Within the party, Xi was telling another story—a somber tale of decay, danger, and potential demise. "Matter must first rot before worms can breed," he warned colleagues, saying the party could crumble under the weight of corruption and ideological deviance.[178] The leadership issued a directive, known as Document Number 9, that demanded efforts to resist the spread of Western values. The party required cadres to watch a six-part documentary that blamed the Soviet Union's collapse not on structural flaws in the communist system but individuals who betrayed the cause.[199] Failure to excise these cancers, Xi said, would eventually destroy the party and ruin the nation.

CHAPTER TWO

GRIPPING IRON
AND LEAVING MARKS

THE PARTY CLEANSES ITSELF

"The party represents unity of will, which precludes all factionalism and division of authority in the party."

—Joseph Stalin, in *The Foundations of Leninism*

"For a party and a country as large as ours, if the party center cannot firmly and effectively exercise centralized and unified leadership, there will be situations where people govern independently and act as they wish, and nothing will get done."

—Xi Jinping

As the novel coronavirus swept through China in January 2020, Kong Lingbao saw little cause for concern. The epidemic seemed far away from his perch in the northeastern rust belt province of Heilongjiang, where authorities had detected just one suspected case of Covid-19, compared to more than four hundred confirmed infections nationwide. The Lunar New Year holiday was nigh and the Communist Party chief of Hengshan, a sleepy district in Jixi city, wanted to go home to see his family, some five hours' drive away in another city. Even though General Secretary Xi Jinping had ordered all-out efforts to contain the virus two days earlier, Kong demurred when a deputy sought permission to prepare for an outbreak. "Let's not make the entire district panic," Kong told the deputy before leaving for home. "I doubt the sky's going to fall."[1]

Provincial leaders launched a full-scale contagion response three days later. Kong returned reluctantly to Hengshan. Still, he told subordinates that "the epidemic isn't that serious," and instructed them to carry out their regular duties. As the severity of what would become a global pandemic became clear, Kong remained lackadaisical and appeared languid at work—a demeanor that investigators later attributed to him staying up late to watch pornography.[2] Hengshan soon suffered a Covid-19 outbreak, accounting for more than half of the cases detected in Jixi. Kong took the fall. The local commission for discipline inspection, as the party's internal watchdogs are known, announced a probe into Kong's alleged dereliction of duty, making him one of the first officials in China to be sacked for mishandling the coronavirus.[3]

Colleagues once regarded Kong as an up-and-comer who'd risen speedily up the local hierarchy. His downfall, at the age of forty-four, was even faster. Within two months, party inspectors transferred his case to state prosecutors, along with evidence detailing a trail of venality over his two decades in public service. By the end of the year, Kong would be expelled from the party and sentenced to ten and a half years in jail for taking millions of yuans' worth of bribes, including cash, cars, premium cigarettes, and hundreds of bottles of liquor. "I regret it, I hate it, I hate that I didn't know how to be content," Kong wrote in his confession. "I am in the prime of life, in the midst of exuberant youth, yet I have to fritter my time away in prison."[4]

Kong's fate was a familiar one for the millions of officials punished since Xi launched his crackdown on corruption in late 2012. But Kong's undoing hadn't been triggered by the usual allegations of criminal misconduct. Party inspectors started probing him not because he was a suspected felon, but because he was a negligent official who failed to execute the party's directives. His disobedience impeded the government's response to a deadly pathogen, and may well have cost lives. "He believed he was capable and bold, refusing to listen to different opinions or tolerate supervision from others," the party's top disciplinary agency said. "The diseasing of the mind is the most serious of ailments."[5]

When Xi first declared war on corruption, his enforcers focused on rapacious officials who took bribes, abused powers, and plundered public money. Politicians and bureaucrats, from top-tier "tigers" to lowly "flies," would become public enemies overnight once the party accused them of "violations of discipline and the law," a euphemism for graft. Cadres and state business executives cut back on lavish spending and travel, spurned banquets and gifts, and some even avoided wearing watches at meetings to avoid suspicion they had ill-gotten riches.[6] The purge stunned party insiders with its intensity, punishing more than 410,000 people in its first two years, including more than 50 officials of at least ministerial rank. It even toppled a retired member of the Politburo Standing Committee, the party's top decision-making body, and a level of seniority once considered untouchable.

The campaign portrayed Xi as a strict disciplinarian determined to put his house in order. Authorities directed breathless news coverage with lurid details of greed and sexual deviance, reinforcing the party's claims that corruption stems from individual degeneracy rather than systemic flaws. Chinese media relished revealing that Zhou Yongkang, the retired Standing Committee member, had fornicated with multiple women and leaked state secrets before getting a life sentence for corruption and abuse of power. News reports chronicled how a top economic planning official, given life imprisonment for taking nearly $6 million in bribes, was turned in by a former mistress.[7] An influential Chinese magazine detailed how a disgraced general, later given a suspended death sentence, owned a lavish home covering nearly five acres, complete with three courtyards, two gardens, one fountain, and a stash of solid gold items, including a bust of Mao Zedong.[8]

For Xi, such depravity is symptomatic of much deeper decay. In public speeches and internal remarks, he speaks of corruption as the result of the party's most fundamental crisis: its collective loss of faith and a breakdown in authority that have sowed disaffection and discord. "Facts have proven, time and again, that the wavering in one's ideals and convictions is the most dangerous form of wavering," Xi said. "I have long been wondering, if we were confronted one day with a complex situation like a 'color revolution,' would our cadres all act resolutely to safeguard the party's leadership and the socialist system?"[9] He prescribed a range of remedies, the most fundamental of which is enforcing compliance and control. "The more complex the situation the party faces and the more arduous the tasks it shoulders, the more we must strengthen discipline and safeguard the party's cohesion and unity," Xi told the party's top disciplinary officials in January 2013. "And we must ensure the entire party has a unified will, acts in concert, and advances in lockstep."[10]

The task fell to the Central Commission for Discipline Inspection, an internal watchdog that polices the conduct of the party's more than 96 million members. Though the commission is often described as an anticorruption body, the label undersells its fearsome reputation for rough justice. It operates outside, arguably above, the formal legal system, able to seize evidence without warrants, detain suspects almost indefinitely, and kill careers with little recourse. Much like how police departments conduct internal affairs probes, the CCDI adjudicates cases in secret, unless the party decides to make selective disclosures that would, as the Chinese saying goes, "kill the chicken to scare the monkeys." And while in theory the commission only supervises party members and can do no worse than expel them, its reach extends over every public servant, along with de facto powers to get errant officials convicted, jailed, or even executed.

Under Xi, the CCDI has transformed from a shadowy agency into an omnipresent tool of governance, tasked with enforcing loyalty to the paramount leader and ensuring compliance with his edicts. Some insiders say the commission has never been more powerful, acting as a parallel bureaucracy that circumvents party and state institutions. Its inspectors routinely burrow into party groups, government departments, and state businesses all over the country, assessing their performance and rebuking those who fail to deliver. Wherever the machinery of state seizes up, CCDI officials swoop in to rectify the faults—be they graft, indolence, or foot-dragging. Many even double up as thought police, probing party members on their ideological zeal.

Xi's crackdown speaks to an old problem for Chinese rulers, often expressed in the ancient verse "the heavens are high and the emperor is far away." Monarchs and mandarins through the ages have bemoaned how distance dilutes imperial authority and allows local officials to abuse their autonomy. Their Communist successors are no exception, struggling to break up vested interests and rein in local fiefs, while lamenting that "government decrees don't go beyond Zhongnanhai," the central leadership compound. Generations of scholars and statesmen grappled with this conundrum but produced no lasting formula, save for a pithy truism still repeated today: "To govern a nation, one must first manage its officials." Guided by this mantra, Xi believes the answers lie in pairing ancient tradition with Leninist hardware, to forge a regiment of ruthless martinets who can keep the party and the nation in line.

ANCIENT TRADITION

HISTORIANS CREDIT QIN SHI HUANG, the first emperor of a unified China, for pioneering an early system of bureaucratic supervision more than 2,200 years ago. He appointed a "chief censor" to his imperial Qin court and vested the official with sweeping powers to police conduct across the government. Outranked only by the grand chancellor, the chief censor could advise the emperor on affairs of the state, formulate policy, impeach officials, and even amend laws.[11] Subsequent dynasties built on the Qin example, creating a corps of censors who served as the emperor's eyes and ears, punishing corrupt mandarins, censuring inept bureaucrats, and executing imperial edicts.

This system reached an apogee during China's last two imperial dynasties. The Ming and Qing each maintained a much feared censorate that effectively operated as an independent arm of government, surveilling the bureaucracy for wayward behavior and enforcing the emperor's policies across his dominions.[12] The tradition of supervision survived the Qing collapse. Sun Yat-sen, the revolutionary revered as the father of modern China, advocated for a Control Yuan to be set up as one of five branches of government in the Chinese republic, responsible for auditing state organs and disciplining officials—an idea his Nationalist Party implemented after winning power in the late 1920s.

The Chinese Communist Party, meanwhile, drew inspiration from the Soviets to create its first control commission in 1927. Early incarnations of this agency were often caught up in factional battles and neglected by Mao, who preferred to enforce his will through purges and rectification campaigns. Under Mao, the party would create (and dissolve) a number of supervisory bodies, including the first CCDI in 1949, but these were generally toothless, thinly staffed, and ultimately dissolved during the Cultural Revolution.

The CCDI was reestablished in 1978, about two years after Mao's death.[13] Its first priorities were to purge Maoist radicals and enforce party rules, though fighting corruption took greater importance as China's economic reforms opened opportunities for graft. But the agency remained relatively feeble in the 1980s, as liberal-minded leaders like Hu Yaobang and Zhao Ziyang tried to set clearer boundaries between the party and state. A separate Ministry of Supervision was resurrected in 1986 to monitor government workers, implicitly bringing them outside the ambit of party inspectors. The leadership also curtailed the CCDI's powers by downgrading the commission chief's party rank and dissolving many party disciplinary groups that were embedded in government agencies.[14]

The 1989 Tiananmen Square protests halted these reforms. Deng Xiaoping resolved to restore the party's authority over state organs, and the CCDI soon regained its watchdog powers over government bodies. In 1993, the commission absorbed the supervision ministry through an arrangement known as "one set of personnel with two signboards," under which officials could switch between party and state identities as circumstances required, though party titles remained more powerful. During this post-1989 restructuring, the CCDI also acquired its most notorious investigative tool—the secretive process of indefinite detention and interrogation known as *shuanggui*, where investigators often subjected suspects to physical and mental abuse with impunity.[15]

As China's economy took off in the 1990s and 2000s, the party designated fighting corruption as a key formal objective. Accordingly, the CCDI switched its focus to investigating official graft, rather than political misconduct and ideological deviance.[16] Corruption may be an ageless scourge, but post-Mao China provided fertile ground for knavish officials and crony capitalists. Pro-market reforms and investment-led growth minted immense wealth and gave officials abundant opportunities to manipulate the allocation of land, capital, and other resources in return for bribes and favors.[17] Government careers promised not just secure employment, known as the proverbial "iron rice bowl," but also under-the-table benefits that dwarfed meager official salaries. A 2008 report released by China's central bank cited estimates suggesting that as many as eighteen thousand corrupt officials and state business executives had fled abroad or disappeared since the mid-1990s, absconding with some 800 billion yuan in assets, equivalent to roughly $120 billion and 2.7 percent of China's gross domestic product that year.[18]

Anticorruption crackdowns pursued by Deng's successors, Jiang Zemin and Hu Jintao, often fizzled after initial fervor. They lasted long enough to eliminate rivals without inflicting too much pain on the political and business elite, who had grown accustomed to greasing palms to sidestep bureaucracy and secure state largesse. A few tigers would be slayed and some flies swatted, but the leadership would ultimately hold off from a broader purge. One fear was that China's economy could seize up without what some believed to be the lubricating effects of corruption—particularly in the form of "access money," or what University of Michigan political scientist Yuen Yuen Ang calls "the steroids of capitalism," whereby businesses offer rewards to officials "not just for speed, but to access exclusive, valuable privileges."[19]

The CCDI targeted mainly mid-level graft and could do little to stem the broader economic forces that were fueling avarice across government ranks. One academic analysis of corruption cases disclosed from 1993 to 2010 indicated that graft committed by higher-ranking officials was less likely to be detected and investigated than that involving junior bureaucrats.[20] In another study, Georgia State University professor Andrew Wedeman presented data suggesting that corrupt officials faced far lower risks of getting caught during the mid-2000s than they had about a decade earlier.[21] Such uneven enforcement "allowed corrupt low-level officials to climb the career ladder and enter the senior ranks," Wedeman wrote. "Flies thus became rats; rats grew into wolves; and wolves morphed into tigers."[22]

The problem stems largely from how the party keeps its enforcers on a tight leash. Before opening cases or meting out punishment, regional and local disciplinary agencies must get approval from party committees at their own level in the hierarchy. The CCDI itself must seek consent from the party leadership. This means the more senior an official is, the harder they are to investigate. The process is highly politicized, structured to prevent the party's bloodhounds from sniffing out skeletons in the darkest closets. Once unleashed, though, there's little stopping them from ripping their prey apart. An investigation against a big-name target was almost certainly party infighting waged under the cover of combating corruption—a convenient fig leaf that departed from how Mao-era officials purged rivals by accusing them of political deviancy.[23]

When Jiang Zemin purged Beijing party boss Chen Xitong on corruption charges in 1995, insiders characterized the case as the moment Jiang established himself as party leader, emerging from the shadows of party grandees who'd installed him as general secretary six years earlier. In 2006, Hu Jintao scored his own win against Jiang's clique, the "Shanghai Gang," when the party sacked Shanghai chief Chen Liangyu for graft. Both cases gripped public attention and unnerved officials who feared being implicated, but neither Jiang nor Hu followed up with a systemic crackdown.

By the time Xi vowed to cleanse the party, many officials thought he was following a well-worn playbook: conduct a short and sharp campaign to consolidate power in the name of fighting graft. But rather than a ritual bloodletting, Xi unleashed a veritable bloodbath. The party has punished more than 4.6 million people in the decade since Xi took power, including some 627,000 in 2021 alone—nearly four times the total in 2012, the final year of Hu's leadership.[24] For Xi, the fight is existential. "Corruption is a cancer of society," he told top CCDI officials in 2013. "If the scourge of corruption worsens, eventually the party and the nation will be ruined."[25]

HUNTERS AND THE HUNTED

THE COMMUNIST PARTY'S TOP DISCIPLINE enforcers operate from a nondescript office tower in central Beijing, roughly ten minutes' drive from the Forbidden City and the former imperial garden of Zhongnanhai. High walls surround the unmarked compound, whose austere gateway features no signs save for the street number, though red flags sometimes flutter above as a hint to the occupants' identity. In the yard, a centuries-old locust tree towers over a stone inscription that exalts the impartial administration of justice.[26]

As the apex agency directing a network of regional and local branches, roving inspection teams, and embedded agents, the Central Commission for Discipline Inspection penetrates all levels of government and supervises every party and state organization across China. In the United States, similar responsibilities would be shared across agencies such as the Justice and Treasury Departments, the Federal Bureau of Investigation, the U.S. Marshals Service, and the Government Accountability Office—all of which are subjected to scrutiny from Congress, the judiciary, and a free media. The CCDI, however, is modeled on Soviet hardware. It answers only to the party, its priorities echo the leadership's agenda, and its work is often used to shape and justify the outcomes of elite power struggles.

CCDI investigators pick up scents in various ways. Sometimes they unearth information in routine audits. Occasionally, misbehaving officials get exposed on viral videos and social media posts. Most trails, however, originate from the copious complaints and anonymous tip-offs that gush through petition offices, web portals, and telephone hotlines. Tipsters even resort to a bit of cloak and dagger, given how complaints have in the past been leaked and invited retaliation. One whistleblower, fearing detection by a corrupt municipal police chief, switched car registration plates three times while driving to meet investigators.[27] In another case, a retired CCDI official recalled how an informant arranged a stealthy liaison in a hotel lobby, where he would read a newspaper as a signal, only to walk away at the last second as an investigator approached. The informant called back later, demanding a new rendezvous at a place without security cameras.[28]

The hunt begins after investigators sift out promising leads and gather enough preliminary evidence to persuade superiors to open a case. Their approval kicks off a more thorough probe, though often by that point the suspect's guilt is all but certain. Proceedings culminate in a "case examination," a sort of closed-door trial where officials assess the evidence and recommend penalties where necessary.[29] Suspects and lawyers can't attend. Errant cadres may receive warnings, lose their party posts, be put on probation, get expelled, or even have their cases transferred to state prosecutors. An accused can ask the commission to reconsider a verdict, but successful appeals are almost unheard of.

If the alleged offenses are severe or sensitive enough, suspects may be spirited away into secret interrogations—the dreaded process known as *shuanggui*, or "dual designation," in reference to how the party summons targets for questioning at a designated time and place. Detainees are held in covert locations without access to lawyers or relatives, typically for up to six months, though extensions can be made. *Shuanggui* detainees have described being held in a variety of locations, ranging from temporary sites such as hotels and villas to purpose-built facilities similar to prisons.

Details about detention facilities are scarce, though state media and scholars have offered glimpses inside. Researchers who visited a county-level detention center in eastern China described a twenty-acre compound in a remote area where no residences existed within a two-kilometer radius. The facility was unmarked, secured by high walls and guards, and featured recreational amenities like basketball and volleyball courts for officials who often stayed on-site for extended periods.[30] To prevent suspects from harming themselves, detention rooms typically feature walls and furniture covered with soft padding, and lack windows or power sockets. At least two officials watch each detainee at all times. The questioning takes place in the holding cells, with a desk and chairs on one side and a bed on the other. Other detention centers, according to official accounts, feature a strong political aesthetic in interrogation rooms, where copies of the party oath and party charter are displayed and used by investigators trying to rehabilitate suspects.[31]

The secrecy shrouding *shuanggui* is meant to shield investigators from undue influence or intervention. In reality, it has facilitated rampant abuse. With the party placing a premium on written confessions, interrogators often try to extract avowals of guilt by means fair or foul. They swing between mildness and menace, offering leniency at one moment and issuing threats the next, such as warning suspects that their family may face consequences unless they cooperate. Investigators in one northeastern city favored breaking down detainees by serving home-cooked food prepared by the suspects' mothers.[32]

With few people watching the watchers, a culture of impunity festered. Wayward inspectors tipped off suspects and manipulated cases for bribes, extorted money from investigation targets, or even tortured suspects to secure confessions. Former detainees describe being tormented through beatings and simulated drowning, though high-ranking officials were less likely to be roughed up. Detainees have died from abuse or suicide. Court officials sentenced six investigators to jail for between four and fourteen years after they drowned a detainee in 2013. Most *shuanggui* cases end with confessions and are sent for prosecution in state courts, where conviction rates exceed 99 percent.[33]

To stop the rot, Xi turned to a skilled political operator and longtime friend, Wang Qishan. A vice premier at the time, Wang boasted a storied career as a policy wonk, banker, and administrator, and impeccable credentials for what many considered a crucial yet unforgiving assignment. Chinese media had nicknamed him "fire brigade chief" in recognition of his crisis management skills, from handling China's largest bankruptcy in the late 1990s to parachuting into Beijing as mayor while the capital reeled from the 2002–2003 SARS outbreak. A princeling through marriage to a party elder's daughter, Wang had a reputation for honesty helped by his lack of children, which supposedly meant he had less incentive to enrich his family. Most crucially, Wang was politically reliable, someone Xi had known since growing up in Beijing and being rusticated to the same province during the Cultural Revolution.[34]

Wang became CCDI secretary in November 2012. Though he ranked sixth in the party's seven-man leadership, he tackled his role with such derring-do that many insiders considered him China's second most powerful official. An avid historian, he asked his staff to read Alexis de Tocqueville's treatise on the French Revolution and write up their views on why the monarchy fell.[35] He called on his investigators to inspire shock and awe, pressing them into working fifteen-hour days and clocking countless overtime hours without weekend or vacation breaks.[36] Wang took his first big scalp just weeks into the job, opening a corruption probe against the deputy party chief for the southwestern province of Sichuan. More than a dozen other "tigers" would be slayed over his first year in charge.

To prevent local authorities from stymieing investigations, Wang stepped up the use of "central inspection teams" to scrutinize regional governments, party organs, and state institutions and assess their compliance with party directives. These teams reported directly to Beijing and were led by retired officials without ties to the regions to which they were sent, minimizing conflicts of interest. Inspectors would move into a local hotel or office building, where they would interview officials, audit accounts, and receive complaints in person, through letters, or over the phone. Wang also harnessed public anger to his advantage, launching an official CCDI website that drew some 24,800 tip-offs in its first month online, or more than 800 a day.[37]

Wang professionalized the investigative process, encouraging officials to rely less on confessions and more on sophisticated technology, such as data analysis to detect misconduct and forensic accounting to trace illicit assets. The CCDI brought in personnel with academic training in finance, law, and technology to tackle complex cases of financial malfeasance. Disciplinary commissions were restructured to separate the powers of investigation, case review, and punishment between different departments, reducing opportunities for graft and abuses of power. Investigators often faced resistance. When a central inspection team visited Henan province in 2014, local officials staked out the team's hotel to try to block whistleblowers from meeting investigators. Some officials in northeastern China provided visiting inspectors with meals that were too salty or spicy to eat, while others arranged for noisy renovation work to take place near the inspection teams' work spaces.[38]

A sense of foreboding, even fear, shrouded the party as Wang stretched his dragnet across government ministries and state companies. Social media lit up with rumors of officials getting detained during work meetings, and in one case, a daughter's wedding.[39] Others reportedly committed suicide before investigators could reach them. State-enterprise executives sometimes disappeared without warning, only to surface later in news reports about a corruption probe.

Wang's targets included party stalwarts whose downfalls were politically helpful for Xi. Zhou Yongkang, the former leadership member who oversaw China's security services, went down with his cronies in the domestic security apparatus and energy sector after an extensive investigation that recuperated at least 90 billion yuan—or $14.5 billion at the time—worth of seized assets, including bonds, stocks, real estate, and artwork.[40] The purge of Ling Jihua, former chief of staff to Hu Jintao, sapped the former leader's influence and capped a clearing out of corrupt officials linked to the coal-rich province of Shanxi. A posse of high-ranking generals close to Jiang Zemin, including two former vice chairmen of the Central Military Commission, were also dismissed, allowing Xi to replace them with his own associates.

Xi actively steered these purges. People familiar with the process say the CCDI had to secure Xi's approval to investigate and punish officials at the vice-ministerial rank or higher. Probes against some high-profile business executives, including an insurance mogul once married to a granddaughter of Deng Xiaoping, proceeded only with Xi's personal sign-off.[41] Such close control over major investigations exposed him to aspersions that he aimed to cashier rivals and accrue more power. Xi seemed to anticipate this criticism and tried to make sure that he remained unimpeachable. In late 2012, members of Xi's immediate and extended family started shedding some assets and investments, a disposal that party insiders say was made at the behest of Xi and his mother.[42]

Xi went one step further in 2014, when authorities reportedly arrested one of his maternal cousins, Ming Chai, for alleged criminal wrongdoing. A former paramilitary policeman who became a naturalized Australian, Chai was doing business in China at the time and often flaunted his family connections while chasing commercial opportunities, according to his friends and associates. One former business partner told me that Chai was someone who enjoyed lavish living and made grandiose promises that he never kept, such as offering to give the partner a tour of Zhongnanhai and arrange a news conference in the Great Hall of the People to promote their business. Nonetheless, there was no indication that Xi did anything to advance Chai's interests, or had any knowledge of his cousin's business dealings.[43]

Many within China's elite circles believed that Xi was trying to demonstrate his incorruptibility through a gesture known as *dayi mieqin*, or destroying one's kin as an act of righteousness. According to Hong Kong political monthly *Front Line*, which first reported the case, Xi personally informed the Politburo Standing Committee about Chai's arrest just a day or two after the CCDI announced a formal probe against Zhou Yongkang.[44] *Front Line* chief editor Lau Tat-man later told me that the magazine was tipped off by a pro-Xi princeling who portrayed the arrest as an example of Xi's upright character.[45] Chinese authorities never publicly acknowledged Chai's case, though party insiders and associates say he stayed in custody for a period of time before resurfacing in Australia by late 2015.[46]

While state media played up Xi's tiger-slaying, he avoided wholesale attacks on China's "red bloodlines," the revolutionary families enmeshed in lucrative sectors of state industry and private business. Xi still needed support from the party elite and attempts to investigate red aristocrats would have faced overwhelming pushback, says Desmond Shum, a former Beijing-based investor who once did business with members of elite political clans. "Red bloodline families are untouchable," he says. "It's like being a made man in the mafia."[47]

Such cold calculations animate discipline inspection commissions at every level. County-level agencies with limited resources, for instance, might consider whether it is worthwhile incurring investigative costs that far exceed the value of assets that might be recovered from a suspect.[48] Politics, above all, are the deciding factor. As the deputy chief of one county disciplinary agency told researchers, inspectors face pressure to meet quotas on the number of officials they should investigate. Exceeding the quota may give the impression that the county suffers from serious corruption, while falling short of it by a large margin could suggest that local investigators are ineffective, the deputy chief said. "Therefore, a process of rational calculation is needed to determine who is to be investigated: there cannot be too many or too few."[49]

Xi too faces a balancing act. While his campaign has been popular with many ordinary Chinese, sustained revelations of high-level graft could erode this goodwill. "The more corruption the campaign reveals, the more it suppresses citizen support for the regime," Harvard political scientist Yuhua Wang and George Washington University professor Bruce Dickson wrote.[50]

The fear that Xi inspired within the party had also become debilitating. Some officials preferred to procrastinate, worried that they could make decisions that ended up putting them at risk of investigation.[51] Others sought safety by engaging in what scholars call "nauseating displays of loyalty" to their paramount leader.[52] For Xi, this pervasive sense of dread is both boon and bane. A feared leader is often a powerful one. But too much fear can paralyze the bureaucracy. And Xi's campaign would prove that both can be true at the same time.

THE PARTY LEADS EVERYTHING

WHEN THE COMMUNIST PARTY REVISED its disciplinary rules in October 2015, perspicacious analysts picked up on a potent new provision tucked inside. Party members would be punished, it said, if they "irresponsibly discuss the party center's policies" and cause damage to "the party's centralized unity."[53] Officials offered few clues at the time on what the new rule meant, but the scope of its power became evident.

Within weeks, the party dismissed the chief editor of the official newspaper in China's northwestern region of Xinjiang, saying he had irresponsibly discussed and contravened official policies on fighting terrorism and religious extremism.[54] Authorities took down one of Beijing's deputy party secretaries two months later for wrongdoing that included irresponsible discussion of party policies, before sacking the governor of the southwestern province of Sichuan for disloyalty and dishonesty to the party.[55]

The purges alarmed some party insiders, who feared that Xi was cracking down on dissent while elite resentment simmered against his anticorruption shake-up and handling of China's slowing economy. CCDI officials soon confirmed those fears, declaring that the new rule against "irresponsible discussion" was meant to punish cadres who sowed confusion and discord by questioning Beijing's decrees.[56] "Discipline inspection commissions are political organs," the CCDI said. Their fundamental duty, the agency explained, was "to resolutely uphold the party center's authority, and ensure that government decrees are thoroughly enforced."[57]

The CCDI was fast becoming an ideological inquisitor. Its inspectors ferreted into government agencies, state enterprises, and universities to conduct "political health checks" and punish those who deviated from Xi's directives. Disciplinary officials censured some of China's most powerful institutions, from the party's propaganda department to the finance and public security ministries, for lacking political loyalty and ideological fervor.[58] The crackdown took on an almost ritualistic quality, as targeted officials resorted to obsequious displays of repentance. In 2016, for instance, after inspectors chastised authorities in the port city of Tianjin for slack leadership and corruption, the municipality's top official promised ruthless remedies and demanded that his subordinates swear unflinching fealty to General Secretary Xi.[59] "Loyalty that isn't absolute is absolute disloyalty," Tianjin's party chief at the time, Li Hongzhong, wrote.[60]

China's Communist leaders, like their imperial forebears, have long struggled to assert control over its vast realms and the legions of functionaries who govern in their name. The party hasn't helped itself by maintaining a jealous monopoly on power, suffocating attempts to build independent institutions and the rule of law. Unfettered by checks and balances like democratic elections and a free press, local officials can wield near-autocratic powers over their domains. Beijing indulged such autonomy as part of Deng's economic reforms, which discarded Marxist orthodoxy, encouraged pragmatism, and brought in technocrats to manage economic and social affairs. Central authorities encouraged lower-level officials to road-test policy ideas that could be rolled out nationally. Local governments engaged in cut-throat competition, chasing investments and growth targets that would help officials win promotion and line their pockets.

The benefits were staggering, as were the pitfalls. Deng-era decentralization had unleashed dynamism that helped China boost its gross domestic product by more than fiftyfold, from less than $150 billion in 1978 to $8.2 trillion by 2012, and bring more than 600 million people out of poverty.[61] After Beijing overhauled the tax structure in the mid-1990s to funnel more revenues directly to the central government, local authorities made up budgetary shortfalls with ever-more rapacious methods, such as expropriating and selling rural land, that stoked public unrest. The economy grew addicted to a debt-fueled, investment-heavy growth model that incentivized unproductive spending, wasting some 42 trillion yuan from 2009 to 2013 by one estimate.[62]

The freewheeling ways of the reform era alarmed Wang Huning, a scholar turned party theorist, who worried that China might come unglued if its rulers failed to rein in a fast-changing society. In a 1995 interview, just weeks before leaving Shanghai's Fudan University to join the party's top policy research office, Wang argued that China needed a centralized political system that could deliver cohesive policy-making in the face of unprecedented challenges, and suppress any social instability kicked up by rapid growth. "In a place without central authority, or a place where central authority has become weakened, the country would be mired in a state of division and chaos," Wang said in one of his last public utterances as an academic. "A strong central authority is the fundamental guarantee for achieving rapid and stable development at a relatively low cost during the process of modernization."[63]

Wang took his ideas to Beijing, where he went on to serve, rather extraordinarily, as a top aide to three successive Chinese leaders, including Xi. The pair started working together after Xi joined the top leadership in 2007 and took charge of a policy committee—of which Wang was a member—that oversaw "party building," an arcane term of art describing efforts to cultivate cohesion and ideological zeal. As leader-in-waiting, Xi echoed Wang's ideas in private conversations, telling people that China needed a strong central leadership to hold the country together.[64] After becoming general secretary in 2012, Xi retained Wang as a key policy adviser and moved to concentrate power.

Xi named himself head of powerful party committees that oversaw key portfolios including economics and finance, national security, foreign affairs, legal affairs, and internet policy. He installed close confidants and trusted associates in key positions. Li Zhanshu, whom Xi had known since their time as county chiefs in Hebei, first served as chief of staff to the general secretary before becoming China's top lawmaker. Liu He, a princeling who grew up alongside Xi in Beijing, became the leading adviser on economic and financial affairs, siphoning off some of Premier Li Keqiang's influence over policy-making.[65] Xi's college roommate Chen Xi took senior roles at the party's Central Organization Department, where he could screen officials and influence personnel appointments.

Those outside Xi's inner circle felt increasingly marginalized. He undermined rivals with hollow promotions to roles with little authority or by switching their portfolios to separate them from their power bases. In some instances, Xi neutralized potential opponents by purging their aides and supporters through disciplinary probes. People familiar with this practice describe a discreet and meticulous process, where Xi would ask trusted disciplinary inspectors to quietly prepare dossiers—often running in the hundreds of pages—on senior officials he wished to undermine. Xi would also authorize investigations against the officials' close associates under the pretext of demonstrating those associates' honesty, making it hard for the targeted officials to block the probes. An early target of this technique was Li Yuanchao, a Politburo member who served as vice president during Xi's first term. Once seen as a contender for higher office, Li stepped down from his party and state roles in 2017 and 2018 respectively after a number of his close associates were detained, even though he was young enough to stay in active politics under the prevailing retirement norms at the time.

Access to the general secretary, a controlled privilege, became scarcer still. Xi once told foreign dignitaries that he didn't have a mobile phone, which meant that most people—apart from his closest advisers—could only reach him through carefully screened meetings, calls, and written submissions.[66] While his predecessors used summer retreats at the seaside resort of Beidaihe for informal policy discussions with party grandees, insiders say Xi has largely discarded this tradition and warned retired leaders against meddling in politics. Some princelings once able to meet Xi privately to discuss affairs of state say they no longer enjoy the privilege, and must go through Xi's chief of staff if they wish to express their views. Xi's relatives have told friends that they will no longer help relay messages to the leader. One princeling who has known Xi for decades told me that the leadership keeps tabs on elite party families through informants within their staff—scrutiny that dissuades many princelings and retired elders from criticizing Xi.

Whereas his predecessors often delegated the finer details of policy-making to specialists, a practice known as "grasping the large, releasing the small," Xi prefers a hands-on approach. He often makes direct requests for policy adjustments and insists that he gets the final call on key decisions. State media credits Xi for personally overseeing the formulation of policies big and small, from major economic plans to campaigns to reduce food waste and improve public toilets.[67] When party inspectors discovered that local officials in Shaanxi province had been illegally building some twelve hundred villas inside nature reserves, Xi issued instructions on six occasions over four years, demanding punishment for the offenders, and stronger protections for the local ecology.[68]

Xi enacted new party rules to "institutionalize" his autocratic style. He ordered senior officials to submit annual accountings of their work, and started a performance review system that graded leaders on political rectitude, alongside other metrics. He directed a relentless rule-making spree, setting party statutes to dictate how every member—from senior leaders to the rank and file—should work and behave, and how they would be punished for any deviance. He set the party's first ever five-year plan for drafting internal regulations, and proceeded to enact or revise far more major ordinances than his recent predecessors.[69] By the party's centenary in 2021, the Xi administration had enacted or revised more than 2,400 sets of party regulations, some two-thirds of all rules in force at the time.[70] Authorities regularly publish guidebooks and explanatory articles to help officials navigate the dizzying array of strictures.

Xi's power-grabbing alarmed officials who believed he was upending the prevailing system of collective leadership and growing overreliant on a small inner circle of advisers. He himself showed awareness of the problem, telling officials to "make more friends at the grassroots who can speak from the heart," so they could better "understand the real situation" facing ordinary people and more accurately gauge the national mood.[71] Even so, he remained committed to his autocratic methods. "Some said we have done enough over the past five years in emphasizing the party's centralized unity, and that we should now focus on promoting intra-party democracy," Xi told senior CCDI officials in January 2018. "The people who utter such strange rhetoric, some are politically confused, some bear ill intentions and have dirty linen, and are trying to muddle their way out of trouble."[72]

Two months later, Xi launched the most extensive reorganization of China's party and state bureaucracies in more than a decade, designed to ensure that "the party leads everything." Party committees overseeing economic reforms, finance, cybersecurity, and foreign affairs were upgraded to commissions, giving their directives more weight in a hierarchy-obsessed system. Some government departments were subsumed into their party equivalents. Others were scrapped entirely, with their responsibilities transferred to a party agency.

The most crucial change, which required a constitutional amendment, established a new anticorruption agency with a mandate to extend party-style discipline over millions of government workers outside the party. Despite its formal status as a state organ, the National Supervisory Commission is essentially the CCDI performing similar functions under another name. Its inaugural director was a deputy chief of the CCDI (and a Xi associate), while its investigative staff are mainly party enforcers double-hatting as government inspectors.

On paper, the NSC enjoys a broad remit to investigate government workers for graft, fraud, and dereliction of duty, and, in some cases, mete out punishment without going through the courts. In practice, rights activists say, the new system provides legal cover for the party's draconian investigative techniques. China's legislature passed a new supervision law in March 2018, in conjunction with the NSC's establishment. The law renamed the notorious *shuanggui* process as *liuzhi*, or "retention in place," and set new rules that cap detentions at six months, though suspects are still denied access to legal counsel and their families.[73] Investigators received new powers to use wiretaps and other electronic eavesdropping techniques that were previously considered off-limits for CCDI probes.

The NSC's inaugural director, Yang Xiaodu, said the new agency plugs gaps in government oversight by tripling the number of people subjected to party supervision.[74] This remit means scrutinizing even the lowliest of workers on government payrolls—including office clerks, elementary-school teachers, and urban sanitation workers—and punishing their misdeeds.[75] In some cases, the pressure has grown so intense that offenders turned themselves in, even though they hadn't been suspected. And that is the goal, Yang said, to "let our contingents of cadres maintain their own purity."[76]

QUALITY CONTROL

PAN LEILEI KNEW NEXT TO NOTHING about Marxism when she joined the Communist Party in 2004. A university sophomore at the time, she hadn't studied much socialist ideology and wasn't politically inclined. As a devout Christian, she shouldn't have been allowed into the officially atheist party at all. Her faith notwithstanding, Pan ticked all the right boxes for membership: she was vice chair of the student council, scored good grades, and was popular among her peers. "For people like us with 'low political consciousness,'" Pan recalls, "joining the party was a matter of having your teacher appreciating your qualities and giving you a recommendation."[77]

Pan was one of 1.37 million people who joined the party that year, when its membership grew by 2 percent. Her new affiliation didn't require much of her, aside from attending seminars and writing essays. After graduation, Pan started working, pursued postgraduate studies in theology, and had forgotten all about the party until early 2016, when an official called Pan's father to ask if his daughter wanted to remain a Communist. It was a question that Xi Jinping was, in effect, asking every party member, when he ordered a nationwide audit to weed out the unworthy and retain only those committed to his cause.[78]

If Pan wanted to stay in the party, she would need to stump up years' worth of unpaid membership dues and recommit to party activities. She declined. A party committee in Pan's hometown struck her name off its registers in August 2017, citing her "slack organizational discipline." Pan hadn't heard about the decision until I asked her about it a few weeks later. "The party has never defined my life," she said. "Leaving the party doesn't mean opposing the party."[79]

Since its founding in 1921 as a scrappy underground group of about fifty people, the Chinese Communist Party has swelled into a sprawling bureaucracy with more than 96 million members. If it were a sovereign state, it would rank well within the world's twenty most populous countries, surpassing the likes of Germany and Turkey. Party members reached into every corner of Chinese society, but among them were plenty of deadweight—inept, indifferent, and work-shy members who joined out of self-interest rather than self-sacrifice.

The problem could be traced to the aftermath of the Cultural Revolution, when Deng Xiaoping wanted to revitalize the party with younger and better educated cadres who could provide a strong technocratic core and drive China's development.[80] Officials expanded the recruitment criteria, favoring urbanites with college degrees while deemphasizing applicants' social class, a traditional gauge of political reliability. The party grew less rigorous in enforcing Marxist orthodoxy over the years, an ideological drift that worsened after the Tiananmen Square protests and the Soviet collapse. Officials and scholars debated alternative political models and, at one point, even contemplated renaming the party to reflect its tilt toward state-led capitalism. But rebranding the party would mean renouncing its revolutionary past and potentially causing an irrevocable split within the ranks, said Li Junru, a former vice president of the Central Party School.[81] The party thus remained professedly communist, while opening its doors to more new ideas, Li said.[82]

In practice, this change meant accepting entrepreneurs into the party and tolerating some political pluralism, such as by allowing independent think tanks and civil society to contribute ideas and provide social services. Party membership more than doubled between 1978 and 2012, reaching some 85 million people, or more than 6 percent of China's population. But as China prospered, party membership came to be seen less as a political commitment and more as a way to boost careers and profit from power. A 2005 survey of private entrepreneurs in China found that 62 percent of respondents preferred to hire a party member over a nonmember, all else being equal.[83] Joanne Song McLaughlin, an economist at the State University of New York at Buffalo, estimated in 2016 that party members earned 7 to 29 percent more than nonmembers.[84] "In a society where networks are still the greatest enabler, the Communist Party offers one of the most complete and extensive ones available," said Kerry Brown, professor of Chinese studies at King's College London. Party membership is "a useful box to tick—something that might give you a slight edge when going for a job or promotion."

With time, many party members stopped attending meetings or paying their dues. Some even found it embarrassing to acknowledge their affiliation publicly, conscious that many peers regarded the party as a band of corrupt and careerist mercenaries. "Imagine that Xi is the new CEO of a company where employees don't show up for work, don't participate in work activities, and can't even articulate what the company's mission statement is," said Jude Blanchette, a China expert at the Washington-based Center for Strategic and International Studies. "That's roughly what Xi faced in late 2012."[85]

Such incohesion was a grave threat for a political system that depends on its officials' loyalty and commitment to implement directives from the top. "For a Leninist party, organizational integrity means the competence to sustain a combat ethos among political office holders who act as disciplined, deployable agents," wrote the Berkeley political scientist Ken Jowitt, who argued that Leninist parties must constantly inspire members with a compelling vision to fight for, or risk decaying toward potential doom.[86]

Xi prescribed a multipronged remedy: preaching the gospel, cracking the whip, and trimming fat. At one of the first Politburo meetings he chaired as general secretary, Xi pledged to control the party's size and forge a more selective and elite organization, whose members were fired with fervor and steeled with discipline.[87] "The party's creativity, cohesion and combativeness directly affect not just the fate of the party, but also the fate of the country, the people, and the nation," Xi said later. "If our party weakens, breaks up, or collapses, what meaning will our political achievements have?"[88]

Xi wielded his China Dream as a rallying cry, calling on cadres to devote themselves to restoring national glory. Cognizant that communist ideals lack cachet in China's increasingly capitalistic society, he extolled ancient culture and soft-pedaled socialist dogma. He celebrated Confucius to inspire virtue among officials and justify authoritarian rule as part of a deep-rooted political tradition, even though the party had traditionally condemned the ancient sage as a feudal relic.[89] Xi also promoted Karl Marx, holding up the German philosopher's egalitarian ideals as a spiritual beacon in a materialistic age, while sidestepping the intellectual substance of Marxist theories.[90]

Mao regained some prominence in public life, as Xi invoked his revolutionary slogans and revived some Mao-era political practices that had fallen out of fashion, including "criticism and self-criticism" sessions where cadres find fault with themselves and each other. But Xi also shunned certain tenets of Maoism, particularly the ideas of class struggle and mass mobilization. Whereas Mao had called on the people to attack what he saw as a decaying party, Xi wanted to save the party from within. In this regard, Xi drew inspiration from Liu Shaoqi, a revolutionary leader who championed the use of political inquisitions and education campaigns to enforce correct thinking among party members. Borrowing from Liu's playbook, Xi ordered mass indoctrination drives that required officials to read his speeches and study party directives to become "qualified party members."

Anthologies of Xi's remarks became required reading for all cadres, along with Liu's most famous treatise, "How to Be a Good Communist." Government agencies, state businesses, and even private companies arranged weekly study sessions for party members, who had to pass quizzes testing their political knowledge or face counseling and reprimand. Participants had to document their activities in a process known as *zhuatie youhen*, or "gripping iron and leaving marks"—writing detailed notes and taking photographs that featured party flags, as proof that the meetings were party-related. "Red tourism" boomed as officials arranged pilgrimages to revolutionary landmarks across China, including the rural village of Liangjiahe, where Xi was rusticated during the Cultural Revolution.[91] At government offices and state enterprises, including airlines, banks, and hotels, party members were told to showcase their identity in public by wearing party flag pins and displaying hammer-and-sickle logos at their workstations.

Such chores became even more ubiquitous after the party launched in 2019 a mobile app known as Xuexi Qiangguo, whose name can translate as "Learn from Xi to Strengthen the Nation." A digital-age equivalent of the "little red book" of Mao quotations, the app supplies users with essays, videos, and quizzes promoting "Xi Jinping Thought," which party members must consume to earn points and meet quotas. The chore became vexing enough for some users to devise work-arounds, using custom-made software to simulate app usage.[92]

At Xi's behest, the party launched a nationwide campaign to collect unpaid membership dues, an effort state media billed as a test of loyalty. In 2016, Tianjin officials reported collecting some 277 million yuan, or about $41 million, in backdated dues from more than 120,000 party members at state-owned companies.[93] Online forums crackled with party members fuming about the hit on their finances. An employee at the China Academy of Space Technology in Beijing posted a poem lamenting how he had to make a lump-sum payment worth "five years of transport expenses or the cost of a half-year's supply of baby formula."

Xi's demands diminished the appeal of a government career.[94] As one local official lamented, "We are now required to work like a superman, live like a Spartan and think like a robot."[95] Bureaucrats quit in droves, many seeking greener pastures in the private sector or even early retirement. Official data showed that roughly twelve thousand civil servants resigned in 2015, some 43 percent more than the preceding year, though some researchers believe the true figure is significantly higher.[96] One former Chinese judge, who quit in 2016 to join the private sector, blamed Xi's political-study campaigns for adding to already onerous workloads and sapping morale in the judiciary. "Even when things get busy, our supervisors will still chair study meetings, asking us if we've paid attention to the party plenums, or watched the evening news bulletins," said the former judge, who presided over criminal cases in a major city. "This is an unreasonable use of our time."[97]

The exodus stoked fears of a brain drain, given that competent cadres were more likely to find new jobs while inept ones stayed behind. "Many officials who resigned were in fact high-performing front runners," wrote Li Lianjiang, a professor at the Chinese University of Hong Kong who studied the phenomenon.[98] Others saw an opportunity to trim a bloated bureaucracy. "If we don't allow unqualified and uncommitted members to leave the party, it will lead to misjudgments about the organization's strength," said Ren Jianming, a professor of clean governance at Beihang University in Beijing.

The party has long grappled with the question of its ideal size. As Xi once warned officials, "the Soviet Communist Party had 200,000 members when it seized power, and had 2 million members when it defeated Hitler, but when it had nearly 20 million members, it lost power."[99] Xi ordered tighter gatekeeping in the recruitment process, and directed the party's personnel department to conduct a nationwide audit in 2016 to track down estranged members and cull those deemed unworthy. The party's membership growth rate dropped from 3.1 percent in 2012 to just 0.1 percent in

2017, the slowest expansion since the party started releasing data annually in the early 1990s.[100] Even so, Xi hasn't allowed a decline, which could dull the party's prestige.

Party regulations state that members are free to leave, and that they are automatically deemed to have withdrawn if they fail to attend party activities, pay dues, or perform their duties for six straight months. In reality, quitting isn't quite so easy. "There are members who don't dare to quit, aren't allowed by the party to quit and are unable to quit in practice," one Marxism professor explained, "because there's an overly politicized interpretation of what it means to quit the party."[101] When a state-owned telecommunications giant ordered employees to catch up on years of unpaid party dues, one of its sales supervisors told me she was stunned by the request and considered quitting the party to avoid paying. In the end, she and her colleagues handed over the money—more than two months' wages in her case—because "we were scared that not paying dues or quitting the party would affect our spouses and jeopardize our children's futures," the supervisor said. "Quitting the party could become a black mark against me."[102]

The more prominent a member is, the more difficult it is to leave. High-profile departures cost more in reputational damage for the party, which also prefers keeping influential figures under the thumb of its disciplinary apparatus. Zhang Ming, a retired politics professor at Beijing's Renmin University, discovered this as he tried to get struck off party registers by declining to pay his dues and telling colleagues not to pay on his behalf. University officials told Zhang that they wouldn't revoke his membership, citing orders from above. "They keep dragging their feet," he said. "I find it frustrating."[103]

RED RITUALS

IN THE SPRING OF 2018, soon after Xi Jinping reiterated his demands for eliminating rural poverty in China, government agencies in the southwestern city of Mianyang were told to devote at least 70 percent of their time and personnel to helping the poor. With inspectors due to appraise their progress in meeting poverty-relief targets, local officials were eager to impress—with flawless paperwork.

Pang Jia, a judicial clerk in her twenties, was roped in to help. She and her colleagues filled out forms certifying compliance, a practice known as "leaving marks" to ensure accountability. They clocked in overtime every day while still doing their day jobs at local courts, but their work was often wasted as higher-ups revised their requests. Sometimes superiors asked for formatting changes in the documents. On other occasions they wanted more forms to be filled out. But even the smallest tweaks would consume dozens of hours, as entire dossiers had to be rewritten.

At one point, aid workers had to scramble when their bosses demanded photographic proof for all home visits to poor households. "Some cadres brought winter coats during summer house visits to make up for the photos they didn't take in winter," Pang recalls. But no sooner had they gathered the required photos, than their bosses changed their minds again, saying the images were no longer needed. "Doing all this repetitive work and dealing with inspections really wore me out," Pang says. "We often joked that, as long as we don't need to fill out forms, we'd be happy to go down and live with rural residents for all 365 days a year!"[104]

For all the pains, it never crossed Pang's mind that she and her colleagues could miss their work targets in Xi's poverty-alleviation campaign, a centerpiece of his China Dream. The notion was unthinkable, for failure would invite punishment for negligence or even dereliction of duty. For many officials, the safest option was simply to "cover one's ass," applying tricks of the bureaucratic trade to please bosses, paper over problems, or deflect blame.

The party denounces such practices as "formalism" and "bureaucratism"—the official epithets for behavior whereby officials perform political rituals that prioritize form over substance. Communist governments have agonized over this problem since the days of Stalin and Mao, who both railed against the ills of bureaucracy and tried to curb them with sweeping purges. The phenomenon has grown even more pervasive under Xi, whose top-down governance has driven officials toward foot-dragging, fraud, and other unproductive practices—so as to satisfy their leader's demands and avoid his wrath.

While the ills of bureaucracy are universal, the way some of these dysfunctions manifest in China are peculiar to the party's Leninist structure and revolutionary roots. Unlike Weberian bureaucracies, which are notionally apolitical and dispassionate, Leninist parties are often powered by ideological zeal and charismatic authority. The party in China has long relied on what political scientists call "campaign-style governance," whereby Beijing mobilizes large volumes of personnel and resources to achieve specific goals within a certain time frame. Mao ran his campaigns by appealing directly to the people, often with disastrous consequences. Deng and his successors avoided mobilizing the masses, relying mainly on party members to implement their campaigns. Once activated, cadres would drop everything to focus on their new priorities, knowing that good results could boost their careers. Party researcher Yang Xuedong calls this arrangement a "pressurized system" of governance, where lower-level officials feel compelled to fulfill targets from superiors who control their professional prospects.[105]

Nonetheless, during the reform era, the central leadership often tolerated a degree of local discretion that rewarded innovation and risk-taking. Beijing's broadly worded directives afforded local officials considerable latitude in deciding how to achieve their objectives, while also allowing the central government to blame front-line cadres for any problems that arise. Xi, however, has upended this dynamic with his emphasis on *dingceng sheji*, or "top-level design," whereby Beijing exerts policy control down to the grassroots, backed by the threat of punishment for those who disobey.

Despite Xi's promises to institutionalize governance, he exerts personal influence over how policies are designed and executed. Party insiders describe Xi as a micromanager. This tendency has stifled debate and sowed confusion, sometimes leading to policies that aren't carefully thought through. Some officials, unsure how far to go with Xi's demands, err on the side of aggressive interpretation—pursuing overly ambitious policies with excessive zeal, only to reverse them later.

In 2021, after Xi asked officials to overhaul China's $100 billion private-tutoring industry—seen as fueling a costly rat race among students chasing scarce placements at top schools—education officials drafted plans that included setting new limits on tutoring for children up to the equivalent of ninth grade. But Xi felt that the measures were too soft, and said so in a one-sentence note to the education ministry. Officials responded by expanding the limits to include students up to twelfth grade, and adding requirements for all private education firms to re-register as nonprofits.[106] The harsher rules sparked panic selling on education companies listed in the U.S. and Hong Kong, wiping out tens of billions of dollars' worth of market value.[107] Chinese regulators scrambled to calm foreign investors and promised that Beijing would consider the market impact when setting future policies.[108] And despite the regulatory shock and awe, private tutoring simply went underground, as parents continued seeking classes for their children and fueled the rise of a thriving black market.[109]

Xi's interventions have also discouraged officials from taking initiative on matters where they worry about making choices with which the top man might later disagree. It's a particularly irksome phenomenon for a leader who, despite his dominance within the party, has often found that his power has limits. "Some only act when the party's central leadership has instructed them to do so," Xi told senior CCDI officials, lamenting that many cadres weren't competent enough to handle complicated issues, and were reluctant to act without direct orders from the top. "I issue instructions as a last line of defense," Xi said. "How can it be the case that if I don't issue instructions, no one would do any work?!"[110]

A key problem, officials say, is that Xi often frames his edicts with the provisos of *jiyao yeyao haiyao*, or "not only, but also, and also." As in, officials must not only achieve policy targets, but also minimize side effects, and also satisfy additional requirements—which may well jeopardize their main goals. For instance, Xi wants state enterprises to not only become more market-oriented and competitive, but also serve the party's interests, and also avoid taking too much risk. He wants his diplomats not only to fight vigorously for Beijing's interests, but also to foster a glowing global image for China, and also ensure stable ties with the West. When the Covid-19 pandemic threatened to disrupt Xi's plans to eradicate rural poverty by the end of 2020, he insisted the party must not only achieve poverty-relief targets on time, but also do so in a sustainable manner, and also stamp out fraud and corner-cutting by officials desperate to meet deadlines.

Xi has repeatedly condemned formalism as a "major enemy" of the party and the people, and ordered the CCDI to spare no effort in curbing such behavior.[111] But some of his remedies only seem to create more bureaucracy. In 2020, after Xi demanded new efforts to curb red tape, a party publisher compiled a 136-page anthology of the general secretary's remarks on "formalism and bureaucratism" that became required reading for all cadres. Government agencies and state businesses arranged seminars for officials to study the text, tying up more of their time in political classes.[112]

Such conundrums became prevalent in Xi's war on poverty, particularly after the party issued a directive in 2015 that linked cadres' promotions to their ability to meet poverty-relief targets and required officials to sign "responsibility pledges" that made them accountable if things went wrong.[113] To avoid punishment, some officials turned to deception. One trick was to designate families with incomes above the poverty line as poor households, while excluding those that were actually below the threshold. Thus, when outside inspectors came to assess progress in poverty relief, the designated "poor" households would satisfy requirements for having "escaped poverty."[114] In the southern city of Yuxi, four poverty-relief workers were punished for defrauding their superiors by documenting phantom house calls and citrus-planting classes that residents said never took place.[115]

Some officials pursued "vanity projects" that gave the appearance of local development without actually improving residents' lives. In 2018, township officials in the eastern city of Fuyang ordered houses in some rural villages to be painted white, hoping to deliver some quick results after their superiors demanded that residents' homes be fixed up within three months. Party investigators later discovered that the "whitewashing" project had cost some 8 million yuan, yet haphazard work left many houses only partially painted. Authorities dismissed Fuyang's party boss and condemned the project as a damaging act of formalism that wasted public funds.[116]

Many officials would set aside their day jobs to clock required hours working in poor rural villages, even if that meant neglecting their primacy duties. After flooding at a coal mine in central China killed seven workers in early 2020, labor activist Han Dongfang called up the local union to ask what was being done to improve safety. Not much, a union official replied, as the cadre handling the incident had gone away to join poverty-relief efforts in the countryside. "It's like a local fire brigade seeing a fire in a neighboring district that's getting more attention, so they ignore the fire burning beside them and rush to join in at the other one, because they can score results there," Han says.[117]

Officials blamed the party's deep-rooted culture of "answering to superiors," whereby bureaucrats focus on satisfying their bosses' demands, often by misrepresenting reality and neglecting the needs of ordinary people.[118] But even when cadres do honest work, they spend most of their time on banal rituals, attending repetitive meetings, and producing mountains of paperwork that could cost as much as tens of thousands of dollars to print and weigh in at hundreds of pounds. "The only thing the party has taught us is how to hold meetings and issue documents," one mid-level official told sociologists studying the phenomenon. "If they take that away, what will we do then?"[119]

The scourge has gone online too, with public servants complaining that their WeChat messaging apps have become inundated by bosses and colleagues texting demands around the clock. Chat rooms created for work discussions often devolve into so-called *kuakuaqun*, or "groups of praise," where subordinates speak sycophantically in support of superiors. Some post emojis depicting genuflection "in order to make superiors happy," while others say fawning things like "boss, you've worked hard" or "boss, you're brilliant," according to a party-published guidebook titled *Combating Formalism*.[120]

The problem grew so alarming that in 2019 Beijing launched a national effort to slash red tape, calling on all levels of government to "ease burdens" on officials by reducing the number of meetings and documents, imposing word lengths on paperwork, and setting time limits on internal confabs. Officials made a show of complying with the campaign, but within months, many cadres found themselves crushed again by "mountains of paperwork and seas of meetings." A year after the campaign began, state media documented complaints from one county chief who had to sit through seventy-one video conferences within a month, and a township cadre worn out from attending nine meetings in a week, each dragging for two to three hours as attendees did little more than recite prepared remarks.[121]

Such indulgence in risk aversion and energy-sapping rituals can have dire consequences. When Covid-19 started spreading in the central city of Wuhan in late 2019, local officials feared sharing bad news with disease-control agencies in Beijing, causing delays to the national response. Central-government officials in turn forbade the publication of any research on the novel coronavirus without approval, while holding back critical information about the contagion from the outside world until unauthorized leaks forced them to acknowledge the data.[122]

Even after Xi acknowledged the crisis and ordered a full-scale response, frontline bureaucrats were consumed with paperwork. Instead of conducting health checks or distributing supplies to residents in home confinement, many officials spent hours each day filling out documents for higher-level agencies, many requesting the same information. The problem grew so exasperating that Xi made a personal intervention at a leadership meeting. "There's actually not much difference in the content of these forms," he said. "But not a single document or a single department has helped villages resolve their urgent need for even a single mask or a single bottle of disinfectant."[123]

Xi's domineering ways didn't help either. In 2021, when some officials suggested that China should consider learning to live with virus and move away from "dynamic zero Covid," a containment strategy centered on strict lockdowns and mass testing, Xi responded in anger, sending a note to subordinates asking if officials were becoming "lax and numbed" in fighting the contagion. Zero-Covid remained in place through most of 2022, even after harsh lockdowns across large cities and entire regions enraged citizens and battered an already weak economy.[124] Spurred by Xi's demands for zero tolerance, local officials adopted what many citizens see as unnecessarily draconian measures—confining millions of residents indoors for weeks, manhandling people into quarantine, killing pets, and requisitioning private apartments as isolation facilities. Even as Xi urged officials to minimize social and economic disruptions, he continued insisting that "dynamic zero Covid" was necessary for protecting lives.[125]

Adherence to strict pandemic controls became a test of political loyalty, despite their mounting costs and questionable efficacy.[126] Even as recurrent lockdowns curbed consumption, throttled industrial output, and fueled unemployment, senior officials ordered the party to act in lockstep with the top leadership and "struggle against all words and deeds that distort, question or repudiate our country's pandemic-prevention policies."[127] The chief of China's National Health Commission name-checked Xi thirteen times in an essay urging stronger efforts to contain Covid-19, and called on all party members to unify their thoughts and actions with their leader's demands.[128]

The government vacillated between easing and tightening pandemic protocols toward the end of 2022, as China's economy sputtered under the weight of zero-Covid. Officials said they would loosen some curbs, raising hopes of a return to normalcy, only to double down on control measures when infections surged.[129] The tipping point came in late November, when a fire in a Xinjiang residential building killed at least ten people. Witnesses alleged that Covid-control barriers had hampered rescue efforts, and the ensuing outrage erupted into street protests against zero-Covid in Beijing, Shanghai, and other major cities—which some analysts called the biggest outbursts of dissent in China since the 1989 pro-democracy movement.[130] Days later, Xi told visiting European officials that the unrest stemmed from frustrations with Covid restrictions, and suggested that the pandemic had entered a less deadly phase.[131]

With his containment strategy overwhelmed by highly transmissible Covid variants while economic and social costs continued to mount, Xi relented.[132] Authorities swiftly dismantled zero-Covid policies, softening their rhetoric on the dangers of the virus and lifting public-health protocols.[133] The sudden switch caught local officials off guard, sending them scurrying to redirect resources from containing outbreaks to managing a surge in infections and deaths—particularly among the elderly, a demographic where Covid vaccination rates had been laggard.[134] Hospitals and pharmacies struggled to deal with swelling demand for intensive care and fever medication, a lack of readiness that physicians privately blamed on the government's funneling of resources toward mass virus testing, quarantine programs, and lockdowns during the first three years of the pandemic.

Health officials estimated that nearly 250 million people may have caught Covid in the first twenty days of December 2022, while some 80 percent of China's population likely had infections by late January.[135] Authorities said they recorded more than 72,500 Covid-related deaths in mainland Chinese hospitals during the first six weeks after they started unwinding pandemic controls—a figure widely seen as an undercount, but still a major spike from the roughly 5,200 deaths reported in the nearly three years prior.[136] Though officials insisted that zero-Covid bought time for China to prepare its transition to normality, Xi ultimately lurched toward a haphazard exit that cost lives and exacerbated economic woes.[137] As one Chinese entrepreneur noted, "The ability to control is different from the ability to govern."[138]

Xi's micromanaging style has worn on many bureaucrats, but his discipline enforcers offer daunting deterrence against dissent. "When loyalty is the critical measure for officials, no one dares to say anything," one official told the *Wall Street Journal*. "Even if the instructions from the great leader are vague and confusing about what to do."[139]

CHAPTER THREE

LAW IS ORDER

THE PARTY WRITES THE RULES

"No country is permanently strong or permanently weak. If those who uphold the law are strong, the country will be strong; if they are weak, the country will be weak."

—Han Fei, Chinese philosopher from the third century B.C.

"The problem now is that our laws are incomplete, with a lot of legislation yet to be enacted. Very often, what leaders say is taken as the law, and any disagreement is deemed as law-breaking."

—Deng Xiaoping

"The question of 'whether the party or the law is more important' is a political trap and a pseudo-proposition. . . . Party leadership and law-based governance aren't opposed to each other, but are in unity."

—Xi Jinping

First her lights went out. Then her internet connection died. Wang Yu could hear someone trying to force open her front door, but when she looked through the peephole, she saw nothing. It was around 3 a.m., just hours after she had bidden goodbye to her husband and teenage son as they left to catch a red-eye flight to Australia, where the boy would attend high school. They were supposed to call her after clearing immigration, but her phone hadn't rung and she couldn't reach them. Now someone was trying to break into her apartment, and she was all alone.[1]

Wang sent a message to her friends. Someone suggested she get a nearby friend to come over. Another asked if her door lock was sturdy. Her husband had just changed it, she replied, because he worried about her safety when she was alone at home. As a human rights lawyer, Wang had often been hauled in by police trying to intimidate her into stopping her legal activism. Perhaps this was another attempt. Wang went up to the door and asked, "Who is it?" The sound stopped. Whoever was outside seemed to have left, Wang told her friends.

A loud noise, like an electric drill, rang through the apartment at around 4 a.m. Wang leapt out of bed and tried calling people. But before she could reach someone, a man broke through her door, his headlamp shining on her face. "Don't move! We're from the Beijing Public Security Bureau," he said. "Who are you?" Wang demanded. "What gives you the right to barge in here? Show me your identification." More people rushed in, shoving her onto her bed, cuffing her hands behind her back, and pulling a black hood over her head. They threw Wang into a van, ignoring her teary pleas for her handcuffs to be loosened.[2] Her husband, a rights activist, and their son didn't make it to Australia. They were detained before they could board the plane.

Wang didn't know it yet, but she was far from alone in her plight. Many friends and fellow lawyers who raised the alarm about her disappearance that summer morning in 2015 soon vanished. Wang's boss was detained too, as were several of her colleagues at the Fengrui Law Firm, a Beijing outfit known for representing defendants in politically delicate cases. Authorities ultimately rounded up and interrogated more than three hundred lawyers and activists in a nationwide sweep known as the "709 crackdown," so named after the date it started, July 9. Many of those detained were part of China's *weiquan*, or "rights defense," movement—a loose collective of legal professionals and intellectuals who sought to protect civil rights through litigation and public advocacy, and help clients seek redress for abuses by the state.[3]

Rights defense advocates numbered just in the hundreds, a tiny fraction of the more than 270,000 licensed lawyers in China at the time. But they were an impassioned lot, taking on politically charged cases involving government abuses and negligence—from illegal land grabs and police brutality to food safety scandals and religious persecution. The most zealous ones called themselves "die-hard" lawyers, known for their combative tactics and dramatic gestures aimed at whipping up public pressure against the government. Their pugnacity had long annoyed the authorities, who condemned these lawyers as provocateurs and sometimes detained them.[4] Even so, there was a tacit acceptance within some corners of the party that such activism, while irksome, helped keep local officials in check.

For decades, Chinese leaders have pledged to build robust legal institutions that can deliver good governance and social stability. In theory, this goal meant the party-state would enact laws to prescribe social norms, regulate economic activity, and provide peaceful means for citizens to resolve disputes, while devolving day-to-day enforcement to dedicated professionals—judges, prosecutors, lawyers, and police officers. But as China's economy took off, its fledgling legal system struggled to keep up with the social distensions kicked up by widening wealth gaps and the spread of corruption.

Rights defense lawyers emerged amid this ferment, providing an outlet for aggrieved citizens trying to right government wrongs. Wang herself, a former commercial attorney, turned against the system after suffering what she describes as a miscarriage of justice. Her epiphany came after an altercation with train station employees in 2008, when she was stopped from boarding despite having a ticket and got beaten up for her troubles. She filed a complaint against police officers whom she blamed for failing to intercede, only to be slapped with assault charges that landed her in jail for two and a half years.

"It was a great awakening for me to the arrogance of state power," recalls Wang, who left prison in 2011 determined to fight back. She reinvented herself as a rights advocate, taking on sensitive cases and defending clients that few others dared to represent, including Uyghur academic Ilham Tohti, who received a life sentence in 2014 on separatism charges, and members of the banned Falun Gong spiritual movement.[5] Though mild-mannered among friends, Wang proved to be a fiery presence in court, sometimes lashing out against judges and prosecutors who she believed had violated her clients' rights.

Rights defense advocates like Wang wanted to pressure authorities into applying the law in ways that restrained the party. And win or lose, they were having an effect. Their work stirred public debate on civil rights and prodded the government into adopting some reforms, such as abolishing in 2013 a controversial "re-education through labor" program that allowed police to send people into gulag-like camps without trial. For liberal-minded Chinese, the rights defense movement showed how civil society can improve governance and spur social change. Xi Jinping and his supporters sensed an attempt to usurp the party's authority.

A month before Wang's detention, state media published a scathing commentary denouncing her as an "arrogant woman with a criminal record" who gabbled hypocritically about human rights while masquerading as a lawyer. The vitriol intensified after the 709 crackdown began, seeking to discredit the rights defense movement as a whole.[6] News reports portrayed Wang and her colleagues as hooligans and con artists who hyped up cases to chase fame and remuneration. A commentary in the *People's Daily* denounced rights lawyers as the "black hands" behind efforts to "pollute" the internet and disturb public order.

Authorities brought criminal charges against more than two dozen people. Wang and several other Fengrui staffers were accused of "inciting subversion of state power," an offense punishable with lengthy prison terms. In August 2016, more than a year after she was nabbed, Wang resurfaced in an online video where she admitted to wrongdoing and disavowed her legal work—remarks she later said she was forced to make.[7] Wang and her husband were released soon after, but remained under state scrutiny that made it hard for them to resume their activism.[8] Some of Wang's colleagues were less fortunate. One received an eight-year jail term. Her boss, sentenced to seven years, used his closing statement in court to declare that "Xi Jinping's rule of law has made China ever stronger."[9]

It was a stunning denouement for a spirited community of legal activists who had believed they could nudge China closer toward its constitutional ideals, and perhaps even something akin to Western-style rule of law that constrains the arbitrary use of state power. Fearing further reprisals, many rights lawyers went underground, abandoned their work, or fled abroad. "The rule of law in China has reached a nadir," Wang says. "I'm not just pessimistic, I'm in despair."[10]

The crackdown killed off any lingering hope among politically minded Chinese that Xi was a closet liberal, biding his time before loosening the party's authoritarian grip. In the fall of 2014, less than a year before mass arrests, Xi had pledged to strengthen the legal system and improve judicial fairness to ensure that the party could effectively govern an increasingly complex and contentious society. Since then, his administration has directed what experts describe as China's most relentless pursuit of dissenters since the crackdown on the 1989 Tiananmen Square protests. Authorities detained, intimidated, or jailed hundreds, perhaps thousands, of people—rights lawyers, labor organizers, women's rights advocates, religious devotees, independent researchers, citizen journalists, and other civil-society figures who tried to operate outside of party oversight.

Many faced lengthy detentions with no access to legal counsel. Some, like

Wang, were coerced into making televised confessions, smeared by state media, and denied fair trials. They had no recourse against these abuses, nor could they expect any. Former U.S. president Richard Nixon, in defending his abuses of power, once insisted that "when the president does it, that means that it is not illegal." In China, it is the Communist Party that exercises this prerogative, insisting that the law is a lever of state power, not a restraint. The party can play judge, jury, or even executioner.

Many legal scholars argue that China practices "rule *by* law," whereby the powers that be use legislation as tools of control and impose few constraints on their own authority, as opposed to the "rule *of* law," where the rulers and the ruled are both treated equally under the same legal standards. In Chinese, both concepts can be expressed as *fazhi*, and official translations typically refer to the "rule of law." Semantics aside, many Western observers have condemned what they see as judicial regression under Xi. In 2021, the Washington-based advocacy group World Justice Report ranked China 98th out of 139 nations on a global rule-of-law index, down from 76th among 99 countries in 2014.[11]

Even so, some experts argue that measuring China's legal reforms by Western standards, while useful in some ways, misapprehends the party's views on the law. Chinese agencies commonly seen as judicial institutions aren't meant to engage in legal activity, but are instead driven by the political goal of maintaining social order, according to Donald Clarke, a George Washington University professor who studies the Chinese legal system. What China has been building since the end of the Mao era, Clarke wrote, is "a system for the maintenance of order and the political primacy of the Chinese Communist Party, not for the delivery of justice."[12]

Chinese courts, prosecutorial agencies, and police forces don't act independently, nor do they provide meaningful checks on one another's powers. Rather, they operate in concert as part of a vast coercive apparatus known as the *zhengfa xitong*, or "political-legal system," named after the party's top body overseeing internal security, the Central Political and Legal Affairs Commission, or *zhengfawei* for short. Collectively controlling yearly budgets that surpass China's declared military spending, they are known in party parlance as the "knife handle"—a Mao-era epithet that kindles images of menacing marauders dealing rough justice.[13] As the name suggests, the political-legal system is guided primarily by politics, and in this regard, there is no greater priority than securing the party's power.

Xi describes the "knife handle" as an indispensable guarantor of Communist rule, on par with the propaganda "pen shaft" and the military "gun barrel." He directed far-reaching purges to tighten his grip on the blade and spared no expense in sharpening its edges, doubling China's annual spending on public security to some $217 billion by 2020. He tapped private-sector expertise and leading-edge technology to bolster the party's formidable surveillance networks, marrying new big-data and artificial intelligence tools with Mao-era tactics to screen suspects, silence dissent, and suppress unrest.

Xi's efforts have yielded a nonpareil system of social control. It features "predictive policing" systems that uses data from social media, online shopping platforms, and facial recognition cameras to assess possible threats. It champions the development of a nascent "social credit" system that tracks people's behavior—both in the real world and online—and tries to influence conduct with carrots and sticks.[14] It promotes the use of mobile apps cajoling citizens to gripe about local grievances and snitch on one another.[15] It relies on police forces bolstered with more personnel and better equipment, including drones and forensic devices for extracting data from laptops and smartphones. It transformed regions with large populations of ethnic minorities, including Xinjiang and Tibet, into test beds for new surveillance and coercion techniques, portending what critics describe as China's dystopian future of "techno-totalitarianism."[16]

Not since the Mao era has the party exerted such dominance over Chinese society. And it was that era that seeded the impulses driving Xi's quest for control, amid the chaos unleashed by China's last totalitarian ruler.

ORDER FROM CHAOS

DURING MAO ZEDONG'S LAST INTERVIEW with American journalist Edgar Snow in December 1970, some four years into the Cultural Revolution, the chairman scoffed at the hero worship that had enveloped him. The personality cult was overdone, Mao said, and the four reverential titles he had been given—Great Teacher, Great Leader, Great Supreme Commander, and Great Helmsman—were a nuisance that would eventually be eliminated. But he would still be known as a teacher, because "Mao had always been a schoolteacher and still was one," Snow later wrote of their conversation, conducted over five hours within the cloistered confines of Mao's study. "As he courteously escorted me to the door, he said he was not a complicated man, but really very simple," Snow recalled. "He was, he said, a lone monk walking the world with a leaky umbrella."[17]

This Mao quotation gained considerable cachet in the Western imagination after Snow's account of their dialogue appeared in *Life* magazine. But some observers, dismayed with Snow's partiality toward Mao, said the journalist failed to recognize the cynical immodesty embedded in the chairman's words. "Snow's command of the Chinese language, even at its best, was never very fluent," wrote Pierre Ryckmans, the Belgian-Australian sinologist better known by his pen name Simon Leys.[18] "It is no wonder that he failed to recognize in this 'monk under an umbrella' evoked by the Chairman, a most popular Chinese joke." Ryckmans explained that the expression Mao used, *heshang dasan*, or "a monk opens an umbrella," forms a riddle typically answered with another four-syllable phrase, *wufa wutian*, or "no hair, no sky," conjuring the image of a bald ascetic sheltering from the elements. The real punchline lies in homophony. *Wufa wutian* can also mean "I know no law, I hold nothing sacred."

For many Chinese who lived through his reign, Mao was the law. His despotic "rule of man" was often a recipe for chaos, unleashing bloody purges and mob justice against class enemies on a grand scale. In the latter half of the 1950s, Mao appealed for constructive criticism of the party—expressed through an ancient verse, "let a hundred flowers bloom, let a hundred schools of thought contend"—only to reverse course after receiving vituperative attacks on his government's deficiencies. He directed an "anti-rightist" purge that persecuted more than a million people for allegedly trying to restore capitalism, including legal specialists who denounced officials for flouting the law and meddling in judicial processes. Some Chinese scholars alleged that Mao had even suggested that "rule of man" was better than the rule of law, saying, "an editorial in the *People's Daily* gets implemented across the country, why is there a need for any laws?"[19]

Mao's megalomania reached a bloody zenith in the summer of 1966, when he launched the Cultural Revolution to reclaim his authority from party grandees who tried to sideline him, and rip up a party bureaucracy that he believed had strayed from its revolutionary roots. Fanatical youth became violent vigilantes known as Red Guards, who tormented "counter-revolutionary" elements with verbal and physical attacks. A *People's Daily* editorial, "In Praise of Lawlessness," urged Mao's supporters to destroy "bourgeois law" that repressed the people.[20] Accusations often amounted to convictions. Children denounced parents, students accused teachers, friends turned on each other. Some of Mao's closest comrades were jailed, tortured, and in some cases, left to die. Millions lost their lives amid a frenzied bloodletting that teetered close to civil war.

The carnage had petered out by the time Mao died, but the specter of chaos still loomed. To prevent a repeat of such mayhem, Deng Xiaoping restored key levers of state power—including law enforcement and the judiciary—and urged political reforms to foster the stable governance that China needed to modernize its economy. "The problem now is that our laws are incomplete, with a lot of legislation yet to be enacted. Very often, what leaders say is taken as the law, and any disagreement is deemed as law-breaking," Deng said. The party must establish a sound legal system, he argued, "to make sure that institutions and laws do not change whenever the leadership changes, or whenever leaders change their views or shift their attention."[21]

Under Deng, the party reestablished the justice ministry, rebuilt courts and procuratorates, reopened law schools closed under Mao, and rehabilitated purged legal specialists into academia and professional practice. Authorities enacted new criminal, civil, and commercial legislation, and launched propaganda campaigns to cultivate public awareness of the law.[22] China adopted a new constitution in 1982, articulating fundamental principles for citizens' rights, including equality before the law and access to open trials.

Officials pressed for political reforms known as *dangzheng fenkai*, or "separating the party and the government," aimed at extricating the party from day-to-day governance and limiting its powers to key areas such as policy formulation and personnel appointments. When drafting the 1982 constitution, officials removed references to the party from the document's main text (while keeping them in the preamble), a symbolic change to connote clearer distinctions between party and state. The goal was to create a more professional civil service less fettered by party politicking. Some liberal-minded reformers even hoped that state institutions would grow strong enough to constrain the party's powers.

But Deng never intended to adopt Western-style rule of law, where the governing and the governed are all held accountable to the same legal standards administered by independent courts. Unlike in many liberal democracies, China's constitution is a largely hollow document—most of its provisions take legal effect only after legislators enact specific laws to implement them. Courts operate under party control and have no power to review laws for their constitutionality. As Deng told a visiting Yugoslav leader in 1987, China's political reforms "can neither borrow from the West's so-called democracy nor copy their three-way separation of powers." And most importantly, he said, they "cannot do without the leadership of the Communist Party."[23]

Such instincts intensified after the 1989 Tiananmen Square protests, a near-death experience for the party that fueled its obsession with *weiwen*, or "stability maintenance," a shorthand for suppressing unrest and other threats to Communist rule. Deng responded by purging liberal reformers and halting further "separation of party and government." He persisted with legal reforms, but stressed that the law shouldn't shackle the party.

Deng's successors followed his lead, introducing the doctrine of *yifa zhiguo*, or "governing the nation in accordance with the law," suggesting the party would develop legal institutions as tools of authoritarian control. Both Jiang Zemin and Hu Jintao enacted new statutes to fill gaps in legislation, built up the private legal sector, and mobilized the criminal justice system to quash dissent. After Jiang ordered the party to crush the Falun Gong spiritual movement in 1999, police and judicial authorities played a leading role in the crackdown—rounding up Falun Gong practitioners, pressuring their lawyers against entering not guilty pleas, and directing courts to do their "political duty" by meting out severe punishment.[24]

Hu ramped up the use of judicial organs for repression as rapid economic growth kicked up social unrest. Promising to create a "harmonious society," he ordered officials to maintain stability by any means necessary, spurring the rise of "securocrats" who proved their worth by keeping the peace while delivering growth.[25] Hu named a former police official as chief justice and promoted a judicial doctrine known as the "three supremes"—judges and prosecutors must uphold "the supremacy of the party's cause, the supremacy of the people's interests, and supremacy of the constitution and laws," in that order.[26] His administration encouraged courts to resolve civil disputes through mediation rather than litigation, a shift that some scholars say "pressured courts to function less as enforcers of the law and more as managers of personal ties and conflicts."[27]

Rather than the "rule of law," the party came to operate by what the late political scientist Mayling Birney called the "rule of mandates," whereby front-line cadres were largely free to bend, ignore, or even break the law as they pursued directives—or "mandates"—assigned by their superiors. "Local officials must pursue high priority political targets but have immense discretion over which laws to implement," Birney wrote. "The implementation of laws is thus conditional on their compatibility with higher priority mandates."[28]

By the time Xi took power, China's legal system had become widely resented for corruption and lack of professionalism, a problem exacerbated by heavy workloads and poor pay in the judiciary that spurred a brain drain to the private legal sector.[29] Public distrust of the courts undermined the party's legitimacy, as ordinary Chinese became more insistent that their government should follow the law and protect citizens' rights.[30] Xi responded with judicial overhauls to restore public faith and mitigate a rise in social ferment.[31] If the judiciary lacks credibility, Xi said, "social justice will be widely questioned, and social harmony and stability will be difficult to guarantee."[32]

Xi's legal reforms took shape in the fall of 2014, when the party's Central Committee convened its first-ever plenary session on the "rule of law" and unveiled broad overhauls for the judicial system.[33] They included the creation of "circuit courts," which would ease workloads on the top court in Beijing, and other measures to curb local government interference in court decisions.[34] Authorities pledged to impose lifetime liability on judges who mishandled cases, and prevent the use of torture and other illegal means to secure evidence and confessions. The party strengthened disciplinary supervision over the judiciary, while boosting pay for judges and prosecutors to help retain talent. China's chief justice apologized for a spate of wrongful convictions, while authorities retried some high-profile capital cases and exonerated defendants.[35]

When discussing legal reforms, Xi often invokes Confucian ideas of moral rectitude and benevolent governance by wise and virtuous noblemen, rooting his vision of "law-based governance" in traditional Chinese culture. In practice, Xi hews more closely to another ancient school of thought known as Legalism, or *fajia* in Chinese, whose proponents advocate harsh autocratic rule as a way to impose order.

Legalism dates back to the Warring States period more than 2,200 years ago, before Qin Shi Huang unified China. Whereas Confucianists see inherent goodness in human nature, Legalists believe that people are covetous and driven by self-interest—qualities that threaten social order. A ruler should therefore harness his subjects' intrinsic selfishness to maintain control, dispensing rewards and punishments to keep his officials and ordinary people in line. Only a strong state buttressed by strict laws and heavy penalties, Legalists argue, can avert chaos.[36]

Xi has shown fondness for Legalist thought since taking power. He spoke admiringly of Shang Yang, an ancient scholar and statesman whose ideas on autocratic rule and draconian justice helped turn a feeble Qin state into a powerful kingdom that established China's first imperial dynasty. In 2014, Xi marked the Chinese legislature's sixtieth anniversary with a telling quote from Han Fei, arguably the most famous Legalist thinker. "If those who uphold the law are strong, the country will be strong," he said. "If they are weak, the country will be weak."[37]

Guided by such advice, Xi became China's codifier-in-chief, enacting new laws at an unprecedented pace and enforcing them rigorously. During Xi's first decade in power, the National People's Congress passed on average close to double the number of bills per year than it had done during Hu's second term, according to data collated by Changhao Wei, a fellow at Yale Law School and the founder of NPC Observer, a website tracking Chinese lawmaking activities.[38] Some statutes set the contours of Xi's authoritarian rule, outlawing threats to China's one-party government and territorial unity, as well as economic, social, and cyberspace interests.[39] Others fortified government powers for policing dissent, regulating commercial activity, and protecting the environment. China also clarified the boundaries of acceptable behavior for all citizens by stitching together its first unified code of civil law, which defines personal and property rights over matters including contracts and marriage.[40]

In keeping with his Legalist leanings, Xi demanded iron-fisted enforcement. His administration brought the full weight of the criminal justice system to bear against civil society, prosecuting activists, shutting down nonprofits, and effectively criminalizing many forms of advocacy work that fell outside party supervision.[41] A new law regulating foreign NGOs, passed in 2016, prompted many groups to scale back their activities in China or pull out entirely.[42] Authorities silenced scholars who called for legal restraints on the state's arbitrary use of power, while amplifying voices that rejected Western-style rule of law. Some Chinese intellectuals, for instance, found favor by championing the ideas of German legal theorist Carl Schmitt, who earned infamy as the "crown jurist of the Third Reich" by supplying the Nazis with arguments for unfettered executive power.[43]

Xi's reforms appeared to pay some dividends. Authorities reported a surge in administrative lawsuits filed by citizens against the government, suggesting that ordinary Chinese were putting more faith in the legal system by spending time and money pursuing claims against the state. Under Xi, the annual total of administrative cases adjudicated in court doubled to nearly 270,000 in 2020, while the volume of administrative litigation reached a record 20 cases per 100,000 people in 2019—far higher than the Hu-era annual average of about 8 cases per 100,000.[44] Plaintiffs' win rates in such lawsuits, which dipped from roughly 30 percent to less than 10 percent under Hu, had recovered to nearly 15 percent by 2016, suggesting that Xi's reforms helped reduce judicial interference.[45] But progress has proved more elusive in the criminal justice system, where corruption and impunity were deeply rooted. For Xi, cleaning up China's contingents of police officers, prosecutors, and judges isn't just a matter of good governance, but also a question of political survival.

GRASPING THE KNIFE HANDLE

Moments before Meng Hongwei, one of China's top cops, disappeared during a work trip to Beijing, he sent a cryptic text to his wife: "wait for my call." He had arrived that day in September 2018 for what was meant to be a routine sojourn—the vice minister of public security often shuttled between the Chinese capital and the French city of Lyon, where he was serving as president of the global police agency Interpol.[46] What followed instead was a flurry of international intrigue that drew global attention to how the Communist Party acts less than scrupulously with due process and the rule of law.

Meng never called his wife. Four minutes later, he sent her an ominous signal: an emoji of a knife. She tried ringing her husband but no one answered. One of the world's most senior police officers had vanished.[47]

At first, Meng's wife waited to see if he might re-emerge. But as days passed and a threatening phone call came in warning that people were coming to Lyon to get her, she called the cops. News of Meng's disappearance flashed across international media, while Interpol officials scrambled to ascertain their president's fate. Only then did Beijing start breaking its silence, sending Interpol a letter purportedly written by Meng, saying that he was resigning voluntarily.[48] Shortly after, China's top anticorruption agency announced that Meng was being investigated for violating the law.[49]

The unusual drama around Meng's downfall belied the almost routine quality that China's purges of senior security officials had taken on under Xi Jinping, who has weeded out scores of high-ranking police officers, prosecutors, judges, and spies, all the while tightening his control over crucial levers of coercive power. By his reckoning, years of moral decay and decentralization had allowed the party's law enforcers to stray from their core mission of maintaining order and upholding Communist rule. "We must cultivate *zhengfa* forces that are loyal to the party, the nation, the people, and the law," Xi said. "And ensure that the knife handle is firmly in the hands of the party and the people."[50]

Under Hu Jintao, Beijing delegated significant autonomy to lower-level authorities in the suppression of civil unrest, allowing local security officials to acquire substantive powers and financial resources that became ripe for abuses such as graft and collusion with organized crime. Zhou Yongkang, who was public security minister and then secretary of the Central Political and Legal Affairs Commission, or *zhengfawei*, under Hu, allegedly built personal cliques within the security forces and used his clout to wage factional fights within the party. Bolstered by bulging budgets, the *zhengfa* system swelled into what some critics called "a state within a state"—a rival power center that Xi couldn't tolerate.

Xi asserted control as party chief. He downgraded the role of *zhengfawei* secretary from the Politburo Standing Committee to the broader Politburo. Xi created a new National Security Commission and named himself chairman, assuming personal authority over China's security forces and overhauling their command structures to tackle long-standing problems of interagency rivalry and poor coordination.[51] He purged the *zhengfa* ranks, discarding the corrupt and disloyal while installing allies in key security posts.[52] Xi directed a nationwide crackdown on organized crime, targeting "underworld groups" and corrupt officials—particularly in police and judicial agencies—who colluded with them.[53] Out went Hu's sloganeering for a "harmonious society," replaced by Xi's calls for "building a peaceful China."[54]

In the early years, Xi's *zhengfa* clean-out appeared to focus on high-ranking "tigers." It took down regional security chiefs, senior prosecutors, a vice president of the Supreme People's Court, as well as deputy ministers at the ministries of public security and state security, the latter being China's top civilian intelligence service.[55] The biggest tiger-slaying came in July 2014, when party inspectors opened a case against Zhou Yongkang for corruption and abuse of power, precipitating a broader hunt for those who enjoyed his patronage while he ran the internal security apparatus.[56]

Meng, the Interpol president, was among them. A veteran police officer, he became vice minister of public security in 2004 and held various portfolios over the years, including stints as coast guard chief and director of China's Interpol branch. Meng won election as Interpol president in 2016 thanks to intense lobbying by Beijing, which hoped to leverage the largely ceremonial post for greater influence over the issuance of "red notices"—formal requests for police forces around the world to detain designated fugitives. Rights activists have accused China of using red notices to hunt dissidents, though Beijing insists it only seeks felons accused of serious crimes like corruption and terrorism. Meng sought more control over Interpol's operations but couldn't deliver the red notices that China wanted. Tensions with his superiors rose to the point that he was making arrangements to live abroad after his four-year tenure was over—a risky plan that likely made him a target.[57]

The party expelled Meng, accusing him of showing political disloyalty, defying party decisions, taking bribes, abusing his powers to get his wife cushy finance-sector jobs, and spending state funds to satisfy his family's "luxurious lifestyle."[58] The public security ministry characterized Meng's case as part of broader efforts to eradicate "Zhou Yongkang's pernicious influence."[59] Meng later confessed in court and was sentenced to thirteen and a half years in jail.[60]

For many party insiders, the Meng case underscored how corruption had pervaded China's security forces, and the immensity of Xi's task in trying to clean it up. Xi's solution was to demand more loyalty, under the threat of punishment. The party issued new internal regulations in 2019 aimed at centralizing control over law-enforcement and judicial agencies, and calling on all *zhengfa* cadres "to resolutely safeguard General Secretary Xi Jinping's core position in the party center."[61] The purges rumbled on. Another vice minister of public security, Sun Lijun, was cashiered in April 2020 and later denounced for wide-ranging misconduct that included corruption, damaging the party's unity, and leading a "political clique" of senior law-enforcement officials that indulged in graft and abused power.[62] The police chief in Chongqing went down in June that year, and was eventually jailed for corruption.[63]

In the summer of 2020, Xi launched his most systematic cleanup of the *zhengfa* apparatus to date. The nationwide "rectification" subjected all members of the police, judicial, and security services to months of disciplinary scrutiny and ideological training.[64] Xi entrusted the effort to a loyalist, Chen Yixin, then secretary-general at the *zhengfawei*, who had earned a reputation for taking on politically fraught assignments, from busting organized crime to marshaling epidemic controls in the city where Covid-19 first emerged.[65] Chen kicked off the purge with a high-profile speech, calling on the *zhengfa* system to "turn the blade inwards and scrape the poison off the bone." Urging officials to emulate the 1942–45 Yan'an rectification movement, a purge that consolidated Mao's control over the party, Chen declared that Xi's latter-day cleansing would produce judges, prosecutors, and police officers who were "absolutely loyal, absolutely pure and absolutely reliable."[66]

Within the first week, party inspectors opened cases against at least twenty-one domestic security and judicial officials. Dozens more would go down, including senior figures later identified as members of Sun Lijun's "political clique"—a former justice minister, a provincial security czar, regional police chiefs, and a top discipline inspector at the Ministry of State Security.[67] The public security ministry revised the oath of honor for police officers, dropping a pledge to "promote social fairness and justice" and adding commitments to "defend political security" and "firmly uphold the absolute leadership of the Chinese Communist Party."[68] Ending what some insiders saw as a quasi-amnesty for errant officials who showed restraint after Xi took power, law-enforcement agencies ordered retrospective reviews of old cases—including organized-crime probes, commuted jail sentences, and parole decisions—going as far back as thirty years, so as to uncover past misconduct by police, prosecutors, judges, and prison officials.[69]

Xi's purges at times cast an uneasy spotlight on local corruption and judicial misconduct. State media credited his crackdown on organized crime—known as *sao-hei chu'e*, or "sweep black and eliminate evil"—for breaking up collusion between officials and mobsters, and anecdotal evidence suggests the campaign has been popular among ordinary Chinese angered by the impunity of local crime rings. But some high-profile scandals also exposed the depth of impunity within local security forces, where some officials have run roughshod over legal procedures to meet quotas for arrests and convictions, or even engaged in organized crime themselves.

Such practices burst into view in the northern industrial city of Baotou, where, amid allegations of police and prosecutorial misconduct, an organized-crime trial collapsed in 2020 and became a cause célèbre for judicial reform. The case centered on Wang Yongming, a moneylender and Baotou native accused of leading an "underworld group" that engaged in loan-sharking, extortion, and blackmail.[70] His daughter, Wang Ran, claimed a local policeman running his own money-lending business framed her father. According to her version of events, the local cop started feuding with her father after one debtor borrowed from both men but only repaid the debts owed to the elder Wang. The policeman then tried to extort money from Wang, before opening a criminal investigation against him as payback.[71]

Lawyers representing Wang and his alleged accomplices accused Baotou authorities of prejudging the outcome at a pretrial meeting, where police, prosecutors, and court officials—according to an account from the local procuratorate—reached agreement on how to manage certain aspects of the case, including its classification as organized crime and the handling of the alleged gang's "illegal gains." The defense also accused Baotou police of accepting fabricated evidence from one of Wang's debtors and wrongfully denying bail to the moneylender, who lawyers believe should have qualified for medical bail on account of his recent leg amputation and kidney transplant.[72]

Irregularities marked the trial from the start. The court restricted public access to the hearings and declined to stream the proceedings online, decisions that defense lawyers said violated rules on judicial transparency. The defense also accused judges of improperly limiting their opportunities to speak. One hearing descended into chaos after defense lawyers accused a prosecutor, Li Shuyao, of soliciting and accepting bribes from Wang's children in return for reclassifying the case under less serious offenses—a promise that Li allegedly reneged on after taking the money. The defense insisted that Li be removed from the trial and wanted to play an audio recording as evidence of the prosecutor's guilt. The court denied their requests.[73]

One defense lawyer, Xu Xin, grew so exasperated that he decided to quit the case. But when Xu approached his client to discuss his decision, a group of bailiffs rushed to confront the lawyer, pointing and shouting at him to stop him from speaking. A photograph of the scene went viral on Chinese social media, where users expressed incredulity at the courtroom drama. "If I keep working on this case, I might die from anger," said Xu, who later succeeded in withdrawing.[74]

By then, the trial had drawn so much bad press that higher-ups decided to step in. Li, whom local officials once praised as an "honest cadre," was placed under investigation by Baotou authorities, who later sacked the prosecutor and sentenced him to four years' jail for corruption.[75] The prosecutors' office for Inner Mongolia, the region where Baotou is located, acknowledged that the mishandling of the case had "severely damaged public trust in the justice system."[76] The region's top court ordered a new trial to take place in another city.[77]

The second trial proceeded with little fuss. Wang was sentenced to fifteen years in jail after pleading guilty to organized crime, fraud, and public disorder offenses, among other charges. His thirteen codefendants received prison terms ranging from six months to fifteen years.

Publicly, the defense team cheered the result, saying their clients received lighter sentences than they would have if the first trial had proceeded. In private, the mood was more circumspect. Some in the legal community believed the Wang case only demonstrated the deep decay in China's criminal justice system, and that Xi's reforms wouldn't amount to much. "It's just a gust of wind," one lawyer told me. "Gone once it blows over."[78]

SURVEILLANCE STATE

ONE CHILLY MORNING IN EARLY 2017, China's top official in Xinjiang, Chen Quanguo, was cruising through the regional capital of Urumqi when he stopped his motorcade and told his aides to call the cops. Heavily armed police and paramilitary officers arrived in just fifty-four seconds, having rushed over from one of the hundreds of small police stations that blanketed the city. Chen praised the officers but demanded better. If security forces "arrive one second earlier," he said, "the safety of the general public increases by one bit."[79]

As the Communist Party chief of Xinjiang from 2016 to 2021, Chen directed a full-throttle campaign to pacify China's northwestern frontier, forcibly assimilating Muslim minorities while building a policing regime unmatched in scale and sophistication. Some critics called him the "hard edge" of Xi Jinping's draconian rule, who blended cutting-edge techniques with traditional tools of repression, and set a template for China's shift toward harsher, technology-driven authoritarianism.

Building on security methods he had developed earlier in his career, Chen installed thousands of high-tech police stations throughout Xinjiang and staffed them with police and paramilitary officers. Security forces screen for threats with facial-recognition cameras and handheld devices that can scan mobile phones for sensitive material among photos, messages, and other data. Networks of surveillance cameras blanket urban areas, supported by big data and "predictive policing" systems that track suspects and identify potential threats on account of their behavior. Authorities collected wide-ranging biometric data from Xinjiang residents aged twelve to sixty-five, including DNA samples, fingerprints, iris scans, and blood types.[80] Some of these methods have filtered to other parts of China, where authorities adapted or copied Xinjiang security techniques to address local policing needs.

Much of the Xinjiang security state runs on commercial software and gadgetry that are ubiquitous in the daily lives of ordinary Chinese. The WeChat mobile app is almost universally used in China for messaging, sharing photos and videos, paying utility bills, hailing cabs, reading news, booking doctors' appointments, and accessing government services. Facial-recognition systems facilitate payments at restaurants and stores and identity verification at office and residential buildings. Chinese internet giants apply big data and artificial intelligence solutions to glean insights into consumer behavior.

The party grasped the potential of these technologies for social control. Security agencies, government censors, and their private-sector partners now use these systems to identify citizens in public spaces, monitor their real-world and online behavior, snoop on social media and mobile-messaging apps to detect malcontents, and even censor subversive speech almost instantaneously. Facial-recognition tools deployed to screen crowds at mass events have helped authorities nab fugitives, including several detained while attending a Hong Kong pop star's concerts.[81] In some regions, authorities deploy voice-pattern analysis systems, cameras capable of creating three-dimensional face images, and DNA sequencers to scoop up biometric data from local residents for policing purposes.

Many of these tools were first tested at scale in Xinjiang, a northwestern frontier region that borders Central Asia and is home to roughly 12 million Uyghurs, a mostly Muslim Turkic people. After China suffered a string of deadly terror attacks in 2014 that authorities attributed to Uyghur separatists, Xi ordered an all-out pacification campaign to suppress anti–Communist Party dissent and end ethnic violence—an effort that has transformed Xinjiang into one of the most heavily policed regions in the world.[82] "In the face of deranged violent terrorists," the party must "unhesitatingly and unwaveringly apply the weapons of the people's democratic dictatorship, and focus energies on delivering a devastating blow," Xi told officials in May 2014. "Do our utmost to leave no gaps in our defenses, and not miss any hidden dangers."[83]

Chen, the man who built the Xinjiang security state, spent much of his career tackling social ferment and refining the party's tactics for suppressing unrest. Born in 1955 into a peasant family, Chen was serving in an army artillery unit when he joined the party as a twenty-year-old in the dying days of the Cultural Revolution. People who knew Chen, whose given name can translate as "whole nation," describe him as ambitious. He distinguished himself as a student leader at Zhengzhou University in the capital of his native Henan province, becoming president of his politics and economics class of roughly 150 people.[84] As a local official in Henan, Chen won promotion faster than many peers and in the late 1980s became the youngest county chief in one of China's most populous provinces, where rural poverty and the spread of Christian and other religious groups tore at party control.

Chen's ascent through the Henan hierarchy coincided with China's rapid economic growth during the reform era, which also stirred up opportunities for crime, corruption, and street protests. To contain such ferment, the party demanded that local officials ensure stability while promoting development. Local administrators needed to provide better social services, deploy closer surveillance, and achieve swifter suppression of dissent and unrest, if they wanted to score good appraisals and promotion.

Chen thrived under these requirements. After Beijing ordered a crackdown in 1999 on the Falun Gong spiritual movement, which party leaders regarded as an "evil cult," Chen participated in the suppression as a senior provincial official, whose roles came with responsibilities over the destruction of the group's pamphlets, books, and CDs. He later oversaw efforts to cleanse Henan party ranks of Falun Gong by re-educating and expelling offenders, according to provincial histories. Every official "knew very clearly that they had to crush Falun Gong with all their might," according to He Sanpu, a former Henan official and Falun Gong believer, who said he was subjected to re-education classes at the time. Toward the end of his Henan stint, Chen became the deputy head of a new provincial party committee on "peace and stability building," coordinating public security work.

In 2009, Chen was named deputy party chief of Hebei, the northern province that surrounds Beijing. During his twenty-two months there, he encountered a new grid-style policing method being tested in the provincial capital, Shijiazhuang. The city built a network of 110 "police services stations" where officers, in addition to regular duties, performed community outreach, fielding queries on municipal services and giving directions and water to elderly folk.[85] The concept stemmed from the party's "grid management" system—first tested in the early 2000s—that divides residential communities into units of several hundred households to facilitate data gathering and local governance. Authorities declared the Shijiazhuang experiment a success, saying these stations maintained a constant police presence on the streets and reduced response times to security incidents. Police agencies from dozens of other localities sent officers to study the new system.[86]

Chen brought that know-how to Tibet, where he was named party chief in 2011—three years after the Himalayan region was rocked by violent protests against government repression of local culture and religious beliefs.[87] His job, in essence, was maintaining stability. Authorities must lay down an "inescapable net" and "ensure that there are no cracks, no blindspots," Chen said. "Across all 1.2 million square kilometers of border territory, the voice and image of the party and government must be heard and seen."[88]

Chen stationed tens of thousands of party members in villages and temples under an outreach program that doubled as a surveillance service for monitoring the restive Buddhist-majority population. He brought in grid-style policing by installing roughly seven hundred "convenience police stations"—small outposts that operated around the clock and doubled as mini community centers, equipped with household tools and cold medications. State television produced a twenty-episode drama series to glamorize these security outposts.[89] While touring the Tibetan capital of Lhasa in 2012, Chen told a local storekeeper that "convenience police stations are the people's guardian angels."[90] But many locals saw it differently. Tibet had "become the world's largest prison," blanketed with security checkpoints and surveillance cameras, said Dhondup Wangchen, a Tibetan filmmaker now exiled in the U.S. "You get anxiety of someone looking at you from different angles all the time."

Chen also tried to dilute the Tibetans' sense of ethnic identity, a precursor to the forced assimilation program he would run in Xinjiang. He promoted education in Chinese instead of in Tibetan, and offered financial and other incentives to encourage interracial marriages. Many Tibetans had their passports confiscated, and thousands of people were forced into re-education classes designed to eradicate the influence of the Dalai Lama, the exiled Tibetan spiritual leader whom Beijing denounces as a separatist.

Rights activists pummeled Chen, but he seemed to pay little attention. U.S. Representative Jim McGovern, who met Chen as part of a congressional delegation visiting Tibet in 2015, recalls the Chinese official as filibustering, taking up most of the two-hour meeting by lecturing his guests on China's economic and environmental policies. "He was not interested in having a real conversation; he was giving a speech," McGovern says. "He seemed totally unsympathetic to concerns over the human-rights situation in Tibet."[91]

Chen's methods won him favor in Beijing, which was looking for a harder-edged approach in Xinjiang as ethnic tensions escalated there. He got the job in August 2016, becoming the first Chinese official to have served as regional chief in both Tibet and Xinjiang. Days after arriving in Urumqi, he visited a police command center to demand all-out efforts to restore order. Officials must infuse themselves with "the philosophy that stability trumps everything," said Chen, who demanded the construction of a security dragnet that has "no blind spots, no cracks, and no gaps."[92]

During Chen's first year or so in charge, Xinjiang advertised some one hundred thousand policing-related jobs and nearly doubled its annual security expenditure in 2017 from the previous year, to 58 billion yuan, or roughly $8.6 billion at the time.[93] He intensified many policing measures that his predecessor had imposed, such as strict curbs on religious practices common among Uyghurs—among them men growing beards and women wearing face veils. Government data indicated that Xinjiang authorities prosecuted more than 533,000 people between 2017 and 2020, at a rate six times higher than the national average during that period.[94]

Chen doubled down on grid-style policing, installing more than 4,900 convenience police stations in his first four months, to create what he called a robust "system of preventive social control." Sited about one thousand to sixteen hundred feet apart in urban areas, these one- to two-floor stations were the most advanced and multifunctional Chen had built to date, featuring amenities for residents including wireless internet, phone chargers, first-aid kits, and in some cases, even lawyers providing legal services.[95] Chen tested his system's efficacy with regular spot checks, appearing unannounced to test officers' response times. By the summer of 2018, he had put at least 7,700 convenience police stations into operation across Xinjiang.[96] Local musicians wrote a song in tribute, with lines such as "Little convenience police stations, speaking of them makes hearts feel warmth."[97]

Chen scaled up networks of security cameras linked with police databases. His government tapped big-data analytics, collecting and sifting through vast pools of personal information—such as individuals' movements, as well as banking, health, and legal records—to try to identify potential threats and anticipate crime, protest, and violence. As one engineer with a state-run defense contractor put it, the idea is to manage urban environments like battlefields and "apply the ideas of military cyber systems to the field of civilian public security."[98] In practice, the indicators used were often dubious. Authorities detained Uyghurs for showing religious piety in public, maintaining ties to relatives living overseas, owning multiple phones, or even claiming to not own any phones.[99]

Xinjiang became a favored proving ground for security techniques. Police agencies across China have sent officers there on exchange programs, during which participants learned new counterterrorism tactics that they would bring back for use in their home regions.[100] Nearby areas with large Muslim populations, such as Qinghai province and the Ningxia region, started replicating Xinjiang's use of convenience police stations.[101] In Tibet, security agencies acquired surveillance and predictive-policing systems that attempted to forecast the activities of targeted persons, such as by reviewing data from bank accounts, social media, and cellphones to build a picture of a person's lifestyle and social circles.[102]

Xinjiang-style security has emerged even in areas that haven't suffered major ethnic violence in recent history, particularly after China's public-security minister in 2018 praised the use of convenience police stations and called for a broader rollout.[103] Nanning, the capital of the southeastern region of Guangxi, introduced dozens of police posts that are connected to the city's digital security-management system and serve as "counterterrorism bridgeheads." In Gansu province, home to roughly 13 million people from the Muslim Hui ethnic group, the capital of Lanzhou created a network of convenience police stations staffed with counterterrorism combat teams. Local authorities called them "urban lighthouses," from which police and paramilitary "guardian angels" watch over the city twenty-four hours a day.[104]

A TANGLED WEB

As COVID-19 TORE THROUGH CHINA in early 2020, Zhou Shaoqing took to Twitter to criticize the government response. As a former censor who scrubbed sensitive speech from some of China's most popular mobile apps, he knew how authorities sought to control information, and thus doubted official statements about the contagion. "The Chinese Communist Party system regards stability as its principle, and in the face of big problems, everyone protects themselves," Zhou, a thirty-year-old single father of two, wrote to his roughly three hundred followers at the time. Hospital and health officials, he said, "would all, intentionally or otherwise, reduce the number of confirmed cases and turn big problems into small ones."[105]

Days later, three men showed up at Zhou's apartment in the northeastern city of Tianjin. Dressed as neighborhood volunteers, they told Zhou that they were doing public outreach on pandemic control measures. When Zhou opened the door, the trio rushed in and pressed him onto the ground. Seven uniformed police officers followed. His young daughter started bawling as she too was held down. "I was stunned, and then I was scared," Zhou recalls. One officer held Zhou's phone to his face and asked if the Twitter account on it was his. "Yes," he replied.[106]

While working as a content moderator at the Chinese internet firm ByteDance, Zhou helped enforce state censorship directives by removing obscene and anti-party material from the company's popular Jinri Toutiao news aggregator app and the video-sharing platform TikTok. In private, though, Zhou was disillusioned with the party and often tweeted about his resentment of authoritarian rule.[107] His posts had earned him a police reprimand in 2018, but after a lull, Zhou resumed tweeting, emboldened by the seeming lack of consequences.

This time there was no let-off. Prosecutors accused Zhou of "picking quarrels and provoking trouble" by publishing and retweeting more than 120 Twitter posts that besmirched China's leaders, its political system, and its Covid-19 response. Zhou confessed and signed a statement of repentance, hoping he could get back to his children sooner. Even so, a local court sentenced him to nine months' jail in November 2020, including time in police custody.[108] The severity of his punishment surprised Zhou, given how small his Twitter following was. "It must have been vindictive," he said. "I felt helpless and indignant."[109]

Authorities who once relied on informants to uncover what people said in private now do so with ease using digital surveillance. Sophisticated algorithms developed by Chinese tech firms can detect sensitive words and images and intercept them mid-transmission, leaving senders and would-be recipients unaware that their conversations have been censored.[110] Ordinary people increasingly face harassment and punishment for imprudent comments made in social media chat rooms and messaging apps, where stray speech to family or friends can be captured as evidence.[111]

While direct criticism of the party and its top leaders have always drawn harsh penalties, authorities have taken an increasingly dim view even of idle backchat about politics. A construction supervisor was detained for five days after cracking jokes on WeChat about a rumored love triangle between a high-ranking Chinese official and a celebrity. An auto mechanic was punished after swearing in a WeChat group while questioning the intelligence of police officers conducting checks in the rain.[112] Li Wenliang, a doctor who used WeChat to raise early alarms about the novel coronavirus in late 2019, was reprimanded by police for allegedly spreading rumors— although the penalty would be rescinded weeks after Li died from Covid-19 in February 2020, amid public outrage over how state censorship had hampered the government's contagion response.[113]

China's zero-tolerance approach to Covid-19 boosted an already formidable state apparatus for corralling citizens.[114] Authorities restricted movement with a ubiquitous smartphone-based "health code" system that classified people by their potential Covid exposure—green, yellow, or red—based on their travel history, test results, and other data. Green codes were required for entry into buildings and public spaces or domestic travel, whereas yellow and red codes typically resulted in restrictions on mobility or compulsory quarantine.[115] What began as a disease-control mechanism became a handy tool for social control, as some security agencies started using health-code data to flush out fugitives and block dissidents from traveling.[116] Some activists, petitioners, and rights lawyers reported instances where their health codes turned yellow or red, forcing them to scrap travel plans or go into quarantine, even though they were staying in areas with no known Covid cases.[117]

This practice sparked controversy in June 2022, when depositors with several rural banks in Henan seeking access to frozen funds were given red health codes as they tried to travel to the provincial capital of Zhengzhou to stage a protest and seek redress. Municipal authorities sent at least dozens of these would-be protesters into quarantine or forced them out of Zhengzhou citing their red codes—an incident that sparked national uproar over the government's apparent abuse of the health-code system.[118]

The party also went after users of foreign social media services, including Twitter and Facebook, even though China blocks such platforms and the vast majority of people in the country can't access them. Chinese users who posted allegedly subversive content—such as criticism of Xi and the party—have been detained by police, sometimes for days or even weeks. Interrogators often also ask these users to delete posts, sign pledges not to re-offend, or shut down their accounts.[119] The toughened enforcement coincided with a noticeable rise in anti–Communist Party discourse on Twitter, amplified by U.S.-based operatives like fugitive Chinese businessman Guo Wengui, who were using social media to fan what many saw as disinformation about China. Beijing's crackdown on Twitter speech forms part of its "long arm" efforts to control global narratives about China, says Yaqiu Wang, a China researcher with the advocacy group Human Rights Watch. "Propaganda only works when it is coupled with censorship of opposing views."

The penalties grew harsher as the crackdown rumbled on. Between 2017 and early 2021, Chinese authorities sentenced more than fifty people to jail for allegedly using Twitter and other foreign social media platforms to criticize the party and its leaders, according to court and government records that I examined for a *Wall Street Journal* report documenting China's increasing use of custodial sentences to punish online dissent.[120] "In the past they only made threats and took statements," said Huang Genbao, an online activist who spent sixteen months in custody after getting detained in 2019 for criticizing the party on Twitter. "This time they were doing things for real, I didn't expect it."

Many of those jailed had modest followings, in the hundreds or low thousands.

Sun Jiadong, a Zhengzhou resident, had just twenty-seven Twitter followers when police detained him in late 2019 for allegedly spreading falsehoods about the party, Hong Kong, Taiwan, and Xinjiang. In one post, Sun said: "Glory to Hong Kong, shame on Communist bandits." Prosecutors said his tweets received 168 likes, retweets from 10 users, and comments from 95 users—enough for the court to sentence Sun to thirteen months in jail.[121]

Even bearing witness to the party's authoritarian ways has become increasingly fraught. An anonymous activist who maintains an online database of Chinese law-enforcement actions against speech offenses says he believes that authorities have been trying to identify him by using technical means. The government also purged information from a state-run repository of judicial documents that had been a key source for the activist's research. The repository, known as China Judgements Online, used to host thousands of court documents related to social media speech offenses, but the majority of such dockets disappeared over the summer of 2021, after the activist's work gained attention through news reports by the *Wall Street Journal* and the *New York Times*. "I personally feel that this was directed at my data-collection work," said the activist, who tweets under the handle @SpeechFreedomCN. Despite the risks, "I will definitely keep doing this work," he told me. "Because there's no turning back."[122]

CHILLING EFFECT

LU YUYU AND HIS GIRLFRIEND thought they were picking up some online shopping on a sunny summer day in 2016 when police ambushed them. It was just past noon in the southwestern city of Dali when the couple arrived at a local courier station on their electric scooter, the rice noodles they'd had for lunch still swirling in their stomachs. Lu waited by the street while his girlfriend, Li Tingyu, went inside. A posse of men surrounded him, wrestling him into a black sedan and sliding a dark shroud over his head. Moments later, he heard Li screaming his name as a group of women pushed her into another car.

"I had imagined countless times before how this day would arrive and how I should react," Lu wrote later of his arrest.[123] "But everything happened too quickly, I had no time to react, no time to fear." The men, who identified themselves as Dali police, drove Lu to his apartment to conduct a search. As the car neared their destination, he caught a glimpse of Li with a shroud over her head. That was the last time he saw her, Lu recalls. "Perhaps the last time in this life."[124]

Lu and Li were a pair of reclusive bloggers who had spent years documenting protests, strikes, and other forms of civil disorder. Their findings, published on social media, provided an invaluable resource for activists, academics, and journalists peering into the social undercurrents coursing through the world's second-largest economy, where data on civil unrest are rare and even considered state secrets. For the Communist Party, however, the couple's work smacked of subversion.

Police accused Lu and Li of "picking quarrels and provoking trouble," a broadly defined offense typically used for disorderly conduct such as brawling and damaging property. A couple of days passed before their friends recognized their social media silence as a sign of trouble, and rights-defense lawyers tracked the couple down to a detention center in Dali. Investigators questioned Lu for weeks, sometimes waving copies of his blog posts and tweets at him. "Why do you collect and publish this information?" one official asked, to which Lu said he was documenting history. "If you're documenting history, you can document it on your own computer. Why publish it?" the official demanded. "History is meant for people to see," Lu replied. "If you don't let people see it, how can you call it history?"[125]

For decades, the party had tolerated a limited role for activists, rights lawyers, and nonprofits to contribute policy ideas, provide social services, and keep local officials on their toes. The number of "social organizations" in China, as the party calls NGOs, had roughly doubled from more than two hundred thousand in 1989 to nearly five hundred thousand by 2012, offering services like disaster relief and welfare for underprivileged people.[126] Allowing civil society some room to operate, so the thinking went, would help authorities detect problems in society before they festered.

Xi discarded this approach, insisting that the party control all aspects of governance. Digital surveillance had made it easier for the government to track social problems on its own, and activists tackling public ills were more and more seen as usurping the party's authority. Initially, authorities went after individual activists and small NGOs, harassing them with well-worn tactics from the Hu era. The pool of targets started widening in spring 2015, when a group of feminists were detained for planning protests against sexual harassment on public transport.[127] Then came the 709 crackdown on rights defense lawyers that summer. By winter, police were rounding up more than a dozen labor activists, many of whom had helped workers engage in "collective bargaining" with employers—a sensitive practice in a country where state-controlled unions are the only legal form of organized labor.[128]

And then they came for foreign NGOs. Swedish activist Peter Dahlin, who ran a China-based group providing funding for local rights lawyers, was detained in January 2016 for allegedly endangering state security, forced to make a televised confession, and then deported.[129] Months later, China enacted a law granting the government sweeping powers to regulate foreign nonprofits and limit the ability of local groups to work with overseas partners and obtain funding from abroad.[130] By 2018, the party came to see even young Marxists as a threat. That year, authorities detained dozens of avowedly Marxist college students who staged protests in support of workers at a Shenzhen factory battling alleged management abuses, while some Chinese universities blocked Marxist groups from re-registering on campus.[131]

Lu and Li seemed unlikely targets even as the dragnet widened around them. The couple kept almost entirely to themselves, and hadn't joined any organized activism. Some of their activist friends had never met them in person. But political red lines were shifting in Xi's China, and even the most cautious dissidents were getting caught.

Lu was born in 1977 in a village outside the southern city of Zunyi, where his father ran a seedling farm. The youngest of three children, Lu was a shy boy, and his parents sent him to live with different families to learn how to interact with people. He struggled with studies and was often bullied in school. Eventually he learned to make friends and fend for himself—skipping class, playing games, and staying out late at night drinking *baijiu*, a fiery liquor made by fermenting sorghum.[132]

Lu enrolled at a local university to study politics and economics, but went to prison, aged nineteen, for wounding someone during a street fight that started, he says, because he was standing up for a friend. During his six years in jail, his mother died and his father's business failed. Lu drifted from job to job after his release, working at factories and building sites. He discovered "dark folk" music, a mix of folk and industrial styles, and came up with his online moniker, "darkmamu," by pairing his musical tastes with the romanized Chinese word for numbness. "I saw no hope in anything and had no direction in life," he says.[133]

In 2011 he came across social media chatter about such Chinese activists as dissident artist Ai Weiwei. Censorship on China's Twitter-like Weibo platform was relatively loose at the time, and users often could debate social issues and question government policies. Inspired by what he read, Lu staged a one-man demonstration in 2012 along a tony shopping street in Shanghai, raising a banner that urged China's leaders to declare publicly their personal assets and called for the right to vote. Police chased him out of the city. When he returned two months later, they detained him for ten days. As social unrest flared across China that year, including high-profile protests against power and copper plant projects, Lu decided to document as many incidents as he could.

He sifted through online chatter, images, and videos of public unrest, posting his findings on Weibo. He sharpened his abilities to cross-check information, corroborating details from various sources and rejecting posts he believed to be false. As the process grew more and more time-consuming, Lu quit his job at a plastics factory and threw himself into documentation work full-time, but the long hours and his dwindling savings led him to question whether his approach was sustainable. He wrote a Weibo post saying he was considering giving up. Friends and acquaintances urged him to reconsider, saying he was producing valuable insight into social conditions.[134]

Among those encouraging him was Li Tingyu, a university student in the coastal city of Zhuhai. Born in 1991 to working-class parents, Li grew up in relative comfort, able to indulge in her love for reading through books and access to the internet. She chose to major in English at university, knowing that English texts were less frequently censored than Chinese ones. Friends knew her as an independent-minded woman with a keen interest in politics and social affairs, who taught classmates how to circumvent China's "Great Firewall" of internet controls.[135]

To Lu, Li was simply Jane. They first met online in early 2013, when Jane reached out to express admiration for Lu's work, and their conversations soon blossomed into long-distance romance. When Lu wavered on his documentation work, Jane persuaded him to keep going. She suggested that Lu solicit donations to fund himself and open a blog and a Twitter account to disseminate his findings. She herself published an interview with him to drum up support. "The Weibo users who publish original posts about these incidents have very few followers," Lu said in the interview. "If I don't search for them, they either get censored or will never see the light of day."[136]

Lu moved to Zhuhai to live with Jane in the summer of 2013. They started working full-time together, living off donations that streamed in from friends, acquaintances, and strangers. Their output caught the eyes of activists and academics studying social unrest in China, and local authorities started paying attention too.[137] Police showed up at the couple's apartment to warn them. Their landlord refused to renew their lease. Strangers knocked on their door and claimed they were the new tenants. Eventually they lost running water.[138]

The couple moved to Dali in early 2014 to escape the harassment, isolating themselves from family and friends. Even though they spent most of their time working at home and minimizing their digital footprints, police still tracked them down. By the time they were arrested in June 2016, the couple had compiled a data set comprising 67,502 protests painstakingly documented with descriptions of participants' grievances, eyewitness accounts, photographs, and videos.[139] Their last blogpost, published about an hour before police detained them, listed ninety-four incidents of unrest, including workers demanding unpaid wages and disgruntled homeowners who said they were cheated by property developers.[140]

During the weeks of interrogation, Lu's thoughts would drift to his girlfriend and their pet tomcat, "Little Yellow Fur." Police and prosecutors pressed Lu to plead guilty in return for a lighter sentence, and even brought his father to persuade him. But Lu refused. When an officer told Lu "you ruined Li Tingyu," he wanted to reply saying it was the government that did so, but held his tongue. "Because if she hadn't gotten to know me, she definitely wouldn't be thrown into jail," he recalls thinking at the time.[141]

Lu tried to keep his spirits up by reading books, studying English, and doing physical exercises like push-ups and sit-ups. One spring day in 2017, after being interrogated and made to watch propaganda videos for a month, he snapped. When a guard ordered him to look down during a cell inspection, he picked up a bottle and threw it at the guard. The guards pressed Lu to the ground, cuffed his wrists and ankles, and started beating him. One guard stepped on Lu's legs. Lu spat in his face. The guard threatened to beat Lu to death. "If you don't kill me," Lu retorted, "I'll look down on you." The guard was dragged away by his colleagues. Lu started a hunger strike, demanding an apology from the guard who stepped on his leg. Officials acquiesced and the guard apologized. Lu started eating again.[142]

Unbeknownst to Lu, Jane had confessed. She received a suspended two-year sentence after a secret trial in April 2017, and was released soon after. Officials showed Lu a portion of the judgment against Jane and urged him to plead guilty as well, in return for leniency, but he refused. Lu stood trial at a Dali court two months later.

It was a one-day affair. Lu returned to the detention center at night, feeling almost relieved. He fell asleep instantly.[143]

Lu was convicted and sentenced to four years in jail. He knew that an appeal would be futile, but he lodged one anyway, so that he could meet his lawyers and maintain contact with the outside world. Near the end of his appeal hearing, the judge asked Lu if he had anything to say. Lu told the court that he had documented about seventy thousand mass incidents in total. "By your standards of sentencing me to four years for eight Weibo posts, my jail sentence ought to be thirty-five thousand years," he said. Laughter rippled through the courtroom. The stone-faced judge adjourned the hearing.

Lu served his sentence in a Dali prison, where he lived in a twelve-man cell and worked ten-hour shifts sewing jeans, skirts, and other apparel to earn the equivalent of a few dollars a month. The tedium wore on Lu, who said he suffered hallucinations and bouts of paranoia. Prison officials offered counseling, but his symptoms persisted.[144]

After his release, Lu settled down in Zunyi, where local police monitored him, visiting and calling him from time to time. He opened a new Twitter account, but the police soon came knocking, censuring him for illegally circumventing internet controls, and temporarily seizing his mobile phone and computer.

Lu tried tracking down Jane. He first reached her mother, who said her daughter had gotten married. A disbelieving Lu insisted on hearing from Jane directly. She called that night, telling Lu that she had started a new life, before breaking down and saying she was sorry. Lu knew then that it was over. He told Jane that he respected her choice.[145]

To clear his mind, Lu started traveling to nearby cities and provinces. He posted photos from his trips on social media, including shots of the lush riverside cliffs, cattle on a grassy mountain, and local dishes that he enjoyed. Police tracked his movements closely. Each time he reached a different city or region, an official would call him and ask, "What are you doing?" Lu knew it was pointless to lie. "It was very obvious he was pretending not to know where I was," Lu recalls. "It's too scary. There's no way to hide." During one trip to the southern city of Guangzhou, local police detained him, extracted data from his phone, and put him on a train back to Zunyi.[146]

Back home, local police would regularly call Lu or summon him for meetings.

One landlord evicted Lu, citing pressure from the government. Even after he moved in 2021 to Dandong, a city in northeastern China that borders North Korea, police in his hometown continued calling him at least once a month, telling him not to tweet anything sensitive. Officers from Zunyi sometimes even made the thirteen-hundred-mile trip to check on Lu in Dandong, taking him out for meals and snapping photos to document their visits.[147]

Lu's experience is common among prosecuted dissidents, who often face psychological pressure and social stigma that extend well after their judicial punishment ends. "Their goal is to make you feel helpless, hopeless, devoid of any support, and break you down so you begin to see activism as something foolish that doesn't benefit anyone, and gives pain to everyone around you," says Yaxue Cao, a Washington-based activist who runs China Change, a human-rights news website. "In so many cases, they are successful."

Jane faced similar scrutiny during her three-year probation. She had to report regularly to local authorities and social workers, attend politics and civics classes, and wear an electronic bracelet that tracked her movements. She found work, first as an English teacher and then a translator, and met a new boyfriend, but struggled to settle into her new life. People who learned about her past often treated her like a former cult member who'd gotten brainwashed into doing bad things. Many of her colleagues expressed pro-party and nationalistic views that jarred with her liberal leanings. "I had to keep lying to them about who I am, what I believe, in order to fit in," she recalls. "My life was made up of lies."[148]

The sense of dissonance drove Jane to leave China. She spent about six months preparing her exit—sorting out travel papers, creating a cover story, and sanitizing her social media presence. She told acquaintances, coworkers, and even her mother that she was going away to study in Germany. She removed sensitive material from her mobile phone, such as software for circumventing internet controls, and filled the device instead with content commensurate with her cover story. The subterfuge paid off. With help from friends and activists, Jane left China without incident in June 2022—her first-ever trip abroad—and arrived in Berlin to start a new life. "I had lost my voice for so many years," Jane says. "Now I want to make use of my new status to say all the things I couldn't say before, and do all the things I couldn't do before."[149]

Lu hasn't been as fortunate. He says he has battled bouts of depression and struggled to find work. When he applied for a passport, authorities barred him from leaving China, but told him they might change their minds if he watched his words online. Lu remains proud of his documentation work, but believes he could never reprise that role. "If you're lucky, they'd detain you within a month, or if you're unlucky, within a week," he says. "You can tell people how brave you are, but in reality you wouldn't achieve anything."[150]

CHAPTER FOUR

CAGING THE ECONOMY

THE PARTY GETS BACK TO BUSINESS

"Invigorating the economy must be done under planned guidance. . . . This is like the rela-
tionship between a bird and a cage. A bird shouldn't be squeezed in one's hand, or it will
die. We must let it fly, but fly only within the cage. Without the cage, it would fly away."

—Chen Yun, Communist Party elder

"Private entrepreneurs should cherish their social image, love the motherland, love the
people, and love the Chinese Communist Party."

—Xi Jinping

In the early summer of 2015, China's stock markets were soaring. The Shanghai and
Shenzhen indices hit their highest levels in seven years, juiced by the government's
appeals for investors to pour money into equities and help indebted companies raise
funds. Greenhorn buyers charged headlong into the fray, many with little more than a
middle-school education and borrowed money.[1] Chinese investors opened more than
30 million new stock-trading accounts over the first five months of the year, some three
times the total added in 2014.[2] The website of the Communist Party's flagship newspaper, *People's Daily*, published a commentary that dismissed concerns about a frothy
market, saying the already prodigious rally was just beginning.[3] Those swept up in the
euphoria scavenged for whatever shares they could find, desperate not to miss out on
what people were calling the "Uncle Xi bull market."

Then, in the middle of June, with markets up by more than 160 percent over the
preceding year, the bubble burst. Stocks slumped on the first trading day after Beijing

signaled it would tighten rules on margin trading, or the buying of stocks with borrowed money. Panicked investors rushed for the exits, turning a dip into a rout. Novices dabbling in stocks on advice from friends, even their hairdressers, watched helplessly as their stakes evaporated.[4] About half of China-listed companies suspended trading on their shares at one point to stem losses.[5] When the central bank loosened controls on the yuan, the Chinese currency took a pummeling that drove more capital out of the country. Hundreds of billions of dollars were wiped off global markets.

The crash spooked China's leadership. In a meeting with economic and financial officials, General Secretary Xi Jinping voiced his dismay at the government's economic management, noting how the *Economist* magazine had splashed the market turmoil on its cover—with an image depicting the Chinese leader with his arms raised trying to hold up a plunging stock index.[6]

To stop the bleeding, officials launched the most heavy-handed state intervention in Chinese stock markets since they debuted a quarter century earlier. A shadowy collective of state-linked investors, known as the "national team," spent hundreds of billions of yuan buying shares to prop up prices. Major investors were told to hold on to their stakes to prevent further selloffs.[7] Regulators suspended new share sales, curbed margin trades, cracked down on investors who bet on stocks to fall, froze suspicious trading accounts, and launched probes into alleged financial misconduct. Authorities introduced a "circuit breaker" mechanism, which suspends trading when shares fall too sharply, only to rescind it days later after it exacerbated losses.[8] The central bank imposed "countercyclical" controls to prop up the yuan and curb capital outflows. Senior financial regulators were ousted, while some high-profile fund managers were detained and punished for market manipulation.[9] For Xi, the implications were clear: the markets had failed, and the state had to save the day.

Less than two years before, the party's elite Central Committee had vowed to give market forces a "decisive role" in allocating resources in the world's second-largest economy.[10] While the November 2013 decision was far from a free-market manifesto, given its affirmation of the state sector's "dominant role," it committed the party to sustaining the reforms China had embarked upon since the late 1970s under Deng Xiaoping—the selective application of capitalist principles that transformed a sterile command economy into a global manufacturing powerhouse, and brought hundreds of millions of people out of poverty.[11] Even while Xi emerged as a political hardliner, some party insiders still hoped he would live up to his record as a business-friendly provincial leader, and honor his father's legacy as a pro-market reformer.

Xi seemed set on economic liberalization early on in his leadership. He promised to overhaul bloated state firms and boost private industry. His administration talked up equity markets, eased controls on the yuan, and even flirted with proposals to allow professional managers to handle day-to-day operations in state businesses—an approach modeled after Singapore's state-investment company Temasek Holdings.[12] Nicholas Lardy, a respected China analyst at the Peterson Institute for International Economics, described this trend in a 2014 book titled *Markets Over Mao*, documenting how private firms superseded a retreating state sector as the dominant driver of China's economy.

The 2015 meltdown upended this trajectory, turning the party's perennial skepticism of market forces into full-blown distrust. For Xi, the capitalist principles that spurred breakneck growth had become too fraught, seeding more disorder than prosperity and overwhelming government overseers. The vagaries of boom-bust cycles and excesses of private capital clashed with Xi's instincts for control, jeopardized social stability, and—if unchecked—could threaten the party's hold on power.

Chen Yun, a revered revolutionary regarded as China's second most powerful leader during the Deng era, once likened the economy to "a bird in a cage." If the cage of state control was too small, the bird would suffocate. But without the cage, the bird would fly away. As Xi saw it, decades of market-oriented reforms had expanded the cage so much that the bird was flying free. Unless he shrunk the cage and restored the party's dominance over the commanding heights of the economy, his China Dream of ennobling a new superpower could come to naught.[13]

Since taking power in late 2012, Xi has discarded his predecessors' hands-off approach to economic management and doubled down on "top-level design," whereby Beijing supervises policy down to the grassroots. He's unveiled grandiose development programs, from the Belt and Road initiative to build global trade infrastructure to his "thousand-year project" to create a new megacity known as the Xiong'an New Area. He declared economic affairs a key component of national security, and demanded compliance with his development agenda as a matter of patriotic duty. State planners sought to engineer economic outcomes, from raw-material prices to stock and currency values. Beijing directed a wave of mergers and acquisitions that turned state-run giants into global behemoths that could dominate sectors such as train manufacturing, shipbuilding, steel, and power utilities.[14] State companies received preferential access to credit, land, and other resources, squeezing out private-sector rivals. Party cells in private firms sought bigger roles in management that allow them to align corporate priorities with government goals. As Xi told a group of business leaders, they must honor the "glorious tradition of listening to the party's words and following the party's path."[15]

That path has led China away from Deng's economic formula, which encouraged bottom-up innovation and integration with global markets, and closer to Xi's principles of top-down control and self-reliance. A bruising trade war and geopolitical tensions with the United States added urgency to Xi's plans, spurring calls for China to become more self-sufficient and, over the long term, challenge America for global supremacy in advanced technology like artificial intelligence, semiconductors, and fifth-generation mobile networks. In totality, Xi wants to roll back China's decades-long drift toward Western-style capitalism and forge a strong, interventionist state—one that hews more closely to Mao's egalitarian ethos.[16]

Echoing how U.S. president Theodore Roosevelt reined in America's robber barons with antitrust actions, Xi denounced Chinese tycoons for pursuing "barbaric growth" and vowed to curb their excesses in the name of delivering "common prosperity"—a populist slogan Mao used to promote collectivized ownership in the 1950s.[17] Insofar as the party had been indifferent to how state-led capitalism was creating wealth unsustainably and spreading it unevenly, Xi promised to shape a more equitable society.[18] He directed regulatory crackdowns against some of China's biggest private companies and vowed to curtail "the disorderly expansion of capital" that could lead to political polarization, populist backlash, and social instability.[19]

Xi's statist approach brought its own risks. The government bureaucracy became increasingly encumbered by inflexibility and indecision, as overzealous officials take Xi's edicts too far, while others dither in fear of punishment for acting without approval. Beijing's reluctance to impose market discipline on state-owned enterprises allowed them to become more heavily indebted while channeling funds into wasteful projects. Credit-starved private firms accounted for a shrinking share of investments in factories, buildings, and other infrastructure. Xi's insistence that entrepreneurs serve the party fostered what critics call a "hyper-politicized" business environment, dampening enthusiasm to invest and innovate. Economists say China could fall into a "middle-income trap," where rising wages erode the country's edge in low-skill manufacturing before it can make the gains in technology and productivity needed to compete with advanced economies.

The party has no easy options for avoiding these pitfalls. Market-oriented reforms can boost efficiency but threaten powerful interest groups that benefit from state largesse. Shutting loss-making factories would reduce excess capacity, but also spur mass layoffs that would fuel unrest. Raising taxes and the retirement age can ease fiscal burdens but also drag consumption and stoke public resentment. Whatever the choices, however, there's only one outcome that matters for Xi: the party must win, and it must always win.

MAO VERSUS MARKETS

As CHIANG KAI-SHEK'S NATIONALIST GOVERNMENT crumbled in the dying months of the Chinese civil war, many of the country's wealthy elite scurried to escape. Mao Zedong had promised to eliminate capitalism in his "new China," and fearful entrepreneurs sought refuge in places such as British Hong Kong and Nationalist-controlled Taiwan. The exodus worried the Communist Party, whose leaders wanted to tap the capitalist class for their money, business nous, and ties with foreign markets, to rebuild their battered nation.[20] Soon after the People's Liberation Army captured Tianjin in early 1949, one of Mao's top lieutenants, Liu Shaoqi, traveled to the port city and met with local businessmen seeking assurances on their fate under Communist rule.

Zhou Shutao, a Tianjin industrialist, confided in Liu his concerns over the morality of expanding his cement and textiles business. A father to two party members, Zhou conceded that he was a part of the exploiting class. He worried that the more factories he opened, the more exploitation would take place, and his sins would become so grave that the party would shoot him if it decided to settle scores. Liu disabused Zhou of his fears. "I said, you want to open a fourth factory, the workers you exploit would increase, does this count as a crime?" Liu said in a speech recounting his conversation with Zhou. "Not only is it not a crime, it would be a meritorious contribution."[21] Citing Marx, Liu defended the "progressiveness" of capitalist exploitation under certain conditions. "Is it better to exploit more workers, or is it better to exploit fewer workers?" he said. "It's better to exploit more."[22]

The party seized power later that year, pledging to build a "united front" with noncommunist groups and work across ideological lines in service of nation building. Entrepreneurs willing to work with the party were given space to operate, and some even received roles in government. They were designated the "national bourgeoisie," distinguishing them from the "bureaucratic capitalists" who had ties to the Nationalists.

Such collaboration was short-lived, as party leaders saw private trade as merely a dispensable tool for building a state-run economy.[23] In 1952, Mao launched the "Five-Antis" campaign against economic crimes—bribery, tax evasion, cheating on government contracts, as well as theft of state property and economic data—that in practice served as a way to appropriate wealth from business owners, who were often publicly denounced and, in some cases, driven to suicide. By the late 1950s, the party had virtually crushed the private sector and seized all major industrial and commercial assets.[24]

Mao's command economy doubled as a tool of totalitarian control. State companies provided an "iron rice bowl" for workers, who enjoyed permanent employment at their work units—*danwei* in Chinese—and could be dismissed only for criminal or political offenses that resulted in imprisonment.[25] Work units took care of people's needs from the cradle to the grave, typically providing their staff with housing, clothing, food, entertainment, and education for their children.[26] Workers' lives revolved around their *danwei*, which monitored every employee; maintained dossiers on their family background, social class, education, and political demeanor; and controlled their ability to travel or even get married.[27] Productivity frequently suffered, as factories were often overstaffed and workers generally content to meet minimum output quotas without concern for the quality or marketability of what they made.[28]

China lurched toward economic disaster in 1958 when Mao launched the Great Leap Forward, a campaign that aimed at catapulting the country toward socialist utopia but ended up causing one of history's deadliest famines. Convinced that mass mobilization could accelerate an agrarian society's development into a modern industrialized state, Mao urged his compatriots to create rural farming and industrial collectives—known as "people's communes"—and channeled vast resources to chasing fanciful production targets. This change led to a deadly cycle of self-deception as officials, afraid of being purged for contradicting Mao, reported inflated agricultural output and delivered nonexistent surpluses by taking from grain stocks needed to feed the rural populace. Food supplies were diverted to the cities at the expense of the countryside, where tens of millions of people died. The party nudged the economy toward a tentative recovery in the early 1960s, only for Mao to wipe out those gains with his Cultural Revolution.

When Mao died in 1976, he left behind an impoverished populace and an economy shattered by mismanagement and isolation from global trade. Deng Xiaoping reoriented the party from revolution to modernization in a program that became known as "reform and opening up." He spurned socialist dogma, advocating a more practical approach to development that tolerated a degree of capitalist excess and inequality.[29] Whereas Mao's planned economy was encapsulated by the slogan "politics in command," Deng's methods put "economics in command," guided by steely pragmatism.[30] "My consistent position is to allow some people and some regions to get rich first," Deng said. "Some regions can develop a little bit faster, and then bring along the majority. This is the shortcut to accelerating development and achieving common prosperity."[31]

Under Deng, the party broke up agricultural collectives and allowed farmers to sell surpluses on open markets. China established "special economic zones" in coastal regions, where local officials could experiment with preferential policies to boost commerce and attract foreign investment. Beijing cut back on central planning, easing price controls and allowing state-owned enterprises, or SOEs, to sell goods at market prices after they satisfied yearly targets. Private businesses emerged again, though entrepreneurs still faced harassment and persecution amid a murky legal environment. Many businesses sought political cover by registering as "red hat collectives," or state firms under the control of local governments.

Deng's reforms proved politically fraught. Corruption and inflation soared in the late 1980s, at times spurring price spikes and panic buying in the cities, and even fueling mass demonstrations. Party infighting over the scope and pace of change intensified, particularly after the 1989 Tiananmen Square protests, and the fall of the Iron Curtain gave conservative elders the opportunity to purge liberal-minded colleagues and block policies they considered too capitalistic. To revive his reformist agenda, Deng embarked upon his "southern tour" in early 1992, inspecting the front lines of economic liberalization—including the cities of Shenzhen, Zhuhai, and Shanghai—and praising their pro-market policies. Party conservatives suppressed state media coverage of the tour for weeks before Jiang Zemin, the general secretary at the time, sided with Deng. Later that year, Jiang declared that China aimed to build a "socialist market economy," enshrining Deng's path as official policy.

Foreign investment poured in, bringing much-needed funds, technology, and expertise that transformed China into the workshop of the world. Total value of exports more than tripled, from about $85 billion in 1992 to $266 billion in 2001, when the country joined the World Trade Organization.[32] Beijing culled the state sector on the principle of "grasping the large, releasing the small," keeping control of major state-owned enterprises while allowing smaller ones to be privatized, restructured, or shut down.[33] Millions were laid off, and by one estimate, employment across state enterprises plunged from a peak of 76 million workers in 1992 to 43 million by 2005.[34] But a booming private sector more than made up for it, fueling a surge in urban employment and soaking up China's growing legions of cheap labor.[35] By 2012, private firms were contributing an estimated 70 percent of the country's gross domestic product and more than two-thirds of its urban labor force.[36] China leapfrogged Britain, France, Germany, and Japan to become the world's second-biggest economy by 2010, trailing only the U.S.[37] Standards of living soared, with GDP per capita in purchasing power terms more than doubling, from about $4,000 in 2002 to roughly $10,300 in 2012, and lifting the People's Republic firmly into the ranks of middle-income nations.[38]

The state sector remained a key asset for the party. Hu Jintao's administration created a specialized agency—the State-owned Assets Supervision and Administration Commission, or Sasac—to manage major SOEs and turn them into "national champions" that could drive China's development as an industrial power. Sasac-controlled SOEs continued receiving preferential treatment, avoided antitrust scrutiny on their acquisitions, and benefited from restrictions that hampered competitors trying to break into key sectors. Beijing tested ways to improve corporate governance at state firms, such as introducing external directors and linking executives' pay to performance. China's big four state banks went public, imposing some market discipline on their lending decisions.

For a time, the strategy seemed to work. China's state juggernauts gained international prominence as they started splashing their cash. More than half of Chinese companies listed in the 2012 Fortune Global 500 were central government–supervised SOEs, including energy and resources giants on a buying binge to satiate China's surging appetite for commodities.[39] By one estimate, Chinese firms grew their value share of global mergers and acquisitions in the oil and natural gas sector from less than 3 percent in 2005 to about 15 percent in 2012.[40] Western observers dubbed them "China, Inc.," portraying a powerful cabal of cash-rich state companies advancing Beijing's interests around the world.

But China, Inc., was far from the fearsome monolith that some imagined. Many state firms remained wastefully inefficient, and instead of working together to support Beijing's industrial strategy, they pursued their own interests and often acted at cross-purposes. Corruption grew rife amid lax oversight. In 2009, a former chairman of state oil giant Sinopec was handed a suspended death sentence—a de facto life term—for taking nearly 200 million yuan in bribes. Graft charges also brought down China National Nuclear Corporation's general manager and a top executive at China Mobile, who were jailed in 2010 and 2011 respectively.

Critics called the Hu era a "lost decade," when China missed its chance to pursue a more sustainable development path—one more reliant on domestic consumption and less on exports and debt-fueled infrastructure spending. Hemmed in by factional squabbling and vested interests, Hu presided over tentative reforms and policy gridlock that kicked economic cans down the road. Beijing's response to the global financial crisis exacerbated the problem. Its massive stimulus program, worth trillions of yuan, indulged China's addiction to easy credit, fueled corruption, and spurred wasteful investments on real estate and heavy-polluting industries. The economy remained vulnerable to shifts in global demand. Excess housing, industrial overcapacity, and debt overhangs weighed on growth, which slipped from a breathless 10 percent per year toward a "new normal" of slowing, single-digit expansion.

The social costs were severe. Pollution and environmental degradation worsened, with dense smog often suffocating Beijing and other major cities. Inequality swelled between rural and urban areas, as well as within cities, where migrant workers from the countryside received far lower wages than registered urban residents. The top 20 percent of households in China controlled more than two-thirds of disposable income, according to research published in 2012 by Chinese economist Gan Li, compared to the one-half held by America's top quintile. Gan's data also showed that China's Gini coefficient, a measure of income inequality scaled from zero to one, whereby zero represents complete equality, had reached 0.61—surpassing the U.S. equivalent of roughly 0.48 at the time.[41] On top of that, China's fast-aging population meant it could grow old before getting rich, while public anger over corruption, pollution, and land grabs chipped away at the party's legitimacy.

Without forceful interventions, the Chinese dynamo could sputter out, unable to boost wages and create enough jobs to sustain a shift toward a more balanced economy. Xi privately blamed a feeble central leadership for the party's failure to address these ills. He promised change, and to do so, he would first put politics back in command.

THE STATE STRIKES BACK

FOR HIS FIRST TRIP OUTSIDE BEIJING since becoming general secretary in 2012, Xi Jinping replicated a famous journey that a revered predecessor had made to spur China's economic miracle. Two decades after Deng Xiaoping's "southern tour," Xi retraced some of those footsteps by traveling to the bustling industrial province of Guangdong, where he laid a wreath before a bronze statue of Deng and paid tribute to the late leader's achievements.[42]

Xi's gesture conveyed a message of continuity, one he followed up with crowd-pleasing promises to dial back government stimulus, reduce debt, and liberalize interest rates. Pro-market reformers saw more positive signals emanating from a 2013 party conclave, known as the Third Plenum, where Xi approved a new economic blueprint calling for markets to play a "decisive" part in allocating resources, an upgrade on past commitments to allow them a "basic" role. But there was a catch. The party also insisted that public ownership would remain dominant, vowing to boost the state sector's influence and vitality. The document, as one foreign analyst noted, "promised something for everyone."[43]

The mixed messaging spurred debate over the merits of state control versus free markets. In the months after the Third Plenum, two prominent economists at the prestigious Peking University jousted over what the party's pronouncements meant. Zhang Weiying, a free-market advocate, called for a hands-off government that limited its role to fostering open, equal, and competitive markets. Justin Yifu Lin, a former World Bank chief economist turned government adviser, countered that the state must mitigate the foibles of capricious markets. The respected financial magazine *Caixin* called the debate "reminiscent of the clashes between John Keynes and Friedrich Hayek that shaped major developed countries' economic policies for most of the last century."[44] And for a time, pro-market advocates seemed to gain ground in this battle of ideas.

Premier Li Keqiang led an early charge to boost private industry and slim a bloated state sector. He promised to help entrepreneurs by reducing taxes, cutting red tape, providing more credit, and using internet technologies to support commerce.[45] He urged efforts to develop the financial sector, such as by encouraging peer-to-peer lending and online insurance sales.[46] Officials touted stock investing as a way to stimulate spending, turn equities markets into a funding vehicle for businesses, and help local governments and companies unwind debt. Policy-makers cut interest rates, gave international investors more access to the Shanghai stock market, and made it easier to trade with borrowed money. Chinese indices surged despite a slowdown in the broader economy, helping indebted companies sell shares and clear up their balance sheets. In early 2015, just months before Chinese stocks collapsed, Li praised regulators for making it easier for companies to get listed, an effort that he credited for creating wealth for the nation and the people. [47]

Li slashed state industry, pledging to eliminate loss-making "zombie enterprises" in sectors such as steel and coal, while applying market mechanisms to unwind ills born from state largesse. Authorities launched a program to introduce mixed ownership for SOEs, hoping that private shareholders could bring in capital and exert pressure on state firms to improve their performances. As mentioned, Beijing even considered adopting the "Temasek model," whereby government-backed investment firms would take ownership of state businesses and appoint professional managers to run them—a move that would all but neuter Sasac, the agency overseeing SOEs, which U.S. officials once described as "the world's largest and most powerful holding company."[48]

Sasac officials battled to persuade Xi that his core political objective—strengthening the Communist Party's dominance—was best served by tightening Beijing's grip on state enterprises and expanding their economic footprint. The alternative, they argued, would slow growth, drive up unemployment, and ultimately destabilize society.[49] The 2015 stock crash reinforced Sasac's warnings, fueling fears that market forces were more agents of chaos than levers of economic efficiency. The internal wrangling reached a crescendo over the summer of 2016, when the Xi and Li camps delivered contradictory messages on how to reform China's state sector. In internal remarks, the general secretary called for "stronger, better, bigger" state enterprises, while the premier stressed the need to "slim down" SOEs and remake them in accordance with market rules.[50]

Xi prevailed. Li, once seen as an advocate for economic liberalization, faded into the background while Liu He, one of Xi's closest advisers, assumed leading roles in economic, financial, and trade affairs.[51] He Lifeng, a confidant whom Xi befriended in Fujian, came out of semiretirement for senior roles at the powerful National Development and Reform Commission, or NDRC, the state economic planning agency. Efforts to impose more market discipline on SOEs petered out. Dozens of Hong Kong–listed SOEs revised their articles of association to add direct references to the Communist Party and give their in-house party committees a more explicit role in decision-making.[52] Sasac's assets swelled to more than 63 trillion yuan by 2019, from 35 trillion yuan in 2013.[53] "Nobody talks about the Temasek model anymore," a Sasac official told the *Wall Street Journal*. "It has been determined that model isn't applicable to China."[54] Lardy, the China analyst who wrote *Markets Over Mao*, reversed his assessment in a new book, titled *The State Strikes Back*.

Open debates over Xi's economic policies became all but taboo. Lou Jiwei, an outspoken technocrat, lost his job as finance minister in 2016 after serving just three and a half years out of a full five-year term. He was ousted again in 2019, when he stepped down as chief of the national social security fund after describing China's industrial policy as a waste of money.[55] Authorities harassed academics, analysts, and journalists who contradicted Beijing's economic narratives, warned them against airing gloomy views, and censored their social media accounts when they disobeyed.[56] The Unirule Institute of Economics, an independent Beijing think tank that had championed pro-market ideas since its founding in 1993, shut down in 2019 under government pressure.[57] Zhang Weiying, the free-market economist, says he has found it harder to get his writings published.[58] His statist colleague, Justin Lin, remained an adviser to the Chinese leadership.

But for all his powers, Xi hasn't always delivered decisive breakthroughs in policy. Even though officials have long promised to raise the statutory retirement age—unchanged since the 1950s—to cope with China's rapidly aging population, the Xi administration missed a self-imposed 2017 deadline to unveil detailed retirement-age reforms, and continued to demur through Xi's second term as general secretary. Beijing has so far also shown little appetite for phasing out China's *hukou* residence permit system, which keeps rural residents from swamping urban areas by denying them subsidized social services unless they hold household registrations, or *hukou*, for urban areas—restrictions that economists say should be dismantled to encourage more urbanization and boost consumption.

Conversely, the state's visible hand has proven too forceful at times. In the fall of 2021, when the NDRC demanded lower energy usage to meet Xi's targets for slashing carbon emissions, local authorities rushed to comply by shutting coal mines, ordering power cuts, and suspending production at factories.[59] Their efforts disrupted global supply chains, drove up coal prices, and threatened to leave millions of people freezing over winter. Beijing was forced to reverse course and call for more coal production. Local governments obliged.[60]

Despite such shocks, Xi sees a strong state as an anchor for the economy—providing jobs, implementing industrial policies, and ensuring stability during spells of volatility. SOEs led the way in Xi's Belt and Road initiative to build global trade infrastructure and the "Made in China 2025" campaign to acquire advanced capabilities in industries like aerospace and robotics. They kept an outsize presence in Chinese markets, accounting for nearly 40 percent of the domestic stock market and the bulk of bond issuances.[61] When President Donald Trump waged a trade war against China, imposing tariffs and curbing Chinese access to American markets and technology, Xi channeled more resources toward the state sector, tasking them to develop indigenous know-how that China needs to become economically self-sufficient.[62] When Covid-19 forced China into lockdown in early 2020, SOEs helped shore up the economy by ramping up investments while private firms pulled back.

Xi still insists that private industry remain a cornerstone of his economic vision. He arranged high-profile meetings with Chinese entrepreneurs, assuring them of his commitment to the non-state economy, while urging private businesses to "proactively take on responsibilities for the nation, and share in the nation's worries."[63] His lieutenants laud the private sector's economic weight with the phrase "56789"—a reference to how it generates 50 percent of tax revenues, 60 percent of GDP, 70 percent of technological innovations, employs 80 percent of urban workers, and accounts for 90 percent of registered companies.[64]

What Xi wants, some experts argue, is a hybrid system that combines central planning with market mechanisms, where state and private enterprises act in concert to advance the party's economic agenda. While Beijing nudges SOEs to become more efficient and profit-driven, the party wants private firms to show more loyalty and work proactively to serve national interests. Jude Blanchette, a China analyst at the Washington-based Center for Strategic and International Studies, dubbed this new model "CCP Inc."—a broad ecosystem comprising state, private, and hybrid-ownership companies that operate across entire value chains, tap international capital markets, and align with the party's industrial strategies. Or as Sasac's party chief put it, "whether they are state-owned or private enterprises, they are all Chinese enterprises."[65] The question of ownership wouldn't matter as long as they sing in tune with the party. Going off key would be costly.

FOLLOWING THE PARTY

DAYS BEFORE JACK MA was to launch the world's largest initial public offering in history, one that would raise more than $34 billion for his financial technology giant Ant Group, the Chinese billionaire was preparing to thumb his nose again at government regulators who had tried and failed to rein in his businesses. The dual listing in Shanghai and Hong Kong, set for November 2020, would be a crowning achievement for one of China's richest entrepreneurs. A self-made business superstar,

Ma was idolized by many Chinese for founding Alibaba Group and turning it from a scrappy e-commerce website into the leading company in the world's largest online-retail market. Along the way, he transformed how Chinese consumers shop and drew comparisons with the likes of Jeff Bezos and Elon Musk.

Ant emerged from the Alibaba empire, first as an online escrow service, before swelling into a financial behemoth in its own right, handling everything from processing digital payments to selling investment products to running China's largest mutual fund. The company runs a highly popular mobile payment app, Alipay, and has become a vital cog in the economy—by extending loans to tens of millions of small businesses and half a billion individuals who otherwise found it hard to borrow from traditional banks.[66] Imbued with Ma's go-getting ethos, Ant pushed regulatory limits and irked officials who worried the firm was saddling China's financial system with excessive risk. With help from powerful backers, Ant got its way for years, fending off government efforts to corral the firm under the tougher regulations and capital requirements that commercial lenders face.

Ahead of the company's mega listing, Ant's rambunctious attitude veered into what critics saw as arrogance. Prospective investors were given limited spaces for meetings with Ant management and were expected to make presentations to persuade the company to accept their investments. When Ant announced that it would trade on the Shanghai Stock Exchange under the ticker 688688, an auspicious set of numbers that symbolize good fortune and prosperity in Chinese culture, netizens marveled at the brazen flexing of corporate clout. A splashy IPO would be a crowning achievement for Ma, and as hype bubbled up before debut day, he couldn't resist basking publicly in his imminent success.

Ma chose his stage for maximum impact—a financial forum in Shanghai attended by China's vice president, top regulators, and senior bankers. Only a small group of subordinates had an inkling of what was to come when he stepped up to the lectern that late October morning. Ma opened with a dash of feigned modesty, describing himself as a "non-official, non-professional person" who felt torn about whether he should address the event. Then, over the next twenty minutes, he tore into China's financial establishment, portraying them as stuffy stewards of a bygone era who must be dragged into the digital age. He accused regulators of stifling innovation with outmoded rules and excessive interventions, contradicting Vice President Wang Qishan's earlier exhortations for more safeguards against systemic risks. Ma chided banks for harboring a "pawnshop mentality"—a reference to industry practice of securing loans with collateral—that impedes businesses from getting capital. "Good innovation doesn't fear being regulated, but it does fear being regulated with yesterday's methods," he said. "We cannot use yesterday's methods to manage the future."

Ma's speech went viral on Chinese social media, where some users cheered his straight-talking jibes. Senior officials, however, recoiled from what they saw as impertinent grandstanding—a "punch in their faces," as one put it.[67] Within hours, Xi ordered regulators to investigate the Ant IPO and officials started compiling reports on Ma's companies, including how Ant used digital financial products to encourage unbridled borrowing and spending.[68] Three days before Ant's trading debut, China's central bank and its securities, banking, and foreign exchange regulators summoned Ma and two top Ant executives for a dressing down.[69] The IPO was suspended the next day.[70]

Ma's public humbling stunned China. The government had indulged the billionaire's brash ways for years, on account of his political connections and national pride in his success. Now, with Ma's defenses breached, regulators rushed to launch probes and enforcement actions against his companies.[71] China's antitrust agency imposed a record $2.8 billion fine on Alibaba for anticompetitive business practices, such as punishing certain merchants who sold goods both on Alibaba and on rival e-commerce platforms.[72] The central bank and the state agencies overseeing securities, banking, and insurance rapped Ant for circumventing financial controls through "regulatory arbitrage" and providing services that saddled consumers with greater risks. Officials who had supported Alibaba started echoing Beijing's priorities in preventing big tech firms from monopolizing credit, and told the company it could no longer count on their backing.[73] Within the Alibaba-Ant empire, dissension flared as employees took to internal discussion boards to attack Ma as "the biggest source of instability" within the firm.

The collapse of the Ant IPO was just the beginning. Beijing directed a wave of regulatory crackdowns against private businesses over subsequent months, investigating and punishing tech firms over issues including antitrust, data security, and financial risks. Ride-hailing group DiDi was hit with cybersecurity probes soon after going public on Wall Street, prompting the company to delist from the U.S. and seek a new listing in Hong Kong.[74] China's lucrative private-tutoring sector, seen as driving up parenting costs, was crippled overnight by new rules that limited the length and scheduling of classes and banned public advertising of such services.[75] Regulators slapped the digital-gaming sector with limits on the number of hours that youth could play online games, citing efforts to battle the gaming addiction that officials blame for distracting people from school and damaging their health.[76]

Ma wasn't the first entrepreneur to face the party's wrath, nor would he be the last. Fearing the emergence of a powerful oligarch class similar to Russia's, China wants to keep its captains of private industry under the party's thumb, and prevent them from building networks that can operate beyond state control or even become rival centers of power. Under Xi, the party had already taken action against some of the biggest names in Chinese business. In 2017, authorities curbed state-bank lending to property developer Dalian Wanda Group, forcing its billionaire founder Wang Jianlin—once China's richest man—to pare back what some officials saw as risky investments.[77] Wu Xiaohui, who turned Anbang Insurance Group into China's third-largest insurer and a global dealmaker, received an eighteen-year jail sentence in 2018 for committing fraud and abusing power.[78] Even so, many Chinese saw Ma's public humbling as a watershed moment.

A former English teacher fond of Chinese martial arts novels, Ma founded Alibaba in 1999 with seventeen others in his apartment in Hangzhou, the capital of Zhejiang province. Starting out as an online marketplace for businesses to sell goods to each other, Alibaba exploded into life by launching its Taobao platform for merchants to sell directly to consumers—success that helped Ma expand into online retail and banking, cloud computing, media, and entertainment. Over time, Alibaba built stakes in or controlled some major Chinese media platforms, including the Weibo microblogging service and Hong Kong's English-language broadsheet *South China Morning Post*.

Ma attained almost divine status within his business empire, revered as a "teacher" by subordinates who regarded each other as "classmates."[79] Legions of young Chinese fans credited Ma for inspiring them to chase opportunities beyond stodgy careers in public service and state firms. He also found favor with party officials, including Xi, who was supportive of startups like Alibaba while he was Zhejiang party boss.[80] Premier Wen Jiabao, during a 2010 visit to Alibaba's Hangzhou headquarters, described himself as a "serious" student of Ma.[81] Ma joined the party too, though his membership wasn't widely known until the *People's Daily* mentioned it in 2018—a revelation that spurred questions about what Ma would do if he, one day, had to choose between party mandates and corporate interests.[82]

Regulators had long wanted to rein in Ma. They believed Alibaba was engaging in consumer unfriendly and anti-competitive practices on its online-retail platforms, while Ant was applying user data to gain an unfair advantage over banks and hampering government efforts to monitor credit risks. But Ma and his businesses held their ground for years. When China's market regulatory agency issued a report in 2015 saying many products sold on Alibaba's Taobao platform were fake, substandard, banned, or they infringed on trademarks, the company threatened to file a complaint, while Ma flew to Beijing to meet with the agency chief, an episode documented by my *Wall Street Journal* colleagues. The regulator soon removed the report from its website and called it an internal memo, not an official document.[83]

Authorities also worried that Alibaba had accrued too much influence over China's news and social media industries, and was trying to use that clout to reshape government policies. In 2020, when rumors about a senior Alibaba executive's involvement in an extramarital affair swirled on Weibo, users complained that their posts about the purported scandal were being censored—a practice common for politically sensitive posts but unusual for celebrity gossip. Internet regulators later found that Alibaba had directed Weibo, in which the e-commerce giant held a roughly 30 percent stake, to suppress the rumors.[84]

Ma's flashy style, once part of his appeal, also started grating on young Chinese who saw him as a symbol of rising inequality and capitalist excess. He earned ridicule for indulging in vanity projects, like a 2017 short film in which Ma played a kung-fu master alongside Chinese action-movie stars. When Ma defended the grueling work hours that permeate China's tech sector, known as "996," or 9 a.m. to 9 p.m. six days a week, social media erupted with anger from young workers denouncing what they saw as exploitation.[85]

Ma also irked Beijing by behaving too much like an American entrepreneur, oozing braggadocio and acting dismissive of the government's authority. He styled himself an informal ambassador for China, traveling to meet world leaders such as French President François Hollande at the Élysée Palace, U.S. President Barack Obama for a private White House lunch, and President-elect Donald Trump in New York.[86] Alibaba's in-house newsletters recounted such trips with language similar to what state media uses for Chinese leaders' foreign visits. When Xi visited the U.S. in 2015, Ma was among a group of American and Chinese executives invited to a meeting with the Chinese leader, where participants each had three minutes to speak. Everyone kept to the allotted time except Ma, who spent ten minutes talking about how China sees the world and what Chinese companies could do to help improve

U.S.-China ties. Xi was reportedly nonplussed by Ma's display, and since then, he hasn't allowed the businessman to speak before him in a group setting.[87]

An early sign of Ma's shifting fortunes came in late 2018, when he wasn't invited to a conference where Xi met fifty leading entrepreneurs—including top executives from tech giants like Tencent, search engine Baidu, and smartphone maker Xiaomi—to discuss the party's policies toward the private sector. Commercial success, Xi told them, is secondary to the primary goal of boosting China's technological security. Shortly after, Tencent CEO Pony Ma pledged to take on the mission of transforming China into an "internet power."[88] Jack Ma, meanwhile, seemed to be falling out of step with the party. His personal office at times sent suggestions to the top leadership through a party office that reported to Xi. Ma got a reply only occasionally. It was "like writing love letters to a loved one, but not getting many responses," a person familiar with the correspondence told the *Wall Street Journal.*[89]

When the time came for Ma to reap the whirlwind, the party didn't hold back. Authorities told Alibaba to slash its sprawling portfolio of media assets, so as to dilute the company's influence over public opinion.[90] Hupan University, an executive business school that Ma established in Hangzhou, was told to suspend enrollment for new students in 2021. "The government thinks Hupan has the potential to organize China's top entrepreneurs to work towards a common goal set by Jack Ma instead of the Communist Party," a person close to the school told the *Financial Times.*[91] When Beijing published an honor roll of "model" contributors to Xi's campaign to eliminate rural poverty, Alibaba joined about fifteen hundred groups and nearly two thousand individuals, including dozens of entrepreneurs, in receiving the accolade. Ma didn't make the list.[92] For many at Alibaba, the message couldn't have been clearer: follow the party, not their founder.

Ma sought to make amends. Alibaba committed to spend 100 billion yuan, or about $15.7 billion at the time, by 2025 in support of Xi's common prosperity campaign.[93] Alibaba assuaged regulators' concerns by allowing users to purchase items on some of its apps via a payment service run by its rival Tencent, while Ant delinked some financial products and services from its core payments platform.[94] Ma stepped away from public view, swapping his jet-setting lifestyle for quieter moments playing golf, reading Taoist texts, and learning oil painting.[95] By early 2023, he had relinquished control over Ant by giving up much of his voting rights over the fintech giant.

Some of his rivals also adapted to new realities. Pony Ma, the Tencent CEO, proposed tighter regulation of internet businesses like his own and volunteered to meet with antitrust authorities.[96] E-commerce firm Pinduoduo's founder left the company, saying he was going to pursue personal interests in life sciences.[97] The founders of ByteDance, the tech firm that developed the TikTok short-video app, and online retail platform JD.com stepped down as chief executives of their respective companies, saying they would focus on longer-term strategy.[98]

Officials insist, in public remarks and private chatter, that the party neither needs nor wants to directly control private companies and their decision-making. What it requires of businesses is for them to conform with the party's interests, or at the very least, do nothing inimical to Beijing's agenda. For the most part, the party relies on Leninist tools to enforce corporate fealty. After the Politburo issued a 2015 directive demanding stronger party leadership over businesses and social groups, officials stepped up enforcement of regulations that mandated the creation of party cells in all organizations with three or more party members. Officially, the party's goal was to reengage members in the private sector, who often joined for career reasons and tended to drift from politics over time. In practice, many executives sensed a campaign to realign corporate practices and decision-making with the party's priorities.

Party cells in private companies serve as de facto human resource departments and listening posts, where members promote the party's priorities, arrange social activities, and gauge worker sentiment. Officials insist that these groups don't interfere in corporate decisions, but instead advise executives on government policies, resolve friction between management and staff, and help cultivate cohesive workforces. Party cells are "pioneers in business development, cradles of talent, and guarantors of business stability," said Han Xu, a regulatory official overseeing party affairs in the private sector.[99]

Already omnipresent in SOEs, party cells have become de rigueur across private businesses. Some 68 percent of non-state enterprises had set up party cells by 2016, up from 54 percent four years earlier, while roughly 74,000 companies in China with full or partial foreign ownership—about 70 percent of the total—had set up party units, compared with 47,000 firms in 2011.[100] Thousands of "party-building consultants" fanned out to "matchmake" between the party and businesses—helping firms set up party cells and recruit new members. As one official told a group of newly appointed consultants, they are the party's "nerve endings" in private companies, who "ensure the party's voice reaches the final meter."[101]

Even major tech startups, long averse to mixing politics and business, started cheering the party on. Smartphone maker Xiaomi, whose executives boast a Western startup vibe and extol minimal hierarchy, established its own party committee in 2015 with about one hundred initial members, and within four years grew those ranks to more than 3,500 people, or more than 15 percent of its workforce.[102] At Shenzhen Bay Venture Plaza, a state-backed industrial park that hosts tech startups, managers installed a sculpture featuring a hammer-and-sickle symbol with inscriptions that say, in Chinese and English: "Follow our party, start your business."

Where entrepreneurs prove less obliging, the party often coerces them. After Xi launched his crackdown on organized crime in 2018, aimed at breaking up collusion between corrupt bureaucrats and mafia-like groups, some prominent industrialists embroiled in disputes with local governments were detained for alleged criminal wrongdoing and had their assets seized. While authorities insisted that these cases were handled lawfully, many within Chinese business circles sensed overreach by overzealous investigators chasing campaign quotas, or self-serving officials who wanted to boost state firms by undercutting private-sector competition.[103]

What makes entrepreneurs especially vulnerable to such tactics is that China's private sector has long been clouded by the notion of "original sin," or the suspicion that many businesses acquired assets and established themselves through illicit means. During the boom years of the 1990s and 2000s, the party struggled to develop a robust regulatory system that could police corporate conduct and protect property rights in a fair and consistent manner. Many companies took advantage of this legal murkiness, resorting to dubious practices—such as bribery, tax evasion, and loan-sharking—to boost their businesses. Others sought patrons in government who can provide deals and protection. Many officials condoned the shady dealings, and some even joined in, accepting bribes to rig tenders and shield companies from criminal probes. What Tsinghua University economist Bai Chong'en described as a "special deal" economy emerged, as local governments—chasing investments and faster growth—competed in dishing out preferential policies to favored private firms.

The question of how to deal with "original sin" is a perennial one.[104] Many Chinese voice outrage over ill-gotten wealth, arguing that those responsible should be punished. Some believe the government should grant some clemency, such as a statute of limitations or tax amnesties, to give past transgressors a chance to turn fully legitimate. Even among entrepreneurs that now conduct business more scrupulously, their past still hangs over them like a Sword of Damocles. Should authorities decide to revisit their misdeeds, companies could face reputational damage, regulatory sanctions, and even criminal prosecution. As it was, Xi's crackdown on organized crime offered incentives for pursuing such cases. Under pressure to deliver results, some officials appeared to build organized-crime probes against entrepreneurs by blurring lines between criminal syndicates and legitimate companies that engage in illegal behavior, according to defendants and lawyers involved in these cases.

Chinese law defines "underworld organizations" broadly. They are described as groups that have clear leadership and a "fairly large" and stable membership, seek economic benefit, repeatedly use violent means, cause severe economic and social harm, and often receive protection from corrupt officials. The problem, however, is that private companies also have an organized hierarchy, seek economic gain, and in some cases, collude with local governments and cause harm to local communities. As Ruan Qilin, a criminal-law professor and an adviser to China's top procuratorial agency, explains, the main difference between an underworld group and a legitimate business lies in the former's propensity for violence. It wouldn't take much for investigators to package what some see as corporate wrongdoing into an organized-crime case.

Such concerns emerged in the public eye when Xi's campaign against organized crime snared Zhang Dewu, a farming tycoon in the central province of Hubei. Born into a peasant family in 1963, Zhang started out selling poultry before setting up Xiangda Group in the early 2000s, eventually growing his animal husbandry business into a conglomerate with interests in chemicals and construction that for a time ranked among China's top five hundred private enterprises.[105] Officials in his home city of Yicheng routinely praised Xiangda as a top contributor to the local economy, while Zhang himself earned recognition from Beijing as a model industrialist.[106]

Zhang also had his brushes with the law. In 2001, he was detained for alleged involvement in organized crime and later sentenced to nine years' jail for offenses that included provoking trouble, firearms possession, and tax evasion—though these convictions were struck down and a retrial acquitted Zhang on most charges.[107]

Authorities detained Zhang again in late 2019, eventually accusing him of running a violent crime ring that disrupted public order, rigged bids, and engaged in loan-sharking.[108] Some of the allegations stemmed from a protest that Zhang arranged in 2016, when hundreds of his employees demonstrated in front of a local court to question a judicial ruling that went against his company.[109] His lawyers said the allegations against him neither fit government definitions of organized crime nor involved serious violence. While acknowledging that some of Zhang's employees used coercive methods to handle business disputes, the lawyers said these employees caused only minor injuries in one instance, and their actions didn't meet the legal criteria of using routine violence to oppress and cause harm to the public.

Zhang's daughter stepped in to run Xiangda but struggled to keep the business going, as employees demurred on making decisions and signing papers that they feared could implicate them in the case against their boss. In June 2021, more than eighteen months after police detained Zhang, his daughter made a dramatic plea: inviting the government to run the company and take over its assets. "It's too bitter and too tough being a Chinese private entrepreneur," Zhang Jianhang wrote in an open letter to provincial leaders, offering to donate Xiangda's assets to the state and allow authorities to manage the firm. A government takeover, she said, would keep Xiangda afloat and ensure that its employees and partners "no longer live in fear everyday."[110]

The letter sparked a furor on social media, where entrepreneurs, lawyers, and ordinary Chinese lamented what they saw as a deteriorating business climate. "The survival of private enterprises is becoming increasingly difficult," Huang Yingsheng, a former judge, wrote in an online post that censors soon blocked. "I hope that the current situation, in which 'entrepreneurs are either in jail or on their way to jail,' can soon change!"[111] Others were less optimistic. For decades, entrepreneurs in China "always thought that tomorrow will be better," but such rosiness has now faded, the founder of a prominent technology company says. "We are all small-time businessmen in the eyes of government officials."[112]

The week after Zhang Jianhang published her letter, the Yicheng municipal party chief visited Xiangda and said the government was committed to helping the company grow and succeed.[113] But the elder Zhang's legal woes didn't go away. Authorities indicted Zhang Dewu for alleged wrongdoing that included "picking quarrels and provoking trouble," loan sharking, bid rigging, and gathering people to assault state organs, though prosecutors didn't proceed with organized-crime charges. In early 2022, a court handed Zhang a thirteen-year jail sentence, which was later reduced to eight and a half years on appeal.[114] As of this writing, the Zhang family continued to control Xiangda.

TAMING BARBARIANS

AT THE WALT DISNEY COMPANY'S theme park in Shanghai, where cartoon mice and preening princesses prance around the Enchanted Storybook Castle, a merry band of Communists work hard to maintain the fantasy. The four hundred or so party members at the Shanghai Disney Resort do everything from running hotels to policing park security, while keeping their political affiliation invisible to visitors. Among colleagues, they showcase their socialist loyalties with pride, displaying hammer-and-sickle insignia on their desks and meeting spaces, even as they serve an icon of American capitalism.

State media extols the Shanghai Disney Resort's Communist Party committee as a fruitful marriage of politics and business. Disney's embrace of the party was crucial in securing Beijing's approval for the $5.5 billion theme park, along with other compromises such as giving their Chinese partners more of the profits and a major role in running the resort.[115] Disney has a minority stake in the resort, but owns 70 percent of the joint venture that runs it.[116] The deal also included a guarantee for the joint venture's right to set up party cells—a demand that Disney, according to its Chinese partner, the state-owned Shendi Group, didn't initially understand but acceded to nonetheless.

When Shanghai Disney Resort celebrated its first anniversary in 2017, state media portrayed the party as a cornerstone of the theme park's success. One report described the resort's party committee as a "bridge of enchantment" between American and Chinese management. The committee, which uses a Disney.com email address, organizes social activities such as singing contests and arranges political seminars at a dedicated party activity center decorated with Mickey Mouse silhouettes. In-house newsletters praise party members as exemplary workers who do their utmost to serve guests and help colleagues.[117] "At the most iconic Sino-foreign joint venture in China," one state media report said, party members "have proved their worth with their actions, and they have shown the world with their hard work that, at all times, the party organization is an indestructible fighting fortress."[118]

But for some Western companies, the compromises that they make to do business in China have become increasingly uncomfortable as Xi has tightened state control over the private sector. Some multinationals have found ways to accommodate the party's presence while keeping them out of public view. Others worry that in-house party groups may try to influence business decisions, and struggle to decide how much party activities they can tolerate to remain in favor with Chinese authorities and business partners, as well as their own local staff. Recently, foreign firms have more often found themselves caught up in geopolitical spats, forced to choose between placating Chinese authorities and consumers and allaying political pressure in their home countries, where resentment against China has risen.

Some of the friction is more prosaic than ideological. Foreign executives tell me they have argued with Chinese counterparts over whether party members should be allowed to meet during work hours, conduct meetings on company premises, or be given time off and receive company funds to conduct party activities. Some foreign businesses worry that party operatives, over time, may gain influence over management decisions or create an alternative power center. Others complain that Chinese executives with party membership spend too much time on their political duties, or are trying to steer corporate decisions in line with Beijing's priorities.[119]

Chinese officials bristle at Western business practices that impair party work. The Beijing Investment Promotion Bureau lamented that the foreign corporate norm of keeping staff salaries secret makes it harder to assess party dues, which are pegged to members' wages. "Party cells at foreign firms face a special work environment," said Xu Ying, a municipal party official in Beijing. "But the political leadership that party cells provide cannot be allowed to weaken."[120]

Foreign executives say openly questioning the party's initiatives would be corporate suicide in a key market, so most companies raise their concerns through business groups. In 2020, after the party issued guidelines on strengthening its links with private businesses, the European Union Chamber of Commerce in China warned that such efforts may force foreign firms to rethink their investments in China. By pushing companies to "incorporate more political calculus into their decisions, instead of just following market forces," the party could "lead companies to reconsider who they partner with," the chamber said.[121]

Some Western multinationals say their Chinese partners have pushed to amend their joint-venture agreements to enshrine formal roles for in-house party groups—a move foreign managers see as the thin end of the wedge. Executives at a major European manufacturer argued with cadres in the company after management tried to set limits on party activities. "We're concerned that the party is pushing the envelope and creeping into the company," one senior executive told me. The company held firm, he said, allowing just three party meetings a year on its premises, and only after business hours.[122] At a 51:49 joint venture between Chinese state energy giant Sinopec and a European firm, promising young staff often went away for weeks to attend classes at a party academy, according to a former executive. "How would you feel if some of your best workers go away for party studies for a month?" he said. "But the Chinese managers were enthusiastic. They see it as a positive."[123]

Even Disney has found itself wrongfooted by its Chinese partner at times, when Shendi went too far in playing up the American firm's support for party activities.

In 2017, Shendi publicized a "party building" meeting with a photograph showing the Shanghai Disney Resort's vice president for public affairs, Murray King, seated beside the theme park's deputy general manager and party chief. Shanghai's official party newspaper, *Jiefang Daily*, quoted King as saying the resort's best employees are mostly party members, and that its party cell helped ensure the theme park's success and created value for shareholders. When the *Wall Street Journal* asked Disney about these reports, the company disputed some quotes attributed to King and said he was speaking at a media briefing arranged by Shendi, rather than a party meeting. What King actually said, according to Disney, was that while some resort employees are party members, Disney doesn't make it a requirement. After I approached Shendi for comment, the party meeting photos disappeared from its website.[124]

Some Western firms have chosen to embrace the party's presence. The Conference Board, a business research association with major U.S. and European brands among its members, advised clients to "know the politics in order to avoid the politics" and demonstrate their "contributions to China." Party members at German engineering firm Bosch Rexroth's Beijing office often spent their Saturdays studying Xi's speeches and policies. French automaker Renault's China joint venture praised its party cell for fostering workplace cohesion, and arranged lectures to teach new foreign staff about the party. The China arm of French cosmetics firm L'Oréal stocked party literature in its Shanghai staff cafeteria and encouraged party members to decorate their desks with stickers saying, "If there's a problem, look for a party member." Party activities create "positive energy and driving forces for the company's healthy development," a L'Oréal China executive said.[125]

But passive acceptance of the party isn't enough. As gatekeepers of the world's largest consumer market, Beijing increasingly called on foreign businesses to echo party narratives and accused uncompliant companies of "hurting the feelings of the Chinese people." The political status of Taiwan, the island democracy which the party claims as Chinese territory, became a key sticking point after an independence-leaning president took office in Taipei in 2016. Chinese officials, media, and netizens denounced any suggestion that Taiwan is a sovereign state, and excoriated foreign airlines, hotel chains, and retailers that listed Taiwan as a country on their websites.[126] Some companies buckled, relabeling the island as a province of China. Others devised workarounds, such as renaming their list of locations from "countries" to "territories," to avoid being seen as caving to Chinese whims.[127]

Hong Kong, a former British colony that returned to Chinese rule in 1997, became a point of contention after anti-Beijing protests rocked the financial center in 2019. The National Basketball Association lost hundreds of millions in sponsorship dollars from China after the then general manager of the Houston Rockets, Daryl Morey, tweeted his support for the protesters with an image showing the words: "Fight for Freedom. Stand With Hong Kong." Though deleted, the post turned the Rockets, widely popular in China for fielding Chinese star Yao Ming from 2002 to 2011, into a target of online scorn and boycott threats in the NBA's biggest international market.[128] When Western governments blasted Beijing for imposing a national-security law on Hong Kong in 2020, foreign multinationals in the city faced pressure to take sides. London-based bank HSBC, which makes most of its profits in mainland China and Hong Kong, had a senior executive sign a petition supporting the security law and publicized his gesture on Chinese social media.[129]

Foreign companies have been buffeted by geopolitical headwinds time and again since Deng welcomed outside capital into China. After the U.S. and European governments sanctioned Beijing for its deadly crackdown on the 1989 Tiananmen Square protests, Western executives grappled with how to abide by the restrictions while trying to resume business in the country. Japanese companies often faced outbursts of nationalist anger when bilateral tensions spiked over territorial disputes and Tokyo's posture on wartime atrocities in China. Such troubles have grown more frequent and intense under Xi. His emphasis on national security, used to justify protectionist practices and demands for control over business data, grated on foreign firms.[130] His calls for China's economic self-sufficiency translated into policies less welcoming toward outside companies that are seen as less helpful to the country's push to acquire high-end technologies. Western multinationals also face pressure from politicians, investors, and consumers at home to avoid complicity with China in rights abuses, such as the suppression of dissent in Hong Kong and the forced assimilation of Muslims in Xinjiang. Hewing to Western opinion would spark anger and threats of boycotts in China, while placating Beijing could incur reputational damage at home.

Some companies balked at these challenges, choosing to trim their China operations or withdraw entirely, citing mounting political risks and a tougher business climate. In 2019, Google confirmed it had scrapped plans to launch a censored search engine in China, after media revelations of the project spurred Western public backlash against the tech firm.[131] Microsoft's LinkedIn closed its China networking service in 2021 and replaced it with a job-board platform without social media features—a change it attributed to "a significantly more challenging operating environment and greater compliance requirements in China."[132] Yahoo pulled out of the country just weeks later, citing similar reasons.[133] Airbnb followed suit in 2022 after struggling to cope with local competition and China's strict Covid lockdowns.[134]

Others tried accommodating Beijing. According to a Reuters report, Amazon .com Inc. complied with Chinese government requests to block customer ratings and reviews on its Chinese site after an anthology of Xi's remarks marketed on the platform received a negative review.[135] Amazon also teamed with a Chinese state propaganda agency to launch a bookselling portal, and gave Beijing information about an internet protocol address used by a fugitive Chinese businessman based in the U.S., the Reuters report said. "Ideological control and propaganda is the core of the toolkit for the communist party to achieve and maintain its success," Reuters quoted an internal Amazon document as saying. "We are not making judgement on whether it is right or wrong."[136] Even so, the American company has struggled to compete with Chinese rivals in their home market, shutting down its China online store in 2019 and pulling its Kindle e-bookstore from the Chinese market.[137]

Foreign businesses also found themselves reckoning with China's policies in the northwestern region of Xinjiang, as human rights watchdogs and Western governments called attention to the Communist Party's efforts to forcibly assimilate Muslim minorities there. Xinjiang plays a sizable role in global supply chains, producing raw materials like cotton used by major clothing brands and nearly half of the world's supply of polysilicon—a key ingredient in making solar panels.[138] Some foreign firms, such as German automaker Volkswagen, have production plants in Xinjiang. The region has also been a major procurer of advanced American technology, from semiconductors to genetic-sequencing gear, that local authorities use to surveil ethnic minorities and suppress dissent.[139] Activists and academics tracked down government documents and eyewitness accounts suggesting that a state-run employment program supplying workers—including former detainees at internment camps—to factories in Xinjiang and around the country amounts to forced labor.

Some multinationals echoed Beijing's narratives to protect their interests in Xinjiang. During a 2019 interview, then Volkswagen CEO Herbert Diess said he was "not aware" of any detention camps in Xinjiang—a remark critics denounced as either a lie or culpable ignorance on the part of a company that used forced labor during the Third Reich.[140] Volkswagen, which at the time was making about 40 percent of its sales and half its profits in China, also resisted calls to close its Xinjiang plant, which started operations in 2013, saying the forced-labor issue didn't arise, because the company directly employed its workers there.[141] Electric car maker Tesla Inc., whose CEO Elon Musk often praised China in meetings with senior Chinese officials, announced a new showroom in Urumqi on the last day of 2021, promising to "launch Xinjiang on its electric journey" and posting photos from the opening ceremony that featured placards reading "Tesla (heart) Xinjiang."[142]

Deviating from Beijing's narratives on Xinjiang can be costly. In early 2021, the world's largest clothing brand, Hennes & Mauritz's H&M, was battered in China after social media users called attention to a statement issued the previous year expressing concern about reports of forced labor and discrimination against ethnic minorities in Xinjiang. In the statement, the Swedish fast-fashion brand said it prohibited forced labor in its supply chain and didn't source products from Xinjiang.[143] State media accused H&M of smearing China, online influencers urged a boycott, its Chinese brand ambassadors cut ties, and major e-commerce platforms blocked searches for the company. The furor also engulfed other major brands like Nike and Adidas, whose membership in the Better Cotton Initiative, a nonprofit that certifies farms on sustainability standards, became a source of controversy when Chinese netizens dug up the group's 2020 decision to suspend licensing of producers in Xinjiang. Chinese brands, meanwhile, enjoyed a surge in sneaker and sportswear sales in China that, in some cases, helped them outperform Western apparel giants.[144]

The government had a hand in stoking outrage. Weeks before consumer anger engulfed H&M, officials from the Chinese foreign ministry and the party's propaganda department met with expert advisers to discuss ways to fight back against Western narratives on Xinjiang.[145] Some said Beijing should refute every false story or statement. Others suggested that the pushback should come from the public and industry, rather than the government.[146] Attacks against H&M and other Western brands unfolded in line with the latter recommendations. According to an analysis by Doublethink Lab, a Taipei-based nonprofit that studies Chinese disinformation operations, the campaign began in March 2021 when a relatively obscure Weibo influencer published screenshots of the H&M statement on Xinjiang cotton and suggested that he would boycott the company.[147] Hours later, the Communist Youth League's official Weibo account republished those screenshots with the caption: "Spreading rumors to boycott Xinjiang cotton while trying to make money in China? Wishful thinking!" Outrage ensued online, and propaganda officials in Beijing quietly celebrated what they saw as a successful counterblow against Western criticism.[148]

Spiraling tensions between China and the West heaped more pressure on multinationals trying to bridge both sides of the geopolitical divide. In the summer of 2021, Beijing fast-tracked an anti–foreign sanctions law into force without public consultation, creating new legal tools for punishing companies whose home governments were deemed to be harming Chinese interests. Washington doubled down with new legislation in December that year, banning imports from Xinjiang over concerns about the use of forced labor in the region.[149] On the day the U.S. Senate passed the law, Intel Corporation published a letter to suppliers asking them to avoid using any labor or sourcing any goods and services from Xinjiang.[150] Though this guidance changed little from what Intel had previously said, Chinese social media lit up with angry users accusing the chip maker of smearing their country. Intel, which counted China as its largest market by revenue, soon revised the letter to remove direct references to Xinjiang, saying the original document had been written to comply with U.S. law and wasn't an expression of the company's position on Xinjiang.[151]

Western multinationals voiced fears that they might become sacrificial pawns in a geopolitical struggle. Surveys by U.S. and European business groups show companies becoming more hesitant about making new investments in China, citing political risks and how ideology has increasingly displaced pragmatism in policy-making.[152] Some investors say they no longer see the world's second-largest economy as a surefire bet, but more of a shorter-term trade—to be bought and sold as policy winds shift. Others, uneasy with the increasing political harassment, have started exploring alternate markets or shifting some assets out of China, even if they can't afford to withdraw entirely. "There's something imperial about how the party leadership treats foreign businesses," says Jörg Wuttke, the president of the EU Chamber, who first visited China in the early 1980s and has lived there for more than three decades. "They want foreign companies to 'tremble and obey.' "[153]

CHAPTER FIVE

GRASPING THE PEN SHAFT

THE PARTY TELLS ITS STORIES

"To destroy a nation, you must first destroy its history."

—Gong Zizhen, Chinese intellectual (1792–1841)

"Use the past to serve the present."

—Mao Zedong

"The future is certain, it is only the past that is unpredictable."

—Old Soviet joke

Over seventeen days in the winter of 1950, a Chinese army surprised, surrounded, and battled bitterly with American-led forces through hellish conditions near a man-made lake in North Korea. Tens of thousands were wounded, killed, or frozen to death in one of the most brutal clashes in modern warfare. Remembered in the United States as the Battle of Chosin Reservoir, the engagement has split historical opinion ever since. Chinese accounts often depict a strategic success, one that helped drive imperialist invaders out of North Korea before the Korean War settled into a bloody stalemate. American narratives portray a moral victory for an outnumbered United Nations force, which avoided annihilation while inflicting horrendous losses on what Beijing called an army of people's volunteers.

Seven decades later, as tensions with the U.S. flared again, China summoned some of its finest filmmakers and spent a record $200 million to dramatize the battle for the big screen. The result was *The Battle at Lake Changjin*, an action-packed epic that earned more than $900 million to become China's highest-ever grossing film. Bristling with jingoism, the movie tracked a Chinese company commander and his jejune younger brother as their unit fought caricatured American troops across snow-swept landscapes. Foreign reception was mixed. Some critics called the film rabble-rousing propaganda, comparable with patriotic Hollywood blockbusters like *Pearl Harbor* and *We Were Soldiers*. South Korean netizens savaged Chinese filmmakers for a one-sided portrayal that excluded Korean voices and whitewashed Pyongyang's culpability in starting the war.

At home, the movie was a smashing success, showered with fulsome praise after hitting theaters on the eve of China's October 1 National Day in 2021. Filmgoers raved over a memorable scene that depicted how a group of Chinese soldiers, eulogized as the "Ice Sculpture Company," froze to death while lying in ambush. "We seem to have become accustomed to watching omnipotent superheroes flying across the big screen and accepting cultural input from the West," one commentator wrote in the party tabloid *Global Times*. "Unlike the illusory superhero stories in the West, China's *The Battle at Lake Changjin* is from real history."[1]

The nationalistic gushing grated with Luo Changping, a former investigative reporter who made his name exposing corruption among senior Chinese officials.[2] A prominent muckraker in a country where few dare pursue the calling, Luo had remained outspoken on social media even after being forced out of journalism in 2014. "Half a century later, our countrymen rarely reflect on the justifiability of the war," he wrote on the Weibo microblogging platform a week after *The Battle at Changjin Lake*'s release in China. "Just like how the soldiers in the Sand Sculpture Company didn't doubt the 'wise decision-making' at the top."[3]

The blowback was instant. Netizens denounced Luo for insulting Chinese martyrs, noting that "sand sculpture" is slang for idiot. Many also condemned him for questioning Beijing's reasons for joining what it calls the "War to Resist U.S. Aggression and Aid Korea" in late 1950, when North Korea was being overrun after its failed invasion of the South. The following day, police detained Luo for allegedly "damaging the reputation and honor of heroes and martyrs"—an amorphous offense set down in 2018 to penalize dissent against official histories.[4] Weibo shut down Luo's account and state media cheered his downfall. A local court later sentenced Luo to seven months in jail and ordered him to make a public apology.[5] The severity of Luo's punishment sent shock waves through scholarly circles and social media. Historians and influencers alike lamented the shifting red lines in public speech and grasped an emphatic message about how Xi Jinping waged battle for China's hearts and minds: to secure the Communist Party's future, he was exerting an iron grip on the past.

While Chinese leaders since Mao had often stressed the importance of controlling historical narratives, Xi enforced party canon with unusual vigor. Just weeks after taking power, he urged vigilance against efforts to topple the party by smearing its past—a threat, known as "historical nihilism," that had corroded the party of Lenin and Stalin and brought down the Soviet Union. "To destroy a nation, you must first destroy its history," Xi said, quoting nineteenth-century Chinese intellectual Gong Zizhen, who lamented the Qing government's weakness in the face of Western power. "Domestic and foreign hostile forces often make hay with China's revolutionary and modern history, sparing no effort in launching attacks, distortions and smears, with the fundamental goal of confusing the people's will."[6] The party of Mao must counter such subversion by telling its stories with verve, Xi argued, and persuade the Chinese people that only Communist rule can steer their teleological path to greatness. "History and reality tell us that only socialism can save China," he said. "This is the conclusion of history, and the choice of the people."[7]

Since then, Xi has directed an all-encompassing struggle to shape China's collective consciousness. Party propagandists revised textbooks and museums to boost Xi's image, while diluting criticism of Mao. State media denounced skeptics of party lore as enemies of the state. Lawmakers prescribed criminal and civil penalties for those who defamed party-approved "heroes and martyrs." Regulators scoured social media and video games for alleged distortions of party and national history, scrubbing dissent and banning errant users. Researchers reported increasing difficulty in accessing Chinese archives and their troves of documents, while censors scrubbed digital academic databases of old articles that contradicted modern political sensibilities. And there was intimidation too, with the banning of books, canceling of classes, and suing of scholars who challenged party canon, as well as ad hominem attacks and denial of visas targeting foreign researchers whose work Beijing disliked. Some Chinese historians, chafing against the party's strictures, moved abroad.

Xi often speaks of wielding the "mirror of history" as a tool of domestic control and foreign policy. He urges officials to "tell the Chinese Communist Party's stories well," and direct national campaigns to propagate official narratives in schools, museums, and across popular culture. Xi himself is one of the biggest beneficiaries, with his life story turned into the centerpiece of a personality cult and propagated with an ardor unseen since the days of Mao. The party rewrote its charter and issued new historical texts to crown Xi as one of China's greatest leaders, a sentiment encapsulated in an oft-quoted refrain: "Mao Zedong built the nation; Deng Xiaoping enriched the nation; Xi Jinping will strengthen the nation."

By portraying the party as an indispensable guarantor of China's ascendancy over a fading West, Xi hopes to secure his own power, and entrench Communist rule for generations to come. "For the party, history is science. Whoever controls what is certified as history controls the truth," says Timothy Cheek, a professor and China historian at the University of British Columbia. "Xi Jinping has to tell a story that's compelling, and his way of telling it is to ensure that nobody else gets to tell another story."

THE PAST SERVES THE PRESENT

DAYS AFTER TAKING OFFICE as general secretary in November 2012, Xi Jinping took his fellow leaders for an excursion just a few hundred yards down the road from their Zhongnanhai leadership compound in central Beijing. Their destination was the National Museum, an austere monolithic complex just east of Tiananmen Square, built in time for the tenth anniversary of the People's Republic in 1959. Curators there had maintained for years a popular exhibition recounting China's modern history, and Xi saw a fitting stage for his first piece of political theater as paramount leader.

Titled *The Road Toward Rejuvenation*, the exhibition begins with the First Opium War of 1839–1842, when a victorious Britain forced the Qing government to open ports for trade and cede the island of Hong Kong. It was a decisive moment of infamy, the first in a series of "unequal treaties" that foreign powers imposed on Beijing, and what many in China consider the start of their nation's "century of humiliation."[8] The displays went on to depict the decline of a proud, preeminent civilization that had dominated Asia before falling laggard to the West and suffering ignominious defeats to imperialist powers, which occupied land, established concessions, and plundered riches on Chinese soil. Featuring more than twelve hundred artifacts and nearly nine hundred photos, the exhibition explained how the Qing dynasty atrophied and collapsed, precipitating decades of civil war and foreign invasion.[9] The Communist Party emerged from this crucible of chaos, so the story goes, inspired by Marxism and steeled by Mao's derring-do as they waged revolution and battled imperialist aggressors before liberating China in 1949.

It is a familiar story for generations of Chinese, drilled into their common consciousness through textbooks, propaganda, and popular culture. The "century of humiliation" forms the spine of the People's Republic's founding mythology, where the party emerged as China's rightful rulers by avenging its indignities and restoring its honor. This narrative is Xi's most valued inheritance, handed down since Mao to successive leaders who tapped its evocative power to justify the party's legitimacy—and their own. It fuels pride and righteous anger that the party uses to defend authoritarian rule, vilify dissent as treasonous, and condemn foreign critics who "hurt the feelings of the Chinese people."[10]

Throughout more than 170 years of trials and tribulations since the Opium War, "the Chinese people have never given in, have struggled ceaselessly, and have finally taken hold of our own destiny and started the great process of building our nation," Xi told his entourage, in remarks aired on national television that evening.[11] Now, he declared, the Chinese people have become more confident and capable than ever of rejuvenating their nation, a goal he called the China Dream. Xi was reaching for the heart of the national mythos, vowing to deliver his nation's resurgence as a great power, as ordained in the party's promise of inexorable progress toward a socialist utopia.[12] "Our generation of Communists should draw on past progress," he said, "and chart a new course for the future."[13]

China's rulers since antiquity have sought to legitimize their power by dictating the past, and the Communist Party is no exception. Mao was a storyteller par excellence. Through speeches, prose, and poetry, he won followers with compelling yarns about the party's struggle to save a suffering China. Though Mao spoke with a thick accent from his native Hunan province that eluded many of his listeners, his speeches would be refined and rendered comprehensible in writing, and disseminated over the airwaves and print. Mao would tell officials to "use the past to serve the present," a saying often interpreted as an appeal to repurpose history to satisfy current exigencies. "Such storytelling enabled the Communists to convert every defeat, retreat, and crisis point into a victory of some sort, a sleight of hand, in which disasters become magical occasions, and failures superhuman accomplishments, a kind of magic realism matched by ruthlessness," Yale political scientist David Apter wrote. "Such fictive truths became self-fulfilling prophecies, enabling the Communists to become virtually miraculous in their own eyes."[14]

History is also *ultima ratio*, the final argument, for settling discord within party ranks. "Like any political figure, Mao needed examples and events to illustrate and if possible validate his preferred strategies as a 'correct line,'" Apter wrote. "Mao became a storyteller precisely because of the practical need to establish his hegemony over others who claimed to be better Marxists than he."[15] In 1945, soon after wrapping up a ruthless purge known as the Yan'an rectification movement, Mao directed the passage of a Central Committee resolution on "certain historical questions." The text recast past events to entrench Mao's dominance, praising his "correct leadership" and excoriating his rivals for their "erroneous" thinking.[16] The party then enshrined "Mao Zedong Thought" as one of its guiding ideologies, alongside Marxism-Leninism, consecrating the Chairman's ideas as part of its holy scriptures.

Deng enacted his own resolution in 1981, this time to draw a line under the Cultural Revolution, repudiate Mao's megalomania, and reset the shattered party onto a reformist path. The document spent more than 34,000 characters condemning Mao's personality cult and arbitrary rule. It discarded dogmatic notions of "class struggle," and urged a restoration of collective leadership and intra-party democracy. Despite heated debates during the drafting process, Deng secured the Central Committee's unanimous approval for his resolution, consolidating his authority as paramount leader—in place of Mao's successor Hua Guofeng—and unifying the party around his platform of pragmatic governance and market-opening reforms.[17]

Work on the 1981 resolution lasted more than one and a half years. Deng reviewed drafts and often requested changes, insisting that the document had to draw a distinction between Mao the person, whose errors must be repudiated, and Mao Zedong Thought, which the party exalted second only to Marxism-Leninism. Whereas the Soviet Union could afford to denounce Stalin, as Nikita Khrushchev did in 1956, Mao commanded such an emotional hold over China that a full-throated renunciation of the man, Deng feared, would erode the party's legitimacy or even topple the entire edifice. The resolution thus proclaimed Mao as a "great Marxist and great revolutionary," whose mistakes were secondary to his successes.

Deng's verdict held sway for the next three decades. Mao's portrait stayed on the facade of Beijing's Tiananmen, the Gate of Heavenly Peace, even as the country embraced the capitalist impulses that he had loathed. Jiang Zemin and Hu Jintao upheld the Dengist canon, celebrating the party's successes while smothering its calamities. In the 1990s, patriotic education became mandatory in schools, where students learned to revere the party for forging a "new China" and righting the

wrongs suffered during the "century of humiliation." Propagandists policed popular culture to ensure its alignment with the party line. Hit television dramas in the
late 1990s and early 2000s depicting the Qing's Kangxi and Yongzheng emperors
featured anachronistic references to how Kangxi "recovered" control of Taiwan,
even though the island hadn't been ruled by any Chinese dynasty preceding the
Qing, which annexed Taiwan in the late seventeenth century. An acclaimed 2003
drama series, *Towards the Republic*, which recounted the Qing collapse and Sun
Yat-sen's troubled efforts to build a constitutional republic, suffered hefty cuts at
the hands of censors, who most glaringly axed the show's final scene—Sun expounding his ideal system of government in a lengthy speech—and replaced it with
twenty minutes of white screen.[18]

Authorities did tolerate some deviation from official canon. Academics could
publish writings and teach classes on the Mao era and the Cultural Revolution, as
long as they didn't question the party's legitimacy. *Yanhuang Chunqiu*, an influential
history magazine founded in 1991 with backing from reformist party elders and
whose evocative name can translate as "China Through the Ages," emerged as a bas-
tion of liberal thought and pushed boundaries with essays that probed the darkest corners of party history, irking conservatives and sometimes suffering sanctions,
while winning fans among party moderates.[19] Yang Jisheng, a former Xinhua News
Agency journalist who documented the 1959–1962 Great Famine in a two-volume
opus titled *Tombstone*, saw his book suppressed in mainland China after its publication in 2008, but was able to speak privately about his work and continue living in
his Xinhua-sponsored apartment in Beijing.[20]

The party's narratives, however, were being stretched to their limits by the time
Xi took power. High-octane growth had fueled economic polarization, which tore at
China's social fabric. The spirit of optimism and opportunity that had powered the
Deng era wore thin with people left behind in an increasingly unequal society, while
those who thrived sought a cleaner break from the Maoist past. Within the party and
beyond, voices of post-traumatic anger with Mao's dictatorship clashed with nostalgia for his bygone egalitarian ethos—a rift that could unravel the party's claims of
being an unimpeachable steward of a rising China.

Xi moved to close the cleavage. Addressing senior officials in January 2013, he
suggested that the party should "correctly evaluate" its early decades in power and
grasp the continuity between the epochs of Mao and Deng. The post-Mao period
shouldn't be used to repudiate the Mao era, and vice versa, he said. As Xi saw it,

China's past struggles had set the stage for its present success, and despite some painful detours, the arc of Chinese history bent toward glory.

As chief narrator, Xi brooked no challenge to his stories. In 2016, party authorities seized control over *Yanhuang Chunqiu* by ousting its top editors and managers, who then declared their twenty-five-year-old magazine defunct, saying they would rather pull the plug than allow their publication to be co-opted by the party.[21] When Yang Jisheng finished writing a history of the Cultural Revolution, titled *The World Turned Upside Down*, officials warned him against publishing or discussing his work, and blocked him from traveling to the U.S.[22] Yang himself came under fire from neo-Maoists and state media.[23] The assault on some of the party's most esteemed chroniclers disturbed some insiders who sensed an ominous turn in the political climate. Whereas Deng had tried to encourage a degree of intellectual curiosity and debate within the party, Xi chose to restrict speech and unify thought, says Yan Huai, a Deng-era official who once assessed Xi's suitability for promotion in the 1980s. "To maintain control, there are only two ways: through the gun barrel and the pen shaft," Yan says, using party-speak for the military and the propaganda apparatus.[24]

Xi's pen shafts spilled considerable ink rewriting established narratives. In 2015, as Xi prepared to mark seven decades since the end of World War II with a military parade, party historians pushed revisionist claims that Mao's Communist forces had played a crucial role in resisting Japanese invaders during the war, challenging the scholarly consensus outside mainland China that Chiang Kai-shek's Nationalist, or Kuomintang, armies did most of the fighting.[25] A Chinese film depicting a 1937 battle in Shanghai, where Kuomintang troops defended a warehouse against Japanese attackers for several days, was shelved just before its scheduled release in 2019, after some party historians accused the film of glorifying the Republic of China flag flown by the Kuomintang—even though it was historically accurate.[26] When the movie came out a year later, viewers noted how the ROC flag was mostly shown from a blurry distance.[27]

Such propaganda hit a crescendo ahead of the party's centenary in 2021. Xi ordered a national campaign to study party history that experts describe as China's largest mass education drive since the Mao era. Pro-party chronicles saturated bookstores, cinemas, television screens, and social media. Officials commissioned concerts with patriotic songs like "Without the Communist Party, There Would Be No New China." Government agencies, state enterprises, and schools organized history-themed field trips, film screenings, and quizzes. Private businesses, law firms, and even a Shanghai temple dedicated to the Chinese god of wealth arranged party history classes for employees. Airlines staged in-flight sing-alongs and poetry recitals to teach passengers about the party's past. China's internet regulator launched web platforms and a telephone hotline for the public to report instances of "historical nihilism," such as content that criticized the party's leaders and policies.

The messaging revived Marxist notions of history proceeding inexorably along a revolutionary trajectory. "Looking back at history, it was in the face of various turbulences and chaos that the Chinese Communist Party was born, grew up and became strong," He Yiting, former executive vice president of Beijing's Central Party School, wrote in a newspaper commentary. A clear-eyed assessment of international affairs, he said, "fully confirms a major judgment made by General Secretary Xi Jinping: the times and trends are on our side."[28]

Xi carved that message into the party gospel in late 2021, becoming only the third party leader to enact a resolution on history.[29] Crafted over seven months under Xi's direct supervision, the document purports to chronicle the party's "major achievements and historical experience" during its hundred-year existence. Even so, it devotes more than two-thirds of its roughly 36,000 characters to exalting Xi's achievements, lionizing him as an epoch-defining figure uniquely suited to steer China through uncertain times.[30] Xi's name appears twenty-two times, surpassing Mao's eighteen mentions and Deng's six. Jiang Zemin and Hu Jintao are each mentioned once.

Unlike Mao and Deng, Xi refrains from overtly attacking rivals or predecessors in his resolution. Still, the document clearly conveys Xi's disapproval, without naming names, with how Jiang and Hu governed China. Before Xi took power, the resolution says, the country faced "problems that have not been resolved for a long time," in particular corruption, unrestrained capitalism, weak control of public opinion on the internet, and dilution of the party's dominance over society. It thus fell to Xi to offer the decisive leadership needed to steer Communist China into its third historical epoch—from "standing up" under Mao and "getting rich" under Deng, to "becoming strong" under Xi.

NEW TESTAMENT

LIKE ITS COUNTERPARTS in the Soviet Union and elsewhere, China's Communist Party has a storied history of unhistory. Censors manipulated photographs to emphasize Mao's presence or excise purged officials. Propagandists revised history texts and museums to diminish, even erase, discussions about policy failures, inconvenient narratives, and alternative pathways. The future is invariably utopian, the past contested ground. "There's a saying that 'all history is contemporary history,'" says Wu Si, a former chief editor of *Yanhuang Chunqiu*. "What you say, what you remove, what you retain—these are all decided in accordance with contemporary interests and concerns."[31]

Such instrumentalist attitudes toward the past go all the way back to the party's roots. When the party started commemorating its founding anniversary in the late 1930s, Mao and another revolutionary who'd attended the inaugural congress could only recall that it took place in July 1921, but not the exact dates. Mao picked July 1 as the anniversary, and although researchers later ascertained that the first congress started on July 23, the party has continued the charade, with many Chinese unaware of the discrepancy.[32] Even Hu Jintao made that mistake as party chief, declaring in his July 1 speech in 2011 that the party was founded "90 years ago today."[33]

Disregard for inconvenient facts aside, the party takes its mythmaking seriously. The creation of party canon is a laborious, painstaking process, often dragging on for years as retired grandees, incumbent officials, and revolutionary families argue over competing narratives. Such squabbling gets most bitter when the party is drafting the most authoritative accounts, and there are none more canonical than the multivolume opus titled *The History of the Chinese Communist Party*. The first volume, published in 1991 and updated a decade later, chronicles the party's struggle for power from its founding in 1921 through to the proclamation of the People's Republic in 1949—a period less encumbered by historical baggage within the party elite, and easily infused with clear heroes and villains.

Work on the second volume, a 1,074-page tome that recounted the three decades up to 1978, was far more fraught. Party historians slogged for sixteen years before the book was published in 2011, including about four years just to complete a first draft.[34] They went through more than ten versions over a series of extensive rewrites, and submitted four drafts to the Politburo before getting approval for the final text.[35] More than one hundred senior officials and experts reviewed drafts, including Xi, who as leader-in-waiting supervised the project as part of his responsibilities over ideological training.[36] Historians say Xi showed keen interest in the book, issuing "clear requests for revisions" and urging them to finish it as soon as possible— a salient concern given that more than a dozen officials and scholars involved died before publication.[37] "I never thought it would take so long," Shi Zhongquan, a senior party historian and an editor on the drafting team, told the *Washington Post*. "Writing history is not easy."[38]

Historians who worked on volume two say they labored most intensely not on the 1966–1976 Cultural Revolution but the decade preceding it, when Mao waged mass campaigns to propel Chinese society toward utopia but wreaked havoc instead. The book tackled some controversial subjects but shied from others. While the text criticized Mao's 1957–1959 "Anti-Rightist" purge of allegedly pro-capitalism dissidents for persecuting innocents and causing grave societal damage, it elided Deng's role as one of the campaign's most energetic enforcers. The book condemned the Great Leap Forward and faulted Mao's complacency and even recklessness in pursuing social and economic change.[39] It avoided the "Great Famine" label but acknowledged that "severe difficulties" during that period caused China's population to fall by 10 million in 1960 due to food shortage and disease. Even then, this figure came in far short of many other estimates, which range between 15 million and 55 million famine-related deaths.

Party researchers had already done more than a decade's worth of preparatory work for volume three of the official history by the time the leadership gave the formal go-ahead in 2013, though little was known about the time period the volume would cover and when it might be published.[40] Meanwhile, the party focused on crafting condensed accounts for general readers—books that skimmed over controversial events, while reaching wider audiences and making more impact in shaping public consciousness about the past.

Among them is an authoritative account of the party's first nine decades, a project Xi launched in 2010 to be published in time for the party's ninety-fifth anniversary.[41] As with volume two of the official history, Xi kept a close eye on the drafting of *Ninety Years of the Chinese Communist Party*. He told party historians to infuse the book with vivid, emotive language that could inspire readers and rouse fervor for the party. The result, published in 2016, raised eyebrows with its diluted criticism of Mao, most notably its omission of references to Mao's "mistakes" in starting the Cultural Revolution—language that had become routine in authoritative party histories. Officials justified the change as a natural shift toward more objective assessments of the past.

Such changes rankled people who sought a reckoning for their suffering under Mao. For decades, the party had discouraged public discussions on subjects like the

Great Leap Forward and the Cultural Revolution, despite having repudiated those events. Grassroots attempts to broach a fuller accounting often ran into state suppression or descended into shouting matches between liberal voices and Maoist groups. When some former Red Guards started publicly confessing to past misdeeds in 2013, they faced criticism from those who felt their apologies were insincere, and others who accused them of smearing Mao.[42] In 2016, when a musical troupe staged a Maoist song-and-dance concert at Beijing's Great Hall of the People ahead of the Cultural Revolution's fiftieth anniversary, princelings and ordinary citizens alike roared their disapproval at what they saw as an attempt to gloss over Mao's errors and build a Xi cult.[43]

A similar backlash erupted when Xi's revisionism reached into high-school classrooms. In 2018, the education ministry's publishing arm introduced a new history textbook that diluted criticism of Mao. Whereas the previous edition, adopted in 2001, had covered the Cultural Revolution in a four-page chapter that said Mao had erred in his judgment, the new edition cut the reference to Mao's mistakes, truncated the Cultural Revolution content, and squeezed it into another chapter innocuously titled "Arduous Exploration and Achievements in Development." Social media users called attention to the changes and accused the People's Education Press of whitewashing history.

The efforts to palliate Mao's legacy help Xi justify his autocratic style and legitimize Communist rule for the long term. Instead of a history where the party can be seen to err, Xi "would benefit greatly from a new narrative in which the party is seen—almost like a religious body—to be on a path to inevitable success," says Rana Mitter, a professor and China historian at Oxford University.

Xi imprinted this narrative in a 2021 book titled *A Short History of the Chinese Communist Party*, an authoritative volume for general audiences that updated earlier editions released in 2001 and 2010. The new text discarded the detailed discussions of Mao's mistakes and elite power struggles that appeared in previous versions, while playing up China's economic and diplomatic achievements under Mao.[44]

Whereas past editions devoted lengthy passages to the Great Leap Forward and concluded that "this bitter historical lesson shouldn't be forgotten," this sentence didn't appear in the 2021 book.[45] The Cultural Revolution no longer appeared as a standalone chapter, but was featured as part of a broader segment titled "The Exploration and Tortuous Developments in Building Socialism." Whereas earlier editions opened the Cultural Revolution chapter by saying the movement "erupted" at Mao's instigation and inflicted "grave disaster upon the party and the people," the 2021 version merely said the movement "happened" due to social and historical factors.

Some of Deng's most famous quotations, which contradict Xi's domineering style, didn't appear in the 2021 *Short History*. Among them was a remark that Deng made in 1989 as he prepared to relinquish his last official leadership post as chairman of the Central Military Commission: "Building a nation's fate on the reputation of one or two people is very unhealthy and very dangerous." Deng's appeal for his compatriots to "hide your light and bide your time," or keep a low profile while accumulating China's strengths, was also cut.

Instead the 2021 book featured new chapters that extolled Xi as a decisive leader and visionary statesman. The book devoted more than a quarter of its 531 pages to Xi's policies and accomplishments, even though his time in power—at that point—accounted for less than a tenth of the party's century-long existence. For China to continue thriving, the book argued, Xi should be vested with unparalleled power. "Amidst ten thousand majestic mountains, there must be a main peak."[46]

THE GOSPEL OF XI

IN THE SPRING OF 2013, a group of prominent princelings and public intellectuals assembled at a Beijing hotel to celebrate the Lunar New Year. It was an annual reunion for these old friends and comrades, many of whom were keen supporters and editors of *Yanhuang Chunqiu*. Among the attendees was Hu Dehua, a son of former party chief Hu Yaobang, a liberal-minded reformer whose death in 1989 sparked the mass mourning that led to the Tiananmen Square protests. A software engineer turned entrepreneur, the younger Hu had flourished in the economic miracle that followed his father's passing, launching successful businesses while earning notoriety for airing irreverent views on political affairs. And so it was on this February day, when his straight talk would again irk the powers that be.

"The current leader is younger than me, and at the time, the education we received was very limited. I only studied up till high school, while Xi Jinping is the same as my younger sister, he attended school only till the first year of junior high," Hu said. "Of course, some people said that I shouldn't say this, your father was also educated till the first year of junior high. But I want to tell everyone something, my father was someone who really loved reading books." The youth of the Cultural

Revolution, who had limited access to books and therefore did little learning, were now leading China, he said. "I just feel very worried."[47]

Within weeks, Xi started raving about his passion for books. "I have many hobbies, the biggest of which is reading. Reading has become a way of life for me," Xi told reporters in March 2013, after name-checking eight Russian writers—including Chekhov, Dostoevsky, and Tolstoy—whose works he claimed to have read.[48] Two months later, Xi charmed Greece's prime minister by saying he read many works by Greek philosophers during his teenage years.[49] When Xi visited France the following year, he boasted about reading Montesquieu, Voltaire, Rousseau, Diderot, Sartre, and more than a dozen other writers.[50] State media feted Xi as an erudite leader, publishing lists of his favorite books and cajoling citizens to emulate his love for learning.

The publicity blitz set tongues wagging across the *Yanhuang Chunqiu* set. Many among them concluded that Xi's outlandish claims of literary prowess betrayed deep-seated insecurity about his lack of a formal education—particularly in contrast with Mao, who wrote poetry, and even Jiang Zemin, who spoke several languages and sang and played music alongside foreign leaders. "Xi is not cultured. He was basically just an elementary schooler," one princeling who has known Xi for decades told me. "He's very sensitive about that."[51]

Mythmaking is a key component of Xi's push for preeminence. Whereas Mao and Deng won adulation through revolutionary exploits and epoch-defining achievements, Xi took power as a relative unknown and had to build his appeal from scratch. He opted for winning favor through populist deeds and folksy branding, drawing on imagery that recalls Mao and on methods that are more Madison Avenue.

The party humanized Xi with marketing on social media. A visit to a Beijing steamed bun shop in 2013 became a viral hit after fellow diners shared images of Xi queuing and paying for lunch. State media nudged netizens into addressing their leader as "Xi Dada," using a term of endearment meaning "daddy" or "uncle" from the Xi clan's home province of Shaanxi. Party-run studios created online videos to play up Xi's credentials, including a 2013 effort—titled *How Leaders Are Made*—likening Xi's ascent to the "training of a kung-fu master," who proved his mettle by governing more than 150 million people over four decades as a local and regional official.[52] Musical odes proliferated online, portraying Xi as a steely man of action, a loving husband, and even an ideal partner for marriage.[53] His songstress wife, Peng Liyuan, added star power by keeping up her charity work and joining Xi on diplomatic engagements, departing from the publicity shyness that China's first ladies had adopted after the Mao era.[54]

Xi also used traditional techniques more familiar to Leninists than millennials. State media plastered Xi's name and image across front pages, websites, and television news bulletins. Party presses published hagiographic accounts of his life from the Cultural Revolution through to his stints in local and regional government. Primary-school textbooks describe "Grandpa Xi Jinping" as an avuncular leader who hoped to see China's children become upstanding citizens, echoing Stalin's self-styled image as the "father of nations."[55] Xi accumulated titles of authority, becoming the party's "core," the military's commander in chief, and the "people's leader"—a designation that echoed Mao's title of "Great Leader."[56] The party rewrote its charter to add an ideological slogan often shortened to "Xi Jinping Thought," giving his words and ideas the power of holy writ. His lieutenants declared that Xi was empowered to *dingyu yizun*, or "decide matters as the highest authority," repurposing a phrase the party once used to warn against unbridled power.[57]

Media controls intensified as Xi insisted that all Chinese news organizations owed their loyalties to the party.[58] He boosted funding for state news outlets, while squelching independent journalism at home with coercion and censorship. Major outlets such as the *People's Daily*, Xinhua News Agency, and China Central Television run "central kitchens" that control and create news content for formats ranging from print to video. Journalists must pass exams testing their knowledge of Xi's policies and Marxist journalistic ideals to secure and renew press credentials.[59] Authorities ramped up internet controls, particularly on the WeChat platform, scrubbing anything that cast aspersions on the party and its leader.

The image-building stretched credulity at times. After a 2017 state television documentary aired old interview footage of Xi saying that he, as a rural laborer during the Cultural Revolution, would carry two hundred *jin* of wheat for ten *li*—roughly two hundred and twenty pounds over three miles—without switching shoulders, some netizens ridiculed what they saw as an implausible feat.[60] Xi's claims to be a sophisticated reader also drew scorn, given his repeated verbal slips in speeches—mispronouncing words and mixing up phrases—that critics attribute to his disrupted education. During a 2021 video conference with leaders of foreign political parties, Xi inadvertently repeated a passage in his speech, prompting an aide to rush over and set him back on track.[61]

Xi's ubiquitous presence has unnerved many Chinese who see shades of a Mao-style dictatorship. But unlike Mao, Xi wants not mass participation but popular support—a source of political capital that he can use to overcome vested interests and bureaucratic inertia. And while Xi enjoys greater popularity than his predecessor, the enthusiasm for his leadership remains a pale shade of the mass veneration that Mao once commanded. At the height of the Mao cult, fanatical students waved "little red books" of the Chairman's quotations at mass gatherings, Mao statues and paraphernalia were omnipresent across public spaces and inside households, and many people worshipped him like a deity.

The party banned personality cults in 1982, and until Xi, its leaders seldom invoked the Great Helmsman beyond perfunctory references to "Mao Zedong Thought." While officials insist that Xi isn't resurrecting a Mao-style cult, the party has gone to great lengths to elevate Xi's stature at the expense of Deng, the man credited for trying to inoculate China against one-man rule. Deng remained a towering figure well after his death in 1997, revered for enriching the nation and transitioning it toward a more stable leadership. This legacy supplies historical tradition and ideological authority that liberal-minded officials can cite to challenge Xi's policies—a potent restraint that the current leader has sought to cast aside.

When the party celebrated the fortieth anniversary of Deng's economic reforms in 2018, the fanfare focused primarily on Xi, even though Deng has long been exalted as the "chief architect" of "reform and opening up." At the national art museum in Beijing, paintings of Xi and his father were displayed prominently at a fortieth anniversary exhibition, overshadowing artwork depicting Deng and other past leaders—in contrast with how Deng imagery had dominated a thirtieth anniversary exhibition at the same museum in 2008. State media credited Xi's stints in Fujian and Zhejiang for those provinces' economic success while omitting Deng, even though Xi—as a provincial official—had cited Deng's policies as a guide for his own.[62]

While Xi hasn't tried to erase or repudiate Deng, the late leader's supporters have been sensitive to any revisionist attempts to dilute his legacy. Such contestation played out vividly in Shenzhen, where Deng is exalted for his role in transforming a sleepy seaside town into a high-tech metropolis. In December 2017, state-owned conglomerate China Merchants Group opened a museum in the city's Shekou district—an early test bed for pro-business policies—to pay tribute to the politicians and entrepreneurs who had spearheaded "reform and opening up." Deng was the most prominent figure featured. Visitors would encounter in the lobby a panoramic frieze depicting Deng's 1984 visit to Shekou, a tribute that curators described as the museum's centerpiece. Deng paraphernalia lined the route—photographs, quotations, calligraphy, as well as a chair that he once sat on during his 1984 tour.[63]

Shenzhen's propaganda chief attended the opening ceremony, declaring that the museum would become a base for patriotic education. Nearly eighty thousand people visited the facility over the first six months, before it suddenly closed for "upgrading" in June 2018. When it reopened two months later, the Shekou Museum of China's Reform and Opening-Up was virtually unrecognizable. The Deng frieze was gone, replaced by two video screens showcasing local development and a beige wall adorned with a Xi quotation: "During the forty years of Reform and Opening Up we have created a new road, a good road by bravely daring to pioneer and boldly undertaking self-reform, realizing a great leap from 'catching up with the times' to 'leading the times.'"[64]

While most Deng-related exhibits remained, the museum added a large volume of photographs, texts, and videos to extol Xi and his father's roles in delivering prosperity to China. Curators removed a border-fence mock-up that highlighted how impoverished Chinese fled to British Hong Kong during the 1970s and 1980s, and replaced it with items showcasing Xi Zhongxun's role in steering economic reforms as Guangdong party chief from 1978 to 1980. The redesigned exhibition concluded with a section on Xi Jinping's Belt and Road infrastructure initiative, splashed with some sixteen photos of the incumbent leader. "Comrade Xi Jinping has raised the banner of reform," read the section's introductory text. "A new era of ideological liberation is sweeping through China."[65]

A museum executive assured me that the redesign, which factored in public and professional feedback, "can stand the test of history." But some visitors weren't impressed. "They should respect history," said Zhao Yanqing, a Shenzhen retiree who saw the museum before and after its revamp. "I feel that we're reviving the cult of personality from Chairman Mao's time. This is too dangerous."

After I described the changes in a *Wall Street Journal* report in August 2018, overseas Chinese media lit up with discussions about what the pro-Xi revisionism suggested about political intrigue in Beijing. Weeks later, Deng's eldest son gave a speech laced with oblique criticisms of Xi, particularly his assertive foreign policy. China "should keep a sober mind and know our own place," Deng Pufang said, echoing his father's famous calls for humble diplomacy. "We should neither be overbearing nor belittle ourselves."[66]

The shadowboxing between the Deng and Xi camps continued at the Shekou museum. Curators tweaked the lobby in September, adding a Deng quotation above Xi's remarks on the wall and displaying Deng images on the video screens. Further renovations in October installed a new Deng frieze similar to the original sculpture torn down months earlier. Then in late December, the museum said it would be permanently closed to the public from Christmas Day—two days short of its first anniversary. A PhD student who was doing research there told me that a skeletal staff maintained the facility for months after its closure, with access limited to China Merchants staff and corporate guests.[67] "Now the exhibition's mission has been fully accomplished," a museum spokeswoman told me. "Therefore it is no longer open."[68]

HONORING HEROES

EIGHT DECADES AFTER HIS GRANDFATHER was killed during the Chinese civil war, Fang Huaqing vowed to defend his ancestor's legacy as a Communist hero, one legal complaint at a time. His crusade started in early 2017, when he came across online articles alleging that his grandfather, a celebrated Chinese Red Army commander, was an unscrupulous bandit who kidnapped and murdered innocent people. Incensed by what he calls malicious slander, the younger Fang has brought civil suits against rumormongers, accused party historians of negligence, and campaigned for a new law to protect heroes and martyrs. "A nation that doesn't uphold its own history has no future," he said.[69]

Fang Zhimin occupies a prominent place in party lore, remembered for his exploits as a revolutionary leader who helped set up an early Communist base in the eastern province of Jiangxi before Kuomintang forces captured and executed him in 1935. His writings in captivity, including an essay titled "Lovely China," prompted Mao to lionize him posthumously as a national hero. In 2005, as Zhejiang party chief, Xi hailed Fang as a martyr and urged party members to honor his example by stepping forward in moments of peril.

Over the years Fang Zhimin has also been dogged by allegations that his troops engaged in kidnappings for ransom. One story blames a military unit from Fang's 10th Red Army for the 1934 kidnap and murder of an American missionary couple, John and Betty Stam. Contemporary American accounts said Communist "bandits" abducted the Stams and sought $20,000 in ransom—a demand John Stam relayed by letter—before executing the couple. After Kuomintang forces captured Fang in early

1935, a Miss C. McFarlane in Jiangxi wrote to a missionary publication describing Fang as "the Communist leader who was said to be responsible for the massacre of Mr. and Mrs. Stam."[70] Some Chinese sources, however, suggest Fang was marshaling his forces elsewhere and wasn't present when the Stams were kidnapped and killed.

Born three decades after his grandfather's death, Fang Huaqing strove to uphold his family's revolutionary pedigree, becoming deputy director of Jiangxi's state archives and an adjunct professor at an elite party academy. The online invective against Fang Zhimin angered the younger Fang, who insisted that "my grandfather would never have done such dirty things." He filed a police report, prompting authorities to punish more than twenty people who had allegedly spread libelous content.[71] He argued that such rumormongering was a symptom of inadequate patriotic education, and lodged objections to the promotion of two local party historians, saying they had neglected their duty to defend the honor of martyrs.[72] Fang also sued a man and a woman for damages against his grandfather, though he later dropped the case after the pair admitted wrongdoing and apologized in person.[73]

Still more had to be done to stop "historical nihilism," said Fang, who joined others in campaigning for new legislation to safeguard the honor of the party's most exemplary servants. In the spring of 2018, China's legislature passed a "Heroes and Martyrs Protection Law" that required all of society to "honor, study and defend" party-approved paragons of virtue. It prescribed criminal penalties and civil liabilities for those who defamed such heroes, and mandated police and state agencies overseeing culture, education, media, and the internet to protect and promote the legacy of Chinese heroes. Fang became one of the first litigants to use the new law, suing a man who disparaged his grandfather on an internet forum.[74]

Heroes and martyrs serve as standard-bearers in Xi's propaganda campaigns, providing moral moorings and rousing patriotic passions for one-party rule. As part of his pursuit of "law-based governance," Xi bolstered the party's legal toolkit for suppressing those who question its history and attack its paragons of virtue. In 2016, a Beijing court ordered a former editor of *Yanhuang Chunqiu* to apologize for questioning elements of the "Five Heroes of Langya Mountain," a World War II legend taught to schoolchildren about how five Chinese soldiers battled Japanese forces to save comrades and nearby villagers before leaping off a cliff to avoid capture.[75] The following year, China's legislature approved a preamble to a civil code of law that provides for civil liabilities related to damage done to the "name, image, reputation, and honor" of heroes and martyrs. The 2018 law then delivered the coup de grâce, effectively criminalizing dissent on historical subjects once open to independent inquiry, public debate, and even a degree of satire.

The government has certified and recorded about 2 million heroes and martyrs, with many listed on a government database that features names from the past century or so. Authorities defined martyrdom in 2011, stipulating that deaths must have occurred in the course of public service, but it is less clear what constitutes a hero. Critics say such expansive lists allow the party to curb debates over wide swaths of Chinese history. After China amended its criminal code in 2021 to prescribe up to three years' jail as punishment for insulting heroes, authorities went after a broad range of targets, including people who allegedly insulted the victims of the 1937 Nanjing massacre perpetrated by Japanese troops; disparaged a Chinese fighter pilot killed in a 2001 midair collision with a U.S. surveillance plane; and spoke ill of Chinese agronomist Yuan Longping, revered in China for his work developing high-yield hybrid rice, after his death in May 2021.[76]

State protection extends even to cultural symbols not formally covered by the law. The "Yellow River Cantata," written in 1939 to rouse Chinese resistance against Japanese invaders, had become a comedic trope in recent years, often performed with spoof lyrics for gala dinners, school proms, and online videos. After one such video went viral in early 2018, the daughter of the cantata's composer lodged complaints, and state media denounced the spoofs as sacrilegious. "Rewriting this signature work that depicts national salvation is clearly an act of historical blasphemy," a *People's Daily* op-ed said.[77] Under orders from the culture ministry, video-streaming sites scrubbed some 3,900 videos and 165 songs that spoofed revolutionary anthems.[78]

Suppression is just half of the formula. Answering Xi's calls to "tell the party's stories well," officials increased funding for academic work that celebrates the party's past and revamped school curricula to emphasize "revolutionary culture," such as by recommending Mao's poetry to students.[79] In Jiangxi, known as the cradle of China's Communist revolution, authorities drafted "red" teaching material for all ages, from nursery rhymes to college lectures. Xiao Fasheng, a party historian and a member of the drafting team, lamented the public's fading memories of their revolutionary forebears. "I had students telling me they didn't know who Zhu De was," he told me, referring to a Chinese marshal regarded as one of the party's greatest military commanders. "We don't include enough revolutionary history in textbooks, nor do we put sufficient emphasis on it in the curriculum."[80]

Xi also sought to commandeer historical scholarship, launching a new research institute in 2019 and tasking it to repackage the past around his priorities. The Chinese Academy of History operates under the aegis of the party's Central Propaganda Department and the state-run Chinese Academy of Social Sciences, or CASS—an unusual arrangement that gives party theorists direct control over its output.[81] Its inaugural director, Gao Xiang, has been a leading historian at CASS, where he wrote influential works on the Qing dynasty. A mild-mannered scholar fond of invoking historical analogies, Gao ventured into politics in 2016, becoming propaganda chief in Fujian province before his appointment as vice minister at the national cyberspace regulator, where he helped oversee China's news and social media industries. "In the information age, all sorts of viewpoints flow together like mud and sand, and some erroneous strands of thought have slipped in through the gaps," including efforts to "distort history and vilify heroes," Gao said in a 2018 speech.[82]

Gao brought his experiences in propaganda and internet affairs to the history academy, where he worked to generate popular appeal for their output. He tapped outside talent with an eye for capturing younger audiences, including fresh-faced presenters and a media producer who attracted attention for writing a rap song selling Karl Marx to Chinese millennials. The academy's social media accounts churn out articles and videos peppered with historical nuggets that celebrate Chinese culture and fan patriotic pride—from promoting new archaeological finds to firing ripostes against Western criticism of China. When Washington pressed Beijing in 2021 over alleged forced labor at Xinjiang cotton farms, the academy published a Weibo post detailing how the American cotton industry was built on slavery. "If cotton is said to be spotlessly white, that would be in China; whereas in the U.S., their cotton has been watered with the blood and tears of black slaves," said the post, which drew more than 1.5 million views. "That was a sinful period of history, one that good people all over the world should never forget."[83]

Academy officials also bust myths that damage the party brand. One persistent rumor has it that Mao's eldest son was killed in a United Nations air strike during the Korean War after giving away his position by firing up a stove to cook some egg fried rice. In November 2020, the academy marked the seventieth anniversary of Mao Anying's death with a myth-busting social media post, citing declassified telegrams and eyewitness accounts that indicated he was killed after the enemy detected radio transmissions from his commander's headquarters. "These rumormongers have tied up Mao Anying with egg fried rice, gravely dwarfing the heroic image of Mao Anying's brave sacrifice," said the post, which has drawn more than 2 million views.

"Their hearts are vicious." The academy traced the fried rice story to the 2003 edition of a Chinese military officer's memoir, but didn't mention that the book was published by the People's Liberation Army's official press.[84]

The academy has missed its mark at times. In late 2020, its Weibo account sparked online anger with an essay that challenged popular condemnation of Mao's "Down to the Countryside Movement" that forced millions of urban youth to live and work in rural villages. The essay described the mass rustication as "a great achievement that advanced the development of society," echoing official portrayals of Xi's seven years as a "sent-down youth" as a transformative experience that taught him to serve the people. Readers, however, vilified the article as leftist nostalgia and worried that it could signal a shift in official attitudes toward Mao's radical campaigns. "One flew over the cuckoo's nest," one Weibo user wrote in response to the essay, which soon vanished. "This is a very scary signal."[85]

The academy also pursues academic work, such as compiling a thirty-volume history of China. It launched a new journal, *Historical Review*, that features scholarly essays that harness historical arguments in support of Xi's agenda. The July 2020 issue, for instance, featured two articles attacking Georgetown University history professor James Millward, who has been a vocal critic of China's forced assimilation campaign against Muslims in Xinjiang. One essay, written by a researcher affiliated with China's Ministry of Culture and Tourism, attacked Millward's writings that characterized Xinjiang, whose name means "new frontier," as an imperial conquest by the ethnic Manchu-led Qing dynasty—an argument that contradicts Beijing's claims that Xinjiang "has long been an inseparable part of Chinese territory."[86] In the other article, Chinese historian Zhong Han accused Millward of being a "political opportunist" who fabricated facts and mischaracterized "vocational-education training centers" in Xinjiang as "political-training centers" that indoctrinate Uyghurs and other Muslim minorities.[87]

When I asked Millward what he thought of the essays, he said the criticism distorted his writings and echoed how Beijing often mischaracterizes foreign censure of its human rights record as attempts to challenge China's sovereignty. "I do know from private conversations with Chinese colleagues that few agree with the kind of approach Zhong Han has taken," Millward said. "But we all know that some Chinese researchers do it sometimes, or have to do it sometimes, when the political climate demands."[88]

Some Chinese historians criticized the academy's methods as undignified and unserious. "These people are doing this to suck up and win promotion," said a prominent history professor in Beijing, who declined the academy's invitation to collaborate on a project. Gao's efforts paid off in 2022, when he was elevated directly to full membership of the party's elite Central Committee and appointed CASS president— telling rewards for a scholar-bureaucrat who dismisses conventional historians' restrained detachment as a dereliction of patriotic duty. "History researchers shouldn't be cold-eyed observers of times and trends," Gao wrote. "Historical research must stand atop the commanding heights of our times," he said, in order to "guide governance and nurture people."[89]

SILENCED STUDIES

A LITERATURE PROFESSOR TURNED HISTORIAN, Pei Yiran wrote prolifically against official narratives that cast the Communist Party as sure-handed stewards steering China's rise. He focused his critiques on the Mao era, drawing on research and his own memories of the Cultural Revolution, when he was forced to work as a construction laborer and schoolteacher in the countryside. His writings appeared in Hong Kong–based political magazines and websites run by overseas Chinese, sometimes with a pen name. "Mao Zedong said 'serve the people,' but in practice it was 'the people serve me,'" Pei wrote in a 2016 essay. "Disclosing Mao's crimes is an act of responsibility toward the nation and history."[90]

Chinese authorities eventually took notice. Officials monitored Pei's communications and asked his colleagues and students to track his activities. His superiors at the Shanghai University of Finance and Economics warned him against expressing subversive views, as did government minders who would call him soon after he discussed ideas with magazine editors over email. Such pressure mounted after Xi came to power. In early 2014, two Shanghai police officials visited Pei's apartment, warning him against crossing bounds of acceptable speech. As they left, one official turned around and said: "Don't engage in historical nihilism."[91]

A frustrated Pei took early retirement, but the interventions continued. In early 2017, university officials pushed him to cancel trips to Hong Kong and the U.S., citing concerns that he could embarrass the party by attending events honoring the victims of Mao's radical campaigns. For Pei, that was the final affront. Months later, he uprooted himself from Shanghai and moved to America, a country he had never visited, hoping to find a haven for his scholarship.

Under Xi, the party tightened its already short leash on free inquiry, flexing legal and technological muscle to monopolize the right to study the past. Officials scrutinized the production chain for historical knowledge—from research to publication—with greater intensity, and punished those who attempted scholarship beyond state supervision.

State archives were among the first targets. Since Xi took office, Chinese and foreign academics say they have found it increasingly difficult to get access into archives across all levels of government—local, regional, and national—and regardless of the subject or era they wish to study.[92] China's foreign ministry archives, first opened in 2004, slashed the amount of material available for perusal after closing their doors in late 2012. Having once offered access to as many as eighty thousand folders' worth of documents, the facility reopened the following spring with only about eight thousand folders accessible, mainly comprising telegrams commemorating holidays, birthdays, and anniversaries that were mostly irrelevant for research on China's international relations.[93]

State archives require researchers to provide introduction letters from Chinese academic institutions, a protocol that can be used to keep out foreign scholars.[94] For many archive officials, demurring on document requests is safer than facilitating research that can yield unflattering accounts of the party, says Thomas Mullaney, a professor of Chinese history at Stanford University, who recalls how a provincial archive told him they didn't have the documents he was looking for, even though he had read those papers at that archive years earlier.[95]

Some of the censorship is much subtler and harder to detect. Online academic libraries have been discreetly pruning impolitic content from their digital collections, leaving researchers oblivious about materials going missing. Efforts to digitize collections at many Chinese archives have also made it easier to omit sensitive documents from online access and monitor researchers who use these repositories. Glenn Tiffert, a China historian at Stanford University's Hoover Institution, found what he called systematic omissions of sensitive articles from digitized versions of two Chinese legal journals from the 1950s.[96] "The providers who control these servers can silently alter our knowledge base at its source without ever leaving their back offices," Tiffert wrote. "For censors, the possibilities are mouthwatering."[97]

Even foreign academic publishers have been press-ganged into the effort. In 2017, Cambridge University Press quietly acceded to requests from Chinese authorities to remove from its Chinese site more than three hundred articles and book reviews from the British academic journal *The China Quarterly*, including material that covered sensitive subjects such as the Cultural Revolution and the 1989 Tiananmen Square protests.[98] When the removal was exposed, the backlash prompted CUP to reverse its decision and rebuff a separate request to censor about one hundred articles from an American journal.[99] Another major academic publisher, Springer Nature, blocked access in China to at least one thousand articles from two journals—a move the company called a "deeply regrettable" action taken to comply with local regulations.[100]

New legislation on data security and protecting state secrets effectively reclassified vast swaths of material, including previously declassified documents, which means that scholars making use of such materials may face repercussions for publishing their work or sharing their findings with others.[101] In Hong Kong, long a haven for publishing books, memoirs, and papers too sensitive to circulate in mainland China, the availability of such material diminished as state scrutiny prompted independent publishers and booksellers to scale down or cease operation. Many cited ebbing sales due to tighter border checks stopping people from bringing sensitive books in to the mainland, as well as concerns over their personal safety—particularly after Chinese authorities detained five Hong Kong booksellers in 2015, and imposed a far-reaching national security law on the city in 2020.

Censors tightened the prepublication review process for history books, journals, and magazines. Some professors say they have run into stiffer obstacles trying to get articles published in Chinese academic journals. An editor at an independent Beijing-based magazine, *Oriental History Review*, told me how they spent three years slogging through the government review process for an issue titled "The Night Before the Collapse," which would feature analyses of the Qing's demise. Two publishing houses dropped plans to publish that edition, citing political sensitivities, before the magazine secured a third publisher. As of this writing, the magazine hasn't published new issues since 2020, and its chief editor has switched his focus to other ventures.

Cross-border academic exchanges have suffered. A group of Chinese and foreign academics collaborating on research on Chinese intellectual history have faced interference from government minders, who blocked them from holding meetings on a Chinese university campus and threatened to bug their discussions, two of the researchers involved told me. Local police sometimes got involved, knocking on Chinese scholars' doors to deliver warnings. These academics switched to meeting in countries such as the U.S., Australia, and Japan, though the Covid-19 pandemic forced them to suspend such trips. "It's not like we're trying to uncover the bank accounts of top officials," one historian lamented. "It feels like the 1980s again," he said, referring to an era when colleagues and friends were often afraid to speak candidly with one another, for fear of being denounced.[102]

Such scrutiny drove some aspiring academics to avoid sensitive subjects. "I used to meet many Chinese graduate students working on the history of China's foreign relations," says Charles Kraus, a historian at the Woodrow Wilson International Center for Scholars in Washington. "Now everyone seems to be writing about U.S. foreign policy history."[103] One Chinese PhD student, who was researching China's diplomatic history at an Asian university, told me he wanted his dissertation published anonymously to avoid repercussions, though the publisher refused. More Chinese scholars are moving abroad to secure more autonomy over their work, one esteemed Chinese historian of the Cold War told me. "I fear a brain drain that may be difficult to reverse."[104]

Sun Peidong, an accomplished historian of Maoist China, was among those who decamped for greener pastures. Born in Shaanxi province just weeks after Mao's death in 1976, Sun says her interest in the Cultural Revolution was first piqued by her parents' "completely opposing" recollections of that period. Her father came from a poor rural household and led a relatively untroubled life during that decade, thanks to what he called his "good social status." But her mother suffered persecution as a child of a landowning family, and often prefaced her recollections of that era by saying, "if only the circumstances of my birth weren't so bad."[105] Puzzled by how such conflicting memories could coexist, Sun decided to figure out for herself "who was right."[106]

Sun earned a master's degree in French literature before switching to sociology, a discipline that taught her how to peer into the lives of ordinary Chinese. After earning doctorates in sociology and law in 2007, she wrote books on Mao-era fashion and parental anxieties over their children's choice of spouse. Sun found signs of dissent in people's sartorial decisions. "People's everyday clothing during that time—a period that has often been regarded as the climax of homogenization and asceticism—became a means of resistance and expression," Sun wrote. "During the Cultural Revolution people dressed to express resistance, whether intentionally or unintentionally, and to reflect their motivations, social class, gender, and region." Her work impressed fellow Mao-era specialists, and in 2013, the party chief of the history department at Shanghai's Fudan University persuaded her to join his team.

Founded in 1905, Fudan ranks among China's most prestigious universities, well regarded for its relatively liberal atmosphere and excellence in humanities, science, and medicine. Sun's first two years there went smoothly. She felt free to do research and teach classes as she liked, even on some sensitive historical episodes like the 1957–1959 Anti-Rightist Campaign and the Great Famine. "We were able to have honest discussions as teachers and students," she recalls. "No one reported me for anything."[107]

Matters changed in 2015. The history department party chief retired and his replacement was far more scrupulous in enforcing party diktats. Officials in Beijing blocked her from attending academic conferences in Britain and France. Two Chinese academic journals scrapped plans to publish articles about the Mao era that they had commissioned Sun to write—decisions that, she later learned, were made at the direction of government officials. Since then, Sun hasn't been able to get any papers published in mainland China, forcing her to seek outlets abroad and write more in English and French.[108] "They were giving me a signal," she says. "I decided that I had to find a new path."

Sun went overseas, first to Cambridge, Massachusetts, in 2016 to spend a year as a visiting scholar at the Harvard-Yenching Institute, before securing a one-year fellowship at Stanford University's Hoover Institution. She was due to start as a visiting scholar at UC Berkeley, but returned to Fudan in 2018 at the behest of her former boss, who had recruited her hoping that she would take on his mantle in studying the Mao era. "I went back to honor a promise," she says.[109]

This time, having tasted academic freedom on American campuses, Sun found the strictures at home even more suffocating. By then Fudan was the only university in mainland China still offering courses on the Cultural Revolution, and even that status seemed under threat. Superiors asked Sun to omit references to the "Mao Zedong Era" in course titles, revise teaching materials, and amend reading lists to include texts published in mainland China—which meant they were already screened by party censors.[110] Even when administrators approved certain foreign texts, faculty and students were expected to treat them with a critical stance and a teacher shouldn't validate the authors' perspectives.[111]

When Sun resisted these demands, the pressure grew in other ways. Inspectors conducted spot checks on her classes, and students seemed less willing than ever to express their views. The scrutiny grew so intense that Sun stopped speaking to students inside her office. Instead they would leave their cellphones behind and go for walks, chatting in open spaces to keep any prying ears at bay. "We weren't discussing anything political, just academic stuff," Sun says. "But the fact that we felt we had to take such precautions showed how the atmosphere on campus had changed."[112]

In early 2019, some students reported Sun for allegedly making politically incorrect remarks and fanning subversion in her classes and on social media. Her accusers posted denunciations and printouts of her Weibo posts on her office door—echoing the "big-character posters" that Red Guards used for accusing class enemies and bourgeois elements during the Cultural Revolution.[113] Abusive and threatening comments against Sun and her family swamped her Weibo account.

But Sun refused to be cowed. In December 2019, when Fudan became one of three universities that revised their charters to remove references to academic independence and freedom of thought, Sun spoke out in protest, telling foreign media that the change dovetailed with the party's efforts to restrict free inquiry.[114] Sun's bosses told her to write a self-criticism, but she refused, as she had decided to quit Fudan and leave China. In her resignation letter, Sun skipped the usual expressions of gratitude to the university and her superiors. "I am thankful to the six years I spent working at Fudan's history department for giving me such an unforgettable experience," she wrote.[115]

Sun left China in February 2020. She returned to her alma mater in Paris, Sciences Po, to work on her books, before moving to Cornell University the following year to become an associate professor of history. Still Sun's minders back home kept tabs on her, warning that she could never escape the party's clutches. A former university classmate, whom Sun hadn't spoken to in two decades, called to remind her that she still had family back home and that she should watch her words. Sun acknowledges that she may never be able to return to China or see her parents again—a heavy price, but one she felt she had to pay. "I just want to simply be a scholar. I want to write whatever I wish to write and produce better research," she says. "If I can't do that in one place, I'll just go somewhere else—it's that simple."[116]

Historians who remain in China continue finding ways to do scholarship. Some devote themselves to translation work and technical analysis, such as verifying the provenance of documents, without explicitly drawing conclusions that could contradict the party line. Others focus on local issues and avoid subjects that pertain directly to the central government, which are more likely to attract state scrutiny. For controversial subjects, some scholars are "writing for the desk drawer," hoping that the political climate may one day improve sufficiently to allow publication.[117] Other researchers continue circulating their work through underground channels, such as samizdat books and magazines.

Foreign researchers too are getting creative. Some scholars are reanalyzing papers in their existing collections, to, as one professor put it, "squeeze more juice out of the lemons they have." More historians have turned toward "garbology," the acquiring of so-called "garbage" documents, pamphlets, letters, and other materials from flea markets, online booksellers, and other dealers. The practice, once disdained as lacking scholarly rigor, has gained currency as a show of resourcefulness, though challenges remain in proving the authenticity and provenance of materials.[118] Academics have started sharing papers and donating them to university libraries so that fellow researchers can read them. David Ownby, a historian at the University of Montreal, teamed up with scholars in China to translate writings by influential Chinese thinkers into English and host them on his website—Reading the China Dream—as an intellectual public service.[119]

"People are keeping their heads down and continuing to do what they can," says Cheek of the University of British Columbia. "Xi's bonfire hasn't sucked out all the oxygen yet."[120]

CHAPTER SIX

ALL UNDER HEAVEN

THE PARTY UNITES THE NATION

"The empire, long divided, must unite; long united, must divide.
Thus it has ever been."

—Opening line in the classic Chinese novel *Romance of the Three Kingdoms*

"To realize the China Dream . . . we must focus on forging a common consciousness of the
Chinese nation."

—Xi Jinping

Wang Fenghe, a former soldier who now works in construction, spent decades chasing jobs across China to supplement the meager takings from his tiny farm. Whenever he is back home in rural Inner Mongolia, a vast stretch of grassland and desert in the country's northeast, he often spends his evenings peering into the future of an island he has never visited, roughly 110 miles off China's southeast coast and claimed by the Communist government in Beijing as a province awaiting liberation—the self-governing democracy of Taiwan.

Wang would tune in after dinner to a nightly news program, *Across the Strait*, for a half-hour update on Taiwan affairs, produced by state broadcaster China Central Television to propagate the party's messaging on its perennial quest to take over the island. Invoking the martial language he has imbibed since his soldiering days, Wang dismisses "Taiwan independence" as a pipe dream and denounces its advocates as separatists. "Taiwan belongs to China," Wang told me one wintry evening as we watched the program in his small farmhouse. "There's no question that we'll recover it one day."

By his own admission, Wang knows little of politics and strategic affairs. Born in 1955, he joined his local farming collective after finishing elementary school, before enlisting, aged nineteen, in the People's Liberation Army to "defend the homeland and protect Chairman Mao." As an infantry radioman, he took part in relief efforts after the devastating Tangshan earthquake of 1976 but saw no combat before being demobilized the following year. He joined a generation of laborers who streamed out of the countryside to build post-Mao China, constructing everything from factories to luxury hotels but never earning enough to avoid working well into their twilight years. Though Wang enjoyed little of the prosperity he helped create, he voices nothing but gratitude for the Communist Party. Posters of Mao and Xi adorn his bedroom walls. "Chairman Xi is a great leader," says Wang, citing Xi's efforts to fight corruption, overhaul the military, and recover the motherland's lost territories. "With him in charge, the great rejuvenation is at hand."

An ardent nationalist, Xi has made no secret of his most treasured ambition: a unified Chinese nation. It is a simple yet compelling idea, one that sits at the heart of his China Dream, and fires the imagination of ordinary Chinese in ways that no economic targets or highfalutin slogans can. It invokes grievances suffered during the "century of humiliation," and promises recovery of the nation's sullied honor. It rouses patriotic fervor into a reservoir of legitimacy for Xi, who can cement his legacy as one of China's most consequential leaders—if he achieves the party's most sacred mission.

Xi's vision of a Chinese renaissance goes beyond mere geography. Through speeches and directives, he has outlined ambitions to build a more centralized state buttressed by a singular identity—a "common consciousness" that unites China's 1.4 billion people. This means stronger central control over areas that notionally enjoy some self-rule, from the former colonies of Hong Kong and Macau to ethnicity-based "autonomous regions" such as Tibet and Xinjiang.[1] It requires a national lingua franca, binding all fifty-six officially recognized ethnic groups with a sense of shared culture, heritage, and purpose centered on the Han Chinese majority. "Xi believes the party must actively forge a shared worldview among its people—whether they be Han, Uyghur, Tibetan, Mongolian, Hong Kongese, or Taiwanese—and if they are not successful, then instability will reign and the country could fall apart," says James Leibold, a professor at Australia's La Trobe University who studies China's ethnic policies.[2]

History dealt Xi a complex hand when he took power in 2012. While the party had largely suppressed ethnic strife in borderlands like Tibet and Inner Mongolia, separatist sentiment still simmered in Xinjiang, the Central Asian frontier region home to millions of ethnic Uyghurs and other mostly Muslim minorities, and where violent attacks against symbols of party authority continued. The former British colony of Hong Kong remained a hotbed of anti-Communist activism well after its return to Chinese control in 1997. Taiwan, the holy grail sought by every Chinese leader since Mao, continued to elude the party's grasp despite decades of pressure and persuasion.

Even so, Xi struck confident tones when expounding on his vision. "To realize the China Dream, we must consolidate China's power—that is the strength from the great unity of all ethnic groups in China," he said in his inaugural speech as president in 2013. "All the nation's ethnic groups must keep their mission firmly in mind, direct their thoughts and actions toward one place, and use the wisdom and strength of 1.3 billion people to assemble an invincible and majestic force."[3]

Such resolve only hardened in 2014, when extremist violence and social unrest struck directly at Xi's vision of national unity. Deadly acts of terror attributed to Uyghur separatists rocked China, including a mass slashing at a train station in the country's southwest and a knife-and-bomb attack that hit Xinjiang's capital just as Xi wrapped up a tour there. In Taiwan, students who resented Beijing's growing economic clout led mass demonstrations that undermined a trade pact with the mainland and galvanized support for a political party that advocated a Taiwanese identity separate from China. Hong Kong dealt another blow to the Chinese leadership months later, when protesters staged a seventy-nine-day street occupation to rebuff a proposal to let the city's residents elect their top official from a pool of Beijing-approved candidates.

Xi responded with force on every front. In Xinjiang, the party directed repressive policing and forced-assimilation programs against Uyghurs and other Muslim minorities that foreign researchers and United Nations experts assessed as rife with human rights abuses. After mass protests rocked Hong Kong in 2019, authorities imposed a broad national security law on the city, rounded up scores of opposition politicians, activists, and independent journalists, and injected nationalist propaganda into local schools. Beijing pressured Taipei by poaching its diplomatic partners, harassing its military with patrols and combat drills, and restricting trade and travel links with the island. Even in regions with no recent history of ethnic strife, the party suppressed minority languages and intensified patriotic education that celebrated Han culture as the core of a Chinese national identity.

Xi's strident style appears to have yielded results, silencing dissent and enforcing order in Xinjiang and Hong Kong. But the battle over hearts and minds is far from over. Resentment still simmers among Uyghurs and Hong Kongers. Efforts to propagate Mandarin Chinese among non-Han ethnic groups has fueled bitterness among communities that the party has long regarded as model minorities. The saber-rattling against Taiwan has stoked anti-China sentiment among the island's more than 23 million people, while prompting the United States and other democracies to strengthen ties with Taipei. Xi's efforts to modernize the military and apply its power in territorial disputes have inflamed regional tensions and raised the specter of armed conflict.

The backlash notwithstanding, Xi has shown no signs of letting up. Having staked his legitimacy on the promise of forging a strong and unified China, Xi has to deliver.

ENGINEERING SOULS

"CHINA IS A CIVILIZATION PRETENDING to be a state," Lucian Pye, the renowned American sinologist, once wrote. "In Western terms the China of today is as if the Europe of the Roman Empire and of Charlemagne had lasted until this day and were now trying to function as a single nation-state."[4] Pye's observations have since become a truism of sorts, cited by academics and journalists who believe that China possesses unique historical and cultural traditions that defy easy comprehension through Western liberal lenses. Others argue the opposite, saying the Communist Party has appropriated the trappings of an ancient civilization to justify its authoritarian rule. "Looking from another angle, we can say that today's China is actually a nation-state masquerading as a civilizational empire," wrote Xu Jilin, a respected historian at Shanghai's East China Normal University. "Because it uses the methods of the nation-state to govern a massive empire."[5]

Whether they believe China constitutes a "civilization state," most scholars agree that the modern concepts of nationalism and the nation-state are relatively new to the country. Revolutionaries and thinkers like Sun Yat-sen and Liang Qichao were among the first to advocate notions of a "Chinese nation," during the late nineteenth and early twentieth centuries, drawing upon notions of ethnicity, culture, and Westphalian sovereignty. It was a departure from the worldview professed by most Chinese rulers since antiquity, that they were ordained by divine right to govern *tianxia*, or "all under heaven," an amorphous concept that broadly refers to the known human world and the universal order.

Sun, in trying to establish a Chinese republic, stoked anger against the Qing's ethnic Manchu rulers and foreign imperialists, while advocating an ethnocentric nationalism whereby the Han majority would assimilate minority groups to forge a cohesive nation.[6] Chiang Kai-shek pushed his own unifying ideology after taking power, launching the "New Life Movement" in the 1930s to promote conservative Confucian-style morality and repel foreign influences that he blamed for corrupting Chinese society.[7]

Mao too stoked patriotism for nation-building. During the early years of the People's Republic, the Communist Party fanned anger against Western imperialism, castigated capitalist decadence, and waged war against "U.S. aggression" toward North Korea. Such sentiment helped Mao mobilize support for his radical land reforms and political purges.[8] Students studied "Mao Zedong Thought," recited the Great Leader's quotations, and sang revolutionary songs lauding his achievements in creating a "new China."

Under Deng Xiaoping, the party focused on purging Mao's radical influence and promoting development. Officials set aside socialist ideology and nativist nationalism to open up China's economy and pursue trade with the West. But the 1989 Tiananmen Square protests stunned party leaders, who grappled with the loss of faith in Marxism-Leninism and sought new ways to inspire loyalty to Communist rule. Some prominent scholars argued that nationalism was the only option. "In an era where ideological confrontation no longer dominates the world, the functions of political integration and cohesion that nationalism provides cannot be replaced by other ideologies," wrote Xiao Gongqin, a Chinese historian and an influential conservative.[9]

The party paid heed. It ramped up patriotic education in the early 1990s, revising the syllabus in ways that rendered the party's fortunes inseparable from those of the Chinese nation. Whereas older history textbooks often recounted the party's successes in waging class struggle and fighting Chiang's Kuomintang, newer course books focused more on how pre-1949 China was bullied by foreign imperialists, from Britain in the 1840s to Japan during the 1930s and 1940s.[10] New museums and monuments, which the party calls "patriotic education sites," sprung up across the country to commemorate the Communist revolution and the war against Japan.[11] The appeal to a national identity was also steeped in ethnic chauvinism, one where the Han majority—who account for more than 90 percent of a highly homogeneous society—are celebrated as the most advanced and prosperous race.

Such efforts yielded mixed results. Surveys suggested that young Chinese generally regarded patriotic education as clumsy and remained politically apathetic, despite an uptick in student-led protests against perceived foreign criticism of their country.[12] Many continued harboring sympathies toward liberal views and hoped to study and work in the West.[13] Harvard professor Alastair Iain Johnston argued in a 2017 paper that younger Chinese tended to be less nationalistic than older citizens, citing survey data dating back to the late 1990s.[14]

Xi, who had lamented how China's economic boom loosened its spiritual moorings and weakened social cohesion, doubled down on patriotic education after taking office. His administration circulated a directive, known as Document Number 9, that demanded greater vigilance against Western ideas that could subvert the party—including liberal notions of human rights, a free press, and an independent judiciary.[15] Hoping to instill pride in what the party proclaims as a five-thousand-year civilization, he promoted Confucius and other classical Chinese thinkers that Mao had once condemned as feudal relics.[16] In 2016, Xi appointed as education minister a former Central Party School vice president who pushed for more patriotic teaching. "Teachers are the engineers of the human soul," Xi told a party conference on education in 2018, borrowing a metaphor that Stalin used to praise writers for shaping the public consciousness.[17] Educators, Xi said, must ensure that "the spirit of patriotism takes root in the hearts of students, and educate and guide students to love and support the Chinese Communist Party."

Beijing centralized control over teaching materials, particularly those related to national sovereignty, ethnicity, and religion, reversing a policy that allowed provincial governments to choose their own textbooks. The government barred elementary and secondary schools from using foreign textbooks, and instead promoted literature espousing Xi's political philosophy.[18] Officials rewrote curricula to amplify nationalistic narratives, such as by adding six years to the official length of China's "war of resistance against Japanese aggression," which now spanned fourteen years, from 1931 to 1945, instead of eight years from 1937.[19]

Schools screened patriotic films and arranged field trips to revolutionary landmarks, while teachers were told to give poor grades to students who voiced unapproved views in essays, such as portraying the government's handling of Covid-19 in unfavorable terms.[20] Authorities encouraged educators to instill culturally conservative values, including a sense of "masculinity" among boys and respect for the military. A kindergarten in the southern city of Guangzhou arranged a ten-day mock boot camp for its pupils, who were taught by PLA personnel to dress in military fatigues, march and perform salutes, sing revolutionary songs, and practice combat drills with toy rifles and rocket launchers.[21]

The internet became a key battleground for hearts and minds. State agencies ran about a quarter-million accounts on three major Chinese social-media platforms as of 2020, and academics estimate that millions of Chinese web users posting pro-party content are paid to do so by the government or are officials themselves.[22] Internet regulators imposed new rules encouraging posts that promote "Xi Jinping Thought" and requiring platforms to adjust their algorithms to favor government and state media content. The party's youth wing, the Communist Youth League, became a leading purveyor of patriotic videos for tens of millions of followers on China's most popular streaming platforms. Many online influencers and live-streamers, part of a swelling industry worth tens of billions of dollars, share nationalistic content to attract attention, sell advertising and products, and earn gifts from fans.[23]

Such fervor can take dark turns. Online mobs harass people who criticize the party or allegedly show disloyalty to China, often hounding them into hiding or even forcing them out of their jobs.[24] Chinese writer Fang Fang, who chronicled how Covid-19 battered her home city of Wuhan, the pandemic's first epicenter, found herself barracked on social media and had rocks thrown into her home by people who resented her online writings that criticized the government's initial mishandling of the coronavirus.[25] A professor who spoke up for Fang Fang was suspended by her university after netizens accused her of being a Japan loyalist and supporter of Hong Kong independence—allegations that she denied.[26]

For all the party's success online, however, officials have struggled to win over minority groups in China's far-flung borderlands, where defiance against the party and the Han majority runs deep. Among them, Xinjiang posed the stiffest challenge, and it is there where Xi demanded compliance in the most draconian ways.

BORDERLANDS

ON THE EVENING OF MARCH 1, 2014, a group of knife-wielding militants stormed through a railway station in China's southwestern city of Kunming, slashing thirty-one people to death and injuring more than a hundred and forty others. The following month, as Xi Jinping wrapped up a four-day tour of Xinjiang, two attackers carried out a suicide bombing at a train station in the regional capital of Urumqi, killing one bystander and injuring about eighty people. Another bomb attack ravaged an Urumqi market weeks later, killing at least thirty-nine people and wounding more than ninety.

The attacks stunned China, a dramatic escalation in Xinjiang's long history of unrest and periodic violence carried out by some militant members of the region's Uyghur community. Xi pledged an iron-fisted response, declaring a "people's war" against religious extremism and separatist violence. "The methods that our comrades have at hand are too primitive," Xi said during his trip in Urumqi, according to internal party documents later leaked to the *New York Times*. "We must be as harsh as them," he said, "and show absolutely no mercy."[27]

Xi has since directed a withering security and assimilation campaign across Xinjiang, creating what some experts describe as a system of near-totalitarian control. In internal speeches later leaked to foreign media and researchers, the Chinese leader warned about the dangers of religious influence and unemployment among minority groups in Xinjiang, and stressed the importance of "population proportion," or the balance between Han Chinese and minorities.[28] Xi's ultimate goal, experts say, is to entrench Han dominance over a restive frontier region where resistance against Beijing has simmered ever since the Qing empire first conquered the territory during the eighteenth century.

Officially, the party celebrates ethnic diversity and harmony across China's fifty-five minority groups. They include traditionally nomadic Tibetans and Mongols, Turkic Muslims, and communities with cultural ties to Southeast Asia, among others, each with their own languages, beliefs, and customs. During the Mao era, the party set up a system of autonomous regions, prefectures, and counties where ethnic minorities took senior posts in local governments, received generous state investments, and were allowed to keep tax revenues for local use. China's constitution provides minorities with the right to speak their own languages and practice their cultures and religions. Members of minority groups were also given bonus points in China's ultracompetitive college entrance examinations and exempted from the one-child policy, the controversial population-control program that lasted three and a half decades before it was officially discontinued in 2016.

Xinjiang has been a focal point for such policies since the early years of the People's Republic. Some 12 million Uyghurs live in this swath of desert and mountains abutting Central Asia that they regard as their homeland, alongside large numbers of Han Chinese and smaller communities of Kazakhs, Kyrgyzs, and other minorities. Xinjiang means "new frontier," so named by the Qing dynasty when it incorporated the region as a province in the nineteenth century. During the 1930s and 1940s, Uyghur nationalists twice established short-lived East Turkestan republics in the area, the second of which was backed by the Soviet Union. The PLA entered Xinjiang in 1949 and Beijing designated it as an autonomous region six years later—a symbolic gesture given that Han officials held overall control.

Separatist sentiment simmered among Uyghurs, who in the early 1950s accounted for 75 percent of Xinjiang's population compared to 6 percent Han.[29] The government encouraged large numbers of Han Chinese to migrate to Xinjiang over subsequent decades, and by 2000, only about 46 percent of the population were Uyghur, while the Han made up close to 40 percent.[30] Widening economic disparities between the two communities fueled Uyghur unrest against what they saw as ethnic discrimination and exploitation by Han Chinese, kicking off a cycle of anti-party violence and state repression. Chinese officials blamed Islamic extremism and separatist agitation. Foreign historians and Uyghur activists pointed to the party's heavy-handed policing, strict curbs on religious activity, and preferential policies for Han and other non-Uyghur settlers.

Beijing showed spells of relative tolerance. Xi's father, Xi Zhongxun, often advocated a softer touch in ethnic policy while serving as a senior official. During the 1950s, the elder Xi argued for coopting local Muslim leaders in China's northwest, and criticized cadres who derided local customs as backward "feudal" practices.[31] When protests broke out in Xinjiang's Kashgar city in the early 1980s, he urged officials to use peaceful means to pacify the unrest and avoid mass persecutions that could inflame tensions.[32] "The more that our policies are tight and inflexible, the more that in practical terms religion is suppressed, things run counter to one's wishes, the exact opposite result occurs," the elder Xi said in 1985.[33]

Deadly riots that rocked Tibet in 2008 and Xinjiang in 2009 forced Beijing to rethink its ethnic policies. Chauvinistic sentiment festered among Han Chinese who saw the unrest as a sign of ingratitude among minorities who benefited from affirmative action and China's prosperity. Academics advocating a more forceful approach to assimilating minorities gained influence in Beijing. They believed the prevailing approach in ethnic affairs would lead to a Soviet-style dissolution of the People's Republic, as minority groups received rights and treatment that could strengthen ethnic identities while undermining national unity.

Hu Angang, a prominent Tsinghua University economist, and Hu Lianhe, a party researcher and specialist in counterterrorism and ethnic policy, were among the leading proponents of more aggressive assimilation. The two Hus, who aren't related, wrote an influential paper in 2011 urging the party to replace its outmoded methods with a "second generation of ethnic policy." Citing the Soviet collapse as a lesson and the American cultural "melting pot" as a model, the pair argued that China should de-emphasize senses of belonging to disparate ethnic identities and instead seek to "intensify the sense of Chinese national identity." They singled out Xinjiang as an example where a "strong ethnic consciousness" and a "weak sense of belonging to the Chinese nation" had allowed separatism to foment.[34]

Xi's accession in 2012 also coincided with a generational shift among officials overseeing ethnic affairs. Whereas older cohorts often sympathized with minority communities, understood their culture, and spoke their languages, many younger officials lacked experience in minority regions, had received a secular education, and equated modernity with secularism, according to Max Oidtmann, a historian at the Ludwig Maximilian University of Munich, who studies China's ethnic minorities. The new generation of ethnic affairs specialists "have much greater faith in the potential for government policy to radically transform social and ideological conditions, and firmly believe in the underlying unity of the Chinese people," Oidtmann says. "It is time, in their view, for peasants, religious folk, and minorities to get with the program, or else."[35]

Within weeks of his 2014 trip to Xinjiang, Xi committed to a hard-line approach to quash the rising violence. He declared that the party's ethnic policies would enter a new phase. Discarding past promises of regional autonomy, officials would focus instead on forging a "common consciousness of the Chinese nation."[36]

Xi's directives led to a far-reaching campaign of ethnic assimilation in Xinjiang. Authorities deployed more police and paramilitary forces across urban centers, tightened restrictions on Islamic customs and practices, and ran intrusive "homestay" programs whereby Han Chinese cadres visited Muslim families and lived with them for several days.[37] Some of the harshest measures emerged after Chen Quanguo, the veteran regional administrator, became Xinjiang's party boss in the summer of 2016, fresh from his five-year stint suppressing ethnic unrest in Tibet.[38] Bringing in techniques honed over his decades managing social tensions, Chen unleashed the party's coercive powers upon Uyghurs and other Muslim minorities, targeting them with mass detentions, political indoctrination, and strict birth controls, as well as policies that resulted in forced labor and family separations.

Chen had help from local experts too. In December 2016, a party-run publisher in Xinjiang released what state media described as the region's first academic monograph on "deradicalization" strategies.[39] Written by Zhu Zhijie, director of a research institute affiliated with Xinjiang's prison administration bureau, the roughly four-hundred-page book recommended promoting loyalty to the party through ideological education and "Chinese cultural infiltration," such as by melding Han traditions with local Islamic customs. "Radicalized attitudes can be changed through counter-brainwashing," Zhu wrote. He proposed that people expressing extremist thoughts and behavior be put through "compulsory correctional methods," while those showing severe symptoms should undergo vigorous indoctrination at "closed-off educational facilities," where they would be taught patriotism and Chinese socialism.[40]

Central-government experts praised Zhu for producing "innovative" research with "important practical significance." While some of his ideas were in use already, Chen ramped up their implementation. His administration blanketed Xinjiang with digital surveillance tools and internment camps for ethnic minorities. Muslim residents were threatened with detention or sent to camps for engaging in routine religious practices such as praying daily and owning a Quran. Officials also demolished Uyghur neighborhoods and tore down thousands of mosques and other religious sites. Some Uyghurs who traveled overseas or contacted relatives abroad were thrown into detention camps or even jailed.[41] Some experts estimated that Xinjiang authorities sent more than a million people into mass detention facilities that Chinese officials euphemistically described as "vocational training centers," where inmates faced political indoctrination that forced them to praise the Communist Party and study Xi Jinping's policies.[42]

Human rights advocates and Western officials have denounced the party's policies in Xinjiang, with some accusing Beijing of committing cultural genocide against Uyghurs. The United Nations human rights agency spent years reviewing the allegations, and after a protracted process issued a report in August 2022 assessing that serious rights abuses have taken placed in Xinjiang, and that Chinese authorities there may have committed "crimes against humanity."[43]

Beijing vehemently denies committing any rights violations in Xinjiang, portraying its policies there as benign efforts to improve the lives of ethnic minorities. They boast of restoring stability to a once-restive region, saying no violent act of terror has taken place there since the end of 2016. "Practice has proven that the party's strategy for governing Xinjiang in the new era is completely correct, and must be sustained for the long term," Xi told party officials in 2020. The next step, he said, is to ensure the "common consciousness of the Chinese nation takes root deep inside people's hearts."[44] Accordingly, Beijing has since assigned Xinjiang a new party chief who brought a greater focus on economic development, and dialed back some of the region's harshest security and assimilation programs—though ethnic minorities there remain under close scrutiny.[45]

The party also tightened ethnic policy across the board. In 2018, lawmakers revised China's constitution to add references to the "Chinese nation," a change some scholars praised as a marker of the party's efforts to forge a singular national identity.[46] Officials stepped up efforts to standardize school curricula, promote interethnic cultural exchanges, and encourage more Han Chinese to work in minority regions—even though such policies had irked many Tibetans and Uyghurs. Some provincial governments announced plans to phase out affirmative action in college entrance exams, meaning ethnic minorities would no longer get bonus points.[47] Officials increasingly refer to standard Mandarin as *guoyu*, or the "national language," when encouraging ethnic minorities to learn China's lingua franca—departing from a decades-old policy of referring to Mandarin as *putonghua*, or "common tongue," to avoid the impression of forcing minorities to adopt Han language.[48]

In Inner Mongolia, where many ethnic Mongols have embraced integration into Chinese society despite lingering resentment over the influx of Han settlers and a deadly anti-Mongol purge during the Cultural Revolution, residents rallied against a 2020 government decision to change the language of instruction in some school classes from Mongolian to Mandarin. Many Mongols believed the shift would dilute their culture, and thousands of people protested, urging authorities to reverse plans to phase out local history, literature, and ethnic textbooks in favor of nationally standardized texts.[49]

In Tibet, long subjected to tough policing and social controls, authorities passed new regulations to promote patriotism, imposed new curbs on Tibetan religion, education, and language, and introduced "military-style" vocational training for rural Tibetans. In the western province of Gansu, home to large populations of Muslim minorities, authorities shut down an Arabic-language school for underprivileged students in 2018, citing its lack of proper approval, even though it had operated for more than three decades with support from local officials. The decision disturbed some locals, who say it targeted Muslims who learned Arabic as part of their religious studies.[50]

The campaign also left visible marks in Ningxia, an autonomous region for Hui Muslims, an ethnic group composed mainly of descendants of Middle Easterners, Central Asians, and Chinese, and a community that Beijing has long regarded as a well-assimilated model minority. Authorities in the regional capital of Yinchuan refurbished a large plaza in the city center known as the "China-Arab Axis" to remove Islamic iconography of Arabic origin—such as domes and crescent-moon sculptures—and replace them with generic Chinese designs. The area was also renamed "Unity Road," just two years after its construction to showcase Ningxia's strategic location astride the ancient Silk Road.[51]

By 2020, Xi had dispensed with any pretense of minority autonomy, installing a Han Chinese official as head of the government body overseeing ethnic affairs—the first time since the 1950s that a non-minority person was in charge of the agency.[52] In his first publicized remarks, the new director of the National Ethnic Affairs Commission reiterated Xi's demands for forging a "common consciousness" through better education and propaganda.[53] "The party leadership reveals that it does not believe that economic growth alone resolves political contradictions or ethnic resentments," says Oidtmann, the Munich-based historian. Instead Xi has inherited Mao's conviction, Oidtmann says, that "ideological transformation will solve political and economic problems."[54]

THE SECOND HANDOVER

HONG KONG HAS LONG BEEN a useful contradiction for the Communist Party. During the Chinese civil war, the British colony sat beyond the reach of Chiang Kai-shek's Kuomintang government, giving Mao's revolutionaries a platform for raising funds and maintaining links with overseas sponsors. Party leaders decided against taking Hong Kong as they seized power on the mainland in 1949, worrying that an invasion could prompt Western powers to intervene militarily.[55]

192 ★ PARTY OF ONE

The Communist government insisted that Hong Kong belonged to China and would be recovered one day. In the meantime, Beijing was content to use the city as a base for earning foreign exchange, developing trade ties, gathering intelligence, and even as leverage over Britain, by issuing implicit threats to destabilize or seize the colony.[56] With the People's Republic off-limits to most Westerners during the Mao years, Hong Kong also became a popular listening post for China watchers of all stripes—diplomats, journalists, spies, and businesspeople—who tapped into local grapevines that stretched as far as Beijing.[57] Deng Xiaoping's market-opening reforms boosted the city's economic value, with foreign businesses tapping Hong Kong as a conduit into a fast-growing mainland economy.

Though Mao, according to a Chinese historian, considered seizing Hong Kong by force in 1967, Beijing preferred a peaceful handover and began formal talks with the United Kingdom in 1982.[58] The British tried to keep Hong Kong beyond 1997, when Britain's lease for land constituting the vast majority of the colony would expire. Deng rebuffed them and secured a 1984 agreement that set the terms of the territory's return to Chinese control. Under the Sino-British Joint Declaration, China would regain sovereignty over Hong Kong in July 1997 and designate it a "special administrative region." Local authorities would enjoy a "high degree of autonomy," and the existing capitalist system and way of life would stay unchanged for fifty years—the cornerstone of Beijing's "one country, two systems" formula.[59]

Deng assured Margaret Thatcher, then British prime minister, that "horses will still run, stocks will still sizzle, dancers will still dance" in Hong Kong after its handover. For the most part, this promise was kept. The city maintained its reputation as one of the world's freest economies, and foreign investors continued funneling money through its capital markets in search of opportunities in China. The Basic Law, Hong Kong's post-handover constitution, provided for freedoms of speech, assembly, and protest that weren't available on the mainland. Activists organized demonstrations criticizing the Communist Party. Falun Gong, the spiritual movement banned by the party in 1999, operated freely. Newspapers, magazines, and books published in Hong Kong carried gossip about political intrigue in Beijing and mocked Chinese leaders. Hong Kongers could access an unfettered internet, while people in mainland China ran up against their government's Great Firewall.

Beijing valued Hong Kong as a gateway to Western finance, but worried that foreign powers were using it as a base for subverting Communist rule. Party leaders recalled how, during the 1989 Tiananmen Square protests, Hong Kongers staged rallies, raised money, and bought supplies for the demonstrators in Beijing before the party crushed what it denounced as "counter-revolutionary riots." During one of British diplomat Percy Cradock's many visits to Beijing in the early 1990s for talks on Hong Kong, the then general secretary, Jiang Zemin, pulled him to a window at the Great Hall of the People and pointed at Tiananmen Square, saying "there were the tents and they were put up with Hong Kong money," Cradock recalled. "And I couldn't deny it. It was a fact."[60]

For Xi Jinping, Hong Kong is also personal. His father, Xi Zhongxun, a top party official in Guangdong from 1978 to 1980, dealt with Hong Kong as he confronted an exodus of mainlanders fleeing to the British colony as economic refugees. To stem the outflows, he cultivated ties with Hong Kong officials and businessmen and tried to narrow the economic gap. He helped set up a "special economic zone" in Shenzhen and encouraged investment from Hong Kong. The elder Xi remained involved in Hong Kong affairs after leaving Guangdong, meeting delegations from the city and facilitating Sino-British talks on the territory's future. Xi Jinping himself visited Hong Kong several times as a local and regional official to drum up investment from the city, which he praised as a globally competitive commercial center worthy of emulation by mainland counterparts.

By the early 2000s, Beijing was starting to see Hong Kong more as a wellspring of trouble. In 2003, when Hong Kong's economy cratered due to a deadly outbreak of SARS (severe acute respiratory syndrome) that started in southern China, the central government took steps to aid the city's recovery, for instance allowing many more mainlanders to visit. Later that year, protests flared in Hong Kong against proposed legislation that would outlaw actions deemed subversive to Beijing, forcing the city's government to withdraw the bill. At the time, the party did little to suppress such defiance, focusing instead on the economic well-being of a key financial hub—and a safe haven where many wealthy Chinese and members of the revolutionary elite, including Xi's relatives, kept their assets.

Xi took on responsibilities over Hong Kong affairs after joining the party's top leadership in 2007, becoming head of the party's coordination group for Hong Kong and Macau policy. In an early sign of his more interventionist approach, Xi appeared to admonish Hong Kong's top official and urged the city's executive, legislative, and judicial branches to cooperate with one another. He oversaw an effort to instill patriotic pride among Hong Kongers, including plans—announced in 2010—to introduce "Moral and National Education" classes into the city's schools, but officials shelved the proposals amid backlash against what many locals denounced as brain-washing.[61] Sentiment toward mainland China also shifted, with opinion polls showing that more residents were identifying as Hong Kongers rather than Chinese.

Xi sensed the rise of a separatist movement, even though only a tiny minority of Hong Kongers advocated independence at the time and in the years since. In July 2012, Xi "issued the party center's first combat order to purge Hong Kong independence elements," and followed up with more demands to stem secessionist sentiment, recalled Chen Zuo'er, a former deputy director of the Chinese government's Hong Kong and Macau Affairs Office.[62] After Xi took power, his administration issued a June 2014 white paper emphasizing that Beijing exercised "comprehensive jurisdiction" over Hong Kong. The document declared that the city's partial autonomy stemmed "solely from the authorization by the central leadership"—implying that the central government could strip Hong Kong of its self-administration powers at any time.[63]

Just two months later, when Beijing announced a plan that would allow Hong Kongers to pick their next top official from candidates screened by the central leadership, hundreds of thousands of protesters rebuffed the proposal by occupying streets outside the city's government headquarters. This extraordinary show of defiance, which became known as the "Umbrella Movement," stunned Beijing.[64] Xi now saw himself as being locked in a "long-term, complex and at times sharp" struggle for control over Hong Kong, recalled Chen, the former official. "The trees want tranquility but the winds won't stop," he quoted Xi as saying.[65]

Beijing responded by tightening its vise on Hong Kong. China's deputy ambassador in London told a U.K. lawmaker that the Sino-British Joint Declaration had become void, irking British officials who believed that the treaty was still binding.[66] Hong Kong authorities jailed a number of protest leaders and disqualified six opposition members of the local legislature. Mainland security agents reportedly entered Hong Kong to abduct a bookseller in late 2015 and Chinese-Canadian financier Xiao Jianhua in early 2017—sparking outcry over the affront to the city's separate British-style legal system. Beijing accelerated plans to integrate Hong Kong economically with major cities in Guangdong and the former Portuguese colony of Macau to form a new megapolis known as the "Greater Bay Area."[67] When Xi visited Hong Kong in 2017 to mark the twentieth anniversary of the city's handover, he brought a warning: any attempt to challenge or subvert the central government would be "an act that crosses the red line, and is absolutely impermissible."[68]

That red line was emphatically breached in the summer of 2019, when mass demonstrations erupted in Hong Kong against the local government's efforts to pass legislation that would allow the extradition of criminal suspects to the mainland.[69] Peaceful marches against what many saw as an erosion of Hong Kong's separate legal system morphed into violent protests that rocked the Asian financial center for months. Black-clad militants armed with bricks, Molotov cocktails, and improvised weapons vandalized symbols of Beijing's authority and battled riot police, wounding officers and pro-Beijing residents (in at least one case fatally).[70] The police applied hard-nosed tactics—firing large volumes of tear gas and rubber bullets, and even the occasional live rounds—that caused injuries to protesters and journalists, and spurred widespread allegations of police brutality.[71]

The 2019–2020 Hong Kong protests stung Xi. Besides the embarrassment caused to his leadership, the unrest exposed deep fissures that belied his China Dream and supplied Western governments with fodder for pressuring Beijing. Chinese officials blamed the turmoil on foreign meddling and economic frustration, though privately some admitted they had failed to appreciate the depth of public resentment.[72] Their solution was a thorough remaking of Hong Kong, to crush dissent, reduce social inequities, and, most crucially, inculcate a stronger sense of Chinese national identity among younger generations.

The party's Central Committee approved this strategy in late 2019, promising broad changes to Hong Kong's political, economic, education, and policing systems.[73] The following summer, Beijing imposed a sweeping national security law on the city that outlawed anti–Communist Party activism and allowed authorities to suppress political dissent with mainland-style policing. In 2021, Chinese lawmakers passed electoral changes to allow only "patriots" to govern Hong Kong, helping pro-Beijing politicians to secure all but one seat in the city's legislature at elections that year—albeit with a record low voter turnout of about 30 percent. Several local news organizations known for critical coverage of the Communist Party and Hong Kong politics closed down after police detained senior media executives and editors for alleged national security offenses.[74] In 2022, Hong Kong named a former law-enforcement chief and veteran police officer, John Lee, as its chief executive—the first time a security specialist had taken the city's top job since the 1997 handover.

National education became a priority. Authorities banned acts of disrespect to the Chinese national flag, and ordered schools to conduct flag-raising ceremonies at least once a week.[75] Teachers who supported anti-government protests were reprimanded or dismissed.[76] Textbooks were rewritten to remove material that could antagonize Beijing and to add more patriotic content. New material included passages promoting national security and asserting that Hong Kong wasn't a British colony because China didn't recognize the unequal treaties that ceded the territory to the U.K.[77] Elementary-school children as young as six are now taught lessons on national security. New teaching material includes a role-play script—titled "Who stole the National Flag?"—that featured a patriotic character saying: "Yes! I love the motherland. I love to collect or buy things with the national flag on it." Another character, named "Destroyer," stomps on the flag and has no friends.[78]

Chinese officials describe the policy overhauls as Hong Kong's "second handover," only this time, Beijing would settle matters once and for all. "As President Xi says, one country is one country," said Ip Kwok-him, a senior pro-Beijing politician in Hong Kong and a member of China's national legislature. "It's no longer about accommodating Hong Kong's needs."[79]

TREASURE ISLAND

IN THE COMMUNIST PARTY'S TELLING, Taiwan was among the sacred pieces of the motherland stolen by foreign imperialists and which must be recovered to restore China's dignity. The Qing empire annexed the island in the 1680s but were forced to cede it, along with other territory, to Japan after losing the 1894–1895 Sino-Japanese war. Some Taiwanese elites opposed the deal and declared an independent Republic of Formosa, but Tokyo crushed the movement and started five decades of colonial rule on Taiwan that lasted until the end of World War II.

Chiang Kai-shek's Kuomintang government took control of Taiwan in 1945 and absorbed the island into the Republic of China. Its administrators imposed brutal authoritarian rule, aiming to root out Communist subversion and pro-Japanese sympathies within the local populace. When Mao seized power in 1949, Chiang withdrew his government to Taiwan, bringing gold reserves and cultural treasures, and spurring an exodus of perhaps a million mainlanders to the island. The influx would fuel decades of tensions between native-born Taiwanese and *waishengren*, as mainlanders who arrived after World War II were known, many of whom were Kuomintang members and supporters.

Successive Communist leaders have since declared their desire to seize Taiwan, which Beijing calls a "treasure island of the motherland." Mao was preparing to assault Taiwan when the Korean War broke out in 1950, prompting the U.S. to join the fighting and send the Seventh Fleet to the Taiwan Strait to forestall an invasion. Beijing sent troops to aid North Korea instead, and over subsequent decades, the Chinese military did little about Taiwan beyond skirmishing with Kuomintang forces and bombarding Taiwanese-held islands just off mainland China. From 1954 to 1978, PLA artillery lobbed high explosives and propaganda leaflets onto the Taipei-controlled Kinmen Islands just a few miles away from Fujian province, including nearly half a million shells fired during a six-week bombardment in 1958.[80] Beijing pushed hard on the diplomatic front, convincing dozens of countries to cut ties with the Kuomintang government and, most crucially, getting the United Nations to unseat Taipei in 1971 and recognize the Communist government as the "only legitimate representatives of China."

Chiang, for his part, hoped to rule China again. While Mao's Great Leap Forward ravaged the People's Republic in the early 1960s, Chiang prepared plans to "retake the mainland."[81] Known as "Project National Glory," it was to be a monumental undertaking, comprising amphibious landings, airborne assaults, and special operations behind enemy lines.[82] But Chiang lost faith after Kuomintang forces suffered a deadly training accident and naval losses against the PLA in 1965. The project was scrapped seven years later.[83] Any lingering hopes of restoring Kuomintang rule on the mainland dissipated with Chiang's death in 1975. His successors focused instead on governing, developing, and defending Taiwan.

Beijing changed tack on Taiwan in the late 1970s. Deng Xiaoping extended conciliatory gestures toward the Kuomintang and normalized relations with the U.S., which cut formal ties with Taipei. Chinese officials halted the shelling of Kinmen and other Taiwanese-controlled islands and pledged to de-escalate tensions. They proposed peaceful unification under the "one country, two systems" concept, whereby Taiwan would keep its existing social and economic system and enjoy significant autonomy from Beijing.[84] Taipei rejected the formula, which Beijing would apply in Hong Kong and Macau when Britain and Portugal returned those territories to China in the late 1990s.

Chiang's son, President Chiang Ching-kuo, took steps to ease hostilities and allow some indirect contacts with the mainland before he died in 1988. Lee Teng-hui, who succeeded Chiang to become Taiwan's first native-born president, followed his predecessor's lead. He walked a careful line at first, insisting the mainland must democratize before unification could occur.[85] Lee ended the Kuomintang government's state of emergency against the "Communist rebellion" in 1991, thereby acknowledging Communist control over the mainland.[86] The following year, Chinese and Taiwanese representatives started talks on opening economic and other ties, while setting aside conflicting claims of sovereignty over China.[87] It was a murky compromise that Kuomintang officials would, years later, call the "1992 consensus"—a tacit understanding that both sides agreed that there is "one China," without defining what that meant.[88]

Even so, Beijing came to loathe Lee for his international travel and remarks that implied Taiwanese nationhood. For instance, he called the Kuomintang an "exogenous regime" in Taiwan, similar to colonial powers like the Netherlands, Spain, and Japan. Lee's 1995 visit to Cornell University, his alma mater, even sparked a military standoff between Washington and Beijing. The PLA practiced amphibious landings and fired missiles near Taiwan, prompting the U.S. to deploy warships to the vicinity. The confrontation stretched into 1996 as Beijing tried to sway Taiwan's first presidential election with more drills and missile-firings, only to see Washington send two aircraft-carrier battle groups—a show of force that China had no answer for. "This was done precisely to send an unambiguous signal to Beijing of our resolve and overwhelming power so as to prevent any miscalculation or accident" that could lead to an armed clash with China, recalls Winston Lord, the U.S. assistant secretary of state for East Asian and Pacific affairs from 1993 to 1997.[89]

The crisis was sobering for China, exposing its weaknesses in the face of American military might. Worse still, Beijing's aggression backfired, riling Taiwanese voters into handing a decisive win to Lee, who became the island's first popularly elected president, with 54 percent of the vote against three challengers. The U.S. intervention in the Kosovo War as part of a North Atlantic Treaty Organization aerial bombing campaign in 1999 also worried Chinese officials, who saw the episode as a sign of Washington's willingness to intervene in a conflict over Taiwan.

Over the next two decades, Taiwan completed a remarkable transition from an authoritarian state toward a multiparty democracy. Lee stepped down as president in 2000, abiding by the term limits he had set, ending fifty-five years of continuous Kuomintang rule in Taiwan. Power was transferred to the independence-leaning Democratic Progressive Party, or DPP, whose candidate eked out a win in a competitive presidential vote. Liberal-minded politicians pushed to dismantle the Kuomintang's coercive machinery, curtail its control over the bureaucracy and news media, and strip down its business empire. Taiwan depoliticized its armed forces—once part of the Kuomintang—and retooled them into a state military. For many mainland Chinese, the island became a mirror of their own hopes and anxieties. Liberals drew inspiration, while Communist leaders saw an object lesson on the fate that might befall their one-party state.

As China's economy took off, Beijing sought to persuade Taiwan that its economic future depended on the mainland. Taiwanese investors poured into the mainland seeking a lower-cost manufacturing base for products from electronics to machinery, while Chinese buyers purchased more Taiwanese goods, like fruit and fish. By the early 2000s, China had replaced the U.S. as Taiwan's most important trading partner, while the island's economy started to mellow from its heyday as a fast-growing "Asian Tiger." Wages eventually climbed too high for some Taiwanese factories, and then stagnated, spurring an exodus of job seekers to the mainland, where more than a million Taiwanese work, according to private-sector estimates. Some of Taiwan's biggest companies, including the iPhone assembler Foxconn, established large production plants in China staffed by mainlanders, who account for the largest share of their overall headcounts.

Along the way, the Kuomintang shed its enmity with the Communist Party, focusing instead on their shared belief that the mainland and Taiwan are part of "one China." Kuomintang politicians advocated warmer relations with Beijing as a way to help Taiwan prosper, and the most prominent among them, Ma Ying-jeou, became president in 2008. He proceeded to expand economic links across the strait, opening the island to Chinese tourists and investors while allowing more Taiwanese capital to flow toward China. Beijing welcomed Taiwanese businesses, workers, and students to the mainland, and used such ties as leverage. When Taipei made positive overtures, Chinese trade and tourists streamed in the other direction. When the island seemed to tilt toward independence, Beijing squeezed the flow of Chinese money and threatened to use military force. And for a time, this strategy appeared to work. As Taiwan became more economically reliant on China, many Taiwanese either accepted that formal independence was impossible, or put off the idea indefinitely.

Xi Jinping extended this approach after taking power. But while his recent predecessors had seemed content to set the unification issue aside indefinitely, he signaled a degree of impatience. In 2013, Xi told a former Taiwanese vice president that political differences between Beijing and Taipei "shouldn't be passed down from generation to generation."[90] His inflection raised eyebrows among seasoned observers, who sensed in Xi an ambition to claim Taiwan within his lifetime, though few believed he would do so by force.

By 2014, however, Beijing's powers of persuasion were reaching their limits. President Ma's brand had become toxic among Taiwanese who resented how China's economic heft was enriching Taiwan's business elite while drawing away jobs and investments. When the ruling Kuomintang tried to expedite the ratification of an unpopular trade agreement with Beijing, students occupied the legislative chambers in Taipei for three weeks and forced Ma to drop the pact.

The backlash boosted the DPP, a group that first emerged in the 1980s as an illegal opposition movement against the Kuomintang, before evolving into a broad church whose members championed a distinct Taiwanese identity and, in some cases, an officially independent Taiwan. Its leader, Tsai Ing-wen, won the 2016 presidential election in a landslide result that irked Beijing, which resented Tsai's refusal to acknowledge the notion that Taiwan is part of "one China." Rather, Tsai and the DPP insist that the Republic of China, Taiwan—as it is formally known—is already an independent sovereign state, complete with its own government, legislature, judiciary, and military. This means, as Tsai argues, there is no need for a formal declaration of independence.[91]

Xi tried pressuring Tsai with military, diplomatic, and economic tools. Beijing deployed warplanes and navy vessels near Taiwan and curtailed Chinese travel to the island. Annual tourist arrivals from mainland China, which peaked at nearly 4.2 million in 2015, fell by more than a third during Tsai's first term as president.[92] China blocked Taiwanese delegates from participating in meetings at United Nations agencies overseeing global aviation and health, and persuaded more countries to cut ties with Taiwan, leaving the island with diplomatic recognition from just fourteen states as of this writing, down from twenty-two when Tsai took office and about seventy more than a half-century ago.

Tsai was running into problems at home too. Some Taiwanese bristled at her perceived mishandling of pension and labor reforms. Others blamed her for Taiwan's tanking trade with the mainland and slow progress in diversifying its economy. The ruling DPP suffered humiliating losses at local elections in late 2018, while a Kuomintang populist, Han Kuo-yu, scored an upset in the mayoral race in the port city of Kaohsiung—a DPP stronghold—in part by pledging to mend trade ties with China.[93] Tsai resigned as DPP chair, and disgruntled party members even questioned whether she should seek re-election in 2020.

But momentum shifted in January 2019, when Xi delivered a major speech on Taiwan that galvanized anti-Beijing views on the island. At a televised ceremony marking four decades since the Communist Party's switch to a strategy of "peaceful unification" with Taiwan, Xi reiterated Beijing's offer to assimilate the island under "one country, two systems," and dangled economic carrots for Taiwanese businesses and youth. He also implicitly denounced Tsai's government as separatists, and stressed that armed unification remained an option.[94] His remarks were received poorly in Taiwan, where "one country, two systems" has never received any significant support. Tsai capitalized, pledging to defend Taiwanese democracy against authoritarian encroachment from China.

Tsai's defiance paid off. When anti-Beijing unrest erupted in Hong Kong that summer, many in Taiwan sympathized with the protesters. Taiwanese activists ran crowdfunding campaigns to buy protective gear for Hong Kong protesters and organized rallies against local politicians seen as too friendly with Beijing. Their main target was Han Kuo-yu, who had become the Kuomintang's presidential candidate and subsequently came under fire for visiting the mainland in early 2019 to meet senior Chinese officials handling Hong Kong and Taiwan affairs.[95] "Taiwan cannot become like Hong Kong," Wu Ma-ko, a Taiwanese pig farmer who brought his wife and son to join an anti-Han march in Kaohsiung, told me. "If we don't speak up ourselves, the international community will come to see us as part of China and won't speak up for us either."[96]

Tsai fanned such sentiment as she chased a second presidential term, casting the January 2020 election as a choice between defending democracy and caving to Beijing for economic benefits. Voters turned out in force, re-electing Tsai with a record 8.17 million ballots and 57 percent of the vote—the highest share ever achieved by a DPP candidate.

Defeat stunned the Kuomintang and sparked a wave of infighting. Younger members called for a tougher tack against Beijing, clashing with establishment figures who held fast to the party's founding aspirations of ruling a unified China.[97] "If the Kuomintang still wants a chance to govern in Taiwan, or even avoid becoming a small fringe party, we must adjust," the party's youth affairs chief wrote on social media.[98] The party agreed at first, electing a new chairman who pledged to rethink the Kuomintang's China-friendly policy and put Taiwanese interests first. But he lasted less than two years, replaced by a party grandee who favored stronger ties with Beijing.[99]

While the Kuomintang struggled with its identity crisis, more Taiwanese were embracing a sense of nationhood. In the three decades since Lee Teng-hui launched democratic reforms, the proportion of citizens who professed a purely Taiwanese identity had grown by more than three times to surpass 60 percent, while the share of those who identified only as Chinese slipped below 3 percent from about one-quarter in 1992, according to surveys by the National Chengchi University's Election Study Center in Taipei.[100] The shift is in large part a generational one. Younger Taiwanese are more likely to emphasize their political and cultural differences with mainland Chinese—a tendency known as "naturally pro-independence." The Covid-19 pandemic has only amplified these views. Many in Taiwan blamed the Communist Party for failing to contain the outbreak in central China, and blocking Taiwanese officials from attending the World Health Organization's annual assembly and technical meetings.[101]

In Beijing, the apparent failure of economic persuasion has fueled bellicose arguments that peaceful unification is a dead end. Though Xi often stressed that the party prefers a cordial solution, some analysts argue he has set implicit deadlines for taking Taiwan—citing his declarations that China should achieve a degree of "socialist modernization" by 2035, and become a "modern socialist power" by 2050. Xie Chuntao, a senior party academic, seemed to confirm such suspicions. "The Taiwan issue would have been resolved" by the mid-twenty-first century, Xie said. "If we can't even achieve national unification, then I think this 'modern socialist power' of ours actually isn't that powerful."[102]

READY TO FIGHT

ONE SWELTERING SEPTEMBER MORNING IN 2015, seven decades after Japan's surrender ended World War II, Beijing shuddered with the rumbling of tanks and rhythmic stomps of goose-stepping soldiers. Fearsome phalanxes of ballistic missiles, drones, and other armaments streamed down the Avenue of Eternal Peace, cheered on by fifty-five thousand spectators while jets and helicopters streaked overhead. The parade was one of China's most extravagant displays of military muscle, and the first time Beijing had hosted such pageantry to celebrate an occasion other than a milestone birthday of the People's Republic.[103]

Dressed in an olive-green Mao suit denoting his status as chairman of the party's

Central Military Commission, Xi Jinping took in the spectacle from atop Tiananmen, the Gate of Heavenly Peace, alongside party grandees and esteemed foreign guests. The event ostensibly commemorated the Allied victory, but no major Western power sent incumbent leaders or troops to participate. Xi kicked off proceedings with dovish remarks that belied the hawkish vibes of the martial display. "We Chinese love peace. No matter how much stronger it may become, China will never seek hegemony or expansion," said Xi, declaring that he would slash the People's Liberation Army ranks by three hundred thousand personnel—the biggest reduction in two decades.

What Xi portrayed as a peaceable gesture was a key step in turning China into a first-rate military power. The PLA may have been the world's largest armed forces, numbering 2.3 million active personnel before Xi's cuts, but its warfighting capabilities were hamstrung by an antiquated command structure, obsolete doctrine, and a lack of combat experience. The People's Republic hadn't waged a full-scale war since 1979, and its leaders could only look on with nervous admiration as Western forces flexed their destructive might across the Middle East, the Balkans, and Afghanistan. If China was to be taken seriously as a global power, as Xi demanded, it needed a military that could challenge its American and European counterparts. "To achieve the great rejuvenation of the Chinese nation," Xi said, "we must ensure unity between a prosperous country and a strong military."[104]

Xi has since pledged to modernize the PLA by 2035 and establish a "world-class fighting force" by the middle of the twenty-first century.[105] Success would secure China's rise, allowing it to challenge American dominance in Asia, prevail in territorial disputes, and protect Beijing's expanding global interests—from raw materials and trade routes to overseas investments and expatriate communities. But the overhauls also risked antagonizing elements within the PLA by stripping away their wealth and prestige, while releasing legions of demobilized soldiers ill-prepared to compete in a bustling labor market.

Mao Zedong once declared that "political power comes from the barrel of a gun," and the PLA has proved as much since its founding in 1927. While modern militaries in democratic systems commit to serving the government of the day, whomever they may be, the PLA exists as the armed wing of China's Communist Party, sworn to "listen to the party's command" and act as the ultimate guarantor of its power.

Even so, there were moments when loyalties wavered, swayed by power struggles or even a sense of moral duty. In 1976, Mao's successor Hua Guofeng secured support from key military leaders before toppling the Gang of Four, who were arrested by the PLA unit responsible for protecting top officials. Deng Xiaoping's orders to crush the 1989 Tiananmen Square protests proved too much for some troops—by one count, 110 officers committed serious disciplinary breaches, while 1,400 soldiers deserted.[106] The commander of the 38th Group Army, Major General Xu Qinxian, refused to lead armed troops into Beijing without clear written orders and reportedly feigned illness—a show of defiance that got him court-martialed, expelled from the party, and jailed.[107]

Every leader since Mao has expended considerable effort to secure control over the proverbial gun. While Deng was often content to govern without formal posts, the veteran revolutionary made sure to hold the chairmanship of the party's Central Military Commission from 1981 to 1989. He sidelined the military from politics, and in return, granted the PLA significant autonomy to manage its affairs and even build businesses—including nightclubs, pharmaceuticals, and real estate—to make up for paltry defense budgets in the 1980s.[108] Encouraged to partake in China's economic boom, the PLA grew increasingly corrupt and distracted from its core duties.

Jiang Zemin and Hu Jintao both tried to modernize the PLA, with mixed success. Jiang started pushing the PLA out of business in 1998, offering budget increases to placate the brass, but many senior officers simply transferred control of these enterprises to their relatives. The military's reluctance to share information or coordinate with civilian authorities also hampered command and control, even embarrassing the leadership at times.[109] When China flight-tested a new stealth fighter in 2011 just hours before Hu met the visiting U.S. defense secretary, the Chinese leader reportedly seemed unaware of the test—fueling speculation that he was having trouble reining in PLA hawks.[110] Combat readiness deteriorated as corruption grew endemic, particularly with the buying and selling of ranks, as well as perks like military registration plates that allowed drivers to flout traffic rules.[111] Securing a general rank reportedly cost more than a million dollars, but the investment would more than pay for itself with bribes and kickbacks.[112]

Xi came to power determined to clean house. He made a stronger PLA a centerpiece of his China Dream, demanding that the armed forces be "ready to fight and win wars." He issued new strategic guidelines calling for a military that could fight digital-age conflicts, deter rival powers, and protect Beijing's interests in Asia and beyond.[113] Chinese strategists cheered his vision, calling it a necessary step in surmounting American attempts to "encircle" China—particularly President Barack Obama's "pivot" to Asia strategy that boosted U.S. military and economic presence in the region.

But before retooling the gun, Xi had to first ensure it was in his grasp. He purged the PLA's senior ranks of corrupt and politically unreliable officers, reorganized its leadership structure, and concentrated command authority in his own hands. Already chairman of the Central Military Commission, Xi claimed the title of "commander in chief" and a direct role overseeing combat operations, often appearing in camouflage fatigues as he toured military facilities.[114] He shrank the eleven-strong military commission to seven members and centralized decision-making under the "CMC chairman responsibility system," whereby Xi himself would decide all major matters—unlike how his recent predecessors delegated day-to-day duties to the CMC vice chairmen, who were professional military commanders.[115] In 2020, lawmakers rewrote legislation to give the Xi-chaired CMC more powers over defense policy, at the expense of the civilian government headed by the premier.

During Xi's first term, authorities investigated more than four thousand corruption cases in the PLA and punished some thirteen thousand people, including more than one hundred high-level officers. Two former CMC vice chairmen were purged, though one died of cancer before his case reached court-martial.[116] Two sitting CMC members also went down, with the PLA's chief of joint staff receiving a life sentence and the general who oversaw political indoctrination committing suicide while under investigation.[117] In their place, Xi brought in commanders whom he deemed more loyal and professional, including a new chief of joint staff who fought with distinction in the 1979 Sino-Vietnamese war. Nearly 90 percent of the PLA delegation to the 2017 party congress were first-time participants, marking a thorough turnover in the military brass.

The purges facilitated an overhaul of the PLA's command structure, removing or cowing officers who might resist change. Before Xi took charge, the PLA Ground Force—as the army is known—accounted for seven of eleven members on the Central Military Commission and some 70 percent of all PLA personnel. The four "general departments" that comprised the PLA leadership—overseeing military operations, political indoctrination, logistics, and equipment maintenance—had decayed into fiefdoms riddled with financial waste and graft.[118] The PLA administered its fighting forces across seven "military regions" that functioned like mini-states, each with its own schools, hospitals, hotels, and newspapers. And while region chiefs commanded army units, air and naval forces were controlled by their own service headquarters, making it harder to conduct integrated operations.[119]

Xi scrapped the four general departments, and redistributed their functions across fifteen smaller departments and offices that reported directly to the Central Military Commission. Also gone were the seven military regions, replaced with five new "theater commands"—covering north, south, east, west, and center—that were each led by a regional chief vested with more direct control over all land, air, naval, and missile forces within their area. Xi also diluted some of the Ground Force's authority, so as to boost the air, naval, and strategic missile forces that are crucial for projecting power beyond China's periphery. A new Rocket Force was created to oversee the PLA's ballistic-missile arsenal, while a new Strategic Support Force took charge of space, cyber, and electronic warfare. Ground forces were hit hardest by Xi's cuts, with the army's share of PLA personnel falling below 50 percent.[120] More than 30 percent of commissioned officers were let go. Noncombat functions—such as song-and-dance troupes—were scaled down.[121]

In some ways, the changes mirror U.S. defense reforms introduced in the late 1980s to reduce rivalry between the armed services and facilitate joint operations. But Xi made sure to retain a Soviet-era feature of political control—the dual leadership system whereby military units are headed by two officers typically of equal grade: a commanding officer, with formal authority over combat decisions, and a political commissar, who would enforce party directives.

Drawing inspiration from the U.S., Xi urged greater "military-civil fusion," whereby the military took advantage of civilian resources to boost its capabilities for waging war. This fusion means tapping civilian advances in science and technology, bringing in civilian contractors to improve military supply chains, and even incorporating military specifications in civilian transport so that they can be easily mobilized for combat use. Defense contractors ramped up the development and production of weapons that could deny U.S. forces access to waters near China's coastline. Beijing built its first overseas military outpost in the African nation of Djibouti, which also hosts U.S. and Japanese bases and has served as a supply stop for Chinese warships on antipiracy patrols in the Gulf of Aden.[122]

Xi's reforms won praise, especially from combat commanders frustrated by graft. There was resentment too, from generals who once controlled large budgets and now ran lower-ranked offices. Senior officers lost some perks and found it harder to supplement salaries with other, sometimes illicit, activities. Demobilized servicemen continued staging protests to vent against the government's perceived failure to give them adequate benefits and new livelihoods.

And a key question remains: How capable is China's new-era military? The PLA has demonstrated improved capabilities under Xi by conducting peacetime operations and combat drills with increasing range, complexity, and frequency. Its navy evacuated hundreds of Chinese nationals from conflict-torn Yemen in 2015, while the air force sent humanitarian aid and Covid-19-related medical supplies across Asia.[123] But insofar as war is the one true test of a military's worth, the PLA has offered few answers since the 1979 Sino-Vietnamese war, when the two sides ground out a bloody stalemate, before waging occasional skirmishes on land and at sea until Beijing and Hanoi normalized relations in 1991.

This relative inexperience was in part a strategic choice. Though the People's Republic largely inherited its boundaries from the Qing dynasty, which conquered Tibet and Xinjiang, annexed Taiwan, and stretched into present-day Mongolia and Russia, the Communist Party willingly gave up large swaths of Qing territory that had fallen into foreign hands. Pursuing these claims would have meant bitter quarrels or even war with China's neighbors, including the Soviet Union. Beijing has thus settled some seventeen of the twenty-three territorial disputes it has been involved in since 1949, often by offering hefty concessions that left it with only modest shares of the land it once claimed.[124]

Most of the outstanding disputes, however, are far more intertwined with China's prestige. In the South China Sea, five Southeast Asian countries and Taiwan assert territorial and maritime claims that overlap with Beijing's broad claims of sovereignty over the strategic waters. Beijing continues to contest Tokyo's control over a group of islands in the East China Sea—known as Diaoyu in Chinese and Senkaku in Japanese—that Japan first claimed in the 1890s and has administered since 1972. The Sino-Indian boundary, meanwhile, has yet to be delimited since the two sides fought a border war in 1962.

These frontiers have become proving grounds for Xi's new-look PLA. Chinese aircraft and warships regularly intercept American counterparts asserting "freedom of navigation" in disputed parts of the South China Sea, occasionally resulting in what Washington calls unsafe encounters caused by risky Chinese maneuvers.[125] Tokyo has reported higher frequencies of PLA warplane sorties that approached close enough for Japan to scramble fighters in response.[126] On China's loosely defined border with India, tensions between the two armies boiled over into physical clashes and even a lethal brawl in June 2020, when at least twenty Indians and four Chinese died in a high-altitude melee fought with rocks, batons, and nail-studded clubs—the first time in three decades that China engaged in a known deadly border skirmish.[127]

The one theater that the PLA has focused on the most is Taiwan, the final piece in China's unification jigsaw. For Chinese war planners, Taiwan serves as a strategic gateway to the Pacific Ocean, thanks to its central location in the "first island chain," off China's east coast, that stretches from Japan to the Philippines—a concept defined as part of a U.S. Cold War strategy to contain the Soviet Union and China by placing American forces in the Western Pacific.[128] General Douglas MacArthur once described Taiwan as an "unsinkable aircraft carrier" that can project power and dominate vital shipping lanes, and Chinese strategists agree.[129] "As long as the Taiwan Strait issue is resolved, the first island chain that blocks and threatens our country will be broken, and our access to the western flanks and the deep-blue Pacific Ocean shall be unimpeded," one retired Chinese general wrote.[130]

Chinese officials and state media often boast that the modernized PLA could capture Taiwan with ease—"within three days," one official claimed—thanks to an overwhelming superiority in troops and technology.[131] But the public bravado belies a circumspection that Chinese strategists often express privately about the prospects of forceful annexation. The PLA's purpose for the time being, some say, is to deter Taiwan from declaring formal independence, a move that China would consider *casus belli.*

Even by Beijing's own assessments, capturing Taiwan is a daunting task. PLA literature acknowledges that an invasion of Taiwan would require complex battle planning.[132] It would feature three main phases, from wearing down Taiwanese defenses with aerial bombing, missile strikes, and naval blockades, to amphibious landings, and then pitched battles on Taiwan itself, before Chinese forces could start transitioning from invasion to occupation.[133] Every stage of the campaign would be fraught with formidable difficulties, such as rough seas in the Taiwan Strait many months of the year, the limited number of beaches suited for amphibious landings, and the logistical challenge of transporting and protecting a massive invasion force across many miles of open water.

China could test the PLA's capabilities through limited campaigns, such as blockading Taiwan or seizing some of its outlying islands, including the Kinmen and Matsu chains just off the mainland or the tiny Pratas in the South China Sea, which are all isolated and hard to defend. After U.S. House speaker Nancy Pelosi defied

Chinese warnings to visit Taipei in August 2022, the PLA encircled Taiwan with rocket and ballistic-missile fire and conducted combat drills near the island—a showcase of its capabilities in cutting off Taiwan from outside help.[134] Analysts say such operations could allow Beijing to squeeze Taipei and secure some territorial gains before Washington can muster a decisive response, though they still risk escalation into a full-blown war, an unpalatable prospect for the party.[135]

In the meantime, Beijing has waged what military experts call "gray-zone warfare" against Taiwan—a campaign of sustained intimidation aimed at wearing down the island's defenses and demoralizing its people.[136] The strategy comprises military operations such as amphibious-assault drills, naval patrols, and warplane sorties, which are paired with non-military pressure including cyber and disinformation attacks, diplomatic pressure, and even the use of sand dredgers to harass residents on Taiwan's outlying islands.[137]

PLA aircraft and warships have maintained an almost constant presence near Taiwan, forcing the island's military to intercept them at an exhausting pace. Over the first nine months of 2020, Taiwanese warplanes scrambled nearly three thousand times against approaching Chinese aircraft, at a cost of almost $900 million.[138] The following year, PLA fighters, bombers, and other planes flew more than 880 sorties near Taiwan's southwestern coast, more than double the roughly 380 sorties flown there in 2020.[139]

Such pressure exerts a heavy toll on Taiwan's air force by raising fuel and maintenance costs, wearing out pilots and planes, and eroding their combat readiness. The PLA can afford such an attritional approach. Its fleet of more than twenty-five hundred fighters, bombers, and other aircraft outnumbers Taiwan's roughly four hundred fighters, which include decades-old airframes that are less reliable and increasingly expensive to maintain.[140] The psychological toll is considerable too, as described by Lee Hsi-min, a retired admiral and Taiwan's top military commander from 2017 to 2019: "You say it's your garden, but it turns out that it is your neighbor who's hanging out in the garden all the time. With that action, they are making a statement that it's their garden—and that garden is one step away from your house."[141]

Lee champions the use of asymmetric warfare to mitigate the PLA's superior numbers and firepower, whereby Taiwan's military would retool itself as a more mobile, resilient, and cost-effective force that can survive Chinese attacks and strike back.[142] Endorsed by many Western strategists, his proposals call for Taiwan to maintain just a small number of high-end armaments to counter China's gray-zone operations and sustain public morale. The bulk of the Taiwanese military, Lee argues, should be rearmed with large volumes of small, cheap, and lethal weapons—including mobile anti-ship and air defense systems, drones, sea mines, and anti-tank missiles—that are easier to disperse and hide, and therefore harder to destroy while they batter an incoming invasion force. Existing reserves should also be reorganized into territorial defense units capable of waging urban and guerrilla warfare. "It is a concept of denial, instead of control," Lee says. "We can't achieve air superiority or control the Taiwan Strait, but we can deny the enemy control over our airspace and waters."[143]

While some in Taiwan's defense establishment remain resistant to Lee's ideas, President Tsai has committed to buying arms suited for such a strategy, alongside big-ticket deals for advanced fighter jets, tanks, and missiles.[144] Taiwanese strategists advocating asymmetric warfare also found validation in Russia's invasion of Ukraine, where Moscow's much-vaunted military—modernized to the tune of hundreds of billions of dollars—suffered heavy losses against smaller Ukrainian forces employing guerrilla tactics, drones, and Western weaponry.

Even so, questions remain over whether Taiwan can field enough qualified and motivated personnel to mount an effective defense.[145] Its military has a solid core of professional officers and regular troops, analysts say, but remains underfunded and lacks adequate reserve forces that would contribute the vast majority of combatants in wartime. As of 2020, Taiwan had about 169,000 active military personnel compared to roughly 2.3 million reservists, who have either received minimal refresher training once every two years or have been completely inactive for more than eight years.[146] The quality of these forces has also declined as authorities reduced the length of mandatory military service for Taiwanese men, whittled down since the early 2000s from a roughly two-year requirement to just four months by the early 2010s.[147] Lacking time for meaningful training, these conscripts often learn little more than basic marksmanship and perform menial duties like moving stores, leaving them ill-prepared for combat.[148]

Taipei has started overhauling its reserves system to provide more frequent and rigorous training. In late 2022, President Tsai announced that the length of mandatory military service would be extended to one year, starting 2024, with better pay and more robust instruction for conscripts.[149] But such changes will take years to take effect, while China's advantage continues to grow.[150] By 2021, Beijing's declared military spending already stood at more than thirteen times that of Taipei's regular defense budget, while PLA ground troops outnumbered the Taiwanese army by more than tenfold.[151] That same year, Taiwan's defense minister warned that China would be capable of launching a full-blown attack on the island with minimal losses by 2025.[152]

Many Western analysts believe a U.S. intervention, or lack thereof, would decide Taiwan's fate in the event of war. The 1979 Taiwan Relations Act, which governed Washington's dealings with Taipei after formal ties were cut, requires the U.S. to ensure that the island can defend itself, and to maintain American capabilities to resist any use of force that threatens Taiwanese security.[153] In practice, this arrangement has meant that successive administrations in Washington have sold arms—including tanks, missiles, and fighter jets—and provided some military training to Taiwan, while avoiding an explicit commitment to intervene by force should China invade.

Both the Trump and Biden administrations stepped up security cooperation with Taipei, sending American military personnel to train Taiwanese counterparts and advise on preparations for combat scenarios against China.[154] Within U.S. defense and foreign policy circles, debates simmered over whether Washington should switch to an open pledge to defend Taiwan, with some arguing that such a commitment could deter Beijing, while others say it would be too provocative and that an American intervention would be futile.[155] President Biden, for his part, kept Beijing guessing with repeated statements that the U.S. would defend Taiwan against a Chinese attack, while his subordinates insisted that Washington hasn't changed its policy.[156]

Some Chinese analysts, meanwhile, argue that the U.S. and other Western powers' refusal to intercede militarily against Russian aggression—including the 2008 war against Georgia, the 2014 annexation of Crimea, and the 2022 invasion of Ukraine—bodes well for Beijing. And while the West rapidly assembled an international coalition to sanction Russia over the Ukraine war, China is better equipped to endure such pressure, thanks to its far larger, more diversified, and globally connected economy.[157]

How U.S. and Chinese forces might fare in direct conflict is unclear. Some analysts say Xi's military modernization appears to have tilted the balance in China's favor in the Western Pacific, where the PLA can outmatch the U.S. in certain scenarios. Beijing has been developing new weapons—such as long-range "carrier-killer" missiles—that could keep American forces at bay while Chinese attackers overwhelm Taiwan. In war games simulating Chinese attempts to invade Taiwan, conducted by

RAND Corporation researchers, the PLA often prevailed against U.S. and Taiwanese forces.[158] Other analysts say the PLA, though well upgraded, must still prove itself through the acid test of war.

Few in Washington are waiting to find out. Since the Trump administration designated China as a "strategic competitor" in 2017, bipartisan support has coalesced behind efforts to bolster American war-fighting capabilities against the PLA. Influential voices in Japan have called for more security cooperation with the U.S. and Taiwan to deter China. While some experts believe that Beijing can afford to wait until its military and economic power becomes so overwhelming that Taipei capitulates peacefully, others warn that the Communist Party may one day find it more desirable to wage war while China still has a military edge, than to risk falling behind the U.S. without securing key prizes.[159]

"Ultimately, Taiwan's fate would depend on how the U.S.-China strategic competition plays out," says Lee Hsi-min, the retired Taiwanese admiral. A critical question is whether the Communist Party would use force to secure its vision of a unified China, a decision that—under current circumstances—would fall to one man. "Beijing prefers peaceful unification, and military means are the last resort, but we cannot really know what Xi is thinking," Lee warns. "Never say never."[160]

CHAPTER SEVEN

WOLF WARRIORS HOWLING

THE PARTY REMAKES THE WORLD

"Diplomacy is the same as military affairs. Diplomacy is just fighting with words."

—Zhou Enlai, Chinese premier and foreign minister

"I am very honored to be called a 'wolf warrior' because there are so many 'mad hyenas' attacking China."

—Lu Shaye, Chinese ambassador to France

"Containment and suppression by the United States are major threats, both in the form of unplanned clashes and protracted warfare."

—Chen Yixin, senior Chinese security official

In the summer of 2019, as Western governments cranked up criticism of China's human-rights abuses against Muslim minorities in Xinjiang, a seasoned Chinese diplomat cried foul against what he saw as rank hypocrisy shown by those berating Beijing. As deputy chief of mission at the Chinese embassy in Pakistan, a mid-level role in one of the world's largest diplomatic corps, Zhao Lijian didn't quite have the standing to front his government's response to foreign censure. But the forty-seven-year-old did boast a personal audience that his colleagues lacked—some 190,000 followers on Twitter—and a penchant for picking fights.[1]

Though Twitter is blocked in China, Zhao had opened an account in 2010 while stationed in Washington. At first he shared travel photos and news reports, before finding his voice skewering foreign politicians, scholars, and journalists who criticized his country. The United States became a frequent target for Zhao, who found American officials especially sanctimonious in castigating China while papering over their own problems with gun violence and racial injustice.

In July 2019, days after twenty-two mostly Western countries—the U.S. excluded—issued a joint statement at the United Nations Human Rights Council urging Beijing to stop persecuting Uyghurs in Xinjiang, Zhao fired off a string of tweets pummeling America for its failure to deal with systemic racism. White residents in Washington, Zhao wrote, would never venture into the capital's southeastern quadrant "because it's an area for the black & Latin."[2] The tweets angered Susan Rice, a former national security adviser to President Barack Obama. "You are a racist disgrace. And shockingly ignorant too," she wrote in response, and called for the Chinese diplomat to be sent home.[3] Zhao bit back. "You are such a disgrace, too. And shockingly ignorant, too," he tweeted at Rice. "Truth hurts. I am simply telling the truth."[4]

Twitter rows are rife in Washington, but trading insults with a Chinese diplomat was unheard of. At first, Zhao seemed to have overstepped. China's then ambassador to the U.S. passed word to Rice indicating that he didn't approve of Zhao's tweets—some of which were soon deleted—and that the younger diplomat's Twitter account didn't reflect China's position.[5] Weeks later, when Zhao said he was returning to Beijing, critics wondered if he would be sidelined.[6]

But Zhao's star was rising fast. State media praised his pugnacity in confronting China's critics, while admirers at the foreign ministry gathered at Zhao's office to cheer his return.[7] After the BBC said Zhao exemplified an emerging "wolf warrior" psyche among Beijing's diplomats, a reference to a popular film franchise about a Rambo-like Chinese soldier who battles Western mercenaries, Chinese nationalists embraced the epithet as praise for their hawkish envoys.[8] The foreign ministry unveiled Zhao as an official spokesperson in a telling appointment. Twitter is dominated by foreigners "badmouthing China," Zhao told an American journalist. "This is a time for Chinese diplomats to tell the true picture."[9]

Using Twitter and news briefings as bully pulpits, Zhao portrayed a conniving West scheming to frustrate China's rise as a global power. When Washington and Beijing bickered over the origins of Covid-19, Zhao promoted conspiracy theories claiming that the coronavirus originated in the U.S. and was brought to China by the American military.[10] After an Australian Defence Force inquiry disclosed war crimes committed by its troops in Afghanistan, Zhao tweeted a Chinese artist's image that depicted an

Australian soldier holding a bloodstained knife against the throat of an Afghan child—prompting Australia's prime minister to condemn Zhao and demand an apology.[11]

Such antics weren't an aberration. As Xi Jinping pushes to reclaim what he sees as China's rightful place in the world, his diplomats are pursuing his vision with bluster and bravado, winning plaudits at home without regard for the anger they stoke abroad. In the year Zhao was promoted, the Chinese ambassador to Canada accused his hosts of "white supremacy," while Beijing's envoy in Stockholm, whose fiery rhetoric got him summoned by the Swedish foreign ministry more than forty times in two years, told local radio that "we treat our friends with fine wine, but for our enemies we have shotguns."[12]

Such bellicosity marks both change and continuity for the Chinese diplomatic corps. Founded in 1949 with a militaristic ethos, the foreign ministry shed its gladiatorial instincts for a more measured style in the post-Mao years, heeding Deng Xiaoping's advice to "hide our light and bide our time," or keep a low profile while accumulating China's strengths. Xi discarded the "hide and bide" philosophy, urging his diplomats to "strive and accomplish things." Whereas the foreign ministry once reserved its truculence for core interests, such as disputed territorial claims and the Dalai Lama's perceived advocacy for Tibetan independence, Xi wants diplomats who "dare to struggle" and enforce Communist Party narratives more vigorously across a much wider range of issues—among them the treatment of Muslim minorities in Xinjiang, the value of Beijing's loans to developing countries, and the efficacy of China's Covid-19 vaccines.

Xi led from the front. He centralized control over foreign policy and styled himself a global statesman, traveling abroad more frequently and widely than any other Chinese leader.[13] He championed bold plans to build global trade infrastructure, poured loans and aid into developing countries, and sought greater influence at international bodies like the United Nations. While President Donald Trump pushed protectionist policies and harangued allies for free-riding under an American security umbrella, Xi cast China as a sober guardian of globalization and a multilateral world order. Above all, Xi strode forth as a nationalist strongman, ready to fight the belligerent West. The Chinese people "will never allow any foreign force to bully, oppress, or enslave us," Xi declared. "Anyone who tries to do so shall be battered and bloodied from colliding with a great wall of steel forged by more than 1.4 billion Chinese people using flesh and blood."[14]

This pugnacity manifested in various ways. Already a prolific exponent of economic statecraft, Beijing increasingly withheld trade, investment, and aid from countries it deemed hostile, while showing munificence to those that acquiesced. The party became more brazen in detaining foreigners as leverage, a practice critics condemned as "hostage diplomacy." Its diplomats now favor bombastic browbeating over subtle persuasion, battling opponents big and small across negotiating tables, in newsprint, and on social media. Beijing wants to coerce and cajole countries into showing automatic deference toward a preeminent China, through what retired Singaporean diplomat Bilahari Kausikan calls an "almost Pavlovian process of conditioning."[15] Or as another Asian diplomat put it: "For China, 'win-win cooperation' means China wins twice."

But Beijing's tactics, built on largesse and intimidation, have yielded diminishing returns. Tensions with the U.S. over trade, technology, and geopolitical influence have galvanized bipartisan support in Washington for a tougher China policy. Other Western countries, including some once eager to curry favor with Beijing, were riled by Chinese efforts to influence their domestic politics, crush dissent in Hong Kong, and prop up Russia's economy amid Western sanctions over the war in Ukraine. Opinion polls show a majority of citizens in many advanced economies distrust China and consider it a threat. Across Asia, a region Beijing considers its backyard, some governments have grown uneasy with what they see as Chinese bullying. These fissures have even stirred talk of a "new Cold War," as liberal democracies promise to band together to resist China.

For Xi, the backlash validates his approach, proving that rivals fear China's rise. Despite misgivings that their government may be acting too obnoxiously, many Chinese take pride in seeing their motherland put smaller neighbors in their place, compete with big powers, and, as Xi says, "look upon the world from an equal footing."[16] Chinese officials often emphasize that "diplomacy is an extension of internal affairs," and therein lies the logic of their often undiplomatic ways. Beijing is stoking and satiating nationalistic fervor, while reshaping the global order in service of Communist Party rule.

FIGHTING WORDS

THE PEOPLE'S REPUBLIC WAS BARELY a month old when its premier and foreign minister, Zhou Enlai, assembled the bulk of his newly constituted diplomatic corps to celebrate the birth of Communist China's foreign ministry. Some 170 people gathered that evening in November 1949 at the ministry's new premises, an elegant European-style guesthouse in central Beijing that once hosted German royalty and the revered revolutionary Sun Yat-sen.[17] Zhou had yet to meet many of his new charges, and the premier wanted to offer a personal welcome, and inspire them for the tasks ahead.[18]

These novice diplomats were a disparate bunch—local officials, university graduates, and peasant soldiers more comfortable with pulling triggers than pushing papers. Many hadn't traveled abroad before and couldn't speak any foreign language. But for Zhou, these were minor issues. Professional skills could be learned, but what every member of the foreign ministry must possess was the gumption to fight. "We must seize the initiative, have no fear, and be confident," Zhou told his audience. Echoing earlier remarks where he declared that "diplomatic cadres are the People's Liberation Army in civilian dress," the premier reiterated his demands for a combative spirit.[19] "Diplomacy is the same as military affairs," he said. "Diplomacy is just fighting with words."[20]

This martial ethos would animate Chinese foreign policy throughout the Mao era, as the Communist government battled for legitimacy in a hostile world. Only nine states had recognized the People's Republic when Zhou spoke that November evening, with most countries still regarding Chiang Kai-shek's Kuomintang regime as the rightful government of China.[21] As the "civilian army" of a fledgling nation-state, Zhou and his foreign ministry shouldered an existential mission: secure international backing for Mao's revolution and keep foreign threats at bay.

The party picked military commanders to lead many of China's new embassies abroad, with twelve of Beijing's first seventeen ambassadors drawn from senior PLA ranks.[22] The aim, as one former diplomat explained, was to have these "ambassador generals" apply their "strategies, tactical ideas and experience in military and political struggles toward the practice of diplomatic struggle," and ensure that "the party and military's fine traditions and style take root in the diplomatic corps."[23] The party also tapped PLA officers for key roles such as political counselors and military attachés, alongside civilian administrators and language specialists.[24] They learned how to dress, dine, and dance, and attended lectures on politics, economics, and international law. Many turned to counterparts from fellow communist states like the Soviet Union and Poland for pointers on protocol and day-to-day embassy work.[25]

Zhou and his team soon proved their mettle. They held their own against the U.S., Britain, and France during post–Korean War talks in Geneva and won friends at the 1955 Bandung Conference, a landmark diplomatic assembly of twenty-nine Asian and African states that laid foundations for the Non-Aligned Movement. Zhou's appeals for peaceful coexistence, mutual noninterference, and solidarity among developing nations persuaded more governments to recognize the People's Republic.

Mao's radical campaigns and antagonism toward the post-Stalin Soviet Union threatened to unravel Zhou's gains. Beijing's split with Moscow rattled other socialist states, many of which sided with the powerful Soviets or tried to stay neutral. Chinese diplomats struggled to maintain a facade of prosperity to the outside world while tens of millions of their countrymen died during the Great Famine. The Cultural Revolution ravaged the foreign ministry, whose officials were excoriated for their alleged bourgeois tendencies—from wearing Western suits to attending lavish parties. To avoid persecution, many Chinese diplomats swapped sophistication for ardor, incanting Mao's maxims, distancing themselves from foreigners, and undermining relationships they had cultivated.

Chinese diplomats still scored significant wins, securing enough votes at the United Nations General Assembly in 1971 to pass a landmark resolution to eject the Kuomintang delegation and recognize the People's Republic.[26] U.S. President Richard Nixon visited China the following year, leading to the establishment of full diplomatic relations in 1979. A surge of countries switched from recognizing Taipei to Beijing, which shared formal ties with some 120 states by the end of the decade.[27]

Deng Xiaoping's "reform and opening up" program boosted China's participation in global governance. By 1989, Beijing had become a member of thirty-seven international organizations—from just one in 1971—and a signatory to more than 125 treaties, compared with just 6 in the first two decades after Mao's victory.[28] But political upheaval would again jeopardize China's standing in 1989, after Deng crushed the Tiananmen Square protests. Foreign leaders, particularly in the West, recoiled at reports of Chinese troops killing hundreds, if not thousands, of people in the June 4 massacre. Beijing confronted a chorus of international condemnation, and the U.S. and Western European powers imposed an arms embargo on China.[29] Some two dozen Chinese embassy staffers defected, reinforcing perceptions that diplomatic personnel were politically unreliable due to regular contact with foreign cultures.[30]

Deng urged patience in rehabilitating China's battered image. "We must stay calm, stay calm, and stay calm; immerse ourselves in practical work and accomplish something—something for ourselves," he said three months after the massacre.[31]

Officials later distilled Deng's advice, dispensed over several years, into a set of principles that would shape Chinese foreign policy for the next two decades: "Observe soberly, hold our ground, face challenges calmly, hide our light and bide our time, remain free of ambitions, never assert leadership, make a difference."[32]

A generation of Chinese diplomats imbibed Deng's dictums. Under Jiang Zemin and Hu Jintao, China focused on integrating itself with the international order and embracing multilateral diplomacy. It cultivated ties with Southeast Asian neighbors and developing countries in Africa and signed major global pacts (but did not necessarily ratify and formally abide by them). Beijing joined the World Trade Organization in 2001, and boosted its influence in the World Bank and International Monetary Fund. To dispel Western concerns over the "China threat," Hu championed the notion of China's "peaceful rise," though he later dialed that down to "peaceful development," to avoid perceptions of his country as a revisionist power shaking up the geopolitical status quo.

But while Jiang offered a jovial presence on the diplomatic stage, famously singing and playing music with his hosts and even dancing with the French president's wife, Hu struck foreign leaders as bland and forgettable. President Obama, in a memoir, recalled Hu as "a nondescript man" who "appeared content to rely on pages of prepared talking points, with no apparent agenda beyond encouraging continued consultation and what he referred to as 'win-win' cooperation."[33] Hu's placid diplomacy disappointed nationalists at home. One infamous vignette within Chinese foreign policy circles recounts how members of the public would mail calcium tablets to the foreign ministry to mock their perceived lack of backbone.[34] Such insults stung, in part because they underscored the foreign ministry's diminished standing within the government—economic and security agencies, the military, and even major state enterprises carried more clout.

The global financial crisis and the Beijing Olympics in 2008 brought China a timely fillip, marking its arrival on the global stage while Western economies faltered. Chinese leaders and diplomats carried themselves with more confidence, even brashness. At the 2009 climate summit in Copenhagen, Chinese premier Wen Jiabao skipped key meetings with Western leaders and sent subordinates in his place, fueling perceptions that Beijing was sabotaging the talks.[35] Xi Jinping flexed this newfound aplomb as vice president. "There are some foreigners who've nothing better to do after eating their fill, pointing fingers at our affairs," Xi told a gathering of Chinese diaspora during a 2009 visit to Mexico. "China, first of all, doesn't export revolution;

second, we don't export hunger and poverty; and third, we don't cause trouble for you. What else is there to say?"[36]

Such hawkishness boiled over at a 2010 gathering of Asia-Pacific foreign ministers in Hanoi, where U.S. secretary of state Hillary Clinton and several Southeast Asian counterparts issued thinly veiled rebukes of Beijing's sovereignty claims in the South China Sea. China's foreign minister, Yang Jiechi, responded with a nearly half-hour tirade, often staring at Clinton as he warned Southeast Asian countries not to get involved with an outside power—a pointed reference to the U.S.[37] At one point, Yang looked at Singapore's foreign minister and said: "China is a big country, and other countries are small countries, and that is just a fact."[38] Yang would later become Xi's top foreign policy adviser and, in 2017, join the Politburo, becoming the first diplomat in fifteen years to hold such high rank.

As paramount leader, Xi extended the hawkish trajectory that began under Hu, but with far more boldness and vigor. Xi unveiled the Belt and Road infrastructure initiative, and launched a new multilateral lender—the Asian Infrastructure Investment Bank—in hopes of eroding Western dominance over development finance. He championed a "new model of major-power relations" with the U.S. based on mutual respect and nonconfrontation, calling on Washington to consider Beijing a peer, rather than a junior partner in global affairs.[39] His administration launched an island-building campaign in the South China Sea, reclaiming land around Chinese-controlled geographical features and fortifying them with military assets—a program that angered neighboring countries with competing territorial claims.[40] Addressing fellow Asian leaders in 2014, Xi declared that "matters in Asia ultimately must be taken care of by Asians," signaling that China would more robustly resist American influence in the region, and stake its claim as Asia's preeminent power.[41]

Xi asserted personal control over China's foreign affairs.[42] He centralized diplomatic decision-making with Communist Party commissions that he chairs, while downgrading the foreign ministry's role in shaping policy. He weighed in on key diplomatic appointments, favoring loyal and combative officials who could channel his demands for muscular diplomacy. He directed a personnel shakeup in the foreign service, ushering in outsiders with more diverse backgrounds and demanding more fighting spirit from his diplomats.[43] By 2019, Xi had nearly doubled Beijing's diplomatic spending to some 62 billion yuan, or roughly $9 billion, and turned the Chinese foreign ministry into the world's largest diplomatic network, with some 276 embassies, consulates, and other missions globally—surpassing that of the U.S. State Department.[44]

Along the way, Xi became China's face to the world. He averaged 14.3 visits to foreign countries a year between 2013 and 2019, eclipsing Jiang and Hu while even surpassing Obama and Trump, who respectively averaged 13.9 and 12.3 visits annually during their presidencies.[45] Xi was also an enthusiastic host, receiving far more foreign leaders in Beijing than his American counterparts did in Washington—until China closed its borders during the Covid-19 pandemic.[46] And unlike his predecessor, Xi carried himself well on the global stage. "Hu could walk into a room with his staffers and you wouldn't know he was the leader, other than the fact that he's standing in front," recalls Ben Rhodes, a former deputy national security adviser to President Obama. "Xi has swagger, the confidence of being the boss."[47]

Such élan permeated China's foreign relations. Just as Zhou Enlai had demanded decades ago, Xi wants his diplomats steeled with discipline and ready to fight. If traditional diplomacy is the art of allowing someone else to have your way, Xi's envoys must insist on their way, or else.

WOLF WARRIORS

WHEN FRENCH NEWS OUTLETS raised questions about China's initial response to the Covid-19 outbreak in early 2020, the Chinese ambassador in Paris rushed to beat back the criticism. A seasoned diplomat with a truculent streak, Lu Shaye scheduled a string of media interviews to counter allegations that the Communist Party had mishandled the first outbreak in central China. His embassy lashed out at Beijing's critics on social media and published online essays excoriating European countries for failing to contain the coronavirus.

"Some mainstream media in the West have seen fit to disguise reality, to make fun of China, to rejoice in its misfortunes and to attack it," Lu told one interviewer.[48] "These misguided propaganda and malicious attacks against China amount to real brainwashing inflicted upon Western public opinion." Weeks later, the Chinese embassy sparked outrage in France by publishing an online essay—attributed to an anonymous Chinese diplomat—that seemed to suggest that French nursing home caregivers were abandoning residents to die from Covid-19. The anonymous diplomat also insinuated that French lawmakers were endorsing racism by voicing support for Taiwan's government, which the essay falsely accused of using a racist slur against the World Health Organization's director general.[49]

France's foreign ministry summoned Lu for a dressing down, prompting the Chinese embassy to remove the essay and clarify that it was neither referring to French caregivers nor accusing French lawmakers of using racist slurs.[50] But far from backing down, Lu and his charges soon unleashed new invectives. "Every time the Americans make an allegation, the French media always report them a day or two later," Lu told a French newspaper days later. "They howl with the wolves, to make a big fuss about lies and rumors about China."[51]

Lu's strident style sealed his reputation as one of Beijing's most prominent "wolf warrior" diplomats. The sobriquet was inspired by a 2017 Chinese action movie *Wolf Warrior 2*, which enthralled domestic audiences with its jingoistic portrayal of a Chinese soldier-turned-security-contractor rescuing compatriots in Africa from local rebels and American-led mercenaries. It raked in more than $850 million to become China's highest-ever grossing movie at the time, and its tagline—"Those who attack China shall be punished however far they are"—became a popular slogan among nationalistic citizens.[52] Lu embraced the "wolf warrior" epithet. "We never provoked anyone. What we do is defend ourselves," he said. "I am very honored to be called a 'wolf warrior' because there are so many 'mad hyenas' attacking China."[53]

Wolf warrior diplomacy was years in the making. When Xi named Wang Yi as foreign minister in early 2013, some old acquaintances welcomed the appointment of an urbane diplomat known for his "subtlety and flexibility."[54] That sophistication soon turned into steeliness as Wang took on a tougher persona to match Xi's. When the Australian foreign minister visited Beijing later that year, Wang skipped the usual pleasantries at the start of formal meetings and—with media still in the room— lambasted Canberra for objecting to China's declaration of an "air defense identification zone" in the East China Sea.[55] It was a stunning breach of etiquette, which a senior Australian diplomat later described as the rudest conduct he had seen in his three-decade career.[56] Wang flashed his hawkish side again during a 2016 visit to Ottawa, where he tore into a local reporter for asking the Canadian foreign minister about China's human rights record. "Your question is full of prejudice against China and an arrogance that comes from I know not where. I find this totally unacceptable," he said. "Do you understand China? Have you been to China?"[57]

Whether such displays are political theater or driven by genuine indignation against the West, Chinese diplomats started taking cues from their boss. They prioritized point scoring over discreet lobbying, which often meant hewing closely to prepared talking points and delivering them with bombast. Many grew reluctant to adapt their messaging or show flexibility, fearing reprimand for doing something impolitic. Foreign diplomats found it harder to get meetings with Chinese counterparts, and when they did, their conversations became increasingly stilted. When a friend of mine arranged dinner with a former Peking University classmate who had joined China's foreign ministry, the former classmate insisted on reporting the meeting to superiors and bringing a colleague, citing guidelines discouraging one-to-one meetings with foreigners.[58]

Even while President Trump antagonized allies and savaged global markets with his "America first" protectionism, Chinese diplomats contrived to squander opportunities for earning goodwill. Beijing's envoy to a 2018 summit of Pacific Island nations stormed out of a session reserved for national leaders after his request to speak was declined.[59] Later that year, at the Asia-Pacific Economic Cooperation summit, an annual gathering of leaders from Pacific Rim economies including the U.S., Chinese negotiators stalled talks over the final communiqué to oppose certain references to "unfair trade practices"—language that they believed was singling Beijing out. Chinese delegates sought facetime with the foreign minister of the host nation, Papua New Guinea, hoping to influence the final wording. The minister declined to meet, only to see the Chinese diplomats barge into his office before security came and got them to leave.[60] When officials announced that talks had collapsed, the first time an APEC summit had failed to produce a joint statement since national leaders started attending in 1993, Chinese negotiators reportedly applauded the news.[61]

Such belligerence grew more prevalent after Qi Yu, a career specialist in cadre training, took over as the foreign ministry's party secretary in January 2019—an unusual appointment to a post traditionally held by a vice foreign minister. A former deputy chief of the party's Central Organization Department, Qi was ranked second in the foreign ministry hierarchy, behind only the foreign minister, even though he lacked prior experience in foreign affairs and received no formal diplomatic title. His job was purely inward-facing, instilling discipline and fervor within the foreign service.

In internal speeches and writings, Qi called for compliance with Xi's demands for a more pugnacious posture in foreign affairs. Chinese diplomats must "firmly counterattack against words and deeds in the international arena that assault the leadership of China's Communist Party and our country's socialist system," Qi wrote, urging the foreign ministry to honor its tradition of being "the People's Liberation Army in civilian dress"—as Zhou Enlai envisioned in the late 1940s. "The demand is for Chinese diplomats to demonstrate greater fighting ability and become more visible," says Wu Xinbo, dean of the Institute of International Studies at Shanghai's Fudan University. "But there are many ways to achieve this—some practice tai chi, others throw Shaolin-style punches."[62]

Verbal jabs were more apparent during preparations for an April 2019 summit centered on Xi's Belt and Road initiative. One mid-level Chinese diplomat said governments that chose to skip the summit wouldn't be missed because there was "a long queue of countries" that wanted to attend.[63] During drafting meetings for the summit communiqué, a senior Chinese negotiator accused foreign counterparts of disrespecting China when they requested revisions to Beijing's proposed text. "Remind me to disinvite your president," the negotiator said to one foreign delegation.[64]

Sometimes the aggression appears mechanistic, performed simply to check bureaucratic boxes. When a senior Chinese foreign ministry official met some European Union diplomats for lunch, ostensibly to discuss China-Europe relations, he spent most of the time criticizing the U.S. with talking points he recited off a hefty dossier. "It was bizarre. We were wondering: Why are you telling us all this? We're not the Americans," one attendee told me later.[65] Some Chinese diplomats, aware that their browbeating behavior is counterproductive, try to assure foreign colleagues that their bluster is all business and nothing personal. One official, while lecturing a European envoy, threw in a dash of humor: "I may be a panda, but I am a kung fu panda."[66]

Qi's calls for combativeness manifested most visibly on social media. After Zhao Lijian's appointment as foreign ministry spokesman in August 2019, Chinese diplomats and embassies rushed to open their own Twitter accounts, including Zhao's boss, Hua Chunying, the ministry's top spokesperson. By the spring of 2020, the number of Chinese diplomatic accounts had risen to at least 137, from 38 a year ago, with the most active among them posting hundreds of tweets a month.[67]

Many of them leapt straight into battle, beating back criticism of Beijing's Covid-19 response as the contagion widened into a global pandemic in early 2020. Chinese diplomats urged other countries not to evacuate their citizens or cut travel links with China, decrying such measures as hostile and unnecessary. The foreign ministry pitched the crisis as a test of friendship and admonished ambassadors whose governments ignored Beijing's pleas. A Chinese vice foreign minister told the Italian envoy that Rome's decision to suspend direct flights between the two countries was an overreaction that ought to be rescinded immediately.[68] "True friendship emerges in times of adversity," said Hua, the ministry spokeswoman.[69]

Critics accused Beijing of hypocrisy, pointing to its treatment of Mexican citizens during an H1N1 swine flu pandemic in 2009, when China forced Mexicans within its borders into quarantine, suspended flights to Mexico, and stopped issuing visas to Mexicans.[70] "China never admitted this was wrong, or apologized," said Jorge Guajardo, Mexico's ambassador to China from 2007 to 2013.[71] Then in March 2020, after Xi declared initial success in containing the domestic spread of Covid-19, China blocked entry for nearly all foreigners and limited international air routes to weekly flights—the kind of border controls that Chinese diplomats told other governments not to impose on China.[72]

Chinese diplomats reserved their worst vitriol for those who accused Beijing of spreading Covid-19 globally. The Chinese embassy in Venezuela lashed out at local officials who referred to the "China coronavirus" by saying they were suffering from a political virus. "Since they are already very sick from this, hurry to ask for proper treatment. The first step might be to wear a mask and shut up," the embassy said.[73] China's embassy in Sri Lanka, meanwhile, took on a local activist who described the Chinese government as "low class" in a tweet criticizing state censorship. "Total death in #China #pandemic is 3344 till today, much smaller than your western 'high class' governments," the embassy tweeted at the activist, who had fewer than thirty followers at the time.[74]

By the time Lu Shaye, the envoy to France, joined the Covid-19 furor, he had already forged a promising career championing a more muscular foreign policy. In a 2013 essay, written while he was the foreign ministry's director general for African affairs, Lu argued that China should be "seizing the right to international discourse" to protect its interests and fulfill its role as a responsible power.[75] Promoted in 2015 to policy research director for the Communist Party's top foreign affairs committee, Lu urged Chinese diplomats to do battle with the West and convince more countries to "accept China, as a major Eastern power, standing at the top of the world."[76]

Lu applied his own advice in Ottawa, where he moved in 2017 to become Beijing's envoy to Canada. He sparred with local media, accusing them of portraying China negatively and frustrating efforts to negotiate a bilateral trade deal. Some Canadian media, Lu said, was "not willing to put China on an equal footing, deeming itself superior to China."[77] When Canada detained a well-connected Chinese telecommunications executive in December 2018, an arrest made at Washington's request, Lu became the face of China's ire. He wrote a fiery newspaper op-ed accusing his hosts of "Western egotism and white supremacy" and defended Beijing's detention of two Canadian citizens—both nabbed soon after the Chinese executive's arrest—as "China's self-defense."[78]

Beijing promoted Lu in summer 2019, appointing him ambassador to France—a senior role handling ties with a permanent member of the United Nations Security Council that customarily came with a vice ministerial rank. A fluent French speaker, Lu pressed hard for attention in Paris, where he and the Chinese embassy racked up more than sixty media engagements in his first year in the job, including interviews, briefings, and op-eds—more than three times as many as his predecessor had logged over a five-year stint.[79] "I hope I don't have to fight against France. The best thing is that we work together," Lu said at his first media briefing in Paris. "But if anything that harms our fundamental interests happens, then I would have to fight."

And fight he did. He and his subordinates attacked China's critics with metronomic pace, dismissing allegations of rights abuses in Xinjiang as "total bullshit" and arguing on Twitter over China's alleged culpability for Covid-19.[80] In one exchange with Paris-based researcher Antoine Bondaz, who tweeted sarcastic remarks about pro-Beijing trolls, the Chinese embassy called him "petite frappe," or "little rascal," earning Lu another dressing down from the French foreign ministry.[81]

Lu defended wolf warrior diplomacy as a legitimate response to foreign slander. "Westerners accuse us of deviating from diplomatic etiquette, but the criteria for assessing our own work aren't how foreigners view us," Lu said. "Whether our people are satisfied or not, whether they agree or not, these are the criteria we use for assessing our work."[82] And by most accounts, Chinese audiences delight in seeing their diplomats unleash lupine instincts. Fan clubs for Hua Chunying and Zhao Lijian sprouted on Chinese social media, where highlight reels showing their acerbic takedowns of Western powers often go viral.

Such displays, however, come with reputational cost. According to polls by the Pew Research Center, unfavorable views of China reached record levels in 2020 across a majority of the fourteen advanced economies surveyed—including the U.S., Britain, and Germany—as Covid-19 swept the world.[83] Negative sentiment toward China would remain elevated in these countries over subsequent years, and in some cases rise to new highs.[84] Scores of legislators, mostly from developed nations, banded together in 2020 to form a coalition, the Inter-Parliamentary Alliance on China, to organize international pressure against Beijing.[85] A think tank affiliated with China's

Ministry of State Security, the top civilian intelligence agency, issued an internal report—presented to Xi and other leaders in April 2020—that concluded that global anti-China sentiment had reached the highest levels since the crackdown on the 1989 Tiananmen Square protests.[86]

Some among China's diplomatic old guard voiced reservations about their successors' lupine tendencies. Fu Ying, a vice foreign minister from 2009 to 2013, wrote a *People's Daily* op-ed stressing that China must pay attention to how its messages are received by international audiences. "A country's power in international discourse relates not just to its right to speak up on the global stage, but more to the effectiveness and influence of its discourse," Fu wrote in April 2020. "Only by winning recognition from audiences and learning from feedback can the influence of our discourse be gradually strengthened."[87] Yuan Nansheng, a former ambassador who became a foreign policy think tanker, offered a starker warning, telling an interviewer: "History proves that when foreign policy gets hijacked by public opinion, it inevitably brings disastrous results."[88]

Opinions were split within the foreign ministry. Some tried to temper the aggression, but feared inviting a nationalistic backlash.[89] "This is a tough job," said one official, citing instructions to avoid behavior that can be perceived as "worshiping America" or "kneeling down before America."[90] Some ministry heavyweights openly rejected any notion of retreat. "The reason why there are 'wolf warriors' is because there are 'wolves' in this world," Liu Xiaoming, China's ambassador to Britain from 2010 to 2021, told state television. "Therefore, we encourage diplomats at all levels to take the initiative to fight."[91] And quite literally too, on rare occasions, most notably in October 2022 when Chinese consulate personnel in the English city of Manchester scuffled with anti–Communist Party protesters, and appeared to drag one demonstrator inside the consulate gates, throw him onto the ground, and punch him—before police broke up the melee.[92]

Xi himself has issued conflicting signals. At a Politburo meeting in May 2021, he called on the party to cultivate a "credible, lovable and respectable" image for China and grow its "circle of friends in international public opinion."[93] But he said officials must keep refining their abilities to wage a "public-opinion struggle"—a demand that senior diplomats distilled as a call to "never step back nor give an inch on matters of principle."[94]

Some prominent nationalist commentators found it hard to tamp down the rah-rah rhetoric. Weeks before Xi's Politburo speech, Chinese social media users hurled abuse at Hu Xijin, then the editor in chief of the nationalistic party tabloid *Global Times*, after he criticized a state-run microblog that had mocked India's Covid-19 crisis. A Weibo account affiliated with the Communist Party's law-enforcement commission published a post—since taken down—that juxtaposed images of a Chinese space rocket launch and an Indian funeral pyre, along with the caption: "China lighting a fire versus India lighting a fire." Hu urged Chinese netizens to "place Chinese society on a moral high ground," only to be inundated with comments calling him a traitor.[95]

Those who found balance between Xi's demands for combativeness and cordiality reaped reward.[96] Qin Gang, a career diplomat who won Xi's trust while accompanying him on diplomatic engagements as the foreign ministry's protocol chief, enjoyed an especially rapid ascent. Appointed vice foreign minister in 2018, Qin forged a reputation among Western diplomats in Beijing as a more nuanced wolf warrior who could project public charm while browbeating foreigners in private, and often asserted hard-line stances that accorded with Xi's priorities. His fighting spirit paid off three years later, when Xi handpicked Qin as envoy to Washington, even though he hadn't previously served as ambassador or handled any portfolios directly related to U.S. affairs. People familiar with the decision said Xi favored Qin over the foreign ministry's preferred candidate, a U.S. specialist whom the Chinese leader saw as too meek to deal with an increasingly hostile American elite.[97]

In Washington, Qin alternated between cordial outreach and steely rhetoric, glad-handing business leaders and regional officials while barking back against perceived U.S. provocations. When he decided to throw punches, he didn't hold back. During one Zoom call hosted by a U.S. nonprofit that promotes exchanges with China, Qin responded bluntly when asked how bilateral ties can be improved: "If we cannot resolve our differences, please shut up."[98]

Qin struggled to secure meaningful engagements with senior policy makers and power brokers in Washington, some of whom were put off by his hawkish image.[99] But his bosses didn't see that as a failure. In the fall of 2022, the Communist Party elevated Qin into its Central Committee, making him the first sitting ambassador to be directly promoted to full membership of the elite body since the Mao era. Xi approved Qin's appointment as foreign minister two months later.[100]

EAST RISES, WEST DECLINES

DAYS AFTER A PRO-TRUMP MOB stormed the United States Capitol in January 2021, a stunning outburst that symbolized the dysfunctions in American democracy,

China's Communist Party elite assembled in Beijing to hear Xi Jinping chart their priorities for the coming year.[101] The general secretary exuded cautious confidence, painting a sanguine picture of his country's prospects while acknowledging that significant challenges lay ahead. "Today's world is going through profound changes unseen in a century," Xi said. "But the times and trends are on our side."

State media published only the gist of Xi's remarks while indulging in schadenfreude over the turmoil in Washington, saying the U.S. had become a "failed state" in the eyes of its allies.[102] A more nuanced appraisal emerged as officials spread Xi's word. "'The East is rising, and the West is declining' is a trend, and developments in the international situation are favorable to us," said Chen Yixin, a senior security official and Xi ally, relaying his leader's appraisal of the geopolitical landscape. Even so, "containment and suppression by the United States are major threats, both in the form of unplanned clashes and protracted warfare," Chen said.[103] One county official cited a starker assessment. "The biggest source of chaos in the world today is the United States," the official quoted Xi as saying. "The United States is the biggest threat to our country's development and security."[104]

Xi's prognosis underscores the dramatic shifts that have unfolded under his watch in the world's most important bilateral relationship, veering from uneasy competition to open hostility. The growing strategic distrust between the U.S. and China has led officials and scholars on both sides to raise the specter of a "new Cold War," or even an armed conflict between two nuclear powers. Harvard political scientist Graham Allison's warnings about a "Thucydides's trap," a theory that rivalries between an emerging power and an incumbent hegemon often lead to war, gained so much currency that former Australian prime minister Kevin Rudd wrote a book on how to prevent "the avoidable war."[105]

Sino-U.S. relations had traced a broadly benign trajectory for decades, with Richard Nixon's China visit in 1972 heralding an era of "engagement" that led to normalized relations and forged political, business, and cultural links that still bind the two nations today.[106] American advocates of engagement believed that the U.S., by expanding bilateral contacts, could help China evolve into a more-open society that hewed closer toward Western norms.[107] Chinese reformers, for their part, wanted to tap foreign expertise to boost economic development.[108] They adapted Western practices for the Chinese context but remained suspicious of U.S. efforts to encourage "peaceful evolution" in China through ideological subversion—a concern that Xi himself, as a local official, had articulated in the wake of the 1989 Tiananmen Square protests.[109]

Engagement endured severe setbacks, particularly U.S. sanctions against Beijing over the June 4 massacre, the 1999 U.S. bombing of the Chinese embassy in Belgrade, and the 2001 collision between a Chinese fighter jet and an American surveillance plane. President Bill Clinton promoted economic ties with Beijing but eased his demands for Chinese progress on human rights, facilitating China's accession to the WTO in 2001. The two economies became so intertwined by the mid-2000s that scholars coined the term "Chimerica" to describe their symbiosis.[110] Boosted by the outsourcing of American manufacturing, and widening access to U.S. markets, China grew its economy into the world's second largest by 2010, trailing only the U.S.

The global financial crisis dispelled any begrudging deference that Beijing might have shown Washington. After years of advice and admonishment from U.S. officials and executives on the merits of American-style capitalism, Chinese leaders could justifiably argue that their system was just as good, if not better. Former U.S. treasury secretary Hank Paulson recalled a 2008 meeting with China's then vice premier Wang Qishan, who conveyed how a stumbling America had lost its luster in the eyes of the Beijing elite. "You were my teacher, but now here I am in my teacher's domain," Wang told Paulson. "And look at your system, Hank. We aren't sure we should be learning from you anymore."[111]

President Obama saw China as a potential partner in tackling global challenges, rather than a predestined adversary. He sought cooperation in areas of mutual interest—restoring global growth, preventing nuclear proliferation in Iran and North Korea, and combating climate change—while sidestepping confrontation over subjects like human rights.[112] "We internalized the view that it is better not to confront China on values-based issues, because that will make them dig in," recalls Ben Rhodes, the former deputy national security adviser to Obama. "I think that was a mistake."[113]

Beijing's perceived intransigence, particularly at the 2009 Copenhagen climate summit and with Yang Jiechi's outburst at the 2010 ASEAN Regional Forum, pushed Washington toward a firmer approach. In 2011, the Obama administration announced a "pivot to Asia," whereby the U.S. would deploy a majority of its military assets to the Pacific, strengthen ties with regional powers like Japan, South Korea, Australia, and India, and negotiate a major trade pact—the Trans-Pacific Partnership—that would pointedly exclude China.[114] Despite Obama's assurances to the contrary, Chinese hawks cited his "pivot" as proof of American intentions to contain China.

Washington saw Xi's ascent as an opportunity for a fresh start. When then vice president Joe Biden went to China in 2011 to size up Xi, he found a seemingly open-minded man who peppered his visitors with questions about U.S. politics while speaking candidly on China's domestic challenges.[115] Though Xi came across as far more confident and forthright than Hu Jintao, American officials assessed that he likely shared Hu's commitment to stable ties with the U.S. and deeper integration into the prevailing international order.[116] Daniel Russel, a senior Obama administration official, recalls suggesting to the Chinese envoy that Xi could make a positive impression during his 2012 visit to the U.S. by giving a talk to American officials and addressing sensitive issues like human rights. And Xi did just that.[117] At this point, "he still appeared to be receptive, flexible and open," Russel says.[118]

People who've interacted with Xi say he doesn't seem to bear any deep-seated animosity toward the U.S., and, in fact, he has shown some affinity for American culture. Xi first visited the U.S. in 1985, when he, then a county chief, led an agricultural study delegation to rural Iowa and home-stayed with a local family—whom he would visit again in 2012.[119] As a municipal and provincial leader, Xi made it a point to interact with American diplomats, with whom he shared his fondness for *Saving Private Ryan* and other Hollywood blockbusters about World War II.[120] In 2010, while he was vice president, Xi sent his daughter and only child to study at Harvard University.[121]

Nonetheless, Xi doesn't speak or read English, "which means that his understanding of America has always been intermediated through official Chinese sources of translation, which are not always known for accuracy, subtlety, or nuance," writes Kevin Rudd, who has met Xi on numerous occasions since the 1980s, when Rudd was an Australian diplomat in China. Xi's views on the United States are likely shaped by latent biases within the Chinese foreign policy and intelligence bureaucracies, as well as the tendency of officials to second-guess what Xi wants to hear, says Rudd, who notes that American leaders face similar problems in trying to understand China.[122]

Xi toughened his demeanor as he took power and grew into the job. By the time Obama hosted Xi for a state visit in 2015, the Chinese leader appeared "much more decisive and much more confident," showing firmness when laying down Beijing's markers on strategic issues like North Korea, Russel recalls.[123] When Obama pressed Xi on China's cyber theft of American technology and efforts to militarize artificial islands in the South China Sea, the Chinese leader seemingly acquiesced by publicly pledging to stop such activities, only for American officials to discover later that the industrial espionage and militarization were continuing unabated.[124]

Trade imbalances, ultimately, tipped the scales in Washington on China. In

2016, Donald Trump won the presidency in part by tapping blue-collar resentment over job losses blamed on cheap Chinese imports, a sentiment he fueled on the campaign trail with claims that China committed "rape" against the U.S. with unfair trade practices. The result stunned Chinese officials, who scrambled to acquaint themselves with Trump's mercurial ways.[125] Despite a honeymoon period in 2017, during which Trump and Xi hosted each other with lavish receptions at the Mar-a-Lago resort in Florida and in Beijing respectively, the U.S. launched a trade war the following year, imposing tariffs on hundreds of billions of dollars' worth of Chinese imports.[126]

As Trump and his advisers saw it, China had misled the U.S. about its long-term goals and reneged on its pledges—as part of its WTO accession—to transition toward a market economy. They believed Xi had not only failed to open China's markets fully, but doubled down on its model of state-led development by protecting key industries, subsidizing exports, stealing foreign technology, and manipulating its currency. White House hawks called for export controls and other curbs that would cut Chinese access to U.S. technology and "decouple" the world's two largest economies.[127] Similar sentiment swept Western capitals that previously flattered Xi with red-carpet treatment. The Chinese leader once could address Australia's parliament, share a ride with Britain's Queen Elizabeth II in her horse-drawn carriage, and receive a grand welcome at the Arc de Triomphe in Paris, but such niceties dried up as those governments started criticizing Beijing for its Covid-19 response, statist industrial policies, and rights abuses in Xinjiang and Hong Kong.[128]

Even longtime advocates of U.S. engagement with China conceded that their approach had become outmoded.[129] Whereas American policy-makers could justify dealing with a one-party state as long as China kept integrating with a rules-based international order and evolved toward political openness, Xi's autocratic turn upended this bargain. "China continues to keep whole sectors of its economy off-limits to U.S. businesses, while expropriating American intellectual property and circumscribing the activities of American civil-society organizations, religious groups, media outlets, think tanks and academics," said Orville Schell and Larry Diamond, lead authors of a 2018 report by prominent China scholars and former officials that urged firmer resistance against Beijing's efforts to influence American society. "Getting China to agree to a new level of fairness and reciprocity may be exceedingly difficult and even create some risks, but it is the only path to a healthier, more durable relationship between the two countries."[130]

Tensions came to a head in December 2018, when Canadian authorities—

acting at Washington's request—detained Meng Wanzhou, the chief financial officer of Chinese telecommunications giant Huawei, while she was transiting through Vancouver. U.S. prosecutors wanted to extradite Meng, a daughter of Huawei's founder, to face wire and bank fraud charges related to alleged violations of American sanctions on Iran. American officials hoped the case would aid their efforts to undercut Huawei, a global leader in developing fifth-generation, or 5G, wireless technology that can deliver ultra-high-speed connectivity, a sector where the U.S. has been laggard. The arrest took place the day when Trump was dining with Xi at a Group of Twenty summit in Buenos Aires, though White House officials made no mention of the case at the time—an omission that struck the Chinese leader as deceptive and insulting when he later learned of the arrest.[131]

For Xi, Trump's trade war only reinforced his belief that China must become economically self-sufficient and globally dominant in strategic technologies.[132] "Unilateralism and trade protectionism are on the rise, forcing us to take the road of self-reliance," Xi said while touring China's northeastern rust belt in 2018. "China ultimately has to rely on itself."[133] He outlined new efforts to boost domestic companies and consumption, with foreign investments and technologies playing a supporting role.[134] His administration reined in private businesses to steer them closer to the party's priorities, while boosting state-owned enterprises with hopes of creating new juggernauts in key industries.

In its broadest strokes, Xi's strategy echoes past analyses by a leading member of his brain trust—Wang Huning, the party theorist who joined the Politburo Standing Committee in 2017.[135] In a 1991 book, *America Against America*, which recounted his observations over six months in the U.S. from 1988 to 1989, Wang concluded that the world's reigning superpower was riven with cultural flaws that could sow the seeds of its decline.[136] American individualism, hedonism, and democracy would eventually blunt the country's competitive edge, he argued, whereas rival nations powered by superior values of collectivism, selflessness, and authoritarianism would rise to challenge American supremacy.[137]

In some ways, China was already pushing ahead. Under Xi, the party poured massive resources into developing advanced digital technologies, aiming to become the world's largest supplier of 5G network gear and create a "Digital Silk Road" lined with countries that use Chinese hardware and adopt its "Great Firewall" approach to managing the internet.[138] Beijing also telegraphed ambitions to supplant the West in setting global industrial standards, and ensure that Chinese norms would shape key technologies of the future like artificial intelligence.[139] By 2019, Chinese officials were leading four of the United Nations' seventeen specialized agencies, with the most recent addition beating Western-backed candidates to take the top job at the Food and Agriculture Organization that year. No other nation had its citizens running more than one U.N. agency at that point, and it took a concerted U.S.-led lobbying campaign to block Beijing's bid in 2020 to secure the leadership of a fifth body, the World Intellectual Property Organization, a role that went to a Singaporean candidate.[140]

U.S. antagonism against China went full throttle by the fourth year of Trump's presidency. Secretary of State Mike Pompeo alleged that Covid-19 originated from a Chinese laboratory, denounced the Communist Party's treatment of Uyghurs as genocide, and urged the Chinese people to alter the party's behavior—remarks that Beijing saw as a call for regime change.[141] Washington sanctioned Chinese officials who allegedly oversaw political repression in Hong Kong and Xinjiang, arranged high-level visits to Taipei, and sent more military forces to challenge Beijing's sovereignty claims in the South China Sea and the Taiwan Strait.[142] The Trump administration also widened its trade war into a broader struggle for technological supremacy, imposing export controls to cut off Huawei from advanced American know-how, excluding the company and other Chinese tech firms from U.S. telecom networks, and blocking Americans from investing in Chinese firms deemed to be aiding the People's Liberation Army.[143]

China responded where it could. In March 2020, Beijing expelled more than a dozen American journalists after the Trump administration forced some sixty Chinese state media staffers to leave the U.S.[144] The Chinese government imposed retaliatory sanctions on American officials seen as antagonizing China over human rights, while Chinese diplomats pushed conspiracy theories that Covid-19 came from a U.S. military laboratory in Fort Detrick.[145] After Washington forced the Chinese consulate in Houston to shut down in July 2020, Beijing ordered the closure of the U.S. consulate in the southwestern city of Chengdu.[146]

Joe Biden's election as president brought little respite for Beijing. He declared that the U.S. would engage in "steep competition" with China, and charted a broad strategy for facing down the People's Republic across economic, military, and diplomatic fronts.[147] He extended some of Trump's punitive measures against Chinese officials and companies, signed a new law aimed at boosting American semiconductor manufacturing, and curbed exports of advanced chips and chip-making equipment to China.[148] Biden also beefed up U.S. security presence in the Indo-Pacific region, and pledged to team up with like-minded countries to pressure Beijing on security, trade, and human rights. Within the Washington beltway, many believe that the impulse to compete with, even contain, China has become an entrenched bipartisan program that will define American foreign policy for decades to come. "The danger for China is their own overreach. That's what got America into trouble," says Rhodes, the former Obama adviser. "The U.S. should figure out how to position itself to take advantage 30 years from now, when China is exhausted and overreached."[149]

Beijing too has braced for a protracted struggle. Though the Chinese elite often deride the U.S. for its political dysfunction, many still accord begrudging respect for American power, and Xi himself has told officials that there are still areas where "the West is strong and the East is weak." Speaking to Biden after his 2020 election win, Xi said he believed that U.S. efforts to rebuild its alliances were meant to "hurt China."[150] Such concerns would drive Xi to continue backing Russia, a strategic partner he had cultivated for years, even after Moscow drew widespread condemnation for invading Ukraine in 2022.[151]

China's top diplomats threw down the gauntlet at their first meeting with Biden administration officials, held in Alaska in early 2021. Yang Jiechi, Xi's foreign policy chief at the time, berated secretary of state Antony Blinken and national security adviser Jake Sullivan with lengthy lectures touting the superiority of China's political system while skewering America for its racial problems and democratic failings. "The United States does not have the qualification to say that it wants to speak to China from a position of strength," Yang said. "Our history will show that one can only cause damages to himself if he wants to strangle or suppress the Chinese people."[152]

Yang's true audience was at home. His remarks went viral on the Chinese internet, where Yang won praise for sticking it to the Americans. State media juxtaposed an image of the Anchorage meeting against a photograph from the signing of the 1901 Boxer Protocol, where Qing officials acquiesced to an unequal treaty with the Eight-Nation Alliance, which comprised the U.S. and other mostly Western powers.[153] The message was clear: China considers itself a peer to the U.S., and the Americans had better do the same.

WHEN ELEPHANTS FIGHT

DURING A LIGHTER MOMENT at a gathering of Asian and European leaders in the summer of 2016, the Mongolian hosts staged cultural performances for their guests.

Chinese premier Li Keqiang settled into a seat beside a fellow Asian leader, while a Mongolian official offered a running commentary on the displays. Wrestlers emerged at one point, dueling in pairs to demonstrate their art. No weight categories applied, and the wrestlers took on opponents of all sizes, the Mongolian official explained. "Sometimes the smaller ones win," he said. Li wasn't impressed, replying, "I don't see any of the smaller wrestlers winning." The Asian leader interjected: "The big are bullying the small."[154]

Though speaking in jest, the Asian leader conveyed a sentiment felt among China's neighbors since Xi Jinping took power. Just days earlier, an international tribunal in The Hague had issued a landmark ruling against Beijing, saying its claims to historic and economic rights over most of the South China Sea have no legal basis.[155] China had snubbed the proceedings since they started in early 2013, insisting that the Permanent Court of Arbitration lacked jurisdiction over the case that the Philippines filed against Chinese sovereignty claims. Rather than fight a risky legal battle, Beijing spent the intervening years changing facts on the ground—reclaiming land around Chinese-controlled geographical features, fortifying these artificial islands with military assets, and using them to project power.[156]

Five Southeast Asian nations assert sovereignty and economic rights in the South China Sea that overlap with Beijing's claims over the strategic waters, traversed by more than half the world's seaborne trade and believed to hold vast energy resources.[157] While some of these countries have also expanded the islands under their control over the years, China's island-building campaign far outstripped any rival effort in pace and scale, adding some 3,200 acres of new land and a formidable array of airfields, air-defense systems, and anti-ship missiles.[158] Some Southeast Asian governments joined the U.S. in accusing Beijing of fueling regional tensions, but Xi doubled down, insisting that islands in the South China Sea "have been China's territory since ancient times."[159]

When the Hague tribunal ruled against Beijing in July 2016, the Chinese government declared the decision "null and void" and continued reinforcing its islands.[160] Rival claimants complained but could do little to compel China to abide by the ruling. Even the U.S., which sent warships and aircraft to challenge Beijing's "excessive territorial claims" and assert "freedom of navigation" in the South China Sea, was otherwise powerless to reverse the fait accompli that Beijing had established. "That paper, in real life, between nations, is nothing," then Philippine president Rodrigo Duterte, whose predecessor sought the arbitration, said of the ruling. "I will throw that away in the wastebasket."[161]

Xi's handling of the South China Sea disputes exemplifies his approach to foreign policy—an uncompromising pursuit of Chinese interests that excites nationalist passions but inflames geopolitical tensions. His style has also asked uncomfortable questions of the many countries that count China as their top trading partner while sheltering under an American security umbrella. As Washington and Beijing battle for preeminence, more governments face difficult reassessments on where they stand in this superpower showdown—whether they can tolerate an assertive China, or push back at the risk of incurring grave costs.

South Korea, a U.S. ally that trades more with China than it does with America and Japan combined, confronted this conundrum in 2017 after deploying an American ballistic missile defense system, known as THAAD, which came with a powerful radar that Beijing believed could glean intelligence on its nuclear weapons.[162] China responded angrily with economic warfare. It blocked shipments of Korean consumer products, denied visas for K-pop artists, disrupted Chinese operations of a South Korean conglomerate that put up a golf course to host the THAAD system, and curtailed travel to South Korea—costing its tourism sector an estimated $7 billion.[163]

Seoul engineered a thaw by telling Beijing that it wouldn't deploy additional THAAD batteries, wouldn't join a U.S.-led missile defense network, and wouldn't form a trilateral military alliance with the U.S. and Japan. At the same time, South Korean officials kept stressing their commitment to strong ties with the U.S.[164] Asking whether South Korea will "choose either China or the United States" is like "asking a child whether you like your dad or your mom," a senior legislator told the *Atlantic* magazine. "We cannot abandon economy for the sake of security, and we cannot abandon security for the sake of economy."[165]

Australia, another U.S. ally reliant on Chinese trade, faced similar repercussions after Canberra blocked Huawei from its 5G networks, called for a global inquiry into the origins of Covid-19, and criticized the political repression in Hong Kong. Beijing fought back with informal sanctions—suspending beef imports from some Australian slaughterhouses, imposing tariffs on Australian barley and wine, and warning Chinese citizens not to travel to Australia.[166] Beijing also detained a China-born Australian journalist working for Chinese state television, citing national security offenses, though her friends suspected that bilateral tensions were to blame.[167] "China is angry," a Chinese embassy official in Canberra told an Australian newspaper. "If you make China the enemy, China will be the enemy."[168]

Canada strayed into the U.S.-China crossfire after arresting Huawei chief financial officer Meng Wanzhou in 2018.[169] Beijing saw her arrest as a provocation and promised "grave consequences" for Canada if Meng wasn't released. Within days, China detained two Canadian citizens, former diplomat Michael Kovrig and entrepreneur Michael Spavor, who were later accused of conspiring to steal state secrets.[170] Weeks later, a Canadian man jailed in northeastern China for smuggling drugs was retried and sentenced to death.[171] Though Chinese officials denied engaging in "hostage diplomacy," Beijing engaged in secret talks with Washington and Ottawa to secure Meng's release in return for freeing Kovrig and Spavor. A deal was agreed to in 2021, and the two Michaels were released after 1,019 days of detention. Meng returned from Canada at the same time after she admitted to some wrongdoing, in exchange for U.S. prosecutors deferring and eventually dropping bank fraud charges against her.[172]

Lithuania suffered China's wrath in 2021, when the tiny Baltic state of less than 3 million people decided to boost ties with Taiwan and withdraw from Beijing's diplomatic platform for engaging with Central and Eastern European countries, known as China-CEEC.[173] Chinese pressure intensified after Lithuania allowed the Taiwanese government to open a representative office—a de facto embassy—in Vilnius under the name of "Taiwan," spurning the usual practice of calling it a "Taipei" office. China recalled its ambassador from Vilnius, declined to renew accreditation for Lithuanian diplomats, blocked Lithuanian companies and products, and even held up customs processing for European goods with Lithuanian-made parts—prompting the EU to launch a WTO case accusing Beijing of discriminatory trade practices.[174]

China's exertions stirred apprehension in parts of Asia and Europe. Opinion polls showed unfavorable views of China reaching or hovering near historic highs across Australia, Canada, and South Korea in 2020 and 2021, mirroring the rise in tensions with Beijing.[175] Australia signed up to a trilateral security partnership with the U.K. and the U.S., known as AUKUS, while the likes of Canada, South Korea, Vietnam, and New Zealand started joining activities arranged under the Washington-led Quadrilateral Security Dialogue, a four-nation platform comprising the U.S., Japan, India, and Australia.[176] In 2022, the Baltic states of Estonia and Latvia followed Lithuania in withdrawing from the China-CEEC platform, reducing what was once informally known as the "17+1" bloc to "14+1."[177] Across Africa, where many countries are major recipients of Chinese loans, citizens have increasingly voiced concerns about their governments' high levels of indebtedness to Beijing.[178]

The contest for superpower proxies has grown particularly intense in Southeast Asia, a region of more than 600 million people sometimes called "the Balkans of

Asia," where great-power interests often intersect over shipping lanes and resources in the South China Sea. Although the U.S. asserts no claims in these waters, Washington has long declared its interests in ensuring peace and freedom of navigation across a key artery of global trade, whereas Beijing senses a hegemonic desire to preserve an American-led security order.

Modern Chinese claims in the area date back to the late 1940s, when Chiang Kai-shek's Kuomintang government published maps featuring an eleven-dash line that enveloped most of the South China Sea. In the years after the Communist Party seized power in 1949, Beijing dropped two dashes around waters off Vietnam, creating what became known as the "nine-dash line," which loops around some 2 million square miles of maritime space—about 22 percent of China's land area—and denotes broad claims that overlap with those of the Philippines, Vietnam, Malaysia, Brunei, and Indonesia.[179] Beijing has neither published coordinates for the line nor explained what it means, and rival claimants can only guess. Does the line represent sovereignty claims over land features like the Spratly and Paracel island chains? Perhaps it demarcates a national boundary, implying that waters within the line are part of China's territorial sea? Or does it reflect "historic" claims over the area and certain economic rights?

The ambiguity is useful for Beijing. "It allows China the flexibility to interpret its position to serve the audience at hand," explained Gregory Poling, an expert on the South China Sea disputes at the Center for Strategic and International Studies in Washington. "Without a defined Chinese position, resolving claims and reconciling positions is not possible."[180] By tying rival claimants down in protracted negotiations, Beijing also buys time to consolidate control over claimed territory in ways that other countries can't challenge or reverse.[181]

China has also frustrated a cohesive Southeast Asian response by playing individual countries off each other. Cambodia and Laos, both recipients of Chinese largesse, often sided with Beijing during discussions on the South China Sea at the Association of Southeast Asian Nations, a ten-member bloc that operates by consensus. Beijing and ASEAN have yet to finalize a code of conduct for the South China Sea after agreeing to draft one in 2002, a delay Southeast Asian officials blame on Beijing's stalling tactics. Even the Philippines, which filed for arbitration against China, reversed course in 2016 after electing a new president, Rodrigo Duterte, who tried to drum up Chinese investment by currying favor with Xi—thus playing into Beijing's preference for facing down rival claimants in one-to-one talks.

The one ASEAN member that has spoken up most consistently on the South

China Sea disputes, however, isn't a claimant state. Singapore, a small island entrepôt turned financial hub that owes its success to maritime trade, insists on punctilious compliance with international law and fervently resists Beijing's "might makes right" approach. For this city-state of 5.6 million people, it is a matter of life and death— without a rules-based international order, where nations big and small abide by the same principles, there can be no guarantees for its existence as a sovereign state.

It is a belief hard-baked into the psyche of Singaporean leaders by their country's troubled birth. Singapore exited the British empire in 1963 to join the new Federation of Malaysia, but the union lasted just under two years before racial violence and political discord drove the city's separation to become an independent state. Lee Kuan Yew, Singapore's founding prime minister, had no illusions about the dangers his country faced—an anomalous Chinese-majority state in a region where most Chinese diaspora are minority groups. There were Cold War sensitivities to navigate too, thanks to the port city's strategic location between the Pacific and Indian Oceans. "It is not due to any special virtue or attractiveness of my people that we receive considerable attention from the Americans, the Soviet Union, the Chinese and the Europeans, who were first there," Lee told a 1973 gathering of national leaders from the British Commonwealth.[182]

When Australian prime minister Gough Whitlam remarked that Soviet ships couldn't go to Singapore because the city-state has a large ethnic Chinese population, "the Soviet Union immediately diverted four Soviet tenders, feeder ships, to Singapore for repairs, to see whether we were Chinese or Singaporeans. We repaired them," Lee said.[183] "The fact is, as the President of Tanzania has said, when elephants fight, the grass suffers," he said. "The thought occurred to me that when elephants flirt, the grass also suffers. And when they make love, it is disastrous."[184]

Despite its anti-communist stance, Singapore started threading a middle path between capitalist America and socialist China, cultivating ties with both powers to advance its own interests. The city-state hosted U.S. military forces passing through the region and bought American arms for its own defense, but never became a formal ally with Washington. Singapore sought wide-ranging cooperation with Beijing, pouring investments into Chinese industrial and real estate projects. Its government encouraged Singaporeans to learn Mandarin—while discarding other Chinese dialects—in part as a language for doing business with China.[185] The city-state has hosted more than fifty thousand Chinese officials for study visits and training programs since the mid-1990s, and maintained regular exchanges with some of the

Communist Party's most powerful and secretive agencies—including its top disciplinary and law-enforcement commissions, and its personnel department.[186] And as
China gained clout on the international stage, Singapore presented itself as a cultural
gateway between East and West, hosting events such as the Shangri-La Dialogue, an
annual security conference that gathers defense chiefs and military brass from the
Asia-Pacific and beyond, including the U.S. and China.

Singapore's insistence on its autonomy has at times sparked spats with the U.S.
and China. The city-state forced out a U.S. diplomat in 1988 for allegedly interfer-
ing in local politics, and caned an American teenager for vandalism in 1994 despite
Washington's pleas for clemency.[187] When Singapore's deputy prime minister Lee
Hsien Loong went to Taiwan on a private trip in 2004, just weeks before he became
premier, Beijing criticized what it saw as a violation of the "one China" principle
and canceled some visits to Singapore, though relations recovered after Lee criticized
advocates of Taiwan independence later that year.[188] "This isn't going to be the last
time our relations with a major friendly power are strained," Lee said in one of his
first major speeches as prime minister.[189]

Beijing sometimes sees Singapore's outspokenness as a nuisance. When Lee
raised the South China Sea disputes at an ASEAN summit, a senior Chinese diplomat told a Singaporean counterpart that "silence is golden."[190] Tensions boiled over
in 2016, when Lee urged compliance with the Hague tribunal ruling. "On the South
China Sea, we have got our own stand, principled, consistent; different from China's,
different from the Philippines or America," he said in a policy speech. "Other countries will persuade us to side with them, one side or the other, and we have to choose
our own place to stand."[191]

Lee's remarks irked Chinese officials who felt that Singapore was acting in concert with Washington. That belief seemed to crystalize at the Non-Aligned Movement summit in September 2016, where ASEAN countries jointly proposed to revise
the final communiqué to include concerns over South China Sea tensions.[192] Chinese
officials came to believe that the Singaporean delegation was lobbying to add references to the Hague ruling, a perception fueled by the fact that a Singaporean diplomat presented the ASEAN proposal, instead of a delegate from Laos, which held the
ASEAN chairmanship at the time.[193]

Days later, the Communist Party–run tabloid *Global Times* published a report
claiming that Singapore had lobbied in vain for references to the tribunal ruling to
be included in the NAM summit communiqué, and that the Singaporean delega-

tion made "hostile attacks" against other countries when its proposal was rejected.[194] Singapore's envoy to Beijing issued a rebuttal, criticizing the *Global Times* for publishing an "irresponsible report replete with fabrications" and pointing out that the proposed changes were collectively drafted by all ASEAN members. The Chinese foreign ministry echoed the *Global Times* account, accusing "individual countries" of trying to insert South China Sea–related content into the communiqué, while the newspaper's chief editor stood by the report and accused Singapore of "damaging China's interests."[195]

Tensions flared higher in November, when Hong Kong customs officials seized nine Singapore army armored vehicles that were being shipped back to the city-state from Taiwan, where the Singaporean military has conducted training since the 1970s. Hong Kong held the vehicles for two months, saying the shipping firm lacked the permits for ferrying military gear. But many Singaporeans suspected ongoing tensions with Beijing had motivated the seizure, at least in part.[196] The spat stirred public debate, with some Singaporeans accusing their government of needlessly antagonizing China—the city-state's biggest trading partner. Politicians and establishment figures took pains to explain how Singapore's interests are sometimes best served by standing up to Beijing. "Our government is not rash but the considerations are not just relations with China," wrote the retired diplomat Bilahari Kausikan, who served as the Singapore foreign ministry's top civil servant from 2010 to 2013. "If we allow ourselves to be intimidated by Beijing what do you think our immediate neighbors will think?"[197]

Bilateral ties have also been complicated by Beijing's perceptions that Singapore is a "Chinese" society. Three-quarters of Singapore citizens are ethnic Chinese, mostly descendants of people who migrated from southern China over the past two centuries or so.[198] Chinese state agencies routinely promote cultural exchanges by arranging for Chinese Singaporeans to visit their ancestral homes and attend classes on Chinese history and calligraphy. Encouraged by Xi to rally the Chinese diaspora behind Beijing's interests, many mainland officials treat their Singaporean interlocutors as distant kin who should show fondness, if not loyalty, toward the motherland. "You're also Chinese," some would say to me when they learn that I'm from Singapore. "You should understand us better."

Singaporean leaders insist that they are a multiracial country, and since Lee Kuan Yew met Mao Zedong in 1976, they have made it a point to speak English in formal engagements with Chinese counterparts. When Deng Xiaoping visited the island in 1978, Lee told him that Chinese Singaporeans were forging their own destiny and didn't see themselves as "overseas Chinese."[199] Singapore was among the last nations in Southeast Asia to establish formal relations with China, doing so in 1990 only after neighboring Indonesia, a Muslim-majority country, restored suspended ties with Beijing.[200] It was a conscious choice, Singaporean leaders say, to avoid being seen as a cat's paw for China.

Ordinary Singaporeans, however, don't necessarily subscribe to their government's delicate balancing act. Public sentiment toward China diverges broadly along cultural, educational, and generational lines. Singapore's colonial heritage, including British-style parliamentary and common law systems, means that many within the English-speaking middle class feel more affinity with the West than the People's Republic, as do members of a ruling elite dominated by graduates of top American and British universities. Younger Singaporeans often grow up on eclectic diets of Western, Japanese, and Korean pop culture and are thus less persuaded by Chinese propaganda.

But China's ethnocentric and anti-Western rhetoric have found an eager audience among older Chinese Singaporeans, many of whom were shaped by Lee Kuan Yew's fiery advocacy of "Asian values" in opposition to Western liberalism. They delight in seeing Asians stand tall on the global stage, partake in a sense of Chinese civilizational pride, and echo Beijing's narratives that reach them through Chinese state television programs and social media apps like WeChat.[201] Many Singaporean entrepreneurs with interests in China sympathize with their Chinese partners' political views. New immigrants from China, who arrived in large numbers over recent years to study and work in Singapore, created lively online communities where pro-Beijing views seep into local discourse. Such narratives often criticize Singapore's strong ties with the U.S. and argue that a Chinese-majority state should be subservient to a "Greater China."

In a 2021 Pew Research study of public opinion in seventeen advanced economies, Singapore was the only country where a majority of respondents—some 70 percent—voiced confidence in Xi's handling of world affairs.[202] Doublethink Lab, a Taipei-based research firm that studies influence and disinformation operations, ranked Singapore second most exposed to Beijing's influence efforts in a 2022 index of thirty-six countries assessed for their susceptibility to Chinese narratives, trailing only Cambodia.[203] China's cachet in one of Asia's most Westernized societies offers a warning for the U.S. and other liberal democracies, that the ideological norms underpinning the American-led world order aren't necessarily self-evident, a former Singaporean diplomat told me. "If those who would champion 'Western' norms—such as rule of law, democracy, and sovereign equality—can't even persuade Singaporeans that their vision of world order is preferable to the Chinese one," he said, "then what chance do they stand with the developing world?"

Singapore has taken steps to counter Chinese interference. In 2017, the city-state expelled Chinese-American academic Huang Jing for allegedly working as an "agent of influence" for an unspecified foreign country—which some local officials privately identify as China, where Huang was born. A professor at Singapore's Lee Kuan School of Public Policy at the time, Huang was accused of working with foreign intelligence agents in trying to sway the city-state's foreign policy and public opinion by passing along purportedly "privileged information" to influential Singaporeans.[204] Huang denied the allegations but acknowledged making "some mistakes, for which I should pay the price."[205] He spent a year working in the U.S. before moving to China to take up academic positions in Beijing and later Shanghai.

The tale took another twist in 2020 when the U.S. jailed one of Huang's former PhD students for spying on Beijing's behalf. Dickson Yeo, a Singaporean national, pleaded guilty to using a fake consulting business as a front for gathering sensitive information for Chinese intelligence services, which recruited him in 2015 while he was studying at the Lee Kuan Yew School.[206] Huang rejected insinuations that he had recruited or "talent spotted" Yeo, telling me that U.S. law enforcement didn't contact him over Yeo's case.[207] Even so, some analysts said the case raised concerns that Chinese spymasters were trying to recruit Singaporeans to take advantage of the country's reputation for neutrality.[208]

Singapore passed an anti–foreign interference law in 2021, granting authorities sweeping powers to force internet service providers and social media platforms to turn over user data, remove content, and block accounts deemed to be participating in "hostile information campaigns."[209] While proposing the legislation, Singapore home affairs and law minister K. Shanmugam described how, during tensions with an unnamed country between 2016 and 2017, the city-state detected a hostile information campaign that tried to undermine its foreign policy with online commentaries and Mandarin-language videos aimed at swaying Singapore's Chinese-speaking population.[210]

Officially, Singapore continued walking a careful line, empathizing with both American and Chinese perspectives while channeling concerns of smaller nations that would suffer most from a superpower conflict. "The status quo in Asia must change. But will the new configuration enable further success or bring dangerous instability?" Prime Minister Lee Hsien Loong wrote in *Foreign Affairs*. "If Washington tries to contain China's rise or Beijing seeks to build an exclusive sphere of influence in Asia—they will begin a course of confrontation that will last decades and put the long-heralded Asian century in jeopardy."[211]

"The prospect of an Asian century," Lee said, "will depend greatly on whether the United States and China can overcome their differences, build mutual trust, and work constructively to uphold a stable and peaceful international order. This is a fundamental issue of our time."

CHAPTER EIGHT

ONE MAN'S FATE

THE PARTY AFTER XI

"When things are going well, people wish 'long life' to the paramount ruler; when they are going badly, people look forward to the arrival of the Grim Reaper."

—Lucian Pye, American political scientist and sinologist

"One of these days Marx is going to call us over. Who knows if our successor might be a Bernstein, a Kautsky, or a Khrushchev?"

—Mao Zedong

"Building a nation's fate on the reputation of one or two people is very unhealthy and very dangerous."

—Deng Xiaoping

During China's last imperial dynasty, Qing emperors held court at the Palace of Heavenly Purity, an imposing edifice of red walls and yellow-glazed roof tiles built upon a white marble platform deep inside Beijing's Forbidden City. The monarch would consult courtiers and receive guests in its lavish main hall—still visible to tourists today—where his "dragon throne" sat on a dais decorated with intricate motifs and cloisonne incense burners. Above the seat of power hangs a horizontal tablet emblazoned with the calligraphy of Shunzhi, the first Qing emperor to reign over China, who wrote, *zhengda guangming*, or as one translation goes, "let the righteous shine." Notwithstanding its appeal for forthrightness, the tablet once concealed the most sensitive of imperial secrets: the identity of the next emperor.[1]

The practice started with Yongzheng, who ascended the throne in 1722 after being named successor at the Kangxi emperor's deathbed. The clandestine choice was born of bitter experience. Even though Kangxi designated a crown prince early in his reign, he vacillated on his decision as his many sons struggled for power, battling one another and even Kangxi himself, and threatening to unravel the Qing court from within. Yongzheng's solution was to anoint his heir in secret. His choice was written on two documents, one kept on the emperor's person and the other sealed in a box and placed behind the *zhengda guangming* tablet. Upon Yongzheng's death, officials would open the box, compare the papers, and unveil the next son of heaven. This way, the monarch could reduce the risks of open conflict between potential heirs, avoid becoming a lame duck, and forestall a ruler-in-waiting from usurping power.

Three centuries later, China's latter-day emperor seems to favor similar secrecy. Xi Jinping, leader of the world's last major communist power, wields preponderant say over who would succeed him and when. But he declined to reveal his hand as he clocked in a third term as Communist Party chief in 2022, packing his leadership bench with allies who lacked the right combination of age and experience that would mark them out as viable successors.[2] By exceeding the ten years he was originally expected to get in office, Xi breathed new life into an old poser in Chinese politics. "Who will be the next leader of China? This question has been a perpetual preoccupation of scholars and journalists for decades, and the reason is clear," Bruce Dickson, a China politics scholar at George Washington University, wrote in 1997. "In one form or another, the succession issue has been the central drama of Chinese politics almost since the beginning of the People's Republic in 1949."[3]

For Xi, this is a mystery by design. Few people, if anyone, and possibly not even Xi himself, know how long he wants to stay in power. Nor has he made clear if, when, or how he would designate an heir. Xi may have a timeline in mind, but changing circumstances could force him to rethink those plans. The uncertainty keeps the party elite on their toes, helping Xi maintain control and buying him time to assess potential successors. But keeping the suspense for too long could backfire, alienating protégés and antagonizing enemies enough to undermine the leader or even sow the seeds for a coup d'état. Xi, whose family suffered the vicissitudes of party infighting, knows this risk all too well.

During Mao Zedong's mercurial rule, one would-be successor was purged and tortured before dying in detention, while another perished in a plane crash after allegedly leading a failed attempt to seize power. The eventual successor, Hua Guofeng, toppled a rival faction led by Mao's wife Jiang Qing—the Gang of Four—before he himself was ousted by Deng Xiaoping. And although Deng developed norms for power-sharing and timely retirement, he ended up purging two protégés and dominating politics until his death in 1997.

For a while, nonetheless, China seemed to have cracked the succession code. Deng's passing spurred an outpouring of emotion but no political turmoil, with his successor Jiang Zemin already well ensconced as party chief. The next two leadership handovers also proceeded with relative calm, despite some intrigue along the way, persuading some scholars that the Communist Party was at last capable of regular, predictable, and peaceful transfers of power.

But the notion of institutionalized succession proved illusory. Since becoming party chief in 2012, Xi has accrued personal clout to a degree unseen since Mao. He designated himself the party's "core" leader and greatest living theorist, ensuring that he would remain China's preeminent politician until he passes on, or as party insiders say, "goes to see Marx." He scrapped term limits on the presidency, and upended retirement norms honed by his predecessors—obliterating the most important political reforms of the post-Mao era.

Succession is a high-stakes game in any political system. As Donald Trump showed with his attempts to overturn Joe Biden's victory in the 2020 U.S. presidential election, leadership changes can prove precarious even in democracies with established procedures for transferring power. In China, the dangers of power struggles remain vivid memories for people who lived through the Mao and Deng eras, as well as the Soviet collapse, which Xi blames in part on bungled successions that allowed the rise of weak leaders not "man enough" to save the regime.[4] A twenty-first-century succession crisis in China—with one of the world's biggest populations, the second largest economy, and one of the most powerful militaries—would unleash global shock waves. It may even bring down the People's Republic.

For Xi, a leader seemingly fixated on his place in history, the ability to engineer a smooth succession could determine whether his vision of a rejuvenated China would survive him. The party exalts Xi as the linchpin in China's renaissance, and justifies his strongman style as a stabilizing force in a tumultuous world. He takes credit for all major policies and every instance of national success. But his top-down control suppressed initiative and flexibility, while encouraging rote compliance and red tape. Although Beijing claimed success in weathering global shocks, including Trump's trade war and the Covid-19 pandemic, the party remained mired in bureaucratic rigidity, impeding decisive solutions for China's long-term challenges. Even Xi himself has complained that progress often doesn't come unless he intervenes with direct orders.[5]

Xi may have delivered the semblance of steady governance, but stability isn't the same as resilience. As demonstrated by the Soviet collapse, which many in the West failed to foresee, a seemingly sturdy government can prove surprisingly fragile.[6] "Our party is the world's largest political party," Xi once told officials. "I think the only ones who can defeat us are ourselves, nobody else."[7] By remaking the party around himself, Xi may have become the weakest link in his quest to build a Chinese superpower.

SUCCESS STRUGGLES

CHINA'S RULERS HAVE GRAPPLED WITH the succession problem since antiquity. Many emperors tried the principle of *dizhangzi* primogeniture, whereby the empress's firstborn male would become the heir. Some picked the worthiest among all their sons, or sometimes younger male relatives. Almost all of them preferred relinquishing power upon their natural deaths, barring assassinations and coups, though a few abdicated voluntarily.[8] A lasting solution, however, would elude Chinese monarchs through the ages, who instead bequeathed a blood-soaked history of power struggles and palace intrigue.

The Qing dynasty tried a mix of succession principles drawn from ancestral practice and shaped by contemporary circumstances. Its ruling clan of Aisin Gioro had followed a tradition of tanistry, whereby prospective heirs competed for power and ensured that only the strongest would reign.[9] Nurhaci, the ruler of the Jurchen people who would establish the Qing, left his dominions to his many sons when he died in 1626, having encouraged them to rule collectively.[10] His eighth son, Hong Taiji, emerged as khan with backing from key princes, renamed his people the Manchu, and proclaimed his realm as the "Great Qing."[11] Hong Taiji's death in 1643 prompted a negotiated succession, whereby a council of Manchu princes settled on his ninth son, five-year-old Fulin. The Manchus captured Beijing the following year, and Fulin reigned over China as the Shunzhi emperor until his death from smallpox in 1661.[12]

Shunzhi's third son, Xuanye, a smallpox survivor, ascended the throne before he turned seven. He took Kangxi as his regnal name and ruled for six decades, beginning a golden era of prosperity and territorial expansion that historians call the "High Qing." Kangxi nodded to Han Chinese customs by designating an heir, naming one-year-old Yinreng as crown prince. But the decision backfired as his sons split into cliques and battled for power, a decades-long struggle enshrined in Chinese folklore as *jiuwang duodi*, or "nine princes seizing the throne." Kangxi twice deposed Yinreng as crown prince over his moral frailties before settling on his final choice in secret, a decision revealed shortly before the emperor expired: the fourth prince, Yinzhen, would succeed him.[13]

Yinzhen reigned as the Yongzheng emperor for nearly thirteen years, though his claim to the throne was shrouded in controversy. Rival brothers questioned his legitimacy, and popular myths—still repeated today—allege that Yinzhen had usurped the throne by doctoring Kangxi's edict to change the successor's identity from the fourteenth prince, Yinti, to himself.[14] The fratricidal conflicts with his brothers scarred Yongzheng, who decided to keep his choice of heir secret. His system helped put the succession issue to rest for well over a century, and marked a useful compromise between Han and Manchu traditions. The emperor got to name his heir, as the Han did, and was free to choose the most worthy one, as the Manchu preferred.

In practice, the secret selection system was never truly tested. Yongzheng's fourth son, Hongli, was the clear favorite and his ascension as the Qianlong emperor came as no surprise. Qianlong outlived his first two choices of successor and became one of the world's longest-reigning monarchs. He abdicated in 1796 as a filial gesture to avoid surpassing Kangxi's sixty-one-year reign, but held on to power for three more years as emperor emeritus, while allowing his fifteenth son to start a new reign. Two more monarchs were named via secret selection, though the latter had only one surviving son, who ruled as the Tongzhi emperor and died—aged eighteen—with no offspring. Tongzhi's mother, Empress Dowager Cixi, installed a nephew as the Guangxu emperor and wielded power as regent. When Guangxu expired childless in 1908, a dying Cixi enthroned a toddler, Puyi, who became the last emperor of China.[15]

The Qing collapse triggered decades of civil conflict, during which the Communist Party was born. These Marxist revolutionaries fared little better at succession than their feudal forebears. The party leadership changed hands many times in the early decades, and often the person holding the party's most senior post wasn't its most powerful leader. Mao seized effective control over the party at a 1935 conference, where he blamed the incumbent leaders for the Red Army's losses against the Kuomintang. Though Mao started chairing the Central Military Commission the following year, he only became the party's top political officeholder in 1943, when he was named chairman of the Politburo.

Mao's twenty-seven-year reign over China was marred by incessant infighting as his radical campaigns ravaged the country. Though he tried to designate a successor, Mao often worried whether his legacy could survive him, having seen what happened after Stalin's death in 1953. Nikita Khrushchev, who won the ensuing power struggle to become Soviet leader, repudiated Stalin and his cult of personality in a 1956 "secret speech" that stunned the communist world. It was an object lesson for Mao—a mishandled succession could destroy his achievements. "One of these days Marx is going to call us over. Who knows if our successor might be a Bernstein, a Kautsky, or a Khrushchev?" Mao told the Vietnamese leader Ho Chi Minh in 1966.[16] Or as Mao told close associates on his seventy-third birthday later that year, the enemies who would betray his revolution lie deep inside the party, for "the fortress is easiest to capture from within."[17]

Mao's first heir apparent was Liu Shaoqi, a veteran revolutionary who became the party's first-ranked vice chairman in 1956 and head of state three years later. But Liu's relationship with Mao soured as they clashed over policy in the early 1960s, and Liu was among the first senior officials to be purged during Mao's Cultural Revolution. The party dismissed Liu as vice chairman, denounced him as a "capitalist roader," and expelled him before he died from maltreatment in 1969.

In Liu's place, Mao promoted Lin Biao, a revered military commander and defense minister, as heir apparent. A Mao loyalist who scored decisive battlefield victories during the Chinese civil war, Lin distinguished himself through obsequious displays of fealty, having popularized the "little red book" of Mao's quotations within the armed forces before it became ubiquitous in the hands of Red Guards. Lin earned a formal designation in the party charter as Mao's "close comrade-in-arms and successor" in 1969, only to die two years later in a mysterious plane crash in Mongolia. The party denounced Lin posthumously as a traitor, saying that he was trying to flee to the Soviet Union after botching a coup attempt against Mao. Some historians have questioned this account, though no conclusive explanations have emerged for the "Lin Biao incident."[18]

Whatever the truth, Lin's death stunned China and sent Mao into a spiral of depression and deteriorating health.[19] Some party insiders believed that Mao would pick a successor from the Gang of Four, who were the Cultural Revolution's most fervent enforcers. But the ailing dictator ultimately went with Hua Guofeng, a former regional administrator who succeeded Zhou Enlai as premier.[20] Mao's death in September 1976 sparked a tense interregnum. Hua and other party elders feared that the Gang of Four would seize power, and so they struck first, arranging for Jiang Qing and her clique to be arrested in a bloodless coup. But Hua didn't last long, outmaneuvered and eased out of power by Deng Xiaoping, whose rehabilitation Hua had approved.

Under Deng, the party elite unified in their desire to prevent another Mao-style dictatorship. "The history of socialism in the past sixty years makes it plain that whenever there is a system of life-tenure for the highest party and state leaders, [a cult of personality] commonly occurs," Yan Jiaqi, a senior party researcher, said in 1979. "Although it begins with an emphasis on collective leadership and the promotion of democracy, it culminates in an arbitrary rule that destroys collective leadership while safeguarding the power of the individual."[21] To forestall such developments, Deng enacted a history resolution to entrench his reformist ideas, encouraged timely retirement for senior leaders, and imposed term limits on the presidency, premiership, and other key state offices. The practice of life tenure "is detrimental for the renewal of leadership and the promotion of younger people," Deng said. "Therefore, we say it would be better for us old comrades to set an example and take an enlightened attitude."[22]

Though Deng declared that "a leader who picks his own successor is perpetuating a feudal practice," he went on to do precisely that.[23] He installed Hu Yaobang as party chief in 1981, but Hu irked party conservatives with his liberal leanings and lost his job after failing to contain student protests in 1986 and 1987. Another Deng protégé, Zhao Ziyang, stepped up as general secretary but he also clashed with hardliners. Party infighting boiled over after Hu died in April 1989, spurring mass mourning on Tiananmen Square that morphed into popular protests demanding greater political freedoms. Zhao opposed calls to forcefully suppress the unrest, and even showed up at the square one early morning in May to make a last-gasp plea for protesters to end a hunger strike. It was his final public appearance, before Deng ordered a military crackdown and purged Zhao.

Forced to designate an heir for the third time, Deng picked Jiang Zemin, then

Shanghai's party boss, as a compromise choice for general secretary. Deng resolved to get things right, urging the party to rally around Jiang as the "core" of its third-generation leadership, while he himself stepped back from front-line politics. "Now it seems that I carry too much weight, which is detrimental to the nation and the party, and one day it would be very dangerous. Many countries have set their China policies on the prospect of my illness or death," Deng told senior officials in June 1989. "Building a nation's fate on the reputation of one or two people is very unhealthy and very dangerous. That's alright as long as nothing goes wrong, but once something happens, the situation can get out of hand."[24]

Deng relinquished his last leadership post, stepping down as chairman of the Central Military Commission. But he remained China's most powerful citizen, revitalizing stalled economic reforms through his "southern tour" in 1992. That year, Deng also approved Hu Jintao's elevation into the Politburo Standing Committee, effectively designating him as Jiang's heir and China's fourth-generation leader. By deciding two successions down the line, Deng was giving the party every chance to make its leadership transitions regular and predictable.

Deng's succession plans survived his death in February 1997, though Jiang tinkered with the process to boost his own authority. At the party congress later that year, Jiang forced a key rival in the Politburo Standing Committee, Qiao Shi, into retirement by insisting that officials aged seventy or older couldn't start a new term in the leadership. Though Jiang was already seventy-one then, he was exempted on the grounds that he was the incumbent leader.[25] Jiang reprised this tactic five years later at the 2002 party congress, lowering the retirement threshold to sixty-eight years to push out another rival, Li Ruihuan, from the Politburo Standing Committee.[26] Insiders dubbed this new precedent *qishang baxia*, or "seven up, eight down," which meant officials aged sixty-seven or younger could start a new term, whereas those aged sixty-eight or older would retire.

Jiang stepped down as general secretary in late 2002 and president in early 2003, handing both posts to Hu. But Jiang stayed on as military commission chairman for two more years. This Deng-style power play allowed Jiang to retain influence and spoke volumes of Hu's tenuous authority. Even so, the handover proceeded smoothly enough to persuade some Western scholars that political succession in China was increasingly bound by rules and norms.[27]

Xi's ascension proved to be the party's cleanest transfer of power to date. Unlike Jiang, Hu relinquished his key posts on time, stepping down as general secretary and military commission chairman at the 2012 party congress and handing over the presidency the following spring. For just the second time, the People's Republic completed a leadership transition triggered neither by the leader's death nor a political crisis. "Succession itself has become a party institution," a pair of China scholars wrote, echoing what was then the broad academic consensus.[28]

Xi upended these expectations in just five years. He declined to elevate a potential successor into the Politburo Standing Committee at the 2017 party congress—the first clear sign that he was preparing to retain power beyond the ten-year leadership cycle that Hu had set. Then Xi repealed presidential term limits the following spring, surprising ordinary Chinese and even party insiders. Just months before, in late 2017, one of China's top constitutional scholars, Han Dayuan, had published an article saying that term limits had effectively curbed the party's problems with life tenure, overconcentration of individual power, and personality cults—the very issues that Xi came to embody.[29] By the 2022 party congress, Xi's authority had grown so entrenched that he was able to completely discard the "seven up, eight down" guideline, claiming his third term as party chief at the age of sixty-nine, forcing rivals into early retirement, and keeping older loyalists in the party's top echelons.[30]

Officials defended Xi's maneuvers as necessary for overcoming bureaucratic stasis, and denied any restoration of life tenure for party and state leaders. These claims offered little comfort for those who feared a return to Mao-style dictatorship. Xi's dominance meant he would be the first leader since Deng to enjoy a free hand in picking his heir. The choice would be pivotal, and Xi was keenly aware of the stakes. "Realizing the great rejuvenation of the Chinese nation," Xi said, "requires cultivating generations upon generations of reliable successors."[31] Unfettered by term limits, he can take as long as he needs to decide.

WHO'S NEXT

FOR CHINA'S RULERS, the question of succession is also a matter of legacy. "No leader, not even a Mao or a Deng, can leave behind statutes that will bind the country to any particular policy course. New rulers bring new policies," the American political scientist Lucian Pye wrote in explaining why debates over succession dominate Chinese politics. "As long as leaders' influence ends at the grave, it is natural for them to try to hold on to power for as long as possible."[32]

Mao did reign till the bitter end, while Deng retained his political preeminence until his death. Xi can follow similar paths, with the party canon of "Xi Jinping Thought" giving his words the strength of holy writ. He could try to keep a formal hold on power for life, like Mao did. Or he may decide to step back and rule from behind the scenes as a regent, à la Deng, whereby he can assess his heir apparent's performance and intervene when necessary, or even pick a new successor altogether.[33]

On paper, the party prohibits life tenure. The party charter states that cadres in leadership positions "do not hold posts for life and can be transferred from or relieved of their posts."[34] The party also has interim regulations that bar officials in leadership roles from staying in the same post beyond ten years, or at the same level of the party for more than fifteen years. But some insiders say these rules don't apply to the top leadership, and in any case, Xi secured a third term as general secretary in 2022 with what officials hailed as unanimous support.[35] Age wasn't the main factor in how the party chose its new leadership that year, according to an authoritative state media account of the process. Rather, it said, top party and state appointments must be decided "in accordance with work requirements, personnel criteria, integrity, and reputation."[36] In essence, Xi can stay on as party chief, military commission chairman, and state president for as long as he wishes.

Xi confronts a timeless conundrum that scholars call the "successor's dilemma." Autocrats prefer installing successors whom they trust to uphold their legacy and protect their interests in retirement. But leaders-in-waiting must start building their own power base ahead of time, if they are to avoid being deposed or rendered ineffectual after taking office. And once a clear successor emerges, the political elite will naturally start realigning their loyalties—a process that can undermine the incumbent leader, who may come to fear that the heir apparent is plotting to usurp power.

Whereas politicians in many democracies are generally confident that they can continue to enjoy personal liberty after leaving office, authoritarian leaders expect grave consequences should they lose power involuntarily. Even autocrats who retire on their own terms have few guarantees for their safety, other than their ability to maintain leverage over their successors. According to a 2010 academic paper that reviewed the fate of more than 1,800 political leaders, some 41 percent of the 1,059 autocrats analyzed suffered exile, imprisonment, or death within a year of leaving office, compared to just 7 percent of 763 democratic leaders.[37]

Xi could mitigate such threats by establishing a framework for relinquishing power. In an authoritarian system that offers clarity on succession timelines, the political elite can calibrate expectations on their career advancement, and thus feel less inclined to challenge the incumbent ruler. If regime insiders see bleak prospects for promotion, or start fearing for their personal safety, they may decide that their best bet is to oust the leader, whether through a procedural challenge or an outright coup. Succession rules "reduce elites' incentives to try to grab power pre-emptively via forceful means," wrote Erica Frantz and Elizabeth Stein in a paper analyzing why autocratic leaders agree to succession rules that could curtail their authority.[38]

Chinese history is rich with succession drama that serves as a guide. Reviewing data on the 282 emperors who reigned across 49 dynasties since Qin Shi Huang unified China, Harvard political scientist Yuhua Wang found that only about 46 percent of them designated a successor, while the rest either didn't have a son or relied on other rules of succession. "Emperors who designated a competent and loyal successor lived longer," Wang wrote, noting that monarchs who anointed heirs apparent were 64 percent less likely to be deposed than those who didn't.[39]

Xi has said little publicly on succession planning, apart from broad platitudes on the need to groom good heirs to the revolution. Having antagonized many within the party elite with his anticorruption crackdown and political purges, he would likely want ironclad guarantees for his safety before stepping down. He could cling on to power for as long as possible without anointing an heir, but that means forsaking his prerogative to install a successor who can protect his legacy. Another possibility is that Xi may struggle to find suitable heirs and end up exiting office—through death or incapacitation—without a successor in place. "Presumably Xi Jinping doesn't want to stay in power forever, and he does want to pick someone that he trusts to replace him, but at the same time, he understands that he could pick the wrong person, and the very act of picking the wrong person could create problems for the system," says Joseph Torigian, a historian at American University who has studied power struggles in China and the Soviet Union. A situation therefore may arise where Xi wants to leave office but he feels that he can't, Torigian says.[40]

Another factor in Xi's succession planning would be how much time he believes he needs to achieve his goals. Although he would be seventy-four by the end of his third term as party chief in 2027, Xi would still be two years younger than Jiang Zemin was when he stepped down as general secretary in 2002. Some party insiders say Xi could choose to stay on until at least 2035, the target date for completing some of his signature initiatives, including economic development and military modernization. Xi would be eighty-two by then, around Biden's age at the end of his first presidential term.

To ensure a smooth transition, Xi would need to prepare potential successors for the stresses of high office. In practice, this means giving them a stint in the Politburo Standing Committee, where they can start learning how to helm the ship of state. Once Xi makes his choice, the heir apparent would then likely be named vice chairman of the Central Military Commission and deputy head of state. If and when Xi feels confident enough to hand over his leadership posts, he could continue exerting influence from behind the scenes, mentoring or even deposing his chosen heir if he sees fit.

Supreme power in China hasn't always been vested in formal titles. Deng famously never held office as the head of the party, government, or state, though as paramount leader he retained a crucial post as chairman of the Central Military Commission. Xi, on the other hand, has placed great premium on leadership titles, in part because he lacked other sources of legitimacy. Unlike Mao and Deng, who boasted revolutionary pedigree and wielded personal clout, Xi exercises power through his formal offices and the institutions those positions command. His successor faces the same problem, something Xi would likely consider in deciding if, when, and how to relinquish his titles. Some party insiders suggest that Xi could resurrect Mao's title of party chairman, possibly as a titular post he could hold for life, while handing over day-to-day responsibilities to his chosen heir.

Who could succeed Xi? Much attention has fallen on senior officials in the party's "post-60" generation, who were born in the 1960s and are expected to take over from Xi and his "post-50" cohort, in accordance with past expectations of a ten-year leadership cycle. Some of Xi's post-60 protégés already hold senior party and government roles, and could emerge as likely successors at the subsequent party congresses in 2027 or 2032. Xi could also skip over the post-60 generation and groom heirs from among younger officials.

Xi has shown little desire to revive dynastic rule in China. His daughter and only child isn't known to be pursuing a political career, which in any case would be challenging in a male-dominated and patriarchal party. Xi does have a nephew—a son of his younger brother—who ventured into public service, becoming the first of Xi Zhongxun's grandchildren known to have entered government. Family friends say Xi Jinping meets the nephew, Qi Mingzheng, from time to time and seemingly trusts him to provide a relatively unvarnished picture of public sentiment. An alumnus of

Georgetown University's School of Foreign Service and Tsinghua, Qi joined China's main antitrust regulator as a junior bureaucrat in 2020 and has taken secondments as a rural official in a poor agricultural county just north of Beijing—echoing Xi's early political career, when he was a county chief in the early 1980s.

Descendants of party elders have joined politics before. Hu Jintao's son, Hu Haifeng, was a municipal party boss as of this writing; a son of former premier Li Peng became transport minister; and Bo Xilai, a son of a revolutionary hero, joined the Politburo before he was purged in 2012. Some liberal-minded princelings say they worry that Qi's budding political career represents a broader attempt to ensure that China will continue to be governed by people with "red genes," contrary to the party's egalitarian values. Regardless, given his relative youth as a millennial born in 1992, Qi must still spend decades proving his mettle and scaling the hierarchy before he can reach the party's top echelons.

Strongman leaders prefer pliant successors who won't outshine or betray them. Whomever Xi chooses as heir may well be a relatively weak ruler who struggles to assert himself. "The death of a strong leader is always followed by a period of oligarchy, usually called 'collective leadership,'" argued Yan Jiaqi, the former party researcher, who went into exile after the 1989 Tiananmen Square protests. The collective would likely be stricken by power struggles, he said, before "a personal dictatorship again emerges from the collective leadership."[41]

GOING TO SEE MARX

WHEN XI JINPING EMBARKED ON a whirlwind tour of Italy, Monaco, and France in early 2019, his hosts feted him with ceremonial welcomes and state banquets—lavish pageantry designed to boost his image as a statesman. For some observers, however, it was his unusual gait that caught the eye. Television footage showed Xi walking with a slight limp while inspecting honor guards and touring local sights.[42] At a meeting with French President Emmanuel Macron in the city of Nice, Xi gripped both arms on his chair to ease himself into his seat.[43]

The images stirred speculation among politically minded Chinese, foreign diplomats, and China watchers, who wondered if Xi had an ailment that was causing him physical discomfort. Guessing games played out on Twitter and overseas Chinese media, offering theories from muscle sprains to gout. In private social media chat rooms, some Chinese intellectuals gossiped about what the videos suggested about Xi's health, a retired politics professor in Beijing told me. "Everyone didn't say much, but there was a tacit mutual understanding."[44]

Speculating about the health of authoritarian leaders is an old sport. For seasoned analysts, the practice goes beyond idle gossip and into the realm of painstaking research, with countless hours spent scrutinizing officials' appearances and remarks for clues on their well-being and their government's inner workings. China specialists often refer to such work as Pekingology—the Chinese equivalent of Kremlinology—or, more evocatively, the art of "tea-leaf reading."

The U.S. Central Intelligence Agency, for instance, prepared detailed studies on the implications of Chinese leadership changes, including analyses on what might happen after the deaths of Mao and Deng. A CIA paper issued in August 1976, the month before Mao died, anticipated that Mao would "soon be totally incapacitated or dead" and mapped out a range of possible scenarios that could follow, including a coup or a tenuous governing coalition between rival factions.[45] A U.S. intelligence report issued in 1986 titled "China After Deng: Succession Problems and Prospects" advised against American efforts to influence the succession process, as such attempts "could probably only affect the succession in a negative way, by destabilizing relations with China."[46]

Foreign intelligence agencies stepped up their scrutiny of Xi's health after he repealed presidential term limits in 2018, according to a researcher who discussed the issue with intelligence officials from two governments. "Their concern is that the party doesn't have a well-thought-out succession plan," the researcher told me. "We can't say we know what would follow if something happens to Xi."[47] Even some of Xi's most fervent supporters have implicitly acknowledged such concerns. "Doesn't the emperor of Japan rule for life? Doesn't the Queen of England rule for life? So why can't our chairman rule for life?" said Chen Jinshi, a real-estate mogul and member of China's legislature. "As long as [Xi's] health is good, what's there to be worried about?"

China's leaders receive the highest standard of healthcare through a dedicated medical system, and their physical conditions are considered state secrets.[48] For Xi, projecting healthy vigor is vital for sustaining his aura of preeminence and keeping potential challengers at bay. As it would be with any system, democratic or authoritarian, information about an official's health can become leverage in palace intrigue.

During the August 1991 coup against the Soviet leader Mikhail Gorbachev, the conspirators issued media reports claiming that Gorbachev had been incapacitated by poor health.[49]

Beijing is therefore highly sensitive to media coverage about Xi's health. After I wrote a report for the *Wall Street Journal* in 2019 discussing speculation about Xi's health and concerns over leadership succession, the Chinese foreign ministry complained to my bureau chief, suggesting that such reports were irresponsible.[50] During a 2020 speech in Shenzhen that was broadcast live, Xi repeatedly coughed and stopped to drink from a cup, prompting state television to cut away from him and show the audience instead—an episode that sparked online chatter about whether Xi was sick.[51] Even an extended absence of Xi images from television news bulletins and *People's Daily* front pages has proved enough to fuel wild rumors on Twitter and overseas Chinese media about Xi's physical and political well-being.

Speculation over Xi's health has simmered from time to time. In September 2012, just months before he took power, Xi canceled meetings with foreign dignitaries and failed to appear in public for about two weeks, prompting rumors that he had a health problem.[52] Details about Xi's physical condition are sparse, apart from some tidbits sprinkled across news reports, old interviews, and the countless photographs and videos taken of him over the years. Even his height has been something of a mystery, though the BBC once concluded that Xi stands roughly five feet and ten inches tall after reviewing photos of him with other world leaders.[53] Xi has gained significant weight since venturing into politics and was known to be a smoker, though Chinese media say he quit while working in Fujian in the 1980s.[54] As paramount leader, Xi works a high-stress job and, according to state media, once told officials that he "feels happiness in exhaustion."[55]

Like many authoritarian one-party states, China lacks clear procedures for filling unplanned vacancies in top posts. The party charter merely states that the Central Committee is responsible for choosing a general secretary, who must also be a member of the Politburo Standing Committee. The Central Committee also decides the membership of the Central Military Commission, though the party charter doesn't specify how the chairperson should be selected.[56] Only the presidency is bound by a line of succession. China's constitution states that a presidential vacancy will be filled by the vice president. Should both positions be vacant at the same time, China's top lawmaker will fill in as acting president until the legislature appoints replacements.[57]

There is no requirement, whether in party regulations or state law, for the new president to also assume the roles of party chief and military commission chairman.

In the United States, the line of succession is defined by law. Under the Presidential Succession Act and the 25th Amendment to the U.S. Constitution, an incumbent president who dies, becomes incapacitated, resigns, or is removed from office would be succeeded—in order—by the vice president, the speaker of the House of Representatives, and the president pro tempore of the Senate, followed by the heads of federal executive departments. In parliamentary democracies, heads of government often designate deputy leaders who can take the helm should the prime minister be incapacitated.

But even established succession procedures can crumble in a crisis. After President Ronald Reagan was shot in 1981, Secretary of State Alexander Haig caused controversy by telling reporters that "I am in control here, in the White House"—implying that he had inherited presidential authority while Vice President George H. W. Bush was returning to Washington from Texas.[58] Some White House officials prepared papers for invoking the 25th Amendment to designate Bush as acting president, but ultimately didn't sign them.[59] The robustness of American presidential transitions was tested again in the wake of the 2020 election, when President Donald Trump refused to concede defeat and tried, unsuccessfully, to challenge the integrity of the vote.

As for China, there are no clear procedures and few precedents to fall back on should Xi leave office suddenly, whether by death, illness, or resignation. In theory, the Central Committee would assemble to select a new party chief and military commission chairman, while the vice president would step up as head of state. In practice, without a designated heir in place with broad support from the party elite, the process of choosing a successor could be politically fraught.

When Vice Premier Huang Ju died of illness in 2007, party elders left his seat on the Politburo Standing Committee vacant until the party congress later that year, when the political elite were due to choose a new leadership bench. But Huang was seen as a relatively weak and inconsequential figure, and replacing him required little fuss. The potential for infighting would be much higher should a sitting leader die or become debilitated. An ideal scenario would see party grandees huddling in backroom negotiations to hash out a name most acceptable to the broader establishment, before submitting their decision for approval by the Central Committee. In most authoritarian regimes, the political elite shares a common interest in maintaining the status quo when the incumbent leader dies—for the surest way to protect their privileged status is to preserve the existing system.

In the case of incapacitation through illness or accident, the government could slip into purgatory while officials hedge between their leader's recovery or death.[60] During the five days that Stalin took to expire from his stroke in 1953, which a *New Yorker* writer described as dying "in installments," members of the Soviet leadership started jockeying for advantage in the succession fight, even as they demonstrated grief and concern over the dictator's well-being.[61] Mao's passing was even more prolonged. As his health and faculties faded in his final years, rival officials schemed against one another as they vied for Mao's favor in hopes of becoming the chosen heir.

Should Xi die or become incapacitated, latent fissures within the senior ranks may erupt. The party elite could splinter into various factions, each backing their own preferred successor. Key constituencies, such as the military and internal security services, would likely play pivotal roles in deciding the outcome. Officials who had been sidelined by Xi may sense an opportunity to reassert their influence. "One leads China by being accepted by one's fellow senior leaders," says Ryan Manuel, managing director of Bilby, a Hong Kong–based artificial-intelligence firm that analyzes party governance.

A prolonged succession crisis could cripple government functions, pummel the economy, and even spark broader turmoil. In a 2016 paper analyzing authoritarian leadership changes, Andrea Kendall-Taylor and Erica Frantz found that personalist regimes, where power is highly concentrated in the hands of one individual, are "more prone to instability following a leader's death than other, more institutionalized autocracies." Reviewing data on nearly five hundred autocrats who left office from 1946 to 2012, they found that 22 percent of personalist regimes fell apart within a year of the leader's death in office—the highest rate among the four types of authoritarian systems the researchers studied, including single-party, monarchic, and military dictatorships.[62]

Nonetheless, "authoritarian regimes have proven to be remarkably resilient when a leader dies," Kendall-Taylor and Frantz wrote. "Even when the institutional channels for handling succession are weak, elites have a strong incentive to rally behind a new leader."[63] But their data also indicated that some 75 percent of personalist dictatorships collapsed within a year of a leadership change triggered by reasons other than death.[64] If an autocrat could be forced out of office, the regime itself may be on shaky ground.

CLIQUES AND FACTIONS

ONE MORNING IN JANUARY 2016, Xi Jinping assembled the Communist Party's top discipline inspectors to issue their marching orders for the year. These enforcers had spearheaded Xi's efforts to combat corruption and accrue personal power, a withering campaign that unsettled many within the party and sparked backlash from some quarters. Such dissent worried Xi, who insisted that any sign of political deviance be crushed at the outset. Once the party leadership has made its decisions, Xi said, the rank and file "must not sing a different tune."[65]

But intraparty discord spilled into the open just weeks later, when a prominent businessman and princeling, Ren Zhiqiang, went online to criticize Xi's demands for fealty from Chinese media.[66] When the media becomes loyal to the party and stops representing the people's interests, "the people will be abandoned in a forgotten corner," wrote the retired property mogul, dubbed "Cannon Ren" for his outspoken views.

Then in early March, as China's political elite gathered in Beijing for an annual legislative session, a mysterious missive calling for Xi's resignation appeared on the website of a state-backed news portal. Signed by "Loyal Communist Party members," the letter criticized Xi for excessively accumulating personal power, endorsing a "personality cult," and causing unprecedented crises for China. "For the sake of ensuring that the party's cause can flourish, for the long-term peace and stability of the country, and for the safety of you and your family," the letter said, "we ask you to resign from all positions of party and state leadership."[67]

The party launched a withering response. Authorities shut down Ren's social media accounts—where he had more than 37 million followers—and suspended his party membership. State media castigated Ren for being "anti-party," a serious political allegation in China.[68] Investigators hunted the authors of the anti-Xi letter, rounding up more than a dozen people affiliated with Wujie, the news portal that published it.[69] Authorities in southern China took away the family of a New York–based Chinese dissident whom they suspected had helped spread the letter. The editor of an overseas Chinese website that first published the letter received harassing phone calls and death threats.[70] Wujie, a media venture partly owned by the Xinjiang regional government, fell silent and soon stopped operating.

For most autocratic leaders, the fear of popular uprisings is perhaps surpassed only by their dread of an elite insurrection. "An overwhelming majority of dictators lose power to those inside the gates of the presidential palace rather than to the masses," wrote Milan Svolik, a Yale political scientist who studies authoritarian systems. "The predominant political conflict in dictatorships appears to be not between the ruling elite and the masses but rather one among regime insiders."[71] After all, in any political system, members of the establishment are best equipped with the knowledge and resources needed to seize key levers of government and mobilize the populace.

Coups are relatively rare in communist regimes, but authoritarian leaders who are forcefully deposed don't fare well, with 73 percent of defeated leaders facing death, jail, or exile, according to one study.[72] And of the 282 Chinese emperors that Harvard's Yuhua Wang analyzed, only about half left office by natural death. Most of the rest were murdered, overthrown, forced to abdicate or commit suicide, or deposed during civil wars, whereas external conflicts dethroned only seven emperors. "The biggest threat was from within the regime rather than from society or foreign countries," Wang concluded.[73]

The specter of a palace coup is well known to Xi, whose family benefited greatly from the Gang of Four's ouster. Xi has warned against internal plots, suggesting that some of the officials he purged had been planning to seize power. "The greater these people's power, the more important their positions, the less seriously they took party discipline and political rules, to the point of becoming unscrupulous and audacious in the extreme," Xi told the party's top discipline inspectors in 2015. "Some of them had inflated political ambitions and, for their personal interests or the benefit of their clique, engaged in political plotting behind the party's back, and carried out politically shady business to damage and split the party!"[74]

Some scholars describe Marxist-Leninist regimes as "leader-friendly" systems, where a sitting ruler wields significant institutional advantages over his opponents. He can call upon a formidable internal security apparatus to sniff and snuff out threats. Rivals who question his policies could expose themselves to allegations of "factionalism" and "antiparty" activities. Even when push comes to shove, most regime insiders would try to cloak their plots with a fig leaf of legitimacy and avoid tactics that could destabilize the party—such as assassination or seizing power through brute force.

Xi maintains close control over key levers of power, including internal security forces and the People's Liberation Army. In 2020, he launched a sweeping purge of China's law-enforcement, judicial, and domestic intelligence agencies that took down dozens of mid- to high-ranking officials, and broke up what the party denounced as a corrupt "political clique" led by a former vice minister of public security.[75] Xi has also purged a number of senior generals with close ties to his predecessors, while promoting PLA officers "whose ethnic, class, and ideological backgrounds make them unlikely to back anti-regime protesters," according to an analysis by Yale University political scientist Dan Mattingly, who reviewed more than ten thousand PLA personnel appointments.[76] Blanket digital surveillance also makes it hard for would-be plotters to evade detection while they communicate with one another and solicit support from the military and security services.

Party enforcers work relentlessly to quash internal dissent. One of their most prominent targets was Ren Zhiqiang, the retired property mogul. Though he had kept a low profile since being punished for his 2016 outburst, Ren resurfaced four years later to criticize what he saw as the party's bungled response to the Covid-19 outbreak. After he wrote an online essay in March 2020 that appeared to excoriate Xi as an imperious clown, party investigators detained Ren and accused him of political deviance and corruption.[77] Ren's pedigree as a son of a senior official, the former chairman of a state enterprise, and a friend to powerful politicians including Vice President Wang Qishan, failed to save him. The party expelled Ren for disloyalty, before a Chinese court sentenced him in September 2020 to eighteen years in jail on charges of corruption, embezzlement, and abuse of power.[78]

Another prominent insider, former Central Party School professor Cai Xia, was forced into exile after she criticized Xi and called the party a "political zombie" in a private talk she gave to friends in 2020.[79] Cai was traveling in the U.S., unable to return to Beijing due to China's Covid-19 travel restrictions, when an audio recording of her talk surfaced online and caused a stir within Chinese political circles. Authorities eventually expelled Cai from the party, revoked her retirement benefits, and froze her bank account. When she sought assurances from the Central Party School about her safety if she were to return home, officials dodged her questions and made vague threats against Cai's daughter and grandchild, who were in China.[80]

The party also went after public intellectuals who could sway elite opinion against Xi. A top legal scholar, Xu Zhangrun, became a target after he published in summer 2018 a scathing jeremiad denouncing Xi's autocratic turn, the first in a series of essays he wrote criticizing the Chinese leader. The following spring, Tsinghua University, where Xu was working as a law professor, suspended him, slashed his pay, and opened an investigation into his writings.[81] Then in July 2020, police detained Xu for six days over allegations that he solicited prostitution, a charge often used against dissidents and one that Xu and his friends condemned as a scurrilous slur. Tsinghua sacked him soon after, citing the solicitation offense and his essays.[82]

China's black-box Leninist system yields few clues about internal power dynamics. Despite frequent murmurings of high-level resentment against Xi, signs of elite struggles may not emerge until a rupture takes place. Authors of the 1986 U.S. intelligence report on Chinese succession politics, for instance, didn't anticipate that Deng would depose his own protégé, Hu Yaobang, as general secretary less than a year later.[83] Even within the party, a lack of reliable intelligence can cause grief for insiders trying to arrange a plot, or an incumbent leader trying to forestall one.

Xi, for his part, has taken few chances in protecting his power. Similar to Mao and Deng, he has sought to dismantle alternative power centers, intimidate potential rivals, and undermine even close colleagues who didn't appear to pose serious threats or have ambitions of challenging the leader. He has used party disciplinary probes against his perceived opponents, sometimes directly, but often simply to undercut them by tearing down their political networks. Those targeted with the subtler approach included former security chief Meng Jianzhu, who saw some of his protégés, including two vice ministers of public security, purged for corruption after he stepped down from the Politburo in 2017. Chen Yuan, a former top banker and an influential son of the revolutionary hero Chen Yun, saw party inspectors open investigations against his wife and more than a dozen of his associates.[84]

Even Wang Qishan, one of Xi's oldest friends, wasn't beyond reach. People close to Wang say he has no ambitions to be leader. He is five years older than Xi and considered too old to be a viable successor. But he still commanded considerable clout of his own, and therefore posed a latent threat.

Wang had stepped down from the party leadership in late 2017, after five years as Xi's anticorruption czar, and in the following spring became vice president, a ceremonial sinecure seen as a reward conferred by Xi. In 2020, the anti-graft enforcers that Wang once led started going after people inside his political and personal circles. The party purged Wang's friend Ren Zhiqiang and opened a corruption probe against one of Wang's longtime aides, Dong Hong—a case that resulted in Dong receiving a de facto life sentence. Officials investigating the bankrupt Chinese conglomerate HNA Group detained its chairman, a friend of Wang's, in the fall of 2021. Wang's nephew-in-law, Yao Qing, was taken into custody the following spring and held for several months as authorities examined the alleged ties that Yao, the grandson of a revolutionary elder, had with HNA. Citing corruption charges, the party then purged a veteran banker who had once worked under Wang.[85]

If elite conflict does break out, the battle lines will likely be messy and personality-driven, with rivals settling scores rather than arguing over ideological and policy differences, according to Joseph Torigian, the historian, who wrote a book analyzing Soviet and Chinese succession struggles that followed the deaths of Stalin and Mao. Elite struggles in Marxist-Leninist regimes are something of a "knife fight with weird rules," where contenders battle yet still seek a veneer of legitimacy and avoid wanton violence that could undermine the ruling party, Torigian says.[86]

The succession fights after Stalin and Mao upended politics in both countries, where the winners repudiated despotism and built new power structures that they hoped wouldn't succumb to one-man rule. Neither Stalin nor Mao, for all their might, could ensure their systems of governance outlived them. The biggest threat to an autocrat's legacy may well be himself.

APRÈS MOI

WHEN THE CHINESE EDUCATOR and political activist Huang Yanpei toured the Communist Party's Yan'an revolutionary base in July 1945, Mao Zedong invited his esteemed visitor into a cave dwelling and probed his thoughts on the future of their war-torn nation. While Huang was impressed by the Communists' collective spirit, he expressed profound pessimism about the party's ability to chart a new course for China.

Huang confided that he could see no escape from the historical cycles that have persisted for millennia, the rise and fall of dynasties that seem as inexorable as the changing of seasons. Time and again, China suffered spells of slack and hubristic rule, as well as instances where a leader's system of governance crumbled after his death, Huang said. "No one has been able to leap out of this cycle."[87]

Mao dismissed Huang's fears. "We have found a new path; we can leap out of this cycle," he replied. "This path is called democracy. Only by letting the people supervise the government, then the government wouldn't dare slacken." And if everyone did their duty, Mao said, there would be no danger of "the leader dies, and his governance ends."[88]

But Mao and his successors didn't bring democracy to China, at least not in the

Western liberal sense. The party imposed iron-fisted control and became a vehicle for the "rule of man," whereby the leader exercises preponderant power—shaping, bending, and breaking norms as he sees fit. Xi embraced this autocratic tradition when he took power, but also gave it his own spin. Where Mao ruled through charisma and used the party as an expendable tool of revolution, Xi governs through the party, calling it an indispensable instrument of governance.

It is in this context that Xi invokes the Huang-Mao dialogue, often citing it as a warning against complacency and decay that could topple the Communist Party.[89] "Looking back on histories of the rise and fall of feudal dynasties, it isn't difficult to see," he said, how past Chinese regimes repeatedly collapsed under the weight of corruption, hedonism, and weak governance. As long as the party steels itself with a sense of collective purpose and ideological zeal, Xi told officials, "we would be able to leap out of the historical cycles of 'rapid rise and rapid fall.'"[90]

A decade into the Xi era, the party appears more in control than ever. It embraces digital authoritarianism and maintains a high-tech security state. It coerces and surveils citizens with internet controls, big data, facial recognition, social-credit systems, and other state-of-the-art tools. Civil society has been all but neutered; activists get imprisoned, muzzled, forced into exile, or coopted by the state. Dissenting voices face police harassment, jail time, and a ravenous online "cancel culture" fueled by party-backed patriotism. The People's Liberation Army increasingly flexes its abilities to wage war and project power. Chinese diplomats charge forth with a more aggressive approach to foreign policy. And above it all, Xi stands supreme, as the face of China's cutting-edge autocracy.

The secret to this success, Xi says, is continuous "self-revolution."[91] He insists the party can escape the dynastic cycles of rise and fall by waging a ceaseless struggle—against its inner demons of greed and indolence, and the outer enemies of Western subversion. He argues that this "self-revolution" can be institutionalized, whereby the party operates by rules and norms, rather than the whims of an individual leader. This means codifying exemplary conduct and enforcing it with a Praetorian Guard of discipline inspectors, whose constant vigilance shall keep the party potent and pure. Through self-revolution, Xi declared, days before taking his third term as general secretary, "we have ensured that the party will never change in nature, change in color, or change in flavor."[92]

Yet Xi's system remains reliant on his personal initiative, as it has been for arguably most Chinese rulers since antiquity. Xi implements major initiatives through top-down campaigns. He takes personal charge over issues he cares about and intervenes often, penning vague instructions that bureaucrats sometimes struggle to decipher. Officials rush to comply, driven less by passion and more by fear. Few dare question Xi's edicts, however confusing or contradictory, sometimes producing policies that seem poorly designed and must be reversed later. If the mark of institutionalized governance is more predictability, Xi appears to have achieved the opposite. "The CCP cannot be institutionalized without destroying what makes it a Leninist party—a hierarchical, mobilizational, task-oriented party," writes Joseph Fewsmith, the Boston University political scientist. What Xi has done, Fewsmith argues, is "to put the Lenin back in the Leninist party."[93]

The risk is that the party of Xi may be so driven by his personality that few of his potential successors—least of all a weak one—could command it effectively in his absence. That's not to say that the party can't survive without Xi. China's Communist rulers have time and again defied prophecies of doom, surviving crises and adapting to new circumstances. A system that appears dysfunctional and wasteful can still operate well enough to keep things going for a long time. But that wouldn't be good enough for Xi's lofty standards.

Xi promised to build a system that could transcend China's feudal past, restore its glories, and seal his place among history's greatest statesmen. But his new-look Communist Party has come to resemble, in some ways, the imperial bureaucracies of old—bigger and better organized, but no less autocratic, rigid, and plagued by succession woes. Just as leaders have died and their governance ended throughout Chinese antiquity, Xi may have become a single point of failure in his China Dream. Whether the party of Xi can hold together without its linchpin leader is perhaps a question only time can answer.

AFTERWORD

"Long-term seclusion and self-isolation made China poor, backward and ignorant. . . . The
lessons of history tell us that if we don't open up, we can't succeed."

—Deng Xiaoping

The Chinese government waited till the last day of my work permit to tell me that I had to leave mainland China. My press credentials and residency visa were due to expire on August 30, 2019, the day before my fifth anniversary as a Beijing correspondent for the *Wall Street Journal*. The foreign ministry had renewed my papers well ahead of expiry in previous years, but this time, they kept an ominous silence on what had been a routine process, and ran the clock down to the final hours.

After a late night of tentative packing, I jolted awake when my phone rang shortly past 8 a.m. "I'm sorry to say that the foreign ministry has told me that they will not be renewing your press card," my bureau chief said. "Right," I replied. "I guess I really have to pack now."

I didn't know it then, but I had become the first *Journal* reporter to be denied a renewal of press credentials by the Chinese government since the newspaper opened its Beijing bureau in 1979, and the sixth foreign journalist to be forced out of mainland China in six years.[1] There was no time to contemplate. My bosses decided that I shouldn't overstay my visa—better to leave first and pick up the pieces later. I spent the next eight hours packing my bags to catch a flight to Hong Kong. Half a dozen colleagues came to my apartment to help box my belongings for shipment later. My bureau chief went to the foreign ministry to make a last-gasp plea, but could only meet junior officials who complained about my coverage and refused to mention my name.

The *Washington Post* broke the news of my expulsion as I headed to the airport late in the afternoon.[2] Calls and text messages poured in from friends and fellow reporters. I had long believed that journalists should report the news and not become the story, yet I was watching myself making headlines one mobile alert at a time. While I was waiting to board my flight, Chinese state media announced that the Communist Party's Central Committee would soon convene its first plenary meeting in more than a year and a half, an unusually long interval. My professional instincts kicked in, my thumbs tapping on my phone to crank out my last story from Beijing, right till the moment the plane lifted off the runway. I hadn't planned on leaving, but if I had to go, I would go out writing.[3]

One month earlier, on July 30, the *Journal* had published an article that I cowrote outlining how Australian law-enforcement and intelligence agencies were scrutinizing one of Xi Jinping's cousins, Ming Chai, as part of broader probes into organized crime, money laundering, and Chinese influence operations. My colleague, Philip Wen, and I reported that Chai had indulged in high-stakes gambling in his adoptive home of Australia, betting tens of millions of dollars at Melbourne's Crown Casino over a number of years—a remarkable outlay that prompted authorities to look into the sources of his money and suspected links to criminal syndicates. We also revealed that Chai had flaunted his familial ties with Xi while seeking business opportunities in China, though there was no indication that Xi had done anything to advance his cousin's interests, or had any knowledge of Chai's business and gambling activities.[4]

China considers the private lives of senior leaders and their families to be off-limits for journalistic inquiry, especially reporting that exposes the enormous gaps between the party's socialist rhetoric and the vast wealth amassed by members of the political elite. When we asked the Chinese foreign ministry to offer comment on the Ming Chai story before publication, ministry officials summoned my bureau chief for a late-night meeting, where they promised "serious consequences" if we went ahead with the report. They also singled me out as being "unfriendly to China," apparently referring to an earlier story I wrote about Xi's health and the party's lack of clear succession plans.[5]

Seven years earlier, when the *New York Times* and Bloomberg News published investigative stories about the wealth of the families of Premier Wen Jiabao and Xi, who was vice president at the time, Beijing retaliated by refusing to grant new journalist visas to both organizations. But the reporters who wrote those stories suffered few direct consequences. One of them, Mike Forsythe, said in a tweet about my expulsion: "In a sign of how things have changed, when Bloomberg published its exposé of the extended Xi family wealth in 2012 (I was one of the reporters), not only was I not expelled but my China journalist visa was renewed for another year, with no fuss."[6]

The party has only tightened its vise around foreign media since my departure. In the spring of 2020, China ejected at least eighteen journalists from three U.S. news organizations—the largest wave of expulsions since the Mao era and a stunning reversal of the efforts by Xi's predecessor to allow more access for foreign press.[7] Three of my colleagues were the first to go. Beijing revoked their visas in February over an allegedly derogatory headline on an op-ed published by the *Journal*'s opinion section, even though they had nothing to do with the article or its headline, which called China the "sick man of Asia"—a highly charged phrase that many Chinese see as a racist insult associated with their nation's "century of humiliation."

Then in March, after the Trump administration decided to force some sixty Chinese state media employees out of the U.S., Beijing revoked press credentials of more than a dozen American reporters working for the *Journal*, the *Times*, and the *Washington Post*. Chinese authorities also forcibly terminated the employment of at least seven Chinese staffers at foreign news outlets, including the *Journal*, the *Times*, and Voice of America.[8] Most of them were "news assistants" or "researchers," the euphemistic labels they adopt to skirt government rules that bar Chinese citizens from working as full-fledged reporters for foreign media. The move sent chills through the small community of Chinese researchers, who form the backbone of every foreign media outlet's operations in mainland China, handling everything from administrative chores to front-line reporting.

Within weeks, the party had gutted the China bureaus of some of the most influential Western news organizations, leaving them with a handful of reporters and researchers to hold the fort. Beijing's message was clear: what few freedoms that foreign media enjoyed in the country were entirely subordinate to the party's interests. The party giveth and the party taketh away.

The expulsions marked the end of an era. While the party has never been particularly welcoming of foreign muckrakers, China had for decades made slow, sometimes bumpy, progress in opening up to outside scrutiny. When Beijing normalized ties with Washington in 1979, it allowed American news organizations to return to the mainland, setting up bureaus and bearing witness as Deng Xiaoping's "reform and opening up" steered China toward capitalist-style modernity. Though conservative elders resisted his efforts, fearing that the influx of foreign influences would erode the party's socialist ideals, Deng was adamant. "Because now for any country that wants to develop, staying isolated is impossible," he told fellow elders in 1984. "The lessons of history tell us that if we don't open up, we can't succeed."[9]

Reporting conditions were far from ideal in the early years. Authorities kept foreign journalists under close surveillance and barred them from venturing beyond Beijing without permission. Reporters were roughed up, denied visas, or expelled for crossing murky political "red lines." The party eventually loosened some shackles as it grew more accustomed to managing Western newshounds, allowing the media to become the "informational lubricant" that helped China interact, trade, and become more economically connected with the outside world.[10] In the run-up to the 2008 Beijing Olympics, China suspended some media controls to allow foreign reporters to travel across the country and conduct interviews without prior state approval, and made these changes permanent after the games concluded.[11] Government harassment persisted, but many foreign correspondents came to believe that China was becoming, bit by bit, a more open society.[12]

That optimism swiftly dissipated under Xi Jinping. The new leader wanted to "tell China's stories well," which first and foremost meant asserting full control over the media and reining in journalists who strayed from the party line. Some of China's most daring news outlets bore the early brunt of Xi's crackdown. *Southern Weekly*, a newspaper in Guangdong province known for hard-hitting coverage, had its 2013 New Year's editorial allegedly rewritten by the provincial propaganda chief, Tuo Zhen, who turned a call for stronger constitutional rights into a celebration of the party's achievements.[13] *Southern Weekly* staffers demanded Tuo's resignation and protests broke out against state censorship, but their defiance did little to impede Xi's campaign to subdue the news industry.

Xi insisted that all media should "bear the surname 'party.'" Regulators ramped up internet censorship and punished a number of prominent Weibo microblog influencers for allegedly spreading rumors—a crackdown that helped tame an increasingly rambunctious online space.[14] Authorities harassed, detained, and jailed journalists who questioned party narratives, and tightened control over commercial news outlets that once prided themselves on producing investigative and explanatory reporting. Party propagandists who did Xi's bidding were well rewarded. Tuo, for instance, was promoted to vice minister at the party's propaganda department, before being named chief editor and president of the *People's Daily*. The pressure on Chinese media grew so suffocating that reporters quit the industry in droves. Some switched to better-paid jobs in public relations, while others left China to pursue graduate degrees. A friend of mine, just before moving to the U.S. for doctoral studies, offered pithy advice to journalist buddies he invited for a farewell dinner: "Watch yourselves."

Foreign media also felt the heat. In late 2013, China threatened to eject nearly two dozen reporters from the *New York Times* and Bloomberg News by withholding renewals for their visas, though Beijing eventually extended their credentials after then vice president Joe Biden raised the matter with Xi during a trip to Beijing.[15] In 2015, the Chinese government declined to renew press credentials for a French newspaper journalist who criticized the party's Xinjiang policies, effectively expelling her.[16] The same thing happened in 2018 to an American reporter for Buzzfeed News who wrote about state surveillance and religious repression in Xinjiang.[17]

Annual surveys by the Beijing-based Foreign Correspondents' Club of China indicated that its members faced increasing intimidation from the government. One poll found that in 2020, nearly 40 percent of reporters surveyed said their sources had been harassed, questioned, or detained for speaking with them, up from 25 percent the year before.[18] Journalists who traveled in Xinjiang independently of government junkets often ran into local officials and police officers blocking them from interviewing residents and intimidating the people who dared speak. Even ordinary Chinese have joined the fray, hounding foreign-media staffers who show up in their communities to cover natural disasters, industrial mishaps, and other mass-casualty events, and accusing them of smearing China.

The intimidation took a chilling turn after the 2020 expulsions. In August that year, authorities detained an Australian reporter working for Chinese state television, Cheng Lei, for allegedly endangering China's national security. State security agents later tracked down two other Australian journalists in connection with the case, prompting Canberra to intervene and help the two reporters leave China—an episode that Chinese state media suggested was retaliation against Australian law-enforcement raids on Chinese journalists.[19] Months later, authorities detained a Chinese citizen working for Bloomberg TV in Beijing, Haze Fan, also for alleged national security offenses (Fan, who was friends with Cheng, was released on bail in January 2022).[20]

In Hong Kong, where the media had long enjoyed more freedoms than on the mainland, authorities tightened press controls in the name of enforcing a 2020 national security law. Police rounded up media executives and journalists for allegedly threatening national security, prompting several local news outlets to shut down. Some reporters at Western organizations had their visa applications held up for months, or rejected outright. The *New York Times* moved its Asia-Pacific news-editing hub to Seoul from Hong Kong, citing the security law and deteriorating conditions for media.[21]

"The Chinese state continues to find new ways to intimidate foreign correspondents, their Chinese colleagues, and those whom the foreign press seeks to interview, via online trolling, physical assaults, cyber hacking, and visa denials," the Foreign Correspondents' Club of China said in a 2022 report. As visa restrictions and rising harassment drive more reporters away, it said, "covering China is increasingly becoming an exercise in remote reporting."[22]

Some news organizations have adapted, and continued producing incisive coverage from long distance. But offshore news gathering, however well done, remains a poor substitute for boots on the ground. Fleshing out stories with journalistic "color," the lucid details that humanize the news and pull in readers, becomes much more difficult. Finding sources and winning their trust is a lot harder without face-to-face contact, and conducting interviews by phone can expose sources to harm. Most journalists would prefer to travel the country, meet people, and experience daily living in the most tactile ways, to keep their fingers on political, economic, and social pulses in one of the world's most consequential nations.

Even remote reporting has gotten harder. While the party has long maintained tight control over information, Xi has taken China to new levels of opacity.[23] His demands for political discipline have made the black box of Chinese politics more inscrutable than ever, as officials grew even more tight-lipped and reluctant to engage with foreigners. His all-encompassing definition of national security spurred authorities to classify a widening range of information as confidential. Beijing enacted a new data-security law in late 2021, subjecting almost all data-related activities to government oversight, including the collection, storage, use, and transmission of information. Officials, scholars, and investors say their traditional playbooks for engaging Beijing and parsing its policies are no longer viable. "It's very difficult to know who has what position within the party, and how decisions flow," one senior Western business lobbyist told me. "There's no clear nexus of decision-making. When you find the government person who's responsible, they'll just read you a document and refuse to engage."[24]

Foreign businesses, investors, and researchers increasingly struggle to get useful and timely information, as Chinese entities err on the side of caution in assessing what constitutes sensitive data. Some financial databases stopped selling information to overseas customers, while ship-tracking services withheld data on vessels in Chinese waters from clients outside the country. Metals suppliers grew reluctant to provide details about their inventory, making it harder for foreign customers to plan production. Chinese regulators and securities-industry groups warned analysts against issuing comments that could trigger instability in the markets or broader society. Several prominent Chinese market strategists had their social media accounts suspended after they posted commentaries contradicting the party's narratives on the economy.[25]

Data sources that foreign officials, activists, and journalists used for highlighting political repression in China have also dried up. Policy directives, procurement papers, and speeches often disappeared from Xinjiang government websites after reporters used them to piece together how the party ran its forced-assimilation campaign against Muslim minorities. In the summer of 2021, a government-run judicial database was purged of thousands of court documents related to cases of political dissent and subversion. Such censorship makes it much harder for outsiders to find information that can be used to pressure Beijing on human rights, says John Kamm, chairman of the Dui Hua Foundation, a San Francisco–based group that advocates for political and religious detainees in China. "The disclosure rate of sensitive political cases is now zero."

Academic and cultural exchanges have suffered too. Chinese universities tightened approval processes for scholars seeking to travel overseas or participate in Zoom calls with foreign counterparts. Strict Covid-19 border controls—which the party maintained until early 2023—disrupted travel into and out of China, drastically reducing opportunities for face-to-face interactions with foreigners. "Excessive management has cut us off from studying advanced ideas, research methods and political experiences from abroad," wrote Jia Qingguo, a former dean of Peking University's School of International Studies.[26]

I tried to warn about some of these consequences after the 2020 journalist expulsions, in the form of an online essay in Chinese ruminating on the impact of the forced exodus. I wrote it as a favor to a friend, who ran a popular WeChat social media account named *qiangzhan waimei gaodi*, or "seizing the foreign media high ground." Often called *qiangwaigao* for short, the account had attracted a dedicated following among current and former Chinese journalists, including many with experience working for foreign media. My friend asked if I wanted to share my thoughts on the expulsions from the perspective of a foreign correspondent. I agreed to write something anonymously.

The result was a roughly 4,100-character essay, written for Chinese readers, in which I lamented the loss of seasoned reporters who can help international audiences learn about China. I explained how differences in Chinese and Western perspectives on the value and social purposes of journalism often lead to misunderstandings on how foreign media operates. Foreign reporters, I wrote, face many constraints in trying to produce balanced and objective coverage, while still ensuring that their stories are appealing, concise, and easily digestible for readers back home, particularly in an era of ever-shortening attention spans.[26] I argued that most foreign reporters who write so-called "negative stories" about China aren't trying to besmirch the country, but, more often than not, are analyzing events through their own perspectives, informed by cultural and social norms in their own countries.

For all their flaws and foibles, Western media correspondents still provide a crucial channel "for the outside world to understand China," I wrote. "Reducing their opportunities to conduct on-the-ground interviews and report in China will only fuel misunderstandings and suspicions about China in the outside world." I cited a Chinese idiom, *huwei biaoli*, that evokes a reciprocal relationship based on mutual accommodation and acceptance. China and the foreign media "should find a way to co-exist," I said. "We live in chaotic times, and may there be an end to this night."[27]

I used a pen name, *dongxie xidu*, which Chinese readers would recognize as a near-homophone for "eastern heretic, western venom"—the noms de guerre for two popular characters created by the famed Chinese martial arts novelist Louis Cha, better known as Jin Yong. Another iteration of this near-homophone translates as "writing in the east, reading in the west," a phrase I use in social media biographies. Several attempts to publish the essay timed out—a typical snag for WeChat posts that feature sensitive content. We tried to sidestep censorship algorithms by replacing certain phrases with subtler alternatives, like "MZD" instead of "Mao Zedong," to no avail. Eventually we gave up and published the essay as a private post, which would be automatically forwarded to readers who sent a certain password to the *qiangwaigao* account.

The essay went live late in the evening of March 22, 2020. Titled "A Letter from a Foreign-Media Reporter," it ran up tens of thousands of clicks within hours, before maxing out the following day at "100,000+ views," the highest tally that WeChat can display.[28] Censors took down one version of the essay, but copies proliferated across Chinese internet forums, where users dissected the essay's arguments. Some dismissed the essay as a self-serving whitewash of Western biases against China. Others sympathized with my views but insisted that Beijing had no choice but to expel American reporters—for anything less would be a dereliction of patriotic duty. "The essay is well-written but it doesn't get to the key of the issue, the core of which is reciprocity" between China and the U.S., one reader said. "Keeps talking about why China shouldn't expel them, why doesn't he talk about what the U.S. did beforehand," another wrote. "Isn't this just double standards?"

The government took notice. Some officials asked Chinese journalists whether they knew the author's identity. One foreign ministry staffer went on social media to criticize the essay for embodying a "holier than thou" attitude that he believed to be prevalent among foreign reporters. Some Chinese media outlets struck back with their own commentaries. *The Paper*, a Shanghai-based news portal, published an op-ed by an unnamed "person from the Chinese media industry," who accused some Western media of perpetuating prejudice against China, and said the Chinese people were capable of discerning well-meaning foreign correspondents from malicious ones.[29] A columnist for the website of the state-run *Economic Daily* newspaper justified the expulsion of American reporters as a reasonable response to Western bullying. "Foreign media should rub their eyes and understand clearly that the era of China 'not fighting back when struck, not shouting back when abused' is over," the columnist wrote. "To foreign media, this is a dark night, an era of chaos. To me, this is the dawn, an era that nurtures order and beckons justice."[30]

Xi's demands on protecting national security and fanning patriotic fervor created a political environment where the outside world is increasingly regarded as hostile and belligerent.[31] It's a potent and self-reinforcing cocktail of digital autocracy and ethnocentric nationalism. State censorship helped stoke patriotic fervor online, often manifesting in a virulent "cancel culture" that drowns out dissenting voices. Ultra-nationalists wage social-media campaigns to boycott foreign brands accused of offending China, denounce dissidents, troll feminist and gay rights activists, and abuse journalists. Popular social media platforms, once seen as public squares that allow a measure of debate, are increasingly dominated by chest-thumping chauvinists, while liberal and moderate users retreat into private chatrooms.

Digital nationalism has become big business. Internet platforms promote patriotic content to drive traffic and rake in advertising fees. Influencers and live-streaming stars monetize their love for China with flag-waving displays.[32] State media and party publicists, chasing clicks to prove their growing reach, indulge in triumphalist tropes that celebrate China's achievements while denigrating other countries. Even academics and public intellectuals have joined in, garnering broad audiences on social media with saber-rattling rhetoric. The online jingoism grew so alarming that an informal collective of anonymous volunteers, known as "the Great Translation Movement," started exposing the toxicity to the outside world by translating ultranationalistic commentary from Chinese social media and publishing it in English and other languages on Twitter—an effort that state media tried to discredit as a smear campaign against China.[33]

Amid such ferment, China's distrust of the West has spilled well beyond the corridors of power and seeped into public discourse, fueling shrill rhetoric that often squeezes out reasoned arguments. Rising anti-China sentiment within Western policy circles also makes it harder for Beijing to offer compromises that many within the party elite and broader society may perceive as weakness. "The party can rein in this nationalism," says Jessica Chen Weiss, a Cornell University scholar who studies the role of nationalism in Chinese foreign policy. "But doing so requires political capital that they may be unwilling or unable to spend." Or as the Chinese saying goes, "If you ride the tiger, it's hard to get off."

Given China's opaque authoritarian system, it is difficult to accurately assess the depth of public support for Xi and the Communist Party. Even so, what glimpses of popular sentiment we get on social media suggest many Chinese care deeply about their nation's global standing, and how they are perceived by outsiders. Positive appraisals are welcomed for affirming China's resurgence as a great power. Negative commentary, well intended or otherwise, is increasingly dismissed as smears by misguided and malicious people.

Xi insists that China will stay the course with "reform and opening up," but where Deng once urged the party to "liberate thoughts," Xi has ordered cadres to "unify thinking" and close their minds to "corrupt" foreign influences. His avowal of a rising East and declining West has become an article of faith within the party and beyond; questioning such views is almost tantamount to disloyalty. Much like how America's "culture warriors" see their struggle in Manichean terms, many nationalistic Chinese embrace the party's claims to leading an existential quest for national dignity and dominance. Compromise is often dismissed as weakness, cooperation derided as collusion.

As the British historian Robert Bickers writes, "nationalism matters in China, and what matters in China matters to us all."[34] Fired by historical grievances and a sense of civilizational destiny, Xi's China is brash but brittle, intrepid yet insecure. It is a would-be superpower in a hurry, eager to take on the world while wary of what may come. It demands to be seen, heard, and respected, but obstructs outsiders who try to peer past the pomp and propaganda. It exerts a global reach with economic and military might, even as its ruling party retreats into an ideological cocoon. Its choices are reshaping the world, and it behooves us to grasp why and how. Understanding this powerful, opaque, and restless China has become harder than ever, but this is why we must try.

ACKNOWLEDGMENTS

Journalism is a collective enterprise. This book is the culmination of the goodwill and generosity of countless people whom I've encountered over my years as a foreign correspondent in China. Political sensitivities and professional discretion prevent me from openly thanking many of them, but I hope they can take some satisfaction from seeing their ideas, insights, and tips appear across these pages.

Jude Blanchette deserves immense credit as the book's most energetic advocate, having first seeded the idea over lunch in Beijing back in 2017. He assured me that I had a compelling story to tell, guided me through the groundwork of crafting a proposal, critiqued my early drafts, and reminded me that "it takes a village to write a book." If I am the village chief in this analogy, then he has been a sterling deputy.

I am greatly indebted to my colleagues and mentors at the *Wall Street Journal*, particularly the denizens of the China bureau, now spread across Beijing, Shanghai, Hong Kong, Taipei, Tokyo, Seoul, Singapore, Washington, and New York. They are the newsroom giants whose shoulders I stand on. Charles Hutzler took a chance in bringing me to Beijing and related the many wisdoms and war stories he accrued over more than two decades in China. The late, great Carlos Tejada was a patient editor and gregarious presence in the bureau. Josh Chin, Liza Lin, and Te-Ping Chen supplied copious advice on how to tackle the vagaries of book-writing. Keith Zhai has been a phenomenal reporting partner, offering a sounding board, sharing contacts, and imparting his vast knowledge on Chinese politics. Kersten Zhang, who navigated the Chinese bureaucracy with an easy charm like no other journalist I know could, was ever so kind when I needed help dealing with officials or eliciting responses from reluctant sources, some of whom are cited in this book. Patrick Barta never failed to distil my arguments and liven up my copy. P. R. Venkat, one of the most resourceful and generous colleagues I've had, taught me many valuable lessons about work and life. Jonathan Cheng and Andrew Dowell offered unflinching support throughout this project.

My deepest thanks goes to the following people, who helped review drafts, correct my misapprehensions, and sharpen my arguments: Ryan Manuel, Yufan Huang, Jeff Khoo, Timothy Cheek, Mark C. Elliott, Max Oidtmann, Joseph Torigian, Changhao Wei, Donald Clarke, Susan Finder, Donald Low, Andrew Collier, Philip Wen, Yang Jie, Yoko Kubota, Lingling Wei, Eva Xiao, James T. Areddy, Liyan Qi, Chao Deng, Joyu Wang, and Clement Tan. I am very grateful as well for the advice and encouragement offered by Gerry Shih, Eva Dou, Yuanjie Zheng, Lun Tian Yew, Jun Mai, Pei Li, Hallie Gu, Sarah Chen, Peidong Sun, Shibani Mahtani, Timothy McLaughlin, Newley Purnell, Stella Xie, Wenxin Fan, Till Lembke, and Nick Marro.

My agent, Howard Yoon, of Ross Yoon Agency, grasped the book's potential immediately, and shepherded this rookie author painlessly through the pitching process. Ben Loehnen of Avid Reader Press edited the manuscript with sharpness and enthusiasm, and managed the production with immense patience.

Lastly, I owe immeasurable gratitude to my family. My late father, who toiled ceaselessly to support our family before his faculties faded; my indefatigable mother, whose quiet sacrifices allowed me to pursue my passions; and my brother and sister, who constantly remind me there's more to life than work. Claire Soon, my wife and best friend, walked with me on every step in this project, reading my manuscript, indulging my foibles, and assuring me that I have the wherewithal to see things through. I dedicate this book to them.

NOTES

EPIGRAPH

1 Author's translation of 《临江仙·滚滚长江东逝水》 ["Immortal by the River · The Yangtze's Roaring Waters Roll Ever Eastward"]. Written by Ming dynasty poet Yang Shen, the verse was later added as an epigraph to the classic Chinese novel *Romance of the Three Kingdoms* by Qing dynasty editors. A son of a top Ming official, Yang won the title of *zhuangyuan* by achieving the best score in imperial examinations. But he was later exiled for his role in the "Great Rites Controversy," during which Yang's father led the opposition against the Jiajing emperor's decision to depart from prevailing succession protocols. Jiajing, who succeeded his heirless cousin, declined to ritually honor his late uncle—the Hongzhi emperor—as his imperial father, and instead declared his own father an emperor posthumously. The full verse and other translations are available here: Wang Xiaohui, "青山依旧在 几度夕阳红——《三国演义》英译品读（一）[But the Lush Hills Remain, and the Scarlet Sunsets Repeat—Appreciating English Translations of *Romance of the Three Kingdoms* (Part One)]," China.org.cn, April 30, 2020, http://www.china.org.cn/chinese/2020-04/30/content_75994782.htm

INTRODUCTION

1 Xi Jinping, "关于坚持和发展中国特色社会主义的几个问题 [Several Issues with Regard to Persevering with and Developing Socialism with Chinese Characteristics]," 《求是》 *Seeking Truth*, March 31, 2019. http://www.qstheory.cn/dukan/qs/2019-03/31/c_1124302776.htm

2 Tian Yipeng, "转型期中国城市社会管理之痛——以社会原子化为分析视角 [The Pains of Chinese Urban Social Management in the Transition Period—From the Perspective of Social Atomization]," 《探索与争鸣》 *Exploration and Free Views*, No. 12 of 2012 (December 2012): 65–69. http://www.tsyzm.com/CN/abstract/abstract909.shtml

3 Yan Lianke, *Serve the People!* (New York: Grove Atlantic, 2008). https://groveatlantic.com/book/serve-the-people/

4 Cheng Min and Jian Jun, "纪念粉碎'四人帮'35周年座谈综述 [A Summary of the Symposium Commemorating the 35th Anniversary of the Smashing of the 'Gang of Four']," 《炎黄春秋》 *Yanhuang Chunqiu*, No. 11 of 2011 (November 2011). https://web.archive.org/web/20190504071106/http://www.yhcqw.com/11/8549.html

5 John Garnaut, "China's Princelings Break Their Silence," *Sydney Morning Herald*, October 17, 2011. https://www.smh.com.au/world/chinas-princelings-break-their-silence-20111016-1lrkh.html

6   Cheng Min and Jian Jun, "纪念粉碎"四人帮"35周年座谈会发言摘要 [A Summary of the Symposium Commemorating the 35th Anniversary of the Smashing of the 'Gang of Four']," 《中国改革》 *China Reform*, No. 11 of 2011 (November 2011): 106–111. https://www.aisixiang.com/data/46123.html

7   Xi Jinping, "跨世纪领导干部的历史重任及必备素质 [The Historical Responsibilities and Necessary Qualities of Cross-Century Leading Cadres]," 《中共福建省委党校学报》 《理论学习月刊》 [*Journal of the Fujian Provincial Committee Party School of the Chinese Communist Party, Theoretical Studies Monthly*], No. 11 of 1991 (November 1991): pp. 32–36. https://xuewen.cnki.net/DownloadArticle.aspx?filename=SWDX199111009&dbtype=CJFD

8   Ronald Reagan, "Speech to the House of Commons," June 8, 1982. https://teachingamericanhistory.org/library/document/speech-to-the-house-of-commons/

9   Kerry Brown, *CEO, China: The Rise of Xi Jinping* (London: I.B. Tauris, 2016), pp. 228–230.

10 Xi Jinping, "紧紧围绕坚持和发展中国特色社会主义 学习宣传贯彻党的十八大精神 [Focus Closely on Upholding and Developing Socialism with Chinese Characteristics; Study, Publicize and Implement the Spirit of the Party's 18th National Congress]," in Xi Jinping, 《习近平谈治国理政》 第一卷 *Xi Jinping: The Governance of China*, Vol. 1(Beijing: Foreign Languages Press, 2014), pp. 6–17.

11 "习近平南巡讲话撮要 [Highlights from Xi Jinping's Southern Tour Speech]," 《前哨》 月刊 *Front Line Magazine*, No. 265 of 2013 (March 2013), p. 162.

12 Richard McGregor, *The Party: The Secret World of China's Communist Rulers* (New York: HarperCollins, 2010).

13 Jane Perlez, "Transcript: On the Trail of Xi Jinping," Harvard Kennedy School Shorenstein Center on Media, Politics and Public Policy, December 18, 2019. https://shorensteincenter.org/transcript-trail-xi-jinping/

14 Mao Zedong, "愚公移山 [Foolish Old Man Moves Mountains]," in Mao Zedong, 《毛泽东选集》 第三卷 *Selected Works of Mao Zedong*, Vol. 3 (Beijing: People's Publishing House, 1991), pp. 1101–1104. Mao Zedong concluded the Communist Party's 7th National Congress in 1945 with a speech that recounted "Foolish Old Man Moves Mountains." The story tells of an old man in northern China, known as "Yugong" or Foolish Old Man, whose house faced two great peaks, Taihang and Wangwu, that blocked his way. Yugong summoned his sons to dig and move the mountains, an effort that a wise old man dismissed as hopelessly misguided. Yugong was undeterred, insisting that his descendants would carry on the task long after his death, until the mountains were moved. Yugong's determination moved God, who tasked two giants to carry the mountains away. In his 1945 speech, Mao couched the fable as analogous to the challenges confronting the Chinese people, who were weighed down by the two mountains of imperialism and feudalism. The Chinese Communist Party, Mao said, had made up its mind to dig up these two mountains, and through perseverance win the hearts of the Chinese people, who would then dig together with the party and clear the mountains away.

15 "习近平的成绩单 [Xi Jinping's Scoresheet]," 人民网 People.cn, October 19, 2014. http://tv.people.com.cn/GB/363018/389906/389978/index.html

1. ASCENDANT XI

1 Huo Xiaoguang, Zhang Xiaosong, Luo Zhengguang, and Zhu Jichai, "人民的信赖 郑重的誓言——记习近平当选国家主席、中央军委主席并进行宪法宣誓 [People's Trust, Solemn Oath—A Chronicle of Xi Jinping's Election as President and Chairman of the Central Military Commission and Swearing-in under Constitutional Oath]," Xinhua News Agency, March 17, 2018. http://www.xinhuanet.com/politics/leaders/2018-03/18/c_1122552249.htm

2 "党政领导干部职务任期暂行规定 [Provisional Regulations on the Terms of Office for Leading Cadres in the Party and Government]," 中共党员网 [Chinese Communist Party Members Net], March 12, 2015. http://news.12371.cn/2015/03/12/ARTI1426126246992108.shtml; Jeremy Page and Lingling Wei, "Xi's Power Play Foreshadows Historic Transformation of How China is Ruled," *Wall Street Journal*, December 26, 2016. https://www.wsj.com/articles/xis-power-play -foreshadows-radical-transformation-of-how-china-is-ruled-1482778917

3 Deng Xiaoping, "党和国家领导制度的改革 [Reform of the Party and State Leadership System]," 《邓小平文选》第二卷 *Selected Works of Deng Xiaoping*, Vol. 2, Second Edition (Beijing: People's Publishing House, 1994), pp. 320–343.

4 Deng Xiaoping, "第三代领导集体的当务之急 [Urgent Tasks for the Third Generation of the Leadership Collective]," 《邓小平文选》第三卷 *Selected Works of Deng Xiaoping*, Vol. 3 (Beijing: People's Publishing House, 1993), pp. 309–314.

5 Geremie R. Barmé, "Introduction: Under One Heaven," in *Shared Destiny: China Story Yearbook 2014* (Australian National University Press, 2015), p. XX, dated November 2014, accessed June 6, 2021. https://www.thechinastory.org/yearbooks/yearbook-2014/introduction-under-one -heaven/

6 Qian Gang, "领袖姓名传播强度观察 [Observations on the Intensity of Propagation of Leaders' Names]," *RTHK Media Digest*, July 11, 2014, accessed August 20, 2021. http://gbcode.rthk.org .hk/TuniS/app3.rthk.hk/mediadigest/content.php?aid=1563

7 Chun Han Wong, "Three Wise Men: Xi Seeks to Join Mao and Deng in China's 'Holy Scripture,'" *Wall Street Journal*, October 20, 2017. https://www.wsj.com/articles/three-wise-men-xi -seeks-to-join-mao-and-deng-in-chinas-holy-scripture-1508491813

8 Chun Han Wong, "China's Communist Party Proposal Sets Stage for Xi to Hold On to Power," *Wall Street Journal*, February 25, 2018. https://www.wsj.com/articles/chinas-communist-party -proposes-scrapping-presidential-term-limits-1519549709

9 Xuan Li, "保证党和国家长治久安的重大制度安排 [Major Institutional Arrangements to Ensure the Long-Term Stability of the Party and the Country]," *People's Daily*, March 1, 2018, p. 3. http://politics.people.com.cn/n1/2018/0301/c1001-29840344.html

10 Chun Han Wong, "Xi Jinping Clear to Rule Indefinitely as China Scraps Presidential Term Limits," *Wall Street Journal*, March 11, 2018. https://www.wsj.com/articles/xi-jinping-clear-to -rule-indefinitely-as-china-scraps-presidential-term-limits-1520757321

11 Nicholas Kristof, "Looking for a Jump-Start in China," *New York Times*, January 5, 2013. https://www.nytimes.com/2013/01/06/opinion/sunday/kristof-looking-for-a-jump-start-in -china.html

12 Joseph Torigian, "Xi Jinping's Tiananmen Family Lessons," *Foreign Policy*, June 4, 2020. https:// foreignpolicy.com/2020/06/04/xi-jinping-tiananmen-lessons-chinese-communist-party/

13 Yang Xiaohuai, "习近平：我是如何跨入政界的 [Xi Jinping: How I Entered Politics]," 人民网 People.cn, January 9, 2015. http://politics.people.com.cn/n/2015/0109/c1001-26356880.html

14 Robert Caro, *The Passage of Power: The Years of Lyndon Johnson* (New York: Alfred A. Knopf, 2012), p. xiv.

15 Official biographies of Xi Jinping state that he was born in June 1953, in keeping with the party's standard practice of not disclosing officials' precise birth dates. Even so, Xi's birth date was reported by Chinese media in 2010, after Laotian leaders marked Xi's birthday on June 15, while he was visiting the Southeast Asian country as China's vice president. Other foreign leaders, including Russian president Vladimir Putin, have wished Xi happy birthday on June 15. Xuexi Xiaozu, a WeChat account run by the *People's Daily* newspaper, has reported that Xi's birthday coincided with China's Dragon Boat Festival, celebrated annually on the fifth day of the fifth lunar month, which in 1953 fell on June 15. See: Xuexi Xiaozu, "Birthday Wishes to Xi from All Across the Country," Xuexi Xiaozu WeChat account, June 3, 2014. https://mp.weixin.qq.com/s/J4xgMqjJFYZwDz5NyDoUKg

16 Yang Jisheng, *The World Turned Upside Down: A History of the Chinese Cultural Revolution* (New York: Farrar, Straus and Giroux, 2021), p. 6.

17 Yang Kuisong, 《中华人民共和国建国史研究》第一卷 [A History of the Founding of the People's Republic of China, Vol. 1] (Nanchang: Jiangxi People's Publishing House, 2009): 445–451.

18 Many of the primary sources that I reviewed while researching Xi Jinping's early life were cited earlier by the historian Joseph Torigian in a 2018 article about Xi's upbringing. See: Joseph Torigian, "Historical Legacies and Leaders' Worldviews: Communist Party History and Xi's Learned (and Unlearned) Lessons," *China Perspectives*, No. 1–2 of 2018 (June 2018): 7–15.

19 Qi Xin, "忆仲勋——纪念习仲勋同志一百周年诞辰 [Remembering Zhongxun—Commemorating the 100th Anniversary of Comrade Xi Zhongxun's Birth]," 《习仲勋纪念文集》 [Xi Zhongxun Commemorative Anthology] (Beijing: Chinese Communist Party History Publishing House, 2013). http://www.sxlib.org.cn/dfzy/rwk/bqjsldr/xzx/qwts/xzxjnwj/201707/t20170719_836128.html

20 "央视《东方时空》省委书记系列专访-浙江省委书记习近平 [CCTV 'Oriental Time and Space' Series of Interviews with Provincial Party Secretaries—Zhejiang Provincial Party Committee Secretary Xi Jinping]," Sina.com, November 14, 2003. http://news.sina.com.cn/c/2003-11-14/13312136924.shtml

21 Yan Huai, 《进出中组部》 [In and Out of the Central Organization Department] (Deer Park, New York: Mirror Books, 2017), p. 219.

22 Hao Ping, "一生信守 '奢靡误国，勤俭兴邦 [A Lifelong Commitment to 'Extravagance Harms the Nation, Hard Work and Frugality Rouses the Nation']," 《习仲勋纪念文集》 [Xi Zhongxun Commemorative Anthology] (Beijing: Chinese Communist Party History Publishing House, 2013), http://www.sxlib.org.cn/dfzy/rwk/bqjsldr/xzx/qwts/xzxjnwj/201707/t20170719_836127.html; Torigian, "Historical Legacies and Leaders' Worldviews: Communist Party History and Xi's Learned (and Unlearned) Lessons."

23 Qi, "Remembering Zhongxun."

24 Zhang Zhigong, 《难忘的二十年：在习仲勋身边工作的日子里》 [*Two Commemorable Decades: The Days Working Under Xi Zhongxun*] (Beijing: People's Liberation Army Press, 2013), p. 216; Torigian, "Historical Legacies and Leaders' Worldviews: Communist Party History and Xi's Learned (and Unlearned) Lessons."

25 Qi Xin, "仲勋，我用微笑送你远行 [Zhongxun, I Send You Off on a Long Journey with a Smile]," in Remembering Xi Zhongxun Editorial Team, 《怀念习仲勋》[*Remembering Xi Zhongxun*] (Beijing: Chinese Communist Party History Publishing House, 2005), pp. 12–33.

26 Xi Zhongxun Biography Editorial Committee, 《习仲勋传》下卷 [*Xi Zhongxun Biography*, Vol. 2] (Beijing: Central Party Literature Press, 2013), p. 634.

27 Xi Zhongxun Biography Editorial Committee, 《习仲勋传》上卷 [*Xi Zhongxun Biography*, Vol. 1] (Beijing: Central Party Literature Press, 2008), p. 1.

28 Editorial Committee, *Xi Zhongxun Biography*, Vol. 1, p. 1.

29 Xiong Fuming, "习仲勋：党的利益在第一位 [Xi Zhongxun: The Party's Interests Come First]," 《学习时报》 *Study Times*, February 20, 2017. https://web.archive.org/web/20210324022318/http://www.dswxyjy.org.cn/n1/2019/0228/c423732-30943304.html

30 "第二批校友名录公示(61届—65届小学毕业 缺62年毕业生名单) [Announcement of the Second Batch of Alumni List (61st–65th primary school graduates, excluding the '62 graduates list)]," Beijing Bayi School Alumni Association, accessed May 25, 2021. http://xyh.bayims.cn/article/88.html and http://xyh.bayims.cn/article/91.html

31 Li Heshun (ed.), 《我心中的八一：献给母校诞辰60周年》[*The Bayi in My Heart: Dedicated to Our Alma Mater's 60th Anniversary*] (Beijing: Unity Publishing House, 2007), pp. 64–81; Torigian, "Historical Legacies and Leaders' Worldviews: Communist Party History and Xi's Learned (and Unlearned) Lessons."

32 Torigian, "Historical Legacies and Leaders' Worldviews: Communist Party History and Xi's Learned (and Unlearned) Lessons."

33 Mi Hedu (ed.), 《當時年少曾輕狂》[*Frivolous When We Were Young*] (Hong Kong: Ruitian Cultural Publishing Co. Ltd., 2015), p. 16; Torigian, "Historical Legacies and Leaders' Worldviews: Communist Party History and Xi's Learned (and Unlearned) Lessons."

34 Wei Mengjia and Zhao Wanwei, "习近平看望北京市八一学校师生回访记 [A Chronicle of Xi Jinping's Visit to Teachers and Students at Beijing Bayi School]," Xinhua News Agency, September 11, 2016. http://www.xinhuanet.com//politics/2016-09/11/c_1119546601.htm

35 Liu Ningzhe and Kai Lei, "师生缘系半世纪，尊师重教情不移 [A Half Century of Teacher Student Ties, Unwavering Respect for Teachers and Education]," 《文匯報》 *Wen Wei Po*, September 10, 2015. http://xyh.bayims.cn/article/105.html

36 Li (ed.), *The Bayi in My Heart*, pp. 97–98.

37 Editorial Committee, *Xi Zhongxun Biography*, Vol. 2, pp. 267–288.

38 Editorial Committee, *Xi Zhongxun Biography*, Vol. 2, p. 282.

39 Author's conversations with Joseph Torigian; Alice Su, "Dreams of a Red Emperor: The relentless rise of Xi Jinping," *Los Angeles Times*, October 22, 2020, https://www.latimes.com/world-nation/story/2020-10-22/china-xi-jinping-mao-zedong-communist-party; Jeremy Page, "How the U.S. Misread China's Xi: Hoping for a Globalist, It Got an Autocrat," *Wall Street Journal*, December 23, 2020, https://www.wsj.com/articles/xi-jinping-globalist-autocrat-misread-11608735769

40 Qi, "Remembering Zhongxun."

41 Mi, *Frivolous When We Were Young*, p. 23.

42 Editorial Committee, *Xi Zhongxun Biography*, Vol. 2, pp. 290–291.

43 Li (ed.), *The Bayi in My Heart*, pp. 231–232; Torigian, "Historical Legacies and Leaders' Worldviews: Communist Party History and Xi's Learned (and Unlearned) Lessons."

44 Jeremy Page, "How the U.S. Misread China's Xi: Hoping for a Globalist, It Got an Autocrat,"

Wall Street Journal, December 23, 2020. https://www.wsj.com/articles/xi-jinping-globalist-auto crat-misread-11608735769

45 Nie Weiping and Wang Ruiyang, 《围棋人生》 [*Life of Go*] (Beijing: China Federation of Literary Art Publishing House, 1999), pp. 124–125.

46 Meng Xiangfeng, "做有志气有作为的一代——习仲勋之子习近平访谈录 [Be a Generation with Ambition and Achievements—An Interview With Xi Zhongxun's Son Xi Jinping]," 《家长》 [*Parents*], No. 2 of 1997, April 15, 1997, p. 4.

47 Yang, "Xi Jinping: How I Entered Politics."

48 Yang Ping, "杨屏:习仲勋与近平的父子情 [Yang Ping: Father-Son Ties Between Xi Zhongxun and Xi Jinping]," Aisixiang.com, accessed August 8, 2021. http://www.aisixiang.com/data /61575.html; Torigian, "Historical Legacies and Leaders' Worldviews: Communist Party History and Xi's Learned (and Unlearned) Lessons."

49 Yang, "Xi Jinping: How I Entered Politics."

50 Yang, "Yang Ping: Father-Son Ties."

51 Page, "How the U.S. Misread China's Xi."

52 Chen Peng, "勤奋 真诚 坦然 尽责——与习近平聊做官与做人 [Diligent, Sincere, Calm, Conscientious—Chatting with Xi Jinping About Being an Official and Being a Person]," 《时代潮》 *Chinese Times*, August 2000, pp. 34–35.

53 "视频: 04年习近平专访 我是延安人 [Video: 2004 Interview with Xi Jinping—I'm a Yan'an Native]," Sina Video, dated June 12, 2014, accessed March 24, 2021. https://video.sina.com.cn /p/news/c/v/2014-06-12/045964024653.html

54 Cheng Li, "Xi Jinping's Inner Circle (Part 1: The Shaanxi Gang)," *China Leadership Monitor*, No. 43 of 2014 (March 14, 2014), accessed April 15, 2021. https://www.brookings.edu/wp-content/ uploads/2016/06/Xi-Jinping-Inner-Circle.pdf

55 Tan Chunping and Qin Liang, "历史的见证者 探访留守延安的北京知青 [Witnesses of History: Visiting the Beijing Rusticated Youth Who Stayed Behind in Yan'an]," 《市场信息报》 [Market Information News], March 26, 2015. https://weibo.com/p/2304189287c5ce0102vl7o

56 北京知青在陕北 [Beijing Rusticated Youth in Northern Shaanxi], 《冷暖人生》, 凤凰卫视 Phoenix TV, aired December 16, 2014. https://www.dailymotion.com/video/x2cp5p6

57 "Video: 2004 Interview with Xi Jinping."

58 Yang, "Xi Jinping: How I Entered Politics."

59 "初心 · 梁家河篇 [Original Aspirations · Liangjiehe Chapter]," China Central Television, March 19, 2017. http://m.news.cctv.com/2017/03/19/ARTI9uhRtfHK8S4sG0nSdLpO170319.shtml

60 Tao Haili, "为群众做实事是习近平始终不渝的信念 [Doing Practical Things for the Masses Is Xi Jinping's Unwavering Belief]," 《习近平的七年知青岁月》 [*Xi Jinping's Seven Years As a Sent-Down Youth*] (Beijing: Central Party School Press, 2017), pp. 70–72. http://cpc.people.com. cn/n1/2017/0306/c64387-29126778.html

61 Editorial Committee, *Xi Zhongxun Biography*, Vol. 2, pp. 332–333.

62 Yang, "Xi Jinping: How I Entered Politics."

63 "Portrait of Vice President Xi Jinping: 'Ambitious Survivor' of the Cultural Revolution," Wikileaks Cable: 09BEIJING3128_a, dated November 16, 2009, accessed April 3, 2021. https://wikileaks.org/plusd/cables/09BEIJING3128_a.html. The leaked U.S. diplomatic cable cited a friend of Xi Jinping identified only as "the professor," but provided key biographical details that matched Yi Xiaoxiong's age, family background, and academic career. Daniel Golden,

a veteran American journalist, named Yi as "the professor" in a 2017 book, *Spy Schools*—an iden- tification that Yi didn't dispute. Yi didn't respond to my requests for comment, while Marietta College, where Yi worked as an academic for more than three decades before retiring in 2021, declined to comment.

64 Yang, "Xi Jinping: How I Entered Politics."

65 "习近平忆延安插队：它教了我做什么 [Xi Jinping Recalls Being Sent Down to Yan'an: What It Taught Me to Do]," 人民网 People.cn, February 14, 2015. http://politics.people.com.cn /n/2015/0214/c1001-26566406.html

66 Yang, "Xi Jinping: How I Entered Politics."

67 Xi Jinping, "我是黄土地的儿子 [I Am a Son of the Yellow Earth]," in Xu Xiaohui and Zeng Yongchen (eds.), 《知青老照片》 [*Sent-Down Youths' Old Photos*] (Tianjin: Hundred Flowers Literature and Art Publishing House, 1998), p. 40.

68 "1975级年级概况 [An Overview of the Class of 1975]," Tsinghua Alumni Association, dated Au- gust 23, 2019, accessed August 11, 2021. https://www.tsinghua.org.cn/xyll/njll/qhdx/a1975.htm

69 Alessandro Russo, "The Conclusive Scene: Mao and the Red Guards in July 1968," *Positions: East Asia Cultures Critique* 13, No. 3 (Winter 2005): 535–574. http://blogs.law.columbia.edu /uprising1313/files/2017/07/project_muse_190199.pdf

70 James C. Hsiung (ed.), *The Xi Jinping Era: His Comprehensive Strategy Toward the China Dream* (New York: CN Times Books, 2015), pp. 60–61.

71 "Portrait of Vice President Xi Jinping: 'Ambitious Survivor' of the Cultural Revolution."

72 Tao, "Doing Practical Things for the Masses," pp. 75–76.

73 Tao, "Doing Practical Things for the Masses," pp. 75–76.

74 Tao, "Doing Practical Things for the Masses," pp. 75–76.

75 Gao Shimeng, Zhou Qiongyuan, Luan Hui, Huang Minmin, and Tang Yong, "Xi Jinping's Men- tor," *Blog Weekly* 《博客天下》, No. 34 of 2013, December 15, 2013, pp. 46–59.

76 The historian Joseph Torigian noted earlier that Xi Jinping and Yang Jiechi were both part of Geng Biao's delegation during his 1979 trip to Europe. Both Xi and Yang appear in a delegation photograph published in an authorized biography of Geng. See: Kong Xiangxiu, 《耿飚传》 下卷 [*Geng Biao Biography*, Vol. 2] (Beijing: People's Liberation Army Press, 2009), p. 418.

77 Gao, Zhou, Luan, Huang and Tang, "Xi Jinping's Mentor," pp. 46–59.

78 "Portrait of Vice President Xi Jinping: 'Ambitious Survivor' of the Cultural Revolution."

79 Gao, Zhou, Luan, Huang and Tang, "Xi Jinping's Mentor," pp. 46–59.

80 "Portrait of Vice President Xi Jinping: 'Ambitious Survivor' of the Cultural Revolution."

81 Xi Jinping, "从政杂谈 [A Discussion on Entering Politics]," in Xi Jinping, 《摆脱贫困》 [*Shak- ing Off Poverty*] (Fuzhou: Fujian People's Publishing House, 1992), pp. 27–28.

82 Yong Huaqi, "习近平回正定 [Xi Jinping Returns to Zhengding]," 《散文百家》 [*Hundred Schools of Prose*], No. 7 of 2009 (July 2009): 4–8.

83 Xi Jinping, 《知之深 爱之切》 [*Knowing Deeply, Loving Profoundly*] (Shijiazhuang: Hebei People's Publishing House, 2015), p. 223.

84 Central Party School Interview Records Editorial Office, 《习近平在正定》 [Xi Jinping in Zhengding] (Beijing: Central Party School Press, 2019), pp. 35–36.

85 "栗战书同志简历 [Comrade Li Zhanshu's Curriculum Vitae]," Xinhua News Agency, March 17, 2018. http://www.gov.cn/guoqing/2018-03/17/content_5275068.htm

86 Chun Han Wong, "Xi's Right-Hand Man Is Message-Bearer in China-U.S. Trade Dispute," *Wall*

Street Journal, August 1, 2018. https://www.wsj.com/articles/xis-right-hand-man-is-message
-bearer-in-china-u-s-trade-dispute-1533121200

87　Yang Jisheng, "前言：特權是'統治階級'的'階級利益' [Foreword: Special Privileges Are
the 'Class Interests' of the 'Ruling Class']," in Yan, *In and Out of the Central Organization Department*, p. 15.

88　Yan, *In and Out of the Central Organization Department*, pp. 216–219; author's interview with
Yan Huai in June 2019.

89　Ding Dong and Li Nanyang (eds.), 《李锐口述往事》[*Li Rui's Oral Accounts of the Past*] (Hong
Kong: Great Mountain Culture Publications, 2013), p. 373.

90　Yan, *In and Out of the Central Organization Department*, p. 218.

91　Qiu Zi, "習仲勳之子談仕途——訪閩寧德地委書記習近平 [Xi Zhongxun's Son Discusses His
Official Career—An Interview with Ningde District Secretary Xi Jinping]," 《大公報》 *Ta Kung
Pao*, April 9, 1989, p. 5.

92　Willy Wo-Lap Lam, *Chinese Politics in the Era of Xi Jinping: Renaissance, Reform, or Retrogression?*
(New York: Routledge, 2015), pp. 43–44.

93　Central Party School Interview Records Editorial Office, 《习近平在福建》上册 [*Xi Jinping in
Fujian*, Vol. 1] (Beijing: Central Party School Press, 2021), pp. 87–101.

94　Ming Hong, "幸福婚姻让她歌声更甜美—彭丽媛谈与习近平的婚姻生活 [A Happy Marriage Makes Her Singing Sweeter—Peng Liyuan Talks About Her Married Life with Xi Jinping],"
《支部建设》 [*Party-Branch Building*] No. 5 of 2003 (May 2003): 54–56.

95　Ming, "A Happy Marriage Makes Her Singing Sweeter"; "这个年轻的副市长与众不同 [This
Young Deputy Mayor Stands Out from the Rest]," 中共党员网 [Chinese Communist Party Members Net], August 4, 2020. http://www.12371.cn/2020/05/25/ARTI1590340088003521.shtml

96　Hsiung (ed.), *The Xi Jinping Era*, p. 103.

97　Desmond Shum, *Red Roulette: An Insider's Story of Wealth, Power, Corruption, and Vengeance in
Today's China* (New York: Scribner, 2021), p. 203; author's interview with Shum in August 2021.

98　Qiu, "Xi Zhongxun's Son Discusses His Official Career—An Interview with Ningde District
Secretary Xi Jinping," *Ta Kung Pao*.

99　Zhang Mingqing, "习近平同志在福建宁德工作时反腐倡廉的生动实践 [Vivid Experiences
from Comrade Xi Jinping's Efforts to Fight Corruption and Promote Honesty While Working
in Fujian's Ningde]," 人民网 People.cn, March 1, 2018. http://politics.people.com.cn/n1/2018
/0302/c1024-29842665.html

100　Zhang Mingqing, "办好一件事 赢得万人心 [Doing One Thing Well and Winning Ten Thousand Hearts]," *People's Daily*, May 21, 1990, p. 5.

101　Xi Jinping, "把握好新闻工作的基点 [Mastering the Fundamentals of Journalism]," in Xi, *Shaking Off Poverty*, p. 69.

102　Editorial Committee, *Xi Zhongxun Biography*, Vol. 2, pp. 642–643.

103　Lan Feng, Zheng Zhao, Lin Wei, and Shan Zhiqiang, "山海情怀 赤子初心——习近平总书
记在福建的探索与实践·党建篇 [An Affinity for Mountains and Seas, Original Aspirations
Like An Innocent Child's—General Secretary Xi Jinping's Exploration and Practice in Fujian,
Party-Building Chapter]," 《福建日报》 *Fujian Daily*, July 13, 2017. http://fjnews.fjsen.com
/2017-07/13/content_19788467.htm

104　John Tkacik, "China's Crown Princeling," *Wall Street Journal*, October 26, 2007. https://www
.wsj.com/articles/SB119334860709572038; *Office Administration*, Interview Group, "实干才能

梦想成真——习近平同志在福州工作期间倡导践行"马上就办"纪实 [Only Hard Work Can Make Dreams Come True—A Chronicle of Comrade Xi Jinping's Advocacy and Implementation of 'Do It Right Away' During His Time Working in Fuzhou," 《秘书工作》 *Office Administration*, No. 2 of 2015 (February 2015): 4–15.

105 Zhao Xin, "从濒临破产到盈利 福州机场的起死回生之谜 [From the Verge of Bankruptcy to Profitability: The Mysterious Revival of Fuzhou Airport]," 《厦门晚报》 [*Xiamen Evening News*], April 16, 2006. http://news.carnoc.com/list/67/67293.html

106 "三坊七巷 收回的背后 [Sanfang Qixiang: Behind the Revocation]," 《东南快报》 *Southeast Express*, December 22, 2005. http://news.sina.com.cn/c/2005-12-22/04017769139s.shtml

107 Xi Jinping, "加强两岸交流 促进祖国统一 [Strengthen Cross-Strait Exchanges, Promote Unification of the Motherland]," 《国防》 [*National Defense*] No. 3 of 2000 (March 2000), p. 10.

108 Xue Zhen, "名城绿海唱大风——记福建省委常委、福州市委书记习近平 [The Famous City of the Green Sea Sings the Great Breeze—Remembering Fujian Provincial Party Standing Committee Member, Fuzhou Municipal Party Secretary Xi Jinping]," 《福建文学》 *Fujian Literature*, No. 4 of 1994, p. 62.

109 Author's interview with Alfred Wu in February 2022.

110 Cheng Li, "China's Fifth Generation: Is Diversity a Source of Strength or Weakness?," *Asia Policy* 1, No. 6 (July 2008): 84–85.

111 "习近平省长强调福建将全力配合中央查处 '远华案' [Governor Xi Jinping Stresses That Fujian Will Fully Cooperate with the Central Government in Investigating the 'Yuanhua Case']," China News Service, January 29, 2000. http://www.chinanews.com/2000-1-29/26/17163.html

112 Yang, "Xi Jinping: How I Entered Politics."

113 "'人民群众是我们力量的源泉'——记中共中央 总书记习近平 ['The People Are the Source of Our Strength'—A Chronicle of Chinese Communist Party Central Committee General Secretary Xi Jinping]," Xinhua News Agency, December 23, 2012. http://www.gov.cn/ldhd/2012-12/25/content_2298338.htm

114 "Xi Jinping Millionaire Relations Reveal Fortunes of Elite," Bloomberg News, June 29, 2012. https://www.bloomberg.com/news/articles/2012-06-29/xi-jinping-millionaire-relations-reveal-fortunes-of-elite

115 Liu Bingrong, 《走近齐锐新》 [*Up Close with Qi Ruixin*] (Beijing: Renmin University of China Alumni Association, 2013), pp. 251 and 532.

116 "Xi Jinping Millionaire Relations Reveal Fortunes of Elite."

117 Interviews by the author and *Wall Street Journal* colleagues with the cousin's friends and associates.

118 "Portrait of Vice President Xi Jinping: 'Ambitious Survivor' of the Cultural Revolution."

119 Yang, "Xi Jinping: How I Entered Politics."

120 Michael Sheridan, "Objection, Mr Xi. Did You Earn That Law Degree?," *Sunday Times*, August 11, 2013, https://www.thetimes.co.uk/article/objection-mr-xi-did-you-earn-that-law-degree-q9vc3nqjbsl; Tom Hancock and Nicolle Liu, "Top Chinese Officials Plagiarised Doctoral Dissertations," *Financial Times*, February 27, 2019, https://www.ft.com/content/2eb02fa4-3429-11e9-bd3a-8b2a211d90d5

121 Edwin Chan, "China's Fujian Governor Flushes Over Rosy Future," Reuters News, July 3, 2002.

122 "Zhejiang Party Secretary Touts Economic Successes and Work Towards Rule of Law at Ambassador's Dinner," Wikileaks Cable: 07BEIJING1840_a, dated March 19, 2007, accessed August 24, 2021, https://wikileaks.org/plusd/cables/07BEIJING1840_a.html; Jeremy Page, Bob Davis, and

Tom Orlik, "China's New Boss," *Wall Street Journal*, November 12, 2012, https://www.wsj.com/articles/SB10001424127887324439804578106860600724862.

123 "Political Pessimism as 60th Anniversary Approaches," Wikileaks Cable: 09SHANGHAI405 _a, dated September 25, 2009, accessed August 9, 2021. https://wikileaks.org/plusd/cables /09SHANGHAI405_a.html

124 James T. Areddy, "Wenzhou's 'Annus Horribilis' Shakes China," *Wall Street Journal*, November 15, 2011. https://www.wsj.com/articles/SB10001424052970204505304577001180665360306

125 Ding and Li (eds.), *Li Rui's Oral Accounts of the Past*, p. 373.

126 "Zhejiang Party Secretary Touts Economic Successes."

127 Du Yan, "浙江省委书记习近平接见季克良袁仁国一行 [Zhejiang Provincial Party Secretary Xi Jinping Meets Ji Keliang, Yuan Renguo and Their Delegation]," 《茅台酒报》 [Moutai News], July 1, 2005, in Luo Shixiang and Yao Hui (eds.), 《百年茅台》 [Hundred Years of Moutai] (Beijing: Chinese Literature and History Press, 2015), p. 226.

128 "贵州茅台酒股份有限公司 酒厂历史 [Kweichow Moutai Co., Ltd. Distillery History]," 中国酒志网 [Chinese Wine History Net], accessed August 25, 2021. http://www.cnjiuzhi.com/ winery/maotai/history.html

129 Cheng Li, "China: Riding Two Horses at Once," Brookings Institution, dated October 23, 2007, accessed August 26, 2021. https://www.brookings.edu/articles/china-riding-two-horses-at-once/

130 Cheng Li, "One Party, Two Coalitions in China's Politics," Brookings Institution, dated August 16, 2009, accessed August 26, 2021. https://www.brookings.edu/opinions/one-party-two -coalitions-in-chinas-politics/

131 Peng You and Ye Jingyu, "浙沪六年 [Six Years in Zhejiang and Shanghai]," 经济观察网 [Economic Observer Net], November 17, 2012. http://www.eeo.com.cn/2012/1117/236222.shtml

132 James T. Areddy, "China Sacks Shanghai's Top Leader," *Wall Street Journal*, September 26, 2006. https://www.wsj.com/articles/SB115916867513772924

133 Dong Qiang and Miao Yirong, "上海召开党政负责干部大会 贺国强、习近平讲话 [Shanghai Convenes Meeting of Responsible Party and Government Officials, He Guoqiang and Xi Jinping Gave Speeches]," 《解放日报》 *Jiefang Daily*, March 25, 2007. http://www.gov.cn/jrzg/2007-03 /26/content_560842.htm

134 Tian Yujue and Sang Xi, "习书记对上海发展的影响是不能用他在上海工作的时间长短来衡量的 [Secretary Xi Jinping's Influence on Shanghai's Development Cannot Be Measured by the Length of Time He Worked in Shanghai]," 《学习时报》 *Study Times*, September 1, 2021, accessed September 1, 2021, p. 3. https://www.ccps.gov.cn/zl/xjpzsh/202108/t20210831_150331 .shtml and https://mp.weixin.qq.com/s/XW7pGZSCZKfzeP7QpuiWuQ

135 Miao Yirong, "习近平回顾在上海7个月工作：重点做了四方面工作 [Xi Jinping Reviews His Seven Months of Work in Shanghai: Focused on Four Aspects of Work]," 《解放日报》 *Jiefang Daily*, October 28, 2007. http://www.chinanews.com/gn/news/2007/10-28/1061285.shtml

136 Miao Yirong, "习近平在瞻仰中共"一大"会址时指出始终坚定理想信念自觉践行党的宗旨 [Xi Jinping Points Out While Paying Homage to the Site of the Chinese Communist Party's First Congress: Always Stay Firm in One's Ideals and Beliefs, Consciously Implement the Party's Purpose]," 《解放日报》 *Jiefang Daily*, March 31, 2007. http://cpc.people.com.cn/GB/64093 /64102/64396/5546082.html

137 Zhu Bin, "上海市委书记习近平会见美国前国务卿基辛格博士 [Shanghai Party Secretary Xi Jinping Meets with Former U.S. Secretary of State Dr. Henry Kissinger]," 《文汇报》 *Wen Wei*

Po, April 5, 2007, http://www.gov.cn/gzdt/2007-04/05/content_572239.htm; "习近平在兴国宾馆分晤日本前首相与瑞典外贸大臣 [Xi Jinping Meets with Former Japanese Prime Minister and Swedish Foreign Minister at Xingguo Hotel]," Shanghai People's Government website, June 15, 2007. http://www.gov.cn/gzdt/2007-06/15/content_649920.htm

138 Brown, *CEO, China*, pp. 4–6.

139 Song Yijun, "新中国成立后中共历届中央领导集体形成始末 [The Formation of the Successive Chinese Communist Party Leadership Collectives Since the Establishment of a New China]," 《世纪桥》 *Bridge of Century*, Nos. 6 and 7 of 2013. http://dangshi.people.com.cn/n/2013/0607/c85037-21775854-16.html

140 "Contacts on New Politburo Standing Committee Member Xi Jinping's Rise, New Leadership Lineup," Wikileaks Cable: 07BEIJING7107_a, dated November 14, 2007, accessed August 25, 2021. https://wikileaks.org/plusd/cables/07BEIJING7107_a.html

141 "领航新时代的坚强领导集体——党的新一届中央领导机构产生纪实 [The Strong Leadership Collective That Navigates the New Era—A Chronicle of the Formation of the Party's Leadership Bodies for a New Term]," Xinhua News Agency, October 26, 2017. http://www.xinhuanet.com/politics/19cpcnc/2017-10/26/c_1121860147.htm; Chun Han Wong, "Xi Jinping Summons 'Red Boat Spirit' of China's Communist Revolutionaries," *Wall Street Journal*, November 1, 2017. https://www.wsj.com/articles/xi-jinping-summons-red-boat-spirit-of-chinas-communist-revolutionaries-1509536096

142 "Contacts on New Politburo Standing Committee Member Xi Jinping's Rise."

143 "2007 10 22 無綫六點半新聞 中共十七大政治局常委亮相 [TVB News at 6:30 Unveiling of the Politburo Standing Committee at the Chinese Communist Party's 17th National Congress]," YouTube, dated January 22, 2017, accessed August 19, 2021. https://youtu.be/yzf_Z9Zg4fU

144 Nicholas Kristof, "China's Genocide Olympics," *New York Times*, January 24, 2008. https://www.nytimes.com/2008/01/24/opinion/24kristof.html

145 "习近平致电慰问因伤退出比赛的刘翔 [Xi Jinping Sends Cable to Console Liu Xiang, Who Withdrew from Competition Due to Injury]," CCTV.com, dated August 18, 2008, accessed August 31, 2021. http://news.cctv.com/china/20080818/108052.shtml

146 PanChinese, "习近平著名的 '吃饱了没事干' 视频 [Xi Jinping's Famous 'Nothing Better to Do After Eating Their Fill' Video]," YouTube video, dated March 25, 2013, accessed July 4, 2021. https://youtu.be/aG903lJtC7M

147 Austin Ramzy, "A Chinese Leader Talks Tough to Foreigners," *Time*, February 13, 2009. https://world.time.com/2009/02/13/a-chinese-leader-talks-tough-to-foreigners/

148 Raymond Li, "Censors Delete Vice-President's Jibe," *South China Morning Post*, February 14, 2009. https://www.scmp.com/article/669939/censors-delete-vice-presidents-jibe

149 Li Yajie, "习近平:加强基层党建工作 促进民族地区繁荣发展 [Xi Jinping: Strengthen Grassroots Party-Building Work, Promote Prosperous Development in Ethnic Regions]," Xinhua News Agency, June 21, 2009, http://www.gov.cn/ldhd/2009-06/21/content_1346519.htm; Shai Oster and Gordon Fairclough, "Deadly Ethnic Riots Pose Fresh Crisis for Beijing," *Wall Street Journal*, July 7, 2009, https://www.wsj.com/articles/SB124685864855299373; Ian Johnson, "Uighurs Lose Economic Ground to Han," *Wall Street Journal*, July 21, 2009, https://www.wsj.com/articles/SB124811293085765891.

150 Jeremy Page, "Internal Security Tops Military in China Spending," *WSJ China Real Time* blog, March 5, 2011, https://www.wsj.com/articles/BL-CJB-13441; Chris Buckley, "China Internal

Security Spending Jumps Past Army Budget," Reuters News, March 5, 2011, https://www.reuters.com/article/us-china-unrest-idUSTRE7222RA20110305

151 Josh Chin, "Top Chinese Propaganda Official Puts Pressure on Microblogs," *WSJ China Real Time* blog, October 15, 2011. https://www.wsj.com/articles/BL-CJB-14487

152 Zhang Cong, "县委书记'进京听训': 仰望星空与接地气的现实期待 [County Party Secretaries 'Head to the Capital for Lectures': Realistic Expectations Between Looking Up to the Stars and Being Connected to the Ground]," 《大地》 *Earth Biweekly*, dated 2008, accessed September 1, 2021. http://cpc.people.com.cn/GB/68742/85928/85931/8658242.html

153 "习近平: 领导干部要加强党性修养 提高综合素质 [Xi Jinping: Leading Cadres Must Strengthen Their Party Spirit and Improve Their Overall Quality]," Xinhua News Agency, March 1, 2009. http://www.gov.cn/ldhd/2009-03/01/content_1247390.htm

154 Author's interview with Daniel Russel in October 2021.

155 Author's interview with Daniel Russel in October 2021.

156 Joe Biden, "Remarks by President Biden at a Democratic National Committee Fundraiser," the White House, dated April 21, 2022, accessed April 26, 2022. https://www.whitehouse.gov/briefing-room/speeches-remarks/2022/04/21/remarks-by-president-biden-at-a-democratic-national-committee-fundraiser-3/

157 Cheng Li and Eve Cary, "The Last Year of Hu's Leadership: Hu's to Blame?," the Jamestown Foundation, dated December 20, 2011, accessed September 3, 2021. https://jamestown.org/program/the-last-year-of-hus-leadership-hus-to-blame/

158 Chris Buckley, "Elite China Think-Tank Issues Political Reform Blueprint," Reuters News, February 19, 2008. https://www.reuters.com/article/us-china-politics-idUSPEK20590720080219

159 Author's interview with Cai Xia in September 2021.

160 Akio Yaita, 習近平: 共産中国最弱の帝王 [*Xi Jinping: Communist China's Weakest Emperor*] (Tokyo: Bungei Shunju, 2012). https://books.bunshun.jp/ud/book/num/9784163749907

161 Michael Wines, "In Rise and Fall of China's Bo Xilai, an Arc of Ruthlessness," *New York Times*, May 6, 2012, https://www.nytimes.com/2012/05/07/world/asia/in-rise-and-fall-of-chinas-bo-xilai-a-ruthless-arc.html; Jeremy Page, "Media Savvy Is Bo Xilai's Wild Card at Trial," *Wall Street Journal*, August 21, 2013, https://www.wsj.com/articles/SB10001424127887323980604579026673432025670.

162 Tom Orlik and Lingling Wei, "Behind a Chinese City's Growth, Heavy Debt," *Wall Street Journal*, April 23, 2012. https://www.wsj.com/articles/SB100014240527023034590045773599726178 62832

163 Jeremy Page, "China Leaders Laud 'Red' Campaign," *Wall Street Journal*, June 20, 2011. https://www.wsj.com/articles/SB10001424052702303936704576395621087173648; https://jamestown.org/program/xi-jinpings-chongqing-tour-gang-of-princelings-gains-clout/

164 Author's interview with Cai Xia in August 2021.

165 Jeremy Page and Lingling Wei, "Bo's Ties to Army Alarmed Beijing," *Wall Street Journal*, May 17, 2012. https://www.wsj.com/articles/SB10001424052702304203604577398034072800836

166 Desmond Shum, *Red Roulette: An Insider's Story of Wealth, Power, Corruption, and Vengeance in Today's China* (New York: Scribner, 2021), pp. 242–243; author's interview with Shum in August 2021.

167 Shum, *Red Roulette*, pp. 242–243; author's interview with Shum in August 2021.

168 Jeremy Page and Andrew Browne, "Chinese Party Chief Falls After Rebuke," *Wall Street Journal*,

March 14, 2012. https://www.wsj.com/articles/SB1000142405270230445980457728075308922
21224

169 Jeremy Page, "Crash Put New Focus on China Leaders," *Wall Street Journal*, October 22, 2012. https://www.wsj.com/articles/SB10000872396390443768804578034290553181894

170 Page, "Crash Put New Focus on China Leaders."

171 SCMP Reporters, "Exclusive: How Crash Cover-Up Threatens Career of Hu's Top Aide," *South China Morning Post*, September 3, 2012. https://www.scmp.com/news/china/article/1028489/exclusive-how-crash-cover-threatens-career-hus-top-aide

172 Monica Langley and Brian Spegele, "U.S.-China Talks Make Little Progress," *Wall Street Journal*, September 5, 2012. https://www.wsj.com/articles/SB10000872396390443571904577631212783313148

173 Bob Davis and Lingling Wei, *Superpower Showdown: How the Battle Between Trump and Xi Threatens a New Cold War* (New York: Harper Business, 2020), pp. 37–38.

174 Author's interview with Desmond Shum in August 2021.

175 Brown, *CEO, China*, pp. 31–35.

176 "'The People Are the Source of Our Strength,'" Xinhua News Agency.

177 Jeremy Page, "For Xi, a 'China Dream' of Military Power," *Wall Street Journal*, March 13, 2013. https://www.wsj.com/articles/SB10001424127887324128504578348774040546346

178 Xi Jinping, "紧紧围绕坚持和发展中国特色社会主义 学习宣传贯彻党的十八大精神 [Focus Closely on Upholding and Developing Socialism with Chinese Characteristics; Study, Publicize and Implement the Spirit of the Party's 18th National Congress]," in Xi Jinping, 《习近平谈治国理政》第一卷 *Xi Jinping: The Governance of China*, Vol. 1 (Beijing: Foreign Languages Press, 2014), pp. 6–17.

179 Jeremy Page, "China Spins New Lesson from Soviet Union's Fall," *Wall Street Journal*, December 10, 2013. https://www.wsj.com/articles/SB10001424052702303755504579207070196382560

2. GRIPPING IRON AND LEAVING MARKS

1 Feng Guogang and Shan Hongfei, "警钟 | 从得志走向沉沦：黑龙江省鸡西市恒山 区委原书记孔令宝腐败案剖析 [Alarm Bells | From Achieving Ambitions to Degradation: An Analysis of the Corruption Case of Kong Lingbao, Former Secretary of the Hengshan District Committee of Jixi City, Heilongjiang Province]," Central Commission for Discipline Inspection and National Supervisory Commission website, dated January 1, 2021, accessed September 14, 2021. https://www.ccdi.gov.cn/jz/202012/t20201231_232994.html

2 Feng and Shan, "Alarm Bells | From Achieving Ambitions to Degradation."

3 Sheng Jixuan and Xue Liwei, "鸡西市恒山区委书记孔令宝因疫情防控失职失责被免职 [Jixi City Hengshan District Committee Secretary Kong Lingbao Dismissed for Negligence in Epidemic Prevention and Control]," 《黑龙江日报》 *Heilongjiang Daily*, February 15, 2020, p. 4. http://epaper.hljnews.cn/hljrb/20200215/460800.html

4 Feng and Shan, "Alarm Bells | From Achieving Ambitions to Degradation."

5 Sun Xianfu, "孔令宝为什么会腐化蜕变 [Why Did Kong Lingbao Degenerate]," Central Commission for Discipline Inspection website, dated January 7, 2021, accessed September 17, 2021. https://www.ccdi.gov.cn/pl/202101/t20210107_233352.html

6   James T. Areddy, "New Frugality Puts Strain on Chinese Firms," *Wall Street Journal*, January 22, 2014. https://www.wsj.com/articles/SB10001424052702304027204579334162357059046

7   "刘铁男与情妇决裂始末: 学历都是情妇帮造 [The Full Story of the Rupture Between Liu Tienan and His Mistress: His Mistress Helped Forge His Academic Qualifications]," 中国共产党新闻网 [Communist Party of China News Net], May 15, 2013. http://fanfu.people.com.cn /n/2013/0515/c64371-21490669.html

8   Jeremy Page, "Scandal Tests Chinese President's Standing With Military," *Wall Street Journal*, February 5, 2014. https://www.wsj.com/articles/SB10001424052702303277704579348142139 463188

9   Xi Jinping, "着力培养选拔党和人民需要的好干部 [Train and Select Good Officials]," in Xi Jinping, 《习近平谈治国理政》第一卷 *Xi Jinping: The Governance of China*, Vol. 1 (Beijing: Foreign Languages Press, 2014), pp. 411 420.

10   Xu Jingyue and Zhou Yingfeng, "习近平在十八届中央纪委二次全会上发表重要讲话 [Xi Jinping Delivers an Important Speech at the 2nd Plenary Session of the 18th Central Commission for Discipline Inspection]," Xinhua News Agency, dated January 22, 2013, accessed September 21, 2021. https://www.ccdi.gov.cn/ldhd/gcsy/201312/t20131222_114953.html

11   Zhang Jinfan (ed.), 《中国古代监察制度史》[*A History of the Supervisory System in Ancient China*] (Beijing: China Fangzheng Press, 2019), pp. 48–50.

12   Charles O. Hucker, "The Traditional Chinese Censorate and the New Peking Regime," *American Political Science Review* 45, No. 4 (December 1951): 1041–1057. https://jstor.org/stable/1951246

13   Wu Meihua, "中国共产党纪检机构的历史沿革及其职能演变 [Historical Evolution of the CPC Organs for Discipline Inspection and Changes in Their Functions]," 《中共党史研究》 [*Chinese Communist Party History Studies*], No. 3 of 2009 (March 2009): 19–25.

14   Chinese Communist Party Central Organizational Department, Central History Research Office and Central Archives (eds.), 《中国共产党组织史资料》第七卷（上）[*Materials on the Chinese Communist Party's Organizational History*, Vol. 7, Part 1], (Beijing: Chinese Communist Party History Publishing House, 2000), pp. 183–184.

15   "'Special Measures': Detention and Torture in the Chinese Communist Party's Shuanggui System," Human Rights Watch, December 6, 2016. https://www.hrw.org/report/2016/12/06/ special-measures/detention-and-torture-chinese-communist-partys-shuanggui-system

16   Ling Li, "The Rise of the Discipline and Inspection Commission, 1927–2012: Anticorruption Investigation and Decision-Making in the Chinese Communist Party," *Modern China* 42, No. 5 (September 2016): 447–482.

17   Andrew Wedeman, "Growth and Corruption in China," *China Currents* 11, No. 2 (December 30, 2012), accessed September 21, 2021. https://www.chinacenter.net/2012/china_currents /11-2/growth-and-corruption-in-china/

18   "我国腐败分子向境外转移资产的途径及监测方法研究 [Research on the Ways That Corrupt Elements in China Transfer Assets Abroad and the Methods for Monitoring Such Transfers]," dated June 2008, accessed September 21, 2021. http://ww2.usc.cuhk.edu.hk/PaperCollection/ webmanager/wkfiles/8152_1_paper.pdf

19   Yuen Yuen Ang, *China's Gilded Age: The Paradox of Economic Boom and Vast Corruption* (Cambridge University Press, 2020).

20   Lin Zhu, "Punishing Corrupt Officials in China," *China Quarterly* 223 (September 2015): 595–617.

21 Andrew Wedeman, "Win, Lose, Or Draw? China's Quarter Century War on Corruption," *Crime, Law and Social Change* 49 (2008): 7–26.

22 Andrew Wedeman, "Flies into Tigers: The Dynamics of Corruption in China," *China Currents* 20, No. 1 (May 27, 2021), accessed October 2, 2021. https://www.chinacenter.net/2021/china_currents/20-1/flies-into-tigers-the-dynamics-of-corruption-in-china/

23 Li, "The Rise of the Discipline and Inspection Commission."

24 Author's calculations using official data from the Central Commission for Discipline Inspection; "中国这十年·系列主题新闻发布 | 十年来中国共产党在革命性锻造中更加坚强 [China in the Past Decade Themed News Briefings | The Chinese Communist Party Has Become Stronger Through Revolutionary Forging Over the Past Decade]," 新华网 Xinhua Net, June 30, 2022. http://www.news.cn/politics/2022-06/30/c_1128791733.htm

25 Chinese Communist Party Central Commission for Discipline Inspection and Central Party History and Literature Research Institute, 《习近平关于党风廉政建设和反腐败斗争论述摘编》 [*Excerpts from Xi Jinping's Discussion on the Construction of Party Style and Clean Government and the Fight Against Corruption*] (Beijing: Central Party Literature Press and China Fangzheng Press, 2015), p. 5.

26 Wang Zhuo, He Tao, Qu Peng, Mao Xiang, and Cheng Wei, "一个多月，看中央纪委国家监委机关转隶干部如何融合——进一家门成一家人 说一家话干一家事 [After More Than a Month, Let's See How the Cadres Transferred from the Central Commission for Discipline Inspection and the National Supervisory Commission Are Integrated—Enter a Family and Become a Family]," 《中国纪检监察报》 *China Discipline Inspection and Supervision Daily*, April 17, 2018, accessed September 12, 2021. https://www.ccdi.gov.cn/yaowen/201804/t20180417_170102.html

27 "官员装探头、编假材料 中央巡视组如何应对干扰？ [Officials Install Secret Cameras and Forge Materials: How Do Central Inspection Teams Deal with Interference?]," 《法制晚报》 *Legal Evening News*, July 26, 2016. http://www.xinhuanet.com/politics/2016-07/26/c_129177502.htm

28 Liu Yancai and Wang Chuchu (eds.), 《传承：我亲历的中央纪委故事》 [*Passing It On: My Personal Stories from the Central Commission for Discipline Inspection*] (Beijing: China Fangzheng Press, 2019), p. 225.

29 China Central Television, "永远在路上 第五集 把纪律挺在前面（"女老虎"吕锡文现身忏悔）[Always on the Road Episode 5 Putting Discipline at the Forefront ('Female Tiger' Lü Xiwen Comes Forward to Express Regret)]," YouTube video, dated October 23, 2016, accessed September 15, 2021. https://youtu.be/F4zI1vt29kw

30 Liao Xingmu and Tsai Wen-hsuan, "Strengthening China's Powerful Commission for Discipline Inspection Under Xi Jinping, with a Case Study at the County Level," *China Journal* 84 (July 2020): 29–50.

31 Wang Xiaoning, "【监察体制改革试点进行时】12项调查措施:在细化中规范 在实践中提升 [[While the Pilot Supervisory-System Reforms Are Underway] 12 Investigatory Measures: Standardize in Refinement and Improve in Practice]," Central Commission for Discipline Inspection website, dated January 25, 2018, accessed September 14, 2021. https://www.ccdi.gov.cn/toutiao/201801/t20180121_162216.html

32 Author's interview with a person briefed on party-discipline inspectors' interrogation techniques.

33 "What Is the Conviction Rate in China?—China Law in One Minute," *China Justice Observer*,

November 16, 2020, accessed September 29, 2021. https://www.chinajusticeobserver.com/a/what-is-the-conviction-rate-in-china

34 Chun Han Wong, "Xi's Right-Hand Man Is Message-Bearer in China-U.S. Trade Dispute," *Wall Street Journal*, August 1, 2018. https://www.wsj.com/articles/xis-right-hand-man-is-message-bearer-in-china-u-s-trade-dispute-1533121200

35 Lingling Wei and Bob Davis, "China's Top Graft Buster, Wang Qishan, Probing Thousands," *Wall Street Journal*, August 20, 2014. https://www.wsj.com/articles/chinas-top-graft-buster-probing-thousands-1408588202

36 "中央纪委西院搬家，办公地合一节省时间多'打虎' [The Central Commission for Discipline Inspection's West Campus Relocates, Combining Work Spaces to Save Time for 'Fighting Tigers']," *The Paper*, September 27, 2014, accessed November 4, 2021. https://www.thepaper.cn/newsDetail_forward_1268843

37 Zhuang Deshui, "各地纪检监察干部热议如何用新媒体发挥正能量 [Discipline-Inspection and Supervision Cadres from All Over Are Discussing How to Use New Media to Exert Positive Energy]," 《中国纪检监察报》 *China Discipline Inspection and Supervision Daily*, January 2, 2014. https://www.ccdi.gov.cn/yaowen/201401/t20140102_130361.html

38 "巡视组长揭入驻单位设障碍：饭菜不是咸就是辣 [Inspection Team Leader Reveals Obstacles to Settling in the Unit: The Food Is Either Salty or Spicy]," 《黑龙江日报》 *Heilongjiang Daily*, January 26, 2016. https://china.huanqiu.com/article/9CaKrnJTsFd

39 Xiaokan Chunshen, "'官员在女儿婚礼上被带走'——纪委该怎样辟谣 ['An Official Was Taken Away at the Daughter's Wedding'—How Should the Disciplinary Committee Refute Rumors]," 新华网 Xinhua Net, March 27, 2015. http://www.xinhuanet.com//politics/2015-03/27/c_127627435.htm

40 Benjamin Kang Lim and Ben Blanchard, "Exclusive: China Seizes $14.5 Billion Assets from Family, Associates of Ex-Security Chief: Sources," Reuters News, March 30, 2014. https://www.reuters.com/article/us-china-corruption-zhou-idUSBREA2T02S20140330

41 Josh Chin, "Xi Jinping's Leadership Style: Micromanagement That Leaves Underlings Scrambling," *Wall Street Journal*, December 15, 2021. https://www.wsj.com/articles/xi-jinpings-leadership-style-micromanagement-that-leaves-underlings-scrambling-11639582426; James T. Areddy, "The Disappearance of a Chinese Deal Maker," Wall Street Journal, June 14, 2017. https://www.wsj.com/articles/the-disappearance-of-a-chinese-deal-maker-1497434038

42 Michael Forsythe, "As China's Leader Fights Graft, His Relatives Shed Assets," *New York Times*, June 15, 2014. https://www.nytimes.com/2014/06/18/world/asia/chinas-president-xi-jinping-investments.html

43 Philip Wen and Chun Han Wong, "Chinese President Xi Jinping's Cousin Draws Scrutiny of Australian Authorities," *Wall Street Journal*, July 30, 2019. https://www.wsj.com/articles/chinese-presidents-cousin-draws-scrutiny-of-australian-authorities-11564500031

44 Feng Yiyan, "习总六亲不认拘捕涉贪表弟 [Boss Xi Disowns His Relatives and Arrests a Cousin Suspected of Corruption]," 《前哨》月刊 *Front Line Magazine*, No. 283 (September 2014): 10–15.

45 Author's interview with Lau Tat-man in September 2019.

46 Wen and Wong, "Chinese President Xi Jinping's Cousin Draws Scrutiny of Australian Authorities."

47 Author's interview with Desmond Shum in August 2021.

48 Liao and Tsai, "Strengthening China's Powerful Commission for Discipline Inspection."

49 Liao and Tsai, "Strengthening China's Powerful Commission for Discipline Inspection."

50   Yuhua Wang and Bruce J. Dickson, "How Corruption Investigations Undermine Regime Support: Evidence from China," *Political Science Research and Methods* (2021): 1–16.

51   Wei and Davis, "China's Top Graft Buster, Wang Qishan, Probing Thousands."

52   Victor Chung-Hon Shih, "'Nauseating' Displays of Loyalty: Monitoring the Factional Bargain Through Ideological Campaigns in China," *Journal of Politics* 70, No. 4 (October 2008): 1177–1192. https://www.journals.uchicago.edu/doi/epdf/10.1017/S0022381608081139

53   "学习贯彻《中国共产党纪律处分条例》 [Studying and Implementing 'Chinese Communist Party Regulations on Disciplinary Actions']," 中共党员网 [Chinese Communist Party Members Net], accessed April 24, 2022. http://www.12371.cn/special/zggcdjlcftl/jlcftl/

54   "新疆日报社原总编辑、副社长赵新尉严重违纪被双开 [Former Editor-in-Chief and Vice President of Xinjiang Daily Zhao Xinyu Was 'Doubly Dismissed' for Serious Violations of Discipline]," 中国共产党新闻网 [Communist Party of China News Net], November 2, 2015. http://fanfu.people.com.cn/n/2015/1102/c64371-27764303.html

55   Li Yuan, "北京市委原副书记吕锡文严重违纪被开除党籍和公职 [Former Deputy Secretary of the Beijing Municipal Party Committee Lü Xiwen Was Expelled from the Party and Public Office for Serious Violations of Discipline]," 中国共产党新闻网 [Communist Party of China News Net], January 5, 2016, http://fanfu.people.com.cn/n1/2016/0105/c64371-28014643.html; Li Yuan, "四川省原省长魏宏受到撤销党内职务、行政撤职处分 [Former Governor of Sichuan Province Wei Hong Was Removed from Party Positions and Administratively Dismissed]," 中国共产党新闻网 [Communist Party of China News Net], February 4, 2016. http://fanfu.people.com.cn/n1/2016/0204/c64371-28111831.html

56   Central Commission for Discipline Inspection, "中央纪委法规室负责人就《党纪处分条例》有关问题回答网友提问 [The Person in Charge of the Central Commission for Discipline Inspection's Regulations Office Answers Netizens' Questions on Issues Related to the 'Regulations on Party Disciplinary Punishments']," Central Commission for Discipline Inspection website, dated November 2, 2015, accessed September 17, 2021. http://v.ccdi.gov.cn/2015/11/01/VIDE1446340741609268.shtml

57   "得益于人民群众支持和参与 [Benefiting from the Support and Participation of the People]," Central Commission for Discipline Inspection website, dated March 7, 2016, accessed September 24, 2021. https://www.ccdi.gov.cn/special/xsjw/series15/201801/t20180102_160820.html#Art5

58   Chun Han Wong, "Today's 'Kings Without Crowns'?—The Growing Powers of Xi's Party Disciplinarians," *WSJ China Real Time* blog, March 2, 2016, accessed September 18, 2021. https://www.wsj.com/articles/BL-CJB-28786

59   "中央第三巡视组向天津市委反馈巡视'回头看'情况 [The No. 3 Central Inspection Team Provides Feedback to the Tianjin Municipal Party Committee on 'Look Back' Inspection Findings]," Central Commission for Discipline Inspection website, October 11, 2016. https://www.ccdi.gov.cn/special/zyxszt/dshilxs_zyxs/fgqg_xs10_zyxs/201610/t20161021_88345.html

60   Li Hongzhong, "做讲政治的知行合一者 [Be a Political Person Who Unifies Thoughts and Deeds]," 《天津日报》 *Tianjin Daily*, October 10, 2016, p. 1.

61   Mark Purdy, "China's Economy, in Six Charts," *Harvard Business Review*, November 29, 2013, accessed September 28, 2021. https://hbr.org/2013/11/chinas-economy-in-six-charts

62   Koh Gui Qing, "China Wasted $6.9 Trillion on Bad Investment Post 2009—Media," Reuters News, November 20, 2014. https://www.reuters.com/article/china-economy-investment-idUSL3N0TA2KP20141120

63 Wang Huning and Chen Mingming, "调整中的中央与地方关系：政治资源的开发与维护 [Central-Local Government Relations in a Period of Adjustment: The Development and Protection of Political Resources]," 《探索与争鸣》 *Exploration and Free Views*, No. 3 of 1995 (March 1995): 33–36.

64 Author's interview with Daniel Russel in October 2021.

65 Cheng Li, "China's New Top Government Leaders," Brookings Institution, dated March 18, 2018, accessed March 26, 2021. https://www.brookings.edu/interactives/chinas-new-top-government-leaders/

66 Author's interview with a China-based foreign diplomat in April 2019.

67 Chin, "Xi Jinping's Leadership Style."

68 Zhao Yinping and Jin Jiaxu, "从六次批示看习近平一抓到底的工作作风 [Looking at Xi Jinping's Work Style Through Six Instructions]," 新华网 Xinhua Net, January 10, 2019. http://www.xinhuanet.com/politics/xxjxs/2019-01/10/c_1123973733.htm

69 Chun Han Wong, "China's Graft Busters Pursue Very Old Cases—and Even the Dead Can't Escape," *Wall Street Journal*, June 3, 2021. https://www.wsj.com/articles/chinas-graft-busters-pursue-very-old-casesand-even-the-dead-cant-escape-11622698787

70 Laws and Regulations Bureau of the Chinese Communist Party Central Committee's General Office, "中国共产党党内法规体系 [The Chinese Communist Party's Internal Party Regulatory System]," *People's Daily*, August 4, 2021. http://dangshi.people.com.cn/n1/2021/0804/c436975-32180618.html

71 "习近平在中央党校（国家行政学院）中青年干部培训班开班式上发表重要讲话 [Xi Jinping Delivers an Important Speech at the Opening Ceremony of the Training Course for Young and Middle-Aged Cadres at the Central Party School (National School of Administration)]," Xinhua News Agency, March 1, 2021. http://www.xinhuanet.com/politics/leaders/2021-03/01/c_1127154621.htm

72 Chinese Communist Party Central Party History and Literature Research Institute (ed.), 《习近平关于全面从严治党论述摘编（2021年版）》 [*Excerpts from Xi Jinping's Remarks on Comprehensively Governing the Party with Strict Discipline* (2021 Edition)] (Beijing: Central Party Literature Press, 2021), pp. 38–39.

73 "New Data Exposes Increased Use of NSC's Liuzhi System," Safeguard Defenders website, July 7, 2021. https://safeguarddefenders.com/en/blog/new-data-exposes-increased-use-nscs-liuzhi-system

74 Chun Han Wong, "China's Communist Party Policing Spreads to Cover All Government Workers," *Wall Street Journal*, March 13, 2018. https://www.wsj.com/articles/chinas-communist-party-policing-spreads-to-cover-all-government-workers-1520943017

75 Wong, "China's Communist Party Policing Spreads to Cover All Government Workers."

76 "【微视频】杨晓渡：国家监察填补对公权力的监督空白 [[Micro video] Yang Xiaodu: State Supervision Fills Gaps in the Supervision of Public Power]," CCTV News, March 5, 2018. http://m.news.cctv.com/2018/03/05/ARTIHaOXpalzxmTxpJ9oRPMZ180305.shtml

77 Author's interview with Pan Leilei in February 2017.

78 Chun Han Wong, "Xi's Next Step: Demand More Fervor from China's Communist Party," *Wall Street Journal*, October 26, 2017. https://www.wsj.com/articles/xis-next-step-demand-more-fervor-from-chinas-communist-party-1509017928

79 Author's interview with Pan Leilei in February 2017.

80 Bruce J. Dickson, "Who Wants to Be a Communist? Career Incentives and Mobilized Loyalty

in China," *China Quarterly* 217 (March 2014): 42–68. http://journals.cambridge.org/abstract_S0305741013001434

81 Transcript from Tsinghua University's April 2018 conference, "China and the World: Dialogue Between Thought Leaders."

82 Chun Han Wong, "Xi Capitalizes on Marx's Legacy to Rally China Around Communist Party," *Wall Street Journal*, May 7, 2018. https://www.wsj.com/articles/xi-capitalizes-on-marxs-legacy-to-rally-china-around-communist-party-1525707225

83 Bruce J. Dickson, *Wealth into Power: The Communist Party's Embrace of China's Private Sector* (New York: Cambridge University Press, 2008), p. 125.

84 Joanne Song McLaughlin, "Does Communist Party Membership Pay? Estimating the Economic Returns to Party Membership in the Labor Market in China," *Journal of Comparative Economics* 45, No. 4 (December 2017): 963–983. https://www.sciencedirect.com/science/article/pii/S0147596716300634

85 Wong, "Xi's Next Step: Demand More Fervor from China's Communist Party."

86 Ken Jowitt, "Soviet Neotraditionalism: The Political Corruption of a Leninist Regime," *Soviet Studies* 35, No. 3 (July 1983): 275–297; Ken Jowitt, *New World Disorder: The Leninist Extinction* (Berkeley: University of California Press, 1992).

87 "习近平主持会议部署加强新形势下党员发展管理工作 [Xi Jinping Chaired a Meeting on Arranging Efforts to Strengthen the Management and Development of Party Members Under the New Situation]," Xinhua News Agency, January 28, 2013. http://www.gov.cn/ldhd/2013-01/28/content_2321165.htm

88 Xi Jinping, "在党的群众路线教育实践活动总结大会上的讲话 [Speech at the Summation Conference of the Party's Mass-Line Education and Implementation Activities]," *People's Daily*, October 9, 2014, p. 2. http://politics.people.com.cn/n/2014/1009/c1024-25792284.html

89 Jeremy Page, "Why China Is Turning Back to Confucius," *Wall Street Journal*, September 20, 2015. https://www.wsj.com/articles/why-china-is-turning-back-to-confucius-1442754000

90 Wong, "Xi Capitalizes on Marx's Legacy to Rally China Around Communist Party."

91 "China's 2019 'Red Tourism' Revenue Tops 400b Yuan," Xinhua News Agency, May 19, 2021. http://english.www.gov.cn/statecouncil/ministries/202105/19/content_WS60a50610c6d0df57f98d9bef.html

92 Shan Li and Philip Wen, "This App Helps You Learn About China, While China Learns All About You," *Wall Street Journal*, October 14, 2019. https://www.wsj.com/articles/china-broadens-data-collection-through-propaganda-app-and-translation-service-11571058689

93 Zhang Jianxin, "天津66家国企12万余名党员干部补交党费2.77亿元 [More than 120,000 Party Members and Cadres from 66 State-Owned Enterprises in Tianjin Paid 277 Million Yuan in Owed Party Dues]," Xinhua News Agency, April 26, 2016. http://www.gov.cn/xinwen/2016-04/26/content_5068180.htm

94 Li Lianjiang, "The Cadre Resignation Tide in the Wake of the 18th Party Congress," *China: An International Journal* 17, No. 3 (August 2019): 188–199.

95 Li, "The Cadre Resignation Tide in the Wake of the 18th Party Congress."

96 Zhang Yan, "商务部辞职的干部去哪儿了？ [Where Are the Cadres Who Resigned from the Ministry of Commerce? Where Did They Go?]," 《中国经济周刊》*China Economic Weekly*, No. 31 of 2018 (August 2018): 50–51. http://www.ceweekly.cn/2018/0806/231143.shtml

97 Wong, "Xi's Next Step."

98 Li, "The Cadre Resignation Tide in the Wake of the 18th Party Congress."

99 Xi Jinping, "推进党的建设新的伟大工程要一以贯之 [We Must Be Consistent in Promoting the New Great Project of Party Building]," 《求是》 *Seeking Truth*, No. 19 of 2019 (2019). http://www.qstheory.cn/dukan/qs/2019-10/02/c_1125068596.htm

100 Neil Thomas, "Members Only: Recruitment Trends in the Chinese Communist Party," Macro Polo, dated July 15, 2020, accessed April 27, 2022, https://macropolo.org/analysis/members -only-recruitment-trends-in-the-chinese-communist-party/; Chun Han Wong, "Party Rules: China's Communist Party Goes for Quality Over Quantity," *WSJ China Real Time* blog, January 5, 2017, https://www.wsj.com/articles/BL-CJB-29703.

101 Gong Xianqing, "建立党员退出常态机制探讨 建立党员退出常态机制探讨 [On Establishing the Normal Exit Mechanism for CPC Membership]," 《中国井冈山干部学院学报》 *Journal of China Executive Leadership Academy Jinggangshan* 9, No. 5 (September 2016): 93–98.

102 Author's interview with the sales supervisor in April 2017.

103 Wong, "Xi's Next Step."

104 Author's interview with Pang Jia in March 2019.

105 Yang Xuedong, "压力型体制：一个概念的简明史 [Pressure System: A Brief History of a Concept]," 《社会科学》 *Journal of Social Sciences*, No. 11 (November 2012): 4–12.

106 Jonathan Cheng, "China's Attempts to Take the Stress Out of Schooling Sparks Its Own Angst," *Wall Street Journal*, August 8, 2021. https://www.wsj.com/articles/chinas-attempts-to-take-the -stress-out-of-schooling-sparks-its-own-angst-11628415001

107 Chong Koh Ping and Quentin Webb, "China's Tutoring Restraint Slams Stocks," *Wall Street Journal*, July 26, 2021. https://www.wsj.com/articles/chinas-tutoring-rules-slam-education -stocks-11627276804

108 Chin, "Xi Jinping's Leadership Style."

109 "China Tried to Ban Private Tutoring. It Created a Huge Black Market," *Sixth Tone*, July 25, 2022, https://www.sixthtone.com/news/1010833/china-tried-to-ban-private-tutoring.-it-created -a-huge-black-market; Coco Feng, "A Year After China's Private Tutoring Crackdown, Classes Have Moved Underground as Companies Struggle to Pivot," *South China Morning Post*, July 29, 2022, https://www.scmp.com/tech/policy/article/3186924/year-after-chinas-private-tutoring -crackdown-classes-have-moved

110 Chinese Communist Party Central Party History and Literature Research Institute (ed.), *Excerpts from Xi Jinping's Remarks on Comprehensively Governing the Party with Strict Discipline*, p. 153.

111 Chun Han Wong, "Xi Jinping's Eager-to-Please Bureaucrats Snarl His China Plans," *Wall Street Journal*, March 7, 2021. https://www.wsj.com/articles/xi-jinpings-eager-to-please-minions-snarl -his-china-plans-11615141195

112 Wen Yan, "力戒形式主义官僚主义，为决胜全面建成小康社会提供坚强作风保证 [Strive to Stop Formalism and Bureaucracy, and Provide a Strong Work Style Guarantee for the Decisive Victory in Comprehensively Building a Moderately Prosperous Society]," *People's Daily*, June 3, 2020, p. 6. http://politics.people.com.cn/n1/2020/0603/c1001-31733056.html

113 "中共中央国务院关于打赢脱贫攻坚战的决定 [The Chinese Communist Party Central Committee and the State Council's Decision on Winning the Battle of Poverty Alleviation]," Xinhua News Agency, December 7, 2015. http://www.gov.cn/xinwen/2015-12/07/content_5020963.htm

114 Chenchen Zhang, "As part of the anti-poverty campaign, mom's danwei (a local govt agency) is liaisoned with a village and all civil servants are responsible for helping designated poor house-

holds. I asked how they help people out of poverty. Mom said, basically, by cheating." Twitter, December 24, 2018. https://twitter.com/chenchenzh/status/1077027530874310656

115 Luo Mei, "人未出现 帮扶工作却干得 "有声有色" 这样的 "痕迹扶贫" 严查 [Even Though Nobody Showed Up, Poverty-Alleviation Work was 'Vividly' Carried Out, Such Instances of 'Poverty-Alleviation By Leaving Traces' Are to Be Strictly Investigated]," Yunnan Provincial Party Discipline-Inspection Commission website, July 2, 2021. http://ynjjjc.gov.cn/html/2020/newcolumn14_0916/99229.html

116 Yuan Haitao, "观察 | 《国家监察》第三集《聚焦脱贫》: 强化监督 护航脱贫攻坚 [Observation | The Third Episode of 'National Supervision' 'Focus on Poverty Alleviation': Strengthening Supervision to Provide Escort for Poverty Alleviation]," Central Commission for Discipline Inspection website, January 15, 2020, https://www.ccdi.gov.cn/yaowen/202001/t20200115_207751.html; "灯没安、路没修，竟斥巨资 '刷白墙'！假脱贫，为了面子，丢了里子 [Lights Weren't Installed, Roads Weren't Repaired, Yet Huge Sums of Money Were Spent to 'Whitewash Walls'! Fake Poverty Alleviation, Saving Face but Losing the Plot]," CCTV News, January 14, 2020, http://m.news.cctv.com/2020/01/14/ARTIRleqgSUSNPLfXFXUalI4200114.shtml; Li Xiaoyang, "敢于斗争 一督到底 以精准监督护航脱贫攻坚 [Dare to Struggle, Supervise to the End, and Provide Escort for Poverty Alleviation with Precise Supervision]," 《中国纪检监察杂志》 China Discipline Inspection and Supervision Magazine, No. 20 of 2020 (October 2020). http://zgjjjc.ccdi.gov.cn/bqml/bqxx/202010/t20201019_227346.html

117 Author's interview with Han Dongfang in September 2021.

118 Zhang Bo, "对下负责才是真正的对上负责 [Being Responsible Down the Hierarchy Is the Real Way to Being Responsible to Superiors]," 《中国纪检监察报》 China Discipline Inspection and Supervision Daily, August 27, 2020, p. 7. https://jjjcb.ccdi.gov.cn/epaper/index.html?guid=1408259401101344769

119 Shaoying Zhang and Derek McGhee, China's Ethical Revolution and Regaining Legitimacy: Reforming the Communist Party Through Its Public Servants (London: Palgrave MacMillan, 2017), p. 153.

120 China Comment Magazine, 《反对形式主义30讲》 Combating Formalism (Beijing: People's Publishing House, 2020), pp. 62–66.

121 Zuo Handi, "住动辄开会发文的惯性 [Stop the Inertial Tendency of Holding Meetings and Issuing Documents at Every Turn]," 《中国纪检监察报》 China Discipline Inspection and Supervision Daily, June 15, 2020, p. 1. https://jjjcb.ccdi.gov.cn/epaper/index.html?guid=1408258957926989825

122 Jeremy Page and Lingling Wei, "China's CDC, Built to Stop Pandemics Like Covid, Stumbled When It Mattered Most," Wall Street Journal, August 17, 2020. https://www.wsj.com/articles/chinas-cdc-built-to-stop-pandemics-stumbled-when-it-mattered-most-11597675108

123 Xi Jinping, "在中央政治局常委会会议研究应对新型冠状病毒肺炎疫情工作时的讲话 [Speech at a Meeting of the Politburo Standing Committee of the Chinese Communist Party's Central Committee to Study the Response to the Novel Coronavirus Pneumonia]," 《求是》 Seeking Truth, No. 4 of 2020 (February 2020). http://www.qstheory.cn/dukan/qs/2020-02/15/c_1125572832.htm

124 Chin, "Xi Jinping's Leadership Style."

125 Stella Xie and Natasha Khan, "Anger Over Covid Lockdowns Mounts in Shanghai," Wall Street Journal, April 15, 2022, https://www.wsj.com/articles/anger-over-covid-lockdowns-mounts-in

-shanghai-11650039314; "习近平在海南考察时强调 解放思想 开拓创新 团结奋斗 攻坚克难 加快建设具有世界影响力的中国特色自由贸易港 [During an Inspection of Hainan, Xi Jinping Emphasizes Emancipating the Mind, Pioneering and Innovating, Working in Unity, Overcoming Difficulties, and Accelerating the Construction of a Free Trade Port with Chinese Characteristics with Global Influence]," CCTV News, April 13, 2022. https://news.cctv.com/2022/04/13/ARTIZrR0dAaonULhxgZ9Fna7220413.shtml

126 Jason Douglas, Stella Yifan Xie, and Selina Cheng, "China's Economy Appears to Be Stalling, Threatening to Drag Down Global Growth," *Wall Street Journal*, May 1, 2022. https://www.wsj.com/articles/china-economy-recession-covid-lockdowns-11651434168

127 "中共中央政治局常务委员会召开会议 习近平主持会议 [The Chinese Communist Party Central Committee's Politburo Standing Committee Held a Meeting, Xi Jinping Chaired the Meeting]," Xinhua News Agency, May 5, 2022. http://www.gov.cn/xinwen/2022-05/05/content_5688712.htm

128 Ma Xiaowei, "坚定不移贯彻 "动态清零" 总方针 坚决巩固疫情防控重大战略成果 [Unswervingly Implement the General Policy of 'Dynamic Zero' and Resolutely Consolidate the Major Strategic Achievements of Pandemic Prevention and Control]," 《求是》 *Seeking Truth*, No. 10 of 2022. http://www.qstheory.cn/dukan/qs/2022-05/16/c_1128649650.htm

129 Austin Ramzy, "China Eases Zero-Covid Rules as Economic Toll and Frustrations Mount," *Wall Street Journal*, November 11, 2022. https://www.wsj.com/articles/china-eases-some-covid-19-rules-even-as-cases-pass-10-000-11668150369

130 Chun Han Wong, "Protests in China: What to Know as Xi Jinping Maintains Covid Controls," *Wall Street Journal*, November 30, 2022. https://www.wsj.com/articles/china-protests-covid-lockdowns-explained-11669735586

131 James T. Areddy, "China's Xi Tells EU Delegation That Protests Reflect Covid Frustration," *Wall Street Journal*, December 2, 2022. https://www.wsj.com/articles/chinas-xi-tells-eu-delegation-that-protests-reflect-covid-frustration-11670009142

132 Lingling Wei and Jonathan Cheng, "Why Xi Jinping Reversed His Zero-Covid Policy in China," *Wall Street Journal*, January 4, 2023, https://www.wsj.com/articles/why-xi-jinping-reversed-his-zero-covid-policy-in-china-11672853171

133 Liyan Qi, "China Officials Soften Tone on Covid Curbs Amid Protests," *Wall Street Journal*, November 30, 2022, https://www.wsj.com/articles/china-officials-soften-tone-on-covid-curbs-amid-protests-11669759134; Chun Han Wong, "China Loosens Covid Restrictions as Public Anger Simmers," *Wall Street Journal*, December 4, 2022, https://www.wsj.com/articles/china-loosens-covid-restrictions-as-public-anger-simmers-11670145430; Selina Cheng, "China Scraps Most Covid Testing, Quarantine Requirements in Policy Pivot," *Wall Street Journal*, December 7, 2022, https://www.wsj.com/articles/china-scraps-most-testing-quarantine-requirements-in-covid-19-policy-pivot-11670398522; Stella Yifan Xie, "China's Zero-Covid Policy Is Ending, but Not Everyone Is Celebrating," *Wall Street Journal*, December 13, 2022, https://www.wsj.com/articles/chinas-zero-covid-policy-is-ending-but-not-everyone-is-celebrating-11670937991

134 Austin Ramzy, "China Records First Deaths after Easing Covid-19 Policy, with Many More Likely," *Wall Street Journal*, December 19, 2022, https://www.wsj.com/articles/china-records-first-deaths-after-easing-covid-19-policy-with-many-more-likely-11671457198

135 Qianer Liu, Cheng Leng, Sun Yu, and Ryan McMorrow, "China Estimates 250mn People Have Caught Covid in 20 Days," *Financial Times*, December 25, 2022, https://www.ft.com/

content/1fb6044a-3050-44d8-b715-80c18ca5c9ab; "China Says 80% of Population Have Had Covid-19, as Millions Travel for Lunar New Year," CNN, January 22, 2023, https://edition.cnn .com/2023/01/22/china/china-covid-80-lunar-new-year-intl-hnk/index.html

136   Keith Zhai, "China Says 60,000 Have Died of Covid Since Controls Were Lifted," *Wall Street Journal*, January 14, 2023, https://www.wsj.com/articles/china-says-60-000-have-died-of-covid -since-controls-were-lifted-11673704125; "China Reports Almost 13,000 New COVID-Related Deaths for Jan. 13–19," Reuters News, January 22, 2023, https://www.reuters.com/world/china/ china-reports-almost-13000-new-covid-related-deaths-jan-13-19-2023-01-22/

137   Chris Buckley, Alexandra Stevenson, and Keith Bradsher, "From Zero Covid to No Plan: Behind China's Pandemic U-Turn," *New York Times*, December 19, 2022, https://www.nytimes .com/2022/12/19/world/asia/china-zero-covid-xi-jinping.html

138   Li Yuan, "With 'Zero Covid,' China Proved It's Good at Control. Governance Is Harder," *New York Times*, December 26, 2022, https://www.nytimes.com/2022/12/26/business/china -covid-communist-party.html

139   Chin, "Xi Jinping's Leadership Style."

3. LAW IS ORDER

1   Wang Yu, "The Nightmare—An Excerpt of Lawyer Wang Yu's Account of 709 Detention and Torture," *China Change*, November 13, 2017. https://chinachange.org/2017/11/13/the -nightmare-an-excerpt-of-lawyer-wang-yus-account-of-709-detention-and-torture/

2   Wang, "The Nightmare."

3   "Five Years After 709 Crackdown, Lawyers Continue to Face Repression and Punishment," Congressional-Executive Commission on China, July 9, 2020. https://www.cecc.gov/publications /commission-analysis/five-years-after-709-crackdown-lawyers-continue-to-face-repression

4   Shen Deyong, "我们应当如何防范冤假错案 [How We Should Prevent Unjust, False and Wrong Cases]," 《人民法院报》 *People's Court Daily*, May 6, 2013, p. 2. http://rmfyb.chinacourt .org/paper/html/2013-05/06/content_65016.htm?div=-1; Shan Renping, "Legal activists must also respect rule of law," *Global Times*, May 8, 2014. https://www.globaltimes.cn/content /859107.shtml

5   Author's interview with Wang Yu in October 2021.

6   Matthew Robertson and Yaxue Cao, "The Vilification of Lawyer Wang Yu and Violence by Other Means," *China Change*, July 27, 2015. https://chinachange.org/2015/07/27/the-vilification-of -lawyer-wang-yu-and-violence-by-other-means/

7   Josh Chin, "Chinese Activist Wang Yu Seen 'Confessing' in Video," *Wall Street Journal*, August 1, 2016. https://www.wsj.com/articles/chinese-activist-wang-yu-seen-confessing-in-video-1470064037

8   Author's interview with Wang Yu in October 2021.

9   Philip Wen, "In Lawyer Trials, China's Courts Have Done Away with Pretence of Due Process," *Sydney Morning Herald*, August 5, 2016, https://www.smh.com.au/world/in-lawyer-trials-chinas -courts-have-done-away-with-pretence-of-due-process-20160805-gqm3fl.html; Jun Mai, "How Chinese Rights Lawyer's Courtroom Mea Culpa Went Off Script," *South China Morning Post*, August 22, 2016, https://www.scmp.com/news/china/policies-politics/article/2006700/how -chinese-rights-lawyers-courtroom-mea-culpa-went

10 Author's interview with Wang Yu in October 2021.

11 World Justice Project Rule of Law Index 2021, accessed October 20, 2021, https://worldjustice project.org/rule-of-law-index/country/China; World Justice Project Rule of Law Index 2014, accessed October 21, 2021, https://worldjusticeproject.org/sites/default/files/documents/Ruleof LawIndex2014.pdf.

12 Donald Clarke, "Order and Law in China," *GW Law Faculty Publications & Other Works*, No. 1506 (August 2020). https://scholarship.law.gwu.edu/faculty_publications/1506/

13 Peng Bo, "习大大说啦: 确保刀把子牢牢掌握在党和人民手中 [Xi Dada Has Spoken: Ensure That the Knife Handle Is Firmly in the Hands of the Party and the People]," 人民日报政文 [People's Daily Political Essays] WeChat account, January 20, 2015. https://mp.weixin.qq.com/s/ MU8EMHra7huUvfrzAwBq_A

14 Chun Han Wong, "'Their Goal Is to Make You Feel Helpless': In Xi's China, Little Room for Dissent," *Wall Street Journal*, November 27, 2020. https://www.wsj.com/articles/their-goal-is-to -make-you-feel-helpless-in-xis-china-little-room-for-dissent-11606496176

15 Jeremy Page and Eva Dou, "In Sign of Resistance, Chinese Balk at Using Apps to Snitch on Neighbors," *Wall Street Journal*, December 29, 2017. https://www.wsj.com/articles/in-sign-of -resistance-chinese-balk-at-using-apps-to-snitch-on-neighbors-1514566110

16 Chun Han Wong, "China's Hard Edge: The Leader of Beijing's Muslim Crackdown Gains Influence," *Wall Street Journal*, April 7, 2019. https://www.wsj.com/articles/chinas-hard-edge-the -leader-of-beijings-muslim-crackdown-gains-influence-11554655886; Salvatore Babones, "Yes, You Can Use the T-Word to Describe China," *Foreign Policy*, April 10, 2021. https://foreign policy.com/2021/04/10/china-xi-jinping-totalitarian-authoritarian-debate/

17 Edgar Snow, "A Conversation with Mao Tse-tung," *Life*, April 30, 1971, pp. 46–48. https://www .bannedthought.net/Journalists/Snow-Edgar/EdgarSnow-Life-1971-April30.pdf

18 Simon Leys, "The Myth of Mao," *Dissent*, Winter 1977. https://www.dissentmagazine.org/article /the-myth-of-mao

19 Shi Bibo, "法治: 建国路上的两难选择 [Rule of Law: A Dilemma on the Path of Nation Building]," 《炎黄春秋》 *Yanhuang Chunqiu*, No. 2 of 2004. https://web.archive.org/web /20191023061505/http://www.yhcqw.com/31/1087.html

20 Xin Wu, "「无法无天」赞 [In Praise of Lawlessness]," *People's Daily*, January 31, 1967, p. 6.

21 Deng Xiaoping, "解放思想, 实事求是, 团结一致向前看 [Emancipate the Mind, Seek Truth from Facts, Unite as One in Looking to the Future]," 《邓小平文选》第二卷 *Selected Works of Deng Xiaoping*, Vol. 2, Second Edition (Beijing: People's Publishing House, 1994), pp. 140–153.

22 Pitman B. Potter, "Review: Legal Reform in China: Institutions, Culture, and Selective Adaptation," *Law & Social Inquiry* 29, No. 2 (Spring 2004): 465–495; Susan Trevaskes, "A Law Unto Itself: Chinese Communist Party Leadership and Yifa Zhiguo in the Xi Era," *Modern China* 44, No. 4 (July 2018): 347–373.

23 Deng Xiaoping, "改革的步子要加快 [The Pace of Reforms Should Be Accelerated]," 《邓小 平文选》第三卷 *Selected Works of Deng Xiaoping*, Vol. 3 (Beijing: People's Publishing House, 1993), pp. 240–242.

24 Amnesty International, "China: The Crackdown on Falun Gong and Other So-Called 'Heretical Organizations,'" March 23, 2000, https://www.refworld.org/docid/3b83b6e00.html; Bryan Edelman and James T. Richardson, "Falun Gong and the Law: Development of Legal Social Control in China," *Nova Religio: The Journal of Alternative and Emergent Religions* 6, No. 2 (April 2003): 312–331.

25 Diana Fu and Greg Distelhorst, "Grassroots Participation and Repression Under Hu Jintao and Xi Jinping," *China Journal* 79 (January 2018): 100–122.

26 "立足中国特色社会主义事业发展全局 扎扎实实开创我国政法工作新局面 [Based on the Overall Development of the Cause of Socialism with Chinese Characteristics, Solidly Create a New Situation in China's Political and Legal Work]," National People's Congress website, December 26, 2007, http://www.npc.gov.cn/zgrdw/npc/wbgwyz/content_1615828.htm; Jerome A. Cohen, "Body Blow for the Judiciary," *South China Morning Post*, October 18, 2008, https://www.scmp.com/article/656696/body-blow-judiciary; Donald Clarke, "He Weifang Versus China's Legal Establishment on the 'Three Supremes,'" Chinese Law Prof Blog, August 12, 2009, https://lawprofessors.typepad.com/china_law_prof_blog/2009/08/he-weifang-versus-chinas-legal-establishment-on-the-three-supremes.html.

27 Taisu Zhang and Tom Ginsburg, "China's Turn Toward Law," *Virginia Journal of International Law* 59, No. 2 (2019): 306–389.

28 Mayling Birney, "Decentralization and Veiled Corruption Under China's 'Rule of Mandates,'" *World Development* 53 (January 2014): 55–67.

29 Zhang and Ginsburg, "China's Turn Toward Law"; Hu Changming, "中国法官职业满意度考察——以2660份问卷文样本的分析 [A Survey of Chinese Judges' Job Satisfaction: An Analysis of 2660 Questionnaires]," 《中国法律评论》 *China Law Review*, No. 4 of 2015 (December 2015): 194–206.

30 Ya-Wen Lei, *The Contentious Public Sphere: Law, Media, and Authoritarian Rule in China* (Princeton: Princeton University Press, 2017), p. 35.

31 Xi Jinping, "习近平：关于《中共中央关于全面深化改革若干重大问题的决定》的说明 [Xi Jinping: Explanation on 'The Chinese Communist Party Central Committee's Decision on Several Major Issues Concerning the Comprehensive Deepening of Reforms']," Xinhua News Agency, November 15, 2013. http://www.xinhuanet.com/politics/2013-11/15/c_118164294.htm

32 Xi Jinping, "习近平：关于《中共中央关于全面推进依法治国若干重大问题的决定》的说明 [Xi Jinping: Explanation on 'The Chinese Communist Party Central Committee's Decision on Major Issues Concerning Comprehensively Promoting the Governance of the Country by Law']," Xinhua News Agency, October 28, 2014. http://www.xinhuanet.com//politics/2014-10/28/c_1113015372.htm.

33 "中共中央关于全面推进依法治国若干重大问题的决定 [The Chinese Communist Party Central Committee's Decision on Several Major Issues Concerning Comprehensively Promoting the Rule of Law]," Xinhua News Agency, October 28, 2014. http://www.gov.cn/zhengce/2014-10/28/content_2771946.htm

34 Zhiqiong June Wang and Jianfu Chen, "Will the Establishment of Circuit Tribunals Break Up the Circular Reforms in the Chinese Judiciary?," *Asian Journal of Comparative Law* 14, No. 1 (July 2019): 91–112. https://www.cambridge.org/core/journals/asian-journal-of-comparative-law/article/abs/will-the-establishment-of-circuit-tribunals-break-up-the-circular-reforms-in-the-chinese-judiciary/265EA667A6EBB5E069D761C25A745AD5

35 Josh Chin, "China Top Judge Apologizes for Wrongful Convictions," *Wall Street Journal*, March 12, 2015. https://www.wsj.com/articles/china-top-judge-apologizes-for-wrongful-convictions-1426184136

36 Youngmin Kim, *A History of Chinese Political Thought* (Cambridge: Polity Press, 2018), p. 59;

Sam Crane, "Why Xi Jinping's China Is Legalist, Not Confucian," *Los Angeles Review of Books: China Channel*, June 29, 2018, https://chinachannel.org/2018/06/29/legalism/

37 Xi Jinping, "在庆祝全国人民代表大会成立六十周年大会上的讲话 [Speech at the Celebrations of the 60th Anniversary of the Founding of the National People's Congress]," 《求是》 *Seeking Truth*, No. 18 of 2019 (September 2019). http://www.qstheory.cn/dukan/qs/2019-09/15/c_1124994844.htm

38 Author's conversations with Changhao Wei between 2021 and 2023.

39 Chun Han Wong, "China Adopts Sweeping National-Security Law," *Wall Street Journal*, July 1, 2015. https://www.wsj.com/articles/china-adopts-sweeping-national-security-law-1435757589

40 Changhao Wei, "2020 NPC Session: A Guide to China's Civil Code (Updated)," *NPC Observer*, May 21, 2020. https://npcobserver.com/2020/05/21/2020-npc-session-a-guide-to-chinas-civil-code/

41 Fu and Distelhorst, "Grassroots Participation and Repression Under Hu Jintao and Xi Jinping."

42 Josh Chin, "New Chinese Law Puts Foreign Nonprofits in Limbo," *Wall Street Journal*, December 14, 2016, https://www.wsj.com/articles/foreign-nonprofits-brace-for-new-regulations-in-china-1481735054; "A Look Back at Foreign NGOs in China in 2020," China NGO Project, dated January 25, 2021, accessed March 29, 2021, https://www.chinafile.com/ngo/latest/look-back-foreign-ngos-china-2020.

43 Flora Sapio, "Carl Schmitt in China," *China Story*, October 7, 2015; Xie Libin and Haig Patapan, "Schmitt Fever: The Use and Abuse of Carl Schmitt in Contemporary China," *International Journal of Constitutional Law* 18, No. 1 (January 2020): 130–146; Ryan Martinez Mitchell, "Chinese Receptions of Carl Schmitt Since 1929," *Penn State Journal of Law & International Affairs* 8, No. 1 (May 2020): 181–263.

44 Data from China's National Bureau of Statistics. https://data.stats.gov.cn/

45 Zhang Yu, "再插手民告官案，拿行政机关 '说事' [Intervening Again in Citizen-Suing-Official Cases, Making Use of Administrative Agencies to 'Say Things']," 《大河报》 *Dahe Daily*, November 5, 2014, p. 11, http://newpaper.dahe.cn/dhb/html/2014-11/05/content_1171751.htm?div=-1; Li Yingfeng, "民告官胜诉率上升释放积极信号 [Rising Win Rates in Citizen-Suing-Official Cases Project Positive Signals]," 《法制日报》 *Legal Daily*, June 15, 2017, http://opinion.people.com.cn/n1/2017/0615/c1003-29340775.html.

46 Drew Hinshaw and Bradley Hope, "China Installed Its Top Cop to Steer Interpol. Then He Disappeared," *Wall Street Journal*, April 26, 2019. https://www.wsj.com/articles/china-installed-its-top-cop-to-steer-interpol-then-he-disappeared-11556304500

47 Hinshaw and Hope, "China Installed Its Top Cop to Steer Interpol."

48 Hinshaw and Hope, "China Installed Its Top Cop to Steer Interpol."

49 "公安部副部长孟宏伟涉嫌违法接受国家监委监察调查 [Vice Minister of the Ministry of Public Security Meng Hongwei Undergoes Supervision and Investigation by the National Supervisory Commission]," Central Commission for Discipline Inspection website, dated October 7, 2018, accessed May 1, 2022. https://www.ccdi.gov.cn/toutiao/201810/t20181007_180936.html

50 "习近平就政法工作作出重要指示 [Xi Jinping Issues Important Instructions on Political and Legal Affairs Work]," Xinhua News Agency, January 20, 2015. http://www.xinhuanet.com/politics/2015-01/20/c_1114065786.htm

51 Yu Xiaohong and Yang Hui, "党政体制重构视阈下政法工作推进逻辑的再审视 [A Re-Examination of the Implementation Logic in Political and Legal Affairs Work from the Perspec-

tive of the Reorganization of the Party and Government]," 《学术月刊》 *Academic Monthly*, No. 11 of 2019 (2019). http://www.cssn.cn/fx/202007/t20200721_5158007.shtml

52 "习近平就政法工作作出重要指示 [Xi Jinping Issues Important Instructions on Political and Legal Work]," Xinhua News Agency, January 20, 2015. http://www.xinhuanet.com/politics /2015-01/20/c_1114065786.htm

53 Chun Han Wong, "China's Xi Jinping Tightens Grip on Domestic Security Forces in First Broad Purge," *Wall Street Journal*, August 18, 2020. https://www.wsj.com/articles/chinas-xi-jinping -tightens-grip-on-domestic-security-forces-in-first-broad-purge-11597773887

54 "郭声琨主持召开平安中国建设协调小组第一次会议 [Guo Shengkun Chaired the First Meeting of the Peaceful China Construction Coordination Group]," 新华网 Xinhua Net, April 20, 2020. http://www.xinhuanet.com/politics/leaders/2020-04/21/c_1125887251.htm

55 Chun Han Wong, "China Antigraft Agency Investigates Intelligence Official," *Wall Street Journal*, January 16, 2015, https://www.wsj.com/articles/china-antigraft-agency-investigates -intelligence-official-1421384788; Chun Han Wong, "Former Chinese Official Linked to Exiled Tycoon Gets Life in Prison," *Wall Street Journal*, December 27, 2018, https://www.wsj.com/ articles/former-chinese-official-linked-to-exiled-tycoon-gets-life-in-prison-11545917102

56 James T. Areddy, "China's Former Security Chief Zhou Yongkang Sentenced to Life in Prison," *Wall Street Journal*, June 11, 2015. https://www.wsj.com/articles/chinas-former-security-chief -zhou-yongkang-sentenced-to-life-in-prison-1434018450

57 Hinshaw and Hope, "China Installed Its Top Cop to Steer Interpol."

58 Chun Han Wong, "China Expels Former Interpol President from Communist Party," *Wall Street Journal*, March 27, 2019. https://www.wsj.com/articles/china-expels-former-interpol-president -from-communist-party-11553694664

59 Cai Changchun, "赵克志主持召开公安部党委(扩大)会议坚决拥护党中央对孟宏伟的处理决定 [Zhao Kezhi Chairs a Meeting of the Party Committee (Expanded) of the Ministry of Public Security, Resolutely Supports the Decision of the Chinese Communist Party Central Committee to Deal with Meng Hongwei]," 《法制日报》 *Legal Daily*, March 28, 2019. http:// cpc.people.com.cn/n1/2019/0328/c64094-31000687.html

60 Eva Dou, "China Sentences Former Interpol President to 13½ Years for Bribery," *Wall Street Journal*, January 21, 2020. https://www.wsj.com/articles/china-sentences-former-interpol -president-to-13-years-for-bribery-11579608588

61 "中共中央印发《中国共产党政法工作条例》 [The Chinese Communist Party Central Committee Issued 'Regulations on the Chinese Communist Party's Political and Legal Affairs Work']," Xinhua News Agency, January 18, 2019, http://www.gov.cn/zhengce/2019-01/18/content _5359135.htm; Chang'an Jun, "陈一新:为你解读政法战线第一部党内法规——《中国共产党政法工作条例》 [Chen Yixin: Interpreting for You the First Intra-Party Regulations on the Political and Legal Front—'Regulations on the Chinese Communist Party's Political and Legal Affairs Work']," 中央政法委长安剑 [Central Political and Legal Affairs Commission Sword of Eternal Peace] WeChat account, February 27, 2019, https://mp.weixin.qq.com/s/a0meJqG SyN6zPaxMLiAlpw

62 "公安部原党委委员、副部长孙力军严重违纪违法被开除党籍和公职 [Former Member of the Ministry of Public Security's Party Committee and Vice Minister Sun Lijun Was Expelled from the Party and Public Offices for Serious Violations of Discipline and Law]," Central Commission for Discipline Inspection website, dated September 3, 2021, accessed April 29, 2022,

https://www.ccdi.gov.cn/toutiao/202109/t20210930_251638.html; Xinhua Net, "公安部原党委员、副部长孙力军涉嫌受贿、操纵证券市场、非法持有枪支被提起公诉 [Former Member of the Ministry of Public Security's Party Committee and Vice Minister Sun Lijun Was Prosecuted for Taking Bribes, Manipulating Securities Markets, and Illegally Possessing Firearms]," Supreme People's Court of China website, dated January 13, 2022, accessed April 29, 2022, https://www.court.gov.cn/fabu-xiangqing-341751.html

63 Fu Jingying, "重庆公安局长邓恢林被查 长期在政法系统任职 [Chongqing Public-Security Bureau Director Deng Huilin Comes Under Investigation, He Held Positions in the Political and Legal Affairs System for a Long Time]," 中国共产党新闻网 [Communist Party of China News Net], June 15, 2020, http://fanfu.people.com.cn/n1/2020/0615/c64371-31746786 .html; "重庆市公安局原局长邓恢林受贿案一审开庭 [First-Instance Trial Against Chongqing Public-Security Bureau Director Deng Huilin Begins]," Xinhua News Agency, September 10, 2021, http://www.news.cn/2021-09/10/c_1127849849.htm; Chun Han Wong, "China Sentences Purged Police Officials as Xi Tightens Grip on Security Forces," *Wall Street Journal*, September 23, 2022, https://www.wsj.com/articles/china-sentences-purged-police-officials-as-xi -tightens-grip-on-security-forces-11663931349

64 Wong, "China's Xi Jinping Tightens Grip on Domestic Security Forces."

65 Jane Cai, "Beijing Pins Hopes on 'Guy with the Emperor's Sword' to Restore Order in Coronavirus-Hit Hubei," *South China Morning Post*, February 12, 2020. https://www.scmp.com/news/china /politics/article/3050087/beijing-pins-hopes-guy-emperors-sword-restore-order-coronavirus

66 "全国政法队伍教育整顿试点启动！陈一新：来一场刀刃向内、刮骨疗毒式的自我革命 [The Pilot Program for the Nation-Wide Education and Rectification Campaign for Political and Legal Contingents Has Been Launched! Chen Yixin: Let's Launch a Self-Revolution by Turning the Blade Inward, and Scraping the Bone to Remove the Poison]," 中国长安网 [China Peace Net], July 8, 2020. http://www.chinapeace.gov.cn/chinapeace/c100007/2020-07/08/content _12369578.shtml

67 "江苏省委常委、政法委书记王立科接受中央纪委国家监委纪律审查和监察调查 [Jiangsu Provincial Party Committee Standing Committee Member and Political and Legal Affairs Commission Secretary Wang Like Undergoes Disciplinary Review and Supervisory Investigation by the Central Commission for Discipline Inspection and the National Supervisory Commission]," Central Commission for Discipline Inspection website, dated October 24, 2020, accessed April 30, 2022. https://www.ccdi.gov.cn/toutiao/202010/t20201024_227860.html; Wong, "China Sentences Purged Police Officials as Xi Tightens Grip on Security Forces."

68 Ministry of Public Security, "《公安机关人民警察誓词》公布 ['Public Security Agencies People's Police Oath' Announced]," Ministry of Public Security website, November 18, 2021, https://www.mps.gov.cn/n2253534/n2253535/c8214599/content.html; "公安部印发修订后的 《人民警察入警誓词》 The Ministry of Public Security Issues the Revised 'People's Police Admission Oath,'" 《人民公安报》 *People's Public Security News*, June 29, 2017, https://mp.weixin .qq.com/s/53KmZUg1-9VOaDhiFQHAGw

69 Chun Han Wong, "China's Graft Busters Pursue Very Old Cases—and Even the Dead Can't Escape," *Wall Street Journal*, June 3, 2021. https://www.wsj.com/articles/chinas-graft-busters -pursue-very-old-casesand-even-the-dead-cant-escape-11622698787

70 Wong, "China's Xi Jinping Tightens Grip on Domestic Security Forces."

71 Author's interviews with Wang Ran and defense lawyers in July and August 2020.

72　Author's interviews with Wang Ran and defense lawyers in July and August 2020.

73　Zhu Lei, "包头纪委监委公布检察官李书耀索贿细节：收钱后又退回 [Baotou Discipline-Inspection Commission and Supervisory Commission Disclose Details on Li Shuyao's Solicitation of Bribery: Accepting Money and then Returning It]," *The Paper*, September 4, 2020, https://www.thepaper.cn/newsDetail_forward_9029548; Chang'an Jun, "检察官被当庭举报'索贿'30万，牵出离任法官！'两高一部'出台两个《意见》源头整治'司法掮客 [Prosecutor Reported in Court for 'Requesting Bribes' of 300,000 Yuan, Implicating a Former Judge! 'Two Supremes and One Ministry' Issued Two 'Opinions' to Rectify the Source of 'Judicial Brokers']," 中央政法委长安剑 [Central Political and Legal Affairs Commission Sword of Eternal Peace] WeChat account, October 28, 2021, https://mp.weixin.qq.com/s/yA6dG_6M _HybPjSneyqFlA

74　Xu Xin, "徐昕：我想退出包头案，'再干下去，可能会被气死' [Xu Xin: I Want to Quit the Baotou Case, 'If I Keep Working on This Case, I Might Die of Anger']," 正义联接 [Justice Connection] WeChat account, July 12, 2020. https://mp.weixin.qq.com/s/_XXY9ttpXnUeviZ 0p75lsA

75　Chang'an Jun, "Prosecutor Reported in Court for 'Requesting Bribes.'"

76　"自治区检察院党组召开会议深入剖析王永明涉黑案办理中存在的问题提出明确要求 [The Party Group of the Autonomous Region Procuratorate Held a Meeting to Deeply Analyze the Problems Existing in the Handling of Wang Yongming's Organized-Crime Case and Put Forward Clear Requirements]," The People's Procuratorate of the Inner Mongolia Autonomous Region, July 27, 2020. http://www.nm.jcy.gov.cn/xwzx/ttxw/202007/t20200727_2883839.shtml

77　Wuda District People's Court in Wuhai City, "自治区高院指定乌海市乌达区人民法院审判王永明案 [The Higher People's Court of the Autonomous Region Appoints the Wuda District People's Court in Wuhai City to Try the Wang Yongming Case]," 内蒙古长安网 [Inner Mongolia Chang'an Net], July 27, 2020. http://www.nmgzf.gov.cn/xwjj/2020-07-27/38303.html

78　Wong, "China's Xi Jinping Tightens Grip on Domestic Security Forces."

79　Yao Tong, "陈全国在乌鲁木齐市和自治区公安厅指挥中心暗访维稳工作时强调 时刻绷紧稳定这根弦打好维稳工作组合拳全力确保大局和谐稳定各族群众生命财产安全 [When Chen Quanguo Made an Unannounced Inspection of Stability-Maintenance Work at the Command Center of Urumqi and the Xinjiang Uyghur Autonomous Region's Public Security Departments, He Emphasized That the Chord of Stability Should Be Tightened at All Times, and Stability Maintenance Work Should Be Combined to Ensure Overall Harmony and Stability]," 《新疆日报》 *Xinjiang Daily*, February 22, 2017. http://cpc.people.com.cn/n1/2017/0222/c64102-29100418.html

80　"China: Minority Region Collects DNA from Millions," Human Rights Watch, December 13, 2017, https://www.hrw.org/news/2017/12/13/china-minority-region-collects-dna-millions; Wenxin Fan, Natasha Khan, and Liza Lin, "China Snares Innocent and Guilty Alike to Build World's Biggest DNA Database," *Wall Street Journal*, December 26, 2017, https://www.wsj.com/ articles/china-snares-innocent-and-guilty-alike-to-build-worlds-biggest-dna-database-1514310353

81　Chun Han Wong, "With Pop Star as Bait, China Nabs Suspects Using Facial Recognition," *Wall Street Journal*, May 22, 2018. https://www.wsj.com/articles/with-pop-star-as-bait-china-nabs -suspects-using-facial-recognition-1527004150

82　Josh Chin, "Leaked Documents Detail Xi Jinping's Extensive Role in Xinjiang Crackdown," *Wall Street Journal*, November 30, 2021. https://www.wsj.com/articles/leaked-documents-detail-xi -jinpings-extensive-role-in-xinjiang-crackdown-11638284709

83 Chin, "Leaked Documents Detail Xi Jinping's Extensive Role"; "The Xinjiang Papers—Document No. 2 Speeches by Comrades Xi Jinping, Li Keqiang and Yu Zhengsheng at the Second Central Xinjiang Work Forum (May 28–30, 2014)," Uyghur Tribunal, first published November 29, 2021, updated December 13, 2021. https://uyghurtribunal.com/wp-content/uploads/2021/11/Transcript-Document-02.pdf

84 Author's interview with a former classmate of Chen Quanguo in September 2018.

85 Yan Mengli and Zhang Linlin, "推进警务机制改革 打造基层警务品牌—河北省石家庄市综合警务服务站高效运行5周年 [Promoting Policing-Mechanism Reforms and Building a Brand of Grassroots Police Service—The Fifth Anniversary of Efficient Operation of Comprehensive Police Service Stations in Hebei Province's Shijiazhuang City]," 《人民法治》 *People · Rule of Law*, No. 8 of 2016 (August 2016): 92–93.

86 Yan and Zhang, "Promoting Policing-Mechanism Reforms."

87 You Lei, "陈全国: 中原治边方法论 [Chen Quanguo: A Theory of Central Plains Boundary Governance]," 《小康》 *Insight China*, No. 3 of 2014 (March 2014): 32–35.

88 Li Chengye, "深入贯彻全国加强和创新社会管理工作座谈会精神统筹推进社会管理维护稳定工作确保西藏长治久安 [Thoroughly Implement the Spirit of the National Symposium on Strengthening and Innovating Social Management Work in a Coordinated Way to Promote Social Management and Maintain Stability to Ensure Long-Term Peace and Stability in Tibet]," 《西藏日报》 *Tibet Daily*, November 30, 2011. http://www.gov.cn/gzdt/2011-11/30/content_2006768.htm

89 He Yuan, "情景喜剧《便民警务站》藏历新年开播 总共20集 [The Sitcom 'Convenience Police Station' Starts Broadcasting in Tibetan New Year With a Total of 20 Episodes]," 《西藏商报》 *Tibet Business Daily*, February 22, 2017. https://www.tibetcul.com/news/movie/28801.html

90 Shi Lei, "陈全国: 让各族群众在稳定祥和的环境中幸福生活 [Chen Quanguo: Let People of All Ethnic Groups Live Happily in a Stable and Peaceful Environment]," 中国长安网 [China Peace Net], August 21, 2012, https://chinapeace.gov.cn/chinapeace/c25061/2012-08/21/content_11890741.shtml; https://web.archive.org/web/20220430082845/https://tjj.xizang.gov.cn/zwgk/ldzc/ldhd/201901/t20190117_58481.html

91 Author's interview with Jim McGovern in October 2018.

92 Yao Tong, "陈全国在自治区公安厅指挥中心检查部署维稳工作 [Chen Quanguo Inspects and Directs Stability-Maintenance Work at the Autonomous Region Public Security Department's Command Center], 《新疆日报》 *Xinjiang Daily*, September 4, 2016. https://web.archive.org/web/20160905131732/http://leaders.people.com.cn/n1/2016/0904/c58278-28689936.html

93 Adrian Zenz and James Leibold, "Securitizing Xinjiang: Police Recruitment, Informal Policing and Ethnic Minority Co-optation," *China Quarterly* 242 (June 2020): 324–348; Xinjiang Uyghur Autonomous Region Finance Department, "关于2017年自治区预算执行情况和2018年自治区预算草案的报告 [Report on the Implementation of the 2017 Autonomous Region Budget and the 2018 Autonomous Region Budget Draft]," 天山网 [Tianshan Net], February 2, 2018, https://www.ts.cn/xwzx/jjxw/201802/t20180202_5972804.shtml.

94 Darren Byler, *In the Camps: China's High-Tech Penal Colony* (New York: Columbia Global Reports, 2021).

95 Wong, "China's Hard Edge."

96 Wong, "China's Hard Edge." I arrived at the figure of 7,700 convenience police stations built across Xinjiang by summer 2018 by tallying official data on such facilities that appeared in

government notices, procurement documents, and state media reports. My calculations accord with a figure that appeared in a leaked transcript from a June 2018 speech by China's then public security minister, Zhao Kezhi, who cited a total of 7,628 convenience police stations. More facilities would have been built after Zhao delivered his speech, a copy of which appeared in a cache of leaked documents—known as the Xinjiang Police Files—that was published in May 2022. https://www.xinjiangpolicefiles.org/key-documents/

97 Wong, "China's Hard Edge."

98 CETC Electronic Science Research Institute, "王鹏达：做电科院文化的传承人 | 身边榜样 [Wang Pengda: Become an Inheritor of the CETC Electronic Science Research Institute's Culture | A Role Model By Your Side]," Sohu.com, dated August 22, 2018, accessed November 17, 2021. https://www.sohu.com/a/249485931_757363

99 Chris Buckley and Paul Mozur, "How China Uses High-Tech Surveillance to Subdue Minorities," *New York Times*, May 22, 2019. https://www.nytimes.com/2019/05/22/world/asia/china-surveillance-xinjiang.html; Adrian Zenz, "The Xinjiang Police Files: Re-Education Camp Security and Political Paranoia in the Xinjiang Uyghur Autonomous Region," *Journal of the European Association for Chinese Studies*, Vol. 3 (May 2022): 1–56. https://journals.univie.ac.at/index.php/jeacs/article/view/7336

100 Chun Han Wong, "China Applies Xinjiang's Policing Lessons to Other Muslim Areas," *Wall Street Journal*, December 23, 2018. https://www.wsj.com/articles/china-applies-xinjiangs-policing-lessons-to-other-muslim-areas-11545566403

101 Wong, "China Applies Xinjiang's Policing Lessons to Other Muslim Areas."

102 Liza Lin, Eva Xiao, and Jonathan Cheng, "China Targets Another Region in Ethnic Assimilation Campaign: Tibet," *Wall Street Journal*, July 16, 2021. https://www.wsj.com/articles/china-ethnic-assimilation-campaign-tibet-xinjiang-11626450702

103 Chen Quanguo, "陈全国书记在自治区干部大会上的讲话 [Speech by Secretary Chen Quanguo at the Autonomous Region Cadres Conference]," June 18, 2018, released in Xinjiang Police Files. https://www.xinjiangpolicefiles.org/key-documents/

104 Eva Xiao, Jonathan Cheng, and Liza Lin, "Beijing Accelerates Campaign of Ethnic Assimilation," *Wall Street Journal*, December 31, 2020, https://www.wsj.com/articles/beijing-accelerates-campaign-of-ethnic-assimilation-11609431781; Lanzhou Municipal Political and Legal Affairs Commission, "24小时守望的 '城市灯塔' [The 'Urban Lighthouses' Keeping Watch for 24 Hours]," 甘肃政法网 [Gansu Political-Legal Net], May 29, 2020. http://www.gszfw.gov.cn/content-15-29282-1.html

105 Zhou Shaoqing, "接上文:2.中共体制以稳为纲，大事面前，人人自保，从医院科室主任、院长、卫健委等官僚角度，都会有意无意削减确诊人数，大事化小，加上病毒"完美"特性，核酸阴性不见得不携带病毒，携带病毒不一定有症状，核酸试剂盒数量有限等原因，主观上各级存在瞒报以自保的可能 [Continued from the above: 2. The CCP's system is based on stability. In the face of major events, everyone protects themselves. From the perspective of bureaucrats such as hospital department heads, hospital directors, and health commissions officials, they will intentionally or unintentionally reduce the number of confirmed cases, and reduce major events to minor ones. In addition, the virus's 'perfect' characteristics—testing negative on nucleic-acid tests doesn't necessarily mean not carrying the virus, carrying the virus doesn't necessarily mean being symptomatic, and the number of nucleic-acid kits is limited, etc.

Subjectively, there is a possibility of concealing reports for self-protection at all levels]," Twitter, February 16, 2020. https://twitter.com/gemingjunlong/status/1229063746858844160

106 Author's interview with Zhou Shaoqing in January 2021.

107 Chun Han Wong, "China Is Now Sending Twitter Users to Prison for Posts Most Chinese Can't See," *Wall Street Journal*, January 29, 2021. https://www.wsj.com/articles/china-is-now-sending -twitter-users-to-prison-for-posts-most-chinese-cant-see-11611932917

108 Author's interview with Zhou Shaoqing in January 2021.

109 Author's interview with Zhou Shaoqing in January 2021.

110 Eva Dou, "China's Stopchat: Censors Can Now Erase Images Mid-Transmission," *Wall Street Journal*, July 18, 2017, https://www.wsj.com/articles/chinas-stopchat-censors-can -now-erase-images-mid-transmission-1500363950; Miles Kenyon, "WeChat Surveillance Explained," The Citizen Lab, May 7, 2020, https://citizenlab.ca/2020/05/wechat-surveillance -explained/

111 Eva Dou, "Jailed for a Text: China's Censors Are Spying on Mobile Chat Groups," *Wall Street Journal*, December 8, 2017, https://www.wsj.com/articles/jailed-for-a-text-chinas-censors-are -spying-on-mobile-chat-groups-1512665007; Kenyon, "WeChat Surveillance Explained."

112 Dou, "Jailed for a Text."

113 Chun Han Wong, "China Rescinds Penalty for Late Doctor Who Warned About Coronavirus," *Wall Street Journal*, March 19, 2020. https://www.wsj.com/articles/china-rescinds-penalty-for -late-doctor-who-warned-about-coronavirus-11584637545

114 Brian Spegele, "China's Surveillance State Pushes Deeper Into Citizens' Lives," *Wall Street Journal*, October 19, 2022. https://www.wsj.com/articles/xi-china-surveillance-covid-11666187151

115 Liza Lin, "China Turns to Health-Rating Apps to Control Movements During Coronavirus Outbreak," *Wall Street Journal*, February 18, 2020, https://www.wsj.com/articles/china-turns-to -health-rating-apps-to-control-movements-during-coronavirus-outbreak-11582046508; Liza Lin, "China's Plan to Make Permanent Health Tracking on Smartphones Stirs Concern," *Wall Street Journal*, May 25, 2020, https://www.wsj.com/articles/chinas-plan-to-make-permanent-health -tracking-on-smartphones-stirs-concern-11590422497.

116 Chris Buckley, Vivian Wang, and Keith Bradsher, "Living by the Code: In China, Covid-Era Controls May Outlast the Virus," *New York Times*, January 30, 2022. https://www.nytimes.com /2022/01/30/world/asia/covid-restrictions-china-lockdown.html

117 Lin Bohong, "中共六中全会强力维稳，异议人士被迫离京 行动受限 [The Sixth Plenum of the Chinese Communist Party Central Committee Prompts Vigorous Stability Maintenance, Dissidents Forced to Leave Beijing and Their Movements Restricted]," *Voice of America*, November 11, 2021. https://www.voachinese.com/a/China-tries-to-silence-activists-as-CCP-Central -Committee-holds-sixth-plenum-in-Beijing-20211111/6307785.html

118 Nectar Gan, "China's Bank Run Victims Planned to Protest. Then Their Covid Health Codes Turned Red," CNN, June 15, 2022, https://edition.cnn.com/2022/06/15/china/china-zheng zhou-bank-fraud-health-code-protest-intl-hnk/index.html; Zhang Yuzhe, "河南村镇银行储户 健康码被赋红码风波始末 [The Full Story Behind Henan Rural Bank Depositors Being Given Red Health Codes]," 《财新》 *Caixin*, June 14, 2022, https://finance.caixin.com/2022-06-14 /101898970.html; Xue Shasha, "追问储户入豫被赋红码：河南如何搜集入豫人员信息， 如何决定赋码 [Following Up with Depositors Getting Red Codes as They Enter Henan: How Does Henan Collect Information on Personnel Entering Henan, and How They Decide What

Codes to Assign]," *The Paper*, June 15, 2022, https://www.thepaper.cn/newsDetail_forward_18584239; Wenxin Fan, "In One Chinese City, Protesters Find Themselves Thwarted by a Red Health Code," *Wall Street Journal*, June 16, 2022, https://www.wsj.com/articles/in-one-chinese-city-protesters-find-themselves-thwarted-by-a-red-health-code-11655437726

119 Paul Mozur, "Twitter Users in China Face Detention and Threats in New Beijing Crackdown," *New York Times*, January 10, 2019. https://www.nytimes.com/2019/01/10/business/china-twitter-censorship-online.html

120 Wong, "China Is Now Sending Twitter Users to Prison."

121 Wong, "China Is Now Sending Twitter Users to Prison."

122 Author's interviews with anonymous free-speech activist from 2021 to 2022.

123 Lu Yuyu, "不正确的记忆 [Incorrect Memories]," Matters.news, August 13, 2020. https://chinadigitaltimes.net/chinese/660629.html

124 Author's interview with Lu Yuyu in September 2020.

125 Author's interview with Lu Yuyu in September 2020.

126 Shen Xinwang and Tao Wangbo, "民政部官员：'社会组织对抗政府'情况没有出现 [Civil-Affairs Ministry Official: 'Social Organizations Opposing the Government' Situations Haven't Appeared]," China News Service, May 21, 2012. http://www.chinanews.com/gn/2012/05-21/3904118.shtml; "2012年社会服务发展统计公报 [Statistical Communiqué on the Development of Social Services in 2012]," Ministry of Civil Affairs of the People's Republic of China, June 19, 2013. http://www.mca.gov.cn/article/sj/tjgb/201306/201306154747469.shtml

127 Andrew Browne, "Xi Turns Back the Clock on Women's Rights in China," *Wall Street Journal*, July 21, 2015. https://www.wsj.com/articles/xi-turns-back-the-clock-on-womens-rights-in-china-1437454619

128 Chun Han Wong, "Chinese Labor Activists Handed Suspended Sentences," *Wall Street Journal*, September 26, 2016, https://www.wsj.com/articles/chinese-labor-activists-handed-suspended-sentences-1474913153; "Labour Activist Meng Han Sentenced to 21 Months," *China Labour Bulletin*, November 4, 2016. https://clb.org.hk/content/labour-activist-meng-han-sentenced-21-months

129 Josh Chin, "China Expels Swedish Activist in Latest Crackdown," *Wall Street Journal*, January 26, 2016. https://www.wsj.com/articles/china-expels-swedish-activist-in-latest-crackdown-1453775331

130 Josh Chin, "China Poised to Approve Crackdown on Foreign NGOs," *Wall Street Journal*, April 26, 2016. https://www.wsj.com/articles/china-crackdown-on-foreign-ngos-about-to-become-law-1461674598

131 Sue-Lin Wong and Christian Shepherd, "China's Student Activists Cast Rare Light on Brewing Labour Unrest," Reuters News, August 15, 2018, https://www.reuters.com/article/uk-china-labour-protests-insight-idINKBN1L0064; "Police Raid Student Group as Support for Shenzhen Jasic Workers Grows," *China Labour Bulletin*, August 24, 2018, https://clb.org.hk/content/police-raid-student-group-support-shenzhen-jasic-workers-grows; Rob Schmitz, "In China, the Communist Party's Latest, Unlikely Target: Young Marxists," NPR, November 21, 2018, https://www.npr.org/2018/11/21/669509554/in-china-the-communist-partys-latest-unlikely-target-young-marxists; Christian Shepherd, "China Police Detain Students Protesting Crackdown on Marxist Group," Reuters News, December 28, 2018, https://www.reuters.com/article/us-china-politics-rights-idUSKCN1OR08M

132 Author's interview with Lu Yuyu in September 2020.

133 Author's interview with Lu Yuyu in September 2020.

134 Author's interview with Lu Yuyu in September 2020.

135 Author's interview with Li Tingyu in September 2022; Huang Simin, "A Chinese Millennial's Crime and Punishment: The Story of Li Tingyu," *China Change*, October 13, 2016. https://chinachange.org/2016/10/13/a-chinese-millennials-crime-and-punishment-the-story-of-li-tingyu/

136 Li Tingyu, Interview with Lu Yuyu, Non News, dated July 15, 2013, http://nonnews.lofter.com/post/1fb414_75ddcf, Internet Archive, accessed May 2, 2022. https://web.archive.org/web/20140918074832/http://nonnews.lofter.com/post/1fb414_75ddcf

137 "Lu Yuyu and Li Tingyu, the activists who put non news in the news," China Labour Bulletin, August 18, 2017. https://clb.org.hk/content/lu-yuyu-and-li-tingyu-activists-who-put-non-news-news

138 Author's interview with Lu Yuyu in September 2020.

139 Han Zhang and Jennifer Pan, "CASM: A Deep-Learning Approach for Identifying Collective Action Events with Text and Image Data from Social Media," *Sociological Methodology* 49, No. 1 (August 2019): 1–57. https://journals.sagepub.com/doi/full/10.1177/0081175019860244

140 "2016-06-13," Wickedonna, dated June 15, 2016, accessed October 18, 2021. https://newsworthknowingcn.blogspot.com/2016/06/2016-06-13.html

141 Lu, "Incorrect Memories."

142 Lu, "Incorrect Memories."

143 Lu, "Incorrect Memories."

144 Lu, "Incorrect Memories."

145 Author's interview with Lu Yuyu in September 2020.

146 Author's interview with Lu Yuyu in September 2020.

147 Author's interview with Lu Yuyu in September 2022.

148 Author's interview with Li Tingyu in September 2022; Chun Han Wong, "A Dissident Escapes Xi Jinping's China and a Life 'Made Up of Lies,'" *Wall Street Journal*, October 12, 2022. https://www.wsj.com/articles/a-dissident-escapes-xi-jinpings-china-and-a-life-made-up-of-lies-11665567002

149 Wong, "A Dissident Escapes Xi Jinping's China."

150 Author's interview with Lu Yuyu in September 2020.

4. CAGING THE ECONOMY

1 Tom Orlik, "China's Big Stock Market Rally Is Being Fueled by High-School Dropouts," Bloomberg News, April 1, 2015. https://www.bloomberg.com/news/articles/2015-03-31/china-s-big-stock-market-rally-is-being-fueled-by-high-school-dropouts

2 Mark Fahey and Eric Chemi, "Three Charts Explaining China's Strange Stock Market," CNBC, July 9, 2015. https://www.cnbc.com/2015/07/09/three-charts-explaining-chinas-strange-stock-market.html

3 Wang Ruoyu, "4000点才是A股牛市的开端 [4000 Points Is Just the Beginning of the A-Share Bull Market]," 人民网 People.cn, April 21, 2015. https://web.archive.org/web/20150424041626/http://finance.people.com.cn/stock/n/2015/0421/c67815-26880528.html

4 Shen Hong, "How Chinese Stocks Fell to Earth: 'My Hairdresser Said It Was a Bull Market,'"

Wall Street Journal, July 6, 2015. https://www.wsj.com/articles/how-chinese-stocks-fell-to-earth-my-hairdresser-said-it-was-a-bull-market-1436165508

5 Gregor Stuart Hunter and Wayne Ma, "China's Market Plunge: Where Only 3% of Firms Could Trade," *Wall Street Journal*, July 21, 2015. https://www.wsj.com/articles/how-china-market-thinned-as-it-plunged-1437472552

6 Lingling Wei, "China Delays Economic Liberalization," *Wall Street Journal*, November 6, 2015, https://www.wsj.com/articles/china-delays-economic-liberalization-1446865113; "China Embraces the Markets," *Economist*, July 11, 2015, https://www.economist.com/weeklyedition/2015-07-11

7 Shen Hong, "The Quiet Side of China's Market Intervention," *Wall Street Journal*, January 13, 2016, https://www.wsj.com/articles/chinas-national-team-plays-defense-when-stocks-decline-1452686207; Shen Hong and Stella Yifan Xie, "That Calm Chinese Stock Market? It's Engineered by the State," *Wall Street Journal*, May 31, 2018, https://www.wsj.com/articles/that-calm-chinese-stock-market-its-engineered-by-the-government-1527775089

8 Lingling Wei, "China Securities Regulator to Suspend New 'Circuit Breaker' Mechanism," *Wall Street Journal*, January 7, 2016. https://www.wsj.com/articles/china-securities-regulator-to-suspend-new-circuit-breaker-mechanism-1452179748

9 Shen Hong and Wei Gu, "In China's Widening Stock Crackdown, It's 'Kill the Chicken to Scare the Monkey,'" *Wall Street Journal*, November 12, 2015, https://www.wsj.com/articles/in-chinas-widening-stock-crackdown-its-kill-the-chicken-to-scare-the-monkey-1447355146; Lingling Wei, "China's Top Securities Regulator Replaced," *Wall Street Journal*, February 19, 2016. https://www.wsj.com/articles/chinas-top-securities-regulator-to-step-down-1455883897.

10 "中共中央关于全面深化改革若干重大问题的决定 [The Chinese Communist Party Central Committee's Decision on Several Major Issues of Comprehensively Deepening Reform]," Xinhua News Agency, November 15, 2013. http://www.gov.cn/jrzg/2013-11/15/content_2528179.htm

11 Bob Davis, "Beijing Endorses Market Role in Economy," *Wall Street Journal*, November 12, 2013. https://www.wsj.com/articles/SB10001424052702304644104579193202337104802

12 Lingling Wei, "China's Xi Approaches a New Term With a Souring Taste for Markets," *Wall Street Journal*, October 16, 2017. https://www.wsj.com/articles/chinas-xi-approaches-a-new-term-with-a-souring-taste-for-markets-1508173889

13 Lingling Wei, "China's Xi Ramps Up Control of Private Sector. 'We Have No Choice But to Follow the Party,'" *Wall Street Journal*, December 10, 2020. https://www.wsj.com/articles/china-xi-clampdown-private-sector-communist-party-11607612531

14 Wei, "China's Xi Ramps Up Control of Private Sector."

15 Xi Jinping, "毫不动摇坚持我国基本经济制度，推动各种所有制经济健康发展 [Unswervingly Adhere to Our Country's Basic Economic System and Promote the Healthy Development of Economies of All Types of Ownership]," State Council Information Office website, dated March 9, 2016, accessed April 21, 2022. http://www.scio.gov.cn/31773/31774/31783/Document/1471430/1471430.htm

16 Lingling Wei, "Xi Jinping Aims to Rein In Chinese Capitalism, Hew to Mao's Socialist Vision," *Wall Street Journal*, September 20, 2021. https://www.wsj.com/articles/xi-jinping-aims-to-rein-in-chinese-capitalism-hew-to-maos-socialist-vision-11632150725

17 David Bandurski, "A History of Common Prosperity," China Media Project, August 27, 2021, https://chinamediaproject.org/2021/08/27/a-history-of-common-prosperity/; Mao Zedong,

"关于农业合作化问题 [On the Cooperativization of Agriculture]," in《毛泽东选集》第五卷 *Selected Works of Mao Zedong*, Vol. 5 (Beijing: People's Publishing House, 1977), pp. 168–191.

18 Wei, "Xi Jinping Aims to Rein In Chinese Capitalism."

19 Lucille Liu, Zhang Xi, Davy Zhu, and Jing Li, "What Xi Means by 'Disorderly Capital' Is $1.5 Trillion Question," Bloomberg News, September 9, 2021. https://www.bloomberg.com/news/articles/2021-09-09/what-xi-means-by-disorderly-capital-is-1-5-trillion-question

20 Mao Zedong, "论人民民主专政 [On the People's Democratic Dictatorship]," in 《毛泽东选集》第四卷 *Selected Works of Mao Zedong*, Vol. 4 (Beijing: People's Publishing House, 1960), pp. 1357–1371. https://www.marxists.org/reference/archive/mao/selected-works/volume-4/mswv4_65.htm

21 Liu Shaoqi, "在全国青年第一次代表大会上的讲话 [Speech at the 1st All-China Youth Congress]," Marxists.org, May 12, 1949, accessed May 15, 2021. https://www.marxists.org/chinese/liushaoqi/marxist.org-chinese-lsq-19490512.htm

22 Liu, "Speech at the 1st All-China Youth Congress."

23 Dorothy J. Solinger, "Socialist Goals and Capitalist Tendencies in Chinese Commerce, 1949–1952," *Modern China* 6, No. 2 (April 1980): 197–224.

24 Dorothy J. Solinger, *Chinese Business Under Socialism: The Politics of Domestic Commerce, 1949–1980* (Berkeley: University of California Press, 1984).

25 Andrew G. Walder, *China Under Mao: A Revolution Derailed* (Cambridge: Harvard University Press, 2015), pp. 92–93.

26 Walder, *China Under Mao*, pp. 92–93.

27 Walder, *China Under Mao*, p. 94.

28 June Teufel Dreyer, *China's Political System: Modernization and Tradition* (New York: Routledge, 2019), p. 156.

29 Bandurski, "A History of Common Prosperity."

30 Stuart R. Schram, "'Economics in Command'? Ideology and Policy Since the Third Plenum, 1978–1984," *China Quarterly*, No. 99 (September 1984): 417–461.

31 Deng Xiaoping, "视察天津时的谈话 [Remarks During an Inspection of Tianjin]," in《邓小平文选》第三卷 *Selected Works of Deng Xiaoping*, Vol. 3 (Beijing: People's Publishing House, 1993), pp. 165–166.

32 "China Trade Summary 1992," World Integrated Trade Solution, World Bank, https://wits.worldbank.org/CountryProfile/en/Country/CHN/Year/1992/Summarytext; "China Trade Summary 2001," World Integrated Trade Solution, World Bank, https://wits.worldbank.org/CountryProfile/en/Country/CHN/Year/2001/SummaryText

33 George Magnus, *Red Flags: Why Xi's China Is in Jeopardy* (New Haven: Yale University Press, 2018), pp. 44–45.

34 Barry Naughton, "The Transformation of the State Sector: SASAC, the Market Economy, and the New National Champions," in Barry Naughton and Kellee S. Tsai (eds.), *State Capitalism, Institutional Adaptation, and the Chinese Miracle* (New York: Cambridge University Press, 2015), pp. 46–71.

35 Nicholas R. Lardy, *Markets Over Mao: The Rise of Private Business in China* (Washington: Peterson Institute for International Economics, 2014), pp. 188–189.

36 Nicholas R. Lardy, *The State Strikes Back: The End of Economic Reform in China?* (Washington: Peterson Institute for International Economics, 2019), p. 13; Lardy, *Markets Over Mao*, p. 90.

37   Tom Orlik, "Charting China's Economy: 10 Years Under Hu," *WSJ China Real Time* blog, November 16, 2012. https://www.wsj.com/articles/BL-CJB-16841

38   World Economic Outlook database, International Monetary Fund, accessed December 2021.

39   Li-Wen Lin and Curtis J. Milhaupt, "We Are the (National) Champions: Understanding the Mechanisms of State Capitalism in China," *Stanford Law Review* 65, No. 4 (April 2013): 697–759.

40   Erica Downs, "Whatever Became of China, Inc.?," Brookings Institution, June 24, 2014. https://www.brookings.edu/articles/whatever-became-of-china-inc/

41   Tom Orlik, "Charting China's Family Value," *WSJ China Real Time* blog, 2012, https://www.wsj.com/articles/BL-CJB-16961; Dexter Roberts, "The Controversial Chinese Economist Uncovering Tough Truths," *Bloomberg Businessweek*, March 23, 2017, https://www.bloomberg.com/news/articles/2017-03-23/the-controversial-chinese-economist-uncovering-tough-truths; Emmanuel Saez, "Striking It Richer: The Evolution of Top Incomes in the United States (Updated with 2013 preliminary estimates)," UC Berkeley, January 25, 2015, https://eml.berkeley.edu/~saez/saez-UStopincomes-2013.pdf

42   "习近平在广东考察时强调：做到改革不停顿开放不止步 [During an Inspection in Guangdong, Xi Jinping Emphasized That Reforms Will Not Stall and Opening Will Not Stop]," 新华网 Xinhua Net, December 11, 2012. http://www.xinhuanet.com//politics/2012-12/11/c_113991112.htm

43   Elizabeth Economy, *The Third Revolution: Xi Jinping and the New Chinese State* (New York: Oxford University Press, 2018), p. 98.

44   Wang Yuqian, "Top Chinese Economists Debate Role of Gov't in Economy," *Caixin Global*, July 11, 2014, https://www.caixinglobal.com/2014-07-11/top-chinese-economists-debate-role-of-govt-in-economy-101013233.html; "张维迎林毅夫激辩．政府之手到底应当放在哪里 [Zhang Weiying and Lin Yifu Argue Passionately: Where Should the Government's Hands Be Placed]," 《财新》 *Caixin*, July 8, 2014, https://opinion.caixin.com/2014-07-08/100700866.html

45   Mark Magnier, "China Plans More Action to Spur Growth," *Wall Street Journal*, March 15, 2015. https://www.wsj.com/articles/china-signals-fresh-moves-for-economy-1426435450

46   James T. Areddy, "China Shakes Up Financial Regulators in Scramble for Stability," *Wall Street Journal*, April 20, 2017. https://www.wsj.com/articles/china-shakes-up-regulators-in-scramble-for-stability-1492678390

47   Lingling Wei, "Chinese Government Struggles in Attempt to Stem Distress in Stock Market," *Wall Street Journal*, July 8, 2015. https://www.wsj.com/articles/chinese-government-struggles-in-attempt-to-stem-distress-in-stock-market-1436362924

48   "2012 Report to Congress," U.S.-China Economic and Security Review Commission, November 2012. https://www.uscc.gov/sites/default/files/annual_reports/2012-Report-to-Congress.pdf

49   Wei, "China's Xi Approaches a New Term with a Souring Taste for Markets."

50   Lingling Wei and Jeremy Page, "Discord Between China's Top Two Leaders Spills into the Open," *Wall Street Journal*, July 22, 2016. https://www.wsj.com/articles/discord-between-chinas-top-two-leaders-spills-into-the-open-1469134110

51   Wei and Page, "Discord Between China's Top Two Leaders"; Chun Han Wong, "Remark by China Premier Li Keqiang Stirs Questions About His Future," *Wall Street Journal*, March 15, 2017, https://www.wsj.com/articles/remark-by-china-premier-li-keqiang-stirs-questions-about-his-future-1489594905

52 Jennifer Hughes, "China's Communist Party Writes Itself into Company Law," *Financial Times*, August 14, 2017, https://www.ft.com/content/a4b28218-80db-11e7-94e2-c5b903247afd; Xianchu Zhang, "Integration of CCP Leadership with Corporate Governance," *China Perspectives*, No. 1 of 2019 (March 2019): 55–63, https://journals.openedition.org/chinaperspectives/8770

53 Hao Peng, "国务院关于2019年度国资系统监管企业国有资产管理情况的专项报告 [State Council Special Report on the Management of State Assets Supervised by the State-Owned Assets System in 2019]," National People's Congress website, October 17, 2020, http://www.npc.gov.cn/npc/c30834/202010/92861cc1660044d0b4c1511083bab902.shtml; "财政部公布2013年全国国有企业财务决算情况 [The Ministry of Finance Announces the Final Accounts for State-Owned Enterprises Nationwide in 2013]," Ministry of Finance of the People's Republic of China, July 28, 2014, http://www.gov.cn/xinwen/2014-07/28/content_2725636.htm

54 Wei, "China's Xi Approaches a New Term With a Souring Taste for Markets," *Wall Street Journal*.

55 Lingling Wei and Jeremy Page, "China Ousts Finance Minister as Xi Jinping Turns to Allies," *Wall Street Journal*, November 8, 2016, https://www.wsj.com/articles/china-replaces-finance-minister-lou-jiwei-in-surprise-reshuffle-1478495917; Jeremy Page, "1989 and the Birth of State Capitalism in China," *Wall Street Journal*, May 31, 2019, https://www.wsj.com/articles/1989-and-the-birth-of-state-capitalism-in-china-11559313717

56 Lingling Wei, "China Presses Economists to Brighten Their Outlooks," *Wall Street Journal*, May 3, 2016, https://www.wsj.com/articles/china-presses-economists-to-brighten-their-outlooks-1462292316; Rebecca Feng, "Outspoken China Strategist Leaves State-Owned Broker After Social-Media Accounts Are Censored," *Wall Street Journal*, May 3, 2022, https://www.wsj.com/articles/outspoken-china-strategist-leaves-state-owned-broker-after-social-media-accounts-are-censored-11651575795

57 Chun Han Wong, "China Finally Snuffs Out a Beacon of Liberal Thought and Democracy," *Wall Street Journal*, August 27, 2019. https://www.wsj.com/articles/china-finally-snuffs-out-a-beacon-of-liberal-thought-and-democracy-11566886519

58 Page, "1989 and the Birth of State Capitalism in China."

59 Stella Yifan Xie, Yang Jie, and Stephanie Yang, "China Power Outages Pose New Threat to Supplies of Chips and Other Goods," *Wall Street Journal*, September 27, 2021, https://www.wsj.com/articles/china-power-outages-pose-new-threat-to-supplies-of-chips-and-other-goods-11632769617; Josh Chin, "Xi Jinping's Leadership Style: Micromanagement That Leaves Underlings Scrambling," *Wall Street Journal*, December 15, 2021, https://www.wsj.com/articles/xi-jinpings-leadership-style-micromanagement-that-leaves-underlings-scrambling-11639582426

60 Chuin-Wei Yap, "China Takes the Brakes Off Coal Production to Tackle Power Shortage," *Wall Street Journal*, October 20, 2021, https://www.wsj.com/articles/china-takes-the-brakes-off-coal-production-to-tackle-power-shortage-11634727835; "Xi's Expanding Power Is a Growing Risk for China's Economy," Bloomberg News, November 8, 2021, https://www.bloomberg.com/news/articles/2021-11-08/xi-s-expanding-power-is-a-growing-risk-for-china-s-economy

61 "The Evolution of China's Bond Market," Seafarer Capital Markets, published March 2019, updated July 2021. https://www.seafarerfunds.com/commentary/the-evolution-of-chinas-bond-market/

62 Lingling Wei, "China's Xi Speeds Up Inward Economic Shift," *Wall Street Journal*, August 12, 2020, https://www.wsj.com/articles/chinas-xi-speeds-up-inward-economic-shift-11597224602; Lingling Wei, "China Stresses Reliance on Its Own Technologies in Five-Year Plan," *Wall Street*

Journal, October 29, 2020; https://www.wsj.com/articles/china-leadership-says-economy-will
-reachmid-level-within-15-years-11603969958

63 Xi Jinping, "在民营企业座谈会上的讲话 [Speech at the Private Entrepreneurs' Symposium],"
Xinhua News Agency, November 1, 2018, http://www.xinhuanet.com/politics/2018-11/01
/c_1123649488.htm; Xi Jinping, "在企业家座谈会上的讲话 [Speech at the Entrepreneurs'
Symposium]," Xinhua News Agency, July 21, 2020, http://www.xinhuanet.com/politics/2020-07
/21/c_1126267575.htm

64 "何立峰谈民营经济 我国民营经济的'56789' [He Lifeng Discusses the Private-Sector Economy, the '56789' of China's Private-Sector Economy]," CCTV News, March 7, 2019. http://
news.cctv.com/2019/03/07/ARTIyYXtrtJ7SYQ6HapQbVsJ190307.shtml

65 "郝鹏接受中央主流媒体采访 谈当前中央企业发展态势 [Hao Peng Accepts an Interview
with Central Mainstream Media to Discuss Current Developmental Trends Among Central En-
terprises]," State-Owned Assets Supervision and Administration Commission, August 11, 2020.
http://www.sasac.gov.cn/n2588020/n2877938/n2879597/n2879599/c15343606/content.html

66 Jing Yang and Xie Yu, "Jack Ma's Ant Group Ramped Up Loans, Exposing Achilles' Heel of China's Banking System," *Wall Street Journal*, December 6, 2020. https://www.wsj.com/articles/jack
-mas-ant-group-ramped-up-loans-exposing-achilles-heel-of-chinas-banking-system-11607250603

67 Keith Zhai, Julie Zhu, and Cheng Leng, "How Billionaire Jack Ma Fell to Earth and Took Ant's
Mega IPO with Him," Reuters News, November 6, 2020. https://www.reuters.com/article/ant
-group-ipo-suspension-regulators-idINKBN27L2GX

68 Jing Yang and Lingling Wei, "China's President Xi Jinping Personally Scuttled Jack Ma's Ant
IPO," *Wall Street Journal*, November 12, 2020. https://www.wsj.com/articles/china-president-xi
-jinping-halted-jack-ma-ant-ipo-11605203556

69 Jing Yang, "Chinese Regulators Summon Ant Leaders Ahead of Gigantic IPO," *Wall Street Journal*, November 2, 2020. https://www.wsj.com/articles/chinese-regulators-summon-ant-leaders
-amid-record-ipo-11604327306

70 Jing Yang and Serena Ng, "Ant's Record IPO Suspended in Shanghai and Hong Kong Stock
Exchanges," *Wall Street Journal*, November 3, 2020. https://www.wsj.com/articles/ant-group-ipo
-postponed-by-shanghai-stock-exchange-11604409597

71 Liza Lin, Lingling Wei, and Chong Koh Ping, "Alibaba, Ant Face Crackdowns from Chinese
Regulators," *Wall Street Journal*, December 24, 2020. https://www.wsj.com/articles/chinese
-regulators-launch-antitrust-investigation-into-alibaba-11608772797

72 Keith Zhai, "Alibaba Hit with Record $2.8 Billion Antitrust Fine in China," *Wall Street Journal*,
April 10, 2021. https://www.wsj.com/articles/alibaba-hit-with-record-2-8-billion-antitrust-fine
-by-chinas-market-regulator-11618018830

73 Keith Zhai and Lingling Wei, "China Lays Plans to Tame Tech Giant Alibaba," *Wall Street
Journal*, March 11, 2021. https://www.wsj.com/articles/china-regulators-plan-to-tame-tech-giant
-alibaba-jack-ma-11615475344

74 Jing Yang, "Didi Global Plans to Delist from New York Stock Exchange," *Wall Street Journal*,
December 15, 2021. https://www.wsj.com/articles/didi-global-plans-to-delist-from-new-york
-stock-exchange-11638495158

75 Jonathan Cheng, "China's Attempts to Take the Stress Out of Schooling Sparks Its Own Angst,"
Wall Street Journal, August 8, 2021. https://www.wsj.com/articles/chinas-attempts-to-take-the
-stress-out-of-schooling-sparks-its-own-angst-11628415001

76   Keith Zhai, "China Limits Online Videogames to Three Hours a Week for Young People," *Wall Street Journal*, August 31, 2021. https://www.wsj.com/articles/china-sets-new-rules-for-youth-no -more-videogames-during-the-school-week-11630325781

77   Lingling Wei and Chao Deng, "Xi's Sign-Off Deals Blow to China Inc.'s Global Spending Spree," *Wall Street Journal*, July 23, 2017. https://www.wsj.com/articles/chinas-latest-clampdown-on -overseas-investing-has-president-xis-approval-1500802203

78   Wayne Ma and Eric Schwartzel, "This Billionaire Had an Oscar Dream, but His Hollywood Ending Was Spoiled by China," *Wall Street Journal*, October 4, 2017, https://www.wsj.com/ articles/how-chinas-capital-clampdown-torpedoed-a-billionaires-oscar-dream-1507109405; James T. Areddy and Stella Yifan Xie, "Anbang Insurance Founder's Stunning Fall Ends with 18-Year Prison Term," *Wall Street Journal*, May 10, 2018, https://www.wsj.com/articles/anbang -insurances-wu-xiaohui-sentenced-to-18-years-in-prison-1525923337

79   Stella Xie Yifan, "Jack Ma: A Showman Who Has Shown China a New Way to Do Business," *Wall Street Journal*, September 10, 2018, https://www.wsj.com/articles/jack-ma-a-showman-who -showed-china-a-new-way-to-do-business-1536584459

80   Keith Zhai, Lingling Wei, and Jing Yang, "Jack Ma's Costliest Business Lesson: China Has Only One Leader," *Wall Street Journal*, August 20, 2021. https://www.wsj.com/articles/jack-mas -costliest-business-lesson-china-has-only-one-leader-11629473637

81   Li Bin, "理想的共鸣——温家宝总理考察阿里巴巴网络有限公司侧记 [The Resonance of Ideals—Side Notes on Premier Wen Jiabao's Visit to Alibaba Network Co. Ltd.]," Xinhua News Agency, June 26, 2010. http://www.gov.cn/ldhd/2010-06/26/content_1638366.htm

82   Shan Li, "It's Official: China's E-Commerce King Is a Communist," *Wall Street Journal*, November 26, 2018. https://www.wsj.com/articles/its official chinas e commerce king is a communist -1543238782

83   Zhai, Wei, and Yang, "Jack Ma's Costliest Business Lesson."

84   Keith Zhai and Lingling Wei, "China Lays Plans to Tame Tech Giant Alibaba," *Wall Street Journal*, March 11, 2021. https://www.wsj.com/articles/china-regulators-plan-to-tame-tech-giant -alibaba-jack-ma-11615475344

85   Yoko Kubota and Shan Li, "Backlash Brews in China's Startup Culture Against Grueling Hours," *Wall Street Journal*, April 30, 2019. https://www.wsj.com/articles/backlash-brews-in-chinas . -startup-culture-against-grueling-hours-11556633929

86   "Magic of Alibaba: Global Leaders Meeting Jack Ma," *China Daily*, June 13, 2016, http://www .chinadaily.com.cn/m/beijing/zhongguancun/2016-06/13/content_26538100_11.htm; Alyssa Abkowitz and Kathy Chu, "Alibaba's Jack Ma to Skip AntiCounterfeiting Conference Amid Fakes Complaints," *WSJ China Real Time* blog, May 18, 2016, https://www.wsj.com/articles /BL-CJB-29205; Kathy Chu, "Trump's Meeting with Jack Ma Comes as U.S. Keeps Eye on Alibaba," *Wall Street Journal*, January 10, 2022, https://www.wsj.com/articles/trumps-meeting -with-jack-ma-comes-as-u-s-keeps-eye-on-alibaba-1484051143.

87   Zhai, Wei, and Yang, "Jack Ma's Costliest Business Lesson."

88   Zhai and Wei, "China Lays Plans to Tame Tech Giant Alibaba."

89   Zhai, Wei, and Yang, "Jack Ma's Costliest Business Lesson."

90   Jing Yang, "Beijing Asks Alibaba to Shed Its Media Assets," *Wall Street Journal*, March 16, 2021. https://www.wsj.com/articles/beijing-asks-alibaba-to-shed-its-media-assets-11615809999

91 Sun Yu and Ryan McMorrow, "Beijing forces elite Jack Ma academy to halt new enrolments," *Financial Times*, April 9, 2021. https://www.ft.com/content/61efaf8b-3bb6-4031-86d8 -09274fcf956b

92 "中共中央国务院关于表彰全国脱贫攻坚先进个人和先进集体的决定 [The Chinese Communist Party Central Committee and the State Council's Decision on Commending Advanced Individuals and Advanced Collectives in the National Fight Against Poverty]," Xinhua News Agency, February 25, 2021. http://www.gov.cn/zhengce/2021-02/25/content_5588864.htm

93 Keith Zhai, "Jack Ma Leaves China for the First Time Since Regulatory Woes Began," *Wall Street Journal*, October 20, 2021. https://www.wsj.com/articles/jack-ma-leaves-china-for-the-first-time -since-regulatory-woes-began-11634714073

94 Zhai, "Jack Ma Leaves China for the First Time Since Regulatory Woes Began."

95 Zhai, Wei, and Yang, "Jack Ma's Costliest Business Lesson."

96 Stephanie Yang, "Tencent Stresses Regulatory Compliance as Profits from Gaming, Payments Surge," *Wall Street Journal*, March 24, 2021. https://www.wsj.com/articles/tencent-stresses -regulatory-compliance-as-profits-from-gaming-payments-surge-11616590055

97 Keith Zhai, "Pinduoduo Founder Colin Huang Steps Down from Company," *Wall Street Journal*, March 17, 2021, https://www.wsj.com/articles/pinduoduo-overtakes-alibaba-to-become-china-s -largest-e-commerce-company-11615978559

98 Liza Lin and Yoko Kubota, "TikTok Parent's Founder Zhang Yiming to Step Down as CEO," *Wall Street Journal*, May 20, 2021, https://www.wsj.com/articles/bytedance-founder-zhang -yiming-to-step-down-as-ceo-11621478797; Liza Lin, "JD.com Billionaire Founder Richard Liu Steps Down as CEO," *Wall Street Journal*, April 2022, https://www.wsj.com/articles/ founder-of-chinas-jd-com-steps-down-as-ceo-11649334972

99 "30年不懈探索党建融入企业运行出版专著 [Publishing a Monograph on 30 Years of Unremitting Exploration of Integrating Party Building into Enterprise Operations]," *Xinhua Daily*《新华日报》, March 29, 2017, pp. 4–5.

100 Zhao Bing, "前沿观察·从严治党 向下延伸：基层战斗堡垒强起来 [Frontier Observations: Strict Party Governance Extending Downwards: Strengthening Grassroots Fighting Fortresses]," *People's Daily*, October 10, 2017, p. 17, http://dangjian.people.com.cn/n1/2017 /1010/c117092-29577263.html; "王京清:在非公企业设立党组织有利企业健康发展 [Wang Jingqing: The Establishment of Party Organizations in Non-Public Enterprises is Conducive to the Healthy Development of Enterprises]," China News Service, November 9, 2012, http:// news.china.com.cn/18da/2012-11/09/content_27062322.htm; "齐玉：七成外商投资企业 建立党组织 [Qi Yu: 70% of Foreign-Invested Enterprises Have Established Party Organizations]," China News Service, October 19, 2017, http://www.china.com.cn/19da/2017-10/19 /content_41758149.htm

101 Zang Ming, "【砥砺奋进的五年】上海13万家实体性非公企业已建党组织 [[Five Years of Hard Work and Endeavor] 130,000 Non-Public Entreprises in Shanghai Have Established Party Organizations]," *The Paper*, June 8, 2017, https://www.thepaper.cn/newsDetail_forward _1704156; "【头条】不留空白 有效服务 增强党建 [[Headline] Leave No Blank Spaces, Serve with Effectiveness, Strengthen Party Building]," 闵行党建 [Minhang Party Building] WeChat Account, November 18, 2016, https://mp.weixin.qq.com/s/Un1GP6k6AQAmpw mZY360Eg?

102 Xu Hui, "小米党建的 "四心" 工作法 [The 'Four Hearts' Work Method of Xiaomi's Party Building]," 《国家电网》 *State Grid*, No. 1 of 2020 (January 2020): 50–51; Shan Renping, "小米成立党委应得到社会的掌声 [Xiaomi's Establishment of a Party Committee Deserves Applause from Society]," *Global Times*, June 29, 2015, https://opinion.huanqiu.com/article /9CaKrnJMuS8

103 Chun Han Wong, "China's Push to Purge Organized Crime Casts Shadow over Private Businesses," *Wall Street Journal*, July 22, 2021. https://www.wsj.com/articles/chinas-push-to-purge -organized-crime-casts-shadow-over-private-businesses-11626960650

104 "Entrepreneurs' 'Original Sin' Unfounded," *China Daily*, February 2, 2007. http://www.china daily.com.cn/bizchina/2007-02/02/content_799604.htm

105 Cui Xiankang, "强拆公安局家属院? 湖北张德武案宣判 [Forced Demolition of the Public-Security Bureau's Family Housing Compound? Judgment in Hubei Zhang Dewu Case]," 《财新》 *Caixin*, January 25, 2022. https://china.caixin.com/2022-01-25/101834765.html

106 "人力资源和社会保障部、中国轻工业联合会、中华全国手工业合作总社关于表彰全国轻工行业先进集体先进工作者和劳动模范的决定 [Decision of the Ministry of Human Resources and Social Security, the China National Light Industry Federation, and the All-China Handicraft Cooperative Association on Commending the National Advanced Collective Advanced Workers and Model Workers in Light Industry]," Legal and Judicial Information Center for China-ASEAN Countries, dated March 27, 2013, accessed April 20, 2022. http://temp .pkulaw.cn:8117/chl/208975.html

107 Li Derong, "企业家千万财产被剥夺的内幕 [The Inside Story of How an Entrepreneur Was Stripped of Assets Worth Tens of Thousands]," 《法治与社会》 *Rule by Law and the Society*, No. 5 of 2005 (May 2005): 33–36. http://www.cqvip.com/QK/80042X/200505/15505216.html

108 Wong, "China's Push to Purge Organized Crime Casts Shadow."

109 Cheng Qian, "被控寻衅滋事等五宗罪 湖北襄大集团董事长张德武案开庭 [Indicted on Five Charges Including Picking Quarrels and Provoking Trouble, Court Proceedings Begin in the Case against Hubei Xiangda Group Chairman Zhang Dewu]," 《财新》 *Caixin*, October 27, 2021, https://china.caixin.com/2021-10-27/101792126.html

110 Wong, "China's Push to Purge Organized Crime Casts Shadow."

111 Wong, "China's Push to Purge Organized Crime Casts Shadow."

112 Wong, "China's Push to Purge Organized Crime Casts Shadow."

113 Yicheng City Convergence Media Center, "郭静调研襄大集团生产运营情况 [Guo Jing Inspects Xiangda Group's Production and Operations]," 宜城发布 [Yicheng Announces] WeChat account, June 12, 2021, https://mp.weixin.qq.com/s/1fo3_hBw6olWSf9lVaKUxg

114 Cui Xiankang and Zhou Xin, "湖北襄大集团张德武案二审落槌 认罪认罚改判8年半 [Gavel Drops in the Second-Instance Trial of Hubei Xiangda Group's Zhang Dewu, Pleaded Guilty and Acknowledged Punishment, Sentence Changed to Eight and a Half Years]," 《财新》 *Caixin*, January 4, 2023, https://china.caixin.com/2023-01-04/101985224.html

115 David Barboza and Brooks Barnes, "How China Won the Keys to Disney's Magic Kingdom," *New York Times*, June 14, 2016. https://www.nytimes.com/2016/06/15/business/international/ china-disney.html

116 Barboza and Barnes, "How China Won the Keys to Disney's Magic Kingdom."

117 Fan Xiping, "申迪集团党委书记、董事长范希平在纪念建党96周年暨 "七一" 表彰大会上的讲话 [Speech by Fan Xiping, Secretary of the Party Committee and Chairman of

Shendi Group, at the Commemoration of the 96th Anniversary of the Party's Founding and the 'July 1st' Commendation Conference]," 上海国际主题乐园和度假区党组织 [Shanghai International Theme Park and Resort Party Organization] WeChat account, August 2, 2017. https:// mp.weixin.qq.com/s/O1tf6mPwnZ3zZms9KXch2g

118 Wang Zhiyan, "迪士尼一周年 | 中美谈判时，中方坚决要将这项条款写进合同，如今老外都竖大拇指 [Disney's 1st Anniversary: During China-U.S. Negotiations, the Chinese Side Insisted on Including This Clause in the Contract, and Now Foreigners Give the Thumbs Up]," 上观新闻 *Shanghai Observer*, June 16, 2017. https://www.jfdaily.com/news/detail?id=56397

119 Chun Han Wong and Eva Dou, "Foreign Companies in China Get a New Partner: the Communist Party," *Wall Street Journal*, October 28, 2017. https://www.wsj.com/articles/foreign -companies-in-china-get-a-new-partner-the-communist-party-1509297523

120 Wong and Dou, "Foreign Companies in China Get a New Partner."

121 "European Chamber Stance on United Front Work in China's Private Sector," European Union Chamber of Commerce in China, October 12, 2020. https://www.europeanchamber.com.cn/en/ press-releases/3291/european_chamber_stance_on_united_front_work_in_china_s_private_sector

122 Wong and Dou, "Foreign Companies in China Get a New Partner."

123 Wong and Dou, "Foreign Companies in China Get a New Partner."

124 Wong and Dou, "Foreign Companies in China Get a New Partner."

125 Wong and Dou, "Foreign Companies in China Get a New Partner."

126 Wayne Ma, "Marriott Makes China Mad with Geopolitical Faux Pas," *Wall Street Journal*, January 11, 2018, https://www.wsj.com/articles/location-location-chinese-officials-slam-marriotts -designation-of-hong-kong-macau-as-countries-1515663854; Wayne Ma, "Marriott Employee Roy Jones Hit 'Like.' Then China Got Mad," *Wall Street Journal*, March 3, 2018, https://www .wsj.com/articles/marriott-employee-roy-jones-hit-like-then-china-got-mad-1520094910; Trefor Moss, "China's Plane 'Nonsense' or Sovereign Right? The Airline Map Flap," *Wall Street Journal*, May 7, 2018, https://www.wsj.com/articles/chinas-plane-nonsense-or-sovereign-right-the-airline -map-flap-1525696597

127 Trefor Moss, "U.S. Airlines Meet Beijing Halfway on Describing Taiwan," *Wall Street Journal*, July 25, 2018. https://www.wsj.com/articles/american-airlines-bows-to-beijing-on-taiwan -issue-1532490608

128 Ben Cohen, Georgia Wells, and Tom McGinty, "How One Tweet Turned Pro-China Trolls Against the NBA," *Wall Street Journal*, October 16, 2019, https://www.wsj.com/articles/how -one-tweet-turned-pro-china-trolls-against-the-nba-11571238943; James T. Areddy and Ben Cohen, "The Houston Rockets Were China's Team. Then a Hong Kong Tweet Happened," *Wall Street Journal*, October 11, 2019, https://www.wsj.com/articles/the-houston-rockets-were-chinas -team-then-a-hong-kong-tweet-happened-11570802945

129 Jing Yang and Simon Clark, "HSBC Throws Support Behind China on Hong Kong Security Law," *Wall Street Journal*, June 3, 2020. https://www.wsj.com/articles/hsbc-throws-support -behind-hong-kong-security-law-11591202105

130 Lingling Wei, "China's New Power Play: More Control of Tech Companies' Troves of Data," *Wall Street Journal*, June 12, 2021. https://www.wsj.com/articles/chinas-new-power-play-more -control-of-tech-companies-troves-of-data-11623470478

131 Ryan Gallagher, "Google Plans to Launch Censored Search Engine in China, Leaked Documents Reveal," *Intercept*, August 1, 2018, https://theintercept.com/2018/08/01/google-china

-search-engine-censorship/; Ryan Gallagher, "Google Faces Renewed Protests and Criticism Over China Search Project," *Intercept*, January 19, 2019, https://theintercept.com/2019/01/18/google -dragonfly-project-protests/; Davey Alba, "A Google VP Told the US Senate the Company Has 'Terminated' the Chinese Search App Dragonfly," Buzzfeed News, July 17, 2019, https://www .buzzfeednews.com/article/daveyalba/google-project-dragonfly-terminated-senate-hearing

132   Liza Lin and Stu Woo, "Microsoft Folds LinkedIn Social-Media Service in China," *Wall Street Journal*, October 14, 2021. https://www.wsj.com/articles/microsoft-abandons-linkedin-in-china -citing-challenging-operating-environment-11634220026

133   Liza Lin, "Yahoo Pulls Out of China, Ending Tumultuous Two-Decade Relationship," *Wall Street Journal*, November 1, 2021. https://www.wsj.com/articles/yahoo-pulls-out-of-china-ending -tumultuous-two-decade-relationship-11635848926

134   Erin Griffith, "Airbnb Shuts Down Its Local Business in China," *New York Times*, May 23, 2022. https://www.nytimes.com/2022/05/23/business/airbnb-china.html

135   Steve Stecklow and Jeffrey Dastin, "Special Report: Amazon Partnered with China Propaganda Arm," Reuters News, December 18, 2021. https://www.reuters.com/world/china/amazon -partnered-with-china-propaganda-arm-win-beijings-favor-document-shows-2021-12-17/

136   Stecklow and Dastin, "Special Report: Amazon Partnered with China Propaganda Arm."

137   Julie Wernau and Yoko Kubota, "Amazon's E-Commerce Adventure in China Proved Too Much of a Jungle," *Wall Street Journal*, April 18, 2019, https://www.wsj.com/articles/for-amazon -chinas-e-commerce-market-proved-too-much-of-a-jungle-11555576769; "Important Notice: Operational Adjustment to Kindle China E-book Store," Amazon Kindle Service WeChat Account, June 2, 2022, https://mp.weixin.qq.com/s/jJG36Hbrw2-ZeUT3aDXKBA

138   Dan Murtaugh, Colum Murphy, James Mayger, and Brian Eckhouse, "Secrecy and Abuse Claims Haunt China's Solar Factories in Xinjiang," Bloomberg News, April 13, 2021. https://www .bloomberg.com/graphics/2021-xinjiang-solar/

139   Paul Mozur and Don Clark, "China's Surveillance State Sucks Up Data. U.S. Tech Is Key to Sorting It," *New York Times*, November 22, 2020, https://www.nytimes.com/2020/11/22/ technology/china-intel-nvidia-xinjiang.html; Sui-Lee Wee, "China Still Buys American DNA Equipment for Xinjiang Despite Blocks," *New York Times*, June 11, 2021, https://www.nytimes .com/2021/06/11/business/china-dna-xinjiang-american.html

140   Timothy Garton Ash, "VW's Dilemma in Xinjiang Shows How the West Is Headed for an Ethical Car Crash," *Guardian*, July 28, 2021. https://www.theguardian.com/commentisfree/2021/jul /28/vw-dilemma-xinjiang-west-ethical-car-crash

141   "*Volkswagen verteidigt Fabrik in Xinjiang*," *Der Spiegel*, April 18, 2021, https://www.spiegel.de/ wirtschaft/unternehmen/volkswagen-verteidigt-fabrik-in-xinjiang-a-8bbc5bf9-20b2-4886-b520 -b8ff050912ae; Yilei Sun and Brenda Goh, "Volkswagen's China Partners Bristle as Carmaker Lavishes Love on New Venture," Reuters News, September 13, 2021, https://www.reuters.com /business/autos-transportation/exclusive-volkswagens-china-partners-bristle-carmaker-lavishes -love-new-venture-2021-09-13/

142   Matthew Campbell, Chunying Zhang, Haze Fan, David Stringer, and Emma O'Brien, "Elon Musk Loves China, and China Loves Him Back—for Now," Bloomberg News, January 13, 2021, https://www.bloomberg.com/news/features/2021-01-13/china-loves-elon-musk-and-tesla -tsla-how-long-will-that-last; Liza Lin, "Tesla Opens Showroom in China's Xinjiang, Region at Center of U.S. Genocide Allegations," *Wall Street Journal*, January 4, 2021, https://www

.wsj.com/articles/tesla-opens-showroom-in-chinas-xinjiang-region-at-center-of-u-s-genocide
-allegations-11641214630

143 "H&M GROUP STATEMENT ON XINJIANG," H&M Group, 2020, Internet Archive, October 23, 2020. https://web.archive.org/web/20201023084759/https://hmgroup.com/ content/dam/hmgroup/groupsite/documents/masterlanguage/CSR/Policies/2020/Xinjiang%20 Statement.pdf

144 Jinshan Hong, Yasufumi Saito, and Adrian Leung, "How Nationalism in China Has Dethroned Nike, Adidas," Bloomberg News, February 16, 2022, https://www.bloomberg.com/graphics /2022-china-nationalistic-online-shoppers/?sref=dwch56hJ; Stu Woo, "Chinese Sportswear Company Anta Gains on Nike, Adidas Over Forced-Labor Issue," *Wall Street Journal*, January 5, 2022, https://www.wsj.com/articles/watch-out-nike-a-chinese-rival-is-on-your-heels-as-forced -labor-issue-divides-brands-11641378781

145 Eva Xiao, "Chinese Propaganda Officials Celebrate Social-Media Attacks on H&M in Counter-ing Forced-Labor Allegations," *Wall Street Journal*, March 31, 2021. https://www.wsj.com/articles /chinese-propaganda-officials-celebrate-social-media-attacks-on-h-m-in-countering-forced-labor -allegations-11617219310

146 Xiao, "Chinese Propaganda Officials Celebrate Social-Media Attacks on H&M."

147 Lee Chafaud and Harpre Ke, "Collab: Uncovering the Chinese Information Operations Behind the H&M Boycott Over Xinjiang Cotton," Doublethink Lab, April 13, 2021. https://medium .com/doublethinklab/collab-uncovering-the-chinese-information-operations-behind-the-h-m -boycott-over-xinjiang-cotton-5e078c0589a9

148 Eva Xiao, "H&M Criticized in China over Xinjiang Forced-Labor Stance," *Wall Street Journal*, March 24, 2021. https://www.wsj.com/articles/h-m-battered-with-criticism-in-china-over -xinjiang-forced-labor-stance-11616598679

149 Natalie Andrew, "Senate Passes Bill Banning Imports from Chinese Region over Treatment of Uyghurs," *Wall Street Journal*, December 16, 2021, https://www.wsj.com/articles/senate-passes -bill-banning-imports-from-chinese-region-over-treatment-of-uyghurs-11639691194; Phred Dvorak and Katherine Blunt, "U.S. Solar Shipments Are Hit by Import Ban on China's Xinjiang Region," *Wall Street Journal*, August 9, 2022, https://www.wsj.com/articles/u-s-solar-shipments -are-hit-by-import-ban-on-chinas-xinjiang-region-11660037401

150 Liza Lin, "Intel Apologizes After Asking Suppliers to Avoid China's Xinjiang Region," *Wall Street Journal*, December 23, 2021. https://www.wsj.com/articles/intel-apologizes-after-asking -suppliers-to-avoid-chinas-xinjiang-region-11640261303

151 Liza Lin, "Intel Erases Reference to China's Xinjiang After Social-Media Backlash," *Wall Street Journal*, January 10, 2022. https://www.wsj.com/articles/intel-erases-reference-to-chinas-xinjiang -after-social-media-backlash-11641808676

152 "European Business in China Business Confidence Survey 2022," European Union Chamber of Commerce in China, June 20, 2022, https://www.europeanchamber.com.cn/en/publications -archive/1020/Business_Confidence_Survey_2022; "USCBC 2022 Member Survey," U.S.-China Business Council, August 2022, https://www.uschina.org/reports/uscbc-2022-member-survey

153 Author's interview with Jörg Wuttke in August 2022.

5. GRASPING THE PEN SHAFT

1   Gong Qian, "'The Battle at Lake Changjin' a Successful Cultural Export to Make the World Begin to Listen to the Voice of China," *Global Times*, October 17, 2021. https://www.globaltimes.cn/page/202110/1236528.shtml

2   Sophie Brown, "How a Chinese Journalist Took on a Corrupt Official," CNN, November 13, 2013. https://edition.cnn.com/2013/11/12/world/asia/china-journalist-profile/index.html

3   Cindy Carter, "Former Journalist Luo Changping Detained for Defaming 'Heroes and Martyrs,'" *China Digital Times*, October 14, 2021. https://chinadigitaltimes.net/2021/10/former-journalist-luo-changping-detained-for-defaming-heroes-and-martyrs/

4   Jiyang Branch of the Sanya Municipal Public-Security Bureau, "Police Matter Bulletin," Hainan Police Weibo account, October 8, 2021. https://weibo.com/5681918507/KBMYDkr2w; "权威发布 | 海南检察机关依法对罗某平批准逮捕 [Authoritative Announcement | Hainan Procuratorate Approved the Arrest of Luo Mouping in Accordance With the Law]," Hainan People's Procuratorate, October 22, 2021. https://mp.weixin.qq.com/s/Ov_p1mVmQMoc9K2FP9M4JA

5   Weibo Administrator, "#微博社区公告# [#Weibo Community Announcement#]," Weibo, dated October 8, 2021, accessed January 31, 2022, https://weibo.com/1934183965/KBNdlbB3o; "国家网信办指导督促网站平台依法处置违法违规'头部账号' [The Cyberspace Administration of China Guides and Urges Website Platforms to Deal With Illegal 'Head Accounts' in Accordance with the Law]," Cyberspace Administration of China, December 15, 2021, http://www.cac.gov.cn/2021-12/15/c_1641167210772273.htm; Xi Danni, Zhang Sai, Wang Wenchang, and Ma Li, "罗昌平侵害英雄烈士名誉、荣誉暨刑事附带民事公益诉讼一案一审宣判 [Judgment Announced for First-Instance Trial of Luo Changping's Infringement Upon the Honor and Reputation of Heroes and Martyrs, as well as Criminal and Civil Public-Interest Litigation]," CCTV News, May 5, 2022, https://news.cctv.com/2022/05/05/ARTIxHPcHcp-2M1TPJLxZzThk220505.shtml; Sun Hang, "罗昌平侵害英雄烈士名誉、荣誉暨刑事附带民事公益诉讼一案一审宣判 [Judgment Announced for First-Instance Trial of Luo Changping's Infringement Upon the Honor and Reputation of Heroes and Martyrs, As Well as Criminal and Civil Public-Interest Litigation]," 《人民法院报》 *People's Court Daily*, May 6, 2022, pp. 1–2.

6   Xi Jinping, "关于坚持和发展中国特色社会主义的几个问题 [Several Issues on Upholding and Developing Socialism with Chinese Characteristics]," 《求是》 *Seeking Truth*, No. 7 of 2019 (April 2019). http://www.qstheory.cn/dukan/qs/2019-04/01/c_1124307480.htm

7   Xi, "Several Issues on Upholding and Developing Socialism with Chinese Characteristics."

8   "为了民族复兴的梦想——《复兴之路》展览巡礼 [For the Dream of National Rejuvenation—'The Road to Rejuvenation' Exhibition Tour]," Xinhua News Agency, December 9, 2012. http://www.gov.cn/jrzg/2012-12/09/content_2286125.htm

9   Li Bin, "习近平：承前启后 继往开来 继续朝着中华民族伟大复兴目标奋勇前进 [Xi Jinping: Inheriting the Past, Ushering in the Future, Continuing to Forge Bravely Ahead Towards the Goal of the Great Rejuvenation of the Chinese Nation]," 新华网 Xinhua Net, November 29, 2012. http://www.xinhuanet.com//politics/2012-11/29/c_113852724.htm

10 William A. Callahan, "China: The Pessoptimist Nation," *China Beat*, August 15, 2008. https://digitalcommons.unl.edu/chinabeatarchive/97/

11 Li, "Xi Jinping: Inheriting the Past, Ushering in the Future."

12 Damien Ma and Neil Thomas, "In Xi We Trust: How Propaganda Might Be Working in the New Era," Macro Polo, September 12, 2018. https://macropolo.org/analysis/in-xi-we-trust/

13 Xi Jinping, "实现中华民族伟大复兴是中华民族近代以来最伟大的梦想 [Realizing the Great Rejuvenation of the Chinese Nation is the Greatest Dream of the Chinese People Since Modern Times]," in Xi Jinping, 《习近平谈治国理政》第一卷 *Xi Jinping: The Governance of China*, Vol. 1 (Beijing: Foreign Languages Press, 2014), pp. 35–37.

14 David E. Apter, "Yan'an and the Narrative Reconstruction of Reality," *Daedalus* 122, No. 2, "China in Transformation" (Spring 1993): 207–232.

15 Apter, "Yan'an and the Narrative Reconstruction of Reality."

16 Wu Jiang (ed.), 《关于若干历史问题的决议》,《关于建国以来党的若干历史问题的决议》 [*Resolution on Certain Questions in History, Resolution on Certain Questions in the History of Our Party since the Founding of the People's Republic of China*] (Beijing: Central Party History Press, 2010).

17 Julian Gewirtz, *Never Turn Back: China and the Forbidden History of the 1980s* (Cambridge, Massachusetts: Belknap Press, 2022), pp. 24–30; Chinese Communist Party Central Committee, "Resolution on Certain Questions in the History of Our Party Since the Founding of the People's Republic of China," June 27, 1981, History and Public Policy Program Digital Archive, translation from the *Beijing Review*, Vol. 24, No. 27 (July 6, 1981): 10–39, accessed April 25, 2021, https://digitalarchive.wilsoncenter.org/document/121344

18 Gotelind Müller, *Representing History in Chinese Media: The TV Drama Zou Xiang Gonghe (Towards the Republic)* (Berlin: Lit Verlag, 2007), pp. 1–23; "Rewriting History," *Economist*, June 21, 2003, https://www.economist.com/asia/2003/06/19/rewriting-history

19 Josh Chin, "Chinese Authorities Shake Up Leadership at Liberal-Thinking Magazine," *Wall Street Journal*, July 15, 2016. https://www.wsj.com/articles/chinese-authorities-shake-up-leadership-at-liberal-thinking-magazine-1468558518

20 Richard McGregor, *The Party: The Secret World of China's Communist Rulers* (New York: Harper Collins, 2010).

21 Josh Chin, "Embattled Magazine Editors Choose to Silence a Liberal Voice," *WSJ China Real Time* blog, July 19, 2016. https://www.wsj.com/articles/BL-CJB-29416

22 Chris Buckley, "Historian's Latest Book on Mao Turns Acclaim in China to Censure," *New York Times*, January 21, 2017. https://www.nytimes.com/2017/01/21/world/asia/china-historian-yang-jisheng-book-mao.html

23 Buckley, "Historian's Latest Book on Mao Turns Acclaim in China to Censure."

24 Author's interview with Yan Huai in June 2019.

25 Julie Makinen, "Communists' Version of China's Wartime Record Frustrates Taiwan," *Los Angeles Times*, September 2, 2015. https://www.latimes.com/world/asia/la-fg-china-taiwan-nationalists-20150901-story.html

26 Qin Chen, "Chinese War Epic Pulled from Festival After Hailing the Wrong Heroes," *Inkstone News*, June 17, 2019. https://www.inkstonenews.com/china/chinese-war-epic-eight-hundred-pulled-shanghai-film-festival-after-hailing-wrong-heroes/article/3014855

27 Steve Rose, "The Eight Hundred: How China's Blockbusters Became a New Political Battleground," *Guardian*, September 18, 2020. https://www.theguardian.com/film/2020/sep/18/the-eight-hundred-how-chinas-blockbusters-became-a-new-political-battleground

28 He Yiting, "民族复兴与百年变局 [National Rejuvenation and Centennial Changes]," 《学习时报》 *Study Times*, April 14, 2021, p. 1.

29 Chun Han Wong and Keith Zhai, "China's Xi Flexes Power with Plan to Rewrite Communist Party History," *Wall Street Journal*, October 18, 2021, https://www.wsj.com/articles/chinas-xi -flexes-power-with-plan-to-rewrite-communist-party-history-11634562713; Keith Zhai, "China's Xi Gains Power as Communist Party Designates Him a Historic Figure," *Wall Street Journal*, November 11, 2021, https://www.wsj.com/articles/chinas-xi-gains-power-as-communist-party -designates-him-historical-figure-11636635312

30 Chinese Communist Party Central Committee, "中共中央关于党的百年奋斗重大成就和历史经验的决议 [The Chinese Communist Party Central Committee's Resolution on the Major Achievements and Historical Experience of the Party's Century-Long Struggle]," Xinhua News Agency, November 16, 2021, http://www.gov.cn/zhengce/2021-11/16/content_5651269.htm; Wu Huanqing, Zou Wei, Zhang Xiaosong, Lin Hui, Zhu Jichai, Wang Min, and Sun Shaolong, "牢记初心使命的政治宣言——《中共中央关于党的百年奋斗重大成就和历史经验的决议》诞生记 [A Political Declaration with Original Aspirations in Mind—The Birth of 'The Chinese Communist Party Central Committee's Resolution on the Major Achievements and Historical Experience of the Party's Century-Long Struggle']," Xinhua News Agency, November 17, 2021, http://www.gov.cn/xinwen/2021-11/17/content_5651466.htm

31 Author's interview with Wu Si in April 2021.

32 Chun Han Wong, "Is China's Communist Party Still Communist?," *Wall Street Journal*, June 30, 2021, https://www.wsj.com/articles/is-chinas-communist-party-still-communist-11625090401; Didi Kirsten Tatlow, "On Party Anniversary, China Rewrites History," *New York Times*, July 20, 2011, https://www.nytimes.com/2011/07/21/world/asia/21iht-letter21.html

33 Hu Jintao, "在庆祝中国共产党成立90周年大会上的讲话 [Speech at the Ceremony Celebrating the 90th Anniversary of the Chinese Communist Party's Founding]," Xinhua News Agency, July 1, 2011. http://www.gov.cn/ldhd/2011-07/01/content_1897720.htm

34 Ji Suping, "党史第二卷出版引关注 编撰人回应敏感历史问题 [The Publication of Party History Volume 2 Draws Attention, an Editor Addresses Sensitive Historical Issues]," China News Service, February 28, 2011, http://www.chinanews.com.cn/gn/2011/02-28/2871169.shtml; Chinese Communist Party Central Party History Research Office, 《中国共产党历史》第二卷 [*The History of the Chinese Communist Party*, Vol. 2] (Beijing: Chinese Communist Party History Publishing House, 2010), pp. 1070–1074.

35 Andrew Higgins, "In China, a Long Path of Writing the Communist Party's History," *Washington Post*, May 26, 2011, https://www.washingtonpost.com/world/in-china-a-long-path-of -writing-the-communist-partys-history/2011/05/16/AGDfMECH_story.html; "中国共产党历史（第二卷）》[The History of the Chinese Communist Party (Volume 2)]," 中共党员网 [Chinese Communist Party Members Net], October 16, 2012, https://fuwu.12371.cn/2012/10 /16/ARTI1350367346060279_all.shtml; Central Party History Research Office, *The History of the Chinese Communist Party*, Vol. 2, pp. 1070–1074.

36 Central Party History Research Office, *The History of the Chinese Communist Party*, Vol. 2, pp. 1070–1074; "习近平:党史部门和党史工作者要搞好党史宣传教育 [Xi Jinping: Party History Departments and Party History Workers Should Do a Good Job in Party History Propaganda and Education]," Xinhua News Agency, http://www.gov.cn/ldhd/2011-02/26/content_1811473.htm

37 Central Party History Research Office, *The History of the Chinese Communist Party*, Vol. 2, pp. 1070–1074.

38 Higgins, "In China, a Long Path of Writing."

39 Central Party History Research Office, *The History of the Chinese Communist Party*, Vol. 2, pp. 318–320.

40 "章百家：《党史》三卷编写工作已准备十年 [Zhang Baijia: Preparations for Drafting Work on 'Party History' Volume Three Have Been Underway for 10 Years]," 中国共产党新闻网 [Communist Party of China News Net], June 8, 2011. https://web.archive.org/web/20130403162541/http://cpc.people.com.cn/GB/164113/14847789.html

41 "中国共产党的九十年 [Ninety Years of the Chinese Communist Party]," 党建网 [Party-Building Net], June 28, 2016. http://www.dangjian.cn/ds/201606/t20160628_3478286.shtml

42 Anthony Kuhn, "Chinese Red Guards Apologize, Reopening a Dark Chapter," NPR, February 4, 2014, https://www.npr.org/sections/parallels/2014/01/23/265228870/chinese-red-guards-apologize-reopening-a-dark-chapter; James T. Areddy, "Ex–Red Guard Offers Fresh Cultural Revolution Apology," *WSJ China Real Time* blog, January 13, 2014, https://www.wsj.com/articles/BL-CJB-20331

43 Chun Han Wong, "Maoist Overtones in Beijing Concert Raise Red Flags," *WSJ China Real Time* blog, May 8, 2016. https://www.wsj.com/articles/BL-CJB-29156

44 Book Writing Team, 《中国共产党简史》 [*A Short History of the Chinese Communist Party*] (Beijing: People's Publishing House and Chinese Communist Party History Publishing House, 2021), pp. 204–206.

45 Book Writing Team, *A Short History of the Chinese Communist Party*.

46 Book Writing Team, *A Short History of the Chinese Communist Party*, p. 474.

47 Lü Yue (ed.), "惹怒高層的《炎黄春秋》新春聯誼會發言 [Speeches at the 'Yanhuang Chunqiu' Lunar New Year Gathering That Provoked High-Level Anger]," 《前哨》月刊 *Front Line Magazine*, No. 268 (June 2013): 30–34; author's interviews with attendees of the 2013 *Yanhuang Chunqiu* Lunar New Year gathering.

48 "习近平接受金砖国家媒体联合采访 [Xi Jinping Gives a Joint Interview to Media from BRICS Countries]," *People's Daily*, March 20, 2013, accessed April 5, 2021. http://cpc.people.com.cn/n/2013/0320/c64094-20845747-3.html

49 "习近平爱读哪些书？ [What Books Does Xi Jinping Love to Read?]," 人民网 People.cn, August 15, 2015, accessed September 9, 2021. http://politics.people.com.cn/n/2015/0815/c1001-27467148-4.html

50 Xi Jinping, "Speech by H.E. Mr. Xi Jinping President of the People's Republic of China at the Meeting Commemorating the 50th Anniversary of the Establishment of China-France Diplomatic Relations," Ministry of Foreign Affairs of the People's Republic of China, dated March 27, 2014, accessed May 26, 2021, https://www.fmprc.gov.cn/mfa_eng/gj hdq_665435/3265_665445/3291_664540/3294_664546/201404/t20140417_575167.html

51 Author's interview with the princeling in August 2019.

52 Chun Han Wong, "Chinese President Xi Jinping's Extreme Makeover," *Wall Street Journal*, May 12, 2016. https://www.wsj.com/articles/xi-jinpings-extreme-makeover-1463069291

53 Liangen Yin and Terry Flew, "Xi Dada Loves Peng Mama: Digital Culture and the Return of Charismatic Authority in China," *Thesis Eleven* 144, No. 1 (April 2018): 80–99.

54 Jeremy Page, "China Swoons Over New First Lady," *Wall Street Journal*, March 22, 2013, https://www.wsj.com/articles/SB10001424127887324103504578376201701604218; Laurie Burkitt and Te-Ping Chen, "China's First Lady Tones Down Star Power," *Wall Street Jour-*

nal, September 25, 2015, https://www.wsj.com/articles/chinas-first-lady-tones-down-star
-power-1443171907

55 Shih-Wen Sue Chen and Sin Wen Lau, "Little Red Children and 'Grandpa Xi': China's School
Textbooks Reflect the Rise of Xi Jinping's Personality Cult," *The Conversation*, November 22,
2021. https://theconversation.com/little-red-children-and-grandpa-xi-chinas-school-textbooks
-reflect-the-rise-of-xi-jinpings-personality-cult-168482

56 Chun Han Wong, "As China's Troubles Mushroom, Xi Collects a Special Title," *Wall Street Journal*, December 28, 2019. https://www.wsj.com/articles/as-chinas-troubles-mushroom-xi-collects
-a-special-title-11577525539

57 David Bandurski, "In the Highest Position," China Media Project, July 31, 2018. https://
chinamediaproject.org/2018/07/31/in-the-highest-position/

58 Chun Han Wong, "In Rare State Media Tour, Xi Jinping Takes the Anchor's Chair," *WSJ China
Real Time* blog, February 19, 2016. https://www.wsj.com/articles/BL-CJB-28715

59 Mia Li and Bree Feng, "Are You Qualified to Be a Journalist in China? Take the Test," *New York
Times Sinosphere* blog, December 23, 2013, https://sinosphere.blogs.nytimes.com/2013/12/23
/are-you-qualified-to-be-a-journalist-in-china-take-the-test/; William Zheng, "Journalists in
Chinese State Media to Be Tested on Loyalty to President Xi Jinping," *South China Morning Post*,
September 19, 2019, https://www.scmp.com/news/china/politics/article/3028152/journalists
-chinese-state-media-be-tested-loyalty-president-xi

60 "初心 · 梁家河篇 [Original Aspirations · Liangjiahe Chapter]," China Central Television,
March 19, 2017, http://m.news.cctv.com/2017/03/19/ARTI9uhRtfHK8S4sG0nSdLpO170319
.shtml; Josh Rudolph, "Drawing the News: Xi's 100 Kilos of Grain [Updated]," *China Digital
Times*, March 20, 2017, https://chinadigitaltimes.net/2017/03/drawing-news-xis-100-kilos
-grain/

61 "习近平：我这说完了吗？ [Xi Jinping: I've Already Finished Saying This?]," YouTube video,
uploaded by Steiner Wu, July 6, 2021, https://www.youtube.com/watch?v=DIG-KLkeH_w;
author's interviews with foreign diplomats who joined the video conference.

62 Chun Han Wong, "China's Museums Rewrite History to Boost Xi," *Wall Street Journal*, August 20, 2018. https://www.wsj.com/articles/sleight-at-the-museum-china-rewrites-history-to
-boost-xi-1534766405

63 Wong, "China's Museums Rewrite History."

64 Author's visit to the Shekou Museum of China's Reform and Opening-Up in August 2018;
@ByChunHan, "When the Shekou Museum of Reform and Opening first opened in December, visitors were greeted by this sculpture depicting a 1984 visit to Shenzhen's Shekou district
by Deng Xiaoping and other senior leaders. 1/," Twitter, August 20, 2018, https://twitter.com/
ByChunHan/status/1031562639082577920

65 Author's visit to the Shekou Museum of China's Reform and Opening-Up in August 2018;
Wong, "China's Museums Rewrite History."

66 Jun Mai, "Deng Xiaoping's Son Urges China to 'Know Its Place' and Not Be 'Overbearing,'"
South China Morning Post, October 30, 2018, https://www.scmp.com/news/china/politics/article
/2170762/deng-xiaopings-son-uses-unpublicised-speech-urge-china-know-its; Chun Han Wong,
"Xi Jinping's Strongman Rule Comes Under Fire as China Celebrates Deng's Reforms," *Wall
Street Journal*, December 18, 2018, https://www.wsj.com/articles/xi-jinpings-strongman-rule
-comes-under-fire-as-china-celebrates-dengs-reforms-11545047738

67 Author's interview with the doctoral student in February 2019.

68 Author's online conversation with a spokeswoman for the Shekou Museum of China's Reform and Opening-Up in December 2018.

69 Author's interview with Fang Huaqing in 2018.

70 Mrs. Howard Taylor, *The Triumph of John and Betty Stam* (Philadelphia China Inland Mission, 1935); China Inland Mission, *China's Millions* 61, No. 1 (January 1935): 67.

71 Ci Aimin and Liu Wentao, "方志敏烈士长孙方华清用法律武器捍卫英烈名誉 [Fang Huaqing, the Eldest Grandson of Martyr Fang Zhimin, Defends the Honor of Martyrs with Legal Weapons]," 党建网 [Party-Building Net], August 6, 2018. http://www.dangjian.cn/djw2016sy/djw2016syyw/201808/t20180806_4784672.shtml

72 Liu Shurong, "江西两干部任前公示遭革命英烈后人质疑: 他们没有维护党的历史声誉 [Two Jiangxi Cadres Called to Question by a Revolutionary Hero's Descendant After the Announcement of Their Next Positions: They Didn't Uphold the Party's Historical Reputation]," 大白新闻 [*Dabai News*], December 12, 2017. https://news.sina.cn/gn/2017-12-12/detail-ifypsvkp2201880.d.html

73 Ci and Liu, "Fang Huaqing, the Eldest Grandson of Martyr Fang Zhimin."

74 Ci and Liu, "Fang Huaqing, the Eldest Grandson of Martyr Fang Zhimin"; Zhang Xibin, "江西网友在网帖中使用侮辱性语言侵害方志敏烈士名誉, 昨公开致歉 [Jiangxi Netizens Publicly Apologized Yesterday for Using Insulting Language to Infringe on the Reputation of Martyr Fang Zhimin]," 大白新闻 [*Dabai News*], October 31, 2019, https://k.sina.cn/article_5996341740_16568e9ec00100lwwk.html?from=news

75 Josh Chin, "In China, Xi Jinping's Crackdown Extends to Dissenting Versions of History," *Wall Street Journal*, August 1, 2016, https://www.wsj.com/articles/in-china-xi-jinpings-crackdown-extends-to-dissenting-versions-of-history-1470087445; Josh Chin, "Lost Appeal: Court Orders a Writer to Apologize Over Wartime Story," *WSJ China Real Time* blog, August 16, 2016, https://www.wsj.com/articles/BL-CJB-29480

76 "中华人民共和国刑法修正案 (十一) [Amendment to the Criminal Law of the People's Republic of China (11)]," National People's Congress website, dated December 26, 2020, accessed February 23, 2022, http://www.npc.gov.cn/npc/c30834/202012/850abff47854495e9871997bf64803b6.shtml; Steven Lee Myers, "Shutting Down Historical Debate, China Makes It a Crime to Mock Heroes," *New York Times*, November 2, 2021, https://www.nytimes.com/2021/11/02/world/asia/china-slander-law.html

77 Li Bin, "别用恶搞毁了艺术 [Don't Ruin Art with Spoofs]," *People's Daily*, January 29, 2018, p. 5.

78 "文化部严肃查处恶搞《黄河大合唱》等红色经典及英雄人物视频 [The Ministry of Culture Seriously Investigates and Punishes Videos Spoofing Red Classics and Heroes Such as 'Yellow River Cantata']," Ministry of Culture of the People's Republic of China, February 2, 2018. https://www.mct.gov.cn/whzx/whyw/201802/t20180202_831119.htm

79 "教育部2017年工作要点 [Main Points of the Ministry of Education's Work in 2017]," Ministry of Education of the People's Republic of China, January 22, 2017. http://www.moe.gov.cn/srcsite/A02/s7049/201702/t20170214_296174.html

80 Author's interview with Xiao Fasheng in 2018.

81 Chun Han Wong and Keith Zhai, "China Repackages Its History in Support of Xi's National Vision," *Wall Street Journal*, June 15, 2021. https://www.wsj.com/articles/china-repackages-history-xi-propaganda-communist-party-centenary-11623767590

82   Gao Xiang, "中央网信办副主任高翔在2018中国网络媒体论坛上的致辞（全文）[Cyber-
     space Administration of China Deputy Director Gao Xiang's Speech at the 2018 China Internet
     Media Forum (Full Text)]," Cyberspace Administration of China, August 7, 2018. http://www
     .cac.gov.cn/2018-09/07/c_1123397126.htm

83   "美国往事：黑奴、红血、白棉花 [American Past: Black Slaves, Crimson Blood, White Cot-
     ton]," Chinese Academy of History Weibo account, March 26, 2021. https://weibo.com/ttarticle
     /p/show?id=2309404618987261788827

84   "戳破谣言、敬悼英魂：毛岸英烈士牺牲的历史真相 [Busting Rumors and Paying Respects
     to a Heroic Soul: The Historical Truth About the Sacrifice of Mao Anying]," Chinese Acad-
     emy of History Weibo account, November 25, 2020. https://weibo.com/ttarticle/p/show?id=
     2309404575043395911782

85   Wong and Zhai, "China Repackages Its History."

86   James A. Millward, *Beyond the Pass: Economy, Ethnicity, and Empire in Qing Central Asia,
     1759–1864* (Stanford: Stanford University Press, 1998); "Historical Matters Concerning Xin-
     jiang," State Council Information Office of the People's Republic of China, July 22, 2019, http://
     english.scio.gov.cn/2019-07/22/content_75017992.htm

87   Liu Shanshan, "歪曲新疆历史别有所图 [Distorting Xinjiang's History to Serve Ulterior Mo-
     tives]," 《历史评论》 *Historical Review*, No. 7 of 2020 (July 2020): 75–78; Zhong Han, "米华
     健是如何捏造事实的? [How Does James Millward Fabricate Facts?]," 《历史评论》 *Historical
     Review*, No. 7 of 2020 (July 2020): 79–85.

88   Email conversation with James Millward in June 2021.

89   Gao Xiang, "新时代史学研究要有更大作为 [Historical Research in the New Era Should Ac-
     complish More]," *People's Daily*, November 4, 2019, p. 9, https://paper.people.com.cn/rmrb/
     html/2019-11/04/nw.D110000renmrb_20191104_2-09.htm

90   Pei Yiran, "裴毅然：穿越史尘评邓、赫 [Pei Yiran: Traveling Through History to Appraise
     Deng, Khrushchev]," 《争鸣》 *Cheng Ming*, No. 468 (October 2016): 87–88. https://www
     .chinesepen.org/blog/archives/69213

91   Author's interview with Pei Yiran in April 2018.

92   Arunabh Ghosh and Sören Urbansky, "Introduction," *PRC History Review* 2, No. 3 (June 2017):
     1–3. http://prchistory.org/wp-content/uploads/2017/06/1_Introduction.pdf

93   Charles Kraus, "Researching the History of the People's Republic of China," Cold War Interna-
     tional History Project Working Paper #79, April 2016. https://www.wilsoncenter.org/publication
     /researching-the-history-the-peoples-republic-china

94   Sarah Mellors Rodriguez, "Researching the PRC in Municipal and Provincial Archives," *PRC
     History Review* 6, No. 3 (September 2021): 10–11.

95   Author's interview with Thomas Mullaney in February 2022.

96   Glenn D. Tiffert, "Peering Down the Memory Hole: Censorship, Digitization, and the Fragility
     of Our Knowledge Base," *American Historical Review* 124, No. 2 (April 2019): 550–568. https://
     academic.oup.com/ahr/article-abstract/124/2/550/5426383

97   Tiffert, "Peering Down the Memory Hole."

98   Te-Ping Chen, "Cambridge University Press Removes Articles from Chinese Website," *Wall Street
     Journal*, August 18, 2017. https://www.wsj.com/articles/cambridge-university-press-removes
     -articles-from-chinese-website-1503073115

99   Te-Ping Chen, "Cambridge University Press to Restore Hundreds of Articles on Chinese Web-

site," *Wall Street Journal*, August 21, 2017, https://www.wsj.com/articles/cambridge-university
-press-to-restore-hundreds-of-articles-on-chinese-website-1503338511; *Journal of Asian Studies*,
"Frequently Asked Questions About the Journal of Asian Studies and Censorship in China,"
Association for Asian Studies, August 23, 2017, https://www.asianstudies.org/frequently-asked
-questions-about-the-journal-of-asian-studies-and-censorship-in-china/

100 Ben Bland, "Outcry as Latest Global Publisher Bows to China Censors," *Financial Times*,
November 1, 2017, https://www.ft.com/content/2d195ffc-be2e-11e7-b8a3-38a6e068f464; Ben
Blanchard, "Springer Nature Blocks Access to Certain Articles in China," Reuters News, November 1, 2017, https://www.reuters.com/article/us-china-censorship-idUSKBN1D14EB

101 Thomas Burnham, "Researching the History of PRC Foreign Relations," *PRC History Review* 6, No. 3 (September 2021): 19–22. http://prchistory.org/wp-content/uploads/2021/09/7_Burnham.pdf

102 Author's interview with the historian in March 2018.

103 Author's email conversation with Charles Kraus in December 2017.

104 Author's interview with the Chinese historian in January 2018.

105 Sun Peidong, 《时尚与政治：广东民众日常着装时尚》 [*Fashion and Politics: Everyday Clothing Choices in Guangdong During the Cultural Revolution*] (Beijing: People's Publishing House, 2013), pp. 11–12.

106 Author's interview with Sun Peidong in January 2022.

107 Author's interview with Sun Peidong in January 2022.

108 Author's interview with Sun Peidong in January 2022.

109 Author's interview with Sun Peidong in January 2022.

110 Author's interview with Sun Peidong in January 2022.

111 Heysun A. Mahboubi, Mary Gallagher, Jia Dalei, Margaret Lewis, Taisu Zhang, Peidong Sun Rory Truex, Shen Kui, and Amy E. Gadsden, "Is There a Future for Values-Based Engagement with China?" *ChinaFile*, July 21, 2020. https://www.chinafile.com/conversation/there-future
-values-based-engagement-china

112 Author's interview with Sun Peidong in January 2022.

113 Sun Peidong, "Love and Passion: Teaching the PRC History in China Today," *PRC History Review* 4, No. 2 (August 2019): 41–43; author's interview with Sun Peidong in January 2022.

114 Philip Wen, "Demand for Absolute Loyalty to Beijing at Chinese Universities Triggers Dissent," *Wall Street Journal*, December 18, 2019, https://www.wsj.com/articles/demand-for-absolute
-loyalty-to-beijing-at-chinese-universities-triggers-dissent-11576674047; Anna Fifield, "In Xi Jinping's China, a Top University Can No Longer Promise Freedom of Thought," *Washington Post*, December 18, 2019, https://www.washingtonpost.com/world/asia_pacific/in-xi-jinpings
-china-a-top-university-can-no-longer-promise-freedom-of-thought/2019/12/18/59f4d21a
-215d-11ea-b034-de7dc2b5199b_story.html; Javier C. Hernandez and Albee Zhang, "Chinese Students Denounce Limits on Free Speech, in a Rare Protest," *New York Times*, December 18, 2019, https://www.nytimes.com/2019/12/18/world/asia/china-protests-universities.html

115 Sun Peidong's resignation letter submitted to Fudan University's history department in October 2019, provided to the author by Sun.

116 Author's interview with Sun Peidong in January 2022.

117 Interviews with China historians in January 2022.

118 Yi Lu, "Garbage Gleanings," *PRC History Review* 6, No. 3 (September 2021): 3–5, http://

prchistory.org/wp-content/uploads/2021/09/2_Yi_Lu.pdf; Matthew Wills, "Problematizing the 'Personal Collection,'" *PRC History Review* 6, No. 3 (September 2021): 6–9, http://prchistory .org/wp-content/uploads/2021/09/3_Wills.pdf; Denise Ho, "Postscript," *PRC History Review* 6, No. 3 (September 2021): 35–36, http://prchistory.org/wp-content/uploads/2021/09/11_Post-script.pdf

119 David Ownby, "About," Reading the China Dream. https://www.readingthechinadream.com/about.html

120 Author's interview with Timothy Cheek in January 2022.

6. ALL UNDER HEAVEN

1   Keith Zhai, "China's Communist Party Formally Embraces Assimilationist Approach to Ethnic Minorities," *Wall Street Journal*, October 8, 2021. https://www.wsj.com/articles/chinas-communist -party-formally-embraces-assimilationist-approach-to-ethnic-minorities-11633702544

2   Author's interview with James Leibold in March 2022.

3   Xi Jinping, "Speech at the First Session of the 12th National People's Congress," Xinhua News Agency, March 17, 2013. http://www.xinhuanet.com//2013lh/2013-03/17/c_115055434.htm

4   Lucian Pye, "China: Erratic State, Frustrated Society," *Foreign Affairs* 69, No. 4 (Fall 1990): 56–74.

5   Xu Jilin, "新天下主义：重建中国的内外秩序 [New Tianxia-ism and China's Internal and External Order]," in Xu Jilin and Liu Qing (eds.), 《新天下主义（知识分子论丛）》 [*New Tianxia, Intellectual Series*] No. 13 (Shanghai: Shanghai People's Publishing House, 2015). https://www.readingthechinadream.com/xu-jilin-the-new-tianxia.html

6   James Leibold, "Positioning 'Minzu' Within Sun Yat-sen's Discourse of Minzuzhuyi," *Journal of Asian History* 38, No. 2 (2004): 163–213.

7   Arif Dirlik, "The Ideological Foundations of the New Life Movement: A Study in Counterrevolution," *Journal of Asian Studies* 34, No. 4 (August 1975): 945–980.

8   Yinan He, "China's Political Trajectory and Foreign Relations Under the Influence of National Identity," The Asan Forum, dated December 20, 2018, accessed March 7, 2022. https:// theasanforum.org/chinas-political-trajectory-and-foreign-relations-under-the-influence-of -national-identity/

9   Xiao Gongqin, "中国民族主义的历史与前景 [History and Prospects of Chinese Nationalism]," 《战略与管理》 *Strategy and Management*, No. 2 of 1996 (April 1996): 58–62.

10 William Callahan, "History, Identity, and Security: Producing and Consuming Nationalism in China," *Critical Asian Studies* 38, No. 2 (2006): 179–208.

11 Chuyu Liu and Xiao Ma, "Popular Threats and Nationalistic Propaganda: Political Logic of China's Patriotic Campaign," *Security Studies* 27, No. 4 (July 2018): 633–664. https://www .tandfonline.com/doi/full/10.1080/09636412.2018.1483632

12 Liqing Li, "China's Rising Nationalism and Its Forefront: Politically Apathetic Youth," *China Report* 51, No. 4 (October 2015): 311–326. https://journals.sagepub.com/doi/abs/10.1177 /0009445515597805

13 Stanley Rosen, "Contemporary Chinese Youth and the State," *Journal of Asian Studies* 68, No. 2 (May 2009): 359–369; Liza Lin, "Xi's China Crafts Campaign to Boost Youth Patriotism," *Wall*

Street Journal, December 30, 2020, https://www.wsj.com/articles/xi-china-campaign-youth-patriotism-propaganda-11609343255

14 Alastair Iain Johnston, "Is Chinese Nationalism Rising? Evidence from Beijing," *International Security* 41, No. 3 (January 2017): 7–43. https://direct.mit.edu/isec/article/41/3/7/12154/Is-Chinese-Nationalism-Rising-Evidence-from

15 Chris Buckley, "China Takes Aim at Western Ideas," *New York Times*, August 19, 2013. https://www.nytimes.com/2013/08/20/world/asia/chinas-new-leadership-takes-hard-line-in-secret-memo.html

16 Jeremy Page, "Why China Is Turning Back to Confucius," *Wall Street Journal*, September 20, 2015. https://www.wsj.com/articles/why-china-is-turning-back-to-confucius-1442754000

17 Wu Jing and Hu Hao, "习近平出席全国教育大会并发表重要讲话 [Xi Jinping Attends the National Education Conference and Delivers an Important Speech]," Xinhua News Agency, September 10, 2018. http://www.gov.cn/xinwen/2018-09/10/content_5320835.htm

18 "教育部关于印发《中小学教材管理办法》《职业院校教材管理办法》和《普通高等学校教材管理办法》的通知 [Ministry of Education Notice on the Issuance of 'Administrative Measures for Primary and Secondary School Teaching Materials,' 'Administrative Measures for Vocational College Teaching Materials,' and 'Administrative Measures for College and University Teaching Materials']," Central People's Government of the People's Republic of China, December 16, 2019, http://www.gov.cn/zhengce/zhengceku/2020-01/07/content_5467235.htm; Xue Yujie, "China Bans Imported Textbooks for Primary, Middle Schools," *Sixth Tone*, January 7, 2020, https://www.sixthtone.com/news/1005052/china-bans-imported-textbooks-for-primary%2C-middle-schools

19 Jie Wenjin, Liu Shuo, and Hu Hao, "改 "8年抗战" 为 "14年抗战", 大中小学教材修改这 一概念有何深意? [What Is the Meaning of the Concept of Revision of Textbooks for Universities, Middle Schools and Primary Schools by Changing the '8-year War of Resistance' to '14-year War of Resistance'?]," Xinhua News Agency, January 11, 2017. http://www.gov.cn/xinwen/2017-01/11/content_5158937.htm

20 Liza Lin, "Xi's China Crafts Campaign to Boost Youth Patriotism," *Wall Street Journal*, December 30, 2020. https://www.wsj.com/articles/xi-china-campaign-youth-patriotism-propaganda-11609343255

21 Xu Guimei and Huang Qiaoqiao, "祖国在我心, 我是小小兵——广州市第一幼儿园爱国主义教育体验营结营活动 [The Motherland Is in My Heart, I Am a Little Soldier——Guangzhou No. 1 Kindergarten Patriotic Education Experience Camp Closing Activities]," 广州市第一幼儿园 [Guangzhou No. 1 Kindergarten] WeChat account, October 23, 2021. https://mp.weixin.qq.com/s/vXMi-fJ0Uj_ZbGDRCQbbJA

22 "The 47th China Statistical Report on Internet Development," China Internet Network Information Center, February 3, 2021, http://www.cnnic.cn/NMediaFile/old_attach/P020210203334633480104.pdf; Chao Deng and Liza Lin, "In Xi Jinping's China, Nationalism Takes a Dark Turn," *Wall Street Journal*, October 22, 2020, https://www.wsj.com/articles/in-xi-jinpings-china-nationalism-takes-a-dark-turn-11603382993

23 Evelyn Cheng, "Chinese Livestreamers Can Rake In Billions of Dollars in Hours. How Long Will It Last?" CNBC.com, November 15, 2021. https://www.cnbc.com/2021/11/16/chinese-livestreamers-can-rake-in-billions-of-dollars-in-hours-how-long-will-it-last.html

24 Deng and Lin, "In Xi Jinping's China, Nationalism Takes a Dark Turn."

25 Chun Han Wong, "A Wuhan Writer Rages Against China's Communist Machine and Becomes an Online Star," *Wall Street Journal*, April 1, 2020. https://www.wsj.com/articles/a-wuhan-writer -rages-against-chinas-communist-machine-and-becomes-an-online-star-11585733403

26 Deng and Lin, "In Xi Jinping's China, Nationalism Takes a Dark Turn."

27 Austin Ramzy and Chris Buckley, "'Absolutely No Mercy': Leaked Files Expose How China Organized Mass Detentions of Muslims," *New York Times*, November 16, 2019. https://www .nytimes.com/interactive/2019/11/16/world/asia/china-xinjiang-documents.html

28 Josh Chin, "Leaked Documents Detail Xi Jinping's Extensive Role."

29 Stanley Toops, "The Population Landscape of Xinjiang/East Turkestan," *Inner Asia* 2, No. 2, Special Issue: Xinjiang (2000): 155–170.

30 Stanley Toops, "Demographics and Development in Xinjiang After 1949," East-West Center Washington Working Papers, No. 1 (May 2004), https://www.eastwestcenter.org/system/tdf /private/EWCWwp001.pdf?file=1&type=node&id=32004; "3-8 主要年份分民族人口数 [3-8 Population by Ethnic Group in Main Years]," Statistic Bureau of Xinjiang Uygur Autonomous Region, dated June 10, 2020, Internet Archive, accessed May 13, 2022, http://web .archive.org/web/20201101133553/http://tjj.xinjiang.gov.cn/tjj/rkjyu/202006/a3217a0ca4d f493c960de1a0e2bcf4fe.shtml

31 Joseph Torigian, "What Xi Jinping Learned—and Didn't Learn—from His Father About Xinjiang," *Diplomat*, November 26, 2019. https://thediplomat.com/2019/11/what-xi-jinping -learned-and-didnt-learn-about-his-father-about-xinjiang/

32 Torigian, "What Xi Jinping Learned—and Didn't Learn—from His Father."

33 Torigian, "What Xi Jinping Learned—and Didn't Learn—from His Father."

34 Hu Angang and Hu Lianhe, "第二代民族政策:促进民族交融一体和繁荣一体 [The Second-Generation Ethnic Policy: Toward Integrated Ethnic Fusion and Prosperity]," 《新疆师范大学学报》(哲学社会科学版) *Journal of Xinjiang Normal University (Social Sciences)* 32, No. 5 (September 2011): 1–12.

35 Author's interview with Max Oidtmann in December 2018.

36 Liza Lin, Eva Xiao, and Jonathan Cheng, "China Targets Another Region in Ethnic Assimilation Campaign: Tibet," *Wall Street Journal*, July 16, 2021. https://www.wsj.com/articles/china-ethnic -assimilation-campaign-tibet-xinjiang-11626450702

37 "China: Visiting Officials Occupy Homes in Muslim Region," Human Rights Watch, dated May 13, 2018, accessed March 7, 2022. https://www.hrw.org/news/2018/05/13/china-visiting -officials-occupy-homes-muslim-region

38 Chun Han Wong, "China's Hard Edge: The Leader of Beijing's Muslim Crackdown Gains Influence," *Wall Street Journal*, April 7, 2019. https://www.wsj.com/articles/chinas-hard-edge-the -leader-of-beijings-muslim-crackdown-gains-influence-11554655886

39 "【新华网】新疆首部去极端化学术专著出版发行 [[Xinhua Net] Xinjiang's First Academic Monograph on Deradicalization Is Published]," Xinjiang Uyghur Autonomous Region Prison Administration Bureau, dated July 20, 2017, accessed March 1, 2022. http://jyglj.xinjiang.gov.cn /jyglj/mtgz/201707/8ff36a3d947b4913a5d1ae8354f648fd.shtml

40 Zhu Zhijie, 《去极端化原理: 思路与方法构建》 [*Deradicalization Principles: The Construction of Reasonings and Methods*] (Yining: Yili People's Publishing House, 2016).

41 Chao Deng, "China Razed Thousands of Xinjiang Mosques in Assimilation Push, Report Says," *Wall Street Journal*, September 25, 2020, https://www.wsj.com/articles/china-razed-thousands

-of-xinjiang-mosques-in-assimilation-push-report-says-11601049531; Nathan Ruser, James Leibold, Kelsey Munro, and Tilla Hoja, "Cultural Erasure," Australian Strategic Policy Institute, September 24, 2020, https://www.aspi.org.au/report/cultural-erasure

42 Gerry Shih, "China's Mass Indoctrination Camps Evoke Cultural Revolution," Associated Press, May 18, 2018, https://apnews.com/article/kazakhstan-ap-top-news-international-news-china -china-clamps-down-6e151296fb194f85ba69a8babd972e4b; Chin, "Leaked Documents Detail Xi Jinping's Extensive Role."

43 "OHCHR Assessment of Human Rights Concerns in the Xinjiang Uyghurs Autonomous Region, People's Republic of China," United Nations Office of the High Commissioner for Human Rights, August 31, 2022, https://www.ohchr.org/sites/default/files/documents/countries/2022 -08-31/22-08-31-final-assesment.pdf; Chun Han Wong and James T. Areddy, "U.N. Report Says China May Have Committed Crimes Against Humanity in Xinjiang," *Wall Street Journal*, September 1, 2022, https://www.wsj.com/articles/u-n-human-rights-agency-issues-report-on -xinjiang-over-chinas-protest-11661986730

44 Chun Han Wong, "Xi Says China Will Continue Efforts to Assimilate Muslims in Xinjiang," *Wall Street Journal*, September 26, 2020, https://www.wsj.com/articles/xi-says-china-will -continue-efforts-to-assimilate-muslims-in-xinjiang-11601133450; "习近平在第三次中央新 疆工作座谈会上发表重要讲话 [Xi Jinping Delivers an Important Speech at the 3rd Central Xinjiang Work Symposium]," Xinhua News Agency, September 26, 2020, http://www.gov.cn/ xinwen/2020-09/26/content_5547383.htm

45 Eva Dou and Cate Cadell, "As Crackdown Eases, China's Xinjiang Faces Long Road to Rehabilitation," *Washington Post*, September 23, 2022. https://www.washingtonpost.com/world/2022/09 /23/china-xinjiang-crackdown-uyghurs-surveillance/

46 Ma Rong, "习近平同志近期讲话指引我国民族工作的方向 [Comrade Xi Jinping's Recent Remarks Guide the Direction of China's Ethnic Work]," 《中央社会主义学院学报》 *Journal of the Central Institute of Socialism*, No. 3 of 2018 (June 2018): 121–126.

47 Zhai, "China's Communist Party Formally Embraces Assimilationist Approach."

48 Zhao Kezhi, "Speech Given While Listening to the Report on Public Security and Stability Work on the Xinjiang Autonomous Region," June 15, 2018, released in Xinjiang Police Files by Victims of Communism Memorial Foundation, https://www.xinjiangpolicefiles.org/wp-content /uploads/2022/05/Zhao-Kezhi-Speech-Given-While-Listening-to-the-Report-on-Public-Security -and-Stability-Work-on-the-Xinjiang-Autonomous-Region.pdf; Yuan Zhongrui, "Guoyu, Putonghua, Huayu," China Language National Language Committee, dated March 10, 2008, http://www.china-language.gov.cn/63/2008_3_10/1_63_3387_0_1205124588468.html, Internet Archive. https://web.archive.org/web/20090426051531/http://www.china-language.gov.cn /63/2008_3_10/1_63_3387_0_1205124588468.html

49 "Schools Are Empty, Students Take Oath to Defend the Mother Tongue," Southern Mongolian Human Rights Information Center, dated September 1, 2020, accessed March 1, 2022, http:// www.smhric.org/news_676.htm; Eva Xiao, "China Cracks Down on Mongols Who Say Their Culture Is Being Snuffed Out," *Wall Street Journal*, September 4, 2020, https://www.wsj.com/articles/ china-clamps-down-on-inner-mongolians-protesting-new-mandarin-language-rules-11599132973

50 Chun Han Wong, "China Applies Xinjiang's Policing Lessons to Other Muslim Areas," *Wall Street Journal*, December 23, 2018. https://www.wsj.com/articles/china-applies-xinjiangs -policing-lessons-to-other-muslim-areas-11545566403

51 Wong, "China Applies Xinjiang's Policing Lessons to Other Muslim Areas."

52 Ren Jiahui, "陈小江任国家民族事务委员会主任 [Chen Xiaojiang Is Appointed Director of the National Ethnic Affairs Commission]," 中国共产党新闻网 [Communist Party of China News Net], December 28, 2020, http://renshi.people.com.cn/n1/2020/1228/c139617-31980752 .html; Zhai, "China's Communist Party Formally Embraces Assimilationist Approach."

53 General Office, "全国民委主任会议在京召开陈小江出席并讲话 [Nationwide Ethnic Affairs Commission Directors Meeting Held in Beijing, Chen Xiaojiang Attended and Delivered a Speech]," National Ethnic Affairs Commission, dated January 21, 2021, accessed March 8, 2022. https://www.neac.gov.cn/seac/xwzx/202101/1144105.shtml

54 Author's email conversation with Max Oidtmann in 2020.

55 Christine Loh, *Underground Front: The Chinese Communist Party in Hong Kong*, Second Edition (Hong Kong: Hong Kong University Press, 2018).

56 Loh, *Underground Front*; William Heaton, "Maoist Revolutionary Strategy and Modern Colonialism: The Cultural Revolution in Hong Kong," *Asian Survey* 10, No. 9 (September 1970): 840–857; Gwynn Guilford and Quartz, "The Secret History of Hong Kong's Democratic Stalemate," *Atlantic*, October 15, 2014, https://www.theatlantic.com/international/archive/2014 /10/the-secret-history-of-hong-kongs-democratic-stalemate/381424/

57 John Gittings, "China-Watching in Hongkong," *Journal of Contemporary Asia* 2, No. 4 (1972): 415–430.

58 Jordan Schneider and Callan Quinn, "Lin Biao: What Really Happened?," *ChinaTalk*, dated February 10, 2022, accessed March 7, 2022. https://chinatalk.substack.com/p/lin-biao-what -really-happened?s=r

59 "China and United Kingdom of Great Britain and Northern Ireland Joint Declaration on the question of Hong Kong," December 19, 1984, United Nations Treaty Series, Vol. 1339, No. 23391, pp. 33–88. https://treaties.un.org/doc/Publication/UNTS/Volume%201399/v 1399.pdf

60 "Secrets and Lies," Four Corners, Australian Broadcasting Corporation, June 23, 1997. https:// web.archive.org/web/20001026034701/https://www.abc.net.au/4corners/stories/s72753.htm

61 Te-Ping Chen, "Protest over 'Brainwashing' Schools," *WSJ China Real Time* blog, September 1, 2012. https://www.wsj.com/articles/BL-CJB-16407

62 Chen Zuo'er, "香港百年沧桑和 "一国两制" 实践 [A Century of Vicissitudes in Hong Kong and the Practice of 'One Country, Two Systems']," 《领导科学论坛》 *The Forum of Leadership Science*, No. 7 of 2017 (July 2017): 3–16.

63 "The Practice of the 'One Country, Two Systems' Policy in the Hong Kong Special Ad-ministrative Region," State Council Information Office of the People's Republic of China, June 2014. http://english.www.gov.cn/archive/white_paper/2014/08/23/content _281474982986578.htm

64 Brian Spegele, Chester Yung, and Isabella Steger, "Beijing Rules Out Open Election in Hong Kong," *Wall Street Journal*, August 31, 2014, https://www.wsj.com/articles/beijing-says-panel-to -name-hong-kong-leader-candidates-xinhua-1409472088; Chester Yung, Jacky Wong, and Jason Chow, "Hong Kong on Edge as Protests Grow," *Wall Street Journal*, September 29, 2014, https:// www.wsj.com/articles/hong-kong-protests-swell-as-riot-police-withdraw-1411979074; Chun Han Wong and Jeremy Page, "For China's Xi, the Hong Kong Crisis Is Personal," *Wall Street*

Journal, September 27, 2019, https://www.wsj.com/articles/for-chinas-xi-the-hong-kong-crisis-is
-personal-11569613304

65 Chen, "A Century of Vicissitudes in Hong Kong and the Practice of 'One Country, Two Systems.'"

66 Danny Lee and Gary Cheung, "Beijing Tells Britain It Has No 'Moral Responsibility' for Hong
Kong," *South China Morning Post*, December 3, 2014. https://www.scmp.com/news/hong-kong/
article/1654603/china-says-british-complaints-over-hong-kong-visit-ban-useless

67 Wendy Wu, Sidney Leng and He Huifeng, "Beijing 'Losing No Time' to Get Input on Blueprint
for 'Greater Bay Area,'" *South China Morning Post*, October 21, 2017, https://www.scmp.com/
news/china/policies-politics/article/2116423/beijing-losing-no-time-get-input-blueprint-greater
-bay; Natasha Khan, "China's New 34-Mile Bridge Links Up 70 Million People in Planned
Megalopolis," *Wall Street Journal*, October 22, 2018, https://www.wsj.com/articles/chinas-new
-34-mile-bridge-to-link-up-70-million-people-in-planned-megalopolis-1540207727; Ned Levin
and Chester Yung, "An Era in Hong Kong Is Ending, Thanks to China's Tight Embrace," *Wall
Street Journal*, September 23, 2016, https://www.wsj.com/articles/an-era-in-hong-kong-is-ending
-thanks-to-chinas-tight-embrace-1474647072.

68 Xi Jinping, "在庆祝香港回归祖国20周年大会暨香港特别行政区第五届政府就职典礼
上的讲话 [Speech at the Celebration of the 20th Anniversary of Hong Kong's Return to the
Motherland and the Inauguration Ceremony of the Fifth Government of the Hong Kong Special
Administrative Region]," Xinhua News Agency, July 1, 2017, http://www.xinhuanet.com//
politics/2017-07/01/c_1121247124.htm; Xi Jinping, "Full Text: Xi's Speech at Meeting Marking
HK's 20th Return Anniversary, Inaugural Ceremony of 5th-Term HKSAR Gov't," Xinhua News
Agency, July 1, 2017, https://www.mfa.gov.cn/ce/cohk//eng/Topics/pth/t1646265.htm

69 Natasha Khan, Joyu Wang, and Wenxin Fan, "Hong Kong Marchers Flood Streets Over Extradition Bill," *Wall Street Journal*, June 16, 2019, https://www.wsj.com/articles/protesters-crowd
-hong-kongs-streets-once-more-11560668928

70 Natasha Khan, "'Hong Kong's Not Right.' Protests Upend Life in a City on Edge," *Wall Street
Journal*, December 27, 2019, https://www.wsj.com/articles/hong-kongs-not-right-protests
-upend-life-in-a-city-on-edge-11577461989; John Lyons and Chun Han Wong, "One Hong
Kong District Becomes a Combat Zone," *Wall Street Journal*, October 1, 2019, https://www.wsj
.com/articles/one-hong-kong-district-becomes-a-combat-zone-11569953252

71 Eun-Young Jeong, John Lyons, and Chun Han Wong, "Hong Kong Protesters Direct Anger at
Police as Violence Flares," *Wall Street Journal*, November 11, 2019, https://www.wsj.com/articles
/hong-kong-protesters-direct-anger-at-police-as-violence-flares-11573499473; Chun Han Wong,
"Beijing's New Hong Kong Protest Strategy: Let 'Em Fight It Out," *Wall Street Journal*, November 21, 2019, https://www.wsj.com/articles/beijings-hong-kong-protest-strategy-let-em-fight-it
-out-11574332204

72 Wong and Page, "For China's Xi, the Hong Kong Crisis Is Personal."

73 Chun Han Wong and Philip Wen, "China Pushes to Integrate Hong Kong Through Patriotic Education, Security Overhauls," *Wall Street Journal*, November 1, 2019. https://www
.wsj.com/articles/china-pushes-to-integrate-hong-kong-through-patriotic-education-security
-overhauls-11572617038

74 Elaine Yu, "Hong Kong's Apple Daily Newspaper Prints Last Edition as Free-Press Era Ends,"
Wall Street Journal, June 23, 2021, https://www.wsj.com/articles/hong-kongs-apple-daily

-will-close-after-government-choked-funds-11624437029; Natasha Khan, "Hong Kong Pro
-Democracy Site Stand News Closes After Arrests, Raid," *Wall Street Journal*, December 29,
2021, https://www.wsj.com/articles/hong-kong-pro-democracy-site-stand-news-closes-after
-arrests-raid-11640771127; Jessie Pang and Edmond Ng, "Hong Kong's Citizen News Says
Closure Triggered by Stand News Collapse," Reuters News, January 3, 2022, https://www
.reuters.com/world/china/hong-kongs-citizen-news-says-closure-triggered-by-stand-news
-collapse-2022-01-03/; "Termination of Operation," FactWire News Agency, June 10, 2022,
https://www.factwire.org/en/termination-of-operation/, Internet Archive, https://web.archive.org
/web/20220610073822/https://www.factwire.org/en/termination-of-operation/; FactWire, "To
every thing there is a season, and a time to every purpose. It has, at last, come time to end our
journey. FactWire will cease operation as of today, Friday, June 10, 2022. Thank you for your
support. Full statement: https://bit.ly/3mAQHHr," Twitter, June 10, 2022, https://twitter.com/
factwirenews/status/1535166134756216833

75 Ng Kang-chung, "Hong Kong Schools Must Hold National Flag Ceremonies At Least Once
a Week Under New Education Bureau Rules," *South China Morning Post*, October 11, 2021,
https://www.scmp.com/news/hong-kong/education/article/3151971/hong-kong-schools-must
-hold-national-flag-ceremonies-least; Cyril Ip and Leung Pak-hei, "New Rule Kicks In for
Hong Kong Schools to Hold Regular Flag-Raising Ceremonies, Some Campuses Seek Training
Help from Police," *South China Morning Post*, January 3, 2022, https://www.scmp.com/news
/hong-kong/education/article/3161963/new-rule-kicks-hong-kong-schools-hold-regular-flag
-raising

76 Natasha Khan, Joyu Wang, and Frances Yoon, "The 11-Year-Old Dissident: Hong Kong's
Schoolchildren Fuel Protests," *Wall Street Journal*, November 15, 2019, https://www.wsj.com/
articles/schoolchildren-propel-hong-kong-protests-11573833842; Joyu Wang and Lucy Craymer,
"Hong Kong Teachers Fired and Afraid as China Targets Liberal Thinkers," *Wall Street Journal*,
July 19, 2020, https://www.wsj.com/articles/hong-kong-teachers-fired-and-afraid-as-china
-targets-liberal-thinkers-11595175839

77 William Yiu, "Hong Kong Was Not British Colony as China Did Not Recognise Unequal Treaties Ceding City to Britain, New Textbooks Reveal," *South China Morning Post*, June 13, 2022.
https://www.scmp.com/news/hong-kong/education/article/3181560/hong-kong-was-not-british
-colony-china-did-not-recognise

78 Joyu Wang and Lucy Craymer, "Hong Kong Wants Young Flag-Waving Patriots So It Scrubbed
Its Schoolbooks," *Wall Street Journal*, February 6, 2021. https://www.wsj.com/articles/hong
-kong-orders-national-security-lessons-for-elementary-students-11612531299

79 Author's interview with Ip Kwok-him in September 2019.

80 "總統出席「823戰役50週年」紀念大會 [President Attends '50th Anniversary of the 823
Battle' Commemorative Ceremony]," Office of the President, Republic of China (Taiwan),
August 24, 2008. https://www.president.gov.tw/NEWS/12527

81 Chang Kuo-cheng, "The Decision Analysis Regarding 'Project National Glory or Project
Guoguang (Chinese: 國光計劃),'" Taiwan Government Research Bulletin, October 31, 2018.
https://www.grb.gov.tw/search/planDetail?id=12227741

82 Cindy Sui, "Taiwan's Plan to Take Back Mainland," BBC News, September 7, 2009. http://news
.bbc.co.uk/2/hi/asia-pacific/8183412.stm

83 Lawrence Chung, "Details of Chiang Kai-Shek's Attempts to Recapture Mainland to Be Made

Public," *South China Morning Post*, April 22, 2009. https://www.scmp.com/article/677614/details-chiang-kai-sheks-attempts-recapture-mainland-be-made-public

84 "Message to Compatriots in Taiwan," China.org.cn, dated January 1, 1979, accessed February 21, 2022, http://www.china.org.cn/english/taiwan/7943.htm; Ye Jianying, "Ye Jianying on Taiwan's Return to Motherland and Peaceful Reunification," China.org.cn, dated September 30, 1981, accessed February 21, 2022, http://www.china.org.cn/english/7945.htm

85 Chun Han Wong, "Lee Teng-hui, Who Guided Taiwan on Its Path to Democracy, Dies at 97," *Wall Street Journal*, July 30, 2020. https://www.wsj.com/articles/lee-teng-hui-who-guided-taiwan-on-its-path-to-democracy-dies-at-97-11596112871

86 Reuters News, "Taiwan Ends Emergency Decree, Opening Way to Closer China Ties," *New York Times*, May 1, 1991. https://www.nytimes.com/1991/05/01/world/taiwan-ends-emergency-decree-opening-way-to-closer-china-ties.html

87 Wong, "Lee Teng-hui, Who Guided Taiwan on Its Path to Democracy, Dies at 97."

88 Ting-I Tsai, "Taiwan and China: The Consensus That Wasn't," *WSJ China Real Time* blog, August 13, 2010, https://www.wsj.com/articles/BL-CJB-10094; Paul Mozur, "Taiwan Opposition Leader Advocates Dumping Old 'Consensus' on China," *WSJ China Real Time* blog, September 6, 2011, https://www.wsj.com/articles/BL-CJB-14299

89 Author's email interview with Winston Lord in June 2020.

90 Du Shangze and Liu Hui, "两岸政治分歧终归要逐步解决不能将这些问题一代代传下去 [Cross-Strait Political Differences Must Eventually Be Resolved and Cannot Be Passed Down from Generation to Generation]," 《人民日报海外版》 *People's Daily Overseas Edition*, October 7, 2013. http://www.people.com.cn/24hour/n/2013/1007/c25408-23112554.html

91 Yang Chia-ying and Tao Ben-ho, "中華民國是獨立主權國家 蔡英文：這件事從來沒動搖過 [The Republic of China Is an Independent Sovereign State, Tsai Ing-wen: This Issue Has Never Wavered]," *ET Today*, December 31, 2016, https://www.ettoday.net/news/20161231/840097.htm; John Sudworth, "China Needs to Show Taiwan Respect, Says President," BBC News, January 14, 2020, https://www.bbc.com/news/world-asia-51104246

92 Data from Taiwan's Ministry of Transportation and Communications, accessed in February 2022.

93 William Kazer, "Taiwan's Voters Say No to Ruling Party," *Wall Street Journal*, November 24, 2018. https://www.wsj.com/articles/taiwans-voters-say-no-to-ruling-party-1543084683

94 Chun Han Wong, "Taiwan Leader Rejects Unification Under Heightened Pressure from China's Xi," *Wall Street Journal*, January 2, 2019. https://www.wsj.com/articles/taiwan-leader-rejects-unification-under-heightened-pressure-from-chinas-xi-11546428688

95 Kristin Huang, "Senior Chinese Officials Give Taiwanese Politician Han Kuo-yu the Red Carpet Treatment on 'Non-Political' Tour of Mainland," *South China Morning Post*, March 25, 2019. https://www.scmp.com/news/china/diplomacy/article/3003186/senior-chinese-officials-give-taiwanese-politician-han-kuo-yu

96 Chun Han Wong and William Kazer, "'Taiwan Cannot Become Like Hong Kong': A Fresh Challenge to China," *Wall Street Journal*, January 8, 2020. https://www.wsj.com/articles/hong-kong-protests-reverberate-in-taiwan-11578506068

97 Chun Han Wong, "Taiwan's Opposition Party Reconsiders Support for Closer China Ties," *Wall Street Journal*, March 8, 2020. https://www.wsj.com/articles/taiwans-opposition-party-reviews-its-support-for-closer-china-ties-11583673325

98 Wong, "Taiwan's Opposition Party Reconsiders Support for Closer China Ties."

99   Liu Kuan-ting, Yeh Su-ping, and Evelyn Kao, "KMT Chairman-Elect Eric Chu Reiterates 1992 Consensus for Ties with China," Focus Taiwan, September 26, 2021. https://focustaiwan.tw/cross-strait/202109260012

100 "Taiwanese / Chinese Identity(1992/06–2021/12)," National Chengchi University Election Study Center, January 10, 2022. https://esc.nccu.edu.tw/PageDoc/Detail?fid=7800&id=6961

101 Chun Han Wong, "Taiwan's Success in Coronavirus Fight Poses Challenge to China," *Wall Street Journal*, April 11, 2020. https://www.wsj.com/articles/taiwans-success-in-coronavirus-fight-poses-challenge-to-china-11586599202

102 Xie Chuntao's remarks at a November 2017 briefing for journalists and diplomats in Beijing.

103 Jeremy Page and Chun Han Wong, "China Flexes Its Military Muscle at World War II Parade," *Wall Street Journal*, September 3, 2015. https://www.wsj.com/articles/china-flexes-its-military-muscle-at-world-war-ii-parade-1441282579

104 Wang Hongshan and Liu Shengdong, "习近平: 富国和强军相统一 巩固国防和强大军队 [Xi Jinping: A Prosperous Country and a Strong Military Unite to Consolidate National Defense and a Strong Military]," Xinhua News Agency, December 12, 2012. http://www.gov.cn/ldhd/2012-12/12/content_2288879.htm

105 Xi Jinping, "决胜全面建成小康社会 夺取新时代中国特色社会主义伟大胜利——在中国共产党第十九次全国代表大会上的报告 [Scoring a Decisive Win in Comprehensively Building a Moderately Prosperous Society and Securing a Great Victory for Socialism with Chinese Characteristics in the New Era—Report at the Chinese Communist Party's 19th National Congress]," Xinhua News Agency, October 27, 2017. http://www.gov.cn/zhuanti/2017-10/27/content_5234876.htm

106 Andrew Jacobs and Chris Buckley, "Tales of Army Discord Show Tiananmen Square in a New Light," *New York Times*, June 2, 2014, https://www.nytimes.com/2014/06/03/world/asia/tiananmen-square-25-years-later-details-emerge; David Shambaugh, "The Soldier and the State in China: The Political Work System in the People' Liberation Army," *China Quarterly* 127 (September 1991): 527–568.

107 Chris Buckley, "30 Years After Tiananmen, a Chinese Military Insider Warns: Never Forget," *New York Times*, May 28, 2019. https://www.nytimes.com/2019/05/28/world/asia/china-tiananmen-square-massacre.html

108 Phillip C. Saunders, Arthur S. Ding, Andrew Scobell, Andrew N.D. Yang, and Joel Wuthnow (eds.), *Chairman Xi Remakes the PLA: Assessing Chinese Military Reforms* (Washington, DC: National Defense University Press, 2019), p. 523. https://ndupress.ndu.edu/Publications/Books/Chairman-Xi-Remakes-the-PLA/

109 Saunders, Ding, Scobell, Yang, and Wuthnow (eds.), *Chairman Xi Remakes the PLA*, p. 523.

110 Sui-Lee Wee, "Analysis: Stealth Flight Sparks China Politics Guessing Game," Reuters News, January 14, 2011. https://www.reuters.com/article/us-china-stealth-military-idUSTRE70D19P20110114

111 Saunders, Ding, Scobell, Yang, and Wuthnow (eds.), *Chairman Xi Remakes the PLA*, p. 6.

112 Jeremy Page, "President Xi Jinping's Most Dangerous Venture Yet: Remaking China's Military," *Wall Street Journal*, April 24, 2016. https://www.wsj.com/articles/president-xi-jinpings-most-dangerous-venture-yet-remaking-chinas-military-1461608795

113 Jeremy Page, "For Xi, a 'China Dream' of Military Power," *Wall Street Journal*, March 13, 2013,

https://www.wsj.com/articles/SB10001424127887324128504578348774040546346; Saunders, Ding, Scobell, Yang, and Wuthnow (eds.), *Chairman Xi Remakes the PLA*, pp. 3–4.

114 Jeremy Page, "China's Xi Adds 'Commander-in-Chief' to His Titles," *Wall Street Journal*, April 21, 2016. https://www.wsj.com/articles/chinas-xi-adds-commander-in-chief-to-his -titles-1461245897

115 James Mulvenon, "The Yuan Stops Here: Xi Jinping and the 'CMC Chairman Responsibility System,'" *China Leadership Monitor*, No. 47 (July 2015). https://www.hoover.org/sites/default/ files/research/docs/clm47jm.pdf

116 Josh Chin, "Retired Chinese General Sentenced to Life in Prison for Corruption," *Wall Street Journal*, July 25, 2016. https://www.wsj.com/articles/retired-chinese-general-sentenced-to-life-in -prison-for-corruption-1469451107

117 Chun Han Wong, "Former Chinese Military Chief Sentenced to Life in Prison for Corruption," *Wall Street Journal*, February 20, 2019, https://www.wsj.com/articles/former-chinese -military-chief-sentenced-to-life-in-prison-for-corruption-11550666372; Chun Han Wong, "Chinese General Under Investigation for Graft Kills Himself," *Wall Street Journal*, November 28, 2017, https://www.wsj.com/articles/chinese-general-under-investigation-for-graft-kills -himself-1511867979

118 Saunders, Ding, Scobell, Yang, and Wuthnow (eds.), *Chairman Xi Remakes the PLA*, p. 6.

119 Saunders, Ding, Scobell, Yang, and Wuthnow (eds.), *Chairman Xi Remakes the PLA*, p. 16.

120 "习近平领航的强军兴军新征程，取得了哪些突破性成果？ [What Breakthrough Achievements Have Been Made in the New Expedition to Strengthen and Rejuvenate the Military Led by Xi Jinping?]," 央视网 [China Central Television Net], July 26, 2017. http://news.cctv.com /2017/07/26/ARTIdR6hECfOsdzBHOmD8MoH170726.shtml

121 Saunders, Ding, Scobell, Yang, and Wuthnow (eds.), *Chairman Xi Remakes the PLA*, p. 9.

122 Jeremy Page, "China Builds First Overseas Military Outpost," *Wall Street Journal*, August 19, 2016. https://www.wsj.com/articles/china-builds-first-overseas-military-outpost-1471622690

123 James T. Areddy, "China Evacuates Citizens from Yemen," *Wall Street Journal*, March 30, 2015, https://www.wsj.com/articles/china-evacuating-citizens-from-yemen-1427689845; "Military and Security Developments Involving the People's Republic of China 2021," Office of the Secretary of Defense, November 3, 2021, pp. 128–129, https://media.defense.gov/2021/Nov/03 /2002885874/-1/-1/0/2021-CMPR-FINAL.PDF.

124 Neville Maxwell, "Settlements and Disputes: China's Approach to Territorial Issues," *Economic and Political Weekly* 41, No. 36 (September 2006): 3873–3881; M. Taylor Fravel, "Regime Insecurity and International Cooperation: Explaining China's Compromises in Territorial Disputes," *International Security* 30, No. 2 (Fall 2005): 46–83, https://www.belfercenter.org/sites/default/ files/files/publication/is3002_pp046-083_fravel.pdf; M. Taylor Fravel, "Mike Pompeo Criticized China for Not Respecting Its Neighbors' Territorial Integrity. What's the Story?," *Washington Post*, February 21, 2020, https://www.washingtonpost.com/politics/2020/02/21/mike-pompeo -criticized-china-not-respecting-its-neighbors-territorial-integrity-whats-story/

125 Gordon Lubold, "Two Chinese Fighters Make 'Unsafe' Interception with U.S. Spy Plane," *Wall Street Journal*, September 22, 2015, https://www.wsj.com/articles/two-chinese-fighters -make-dangerous-interception-with-u-s-spy-plane-1442957904; Ryan Browne, "US Navy Has Had 18 Unsafe or Unprofessional Encounters with China Since 2016," CNN, Novem-

ber 3, 2018, https://edition.cnn.com/2018/11/03/politics/navy-unsafe-encounters-china/index.html

126 Kyodo News, "Japan's Total Number of Fighter Jet Scrambles Reaches 30,000," *Japan Times*, July 21, 2021, https://www.japantimes.co.jp/news/2021/07/21/national/fighter-jet-scrambles/; "Statistics on Scrambles Through FY2020," Japan Ministry of Defense, April 9, 2021, https://www.mod.go.jp/js/Press/press2021/press_pdf/p20210409_03.pdf

127 Niharika Mandhana, Rajesh Roy, and Chun Han Wong, "The Deadly India-China Clash: Spiked Clubs and Fists at 14,000 Feet," *Wall Street Journal*, June 17, 2020, https://www.wsj.com/articles/spiked-clubs-and-fists-at-14-000-feet-the-deadly-india-china-clash-11592418242; Chun Han Wong, "India-China Border Clash Shows Rising Risk in Beijing's Territorial Push," *Wall Street Journal*, June 19, 2020, https://www.wsj.com/articles/india-china-border-clash-shows-rising-risk-in-beijings-territorial-push-11592585381

128 Ian Easton, *The Chinese Invasion Threat: Taiwan's Defense and American Strategy in Asia* (Arlington: Project 2049 Institute, 2017); Andrew S. Erickson and Joel Wuthnow, "Why Islands Still Matter in Asia," *National Interest*, February 5, 2016, https://nationalinterest.org/feature/why-islands-still-matter-asia-15121

129 Douglas MacArthur, "Memorandum on Formosa, by General of the Army Douglas MacArthur, Commander in Chief, Far East, and Supreme Commander, Allied Powers, Japan," U.S. Department of State website, June 14, 1950. https://history.state.gov/historicaldocuments/frus1950v07/d86

130 Wang Hongguang, "从历史看今日中国的战略方向 [Assessing the Strategic Direction of Today's China from a Historical Perspective]," 《同舟共进》 [*Tongzhou Gongjin*], No. 3 of 2015 (March 2015). 44–50. https://www.gdszx.gov.cn/zxkw/tzgj/2015/03/content/post_13511.html

131 Wang Hongguang, "为什么统一的炮声一响，"台独"顶多撑三天！ [Why 'Taiwan Independence' Can Last At Most Three Days Once the Cannons of Unification Are Sounded!]," Huanqiu.com, dated March 29, 2018, accessed March 13, 2022. https://mil.huanqiu.com/article/9CaKrnK78gP

132 Easton, *The Chinese Invasion Threat*.

133 Easton, *The Chinese Invasion Threat*.

134 Brian Spegele, Chun Han Wong, and Joyu Wang, "As Pelosi Leaves Taiwan, China's Military Looms Larger," *Wall Street Journal*, August 3, 2022, https://www.wsj.com/articles/as-pelosi-leaves-taiwan-chinas-military-looms-larger-11659531357; Wenxin Fan, Chun Han Wong, and Joyu Wang, "China Launches Live-Fre Drills, Missiles Around Taiwan After Pelosi Visit," *Wall Street Journal*, August 4, 2022, https://www.wsj.com/articles/chinas-military-launches-live-fire-exercises-around-taiwan-11659600560; Chun Han Wong, "China's War Games Showcase New Tools to Intimidate Taiwan," *Wall Street Journal*, August 7, 2022, https://www.wsj.com/articles/chinas-war-games-showcase-new-tools-to-intimidate-taiwan-11659872354

135 David Lague and Maryanne Murray, "T-DAY: The Battle for Taiwan," Reuters News, November 5, 2021. https://www.reuters.com/investigates/special-report/taiwan-china-wargames/

136 Yimou Lee, David Lague, and Ben Blanchard, "China Launches 'Gray-Zone' Warfare to Subdue Taiwan," Reuters News, December 10, 2020, https://www.reuters.com/investigates/special-report/hongkong-taiwan-military/; Lague and Murray, "T-DAY: The Battle for Taiwan."

137 Yimou Lee, "China's Latest Weapon Against Taiwan: the Sand Dredger," Reuters News, February 5, 2021. https://graphics.reuters.com/TAIWAN-CHINA/SECURITY/jbyvrnzerve/

138 Yu Kai-hsiang, "共機侵擾空域 國軍近3千架次攔截耗費255億元 [Communist Aircraft Airspace Intrusions, National Military Spent 25.5 Billion Yuan Launching Nearly 3,000 Interception Sorties]," Central News Agency, October 7, 2020, https://www.cna.com.tw/news/firstnews/202010075002.aspx; Ben Blanchard, "Taiwan Says Has Spent Almost $900 Million Scrambling Against China This Year," Reuters News, October 7, 2020, https://www.reuters.com/article/us-taiwan-security-idUSKBN26S0K6

139 Fu Chao-wen, "我國防空識別區相關問題之淺析 [A Brief Analysis of Issues Related to Our Country's Air-Defense Identification Zone]," Legislative Yuan, Republic of China (Taiwan), February 22, 2022. https://webcache.googleusercontent.com/search?q=cache:Mvqwsg4PnPoJ:https://www.ly.gov.tw/Pages/Detail.aspx%3Fnodeid%3D6590%26pid%3D217318+&cd=1&hl=en&ct=clnk&gl=jp

140 Office of the Secretary of Defense, "Military and Security Developments Involving the People's Republic of China 2021," United States Department of Defense, November 3, 2021. https://media.defense.gov/2021/Nov/03/2002885874/-1/-1/0/2021-CMPR-FINAL.PDF

141 Lee, Lague, and Blanchard, "China Launches 'Gray-Zone' Warfare to Subdue Taiwan."

142 Lee Hsi-min and Eric Lee, "Taiwan's Overall Defense Concept, Explained," *Diplomat*, November 3, 2020, https://thediplomat.com/2020/11/taiwans-overall-defense-concept-explained/; Joyu Wang, "In Taiwan, Russia's War in Ukraine Stirs New Interest in Self-Defense," *Wall Street Journal*, March 4, 2022, https://www.wsj.com/articles/in-taiwan-putins-war-in-ukraine-stirs-new-interest-in-self-defense-11646402103; Ben Blanchard, "Analysis: Taiwan Studies Ukraine War for Own Battle Strategy with China," Reuters News, March 9, 2022, https://www.reuters.com/business/aerospace-defense/taiwan-studies-ukraine-war-own-battle-strategy-with-china-2022-03-09/

143 Author's interview with Lee Hsi-min in March 2022.

144 "Transcript: President Tsai Ing-wen Discusses the Diplomatic, Security, and Economic Challenges Facing Taiwan," Hudson Institute, dated August 12, 2020, accessed March 13, 2022. https://www.hudson.org/research/16300-transcript-president-tsai-ing-wen-discusses-the-diplomatic-security-and-economic-challenges-facing-taiwan

145 Paul Huang, "Taiwan's Military Has Flashy American Weapons but No Ammo," *Foreign Policy*, August 20, 2020. https://foreignpolicy.com/2020/08/20/taiwan-military-flashy-american-weapons-no-ammo/

146 Office of the Secretary of Defense, "Military and Security Developments Involving the People's Republic of China 2021," United States Department of Defense; "2021 Report to Congress of the U.S.-China Economic and Security Review Commission," U.S.-China Economic and Security Review Commission, p. 405, https://www.uscc.gov/sites/default/files/2021-11/2021_Annual_Report_to_Congress.pdf; Kuo Hsien-chung, "志願役後備軍人選充率漸增之問題淺析 [A Brief Analysis on the Problem of Increases in Selection and Filling Rates for Volunteer and Reserve Soldiers]," Legislative Yuan, Republic of China (Taiwan), June 3, 2020, https://www.ly.gov.tw/Pages/Detail.aspx?nodeid=6590&pid=196348

147 Office of Information Services, "Regulatory Revisions for Volunteer Military Service Approved," Republic of China (Taiwan) Executive Yuan website, October 18, 2012, https://english.ey.gov.tw/Page/61BF20C3E89B856/9987a7cf-4850-4041-8785-4e5b66ce2601

148 Joyu Wang and Alastair Gale, "Does Taiwan's Military Stand a Chance Against China? Few Think So," *Wall Street Journal*, October 26, 2021, https://www.wsj.com/articles/taiwan-military-readiness-china-threat-us-defense-11635174187

149 Joyu Wang, "Taiwan to Extend Mandatory Military Service in Face of Chinese Pressure," *Wall Street Journal*, December 27, 2022, https://www.wsj.com/articles/taiwan-to-extend -mandatory-military-service-11672129529

150 2021 National Defense Report Editorial Committee, *ROC National Defense Report 2021* (Taipei: Ministry of National Defense of the Republic of China, October 2021). https://www .mnd.gov.tw

151 Joyu Wang, "Taiwan Plans to Bulk Up Military Budget to Contend with Chinese Pressure," *Wall Street Journal*, September 16, 2021. https://www.wsj.com/articles/taiwan-plans-to-bulk-up -military-budget-to-contend-with-chinese-pressure-11631787522

152 Josh Chin and Chao Deng, "China Would Be Able to Launch Attack on Taiwan by 2025, Island's Defense Minister Warns," *Wall Street Journal*, October 6, 2021. https://www.wsj.com /articles/china-would-be-able-to-launch-attack-on-taiwan-by-2025-islands-defense-minister -warns-11633525206

153 "H.R.2479—Taiwan Relations Act," Congress.gov, Library of Congress, April 10, 1979. https:// www.congress.gov/bill/96th-congress/house-bill/2479/

154 Jack Detsch and Zinya Salfiti, "The U.S. Is Getting Taiwan Ready to Fight on the Beaches," *Foreign Policy*, November 8, 2021. https://foreignpolicy.com/2021/11/08/us-taiwan-military -presence-china-biden-porcupine/

155 Graham Allison and Jonah Glick-Unterman, "The Great Military Rivalry: China vs the U.S.," Belfer Center for Science and International Affairs, Harvard Kennedy School, December 16, 2021. https://www.belfercenter.org/sites/default/files/files/publication/GreatMilitaryRivalry _ChinavsUS_211215_1.pdf

156 Charles Hutzler, Joyu Wang, and James T. Areddy, "Biden's Pledge to Defend Taiwan Chips Away at Longstanding U.S. Policy," *Wall Street Journal*, September 23, 2022. https://www .wsj.com/articles/bidens-pledge-to-defend-taiwan-chips-away-at-longstanding-u-s-policy -11663962151

157 Alastair Gale, "China, Eying Taiwan, Gets Lesson from Ukraine's Stiff Resistance," *Wall Street Journal*, March 2, 2022. https://www.wsj.com/articles/china-eying-taiwan-gets-lesson-from -ukraines-stiff-resistance-11646226559

158 Dan De Luce and Ken Dilanian, "China's Growing Firepower Casts Doubt on Whether U.S. Could Defend Taiwan," NBC News, March 27, 2021, https://www.nbcnews.com/politics/ national-security/china-s-growing-firepower-casts-doubt-whether-u-s-could-n1262148; Sydney J. Freedberg Jr., "US 'Gets Its Ass Handed to It' in Wargames: Here's A $24 Billion Fix," *Breaking Defense*, March 7, 2019, https://breakingdefense.com/2019/03/us-gets-its-ass-handed-to-it-in -wargames-heres-a-24-billion-fix/.

159 Hal Brands and Michael Beckley, "China Is a Declining Power—and That's the Problem," *Foreign Policy*, September 24, 2021. https://foreignpolicy.com/2021/09/24/china-great-power-united-states/

160 Author's interview with Lee Hsi-min in March 2022.

7. WOLF WARRIORS HOWLING

1 Adam Taylor, "A Chinese Diplomat Had a Fight About Race in D.C. with Susan Rice on Twitter. Then He Deleted the Tweets," *Washington Post*, July 15, 2019, https://www.washingtonpost.com/

world/2019/07/15/responding-uighur-criticism-chinese-diplomat-points-racial-segregation-dc/; "CV of Foreign Ministry Spokesperson Zhao Lijian," Ministry of Foreign Affairs of the People's Republic of China, February 24, 2020, https://www.fmprc.gov.cn/mfa_eng/xwfw_665399/s2510_665401/zlj/

2   Zhao Lijian, "If you're in Washington, D.C., you know the white never go to the SW area, because it's an area for the black & Latin. There's a saying 'black in & white out', which means that as long as a black family enters, white people will quit, & price of the apartment will fall sharply," Twitter, July 13, 2019, Internet Archive. https://web.archive.org/web/20190715084640/https://twitter.com/zlj517/status/1150248934020960256

3   Susan Rice, "You are a racist disgrace. And shockingly ignorant too. In normal times, you would be PNGed for this. Ambassador Cui, I expect better of you and your team. Please do the right thing and send him home. https://twitter.com/zlj517/status/1150248934020960256," Twitter, July 15, 2019. https://twitter.com/AmbassadorRice/status/1150584069354414080

4   Global Times, "Should Zhao Lijian @zlj517 be labeled a 'racist' simply because he told the truth about southeast Washington DC where 'the whites never go?' No. Ms Susan Rice @AmbassadorRice picked on wrong person. Some in US deserve 'racist disgrace' more than others. http://bit.ly/2ll6b63," Twitter, July 15, 2019. https://twitter.com/globaltimesnews/status/1150744476593377280

5   "China Finds A Use Abroad for Twitter, a Medium It Fears at Home," *Economist*, February 20, 2020. https://www.economist.com/china/2020/02/20/china-finds-a-use-abroad-for-twitter-a-medium-it-fears-at-home

6   Zhao Lijian, "I am leaving Pakistan with a heavy heart, because Pakistan has stolen my heart, and I have to leave now," Twitter, August 9, 2019, https://twitter.com/zlj517/status/1159644089991782400; Zhao Lijian, "New DCM Ms Pang Chunxue said she will pick up thread where Lijian Zhao left. Though Zhao is departing for Beijing, it's heartening to note that he is leaving behind a legacy of CPEC and Twitter diplomacy and is being replaced by another friend of Pakistan. https://diplo-mag.com/pakistan-says-zaijian-to-chinese-envoy-lijian-zhao/," Twitter, August 9, 2019, https://twitter.com/zlj517/status/1159661385963462656

7   "社评：赵立坚们没说错，赖斯们的表现太无理 [Editorial: The Likes of Zhao Lijian Are Right, Rice's Behavior Is Too Unreasonable]," *Global Times*, July 17, 2019, https://opinion.huanqiu.com/article/9CaKrnKlB5G; Keith Zhai and Yew Lun Tian, "In China, a Young Diplomat Rises as Aggressive Foreign Policy Takes Root," Reuters News, March 31, 2020, https://www.reuters.com/article/us-china-diplomacy-insight/in-china-a-young-diplomat-rises-as-aggressive-foreign-policy-takes-root-idUSKBN21I0F8

8   "中美外交官推特骂战再起，中国外交愈趋"战狼化"？ [Chinese and American Diplomats Resume Twitter War of Words, China's Diplomacy Is Taking On a More 'Wolf Warrior' Quality?]," BBC News Chinese, July 17, 2019. https://www.bbc.com/zhongwen/simp/world-49012321

9   Ben Smith, "Meet the Chinese Diplomat Who Got Promoted for Trolling the US on Twitter," Buzzfeed News, December 3, 2019. https://www.buzzfeednews.com/article/bensmith/zhao-lijian-china-twitter

10 Ben Westcott and Steven Jiang, "Chinese Diplomat Promotes Conspiracy Theory That US Military Brought Coronavirus to Wuhan," CNN, March 14, 2020, https://edition.cnn.com/2020/03/13/asia/china-coronavirus-us-lijian-zhao-intl-hnk/index.html; James T. Areddy, "Coronavirus Conspiracy Theory Claims It Began in the U.S.—and Beijing Is Buying It," *Wall Street*

Journal, March 26, 2020, https://www.wsj.com/articles/canadian-writer-fuels-china-u-s-tiff-over-coronaviruss-origins-11585232018; Zhao Lijian, "2/2 CDC was caught on the spot. When did patient zero begin in US? How many people are infected? What are the names of the hospitals? It might be US army who brought the epidemic to Wuhan. Be transparent! Make public your data! US owe us an explanation!," Twitter, March 12, 2020, https://twitter.com/zlj517/status/1238111898828066823; Zhao Lijian, "This article is very much important to each and every one of us. Please read and retweet it. COVID-19: Further Evidence that the Virus Originated in the US. https://globalresearch.ca/covid-19-further-evidence-virus-originated-us/5706078," Twitter, March 13, 2020, https://twitter.com/zlj517/status/1238269193427906560

11 David Winning, "Chinese 'Wolf Warrior' Diplomat Enrages Australia with Twitter Post," *Wall Street Journal*, November 30, 2020, https://www.wsj.com/articles/chinese-wolf-warrior-diplomat-enrages-australia-with-twitter-post-11606731906; Jason Scott, Colum Murphy, and James Magyer, "Australia Demands China Apology for 'Repugnant' Afghan Tweet," Bloomberg News, November 30, 2020, https://www.bloomberg.com/news/articles/2020-11-30/australia-demands-china-apologize-after-repugnant-afghan-tweet?sref=dwch56hJ

12 Lu Shaye, "China's Ambassador: Why the Double Standard on Justice for Canadians, Chinese?," *Hill Times*, January 9, 2019, https://www.hilltimes.com/2019/01/09/double-standard-justice-canadians-chinese/182367; "How Sweden Copes with Chinese Bullying," *Economist*, February 20, 2020, https://www.economist.com/europe/2020/02/20/how-sweden-copes-with-chinese-bullying

13 Neil Thomas, "China Overtakes America in Presidential Diplomacy," *Interpreter*, June 9, 2021, https://www.lowyinstitute.org/the-interpreter/china-overtakes-america-presidential-diplomacy; Neil Thomas, "Far More World Leaders Visit China Than America," *Interpreter*, July 28, 2021, https://www.lowyinstitute.org/the-interpreter/far-more-world-leaders-visit-china-america

14 Chun Han Wong and Keith Zhai, "Xi Jinping Warns China Won't Be Bullied as Communist Party Marks 100 Years," *Wall Street Journal*, July 1, 2021. https://www.wsj.com/articles/xi-jinping-warns-china-wont-be-bullied-as-communist-party-marks-100-years-11625122870

15 Bilahari Kausikan, "Dealing with an Ambiguous World Lecture III: ASEAN & US-China Competition in Southeast Asia," Lee Kuan Yew School of Public Policy Institute of Policy Studies, March 30, 2016. https://lkyspp.nus.edu.sg/docs/default-source/ips/mr-bilahari-kausikan-s-speech7d7b0a7b46bc6210a3aaff0100138661.pdf?sfvrsn=cec7680a_0

16 Zhong Sanping, "平视世界，习近平说中国的'势'与'事' [Looking the World in Its Eyes, Xi Jinping Talks About China's 'Momentum' and 'Deeds']," China News Service, March 10, 2021. http://www.chinanews.com.cn/gn/2021/03-10/9429030.shtml

17 Guan Zongshan, "外交部成立初期往事回顾 [A Review of the Early Years of the Ministry of Foreign Affairs]," 《纵横》 *Across Time and Space*, No. 2 of 2018 (February 2018).

18 Xu Jingli, 《另起炉灶: 崛起巨人的外交方略》 [*Starting from Scratch: The Diplomatic Strategy of Rising Giants*] (Beijing: World Knowledge Press, 1997), pp. 187–201; Guan, "A Review of the Early Years of the Ministry of Foreign Affairs."

19 Ling Qing, 《从延安到联合国：凌青外交生涯》 [*From Yan'an to the United Nations: Ling Qing's Life in Diplomacy*] (Fuzhou: Fujian People's Publishing House, 2008), pp. 64–65.

20 Zhou Enlai, "新中国的外交 [The Diplomacy of New China]," in The Ministry of Foreign Affairs of the People's Republic of China and the Chinese Communist Party Central Literature Research Office (eds.), 《周恩来外交文选》 [*Selected Works of Zhou Enlai on Diplomacy*] (Beijing:

Central Party Literature Press, 1990), pp. 1–7; "November 8th 11月8日," Foreign Ministry of the People's Republic of China. https://www.fmprc.gov.cn/web/ziliao_674904/historytoday _674971/200311/t20031108_9284670.shtml

21 Zhou, "The Diplomacy of New China."

22 Liu Xiaohong, *Chinese Ambassadors: The Rise of Diplomatic Professionalism Since 1949* (Seattle and London: University of Washington Press, 2001), pp. 14–18.

23 Zhou Yihuang, "将军大使们 [Ambassador Generals]," 《人民之声》 [*People's Voice*], No. 1 of 2004 (January 2004): 47–48.

24 Peter Martin, *China's Civilian Army: The Making of Wolf Warrior Diplomacy* (New York: Oxford University Press, 2021), pp. 49–51.

25 Liu, *Chinese Ambassadors*, pp. 21–23.

26 "2758 (XXVI). Restoration of the lawful rights of the People's Republic of China in the United Nations," United Nations Documents. https://undocs.org/en/A/RES/2758(XXVI)

27 "第三次建交高潮 [The Third Wave in Establishing Diplomatic Relations with Other Countries]," Ministry of Foreign Affairs of the People's Republic of China. https://www.fmprc.gov.cn/ web/ziliao_674904/wjs_674919/2159_674923/200011/t20001107_10251006.shtml

28 Samuel S. Kim, "China's International Organizational Behaviour," in Thomas W. Robinson and David Shambaugh (eds.), *Chinese Foreign Policy: Theory and Practice* (Oxford: Clarendon Press, 1994), pp. 405–407.

29 Tyler Marshall, "West Europe Follows U.S. Lead, Suspends Normal China Ties," *Los Angeles Times*, June 28, 1989. https://www.latimes.com/archives/la-xpm-1989-06-28-mn-4182-story .html

30 Martin, *China's Civilian Army*, pp. 148–149.

31 Deng Xiaoping, "改革开放政策稳定，中国大有希望 [With Stable Policies of Reform and Opening Up, China Can Have Great Hopes]," in 《邓小平文选》第三卷 *Selected Works of Deng Xiaoping*, Vol. 3 (Beijing: People's Publishing House, 1993), pp. 315–321.

32 Chinese Communist Party Central Party History Research Office, 《中国共产党的九十年》 [*Ninety Years of the Chinese Communist Party*] (Beijing: Chinese Communist Party History Publishing House and Party Building Books Publishing House, 2016), pp. 777–780.

33 Barack Obama, *A Promised Land* (New York: Crown, 2020), p. 338.

34 Author's interviews with diplomats and Chinese foreign-policy scholars in Beijing.

35 Mark Lynas, "How do I know China wrecked the Copenhagen deal? I was in the room," *Guardian*, December 22, 2009, https://www.theguardian.com/environment/2009/dec/22/copenhagen -climate-change-mark-lynas; Obama, *A Promised Land*, pp. 510–515; Shai Oster, "After Copenhagen: Hot Air in China," *WSJ China Real Time* blog, December 25, 2009, https://www.wsj.com /articles/BL-CJB-6487

36 PanChinese, "习近平著名的 '吃饱了没事干' 视频 [Xi Jinping's Famous 'Nothing Better to Do After Eating Their Fill' Video]," YouTube video, dated March 25, 2013, accessed July 4, 2021. https://youtu.be/aG903lJtC7M

37 Hillary Rodham Clinton, *Hard Choices* (New York: Simon & Schuster, 2014), pp. 70–71; Jeffrey A. Bader, *Obama and China's Rise: An Insider's Account of America's Asia Strategy* (Washington, DC: Brookings Institution Press, 2012), pp. 104–106.

38 John Pomfret, "U.S. Takes Tougher Stance with China; Strategy Acknowledges Beijing's Rise in Power But Lays Down Markers," *Washington Post*, July 30, 2010.

39 Chang Hong, Kang Denghui, and Chen Bingjie, "综述：习近平的"新型大国关系"外交战略是这样炼成的 [Summary: This Is How Xi Jinping's Diplomatic Strategy of 'New Model of Major-Power Relations' Is Made]," 人民网 People.cn, February 13, 2016. http://world.people.com.cn/n1/2016/0213/c1002-28120530.html

40 Gordon Lubold and Adam Entous, "U.S. Says Beijing Is Building Up South China Sea Islands," *Wall Street Journal*, May 9, 2015. https://www.wsj.com/articles/u-s-says-beijing-building-up-south-china-sea-islands-1431109387

41 Xi Jinping, "积极树立亚洲安全观 共创安全合作新局面——在亚洲相互协作与信任措施会议第四次峰会上的讲话 [Actively Establish the Asian Security Concept and Jointly Create a New Situation of Security Cooperation—Speech at the Fourth Summit of the Conference on Interaction and Confidence Building Measures in Asia]," Xinhua News Agency, May 21, 2014, http://www.xinhuanet.com//world/2014-05/21/c_126528981.htm; "China President Speaks Out on Security Ties in Asia," BBC News, May 21, 2014, https://www.bbc.com/news/world-asia-china-27498266

42 "习近平出席中央外事工作会议并发表重要讲话 [Xi Jinping Attends the Central Foreign Affairs Work Conference and Delivers an Important Speech]," Xinhua News Agency, November 29, 2014. http://www.xinhuanet.com//politics/2014-11/29/c_1113457723.htm

43 Chun Han Wong and Keith Zhai, "China's Xi Jinping Set to Give 'Wolf Warrior' Diplomacy More Bite," *Wall Street Journal*, October 26, 2022. https://www.wsj.com/articles/chinas-xi-jinping-set-to-give-wolf-warrior-diplomacy-more-bite-11666784679

44 Author's calculations using data from China's Ministry of Finance; "2019 Lowy Institute Global Diplomacy Index," Lowy Institute, accessed March 21, 2022, https://globaldiplomacyindex.lowyinstitute.org/

45 Neil Thomas, "China Overtakes America in Presidential Diplomacy."

46 Neil Thomas, "Far More World Leaders Visit China Than America."

47 Author's interview with Ben Rhodes in January 2022.

48 "视频 (双语版):《大使视界》：卢沙野大使纵论新冠疫情 [Video (Bilingual Version): 'Ambassador's Vision': Ambassador Lu Shaye on the Covid-19 Pandemic]," Mandarin TV, March 14, 2020, https://www.mandarintv.fr/video_detail.php/documentairesetreportages/5789; "*Entretien de l'Ambassadeur Lu Shaye sur l'émission 'Parole d'Ambassadeur' de Mandarin TV*," Embassy of the People's Republic of China in the French Republic, dated March 15, 2020, http://www.amb-chine.fr/fra/zfzj/202003/t20200315_2575006.htm

49 "把颠倒的事实再颠倒过来——一名中国驻法国使馆外交官对新冠肺炎疫情的观察（之四）[Turn Inverted Facts Right-Side Up—Observations of a Chinese Diplomat in the French Embassy on the Coronavirus Pandemic (Part 4)]," Embassy of the People's Republic of China in the French Republic, dated April 12, 2020, Internet Archive. https://web.archive.org/web/20200415230604/http://www.amb-chine.fr/chn/ttxw/t1768710.htm

50 "Interview given by M. Jean-Yves Le Drian, Minister for Europe and Foreign Affairs, to the newspaper Le Monde (20 Apr. 20)," Ministry for Europe and Foreign Affairs of the French Republic, dated April 20, 2020, Internet Archive, accessed February 9, 2023. https://web.archive.org/web/20200425182336/https://www.diplomatie.gouv.fr/en/our-ministers/jean-yves-le-drian/press/article/interview-given-by-m-jean-yves-le-drian-minister-for-europe-and-foreign-affairs

51 "*Interview accordée par l'Ambassadeur Lu Shaye à L'Opinion*," Embassy of the People's Republic of China in the French Republic, April 29, 2020. http://www.amb-chine.fr/fra/zfzj/202004/t20200429_10010820.htm

52 Ashley Rodriguez, "China's Box Office Is Setting New Records—With A Bit Of Hollywood Help," *Quartz*, November 22, 2017. https://qz.com/1134905/wolf-warrior-2-helped-chinas-box -office-to-new-records-in-2017/

53 *"Interview accordée par l'Ambassadeur Lu Shaye à l'Opinion,"* Embassy of the People's Republic of China in the French Republic, June 18, 2021, http://www.amb-chine.fr/fra/zfzj/202106/ t20210618_9007058.htm

54 Peter Ford, "The New Face of Chinese Diplomacy: Who Is Wang Yi?," *Christian Science Monitor*, March 18, 2013. https://www.csmonitor.com/World/Asia-Pacific/2013/0318/The-new-face-of -Chinese-diplomacy-Who-is-Wang-Yi

55 Jade Macmillan, "Julie Bishop Recalls Meeting with Her Chinese Counterpart After Diplomatic Dispute," Australian Broadcasting Corporation, August 13, 2019. https://www.abc.net.au/news /2019-08-14/julie-bishop-recalls-meeting-with-her-chinese-counterpart/11411462

56 David Wroe, "China's Rebuke of Julie Bishop 'Rudest' Conduct Seen in 30 Years, Says Senior Foreign Affairs Official," *Sydney Morning Herald*, February 27, 2014. https://www.smh.com .au/politics/federal/chinas-rebuke-of-julie-bishop-rudest-conduct-seen-in-30-years-says-senior -foreign-affairs-official-20140227-33jid.html

57 CBC News, "China's Foreign Minister Criticizes Canadian Reporter for Her Question," YouTube video, June 2, 2016, https://www.youtube.com/watch?v=qikBsQ1h4S8; Mike Blanchfield, "Chinese Foreign Minister Berates Canadian Reporter for Asking About Human Rights," *Canadian Press*, June 1, 2016, https://www.cbc.ca/news/politics/chinese-foreign-minister-berates -reporter-1.3611510

58 Author's conversations with Beijing-based foreign diplomats and officials.

59 Ben Doherty and Helen Davidson, "Chinese Envoy Walks Out of Meeting After Row with Nauru President Amid 'Bullying' Claims," *Guardian*, September 5, 2018, https://www.theguardian.com /world/2018/sep/05/chinese-envoy-walks-out-of-meeting-after-row-with-nauru-president-amid -bullying-claims; Charlotte Greenfield and Tom Westbrook, "Nauru Blasts 'Insolent' China for Speaking Out of Turn at Meeting," Reuters News, September 5, 2018, https://www.reuters.com/ article/us-pacific-forum-china-idUSKCN1LL0AC

60 Natalie Whiting and Stephen Dziedzic, "APEC 2018: Chinese Officials Barge into PNG Foreign Minister's Office After Being Denied Meeting," Australian Broadcasting Corporation, November 18, 2018, https://www.abc.net.au/news/2018-11-18/chinese-officials-create-diplomatic-storm -at-apec/10508812; "Police Called on Diplomats as APEC Summit Tensions Boil Over," Agence France Presse, November 18, 2018. https://www.yahoo.com/news/police-called-diplomats-apec -summit-tensions-boil-over-050420060.html

61 Jason Scott, Dandan Li, and Toluse Olorunnipa, "APEC Ends in Disarray After U.S.-China Dispute over Final Statement," Bloomberg News, November 18, 2018. https://www.bloomberg .com/news/articles/2018-11-18/apec-fails-to-agree-on-joint-statement-amid-u-s-china-tensions ?sref=dwch56hJ

62 Author's interview with Wu Xinbo in January 2021.

63 Author's interviews with foreign diplomats who heard the remark.

64 Author's interviews with foreign diplomats who attended the negotiations.

65 Author's interview with a European diplomat in January 2021.

66 Author's interview with a European diplomat in October 2021.

67 Wong and Deng, "China's 'Wolf Warrior' Diplomats Are Ready to Fight."

68   "Vice Foreign Minister Qin Gang Requires the Italian Side to Suspend the Decision to Cancel Direct Flights Between Italy and China, The Italian Side Agrees to Resume Some Commercial Flights," Ministry of Foreign Affairs of the People's Republic of China, February 7, 2020. https:// www.fmprc.gov.cn/mfa_eng/wjb_663304/zzjg_663340/xos_664404/gjlb_664408/3311_664600 /3313_664604/202002/t20200208_577353.html

69   Chun Han Wong, "Fighting Outbreak, China Urged Open Borders. Even Allies Are Resisting," *Wall Street Journal*, March 16, 2020. https://www.wsj.com/articles/fighting-outbreak-china -urged-open-borders-even-allies-are-resisting-11581681602

70   Andrew Browne, "China Forces Dozens of Mexican Travelers into Quarantine," *Wall Street Journal*, May 4, 2009. https://www.wsj.com/articles/SB124137876507580987

71   Jorge Guajardo, "In 2009 H1N1, against WHO recommendation, China: - Placed all Mexican nationals in China under quarantine. - Cancelled direct flights to Mexico. - Stopped issuing visas to Mexicans. - Closed consulates in Mexico. China never admitted this was wrong, or apologized," Twitter, February 1, 2020. https://twitter.com/jorge_guajardo/status /1223618829839978497

72   "中华人民共和国外交部、国家移民管理局关于暂时停止持有效中国签证、居留许可的 外国人入境的公告 [Ministry of Foreign Affairs of the People's Republic of China, National Immigration Administration Announcement on the Temporary Suspension of Entry by Foreign Nationals Holding Valid Chinese Visas or Residence Permits]," Ministry of Foreign Affairs of the People's Republic of China, March 26, 2020. https://www.mfa.gov.cn/wjbxw_new/202201/ t20220113_10491272.shtml

73   "*Declaración del Portavoz de la Embajada de China en Venezuela*," Embassy of the People's Republic of China in Venezuela, March 19, 2020. https://www.mfa.gov.cn/ce/ceve//esp/sgxx/ t1757897.htm

74   Chinese Embassy in Sri Lanka, "You are right that the 'low class' Chinese government are serving 1.4billion Chinese people, even the grass root or the 'lowest class' included. Total death in #China #pandemic is 3344 till today, much smaller than your western 'high class' governments. Who are cursed?," Twitter, April 9, 2020. https://twitter.com/chinaembsl/status /1248168334899712002

75   Lu Shaye, "中国和平发展的 "溢出效应" —— 以非洲为例 [The 'Spillover Effect' of China's Peaceful Development: Taking Africa as An Example]," 《中国党政干部论坛》 *China Cadres Tribune*, No. 7 of 2013 (July 2013): 90–93.

76   Lu Shaye, "中国特色大国外交:要素、原则和思路 [Major Power Diplomacy with Chinese Characteristics: Elements, Principles and Ideas]," 《公共外交季刊》 *Public Diplomacy Quarterly*, No. 1 of 2016 (Spring 2016): 7–15.

77   "Transcript of Ambassador H.E. Lu Shaye's Interview with the Canadian Press," Embassy of the People's Republic of China in Canada, July 3, 2017. http://ca.china-embassy.org/eng/dsxx/dsjh /201707/t20170704_4898824.htm

78   Lu, "China's Ambassador: Why the Double Standard on Justice for Canadians, Chinese?," *Hill Times*; "Ambassador Lu Shaye Published a Signed Article," Embassy of the People's Republic of China in Canada, January 10, 2019, http://ca.china-embassy.org/eng/sgxw/201901/t20190110 _4614200.htm

79   Author's calculations based on notices published on the website of the Chinese embassy in France.

80 "*Déclaration du porte-parole de l'Ambassade de Chine en France au sujet des mensonges récemment apparus sur le Xinjiang*," Embassy of the People's Republic of China in the French Republic, July 23, 2020. http://www.amb-chine.fr/fra/zfzj/202007/t20200723 _2575085.htm

81 "Wolf Warriors and a 'Crazed Hyena': French Researcher 'Not Intimidated' After Clash with China Envoy," *France 24*, March 23, 2021. https://www.france24.com/en/europe /20210323-wolf-warriors-and-a-crazed-hyena-french-researcher-not-intimidated-after-clash -with-china-envoy

82 Lu Shaye and Zheng Ruolin, "郑若麟对话驻法大使卢沙野："我们现在外交风格变了，你们要适应我们的新风格' [Zheng Ruolin Talks to Ambassador to France Lu Shaye: 'Our Diplomatic Style Has Changed Now, You Have to Adapt to Our New Style']," 观察者网 [Guanchazhe Net], June 16, 2021. https://www.guancha.cn/lushaye/2021_06_16_594555.shtml

83 Laura Silver, Kat Devlin, and Christine Huang, "Unfavorable Views of China Reach Historic Highs in Many Countries," Pew Research Center, October 6, 2020, https://www.pewresearch.org /global/2020/10/06/unfavorable-views-of-china-reach-historic-highs-in-many-countries/; Laura Silver, Kat Devlin, and Christine Huang, "Large Majorities Say China Does Not Respect the Personal Freedoms of Its People," Pew Research Center, June 30, 2021, https://www.pewresearch .org/global/2021/06/30/large-majorities-say-china-does-not-respect-the-personal-freedoms-of-its -people/

84 Laura Silver, Christine Huang, and Laura Clancy, "How Global Public Opinion of China Has Shifted in the Xi Era," Pew Research Center, September 28, 2022. https://www.pewresearch.org/ global/2022/09/28/how-global-public-opinion-of-china-has-shifted-in-the-xi-era/

85 Sha Hua, "Global Coalition of Legislators Faces Challenges Countering China," *Wall Street Journal*, June 12, 2020. https://www.wsj.com/articles/global-coalition-of-legislators-faces-challenges -countering-china-11591980969

86 Reuters Staff, "Exclusive: Internal Chinese Report Warns Beijing Faces Tiananmen-Like Global Backlash Over Virus," Reuters News, May 4, 2020. https://www.reuters.com/article/%20u s-health-coronavirus-china-sentiment-ex-idUSKBN22G19C

87 Fu Ying, "在讲好中国故事中提升话语权 [Raising Discourse Power by Telling China's Stories Well]," *People's Daily*, April 2, 2020, p. 9. http://opinion.people.com.cn/n1/2020/0402/c1003 -31658143.html

88 Yuan Nansheng and Ma Guochuan, "袁南生：疫情改变世界秩序，防止发生战略误判以避免最坏的局面发生 [Yuan Nansheng: The Epidemic Has Changed the World Order, Prevent Strategic Misjudgment to Avert the Worst Situation]," 钝角网 [Dunjiao Net], April 26, 2020. http://www.dunjiaodu.com/top/2020-04-26/5898.html

89 Keith Zhai and Chun Han Wong, "China's Effort to Tame 'Wolf Warrior' Diplomats Is Stymied by Nationalism," *Wall Street Journal*, June 29, 2021. https://www.wsj.com/articles/china-wants -howling-diplomats-to-quiet-down-but-nationalism-gets-in-the-way-11624962559

90 Zhai and Wong, "China's Effort to Tame 'Wolf Warrior' Diplomats."

91 "驻英大使刘晓明：之所以有'战狼'是因为这个世界有'狼' [Ambassador to Britain Liu Xiaoming: The Reason Why There Are 'Wolf Warriors' Is Because There Are 'Wolves' in This World]," China Central Television, May 25, 2020. http://m.news.cctv.com/2020/05/24/ ARTI8BYmADeqivsgNvMiMRF4200524.shtml

92 Selina Cheng, "British Police Investigate Attack on Pro-Democracy Protester at Chinese Consul-

ate," *Wall Street Journal*, October 17, 2022, https://www.wsj.com/articles/british-police
-investigate-attack-on-pro-democracy-protester-at-chinese-consulate-11666011193; James T.
Areddy, "Chinese Diplomats Leave U.K. Ahead of Questioning Over Clash with Protesters,"
Wall Street Journal, December 14, 2022, https://www.wsj.com/articles/chinese-diplomats-leave
-u-k-ahead-of-questioning-over-clash-with-protesters-11671037009

93 "习近平在中共中央政治局第三十次集体学习时强调 加强和改进国际传播工作 展示真
实立体全面的中国 [During the 30th Collective Study Session of the Chinese Communist
Party Central Committee's Politburo, Xi Jinping Emphasizes Strengthening and Improving
International Communication Work and Showcasing a True, Three-Dimensional and Comprehensive China]," Xinhua News Agency, June 1, 2021. http://www.xinhuanet.com/2021-06/01/c
_1127517461.htm

94 "During the 30th Collective Study Session of the Chinese Communist Party Central Committee's Politburo"; Ministry of Foreign Affairs Party Committee, "以习近平外交思想为引领开创
新时代外交工作新局面 [Using Xi Jinping Thought on Diplomacy as the Guide for Creating a
New Situation for Diplomatic Work in a New Era]," Ministry of Foreign Affairs of the People's
Republic of China, December 7, 2021. https://www.mfa.gov.cn/web/wjb_673085/zygy_673101
/qy/xgxw_673105/202112/t20211207_10463376.shtml

95 Zhai and Wong, "China's Effort to Tame 'Wolf Warrior' Diplomats."

96 Keith Zhai and Chun Han Wong, "China Likely to Name U.S. Specialist as Next Ambassador
to Washington," *Wall Street Journal*, January 11, 2023, https://www.wsj.com/articles/china-likely
-to-name-u-s-specialist-as-next-ambassador-to-washington-11673441348

97 Chun Han Wong and Keith Zhai, "China's Xi Jinping Set to Give 'Wolf Warrior' Diplomacy
More Bite," *Wall Street Journal*, October 26, 2022, https://www.wsj.com/articles/chinas-xi
-jinping-set-to-give-wolf-warrior-diplomacy-more-bite-11666784679

98 Jimmy Quinn, "New Chinese Ambassador Snaps at U.S.: 'Please Shut Up,'" *National Review*,
September 10, 2021, https://www.nationalreview.com/corner/new-chinese-ambassador-snaps-at
-u-s-please-shut-up/

99 Phelim Kine, "Biden Froze Out China's Ambassador. He May Regret That," *Politico*, November 2, 2022, https://www.politico.com/news/2022/11/02/biden-froze-out-chinas-ambassador-he
-may-regret-that-00064688

100 Chun Han Wong, "China Promotes U.S. Ambassador to Foreign Minister," *Wall Street
Journal*, December 30, 2022, https://www.wsj.com/articles/china-promotes-u-s-ambassador
-to-foreign-minister-11672409545

101 "习近平在省部级主要领导干部学习贯彻党的十九届五中全会精神专题研讨班开班式上发
表重要讲话 [Xi Jinping Delivers an Important Speech at the Opening Ceremony of the Seminar
on the Study and Implementation of the Spirit of the Fifth Plenary Session of the Chinese Communist Party's 19th Central Committee for Provincial and Ministerial-Level Leading Cadres],"
Xinhua News Agency, January 11, 2021, http://www.xinhuanet.com/politics/leaders /2021-01
/11/c1126970918.htm

102 Wu Liming, "新华国际时评：论美国'灯塔'的倒掉 [Xinhua International Commentary:
On the Fall of the American 'Beacon']," Xinhua News Agency, January 12, 2021. http://www
.xinhuanet.com/world/2021-01/12/c_1126973955.htm

103 Chang'an Jun, "新发展阶段新在哪里？陈一新从八个方面进行阐释 [Where Is the New Stage
of Development? Chen Yixin Explains Through Eight Aspects]," 中央政法委长安剑 [Central

Political and Legal Affairs Commission Sword of Eternal Peace] WeChat account, January 15, 2021. https://mp.weixin.qq.com/s/1aJCjiKE7LBZXUtySBMghw

104 He Bin, "在县级领导干部学习贯彻党的十九届五中全会专题研讨班上的发言 [Speech at the Special Seminar for County-Level Leading Cadres to Study and Implement the Fifth Plenary Session of the 19th Central Committee of the Chinese Communist Party]," 祁连新闻网 [Qilian News Net], February 25, 2021, Internet Archive. https://web.archive.org/web/20210226222555/http%3A%2F%2Fwww.qiliannews.com%2Fsystem%2F2021%2F02%2F25%2F013341147.shtml

105 Graham Allison, *Destined for War: Can America and China Escape Thucydides's Trap?* (Boston and New York: Houghton Mifflin Harcourt, 2017); Kevin Rudd, *The Avoidable War: The Dangers of a Catastrophic Conflict Between the US and Xi Jinping's China* (New York: Public Affairs, 2022).

106 Orville Schell, "The Death of Engagement," The Wire China, June 7, 2020. https://www.thewirechina.com/2020/06/07/the-birth-life-and-death-of-engagement/

107 Orville Schell and Larry Diamond, "China Gets Its Message to Americans but Doesn't Want to Reciprocate," *Wall Street Journal*, December 21, 2018. https://www.wsj.com/articles/china-gets-its-message-to-americans-but-doesnt-want-to-reciprocate-11545407490

108 Julian Gewirtz, *Unlikely Partners: Chinese Reformers, Western Economists, and the Making of Global China* (Cambridge, Massachusetts: Harvard University Press, 2017).

109 Xi Jinping, "跨世纪领导干部的历史重任及必备素质 [The Historical Responsibilities and Necessary Qualities of Cross-Century Leading Cadres]," 《中共福建省委党校学报》 《理论学习月刊》 [*Journal of the Fujian Provincial Committee Party School of the Chinese Communist Party, Theoretical Studies Monthly*], No. 11 of 1991 (November 1991): 32–36.

110 Niall Ferguson and Moritz Schularick, "'Chimerica' and the Global Asset Market Boom," *International Finance* 10, No. 3 (Winter 2007): 215–239.

111 Henry M. Paulson, *Dealing With China: An Insider Unmasks the New Economic Superpower* (New York: Twelve, 2015).

112 Jane Perlez, "Pressing Asia Agenda, Obama Treads Lightly on Human Rights," *New York Times*, September 7, 2016, https://www.nytimes.com/2016/09/08/world/asia/obama-asia-human-rights.html; Ben Rhodes, *After the Fall: Being American in the World We've Made* (New York: Random House, 2021).

113 Author's interview with Ben Rhodes in January 2022.

114 Hillary Clinton, "America's Pacific Century," *Foreign Policy*, October 11, 2011. https://foreignpolicy.com/2011/10/11/americas-pacific-century/

115 Author's interview with Daniel Russel in October 2021; Richard McGregor, *Xi Jinping: The Backlash, A Lowy Institute Paper* (Penguin Random House Australia, 2019).

116 Jeremy Page, "How the U.S. Misread China's Xi: Hoping for a Globalist, It Got an Autocrat," *Wall Street Journal*, December 23, 2020. https://www.wsj.com/articles/xi-jinping-globalist-autocrat-misread-11608735769

117 "Remarks by Vice President Biden and Chinese Vice President Xi at the State Department Luncheon," Archived Obama White House website, February 14, 2012. https://obamawhitehouse.archives.gov/photos-and-video/video/2012/02/14/state-department-lunch-honoring-vice-president-xi-jinping-china#transcript

118 Author's interview with Daniel Russel in October 2021.

119 Owen Fletcher, "In Iowa, a Reunion with Old Friends," *Wall Street Journal*, February 16, 2012. https://www.wsj.com/articles/SB10001424052970204792404577225153739170874

120 John Tkacik, "China's Crown Princeling," *Wall Street Journal*, October 26, 2007, https://www
.wsj.com/articles/SB119334860709572038; "Zhejiang Party Secretary Touts Economic Successes
and Work Towards Rule of Law at Ambassador's Dinner," Wikileaks Cable: 07BEIJING1840
_a, dated March 19, 2007, accessed August 24, 2021. https://wikileaks.org/plusd/cables/07BEI
JING1840_a.html

121 Jeremy Page, Nathan Hodge, and Brian Spegele, "China Visit Starts with a Dinner, Protests on
Tibet," *Wall Street Journal*, February 14, 2012. https://www.wsj.com/articles/SB1000142405297
02040627045772206609238188388

122 Rudd, *The Avoidable War.*

123 Author's interview with Daniel Russel in October 2021.

124 Damian Paletta, "U.S., China in Pact over Cyberattacks That Steal Company Records," *Wall
Street Journal*, September 25, 2015, https://www.wsj.com/articles/u-s-china-agree-over-cyber
attacks-that-steal-company-records-1443205327; Jeremy Page, Carol E. Lee, and Gordon
Lubold, "China's President Pledges No Militarization in Disputed Islands," *Wall Street Journal*,
September 25, 2015, https://www.wsj.com/articles/china-completes-runway-on-artificial-island
-in-south-china-sea-1443184818; Chun Han Wong and Gordon Lubold, "U.S.-Beijing Spat
Escalates Over South China Sea," *Wall Street Journal*, February 17, 2016, https://www.wsj.com
/articles/south-china-sea-missile-deployment-entrenches-u-s-chinese-positions-1455729019;
Dustin Volz, "China Violated Obama-Era Cybertheft Pact, U.S. Official Says," *Wall Street
Journal*, November 8, 2018, https://www.wsj.com/articles/china-violated-obama-era-cybertheft
-pact-u-s-official-says-1541716952

125 Jiayang Fan, "China Tries to Make Sense of Donald Trump," *New Yorker*, November 12, 2016,
https://www.newyorker.com/news/daily-comment/china-tries-to-make-sense-of-donald-trump;
Bob Davis and Lingling Wei, *Superpower Showdown: How the Battle Between Trump and Xi
Threatens a New Cold War* (New York: HarperCollins, 2020), pp. 162–163.

126 Louise Radnofsky and Jeremy Page, "U.S., China Make Limited Headway During Summit,"
Wall Street Journal, April 7, 2017, https://www.wsj.com/articles/u-s-china-make-limited
-headway-during-summit-1491611582; Jeremy Page, Michael C. Bender, and Chun Han
Wong, "In China, Trump Employs Tough Talk, Flattery with Xi," *Wall Street Journal*, November 9, 2017, https://www.wsj.com/articles/in-china-trump-walks-fine-line-on-trade-north
-korea-1510218443; Davis and Wei, *Superpower Showdown.*

127 Grep Ip and Yoko Kubota, "Can This Marriage Be Saved? Chinese-U.S. Integration Frays," *Wall
Street Journal*, May 9, 2019, https://www.wsj.com/articles/can-this-marriage-be-saved-chinese
-u-s-integration-frays-11557414600; Stephen A. Myrow, "China Finds It Can Live Without the
U.S.," *Wall Street Journal*, September 3, 2019, https://www.wsj.com/articles/china-finds-it-can
-live-without-the-u-s-11567551458

128 "Xi Jinping Delivers Important Speech at Federal Parliament of Australia Entitled 'Pursuing Chinese and Australian Development Dreams Hand in Hand and Achieving Regional Prosperity and
Stability Shoulder to Shoulder,'" Ministry of Foreign Affairs of the People's Republic of China, November 17, 2014, https://www.fmprc.gov.cn/mfa_eng/wjb_663304/zzjg_663340/bmdyzs_664814
/gjlb_664818/3377_664820/3379_664824/201411/t20141119_586151.html; Jenny Gross,
"China's Xi Meets Royals, Officials on First U.K. State Visit," *Wall Street Journal*, October 20,
2015, https://www.wsj.com/articles/chinas-xi-jinping-to-meet-royals-politicians-on-first-u-k-state
-visit-1445335945; "Xi Jinping Holds Talks with President Emmanuel Macron of France," Minis-

try of Foreign Affairs of the People's Republic of China, March 26, 2019, https://www.fmprc.gov
.cn/mfa_eng/topics_665678/2019zt/xjpdydlmngfggsfw/201903/t20190327_710505.html

129 Larry Diamond and Orville Schell, "China's Influence & American Interests: Promoting Constructive Vigilance," Hoover Institution, November 29, 2018. https://www.hoover.org/research/
chinas-influence-american-interests-promoting-constructive-vigilance

130 Schell and Diamond, "China Gets Its Message to Americans."

131 Drew Hinshaw, Joe Parkinson, and Aruna Viswanatha, "Inside the Secret Prisoner Swap That
Splintered the U.S. and China," *Wall Street Journal*, October 27, 2022. https://www.wsj.com/
articles/huawei-china-meng-kovrig-spavor-prisoner-swap-11666877779

132 Lingling Wei, "China Stresses Reliance on Its Own Technologies in Five-Year Plan," *Wall Street
Journal*, October 29, 2020. https://www.wsj.com/articles/china-leadership-says-economy-will
-reachmid-level-within-15-years-11603969958

133 Zhang Xiaosong, "习近平：装备制造业练好"内功"才能永立不败之地 [Xi Jinping: Only
by Practicing 'Internal Skills' in the Equipment-Manufacturing Industry Can We Remain
Invincible Forever]," 新华网 Xinhua Net, September 26, 2018, http://www.xinhuanet.com/
politics/2018-09/26/c_1123486536.htm; Neil Thomas, "Mao Redux: The Enduring Relevance
of Self-Reliance in China," Macro Polo, April 25, 2019, https://macropolo.org/analysis/china-self
-reliance-xi-jin-ping-mao/

134 Lingling Wei, "China's Xi Speeds Up Inward Economic Shift," *Wall Street Journal*, August 12,
2020. https://www.wsj.com/articles/chinas-xi-speeds-up-inward-economic-shift-11597224602

135 Chang Che, "How a Book About America's History Foretold China's Future," *New Yorker*,
March 21, 2022. https://www.newyorker.com/books/second-read/how-a-book-about-americas
-history-foretold-chinas-future

136 Wang Huning, 《美国反对美国》 [*America Against America*] (Shanghai Literature and Art
Publishing House, 1991).

137 Wang, *America Against America*, pp. 384–390.

138 Josh Chin, "The Internet, Divided Between the U.S. and China, Has Become a Battleground,"
Wall Street Journal, February 9, 2019. https://www.wsj.com/articles/the-internet-divided-between
-the-u-s-and-china-has-become-a-battleground-11549688420

139 Valentina Pop, Sha Hua, and Daniel Michaels, "From Lightbulbs to 5G, China Battles West
for Control of Vital Technology Standards," *Wall Street Journal*, February 8, 2021. https://
www.wsj.com/articles/from-lightbulbs-to-5g-china-battles-west-for-control-of-vital-technology
-standards-11612722698

140 Yaroslav Trofimov, Drew Hinshaw, and Kate O'Keeffe, "How China Is Taking Over International Organizations, One Vote at a Time," *Wall Street Journal*, September 29, 2020. https://
www.wsj.com/articles/how-china-is-taking-over-international-organizations-one-vote-at-a-time
-11601397208

141 James T. Areddy, "Chinese Media Denounce Pompeo Allegation That Coronavirus Can Be
Traced to Wuhan Lab," *Wall Street Journal*, May 4, 2020, https://www.wsj.com/articles/
chinese-media-denounce-pompeo-allegation-that-coronavirus-can-be-traced-to-wuhan-lab
-11588617734; Michael R. Gordon and Eva Xiao, "U.S. Says China Is Committing Genocide
Against Uighur Muslims," *Wall Street Journal*, January 19, 2021, https://www.wsj.com/articles
/u-s-declares-chinas-treatment-of-uighur-muslims-to-be-genocide-11611081555; Kate O'Keeffe
and William Mauldin, "Mike Pompeo Urges Chinese People to Change Communist Party," *Wall*

Street Journal, July 23, 2020, https://www.wsj.com/articles/secretary-of-state-pompeo-to-urge -chinese-people-to-change-the-communist-party-11595517729

142 William Mauldin, "U.S. Sanctions Chinese Officials Over Alleged Human Rights Abuses in Muslim Xinjiang Region," *Wall Street Journal*, July 9, 2020, https://www.wsj.com/articles /u-s-sanctions-chinese-officials-over-alleged-human-rights-abuses-in-muslim-xinjiang -region-11594313641; Andrew Restuccia and Lindsay Wise, "Trump Signs Hong Kong Sanctions Bill, Pivots to Criticizing Biden," *Wall Street Journal*, July 14, 2020, https://www.wsj.com /articles/trump-signs-hong-kong-sanctions-bill-11594762613; Ian Talley, "U.S. Adds Senior Chinese Lawmakers to Hong Kong Sanctions Blacklist," *Wall Street Journal*, December 7, 2020, https://www.wsj.com/articles/u-s-adds-senior-chinese-lawmakers-to-hong-kong-sanctions -blacklist-11607370603; Chun Han Wong, "Health Secretary Alex Azar Renews Swipes at China Over Coronavirus in Taiwan Visit," *Wall Street Journal*, August 11, 2020, https://www .wsj.com/articles/health-secretary-alex-azar-renews-swipes-at-china-over-coronavirus-in-taiwan -visit-11597149880

143 Gordon Lubold and Dawn Lim, "Trump Bars Americans from Investing in Firms That Help China's Military," *Wall Street Journal*, November 12, 2020. https://www.wsj.com/articles/trump -bars-americans-from-investing-in-firms-that-help-chinas-military-11605209431

144 "China Banishes U.S. Journalists from Wall Street Journal, New York Times and Washington Post," *Wall Street Journal*, March 18, 2020, https://www.wsj.com/articles/china-bans-all-u-s -nationals-working-for-the-wall-street-journal-new-york-times-washington-post-whose-press -credentials-end-in-2020-11584464690; Katrina Northrop, "The Great Expulsion," The Wire China, February 14, 2021, https://www.thewirechina.com/2021/02/14/the-great-expulsion/

145 Yew Lun Tian, "China Sanctions U.S. Lawmakers in Dispute over Uighur Muslims," Reuters News, July 13, 2020, https://www.reuters.com/article/us-china-usa-xinjiang-idUSKCN24E0NU; Jeremy Page and Drew Hinshaw, "China Says Covid-19 Origin Probe Should Shift Focus to Other Countries," *Wall Street Journal*, March 31, 2021, https://www.wsj.com/articles/china-says -covid-19-origin-probe-should-shift-focus-to-other-countries-11617186625

146 Chun Han Wong, Liza Lin, and William Mauldin, "China Orders U.S. to Close Chengdu Consulate as Payback for Houston Move," *Wall Street Journal*, July 24, 2020. https://www.wsj .com/articles/china-orders-u-s-to-close-chengdu-consulate-in-retaliation-to-houston-move -11595564849

147 Kurt M. Campbell and Rush Doshi, "How America Can Shore Up Asian Order," *Foreign Affairs*, January 12, 2021, https://www.foreignaffairs.com/articles/united-states/2021-01-12/how -america-can-shore-asian-order; Rush Doshi, *The Long Game: China's Grand Strategy to Displace American Order* (New York: Oxford University Press, 2021).

148 Natalie Andrews, "House Passes Chips Act to Boost U.S. Semiconductor Production," *Wall Street Journal*, July 28, 2022, https://www.wsj.com/articles/house-passes-chips-act-to-boost-u -s-semiconductor-production-11659035676; Jeanne Whalen, "A New Era of Industrial Policy Kicks Off with Signing of the Chips Act," *Washington Post*, August 9, 2022, https://www .washingtonpost.com/us-policy/2022/08/09/micron-40-billion-us-subsidies/; John D. McKinnon and Asa Fitch, "U.S. Restricts Semiconductor Exports in Bid to Slow China's Military Advance," *Wall Street Journal*, October 7, 2022, https://www.wsj.com/articles/u-s-restricts-sem iconductor-exports-in-bid-to-slow-chinas-military-advance-11665155702; Dan Strumpf and Liza Lin, "U.S. Chip Curbs Threaten China's Emerging Manufacturers," *Wall Street Journal*,

October 10, 2022, https://www.wsj.com/articles/u-s-chip-curbs-threaten-chinas-emerging-manufacturers-11665407496

149 Author's interview with Ben Rhodes in January 2022.

150 Joe Biden, "Remarks by President Biden at a Democratic National Committee Fundraiser," The White House, dated April 21, 2022, accessed April 26, 2022. https://www.whitehouse.gov/briefing-room/speeches-remarks/2022/04/21/remarks-by-president-biden-at-a-democratic-national-committee-fundraiser-3/

151 Lingling Wei, "China Adjusts, and Readjusts, Its Embrace of Russia in Ukraine Crisis," *Wall Street Journal*, February 25, 2022. https://www.wsj.com/articles/china-adjusts-and-readjusts-its-embrace-of-russia-in-ukraine-crisis-11645805266

152 "Secretary Antony J. Blinken, National Security Advisor Jake Sullivan, Director Yang and State Councilor Wang at the Top of Their Meeting," U.S. Department of State website, dated March 18, 2021, accessed April 1, 2022, https://www.state.gov/secretary-antony-j-blinken-national-security-advisor-jake-sullivan-chinese-director-of-the-office-of-the-central-commission-for-foreign-affairs-yang-jiechi-and-chinese-state-councilor-wang-yi-at-th/; "U.S.-China Summit in Anchorage, Alaska," C-SPAN, dated March 18, 2021, accessed April 1, 2022, https://www.c-span.org/video/?510091-1/secretary-blinken-chinese-foreign-minister-clash-meeting-anchorage-alaska.

153 Lingling Wei and Bob Davis, "China's Message to America: We're an Equal Now," *Wall Street Journal*, April 12, 2021, https://www.wsj.com/articles/america-china-policy-biden-xi-11617896117; David Bandurski, "Multiplayer Diplomacy," China Media Project, dated March 19, 2021, accessed April 3, 2022, https://chinamediaproject.org/2021/03/19/multiplayer-diplomacy/

154 Author's interviews with people familiar with the exchange.

155 "The South China Sea Arbitration (The Republic of Philippines v. The People's Republic of China)," Permanent Court of Arbitration, accessed April 5, 2022, https://pca-cpa.org/en/cases/7/; Jeremy Page, "Tribunal Rejects Beijing's Claims to South China Sea," *Wall Street Journal*, July 12, 2016, https://www.wsj.com/articles/chinas-claim-to-most-of-south-china-sea-has-no-legal-basis-court-says-1468315137

156 Bonnie Glaser, "On the Defensive? China Explains Purposes of Land Reclamation in the South China Sea," Asia Maritime Transparency Initiative, dated April 20, 2015, accessed April 6, 2022, https://amti.csis.org/on-the-defensive-china-explains-purposes-of-land-reclamation-in-the-south-china-sea/; Gregory B. Poling, "The Conventional Wisdom on China's Island Bases Is Dangerously Wrong," *War on the Rocks*, dated January 10, 2020, accessed February 16, 2022, https://warontherocks.com/2020/01/the-conventional-wisdom-on-chinas-island-bases-is-dangerously-wrong/

157 Andrew Browne, "China's Line in the Sea," *Wall Street Journal*, April 1, 2014. https://www.wsj.com/articles/SB10001424052702303978304579474570220330370

158 Mira Rapp-Hopper, "Before and After: The South China Sea Transformed," Asia Maritime Transparency Initiative, February 18, 2015. https://amti.csis.org/before-and-after-the-south-china-sea-transformed/

159 Xi Jinping, "习近平在新加坡国立大学的演讲（全文）[Xi Jinping's Speech at the National University of Singapore (Full Text)]," 新华网 Xinhua Net, November 7, 2015. http://www.xinhuanet.com//politics/2015-11/07/c_1117071978_2.htm

160 "Statement of the Ministry of Foreign Affairs of the People's Republic of China on the Award of 12 July 2016 of the Arbitral Tribunal in the South China Sea Arbitration Established at the Request of the Republic of the Philippines," Ministry of Foreign Affairs of the People's Republic

of China, dated July 12, 2016, accessed April 6, 2022, https://www.fmprc.gov.cn/mfa_eng/wjdt _665385/2649_665393/201607/t20160712_679470.html; Wang Yi, "Remarks by Chinese Foreign Minister Wang Yi on the Award of the So-called Arbitral Tribunal in the South China Sea Arbitration," Ministry of Foreign Affairs of the People's Republic of China, dated July 12, 2016, accessed April 6, 2022, https://www.fmprc.gov.cn/mfa_eng/wjb_663304/wjbz_663308/2461 _663310/201607/t20160712_468631.html; "Build It and They Will Come," Asia Maritime Transparency Initiative, August 1, 2016, https://amti.csis.org/build-it-and-they-will-come/; "Update: China's Continuing Reclamation in the Paracels," Asia Maritime Transparency Initiative, dated August 9, 2017, accessed April 6, 2022, https://amti.csis.org/paracels-beijings-other-buildup/

161 Neil Arwin Mercado, "Duterte on PH Court Win over China: 'That's just paper; I'll throw that in the wastebasket,'" *Philippine Daily Inquirer*, May 6, 2021. https://newsinfo.inquirer.net /1427860/duterte-on-ph-arbitral-win-over-china-papel-lang-yan-itatapon-ko-yan-sa-waste-basket

162 Ethan Meick and Nargiza Salidjanova, "China's Response to U.S.-South Korean Missile Defense System Deployment and Its Implications," U.S.-China Economic and Security Review Commission, July 26, 2017. https://www.uscc.gov/sites/default/files/Research/Report_China's%20 Response%20to%20THAAD%20Deployment%20and%20its%20Implications.pdf

163 Jonathan Cheng, "Chinese Retaliation Over Antimissile System Has South Korea Worried," *Wall Street Journal*, March 3, 2017, https://www.wsj.com/articles/in-south-korea-jitters-grow-that -china-is-punishing-it-1488519202; Chun Han Wong, "Conglomerate Feels Heat from China's Anger at South Korea," *Wall Street Journal*, March 10, 2017, https://www.wsj.com/articles/ conglomerate-feels-heat-from-chinas-anger-at-south-korea-1489161806; "Damage from China's Ban on S. Korean Tours Estimated at 7.5 tln Won," Yonhap News Agency, December 3, 2017, https://en.yna.co.kr/view/AEN20171203004100320

164 Park Byong-su, "South Korea's 'Three No's' Announcement Key to Restoring Relations with China," *Hankyoreh*, November 2, 2017, https://english.hani.co.kr/arti/english_edition/e _international/817213.html; Moon Chung-in, "[Column] Controversy over 'Three Noes' on THAAD and National Interest," *Hankyoreh*, August 9, 2021, https://english.hani.co.kr/arti/ english_edition/e_editorial/1007006.html

165 Uri Friedman, "How to Choose Between the U.S. and China? It's Not That Easy," *Atlantic*, July 26, 2019. https://www.theatlantic.com/politics/archive/2019/07/south-korea-china-united -states-dilemma/594850/

166 Rachel Pannett, "China's Clout Loses Punch as Trading Partners Push Back Over Coronavirus," *Wall Street Journal*, May 14, 2020, https://www.wsj.com/articles/chinas-clout-loses-punch-as -trading-partners-push-back-over-coronavirus-11589448604; Nathaniel Taplin, "Australia Is Getting Dragged into the Trump-Xi Trade War," *Wall Street Journal*, May 21, 2020, https://www .wsj.com/articles/australia-is-getting-dragged-into-the-trump-xi-trade-war-11590056788; Alice Uribe, "China Warns Citizens Not to Travel to Australia," *Wall Street Journal*, June 6, 2020, https://www.wsj.com/articles/china-warns-citizens-not-to-travel-to-australia-11591446223; Stuart Condie, "China Escalates Australia Trade Dispute with Wine Tariffs," *Wall Street Journal*, November 27, 2020, https://www.wsj.com/articles/china-escalates-australia-trade-dispute-with -wine-tariffs-11606472504

167 Stuart Condie, "Australian Journalist Detained in China as Relations Sour," *Wall Street Journal*, August 31, 2020. https://www.wsj.com/articles/australian-journalist-detained-in-china-as -relations-sour-11598886544

168 Jonathan Kearsley, Eryk Bagshaw, and Anthony Galloway, "'If you make China the enemy, China will be the enemy': Beijing's Fresh Threat to Australia," *Sydney Morning Herald*, November 18, 2020. https://www.smh.com.au/world/asia/if-you-make-china-the-enemy-china-will-be-the-enemy-beijing-s-fresh-threat-to-australia-20201118-p56fqs.html

169 Kate O'Keeffe and Stu Woo, "Canadian Authorities Arrest CFO of Huawei Technologies at U.S. Request," *Wall Street Journal*, December 5, 2018. https://www.wsj.com/articles/canadian-authorities-arrest-cfo-of-huawei-technologies-at-u-s-request-1544048781

170 Chun Han Wong, John Lyons, and Josh Chin, "'No Coincidence': China's Detention of Canadian Seen as Retaliation for Huawei Arrest," *Wall Street Journal*, December 12, 2018, https://www.wsj.com/articles/no-coincidence-chinas-detention-of-canadian-seen-as-retaliation-for-huawei-arrest-11544619753; Chun Han Wong, "Two Canadians Detained in China Indicted on Espionage Charges," *Wall Street Journal*, June 19, 2020, https://www.wsj.com/articles/two-canadians-detained-in-china-indicted-on-espionage-charges-11592545373

171 Chun Han Wong, "Canadian's Appeal of Chinese Drug-Smuggling Charges to Get Public Hearing," *Wall Street Journal*, December 27, 2018, https://www.wsj.com/articles/canadians-appeal-of-chinese-drug-smuggling-charges-to-get-public-hearing-11545891748; Eva Dou, "China to Retry Long-Held Canadian on Drug Charges," *Wall Street Journal*, December 31, 2018, https://www.wsj.com/articles/china-to-retry-long-held-canadian-on-drug-charges-11546100231; Eva Dou and Paul Viera, "Chinese Court Sentences Canadian National to Death for Drug Crimes in Retrial," *Wall Street Journal*, January 14, 2019, https://www.wsj.com/articles/chinese-court-sentences-canadian-national-to-death-for-drug-crimes-in-retrial-11547470636

172 Aruna Viswanatha, Dan Strumpf, and Jacquie McNish, "Huawei Executive's Return to China: How the Deal Came Off," *Wall Street Journal*, September 25, 2021, https://www.wsj.com/articles/justice-department-reaches-deal-with-huawei-executive-11632494001; Aruna Viswanatha, Dan Strumpf, Jacquie McNish, and James T. Areddy, "Huawei Executive's Return to China: How the Deal Came Off," *Wall Street Journal*, September 27, 2021, https://www.wsj.com/articles/huawei-executives-return-to-china-how-the-deal-came-off-11632784295

173 Stuart Lau, "Lithuania Pulls Out of China's '17+1' Bloc in Eastern Europe," *Politico*, May 21, 2021. https://www.politico.eu/article/lithuania-pulls-out-china-17-1-bloc-eastern-central-europe-foreign-minister-gabrielius-landsbergis/

174 Laurence Norman and Drew Hinshaw, "China Presses EU over Taiwan by Targeting One of Smallest Members," *Wall Street Journal*, December 15, 2021, https://www.wsj.com/articles/china-presses-eu-over-taiwan-by-targeting-one-of-smallest-members-11639579784; Daniel Michaels and Drew Hinshaw, "EU Hits Back at China over Trade Limits, Taking Lithuania Fight Global," *Wall Street Journal*, January 27, 2022, https://www.wsj.com/articles/eu-takes-china-to-wto-over-lithuania-trade-restrictions-11643271938

175 Silver, Devlin, and Huang, "Large Majorities Say China Does Not Respect the Personal Freedoms of Its People."

176 Gordon Lubold, "U.S. to Share Nuclear Submarine Technology with Australia in New Pact," *Wall Street Journal*, September 15, 2021, https://www.wsj.com/articles/u-s-forms-a-new-security-alliance-for-asia-with-the-u-k-and-australia-11631741734; Anirudh Bhattacharyya, "Canada Joins Quad Joint Naval Exercise in Pacific Ocean," *Hindustan Times*, January 25, 2021, https://www.hindustantimes.com/india-news/canada-to-join-quad-joint-naval-exercise-in-pacific-ocean-101611556512917.html; Susannah Patton, "Does the Quad Plus Add Up?,"

Lowy Institute, dated March 21, 2022, accessed April 8, 2022, https://www.lowyinstitute.org/the-interpreter/does-quad-plus-add

177 Stuart Lau, "Down to 14 + 1: Estonia and Latvia Quit China's Club in Eastern Europe," *Politico*, August 11, 2022. https://www.politico.eu/article/down-to-14-1-estonia-and-latvia-quit-chinas-club-in-eastern-europe/

178 Josephine Appiah-Nyamekye Sanny and Edem Selormey, "Africans Welcome China's Influence but Maintain Democratic Aspirations," Afrobarometer, November 15, 2021. https://www.afrobarometer.org/wp-content/uploads/migrated/files/publications/Dispatches/ad489-pap3-africans_welcome_chinas_influence_maintain_democratic_aspirations-afrobarometer_dispatch-15nov21.pdf

179 Kevin Baumert and Brian Melchior, "Limits in the Seas No. 143—China: Maritime Claims in the South China Sea," Office of Ocean and Polar Affairs, Bureau of Oceans and International Environmental and Scientific Affairs, U.S. Department of State, December 5, 2014. https://2009-2017.state.gov/documents/organization/234936.pdf

180 Gregory B. Poling, "Time to End Strategic Ambiguity in the South China Sea," Center for Strategic and International Studies, dated July 6, 2012, accessed February 21, 2022. https://www.csis.org/analysis/time-end-strategic-ambiguity-south-china-sea

181 Dan Altman, "By Fait Accompli, Not Coercion: How States Wrest Territory from Their Adversaries," *International Studies Quarterly* 61, No. 4 (December 2017): 881–891, https://doi.org/10.1093/isq/sqx049; Dan Altman, "What the History of Modern Conquest Tells Us About China and India's Border Crisis," *War on the Rocks*, dated July 9, 2020, accessed February 15, 2022, https://warontherocks.com/2020/07/what-the-history-of-modern-conquest-tells-us-about-china-and-indias-border-crisis/

182 Lee Kuan Yew, "Excerpts of Address by Singapore's Prime Minister, Mr. Lee Kuan Yew, on the Change in Great Power Relations at the Commonwealth Heads of Government Meeting in Ottawa on Friday, August 3, 1973," National Archives of Singapore. https://www.nas.gov.sg/archivesonline/data/pdfdoc/lky19730803.pdf

183 Lee, "Excerpts of Address"; Lee Kuan Yew, *From Third World to First: The Singapore Story: 1965–2000* (New York: HarperCollins, 2000), p. 395.

184 Lee, "Excerpts of Address."

185 Patrick Chin Leong Ng, *A Study of Attitudes of Dialect Speakers Towards the Speak Mandarin Campaign in Singapore, Springer Briefs in Linguistics* (Singapore: Springer, 2017).

186 "People's Republic of China," Ministry of Foreign Affairs Singapore, accessed May 6, 2022. https://www.mfa.gov.sg/SINGAPORES-FOREIGN-POLICY/Countries-and-Regions/Northeast-Asia/Peoples-Republic-of-China

187 Henry Gottlieb, "U.S. Withdraws Diplomat from Singapore with 'Deep Regret,'" Associated Press, May 8, 1988, https://apnews.com/article/24c180ef76a9a422944efce99392a613; Charles P. Wallace, "Decision on Caning Disappoints White House: Asia: Clinton Aide Says Singapore's Reduction of U.S. Teen's Sentence Is Still 'Out of Step' with Crime. Youth's Mother Thinks Flogging Is Imminent," *Los Angeles Times*, May 5, 1994, https://www.latimes.com/archives/la-xpm-1994-05-05-mn-54203-story.html; Valerie Chew, "Michael Fay," Singapore Infopedia, dated 2009, accessed April 7, 2022, https://eresources.nlb.gov.sg/infopedia/articles/SIP_1554_2009-08-06.html

188 Lee Hsien Loong, "National Day Rally 2004," Prime Minister's Office website, dated August 22,

2004, accessed April 3, 2022. https://www.pmo.gov.sg/Newsroom/prime-minister-lee-hsien
-loongs-national-day-rally-2004-english

189 Lee, "National Day Rally 2004."

190 Kausikan, "Dealing with an Ambiguous World Lecture III."

191 Lee Hsien Loong, "National Day Rally 2016," Prime Minister's Office, August 21, 2016. https://
www.pmo.gov.sg/Newsroom/national-day-rally-2016

192 Stanley Loh, "Full text of Ambassador Stanley Loh's letter to Global Times Editor-in-Chief Hu
Xijin, in response to an article by *Global Times* (Chinese) dated 21 September 2016," Ministry
of Foreign Affairs Singapore, September 21, 2016. https://www.mfa.gov.sg/Overseas-Mission/
Beijing/Consular-Services/Consular-Updates/2016/09/global_times

193 Author's interviews with current and former diplomats familiar with the summit.

194 Wang Panpan, "不结盟运动首脑会闭幕 新加坡不顾反对妄提南海仲裁 [Non-Aligned
Movement Summit Closes, Singapore Raises South China Sea Arbitration Despite Opposition],"
Global Times, September 21, 2016. https://world.huanqiu.com/article/9CaKrnJXInM

195 Chun Han Wong, "Chinese Tabloid Riles Singapore in South China Sea Spat," *WSJ China Real
Time* blog, September 29, 2016, https://www.wsj.com/articles/BL-CJB-29561; "Foreign Minis-
try Spokesperson Geng Shuang's Regular Press Conference on September 27, 2016," Consulate-
General of the People's Republic of China in Mumbai, dated September 27, 2016, accessed
April 8, 2022, https://www.mfa.gov.cn/ce/cgtrt//eng/fyrthhz/t1401306.htm

196 Bernard F W Loo, "Making Sense of the Terrex Incident," *Today*, dated December 6, 2016,
updated July 9, 2020, https://www.todayonline.com/commentary/making-sense-terrex-incident;
Minnie Chan, "How Singapore's Military Vehicles Became Beijing's Diplomatic Weapon,"
South China Morning Post, December 3, 2016, https://www.scmp.com/week-asia/politics/article
/2051322/how-singapores-military-vehicles-became-beijings-diplomatic

197 Bilahari Kausikan, "Our government is not rash but the considerations are not just relations
with China. If we allow ourselves to be intimidated by Beijing what do you think our immediate
neighbours will think?" Facebook comment, November 26, 2016. https://www.facebook.com/
bilahari.kausikan/posts/1836788019911952

198 National Population and Talent Division, Strategy Group, Prime Minister's Office Singapore;
Department of Statistics; Ministry of Home Affairs; Immigration & Checkpoints Authority and
Ministry of Manpower, "Population in Brief 2021," Population.gov.sg, September 2021. https://
www.population.gov.sg/files/media-centre/publications/Population-in-brief-2021.pdf

199 Chai Kim Wah, "China Ties Come After Long Period of Gestation," *Straits Times*, October 4, 1990,
p. 35. https://eresources.nlb.gov.sg/newspapers/Digitised/Article/straitstimes19901004-1.2.44.6

200 Chai, "China Ties Come After Long Period of Gestation"; "Singapore Establishes Formal Diplomatic Relations with China," HistorySG. https://eresources.nlb.gov.sg/history/events/4181dd20
-df08-4ff5-8d93-620350b639fd

201 Silver, Devlin, and Huang, "Large Majorities Say China Does Not Respect the Personal Freedoms of Its People."

202 Silver, Devlin, and Huang, "Large Majorities Say China Does Not Respect the Personal Freedoms of Its People."

203 "China Index," Doublethink Lab, accessed May 5, 2022. https://china-index.io/

204 "Cancellation of Singapore Permanent Residence (SPR) Status—Huang Jing and Yang Xiuping,"
Singapore Ministry of Home Affairs, August 6, 2017. https://www.mha.gov.sg/mediaroom/press

-releases/cancellation-of-singapore-permanent-residence-spr-status—huang-jing-and-yang
-xiuping

205 Tashny Sukumaran, "Huang Jing, Chinese-American Academic Expelled by Singapore, Is
Working in Beijing and Has 'No Hard Feelings,'" *South China Morning Post*, June 17, 2019.
https://www.scmp.com/news/asia/southeast-asia/article/3014872/huang-jing-chinese-american
-academic-expelled-singapore

206 Michael Yong, "How a Singaporean Man Went from NUS PhD Student to Working for Chinese
Intelligence in the US," CNA, July 25, 2020, https://www.channelnewsasia.com/singapore/
dickson-yeo-us-china-intelligence-singapore-nus-phd-711701; United States District Court for
the District of Columbia, *United States of America v. Jun Wei Yeo*, also known as *Dickson Yeo*,
United States Department of Justice, July 15, 2020, https://www.justice.gov/usao-dc/press-release
/file/1297451/download; Office of Public Affairs, "Singaporean National Pleads Guilty to Acting
in the United States as an Illegal Agent of Chinese Intelligence," United States Department of
Justice, July 24, 2020, https://www.justice.gov/opa/pr/singaporean-national-pleads-guilty-acting
-united-states-illegal-agent-chinese-intelligence

207 Colum Murphy, Tom Mackenzie, David Ingles, and Jing Li, "Singaporean's Ph.D Adviser
Says He's Glad Ex-Student Caught for Spying," Bloomberg News, July 27, 2020, https://www
.bloomberg.com/news/articles/2020-07-27/singapore-agent-s-ph-d-adviser-says-he-s-glad-ex
-student-caught; Maria Siow, "Chinese-American Academic Huang Jing Denies Spy Recruitment
of Singaporean Jun Wei Yeo," *South China Morning Post*, July 27, 2020, https://www.scmp.com
/week-asia/politics/article/3094913/nonsense-chinese-american-academic-huang-jing-denies
-recruiting

208 Bilahari Kausikan, "One fool like this can get all Singaporeans suspected. This guy used to be a
PhD student at the LKYSPP where Huang Jing who was expelled and banned from SG in 2017
for being a Chinese agent of influence also worked. It is not unreasonable to assume he was
recruited or at least talent spotted by the MSS there. After note: just learnt Huang Jing was Dickson's PhD supervisor until we threw him out," Facebook, July 25, 2020, https://www.facebook
.com/bilahari.kausikan/posts/2760980700826008; John Geddie and Aradhana Aravindan,
"Singapore Spy Case Reawakens Fears China Recruiting on Island State," Reuters News, July 28,
2020, https://www.reuters.com/article/us-usa-china-spy-singapore-idUSKCN24T0ZV

209 Hariz Baharudin, "Proposed Law Seeks to Counter Foreign Interference in S'pore Politics,
Measures Include Take-Down and Blocking Orders," *Straits Times*, September 13, 2021, https://
www.straitstimes.com/singapore/politics/proposed-law-seeks-to-counter-foreign-interference-in
-spore-politics-measures; Vanessa Lim, Ang Hwee Min, and Jalelah Abu Baker, "Parliament
Passes Bill to Deal with Foreign Interference After 10-Hour Debate," CNA, October 5, 2021,
https://www.channelnewsasia.com/singapore/fica-parliament-singapore-foreign-interference
-countermeasures-bill-2221236

210 Singapore Parliamentary Debates, Official Report (04 October 2021), Vol. 95, No. 39, Singapore Parliament, accessed April 10, 2022, https://sprs.parl.gov.sg/search/#/fullreport?sittingdate
=04-10-2021

211 Lee Hsien Loong, "The Endangered Asian Century: America, China, and the Perils of Confrontation," *Foreign Affairs* 99, No. 4 (July/August 2020). https://www.foreignaffairs.com/articles/asia
/2020-06-04/lee-hsien-loong-endangered-asian-century

8. ONE MAN'S FATE

1 "The Reign of the Yongzheng Emperor (approx. 1723–1735)," The Palace Museum, accessed April 15, 2022. https://en.dpm.org.cn/EXPLORE/ming-qing/2015-02-06/16.html

2 Keith Zhai and Chun Han Wong, "China's Xi Claims Third Term as Communist Party Leader," *Wall Street Journal*, October 23, 2022. https://www.wsj.com/articles/chinas-xi-claims-third-term -as-communist-party-leader-11666499842

3 Bruce J. Dickson, "Unsettled Succession: China's Critical Moment," *National Interest*, September 1, 1997. https://nationalinterest.org/article/unsettled-succession-chinas-critical-moment-785

4 Xi Jinping, "We Must Be Consistent in Promoting the New Great Project."

5 The Chinese Communist Party Central Party History and Literature Research Institute, 《习近平关于全面从严治党论述摘编》 [*Excerpts from Xi Jinping's Remarks on Comprehensively and Strictly Governing the Party*] (Beijing: Central Party Literature Press, 2021), p. 153.

6 Leon Aron, "Everything You Think You Know About the Collapse of the Soviet Union Is Wrong," *Foreign Policy*, June 20, 2011. https://foreignpolicy.com/2011/06/20/everything-you -think-you-know-about-the-collapse-of-the-soviet-union-is-wrong/

7 Xi, "We Must Be Consistent in Promoting the New Great Project."

8 Yuhua Wang, "Can the Chinese Communist Party Learn from Chinese Emperors?," in *The China Questions: Critical Insights into a Rising Power* (Cambridge, Massachusetts: Harvard University Press, 2018), pp. 58–64.

9 Joseph Fletcher, "Turco-Mongolian Monarchic Tradition in the Ottoman Empire," *Harvard Ukrainian Studies* ¾ (1979–1980): 236–251.

10 Frederic Wakeman, Jr., *The Great Enterprise: The Manchu Reconstruction of Imperial Order in Seventeenth-Century China* (Berkeley: University of California Press, 1985), pp. 157–158.

11 Mark C. Elliott, *The Manchu Way: The Eight Banners and Ethnic Identity in Late Imperial China* (Stanford: Stanford University Press, 2001), pp. 39–88; Gertraude Roth Li, "State Building Before 1644," in Willard J. Peterson (ed.), *The Cambridge History of China*, Volume 9, Part One: *The Ch'ing Empire to 1800* (Cambridge: Cambridge University Press, 2002), pp. 9–72.

12 Jerry Dennerline, "The Shun-chih Reign," in Peterson (ed.), *The Cambridge History of China*, Volume 9, Part One, pp. 73–119.

13 Silas H. K. Wu, *Passage to Power: K'ang-hsi and His Heir Apparent, 1661–1722* (Cambridge, Massachusetts: Harvard University Press, 1979), pp. 179–183.

14 Wu, *Passage to Power*, pp. 185–186; Shangguan Yun, "雍正到底改没改亲参康熙遗诏？历史悬案有答案了！ [Did Yongzheng Doctor His Father Kangxi's Edict? There's an Answer to This Historical Mystery!]," 中新网 [China News Service Net], December 5, 2019, https://www .chinanews.com.cn/cul/2019/12-05/9025775.shtml

15 William T. Rowe, *China's Last Empire: The Great Qing* (Cambridge, Massachusetts and London: Harvard University Press, 2009).

16 Chinese Communist Party Central Committee Documentary Research Office (ed.), 《毛泽东年谱：1949-1976 第5卷》 [*Chronology of Mao Zedong: 1949–1976, Volume 5*] (Beijing: Central Party Literature Press, 2013), p. 592.

17 Wang Li, 《現場歷史：文化大革命紀事》 [*Live History: A Chronicle of the Cultural Revolution*] (Hong Kong: Oxford University Press, 1993), pp. 100–110.

18 Roderick MacFarquhar and Michael Schoenhals, *Mao's Last Revolution* (Cambridge, Massachusetts: Harvard University Press, 2006), pp. 333–336; Andrew G. Walder, *China Under Mao: A Revolution Derailed* (Cambridge, Massachusetts: Harvard University Press, 2015), pp. 286–287; Jonathan D. Spence, *The Search for Modern China*, Second Edition (New York: W. W. Norton, 1999), pp. 584–586.

19 MacFarquhar and Schoenhals, *Mao's Last Revolution*, pp. 338–339.

20 Joseph Torigian, *Prestige, Manipulation, and Coercion: Elite Power Struggles in the Soviet Union and China After Stalin and Mao* (New Haven: Yale University Press, 2022), pp. 114–123.

21 Yan Jiaqi, *Towards a Democratic China: The Intellectual Biography of Yan Jiaqi*, translated by David S. K. Hong and Denis C. Mair (Honolulu: University of Hawaii Press, 1992), p. 52.

22 Deng Xiaoping, "答意大利记者奥琳埃娜 · 法拉奇问 [Answers to the Italian Journalist Oriana Fallaci]," 《邓小平文选》第二卷 *Selected Works of Deng Xiaoping*, Vol. 2, Second Edition (Beijing: People's Publishing House, 1994), pp. 344–353.

23 Deng, "Answers to the Italian Journalist Oriana Fallaci."

24 Deng Xiaoping, "第三代领导集体的当务之急 [Urgent Tasks of China's Third Generation of Collective Leadership]," in 《邓小平文选》第三卷 *Selected Works of Deng Xiaoping*, Vol. 3 (Beijing: People's Publishing House, 1993), pp. 309–314.

25 Richard Baum, "The Fifteenth National Party Congress: Jiang Takes Command?," *China Quarterly*, No. 153 (March 1998): 141–156.

26 John Pomfret and Philip P. Pan, "In China's Transfer of Power, Jiang Retires and Ousts Liberal Rival," *Washington Post*, November 14, 2002, https://www.washingtonpost.com/archive/politics/2002/11/14/in-chinas-transfer-of-power-jiang-retires-and-ousts-liberal-rival/8acaa37f-f897-435b-a3d7-aca377a1a38b/; Ewan Smith, "On the Informal Rules of the Chinese Communist Party," *China Quarterly*, No. 248 (November 2021): 141–160.

27 Andrew J. Nathan, "China's Changing of the Guard: Authoritarian Resilience," *Journal of Democracy* 14, No. 1 (January 2003): 6–17.

28 Zhengxu Wang and Anastas Vangeli, "The Rules and Norms of Leadership Succession in China: From Deng Xiaoping to Xi Jinping and Beyond," *China Journal* 76 (July 2016): 24–40. https://www.journals.uchicago.edu/doi/10.1086/686141

29 Han Dayuan, "任期制在我国宪法中的规范意义——纪念1982年《宪法》颁布35周年 [The Normative Significance of the Term System in My Country's Constitution: Commemorating the 35th Anniversary of the Promulgation of the 1982 'Constitution']," 《法学》 *Legal Science*, No. 11 of 2017 (November 2017): pp. 3–8. http://www.calaw.cn/article/default.asp?id=12543

30 Chun Han Wong and Keith Zhai, "China's Xi Jinping Moves to Extend Rule as Top Communist Party Rivals Retire," *Wall Street Journal*, October 22, 2022, https://www.wsj.com/articles/chinas-xi-jinping-moves-to-extend-rule-as-top-communist-party-rivals-retire-11666418847; Zhai and Wong, "China's Xi Claims Third Term as Communist Party Leader."

31 "习近平: 切实贯彻落实新时代党的组织路线 全党努力把党建设得更加坚强有力 [Xi Jinping: Effectively Implement the Party's Organizational Line in the New Era, the Entire Party Striving to Build a Stronger Party]," Xinhua News Agency, July 4, 2018. http://www.xinhuanet.com/politics/leaders/2018-07/04/c_1123080079.htm

32 Lucian Pye, "China: Erratic State, Frustrated Society," *Foreign Affairs* 69, No. 4 (Fall 1990): 56–74.

33 Jiangnan Zhu and Nikolai Mukhin, "The Modern Regency: Leadership Transition and Authoritarian Resilience of the Former Soviet Union and China," *Communist and Post-Communist Studies* 54, No. 1–2 (March-June 2021): 24–44.

34 "中国共产党党章 [Constitution of the Communist Party of China]," 中共党员网 [Chinese Communist Party Members Net], dated October 28, 2017, accessed August 25, 2021. https://www.12371.cn/2017/10/28/ARTI1509191507150883.shtml

35 "党政领导干部职务任期暂行规定 [Provisional Regulations on the Terms of Office for Leading Cadres in the Party and Government]," 中共党员网 [Chinese Communist Party Members Net], March 12, 2015, http://news.12371.cn/2015/03/12/ARTI1426126246992108.shtml; Jeremy Page and Lingling Wei, "Xi's Power Play Foreshadows Historic Transformation of How China is Ruled," *Wall Street Journal*, December 26, 2016, https://www.wsj.com/articles/xis -power-play-foreshadows-radical-transformation-of-how-china-is-ruled-1482778917

36 Zhao Cheng, Huo Xiaoguang, Zhang Xiaosong, Lin Hui, and Hu Hao, "领航新时代新征程新辉煌的坚强领导集体——党的新一届中央领导机构产生纪实 [The Strong Leadership Collective Navigating the New Era, the New Expedition, and New Glories—Documenting the Selection of the Party's New Central Leadership Body]," Xinhua News Agency, October 2022. http://www.news.cn/politics/cpc20/2022-10/24/c_1129077854.htm

37 Alexandre Debs and H. E. Goemans, "Regime Type, the Fate of Leaders, and War," *American Political Science Review* 104, No. 3 (August 2010): 430–445.

38 Erica Frantz and Elizabeth A. Stein, "Countering Coups: Leadership Succession Rules in Dictatorships," *Comparative Political Studies* 50, No. 7 (June 2017): 935–962. https://journals.sagepub .com/doi/abs/10.1177/0010414016655538

39 Wang, "Can the Chinese Communist Party Learn from Chinese Emperors?"

40 Joseph Torigian's talk on Soviet and Chinese succession struggles in April 2022.

41 Yan Jiaqi, "The Nature of Chinese Authoritarianism," in Carol Lee Hamrin, Suisheng Zhao, and A. Doak Barnett (eds.), *Decision-Making in Deng's China: Perspectives from Insiders* (New York: Routledge, 1995), pp. 3–14.

42 LA SICILIA, "*Xi Jinping a Palazzo dei Normanni*," YouTube video, March 24, 2019, https://www .youtube.com/watch?v=OZFHO2fzmi8; Associated Press, "Welcome ceremony for Xi at Arc De Triomphe," YouTube video, March 30, 2019, https://www.youtube.com/watch?v=z2cRL_imI6k

43 AFP, "*Macron accueille le président Xi Jinping à la Villa Kérylos 2/2 l AFP Images*," YouTube video, March 25, 2019. https://www.youtube.com/watch?v=H7Bv2qMmqsE

44 Author's conversation with the retired politics professor in April 2019.

45 Central Intelligence Agency, Directorate of Intelligence, Office of Political Research, "After Mao: Factors and Contingencies in the Succession," Central Intelligence Agency Freedom of Information Act Electronic Reading Room, August 1976. https://www.cia.gov/readingroom/docs /CIA-RDP79T00889A000800060001-5.pdf

46 Director of Central Intelligence, "China After Deng: Succession Problems and Prospects," Central Intelligence Agency Freedom of Information Act Electronic Reading Room, May 1986. https://www.cia.gov/readingroom/document/cia-rdp90r00961r000200060001-2

47 Chun Han Wong, "Xi's Unsteady Steps Revive Worries Over Lack of Succession Plan in China," *Wall Street Journal*, April 23, 2019. https://www.wsj.com/articles/xis-unsteady-steps-revive -worries-over-lack-of-succession-plan-in-china-11556011802

48 Wen-Hsuan Tsai, "Medical Politics and the CCP's Healthcare System for State Leaders," *Journal of Contemporary China* 27, No. 114 (July 2018): 942–955.

49 Michael Dobbs, "Close Aides Oust Gorbachev," *Washington Post*, August 19, 1991. https://www .washingtonpost.com/archive/politics/1991/08/19/close-aides-oust-gorbachev/c6e16efc-a073 -4c31-a419-6665ef3fecad/

50 Wong, "Xi's Unsteady Steps Revive Worries."

51 James Griffiths, "What the Reaction to Chinese President Xi Jinping Coughing During a Speech Says About East Asia Right Now," CNN, October 15, 2020, https://edition.cnn.com/2020/10 /15/asia/xi-jinping-shenzhen-speech-cough-intl-hnk/index.html; CGTN, "Live: Celebrate the 40th anniversary of the establishment of Shenzhen SEZ," YouTube video, October 14, 2020. https://www.youtube.com/watch?v=0UuukZvAxOo&t=6127s

52 Jeremy Page, Flemming Emil Hansen, and Josh Chin, "China Mystery: Where Is Xi Jinping?," *Wall Street Journal*, September 11, 2012, https://www.wsj.com/articles/SB10000872396390443 9215045777643580141787056; Russell Leigh Moses, "Xi's Back, Now Let the Chinese Political Battle Begin," *WSJ China Real Time* blog, September 17, 2012, https://www.wsj.com/articles/ BL-CJB-16495

53 James Melley, "How Tall is Xi Jinping?," BBC News, October 21, 2015. https://www.bbc.com/ news/magazine-34592196

54 Zhuang Pinghui, "Model Quitter: President Xi Jinping's Decision to Give Up Smoking Deserves Praise, WHO Chief Says," *South China Morning Post*, August 2, 2016, https://www.scmp.com/ news/china/policies-politics/article/1997897/model-quitter-president-xi-jinpings-decision-give; "点赞！世卫组织称习大大是戒烟'好榜样' [Giving a Like! The World Health Organization Says Xi Dada Is a 'Role Model' for Quitting Smoking]"《健康时报》 *Health Times*, August 3, 2016. http://www.jksb.com.cn/html/news/hot/2016/0803/101663.html

55 Guan Jintai, "【政情】记者亲历：跟访习近平一天 [[Political Affairs] A Reporter's Personal Experience: Trailing Xi Jinping for a Day During a Visit]," 上观新闻 *Shanghai Observer*, October 25, 2014. https://m.jfdaily.com/wx/detail.do?id=2141

56 "中国共产党章程 [Constitution of the Communist Party of China]," 中共党员网 [Chinese Communist Party Members Net], accessed April 11, 2022. https://www.12371.cn/special/ zggcdzc/zggcdzcqw/

57 "中华人民共和国宪法 [The Constitution of the People's Republic of China]," Central People's Government of the People's Republic of China, dated March 22, 2018, accessed April 11, 2022. http://www.gov.cn/guoqing/2018-03/22/content_5276318.htm

58 "Who's in Charge? The 25th Amendment and the Attempted Assassination of President Reagan," Reagan Library Education Blog, dated January 8, 2021, accessed April 12, 2022. https://reagan .blogs.archives.gov/2021/01/08/whos-in-charge-the-25th-amendment-and-president-reagans -assassination-attempt/

59 "The 25th Amendment: Section 4 and March 30, 1981," Reagan Library Education Blog, dated July 26, 2017, accessed April 12, 2022. https://reagan.blogs.archives.gov/2017/07/26/the-25th -amendment-section-4-and-march-30-1981/

60 Richard McGregor and Jude Blanchette, "After Xi: Future Scenarios for Leadership Succession in Post-Xi Jinping Era," Center for Strategic and International Studies and Lowy Institute, April 2021.

61 A. J. Liebling, "The Wayward Press: Death On The One Hand," *New Yorker*, March 28, 1953. https://www.newyorker.com/magazine/1953/03/28/death-on-the-one-hand-wayward-press

62 Andrea Kendall-Taylor and Erica Frantz, "When Dictators Die," *Journal of Democracy* 27, No. 4 (October 2016): 159–171.

63 Kendall-Taylor and Frantz, "When Dictators Die."

64 Kendall-Taylor and Frantz, "When Dictators Die."

65 Xi Jinping, "习近平在中纪委第六次全体会议上的讲话（全文）[Xi Jinping's Speech at the Sixth Plenary Session of the Central Commission for Discipline Inspection (Full Text)]," 新华网 Xinhua Net, dated May 3, 2016, accessed April 21, 2022, http://www.xinhuanet.com//politics /2016-05/03/c_128951516_2.htm; Chun Han Wong, "China's Xi Jinping Puts Loyalty to the Test at Congress," *Wall Street Journal*, March 1, 2016, https://www.wsj.com/articles/chinas-xi -jinping-puts-loyalty-to-the-test-at-congress-1456853257

66 Josh Chin, "China Muzzles Outspoken Businessman Ren Zhiqiang on Social Media," *Wall Street Journal*, February 28, 2016, https://www.wsj.com/articles/china-muzzles-outspoken-business man-ren-zhiqiang-on-social-media-1456712781; Chun Han Wong, "Chinese Communist Party Suspends Critic Ren Zhiqiang's Membership," *Wall Street Journal*, May 3, 2016, https://www.wsj .com/articles/chinese-communist-party-suspends-critic-ren-zhiqiangs-membership-1462199602

67 "关于要求习近平同志辞去党和国家领导职务的公开信 [Open Letter Calling on Comrade Xi Jinping to Resign from Party and State Leadership Roles]," Wujie News, dated March 4, 2016, http://www.watching.cn/show-2-76713-1.html, Internet Archive. http://web.archive.org/web /20160304150122/http:/www.watching.cn/show-2-76713-1.html

68 Wong, "Chinese Communist Party Suspends Critic Ren Zhiqiang's Membership."

69 Chun Han Wong, "China Hunts Source of Letter Urging Xi to Quit," *Wall Street Journal*, March 27, 2016, https://www.wsj.com/articles/china-said-to-cast-net-after-online-letter-urges -president-xi-jinping-to-quit-1459081193; Chun Han Wong, "Future of China's Wujie Media in Doubt After Letter Calling on Xi to Quit," *WSJ China Real Time* blog, March 28, 2016, https:// www.wsj.com/articles/BL-CJB-28943

70 Wong, "China Hunts Source of Letter Urging Xi to Quit."

71 Milan W. Svolik, *The Politics of Authoritarian Rule* (New York: Cambridge University Press, 2012), p. 5.

72 Frantz and Stein, "Countering Coups."

73 Wang, "Can the Chinese Communist Party Learn from Chinese Emperors?"

74 Chinese Communist Party Central Commission for Discipline Inspection and Chinese Communist Party Central Party History and Literature Research Institute, 《习近平关于严明党的纪律 和规矩论述摘编》 [Excerpts from Xi Jinping's Remarks on Strictly Enforcing Party Discipline and Regulations] (Beijing: Central Party Literature Press and China Fangzheng Press, 2016). http://cpc.people.com.cn/xuexi/n1/2016/0106/c385474-28018287.html

75 Chun Han Wong, "China's Xi Jinping Tightens Grip on Domestic Security Forces in First Broad Purge," *Wall Street Journal*, August 18, 2020, https://www.wsj.com/articles/chinas-xi-jinping -tightens-grip-on-domestic-security-forces-in-first-broad-purge-11597773887; Chun Han Wong, "China Sentences Purged Police Officials as Xi Tightens Grip on Security Forces," *Wall Street Journal*, September 23, 2022, https://www.wsj.com/articles/china-sentences-purged-police -officials-as-xi-tightens-grip-on-security-forces-11663931349

76 Dan Mattingly, "How the Party Commands the Gun: The Foreign-Domestic Threat Dilemma in China," *American Journal of Political Science* (2022). https://onlinelibrary.wiley.com/doi/10.1111 /ajps.12739

77 Chun Han Wong, "Chinese Mogul Faces Probe for Essay Critical of President Xi's Coronavirus Handling," *Wall Street Journal*, April 7, 2020. https://www.wsj.com/articles/chinese-mogul-faces -probe-for-essay-critical-of-president-xis-coronavirus-handling-11586283853

78 Chun Han Wong, "Chinese Tycoon Kicked Out of Communist Party, Faces Prosecution After Criticizing Xi," *Wall Street Journal*, July 23, 2020, https://www.wsj.com/articles/chinese-tycoon -kicked-out-of-communist-party-faces-prosecution-after-criticizing-xi-11595526273; Chun Han Wong, "China Sentences Xi Critic Ren Zhiqiang to 18 Years in Prison," *Wall Street Journal*, September 22, 2020, https://www.wsj.com/articles/china-sentences-xi-critic-ren-zhiqiang-to -18-years-in-prison-11600755598

79 "Translation: Former Party Professor Calls CCP a 'Political Zombie,'" *China Digital Times*, June 12, 2020. https://chinadigitaltimes.net/2020/06/translation-former-party-professor-calls -ccp-a-political-zombie/

80 Author's conversations with Cai Xia from 2020 to 2022; Cai Xia, "The Party That Failed: An Insider Breaks with Beijing," *Foreign Affairs* 100, No. 1 (January/February 2021): 78–96, https:// www.foreignaffairs.com/articles/china/2020-12-04/chinese-communist-party-failed

81 Chris Buckley, "A Chinese Law Professor Criticized Xi. Now He's Been Suspended," *New York Times*, March 26, 2019, https://www.nytimes.com/2019/03/26/world/asia/chinese-law -professor-xi.html; Echo Xie and Su Xinqi, "Tsinghua University Suspends Xu Zhangrun, Chinese Law Professor Who Criticised Xi Jinping," *South China Morning Post*, March 27, 2019, https://www.scmp.com/news/china/politics/article/3003397/tsinghua-university-suspends -chinese-law-professor-who

82 Xu Zhangrun, "许章润: 我们当下的恐惧与期待 [Xu Zhangrun: Our Imminent Fears and Immediate Hopes]," Unirule Institute of Economics, dated July 24, 2018, accessed April 21, 2022, http://unirule.cloud/index.php?c=article&id=4625; Chun Han Wong, "Chinese Begin to Vent Discontent with President Xi and His Policies," *Wall Street Journal*, August 15, 2018, https://www.wsj.com/articles/chinese-begin-to-vent-discontent-with-president-xi-and-his -policies-1534350856; Chun Han Wong, "Chinese Law Professor Who Criticized Xi Jinping to Fight Charge and Dismissal," *Wall Street Journal*, July 29, 2020, https://www.wsj.com/articles/ chinese-law-professor-who-criticized-xi-jinping-to-fight-charge-and-dismissal-11596032995

83 Director of Central Intelligence, "China After Deng."

84 Chun Han Wong, "Xi Jinping's Quest for Control over China Targets Even Old Friends," *Wall Street Journal*, October 16, 2022. https://www.wsj.com/articles/xi-jinping-china -anticorruption-11665925166

85 Wong, "Xi Jinping's Quest for Control over China."

86 Torigian, *Prestige, Manipulation, and Coercion*, pp. 1–4.

87 Huang Yanpei, 《延安歸來》 [*Return from Yan'an*] (Chongqing: Chongqing Guoxun Bookstore, 1945), pp. 64–65.

88 Huang, *Return from Yan'an*, pp. 64–65.

89 "学习关键词 | 总书记为何多次提到'窑洞对'？ [Studying Key Words | Why Did the General Secretary Repeatedly Mention the 'Cave Dwelling Dialogue'?]," CCTV News, January 16, 2022. http://news.cctv.com/2022/01/16/ARTITg2N3w7f4wCZEnyB8WmF220116.shtml

90 Xi, "We Must Be Consistent in Promoting the New Great Project."

91 Chun Han Wong, "China's Xi Jinping Stakes Out Ambitions, with Himself at the Center,"

Wall Street Journal, October 17, 2022. https://www.wsj.com/articles/chinas-xi-jinping-hails-communist-partys-self-revolution-in-bid-to-extend-rule-11665894731

92 "中国共产党第二十次全国代表大会开幕会 [The Opening of the Chinese Communist Party's 20th National Congress]," 新华网 Xinhua Net, October 16, 2022. http://www.news.cn/politics/cpc20/zb/xhwkmh1016/index.htm

93 Joseph Fewsmith, *Rethinking Chinese Politics* (Cambridge: Cambridge University Press, 2021), p. 22.

AFTERWORD

1 Charles Hutzler, "Wall Street Journal Reporter Forced to Leave China," *Wall Street Journal*, August 30, 2019, https://www.wsj.com/articles/wall-street-journal-reporter-forced-to-leave-china-11567161852; "AWSJ Through the Years," *Wall Street Journal*, September 2, 1996, https://www.wsj.com/articles/SB841288562488934500

2 Gerry Shih, "China Expels Wall Street Journal Reporter over Coverage of Xi's Family," *Washington Post*, August 30, 2019. https://www.washingtonpost.com/world/asia_pacific/china-expels-wall-street-journal-reporter-over-coverage-of-xis-family/2019/08/30/69a0e77e-caf7-11e9-9615-8f1a32962e04_story.html

3 Philip Wen and Chun Han Wong, "After Lengthy Delay, China's Communist Party to Meet in October," *Wall Street Journal*, August 30, 2019. https://www.wsj.com/articles/after-lengthy-delay-chinas-communist-party-to-meet-in-october-11567182539

4 Philip Wen and Chun Han Wong, "Chinese President Xi Jinping's Cousin Draws Scrutiny of Australian Authorities," *Wall Street Journal*, July 30, 2019. https://www.wsj.com/articles/chinese-presidents-cousin-draws-scrutiny-of-australian-authorities-11564500031

5 Chun Han Wong, "Xi's Unsteady Steps Revive Worries Over Lack of Succession Plan in China," *Wall Street Journal*, April 23, 2019. https://www.wsj.com/articles/xis-unsteady-steps-revive-worries-over-lack-of-succession-plan-in-china-11556011802

6 Mike Forsythe, "In a sign of how things have changed, when Bloomberg published its expose of the extended Xi family wealth in 2012 (I was one of the reporters), not only was I not expelled but my China journalist visa was renewed for another year, with no fuss," Twitter, August 30, 2019. https://twitter.com/pekingmike/status/1167389704444100608

7 Foreign Correspondents' Club of China, "2/ Visas remained a chokepoint: In the first half of 2020, China expelled at least 18 foreign journalists from @WashPo @NYT @WSJ . One fourth of respondents reported getting visas valid for less than a year, the standard length," Twitter, March 21, 2021. https://twitter.com/fccchina/status/1366253377726808064

8 Sarah Zheng, "Beijing Revokes Work Permits for Chinese Assistants Working for US Media Organisations," *South China Morning Post*, March 20, 2020, https://www.scmp.com/news/china/diplomacy/article/3076082/beijing-revokes-work-permits-chinese-assistants-working-us; "Beijing Dismisses Chinese News Assistants Working for U.S. Bureaus," Committee to Protect Journalists, March 20, 2020, https://cpj.org/2020/03/beijing-orders-us-news-bureaus-to-dismiss-chinese/

9 Deng Xiaoping, "在中央顾问委员会第三次全体会议上的讲话 [Speech at the Third Plenary

376 ★ NOTES

Meeting of the Central Advisory Commission]," in 《邓小平文选》 第三卷 *Selected Works of Deng Xiaoping*, Vol. 3 (Beijing: People's Publishing House, 1993), pp. 83–93.

10 Orville Schell, "How Journalism Helped China Open Up," *Wall Street Journal*, August 14, 2020. https://www.wsj.com/articles/how-journalism-helped-china-open-up-11597433061

11 "China Eases Rules for Foreign Media," Associated Press, October 17, 2008. https://www.nytimes.com/2008/10/18/world/asia/18china.html

12 Katrina Northrop, "The Great Expulsion," The Wire China, February 14, 2021. https://www.thewirechina.com/2021/02/14/the-great-expulsion/

13 Josh Chin and Brian Spegele, "Censorship Protest Gains Support in China," *Wall Street Journal*, January 8, 2013. https://www.wsj.com/articles/SB10001424127887323707045782275028419 25808

14 Josh Chin and Paul Mozur, "China Intensifies Social-Media Crackdown," *Wall Street Journal*, September 19, 2013. https://www.wsj.com/articles/SB10001424127887324807704579082940411106988

15 Mark Landler and David E. Sanger, "China Pressures U.S. Journalists, Prompting Warning from Biden," *New York Times*, December 4, 2013. https://www.nytimes.com/2013/12/06/world/asia/biden-faults-china-on-foreign-press-crackdown.html

16 Tom Phillips, "French Journalist Accuses China of Intimidating Foreign Press," *Guardian*, December 26, 2015. https://www.theguardian.com/world/2015/dec/26/china-ursula-gauthier-french-journalist-xinjiang

17 Emma Graham-Harrison, "China 'Ejects' US Journalist Known for Reporting on Xinjiang Repression," *Guardian*, August 22, 2018. https://www.theguardian.com/world/2018/aug/22/china-ejects-us-journalist-known-for-reporting-on-xinjiang-repression

18 "Track, Trace, Expel: Reporting on China Amid a Pandemic," Foreign Correspondents' Club of China, March 1, 2021. https://twitter.com/fccchina/status/1366253375646433280

19 Stuart Condie, "Australian Journalist Detained in China as Relations Sour," *Wall Street Journal*, August 31, 2020, https://www.wsj.com/articles/australian-journalist-detained-in-china-as-relations-sour-11598886544; Chao Deng and Rachel Pannett, "Australian Reporters Flee China After Late-Night Visits from State Security," *Wall Street Journal*, September 8, 2020, https://www.wsj.com/articles/australian-reporters-flee-china-after-late-night-visits-from-state-security-11599590728

20 "'Press Freedom' Should Not Become a Pretext for Interference in Other Countries' Judicial Sovereignty," Embassy of the People's Republic of China in the United States of America, May 6, 2022, http://us.china-embassy.gov.cn/eng/lcbt/sgfyrbt/202205/t20220506_10682082.htm; Chun Han Wong, "China Releases Bloomberg News Staffer Detained on National-Security Grounds," *Wall Street Journal*, June 14, 2022, https://www.wsj.com/articles/china-releases-bloomberg-news-staffer-detained-on-national-security-grounds-11655218147

21 Michael M. Grynbaum, "New York Times Will Move Part of Hong Kong Office to Seoul," *New York Times*, July 14, 2020, https://www.nytimes.com/2020/07/14/business/media/new-york-times-hong-kong.html; Zanny Minton Beddoes, "Statement from The Economist's Editor-in-Chief," *Economist*, November 12, 2021, https://press.economist.com/story/15283/statement-from-the-economist

22 "Media Freedoms Report 2021: 'Locked Down or Kicked Out,'" Foreign Correspondents'

Club of China, January 31, 2022. https://fccchina.org/2022/01/31/media-freedoms-report -2021-locked-down-or-kicked-out/

23 "习近平在中共中央政治局第三十次集体学习时强调 加强和改进国际传播工作 展示真实 立体全面的中国 [During the 30th Collective Study Session of the Chinese Communist Party Central Committee's Politburo, Xi Jinping Emphasizes Strengthening and Improving International Communication Work and Showing a True, Three-Dimensional and Comprehensive China]," Xinhua News Agency, June 1, 2021. http://www.xinhuanet.com/politics/leaders/2021 -06/01/c_1127517461.htm

24 Chun Han Wong and Liza Lin, "China's Opaque Decision-Making Confounds Business, Governments," *Wall Street Journal*, January 9, 2023, https://www.wsj.com/articles/chinas -opaque-decision-making-confounds-business-governments-11673269970

25 Rebecca Feng, "Outspoken China Strategist Leaves State-Owned Broker After Social-Media Accounts Are Censored," *Wall Street Journal*, May 3, 2022. https://www.wsj.com/articles /outspoken-china-strategist-leaves-state-owned-broker-after-social-media-accounts-are -censored-11651575795

26 Jia Qingguo, "贾庆国委员：让中国人的声音更便捷、更有效地向世界传播 [Committee Member Jia Qingguo: Let the Voices of the Chinese People Be Propagated to the World in a More Convenient and Effective Manner]," Charhar Institute WeChat account, March 5, 2021. https://mp.weixin.qq.com/s/C42O0Q1sTIQfBN3IgvzAdw

27 Dongxie Xidu, "一个外媒记者的来信 [A Letter from a Foreign-Media Reporter]," 抢占外媒 高地 [Seizing the Foreign Media High Ground] WeChat account, March 22, 2020. https:// mp.weixin.qq.com/s/VqQQpAUUah0xIa2KbJzfTQ

28 Dongxie Xidu, "A Letter from a Foreign-Media Reporter."

29 Dongxie Xidu, "A Letter from a Foreign-Media Reporter."

30 Lai Si, "来论 | 中国人分得清善恶虚实：也谈《一个外媒记者的来信》 [Come and Speak | Chinese People Can Distinguish Between Good and Evil: Let's Also Discuss 'A Letter from a Foreign-Media Reporter']," *The Paper*, March 25, 2020. https://www.thepaper.cn/newsDetail _forward_6680151

31 Zhong Jiahu, "对于《一个外媒记者的来信》我有话说 [Regarding 'A Letter from a Foreign- Media Reporter,' I Have Something to Say]," 中国经济网 [China Economic Net], March 25, 2020. http://www.ce.cn/xwzx/gnsz/gdxw/202003/25/t20200325_34555733.shtml

32 Liza Lin and Chun Han Wong, "China Increasingly Obscures True State of Its Economy to Outsiders," *Wall Street Journal*, December 6, 2021. https://www.wsj.com/articles/china-data-security -law-ships-ports-court-cases-universities-11638803230

33 China Team, "China's Nationalistic Cancel Culture Is Out of Control," Protocol, December 30, 2021, https://www.protocol.com/china/china-nationalism-cancel-culture; China Team, "Red Vs Are After China's Queer Community," Protocol, July 13, 2021, https://www.protocol.com/china /china-wechat-delete-lgbt-accounts

34 Timothy McLaughlin, "The Volunteer Movement Enraging China," *Atlantic*, May 21, 2022, https://www.theatlantic.com/international/archive/2022/05/great-translation-movement -china-censorship-firewall/629914/; GT Staff Reporters, "GT Investigates: Behind the Online Translation Campaign Are a Few Chinese-Speaking Badfaith Actors Fed by Antagonistic Western Media," *Global Times*, March 24, 2022, https://www.globaltimes.cn/page/202203/1256769.

shtml; Wang Qiang, "'Great Translation Movement' a Despicable Anti-China Smear Campaign," *Global Times*, March 31, 2022, https://www.globaltimes.cn/page/202203/1257320.shtml; Huang Lanlan and Lin Xiaoyi, "Twisted in Translation: Western Media, Social Groups Set Up Language Barriers by Intentionally Misreading, Misinterpreting Chinese Materials," *Global Times*, April 14, 2022, https://www.globaltimes.cn/page/202204/1259372.shtml

35 Robert Bickers, *Out of China: How the Chinese Ended the Era of Western Domination* (Cambridge, Massachusetts: Harvard University Press, 2017), p. XXXI.

INDEX

ABOUT THE AUTHOR

Chun Han Wong has covered China for the *Wall Street Journal* since 2014. He was part of a team of reporters named as Pulitzer Prize finalists for their coverage of China's autocratic turn under Xi Jinping. As a *Journal* correspondent in Beijing and Hong Kong, Wong has written widely on subjects spanning elite politics, Communist Party doctrine, human and labor rights, as well as defense and diplomatic affairs. Born and raised in Singapore, Wong is a native speaker of English and Mandarin Chinese. He studied international history at the London School of Economics, where he graduated with first-class honors and won the Derby Bryce Prize.